The Shape of the Soul

The Shape of the Soul

What Mystical Experience Tells Us
about Ourselves and Reality

PAUL MARSHALL

ROWMAN & LITTLEFIELD
Lanham • Boulder • New York • London

Published by Rowman & Littlefield
An imprint of The Rowman & Littlefield Publishing Group, Inc.
4501 Forbes Boulevard, Suite 200, Lanham, Maryland 20706
www.rowman.com

6 Tinworth Street, London SE11 5AL, United Kingdom

British Library Cataloguing in Publication Information Available

Library of Congress Cataloging-in-Publication Data Available
ISBN 978-1-5381-2477-2 (hardcover)
ISBN 978-1-5381-2478-9 (electronic)

♾️™ The paper used in this publication meets the minimum requirements of American
National Standard for Information Sciences—Permanence of Paper for Printed Library
Materials, ANSI/NISO Z39.48-1992.

Printed in the United States of America

For my parents

Contents

Preface

> For he who knows himself
> will perceive first of all that
> he possesses something divine.
>
> —Cicero

THERE ARE MOMENTS OF SELF-DISCOVERY in which consciousness of the world is radically transformed by unity, knowledge, light, and love. Quite a few years ago, when I was a young man, I had such an experience, and it seemed to me in that all-too-brief interlude of clarity that I was both much less and much more than I had previously imagined. It was now plain that a good deal of what I had taken myself to be was relatively unimportant and insubstantial, dependent on something far more alive and profound. That "much more" was of the nature of mind, intensely perceptual and knowing, holding the universe in its compass, and disposed toward the most inclusive love. Yet it was not other than myself, and if true of me then true of each and every one of us.

No doubt many will put the experience down to a neuropsychological quirk or an overexcited imagination, but I am inclined to think that it was genuinely revelatory. For one thing, the sheer clarity and the depth of knowing and feeling it brought are hard for me to brush aside. I have been sufficiently impressed by the experience to approach it at face value as an authentic self-revelation, a glimpse into the deeper nature of things. In the present book, I describe the experience as best I can and draw on a variety of sources, religious, philosophical, and scientific, to inquire into its possible significance and the greater dimension of self it appeared to reveal. Inquiry into the self, a central undertaking of the present study, is of course a very

old preoccupation, traditionally framed as the pursuit of self-knowledge—
the endeavor to "know thyself." It has also been the quest for the soul, the
immortal "pearl" concealed in perishable flesh, and in these pages we shall
indeed come across sightings of that elusive essence that was believed to
survive bodily death. While talk of "soul" is largely out of fashion within
intellectual circles, and so too belief in postmortem survival, there is a case
for preserving the term, especially if it can be rescued from its customary
vagueness, as I hope to do here.

In modern, secular contexts, "mind" is now the preferred term for the
perceiving, thinking, feeling, willing part of the human constitution, and it is
appropriate too for the superhuman dimension of self I seemed to encounter
in my experience, for it was perceptual and knowing, although in a way that
far exceeded ordinary mentality. In this work, I try to understand how mind
could have such unsuspected depths, and in so doing I sketch the outlines
of a philosophy for which *mind is fundamental*. I edged my way toward
this understanding in the wake of the experience, but it turns out to have a
distinguished history: "idealist" thinkers have long argued that mind is more
basic than matter, that it is not only integral to the universe but constitutes
its very nature and is the source from which all things derive, including our
human minds and brains. The common view in modern times has been
essentially the opposite: it is usually assumed that experience, mind, and
consciousness, far from being fundamental, are simply "emergent properties" of the material brain, arising only when evolution has yielded biological
processes of sufficient complexity to generate them.

Undoubtedly mind and body are intimately related, but this is not to
say that brain creates experience, for it is far from obvious how material
structures and processes could do so if matter is defined as lacking basic
experiential qualities, such as those of color and sound. In recent years,
there has been much discussion of this "mind–body problem," with renewed
interest in philosophies that give mind a more integral place in the scheme
of things. These approaches, which are quite varied, include types of *panpsychism*, for which the basic units of matter do possess some degree of
consciousness, if only very primitive.[1] They also include types of *idealism*
of the kind intimated above, for which mind is more fundamental than
matter.[2] The outlook I develop here combines these two approaches, finding
consciousness in the basic units of nature and taking mind to be primary. As
such, it is a contribution to the consciousness-centered type of philosophy
that is reasserting itself after the long dominance of materialism. It is also
a contribution to the study of the soul, for the kind of idealism I propose
here furnishes a very specific understanding of soul, giving it more shape

and substance than is ordinarily the case. Some contemporary thinkers have defended the concept of soul by upholding various kinds of dualism that distinguish soul from matter.[3] I aim for a more unified picture, favoring an idealism that absorbs the material world into the soul as the contents of its perceptions. There is no material world outside these perceptions.

The present book, however, is not a conventional work of philosophy, for it draws its inspiration from sources often passed over as unimportant or irrelevant, and its speculative ambition is not typical of much contemporary, mainstream philosophy. As already indicated, I take as my starting point a kind of experience that seems to reveal hidden depths of reality. These experiences, nowadays often called "mystical," occur in a variety of circumstances, including the beauty of nature, meditation, mental distress, and near-death crisis. While they have received some philosophical attention over the years, especially in connection with issues of knowledge, logic, language, and ethics, their metaphysical claim to be revelatory of reality has not been of great interest to philosophers, in part because metaphysics itself had been rather unfashionable for a long time and also because it is no easy matter to navigate the difficulties that such inquiry faces. One of these challenges is the cross-cultural diversity of mystical teachings, that is, the lack of metaphysical consensus among spiritual traditions supposedly informed by mystical experience. Why should there be significant doctrinal differences if these traditions draw on mystical insights into the nature of reality? I have considered this and other challenges elsewhere, and shall not repeat my observations, other than to reiterate my conclusions that the difficulties are not insurmountable and that there is a place for inquiry into the claim of mystical experience to be revelatory of reality, if conducted circumspectly and directed in the first place not at mystical doctrines but at unadorned, descriptive accounts of mystical experiences.[4]

Another somewhat unusual inspiration behind the present book is a philosophical system well known to scholars but viewed more often as a historical curiosity than a serious constructive metaphysics for our times, namely the theory of monads or *monadology* formulated by philosopher and mathematician Gottfried Wilhelm Leibniz around the beginning of the eighteenth century. According to Leibniz, the fundamental units of nature are the monads, perceptual beings who express the entire universe from their unique points of view as they shift from state to state, driven onward by an inherent striving or "appetition." In more developed form, these monads are souls and minds. Over the centuries, Leibniz's system has caught the imagination of several thinkers who have modified and updated it to suit their concerns. For example, in the early twentieth century, A. N. Whitehead,

Bertrand Russell, and several British idealists were inspired by monadology.[5] I am no exception here, taking up the philosophy and adapting it to address not only the mind–body problem but also some of the puzzles of mystical experience and modern science. I have not been alone in thinking that monadology may shed light on relativistic and quantum physics, and offer a framework in which a deeper understanding of evolution can be had, one that is true to our experience as conscious, purposive beings.

The book proceeds as follows. In CHAPTER 1, I introduce mystical experiences, specifically those that bring transformations of self-understanding through discovery of a profound connection with the natural world, a sense that one is not really separate from other human beings, animals, plants, inanimate objects, even the entire universe. These "unitive" or "nondual" states, distinguished from everyday, dualistic consciousness, have a claim to be the key to self-knowledge, an antidote to self-identifications that are misleading because they are too narrow and exclusive. I give a few examples of these unitive experiences and briefly set out their characteristics and the circumstances in which they take place, drawing on a more detailed overview in my earlier study *Mystical Encounters with the Natural World*,[6] but now advancing the discussion a little further. I offer a classification of mystical experiences according to whether they embrace the natural world, some other world, or no world at all, and I give more prominence to a distinction between mystical perceptions of the world that remain tied to the ordinary senses and those that seem to go beyond them. I also discuss the structure of dualistic consciousness, and I introduce the mystical intuition that the entire universe can be found within, in the self or soul.

In order to take the discussion further, I find it necessary to describe my own experience of cosmic wholeness, mentioned in the opening paragraph. This took place one morning about thirty-five years ago, while I was asleep. I probably would not have been induced to publish an account of this personally meaningful experience were it not for a peculiar, potentially important detail to be noted shortly, one not often reported in contemporary mystical accounts. In CHAPTER 2, I describe the mystical experience and its background, and highlight several features, some of which receive detailed consideration in the chapters that follow. I also pay attention to the curious fact that when I awoke from sleep I was able to remember two dreams but not the core experience sandwiched between them. There are notable precedents to the forgetting and remembering of profound truths, going back to the ancient Platonic doctrine of *anamnēsis* or "recollection" of forgotten knowledge, and illustrated by modern examples, particularly pronounced in anesthetic intoxication, which interestingly has brought idealist insights too.

It is noteworthy that my experience was similar to those associated with life-threatening physical traumas such as cardiac arrests and traffic-accident injuries, that is to say, the near-death experiences that have attracted much attention in recent decades. In my case there was, as far as I can tell, no such threat to life, for at the time I was fast asleep in bed and out of harm's way. However, the experience was preceded by dream imagery suggestive of a journey into death, and the experience itself can be understood as a kind of death of the ordinary self, if only a partial and temporary one. Thus, in CHAPTER 3, I treat the mystical journey as an excursion into the realm of the dead, which paradoxically is the land of the truly living, a journey that brings threats to the ego, moments of self-judgment in the face of overwhelming love, and revelations of deeper identity. As we shall see, the idea that near-death and postmortem judgments are self-judgments, rather than those of an external arbiter, should not be dismissed too quickly as a modern psychological reading, for it has significant historical precedents.

Self-knowledge as revelatory of an identity over and above the familiar one—or "the Human as Two" as scholar of religions Jeffrey J. Kripal has called it—becomes the focus of interest in CHAPTER 4. If there is a hidden dimension of self, how far does it extend toward the center of things, and what is its relation to the everyday sense of self? Is it, indeed, appropriate to apply "self" terminology to deeper facets of reality? Mystical experiences undoubtedly bring dramatic transformations of self-experience, but it is open to debate whether the deeper aspects of self they sometimes reveal are genuine, and I do not expect to reach any firm conclusions on this thorny issue. After all, it is notable that such experientially informed, philosophically astute religious traditions as Hinduism and Buddhism are often thought to have very different positions on the reality of the self.[7] Although the present book raises the possibility of hidden depths of self, it does not pretend to give a rigorous analysis of "self" and its metaphysical status.[8] Rather, the book is experience-oriented and speculative in approach, taking as a starting point mystical experience and proceeding to some tentative reflections. What the study lacks in detailed philosophical analysis is hopefully offset by some worthwhile lines of inquiry opened up by mystical experience, my own included.

My suspicion is that even if "self" terminology is not quite right for the very essence of reality (if that reality transcends all subject–object discrimination), it can still be applied in a meaningful way to the level of knowing and feeling that I accessed during my cosmic episode, for the experience had a social character, involving a community of beings. The expansive mind was not a solitary intellect but a vast, communing soul, one among many, cognizant of its distinctness from the others, yet aware that it was intimately related to them by virtue of shared identity with the whole. This realization stemmed from the peculiar detail I have not found commonly reported in present-day accounts of mystical experience, although it has parallels in mystical traditions. Within the cosmic mind I had discovered myself to be, I was able to discern other minds or "knowers" who were likewise cosmic in scope, yet they were very tiny things, and it was puzzling to me that these little beings, circular in shape and capable of igniting the most powerful, all-inclusive love, also embraced the world in their comprehensions. In fact, this detail was so baffling that I pushed it to the back of my thoughts for several years and did not pay much attention to it. Yet it was perhaps one of the most important features of the experience, and the enigma it presented to me has been the inspiration behind *The Shape of the Soul*. Who were those beings? Why were they circular in shape? How could such diminutives hold the great universe within their comprehensions?

I begin to address these questions in CHAPTER 5 by taking a look at references to circular and spherical forms both in modern-day accounts of altered states of consciousness and in the older religious and philosophical literature. It turns out that sphericity has been attributed to the soul for a long time, figuratively or literally. One particularly rich example is to be found in Hildegard of Bingen's visionary writings, which describe fiery soul-globes. But it has been suggested that Hildegard suffered from migraine, and so the question arises whether her visions of globes can be put down to the visual auras that sometimes attend the medical condition. More generally, it can be asked whether "entoptic" light phenomena, believed to originate in the eyes and nervous system, and related to the migraine aura, are the source of some visionary contents. Entoptics can certainly be a feature of altered states of consciousness, but do they account for the details of my own experience?

I find the entoptics approach interesting but unsatisfactory, for the "rings" I experienced were not just visual forms: they were recognizable as all-encompassing, living beings equivalent to myself. Thus, in CHAPTER 6, I work toward an alternative understanding, drawing upon and adapting the philosophies of Plotinus and Leibniz. Both thinkers explained how it is possible for a mere part to contain within itself the entire whole. It turns out that the world may consist of a plurality of distinct, all-encompassing, self-evolving yet mutually representative experiences, so that it is in effect a communal enterprise and a "social construction" in the strongest sense of the term.[9] The universe and its material constituents are then a social reality in their organization and development, and consciousness at this level is truly a "knowing with others," a "knowing together."

Each of these all-inclusive wholes or monads has complete perceptions of the universe organized from its own point of view, representing within itself all the other cosmic perspectives in such a way that the representations form the basis of material structure. As a perception, each monad is an experiential continuum, an undivided whole, but it represents within itself all the other discrete wholes, and these representations are the fundamental units of *matter*. Leibniz's philosophy of monads shows how one can go about understanding the nature of matter in a universe that is experiential in nature, an achievement rarely emulated by other philosophies that regard mind, experience, or consciousness as primary and matter as derivative. Interpreted as an idealist solution to the mind–body problem, the monadology not only explains in general terms how mind and matter can be reconciled but also lays the foundation for a detailed understanding of matter. Furthermore, it is a metaphysics well suited to the explication of mystical experiences and certain parapsychological phenomena, such as telepathy and precognition. I do not attend to these "psi" phenomena here, but I have discussed their relation to mystical experience elsewhere,[10] and I have suggested how monadological ideas can be applied to them.[11]

Arguably, Plotinus and Leibniz were the most gifted philosophers of their ages, but their eminence as thinkers does not guarantee that their ideas, however admirable, tally with the way things are. What evidence is there for a universe organized in the manner indicated above, from multiple centers of perception? In CHAPTER 7, I look at the mystical evidence but observe that it is not as plentiful as I would have hoped. One explanation for the comparative dearth of relevant accounts is that the state of consciousness in question is not easily accessed, for the necessary depth of insight seems to require a deathlike subjugation of the everyday self, an "ego-death" that is a formidable obstacle to progress into the cosmic hinterlands of consciousness. Furthermore, it can be difficult to remember and describe such excursions when they do take place, as I myself can attest. Nevertheless, we shall see that experiences which fail to reach the requisite depth can still hint at a world organized along monadological lines by bringing into view a "guardian of the threshold" who blocks the way to deeper realizations yet displays telltale signs of the reality it guards, such as luminosity, sphericity, and multiple but interconnected centers of perception.

Scientific support for a universe organized in monadological fashion takes center stage in CHAPTER 8. This is no less than the two great pillars of modern physics, the relativistic and quantum theories, both of which have stood up well to rigorous experimental testing over the years. Each of these theories on its own can be regarded as suggestive of a universe organized along monadological lines, but taken in combination the evidence they provide is even more compelling. Surely it is significant that each of these fundamental theories points in its own way to the same conclusion? It is even possible that their much anticipated union in a "theory of everything" may be achievable in a monadological framework, which effortlessly combines the seeming contraries of the continuous and the discrete. The former is a feature of general relativity, with its account of large-scale structure dominated by gravitation; the latter is a feature of quantum theory, with its discontinuities at small scales. Monadology naturally combines the continuous and discontinuous, and also the large and the small, by having the cosmically inclusive monads, which are discrete continua, represented in the microstructure of one another. The territory was explored in my first book, *The Living Mirror*,[12] but now it receives a less physical, more philosophical treatment, drawing on Einstein's helpful distinction between "theories of principle" and "constructive theories" to suggest that physics is in need of a metaphysics and that monadology may fit the bill.

The study draws to a close with chapters on origins, destinations, and journeys: where do we come from, where are we going, and how do we get there? A world of harmonized perceptions points to a common source, one that generates, coordinates, and supports the cosmic multiplicity. But how do the Many come forth from this supernal One, the origin and essence of all things, the ultimate center of centers? If the universe truly consists of mutually representative cosmic perceptions, then it must come into being through the generation of a multiplicity of subjects who take one another as their objects. Thus, in CHAPTER 9, the question of origins draws us back to the separation of subject and object with which the book opened, the apprehension of the other as distinct from oneself. It is possible that the separative discriminations that mark our everyday range of experiences are not just a peculiarity of creatures such as ourselves, with our highly developed conceptual-linguistic abilities and somewhat alienating ways of life, but are far more widespread. Indeed, they may stem from subject–object discriminations intrinsic to the process of world manifestation itself and so are woven into the fabric of things. According to some mystically informed schools of thought, including Plotinian philosophy and nondual Kashmir Shaivism, the world of multiplicity comes forth from its luminous source through the emergence of a subject who seeks an object and in so doing generates a world of subject–object perceptions that are subtly dualistic at a cosmic level and grossly dualistic at the sensory level. The assertion of a subject ("Ego") and associated want of an object ("Eros") set up a dynamic that drives all that follows, powering cycles of self–other differentiation and unification, dominated alternately by duality and unity, revolutions of luminous consciousness out of which manifest existence is spun.

With the journey now well underway, the role played by biological evolution comes into view. CHAPTER 10 begins with the old idea of a "ladder of nature." Leibniz's monadology describes a hierarchy of organisms with increasingly sophisticated bodies, perceptions, and mental functioning. This ladder stretches from the most basic organisms through plants, animals, humans, and superhumans toward God, but it is not really possible to climb up it, even though Leibniz's system of nature works toward the achievement of greater perfection. A comparable ladder of nature in the ancient Indian religion of Jainism is traversable because transmigration of souls across species is recognized there. It is possible to scale the ladder through rebirths into more favorable bodies and environments. Leibniz did not accept transmigration as such, but it can be a natural extension of his system, and already in Leibniz's time monads and reincarnation had been brought together in a limited fashion by Leibniz's friend Francis Mercury van Helmont. But it was only after the rise of biological evolutionism in the eighteenth and nineteenth centuries that the integration could come of age. Evolutionary theory added a new idea to the mix: it turns out that the static ladder of nature is actually an escalator, or better, a growing, branching "tree of life." Evolution makes available new kinds of bodies and mental capacities through which monads can pursue their developmental journeys.

No doubt the path is long and difficult, bringing much pain and suffering on the way, and the question arises whether the journey and goal are worthwhile. Attention therefore turns in CHAPTER 11 to the problem of evil, including John Hick's "soul-making" approach to suffering, a Christian theodicy that takes on board biological evolutionism and which meshes well with monadology. In fact Hick's approach would benefit from relocation into a framework of evolutionary monadology, for some difficulties it faces are eased there. The concept of God also receives attention, since the evils of the world raise formidable difficulties for a God conceived along traditional lines. This is an appropriate topic on which to conclude since the concept of God has a bearing on the puzzle that runs through the book, the question of self-identity—who we are and what we may be. The outcome of these final reflections is a concept of God-in-the-making who contains the world but also transcends it, a divinity who we all are at heart.

Finally, I would like to highlight in advance where I believe the present book makes some distinctive and innovative contributions:

1. Unusually for a contemporary study, the claim of mystical experience to be revelatory of deeper realities is taken seriously. I am therefore willing

to draw on mystical testimonies as a resource for exploring questions about self, mind, time, suffering, and other enigmas.

2. Although I take the reality claim of mystical experience seriously, I do so cautiously, mindful of alternative explanations. Previously, in *Mystical Encounters*, I discussed several competing theories of mystical experience, including neuropsychological and social-psychological ones, and now I give the migraine theory special attention, since luminous phenomena feature prominently in the current study.

3. I draw on a wide range of mystical sources, traditional and modern, and offer novel perspectives on several mystics, including Thomas Traherne and Hildegard of Bingen, and on visionary glimpses of circular and spherical forms. I use my own experience as a starting point, and, if the present study does nothing else, it adds a detailed account of my experience to the mystical literature.

4. I develop an idealist metaphysics based on Leibniz's philosophy of monads, refashioned in the light of mystical experience and the philosophy of Plotinus. Unlike many reformers of monadology I leave intact the cosmic completeness of monads, and in a radical move I make their cosmic perceptions fully distinct, like those of Plotinian intellects.

5. My adoption of monadology allows me to give more substance to the concept of the soul. Moreover, my upgrading of monads to fully fledged cosmic minds means that the idea of a higher level of soul can be supported, for each monad in its totality now constitutes such a higher level, indeed, a communal level of soul, a social self, a "One-Many." Thus, the soul is at least twofold, comprising the everyday self and the monadic mind of which this limited, everyday self is just a small part.

6. The proposed metaphysics incorporates a traditional dualist theory of perception but makes it idealist: the "external world" represented in our sense perceptions is now understood to be internal to our monadic minds. Thus, two basic kinds of perception are distinguished, one sensory and limited, the other monadic and all-inclusive.

7. These philosophical innovations are, I think, significant in their own right, but they are even more interesting if monadological thought provides a framework in which relativistic physics and quantum physics become more comprehensible, as I suggest it does.

8. Leibniz has little to say about the origin of monads, and so I turn again to Plotinus for inspiration and trace the origin and striving of monads to the productive, reflexive activity of their source. There is, I think, justification for this move, since my reconstructed monads are somewhat like Plotinian intellects (although significantly different too, as I shall explain).

9. Taking the idea further, I describe cycles of cognition and feeling that swing between subject–object duality and unity, powered by an *egoic* pull toward differentiation and an *erosic* pull toward unification. In this way, dualistic and nondual consciousness are partnered in creative interplay. My speculations here provide a new angle on earlier concepts of two dynamic principles at work in the human psyche and the world at large, such as the Chinese *yang* and *yin*, and the Jungian Logos and Eros.

10. Leibniz's monadology predates the emergence of evolutionary science, but its developmental vision, which has monads striving to actualize their potential, is readily modified to incorporate biological evolutionism. I draw attention to this evolutionary form of monadology, which brings together scientific and spiritual concepts of evolution, uncover some of its history, and endeavor to retrieve it from esoteric expositions that were inventive but overly fanciful.

11. I suggest that soul-making theodicy, which attempts to reconcile the world's ills with the existence of a benign creator God, has a natural home in evolutionary monadology. Logical arguments, however, only go so far in addressing the problem of evil, for raw experiences of suffering can make theoretical attempts to grapple with the problem look very hollow indeed. While the experiential problem of evil remains as challenging as ever, I draw attention to experiences that bear witness to meaning in suffering and so give some ground for faith in the basic goodness of the world process, despite many indications to the contrary.

12. The problem of evil has led some thinkers to reconsider the nature of God, and I too look for an alternative understanding, one more deeply integrated with the evolutionary monadology I describe. I suggest that divine consciousness evolves through the cosmic odyssey of monads, yet is available fully developed at each step of the journey if all of time is present in each moment.

A book in the making for as long as this one incurs many debts, and here I can mention just a few. The speculative reach of the work has been greatly enlarged through my participation in seminars at Esalen Institute's Center for Theory and Research (CTR) in the beautiful setting of Big Sur, California. I was encouraged by these seminars to extend the idealist framework I had previously developed to further areas of concern, namely evolution, post-mortem survival, the nature of God, and psi phenomena. The first three are central to the final chapters of the present book, while the fourth received my attention in *Beyond Physicalism*, a multiauthored volume that emerged out of CTR's "Sursem" or Survival Seminar series, which I joined toward the end of its fifteen-year run. I am most grateful to the hosts of the various seminars

I attended, including Harald Atmanspacher, Gregory Shaw, and especially Michael Murphy, whose vision of human flourishing has guided the work of CTR and Esalen, Jeffrey J. Kripal, who first introduced me to CTR, and Edward F. Kelly, who invited me to take part in Sursem. Ed and Jeff have been immensely supportive of my work over the years, and my very special thanks go to them. I also thank CTR colleagues Loriliai Biernacki, Bernard Carr, and Robert Rosenberg, who read parts of the book or offered advice, G. William Barnard for his advocacy of metaphysical inquiry in mystical studies (a concern dear to my heart), and Eric M. Weiss for impressing on me the relevance of Whitehead's philosophy. More generally, CTR provided an opportunity to meet many knowledgeable and inspiring people, too many to name individually. They gave an independent researcher a rare collegial experience—my thanks to you all.

Outside Esalen, I am deeply indebted to Linda Marshall and Alan Hunter, who offered insightful comments on a draft version of *The Shape of the Soul*, making the book far better than it would otherwise have been. I also thank the editorial staff at Rowman & Littlefield, the four anonymous readers for the publisher, David Lawton and Steve Taylor for stimulating conversations, Keiron Le Grice for reading a chapter of the book, and John Franklin for encouraging a closer look at the classification of mystical experiences. Over the years I have been approached by several persons who have had profound mystical experiences, and I am grateful to them for sharing their stories with me: as a researcher too often caught up in details, I can miss the forest for the trees and forget the lived reality of the experiences. It is helpful to be reminded now and again of their power and mystery.

Finally, I am grateful to the Alister Hardy Trust and the Alister Hardy Religious Experience Research Centre, University of Wales Trinity Saint David, Lampeter, UK, for permission to quote extensively from their archive of spiritual accounts. Other sources and individuals are acknowledged in the main text and Notes.

1

Mystical Perceptions

All mean egotism vanishes.
I become a transparent eye-ball.
I am nothing. I see all.

—Ralph Waldo Emerson

THERE IS A TRADITION among poets and artists that we, as jaded adults, have become estranged from the world—cut off from nature, from one another, even from ourselves—through deeply ingrained habits of mind that prevent us from seeing things as they really are. Familiarity has bred a lack of awareness, a haze of inattention that conceals the wonder of the here and now, while separative thoughts and evaluations make the world appear fragmented, a heap of isolated pieces divided from one another and from ourselves. But on occasion the fog lifts a little, bringing moments of clarity, reconnection, and wholeness.

So it was that the Romantic poets aspired to see the world anew, vivid, luminous, unified, as some of them had known it in childhood. Wordsworth recounts that as a boy he would at times feel the outside world to be insepa-rable from himself: "I communed with all that I saw as something not apart from, but inherent in, my own immaterial nature."[1] The young Shelley may have known the feeling too, as suggested by his recollections in adulthood of the state of childhood:

> Let us recollect our sensations as children. What a distinct and intense apprehension had we of the world and of ourselves. . . . We less habitually distinguished all that we saw and felt from ourselves. They seemed as it were to constitute one mass.[2]

Shelley explained that the sense of unity is all too easily lost as we grow up. Thinking and feeling become fixed into routines, turning us into automatons, into "mechanical and habitual agents." Appreciation of the miracle of existence is lost: "The mist of familiarity obscures from us the wonder of our being."[3] Some, however, remain childlike in their susceptibility to the feeling of unity: "Those who are subject to the state called reverie feel as if their nature were dissolved into the surrounding universe, or as if the surrounding universe were absorbed into their being. They are conscious of no distinction."[4] More commonly, the feeling goes away as childhood is left behind, but according to Shelley all is not lost: he believed that poetry, as the exercise of the imagination, has the power to strip away the veil of deadening familiarity.[5] Among the Romantics, the recovery of the vision was generally viewed not as a regression to a state of innocence but as an advance, with unity now established in the mature mind, instructed by the lessons of experience. Consciousness develops not along a circle, from unity through division back to the old unity, but along a spiral, from unity to division to a higher unity, with the fall into the stage of alienation making advancement possible. The journey home leads to Jerusalem, not back to Eden.

It is unclear whether any of the Romantics attained the higher unity in an enduring fashion, but one poet and spiritual thinker does appear to have reached the longed-for condition. Thomas Traherne (ca. 1637–1674), writing over a century before the Romantic movement was properly underway, recalled the loss of his own infant "pure and virgin apprehensions," attributing the deprivation to several factors: the poor examples set by others, a host of distractions, and an education that neglected to "foster and cherish" the vision. Like "grit in the eye" or "yellow jaundice," these had worked to cloud his sight (CM III.5).[6] Without clear vision, we are like dead "Puppets" and "Statues"—or worse, we are alive, but dead to the wonders of nature and ourselves.[7] However, Traherne was to recover the vision, and he set out to communicate it to others and show them the way to their infinitely precious birthright, the divine Image, the soul restored to the likeness of God.

Traherne, the Romantics, and assorted proponents of "nonduality" look upon our ordinarily confused, divided state of consciousness with regret.[8] The case can be put as follows, although nondualist thinkers will disagree over the details and some major points too. While the discriminations by which we distinguish ourselves from others are often based on real differences and so are largely justified, they are usually applied too severely, taken too far, with the result that the world is construed as a heap of bits and pieces separate from oneself, rather than as an unbroken whole of which all things, including one's thoughts, feelings, and body, are parts and modifications. The tendency toward conceptual fragmentation of the universe, reinforced by the naming of things, and exacerbated by certain atomizing and materializing trends in the history of philosophical and scientific thought, could be called, rather grandly, the *miscognition of the continuum as radically discontinuous*. The universe so divided is structured dualistically into "myself" and "not-myself," with the two sharply distinguished, a tendency that could be called, equally grandly, *exclusive identification with a fragment*. In short, "divide and misidentify." But sometimes the conceptual impositions cease to dominate, and the world is apprehended in its integrality, with self no longer delimited to a fragment and divorced from the whole.

The important point to appreciate is that the universe is an undivided whole and can be so *only if it is experiential in nature*, for only an experience can hold together a multiplicity in a true unity. But we habitually misconstrue the world by fragmenting it in our thoughts and feelings into discrete, nonexperiential bits and pieces radically separate from one another. Unlike trees rooted in the soil, we human beings are free to wander about our environments and stake out our little patches. Moreover, being endowed with nervous systems that help define our interiors and surfaces with sensations of various kinds, including pleasures and pains, we very naturally distinguish our bodies sharply from the rest of the world. All this provides the groundwork for highly developed conceptual, linguistic, social, economic, legal, political, scientific, philosophical, and religious ways of carving up the world and setting ourselves apart from it and one another.

This, at least, is one version of the story, and an oft-told story it is too, set forth in the spiritual writings of several cultures, reinvigorated and disseminated by the Romantics, and repeated in modern times with varying degrees of competence by teachers of nonduality. It is sometimes expressed in rather abstract terms but is brought vividly to life by accounts of mystical experience that give a sense of what it is like to apprehend the universe as it truly is, a highly differentiated but nonetheless undivided whole.

How, then, might the world look if the veils of habit, mental distraction, and separative, dualistic mindset were to lift? What kind of perceptual, intellectual, and emotional transformations would clarified engagement with the world bring? Hints can be found in modern-day reports of extraordinary experiences in which barriers between self and world melt away. Surveys have suggested that feelings of unity with the natural world are fairly common. In Andrew Greeley's 1973 US survey, one person in ten had known "a sense of the unity of everything and my own part in it."[9] In a 1987 UK survey, one in twenty reported "experiencing that all things are one."[10] However, studies of this kind have not inquired into the depth and intensity of the feelings, and it is likely that many such experiences are mild compared with the rather dramatic instances I cite below. These examples will illustrate some common features of the more intense experiences but also bring out significant differences. In particular, it is noticeable that some experiences involve perceptual transformations of comparatively limited extent, restricted to the immediate surroundings, whereas others seem to bring expansions of much greater scope and even shifts of consciousness out of the body. Although it is difficult to place these varied experiences into neat categories, a useful distinction can be made between transformed perceptions of the world that continue to draw on the ordinary senses ("sensate") and those that seem to reach beyond the senses ("trans-sensate"). By withdrawing from sensory perception of the world, by turning "inward" so to speak, one can find the world again but in a "richer manner" as Traherne put it, recalling his own discovery of the universe within the soul.

To See the World Anew

Transfigured perceptions of the natural world often take place when some influence works to quieten or interrupt the restless activity of the mind. Ordinarily, the flow of consciousness is made turbulent by eddies of thoughts and feelings, but sometimes the stream becomes calm, and the normally sharp distinctions between self and other relax to some extent. Meditative practices can have this tranquillizing and unifying effect, but frequently it occurs without any special intention or effort, brought about, for example, by exposure to some object or scene, often beautiful, that draws the attention in a gentle, absorbing way. For instance, the focus of attention might be a flower, tree, animal, crystal, mountain, water wave, cloud, patch of sunlight, work of art, or musical performance; typical scenes include the countryside, mountains, coast, sunrise and sunset, and the night sky.

William Blake scholar and poet Kathleen Raine (1908–2003) recounts such an experience. One quiet evening, Raine was sitting by a table at which she would write her poems. She was looking at a hyacinth on the table, and, as she gazed at the petals and "eye-like hearts" of the flowers, she suddenly experienced a shift in consciousness:

> I found that I was no longer looking *at* it, but *was* it; a distinct, indescribable, but in no way vague, still less emotional, shift of consciousness into the plant itself. Or rather I and the plant were one and indistinguishable; as if the plant were a part of my consciousness. I dared scarcely to breathe,

held in a kind of fine attention in which I could sense the very flow of life in the cells. I was not perceiving the flower but living it. I was aware of the life of the plant as a slow flow or circulation of a vital current of liquid light of the utmost purity. . . . There was nothing emotional about this experience which was, on the contrary, an almost mathematical apprehension of a complex and organized whole, apprehended *as* a whole. This whole was living; and as such inspired a sense of immaculate holiness. Living form—that is how I can best name the essence or soul of the plant. . . . The experience lasted for some time—I have no idea how long—and I returned to dull common consciousness with a sense of diminution. I had never before experienced the like, nor have I since in the same degree; and yet it seemed at the time not strange but infinitely familiar, as if I were experiencing at last things as they are, was where I belonged, where in some sense, I had always been and would always be. That almost continuous sense of exile and incompleteness of experience which is, I suppose, the average human state, was gone like a film from sight.[11]

Here Raine describes some common features of this type of experience: unity, enhanced attention and perception, a special luminosity, vitality, the novelty of the occurrence yet its underlying familiarity, as if the condition were a natural but forgotten state.

A benevolent, loving, or compassionate attitude also encourages the experiences, as the following case illustrates, again involving a plant:

I was standing at my kitchen sink one evening, looking at the various plants I have on the window-sill, one of which is a spider plant. I was feeling particularly pleased about it because I had managed to salvage it from a much larger one, which had given up the ghost after my mother died.

I began to mentally praise it, when I suddenly became aware that there was a wonderful feeling coming out from the plant and I felt that it was 'loving' me. In fact, I felt that I became it and it became me and that we were all one with the universe. We seemed to be surrounded with 'waves' of 'love', which is the only way I can describe the feeling. It lasted about half a minute and was like nothing else I have ever experienced.[12]

In this account, there is no mention of any perceptual expansion (such as Raine's visual sense of the inner life of the plant), but strong feelings of unity and love are reported.

Sometimes the experiences follow periods of unhappiness and searching, and perhaps look back to an earlier, more unified way of experiencing the world known in childhood, in line with the Romantic perspective. Anne Bancroft (b. 1923), author of several books on spirituality and mysticism, recalls that in her early years she had been aware of a wonder and mystery in nature and also a meaning that she could not grasp, a meaning that had something to do with "belonging to the world" and the feeling of a presence in the fields and woods. At the age of sixteen, she withdrew from this side of herself, partly in fear, partly as a result of attractions in the outer world, but then years later, at a time of dissatisfaction and depression, she began to have glimpses again, first a blackbird seen with new significance and reality, and shortly afterward a flower:

> One evening I was looking at a branch of rhododendron which I had put in a vase. As I looked, enjoying its beauty but without any purpose in my mind, I suddenly felt a sense of communication with it, as though it and I had become one. It seemed to come from my forehead and the feeling was immeasurably happy and strong. It came to me then that the whole mystery of existence – that mystery which I was so aware of in my childhood – was not far away from me but very close at hand. And that somehow the secret lay in my relationship with everything about me. That strange sense of oneness with the rhododendron seems to have come about because I was still, and not wanting anything, and therefore somehow free to see it properly and know it as itself.[13]

Here Bancroft describes a unity, a joyful oneness with a beautiful object in her vicinity. She links the new way of seeing with her childhood sense of mystery. She was left with a desire to know everything in this way, to gaze and listen with a loving openness to all of life. Another experience followed several days later:

> It was in the morning and I switched on the wireless to hear a concert. As the first note of music sounded, there was an almost audible click in my mind and I found that everything was transformed. I was in a different state of consciousness altogether. It was as though the separate feeling of 'me' which we all feel had gone, clicked away, and instead there was a great sense of clarity, of utter beneficent, wonderful emptiness. And in that emptiness there were no barriers. The stones on the road were exquisitely beautiful and as significant as a person. An upright, old-fashioned bicycle propped up by the road was wonderfully funny. It was as though my mind could now embrace, without reserve, all that it encountered whether people or animals or things, because it was living in clearness and emptiness.[14]

This condition of unity, clarity, and "emptiness" faded after three days, and Bancroft was left "desolate" by the loss, but it gave her the impetus to explore further, and she became attracted to Buddhist teachings and practice aimed at revealing things in their "suchness" (*tathatā*), in their actuality.

A similar story of adolescent alienation and recovery in a unifying perception that embraced all things is told by Flora Courtois (1916–2000). As a small child, she had felt in "magic communion with other living things," but by her teenage years she had grown self-conscious, nervous, isolated, and wrapped up in the need to be liked by her peers.[15] At sixteen, while under ether, she experienced a "whirling spiral of light," the center of which promised to bring complete understanding as it approached. Then, from seventeen, Courtois went through a period of doubt and restless searching, although she was to gain some relief and direction from a unitive experience:

> Standing at the kitchen window one day, and looking out at where a path wound under some maple trees, I suddenly saw the scene with a freshness and clarity that I'd never seen before. Simultaneously, as though for the first time, I fully realized I was not only on the earth but of it, an intimate part and product of it.[16]

Now she became intent on finding reality in the immediacy of sensation, a secret quest that brought further isolation and some "messianic" impulses, with the attendant danger that she would go off the rails. But her solitary efforts did have results. One day, gazing at her desk with a mind clear of thoughts, she experienced a momentary turnaround in her experience of the world:

> The small, pale green desk at which I'd been so thoughtlessly gazing had totally and radically changed. It appeared now with a clarity, a depth of three-dimensionality, a freshness I had never imagined possible. At the same time, in a way that is utterly indescribable, all my questions and doubts were gone as effortlessly as chaff in the wind. I knew everything and all at once, yet not in the sense that I had ever known anything before.[17]

Over the next few months, the new way of perceiving things (which Courtois called "Open Vision") developed further, bringing a release of tension and a joyous unity with the universe:

> It was as if, before all this occurred, "I" had been a fixed point inside my head looking out at a world out there, a separate and comparatively flat

world. The periphery of awareness had now come to light, yet neither fixed periphery nor center existed as such. A paradoxical quality seemed to permeate all existence. Feeling myself centered as never before, at the same time I knew the whole universe to be centered at every point. Having plunged to the center of emptiness, having lost all purposefulness in the old sense, I had never felt so one-pointed, so clear and decisive. Freed from separateness, feeling one with the universe, everything including myself had become at once unique and equal. If God was the word for this Presence in which I was absorbed, then everything was either holy or nothing; no distinction was possible. All was meaningful, complete as it was, each bird, bud, midge, mole, atom, crystal, of total importance in itself. As in the notes of a great symphony, nothing was large or small, nothing of more or less importance to the whole. I now saw that wholeness and holiness are one.[18]

The clear perception and equalizing comprehension, which involved a sense of the eternal in the present moment and a greater sensitivity to the sufferings of others, had suffused into everyday life, but it appears to have faded to some extent as Courtois became involved in graduate psychology studies. After many years, however, she came into contact with Zen meditation, which enabled her to reconnect with her earlier experience and place it in the context of a religious tradition that could help her to understand what had happened.

Expansions of Consciousness

The experiences described above brought significant transformations of consciousness, yet they retained some continuity with the everyday way of perceiving the world. Perceptions of objects, such as Raine's hyacinth and Bancroft's rhododendron, were clarified or augmented in some way, through heightened awareness, unity, knowledge, luminosity, or love, but the perceptions by and large continued to be organized from the usual vantage point, and there was no loss of sensory contact with the environment. Sometimes the experiences involve more dramatic transformations, including what appear to be immense expansions of consciousness and even displacements of awareness, as if the perceptual vantage point has moved out of the body. In some cases, the experiences occur when normal visual contact with the world has been excluded because the eyes have been closed or waking consciousness has been lost through sleep or trauma.

Simple Expansions

In the following example, a woman experienced a cosmic expansion of consciousness, bringing a unity of mind and universe that challenged her "atheist and materialist" outlook:

> It came upon me in the form of a mood, growing in intensity until it took hold of me completely. Although fully aware that my consciousness was undergoing a considerable change I was, all the same, quite unable to control the situation.
>
> It was as though my mind broke bounds and went on expanding until it merged with the Universe. Mind and universe became *one within the other*. Time ceased to exist.
>
> It was all one thing and in a state of infinity. It was as if, willy-nilly, I became directly exposed to an entity within myself and nature at large.
>
> I seemed to be "seeing" with another sight in another world.
>
> This event left an impressive afterglow which lasted many days but, eventually, it faded away as mysteriously as it had come. The familiar world returned.[19]

Some details of the account are open to interpretation, but it appears that the woman's consciousness became one with the universe, and that this universal consciousness was the "entity" that she discovered both in herself and in the world in general, conferring upon her a form of perception very different from the familiar way of seeing things.

A man became convinced of "the oneness of the cosmos" as a result of two unusual experiences. In the less expansive one, he felt as though "his real self were as much in the surrounding natural scene" as in his own physical body, and he found that the world about him was "suffused with an unnatural brilliance and vitality." In the other experience, his self was even more expansive:

> It was a slightly frosty night and the sky was very clear. On such nights I was in the habit of ranging the sky for the few constellations I could recognize. On reaching the particular spot something happened which I am sure I shall find great difficulty in describing. If you can imagine yourself not as a photographic flash bulb but as the light from that bulb and that the light is sentient, that is the nearest I can get to explaining how I felt at that moment. I was perfectly conscious of where I was and of my immediate physical surroundings, but for that brief moment it was as though my

whole self was able to expand to and encompass the furthermost star. It was an influx of a certain knowledge in that one flash, that somewhere in the make-up of the cosmos is a factor which transcends time and distance.[20]

Such expansions of consciousness and self are sometimes expressed in terms of an enlargement of the body, and of the head in particular, presumably because the head is the part of the body most readily associated with seeing, knowing, self, and mind. For example, Karl Kunst described an expansion induced by ingestion of morning glory seeds:

all of a sudden I felt that there was an inward explosion, kind of, in the Self. And it felt like all the pieces of the "I" were rushing away from each other at an incredible rate, until they filled all space. And then it stopped! It was this tremendous "whoosh," and then everything was quiet, and there it was, you know, kind of hanging, this tremendous expanded state. . . . All I can say is that my head felt like it was 30,000 miles across, embracing everything.[21]

Despite the enormous self-expansion, awareness of the surroundings was not lost: "I saw the room absolutely clearly, and saw everyone clearly."[22]

Children, more so than adults, are likely to express their expansions of consciousness in bodily terms, rather than employ the less concrete vocabulary of "consciousness" and "mind." A woman who had been prone to unusual experiences from an early age recalled the following phenomenon:

I would at night sometimes wake up to feel what I called a huge bigness, when I seemed to stretch and be very, very big, as big as all England or even bigger. It made me feel nervous, and I would try to fight my way back to littleness, and make the sensation stop. It was frightening. My head seemed to go outside my skull, and feel magnetic and dense and enormously big, perhaps sixty miles or so all around me, even down into the earth. I knew I was on my bed, and only me and my body, and yet this hugeness was certainly also me, but with no edge.[23]

In itself, the experience described here is fairly basic, consisting solely of the feeling of "head" expansion and the anxiety it would bring, and it may not be the kind of consciousness expansion that concerns us here. However, the author describes other unusual experiences, some of which may indicate a tendency toward genuine mystical experience. From the age of seven, she found that she could see a sparkling luminosity if she looked at objects in a particular way, by gently staring at them. Rocks would begin to "shimmer and tremble"; grass would appear brighter. She found this "special looking" relatively pleasant and could stop it whenever she wanted. Many years later, she read a book about LSD and came to the opinion that the drug can produce similar effects.

She would also sometimes hear a frightening noise, a "clanging" or "hum" in her ears, as if a "cosmic dynamo" were creating "primal music" in her head. The noise would bring with it a loss of the ordinary sense of self. She would resist this feeling because she found it unpleasant, indeed even more frightening than the sense of "hugeness." But beyond these strange and disconcerting experiences, there was one she really valued, which she called "a kind of insight," an experience of "intense reality and knowing," a feeling of seeing and knowing things as they are "underneath appearances":

> I saw the ordinary world very clearly and in infinite detail, and knew it to be all joined up, and all made of one substance or life force, which force whipped up the poles of duality: this produced electricity and polarity, and thus was formed every atom and every material thing. I could see how we all are one substance and interdependent, and all joined: and how in reality nothing has a fixed immovable edge or skin, but all things merge into their surroundings.[24]

These experiences of insight and nonduality, which seemed to be the "least dependent on the senses," became more frequent as she grew older. Indeed, she acquired the ability to access them whenever she pleased, "entering at will into the rolling awareness of the unity and edgelessness of reality," as she beautifully put it.

Displacements from the Body

Expansions of consciousness are sometimes accompanied by apparent shifts out of the body. These are not ordinary out-of-body experiences, for they involve some kind of unity, such as the feeling that everything is contained within. For instance, in another case of "head" expansion, a young girl observed her reclining body:

> It was a hot summer evening. I lay on the lawn in the back garden trying to get cool. The sun had almost set and I watched the planets appear. Suddenly I felt my head swelling. It seemed to increase in size until it contained

the whole world: all the stars too. Everything that had ever happened or would happen was within myself. I was in my eighth year at the time, so knew little of history and nothing of religion. I saw many things, events I later learned about, also much I have as yet been unable to discover from any physical source. After what seemed untold ages I became aware of my mother telling me to come inside. There was a brief glimpse of my body lying on the grass with my mother bending over it. Then I was awake feeling very bewildered. It was some time before I recovered.[25]

There seems to have been a displacement of the center of perception into the environment, for the girl was able to observe her body on the grass. Note also that the expansion of consciousness appears to have had a temporal as well as a spatial dimension, for the girl found that she now included in herself all events, everything that had happened and would happen.

In another case of out-of-body displacement and expansion, it was as if consciousness exited through the top of the head:

> One afternoon while I was at home alone, just relaxing, I started thinking about the universe, how big it must be, perhaps never ending. I was wondering about that. How could something never end? Suddenly, it was as if a funnel was in the top of my head and my consciousness went out into it, spreading wider and wider as it went. This went on for quite some time until I suddenly realized that I was conscious of everything that is, and that I was part of it all. Then I became aware of it from a different aspect. I was everything that is.[26]

This out-of-head shift of consciousness was clearly not an ordinary out-of-body experience, for it brought a feeling of unity with the universe, which is not typical of run-of-the-mill out-of-body experiences. In a similar vein, a girl aged eleven or twelve felt that she came to know everything after "something" shot out of herself and momentarily expanded:

> Suddenly something seemed to whip from me as though shot by a bow; it whizzed up to the sky, exploded and pieces shot back. That is how I remember the experience; and how I thought at the time something that mystics often think: if I could remember what I knew then, I'd know everything.[27]

In these last two cases, the shift out of the body preceded the great expansion of consciousness, perhaps indicating that embodiment ordinarily imposes limitations on consciousness. The idea that perceptions are restricted by embodiment, by the "veil of flesh," is an old idea that will surface again when some historical reports of near-death experience are raised in chapter 5.

Expansions Beyond the Senses

Sometimes the expansions of consciousness take place when visual contact with the environment has been left behind, as for instance when the eyes have been closed or during the apparent "unconsciousness" of near-death emergencies. My own experience, described in the next chapter, was of this type, for it took place when I was asleep and therefore when sensory contact with my surroundings had been greatly reduced. Another experience of this kind is described by H. Warner Allen (1881–1968), journalist, wine expert, and crime writer.[28] Approaching the age of fifty, Allen realized that he had not found any "pattern or rational purpose" in life, and he vaguely supposed that the mystery had to remain unsolved for interest in life's adventure to continue. The rationalization was to prove unsatisfactory, for the appearance of a very bright light in a dream began a period of introspection that led "through paths of unforeseen darkness and danger."[29] Within a year, an answer to his searching emerged in the form of a momentary experience that took place when he closed his eyes at a concert:

> Rapt in Beethoven's music, I closed my eyes and watched a silver glow which shaped itself into a circle with a central focus brighter than the rest. The circle became a tunnel of light proceeding from some distant sun in the heart of the Self. Swiftly and smoothly I was borne through the tunnel and as I went the light turned from silver to gold. There was an impression of drawing strength from a limitless sea of power and a sense of deepening peace. The light grew brighter, but was never dazzling or alarming. I came to a point were time and motion ceased. In my recollection it took the shape of a flat-topped rock, surrounded by a summer sea, with a sandy pool at its foot. The dream scene vanished and I am absorbed in the Light of the Universe, in Reality glowing like fire with the knowledge of itself, without ceasing to be one and myself, merged like a drop of quicksilver in the Whole, yet still separate as a grain of sand in the desert. The peace that passes all understanding and the pulsating energy of creation are one in the centre in the midst of conditions where all opposites are reconciled.[30]

Allen distinguished three stages of the experience and its aftermath. The first, the event itself—"Union with God" or "Mystic Union" as Allen came to call it—was instantaneous, a "timeless moment" seemingly interposed between two notes of Beethoven's Seventh Symphony. The second stage, "Illumination," was the immediate reaction to the experience, consisting of a "*wordless* stream of complex feelings," with thoughts beginning to take form in a chaotic fashion. Allen attempted to convey a sense of these "dawning thoughts" in a series of exclamations:

> Something has happened to me—I am utterly amazed—can this be that? (*That* being the answer to the riddle of life)—but it is too simple—I always knew it—it is remembering an old forgotten secret—like coming home—I am not "I", not the "I" I thought—there is no death—peace passing under-standing—yet how unworthy I——[31]

Lastly, there followed "Enlightenment," the considered expression of the experience, the subsequent intellectual recollection expressed at leisure in words and images. It is, in effect, Allen's attempt to describe and understand the experience in his mystical trilogy *The Timeless Moment* (1946), *The Happy Issue* (1948), and *The Uncurtained Throne* (1951). Allen's core experience, in so far as it can be extracted from his descriptions, seems to have been an apprehension of the universe as a timeless whole in which knower and known are united and a higher identity is rediscovered, a greater Self that does not obliterate the individuality of the ordinary self.

David Spangler (b. 1945), spiritual thinker and early contributor to the Findhorn community in Scotland, also describes an experience of the universe in connection with the rediscovery of a higher identity. Again, the vision seems to have been independent of the usual sensory channels, in this case taking place after a shift of consciousness out of the body. At the age of seven, Spangler was sitting in the back of his parents' car on a shopping trip to Casablanca, "idly watching the scenery go by," when he suddenly experienced a peculiar form of out-of-body experience in which he was simultaneously outside his body and also around it, enclosing it within his expanding self:

> All at once I am filled with a feeling of energy coursing through my body and a sensation as if I am expanding like a balloon. Before I can think about what is happening, I find myself somehow outside my body but envelop-ing it. Looking down and in some fashion within at the same time, I see my physical form, my parents and our automobile, tiny objects rapidly shrinking out of view. When they are gone, I am alone in an unbroken field of white light.[32]

Spangler felt joy and release as he experienced a change in his understanding of self: he was reawakening to an identity that was one with the circumambient light and with creation. When the light cleared, he saw himself as a pattern of lives and experiences, both past and future, and experienced flashes of memory of previous births and deaths, which brought a sense of the "eternity of the soul." Then, after the pattern and the surrounding light had faded, Spangler felt a presence in which all things seemed to exist in oneness, love, power, and serenity. Taking on the perspective of this all-encompassing presence and momentarily becoming one with it, Spangler had a cosmic vision:

> As if a curtain were drawn aside, I had a visual impression of the universe, a great wheel of stars and galaxies, suffused with the golden glow of billions of suns, floating in a sea of spirit. It was as if I were seeing as this presence saw, and for one instant we were as one. In that instant, it was as if I were one with everything that existed, every atom, every stone, every world, every star, seeing creation not from some great distance but from the inside out as if it were my very body and being.[33]

There was also a sense of creative flow through everything, like music and dancers, creating unfolding and ever-changing patterns.

The experience developed a little further, with Spangler conscious of his intent to be born into his current life, and feeling love toward all the other beings who had made similar choices and are taking part in the cosmic drama. He then found himself back in his body, a seven-year-old boy staring out of a car window.

This-worldly Mysticism

The experiences described above differ from one another in various ways, but they have in common a new perception or understanding of the world through some combination of unity, knowledge, vision, and love, and several share the sense of return to a condition that has been lost or forgotten. In modern times, experiences of this kind have often been called "mystical."[34] The term derives from the Greek *muein*, to close one's mouth or eyes, hence the adjective *mustikos* (μυστικος, Latin *mysticos*), indicating lips sealed, and so to keep secrets. It seems that in the context of the ancient Mystery Religions, *mustikos* referred to the secrecy to which initiates were sworn: they were not to divulge the details of their rituals.[35] With the early

Church Fathers, "mystical" came to refer to the hidden meanings that can be extracted from the Bible by allegorical interpretation, particularly with regard to divine realities such as Christ and the Trinity, and the word came to be applied to the sacramental mystery of the Eucharist, and also to the experiential knowledge of God that Scripture has revealed. In modern times, "mystical" and "mysticism" have become ever more associated with the experiential dimension of religion, irrespective of any connection with revealed texts, and nowadays the term "mystical" is often applied to intense spiritual experiences characterized by one or more of the following:

- KNOWLEDGE—a sense of profound, intuitive knowledge
- UNITY—a sense of unity, oneness, wholeness
- REALITY—a sense of contact with deeper realities

However, there is no consistency or consensus over the use of the term. Some scholars have emphasized knowledge, others unity, and still others contact with deeper realities. For example, a textbook definition of mystical experience by Robert Ellwood highlights reality and unity, and the seeming directness of the experience:

> Mystical experience is experience in a religious context that is immediately or subsequently *interpreted* by the experiencer as a direct, unmediated encounter with ultimate divine reality. This experience engenders a deep sense of unity and suggests that during the experience the experiencer was living on a level of being other than the ordinary.[36]

There is no mention here of the sense of profound, intuitive knowledge, the "noetic quality" of mystical experience, and contact is said to be with "ultimate divine reality." I have offered a broader definition, one that does not limit contact to ultimate reality, and which has a place for the noetic quality:

> experiences are "mystical" if they bring a sense of deepened contact with reality, the contact consisting of unity or at least intimate connection or presence, and often an intuitive type of knowing.[37]

Contact here can be with aspects of reality that are not ultimate yet have a claim to be "real," such as the natural world, fellow human beings, other-worldly realms, and various spiritual entities.

Scholars tend to define mysticism to suit the specific traditions or mystics they are studying. For instance, Bernard McGinn, in a study of Christian mysticism, points out that if mystical experience is defined in terms of union or identity with God, then much of Christian mysticism would be excluded. He therefore prefers a weaker definition that refers to a consciousness of the *presence* of God, rather than union with God.[38] Several types of mystical experience have been distinguished. For example, R. C. Zaehner famously identified three types: *theistic* (union with the personal God); *monistic* (identity with the impersonal Absolute); *natural* (unity with the natural world).[39] He understood these to be distinct categories of mystical experience, but a case can be made for overlap between them. A natural mystical experience would also be a theistic one if the mystic sensed the presence of God in nature or felt unity with God as creator of the world. For example, a woman had been going through a period of deep, isolating depression when the scales fell from her eyes and she "saw the world as it truly was":

> It was as if the cocoon had burst and my eyes were opened and I saw the world was infinitely beautiful, full of light as if from an inner radiance. Everything was alive and God was present in all things, in fact the earth, all plants and animals and people seemed to be made of God. All things were one, and I was one with all creation and held safe within a deep love. I was filled with peace and joy and with a deep humility, and could only bow down in the holiness of the presence of God.[40]

Zaehner dogmatically asserted that mention of God's presence in such accounts must be an interpretative error on the part of the mystic, for he could not believe that God has a presence in nature, which in Zaehner's estimation is indifferent, inhospitable, purely material, devoid of God. Only in the theistic mystical experience, the type of mystical experience Zaehner valued, does the mystic really come into contact with God. Zaehner's negative attitude toward natural mystical experience was colored by his own acquaintance with it, for as a student at Oxford, in 1933, he had such an experience himself and found it to be in keeping with his outlook at the time, which was atheistic (this was prior to his conversion to Roman Catholicism in the 1940s).[41]

Over the years, mystical experiences of the natural world have been given a variety of names, including the following:

- nature mystical experience
- cosmic consciousness (R. M. Bucke and Edward Carpenter)
- objective mystical experience (W. R. Inge)
- unifying vision (Rudolf Otto)

- oceanic feeling (Romain Rolland and Sigmund Freud)
- natural or panenhenic mystical experience (R. C. Zaehner)
- extrovertive mystical experience (W. T. Stace)
- unitive mystical state (Robert K. C. Forman)

In academic contexts, Walter Stace's term *extrovertive mystical experience* is often used. Here "extrovertive"—literally "outward-turning"—refers to mystical experience that has the natural world as its object, contrasted with "introvertive" ("inward-turning") mystical experience, which Stace took to be a consciousness completely empty of contents, no sensations, no concepts, no feelings, just a pure consciousness. Stace's categorization of mystical experiences into these two types has its problems, and scholars often have difficulty reconciling it with the mystical traditions they study. In the past, I have often used "extrovertive mystical experience" as a convenient label for mystical experiences of the natural world. However, to avoid some of the confusions and assumptions that surround Stace's typology, including his claim that extrovertive experience is always directed "outward" through the sense organs, I shall introduce a slightly more elaborate classification better suited to the study of world-oriented mystical experiences. This classification will have the advantage of carrying no assumptions about the "outwardness" of such experiences, their dependence on sense organs. Let us suppose that mystical experiences can be *this-worldly* (T), *other-worldly* (O), *no-worldly* (N), or some combination (TO, TN, ON, TON).

1. *This-worldly mystical experience* (T): mystical experience of the natural world or some region or content of it, whether or not experienced through the familiar senses.

This category covers mystical experiences of the natural world, including experiences of limited range as well as the more expansive and cosmic experiences, and also experiences of ordinarily hidden entities considered to be part of the natural order, such as nature spirits. In this-worldly experiences, the world or some part of it is a focus of the mystical knowledge, unity, and sense of reality. The mystic may feel united with the world as a whole or with particular objects or beings within it, and may discern a unity and interconnectedness in the world. It may seem that everything is known and understood, including the meaning of it all. It can seem as if, at long last, the world is perceived as it truly is.

But mystics sometimes claim that they have experienced realms that are radically different from the one we ordinarily know:

2. *Other-worldly mystical experience* (O): mystical experience of a world or some its contents (e.g., places, beings, objects) fundamentally distinct from our familiar universe.

For instance, in philosophical traditions inspired by Plato, a firm distinction has often been made between the sensible universe and a higher, more perfect, intelligible world of Forms. Mystical experience of the latter would be an example of an exclusively other-worldly experience. But a combination of other-worldly and this-worldly contents in one experience is conceivable. If the Forms were apprehended as partly immanent in the natural world, then the experience would also have a this-worldly character. So too would an experience in which an other-worldly being was observed to operate in our world. There is, therefore, a category (TO) of experiences that may combine this-worldly and other-worldly elements. If such experience were so comprehensive that it encompassed all realms, this-worldly and other-worldly, it could be called *all-worldly mystical experience*. Such inclusive experience, taking in all realms—mundane, heavenly, and hellish—has sometimes been attributed to those highly realized beings who have attained omniscience in the full sense of the word, such as the liberated souls of the Jaina tradition.

By contrast, some mystical experiences are not centered on a world at all, neither this world nor another world, having instead as their object something that transcends all worlds, all systems, perhaps because it is the source or creator of those worlds:

3. *No-worldly mystical experience* (N): mystical experience of something beyond all worlds, this-worldly and other-worldly, and all their contents.

The "no-worldly" or "world-transcendent" category includes experiences of spiritual beings considered distinct from the world, such as the supreme God, Absolute, One, or Self of some religious traditions, if these experiences do not involve any sense of a world. The category also includes experiences deemed contentless or empty, such as the pure consciousness that Stace labeled "introvertive" and Robert Forman's "pure consciousness event." By definition, there is no sense of the world in these experiences: they are said to consist of an awareness that has no object, other than perhaps itself. It is open to debate whether certain states described in religious traditions are of the "pure consciousness" type. Among various possibilities, Forman mentions the condition of *turya* (or *turīya*) described in the *Upaniṣads*, a fourth state of consciousness beyond waking, dreaming, and deep sleep revealed by practices that encourage a withdrawal from thought, emotion, and sensation.[42]

Again, mixed experiences are conceivable, bringing together the seeming contraries of worldly and no-worldly experiences, with this-worldly or other-worldly contents experienced in conjunction with something that seems to transcend all realms. For example, some mystical experiences of the natural world bring the sense of presence of a transcendent reality. If one were to intuit a transcendent God, Self, or pure consciousness as partly immanent in the world or as the creative force behind it, or to feel simultaneously united with the world and in communion with its source, then the experience would combine this-worldly and no-worldly elements (TN). Likewise, an experience of the Neoplatonic realm of Forms emanated from its transcendent source, the One, would combine the other-worldly and the no-worldly (ON). The most encompassing experience would combine the all-worldly and the no-worldly (TON), with all realms (and perhaps all universes, if more than one should exist) experienced in relation to their creator, source, or ground. Such maximally inclusive experience has sometimes been attributed to the supreme deity and those who realize their unity with it.

Let us now look more closely at mystical experiences that have a pronounced this-worldly quality. Some commonly reported characteristics of these are listed in the Box, "This-worldly mystical experience." The experiences can be quite varied, with some exhibiting just two or three of the features listed, others showing many more characteristics and being rather complex in development. For instance, a simple experience might involve just unity with the immediate surroundings, a feeling of elation, and perhaps a special light that suffuses objects, whereas a more complex one (such as David Spangler's described above) might develop through several stages into, say, a vision of cosmic scope, all-encompassing love, the sense that everything is known and understood, and a transformed experience of time. Some this-worldly experiences also develop into no-worldly (N) experience or the mixed experiences in which the universe is experienced in relation to its creator or source (TN).

Several kinds of unity are described in reports of this-worldly mystical experience:[43]

- *integral* unity: the universe experienced as an unbroken whole, with no real gaps or empty spaces between things

The universe is found to be an undivided whole, a continuum, as the etymology of "universe" hints it is: *uni-versus*, all things "turned into one."

❧ This-worldly mystical experience ❧

UNITY: A feeling of unity with the world or some of its parts. Everything seems to be contained within. Things appear interconnected. A deep sense of community. Unity of world and its source.

SELF-EXPERIENCE: Boundaries that separate self from other persons, animals, plants, objects, even the entire cosmos, relax or melt away. It can seem that a greater self is discovered or rediscovered.

KNOWLEDGE: All-inclusive knowledge that fades when the experience ends. Understanding of the meaning of existence, life, and suffering, often difficult to recall afterward. Insights into the order, harmony, and life of the world, and the significance of love. The sense that everything is fundamentally "all right." A recognition that one has "come home." Occasionally an intuition of "other lives." Insights into the natural world.

LOVE: Powerful feelings of love and/or being deeply loved oneself.

BEAUTY: Objects are extraordinarily and equally beautiful.

MISCELLANEOUS FEELINGS: A variety of emotional feelings and reactions, some pleasant, some challenging, including joy, bliss, elation, peace, relief, gratitude, wonder, power, fearlessness, humor, surprise, insignificance, humility, unworthiness, awe, and discomfort with sheer intensity.

TIME-EXPERIENCE: Often lasts only seconds or minutes but seems a long time or has a "timeless" quality. Time seems to stop, or past, present, and future contained in an "eternal" moment. If flow of time persists, it can seem to do so in a harmonious fashion, as if the transforming world is a cosmic dance.

REALITY: It is felt that the world has been experienced as it is in reality, in its unity, wholeness, life, eternity, love, and rightness.

REALNESS: The experience feels very real, far more vivid than everyday experience. By comparison, the latter can seem unreal, flat, dreamlike.

LIFE: Everything is animated with "life," "consciousness," "energy," and things once thought living may now seem lifeless in comparison.

PRESENCE: Sense of a "presence" or "power" in the immediate vicinity or in nature in general.

ATTENTION: Heightened awareness of objects in the environment.

PERCEPTION: An obscuring light that fades, sometimes leaving enhanced vision of the environment. More often a light that is clear, or hazy but not totally obscuring. White and golden colors are common. The light can be indistinguishable from the knowledge, love, and bliss. Vision can seem to extend into and through things, even acquiring a cosmic reach. In contrast, auditory perception is more likely to diminish—a silence or "hush." Extrasensory and out-of-body perceptions.

BODY CHANGES: Sensations felt through the body or at places along the spine. Consciousness seems to leave the body, or the body itself seems to expand.

© Paul Marshall, 2005, p. 27, Table 1.1 (modified), from ch. 1, *Mystical Encounters with the Natural World: Experiences and Explanations*. By permission of Oxford University Press.

Experience of integral unity, of wholeness, provides an antidote to one of the basic misapprehensions characteristic of the "dualistic" frame of mind, namely "miscognition of the continuum as radically discontinuous" as I styled it above, or more simply, FRAGMENTATION. This tendency to fragment the world in our thoughts and feelings is challenged too by a more specialized unity described in some mystical accounts:

- *interconnective* unity: things observed to be linked by visible or invisible bonds or a common nature

For instance, objects that formerly appeared separate are now found to be joined by causal connections or networks of luminosity.

The other dualizing misapprehension highlighted above, "exclusive identification with a fragment," or EXCLUSIVE IDENTIFICATION for short, is undermined by further kinds of unity, those that transform sense of self by bringing "myself" and "not-myself" together in some profound way:

- *immersive* unity: experience of oneself as part of the whole
- *identificatory* unity: identification of the universe or some of its contents with oneself
- *incorporative* unity: experience of the universe or some its contents as internal to oneself
- *communal* unity: a sense of connection or kinship with others through mutual identity, empathy, love, community

Self no longer feels separate from nature and other selves, is no longer an isolated individual. Incorporative unity works to overcome a logical counterpart of exclusive identification, namely "miscognition of the rest of the universe as not oneself," or EXTERNALIZATION. If I am just this little being, then the rest of the universe is not I. It is external to self and consciousness. Incorporative unity challenges this view by placing the world internal to self and consciousness. I shall have more to say about the incorporative unity in the following section. Communal unity, often linked with love and compassion, is the most important of the unities from the viewpoint of ethics and spiritual development, and it will come to the fore in later chapters.

One further kind of unity also has implications for self-understanding:

- *source* unity: the universe and its contents, including oneself, experienced in unitive relation to their creator, ground, or source, whether God, the Absolute, the Self, or suchlike

This unity belongs to the "mixed" types of experiences I labeled TN and TON in my classification of experiences according to their this-worldly (T), other-worldly (O), and no-worldly (N) orientations. Note that many of the unities, source unity included, can be experienced simultaneously or sequentially over the course of one experience. For instance, it is possible to experience the world as an undivided whole (integral unity) and oneself as part of that whole (immersive unity), while at the same time intuiting that multiple things are linked together (interconnective unity) and derive from one's own essential nature (source unity). Even immersive and incorporative unities can occur together—one can feel oneself to be both a part of the whole and the whole itself, a "twofoldness" of self (see chapter 4).

The dualizing tendencies I have distinguished so far—fragmentation, exclusive identification, externalization—work in conjunction with one another and therefore are not independent: fragmentation of the whole is a precondition for exclusive identification with a fragment and its complement, externalization. They are all facilitated by another tendency, which again is challenged by mystical experience. This tendency can be called "nonrecognition of the experientiality of things," or NONEXPERIENTIALITY for short. In our everyday dealings with the world, we do not ordinarily stop to take note that what we have is *experience*. The world as we know it is a world of experience, of colors, sounds, flavors, emotions, thoughts. To lose sight of the experientiality of things is to create abstractions and ultimately concoct philosophies and sciences of nonexperiential matter, space, and time. In so doing, the unity that experience naturally brings is lost, for experience is able to hold together a multiplicity and variety of contents in a seamless whole. In summary, nonexperientiality encourages fragmentation, and fragmentation supports exclusive identification and externalization.

When I stated that this-worldly mystical experiences have the natural world as a mystical focus, I used the term "natural world" in a very broad sense to indicate the entire universe or any of its contents (fig. 1.1). The "natural world" and "nature" understood in this way cover not only untamed wilderness, mountain, desert, jungle, coast, sea and sky, but also the human realms of city, town and village, as well as transitional places between the two, such as gardens, parks and the countryside. It also includes human beings, at least in so far as they are considered to be part of the universe (I add this qualification because it is open to discussion whether human beings are entirely situated within the world: they may have a transcendent dimension too). Furthermore, nature in this comprehensive sense encompasses those domains that ordinarily go unperceived because they are too small or too far away, or are imperceptible for some other reason.

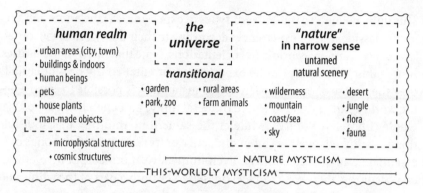

Figure 1.1 Broad sense of "nature"—the entire natural world, all objects and processes in the universe, including human beings and their works.

Admittedly, there is still considerable room for debate here. For one thing, modern cosmology entertains the idea of multiple universes or "the multiverse," but as long as these universes form one ordered whole they can be regarded as a single system, "the universe." It is also open to debate whether certain kinds of things should be regarded as this-worldly, as contents of the universe, or as other-worldly, as contents of some other realm of reality. For example, we can ponder whether numbers should be regarded as fully part of the universe or as having some other-worldly existence, say, as ideas or archetypes in a "Platonic" mathematical realm. Similarly, questions can be raised about whether certain intelligible, heavenly, or imaginal realms described in religious literature or encountered in altered states (including out-of-body and near-death experiences) should be regarded as distinct, other-worldly realities or as ordinarily unperceived regions of the familiar universe. Understood very broadly, "universe" as an all-encompassing term might include such "other-worldly" entities and realms; understood more narrowly, "universe" would exclude them. The distinction between "this-worldly" and "other-worldly" has its problems.

This-worldly mystical experiences do not necessarily take place amid beautiful or awe-inspiring nature scenery, that is, amid "nature" in the narrow sense. They are not limited to the "communing with nature" type of experience often associated with Wordsworth and the Romantics (so-called nature mysticism). Certainly, very many this-worldly experiences do take place in beautiful nature scenery or in the transitional zones of countryside, park, and garden, but more generally the circumstances are quite varied. They range from calm states of mind facilitated by natural beauty and contemplative techniques to chemically induced disruption of brain processes and to distressed states of mind:

- scenic nature
- psychological distress
- concern, compassion, love
- thoughts about profound matters
- spiritual practices, including meditation
- literature, art

- music, dance
- sleep
- lovemaking
- childbirth
- near-death emergencies
- psychedelics & dissociative anesthetics
- mental and physical illness[44]

If scenic nature is the most commonly reported circumstance, psychological distress is probably the second. The experiences often occur during times of suffering, whether worry, depression, existential angst, bereavement, moments of crisis, or when a prayer for help is uttered. It can seem as if the experience intervenes to bring some relief or to show a way out of the difficulty, perhaps by placing the troubling matter in perspective or by giving insight into the meaning of suffering, or by pointing to a new way of relating to the world.[45] Scenic nature and psychological distress sometimes work together: a tense state of mind in combination with exposure to the uplifting or calming influence of nature may lead to a mystical expansion. Perhaps the most controversial circumstances are lovemaking, psychoactive drugs, and mental and physical illnesses. Some scholars fear that if they admit that mystical experiences take place in such circumstances, then mysticism will be explained away by skeptics as mere sexual elation or disturbed brain chemistry. However, these reductive conclusions are not inevitable: it is possible that sex, drugs, and illnesses, like some other circumstances, facilitate the experiences because they work to break down the psychological and biological barriers that ordinarily reduce contact with deeper realities, for instance, by interrupting the flow of distracted thought.

The aftereffects of the experiences also show some variation. At the very least, persons find the experiences memorable. They are not easily forgotten, at least in broad outline, and for some, the experiences are the most significant happenings in their lives. In some cases, the impact seems to be negligible, but in other cases—particularly with the more powerful experiences—there are significant consequences, very similar to those reported of near-death experiences. Immediate aftereffects can include heightened perceptions, and feelings of unity, love, happiness, and peace, that last for minutes, hours, and even weeks. Surprise and puzzlement are common.

Although this-worldly mystical experiences are generally positive, they can, like other unusual or intense experiences, bring problems. The experiences can be disturbing, leading to difficult emotions, confusion, eccentric

interpretations, and self-inflation or deflation. The more intense and prolonged experiences can be particularly challenging, especially when the
experiences come to an end. After the blissful state of unity, knowledge, and
love, the return to everyday limitations can feel like imprisonment or a fall
from heaven. There can be feelings of loss and depression, and a longing for
the experience to return. There can be a sense of isolation from others, who
more likely than not will fail to understand if told about the experience. It
may be feared, with good reason, that others will think one mad, or it may be
felt that such experiences are too private and precious to discuss openly—to
talk about them would be to devalue and disempower them. Sometimes the
experiences stimulate interest in philosophy, religion, and mysticism. They
can lead to the conviction that the depths of reality were glimpsed, and to
beliefs in the fundamental "all-rightness" of the world and the importance
of love, and they can act as a spur toward humanitarian concern and action.

Historically, there has at times been a link between mystical experience
and a radical sociopolitical outlook, and this has been true of the this-
worldly variety—which is not to say that mysticism cannot be conservative,
self-absorbed, and blind to social issues. "To see the world as it truly is"
involves rather more than heightened attention and vivid, sparkling colors.
The "clarified perceptions" of this-worldly mystical experience can include
equalizing revelations about self and other, a realization of loving communion with others, nonhuman as well as human, a discovery of profound
mutuality, encouraging deep empathy and a sensitivity to the numerous ways
in which the conditions of society, economics, and politics can work against
equality and love. In this manner, mystical vision has the power to inspire
and expand social and political vision, as appears to have been the case for
some Romantic thinkers in whom radical politics and mystical tendencies
came together, including Blake and Shelley. Perhaps Shelley's radicalism
was driven in part by an epiphany during his school days: estranged from
and victimized by his fellows, he experienced release in a vision of Beauty
manifest in nature, a revelatory moment and a revolutionary call that apparently inspired the youngster to dedicate himself to the pursuit of beauty,
justice, and freedom.[46]

Infinitely Wide on the Inside

This-worldly mystical experiences often take place without any break in
sensory contact with the world, but it seems that they can also occur when
such contact has been left behind. Whereas Raine and Bancroft maintained

sensory awareness of their surroundings during their experiences, Allen and Spangler appear to have had their cosmic visions after a disengagement from visual contact with their environments. Stace assumed that mystical experiences of the natural world invariably take place through the senses, "with the eyes open," but it seems that some of the more expansive ones, the truly cosmic mystical experiences, are more likely to occur when sensory input has been shut out. Allen had withdrawn from visual contact with the world by closing his eyes, yet he seemed to make contact with the world again at a deeper level, now experienced as a luminous whole. Spangler expanded upward and outward from his body and then had his visual field filled with white light before his cosmic experience commenced. Thus, it should be emphasized that although this-worldly experiences are extrovertive in *content*, they can be introvertive in *circumstance* or *method*. The introvertive exclusion of everyday perception and cognition can lead to all-encompassing cosmic experience. It seems that the world without can be found by turning within: "interiorization is universalization," to paraphrase Pierre Hadot on the contemplative withdrawal to the self advocated by certain ancient philosophers, Platonic and Stoic.[47] In the Indian sphere, the encounter with the universe in the self was expressed at an even earlier date in the *Chāndogya Upaniṣad*, perhaps as early as the seventh century BCE:

> As vast as the space here around us is this space within the heart, and within it are contained both the earth and the sky, both fire and wind, both the sun and the moon, both lightning and stars. What belongs here to this space around us, as well as what does not—all that is contained within it.[48]

In the human heart there is a small space that contains everything, a space that is the true, imperishable self or soul (*ātman*).

Thomas Traherne gives personal testimony to the interior discovery of the world through a withdrawal from sense perception:

> When I retire first I seem to com in my selfe to a centre, in that centre I find Eternitie and all its Riches. By leav[ing] things as they Stand without, I find them within in a richer Manner.[49]

Being akin to God, the soul is infinitely wide on the inside, with all things perceptible within. Traherne understands this inward apprehension of the world to be the more natural, original form of perception, a divine way of seeing that predates sensory vision. It is liable to be covered over as we grow up and are corrupted by the ways of the world:

Till custom and Education had bred the Difference: it was as obvious to
me to see all within us, as It was without. As easy and as natural to be
Infinitly wide on the Inside, and to see all Kingdoms Times and persons
within my Soul, as it is now to see them in the open world. Nay verily it
was more natural, for there was a comprehensiv Spirit, before ther was an
Eye. And my Soul being Like him, did first expect to find all things in it
Selfe, before it learned to See them without it.[50]

In chapter 6, I shall suggest that the "inward" type of perception is indeed the
more fundamental of the two, and that our everyday "outward," sensory type
of perception is a *specialized* form of the inward one. The world we ordinarily take to be outside ourselves is in fact our interior universe apprehended
dimly and very incompletely through representations mediated by the bodily
senses. All perceptions are actually inward. Within the mind there exists
the entire universe, including the body's sense organs and all the objects to
which they provide sensory access.

It may, then, be appropriate to distinguish types of this-worldly mystical
experience according to their mode of contact with the world:

1. *Sensate:* sensory experience of the environment is maintained,
   often transfigured by a special unity, clarity, depth, or luminous
   quality (e.g., Bancroft).
2. *Trans-sensate:* the universe is perceived in a way that seems to
   be independent of the ordinary senses (e.g., Allen).

Some this-worldly mystical experiences appear to be a blend of the above
two types. Sensory contact with the everyday world is maintained, but there
is also a more expansive or penetrating mode of perception alongside it:

3. *Mixed:* sensory contact with the environment persists, transfigured in some way, but supplemented by what seems to be a
   trans-sensory form of awareness of the world.

For example, Gopi Krishna recounts an experience in which perception of his
immediate environment, transfigured by a silvery luminosity, was retained
alongside a vastly expanded awareness of the universe that brought with it
a sense of higher identity:

Although linked to the body and surroundings I had expanded in an
indescribable manner into a titanic personality, conscious from within of

an immediate and direct contact with an intensely conscious universe, a wonderful inexpressible immanence all around me. My body, the chair I was sitting on, the table in front of me, the room enclosed by walls, the lawn outside and the space beyond, including the earth and sky appeared to be most amazingly mere phantoms in this real, interpenetrating and all pervasive ocean of existence which, to explain the most incredible part of it as best I can, seemed to be simultaneously unbounded, stretching out immeasurably in all directions, and yet no bigger than an infinitely small point.[51]

The passage is open to interpretation, but it may describe dual contents, with sensory perception of the transient world transfigured and resting in a vision of an eternal universe, the "ocean of existence." Gopi Krishna had difficulty describing this ocean, for it was at the same time cosmically vast and infinitely small, perhaps like the luminous Self (ātman) of the Upaniṣads, the space within the heart that is smaller than a mustard seed or millet kernel, yet larger than earth and sky (Chāndogya Upaniṣad, 3.14). As a tiny point, this oceanic self was experienced as a source that radiated the world of phenomenal experience, a projected "material world" that had the appearance of a mere "layer of foam" on the "ocean of life," the "mighty universe" of consciousness on which it floats.[52]

An experience described by Irina Starr might also be of the mixed type, with sensory experience maintained alongside a special faculty of vision, although here there is no sense of the cosmic expansiveness that marks Gopi Krishna's experience:

Everything around me had come to life in some wondrous way and was lit from within with a moving, living radiance. It was somewhat as it must be with one blinded, whose vision is restored. I was obviously seeing with vision other than the purely physical, but what I saw did not conflict with what my ordinary vision registered . . . . I saw objects in the ordinary way as well as with some extraordinary extension of the visual faculty; I saw into them with an inner vision and it was this inner sight which revealed the commonplace objects around me to be of the most breathtaking beauty.[53]

It is also possible that Flora Courtois's experience, noted above, belongs to the mixed category, for she mentions an "inner vision" connected with but distinguishable from her ordinary sight. It is interesting that Courtois describes this mode of awareness as omnidirectional, a "spherical" or "panoramic" kind of perception that will receive attention in chapter 5:

It was as if some inner eye, some ancient center of awareness, which extended equally and at once in all directions without limit and which had been there all along, had been restored. This inner vision seemed to be anchored in infinity in a way that was detached from immediate sight and, yet at the same time, had a profound effect on sight.[54]

The experiences of Starr and Courtois are unusual not only for the power of dual vision they appear to have conferred. Whereas most experiences last for only seconds, minutes, or hours, theirs continued for much longer, Starr's persisting for four days and Courtois's considerably longer.

I present the sensate–trans-sensate distinction as only a makeshift attempt at classification, one that will probably have to be refined if it is to deal adequately with the full range of world-oriented mystical experiences that have been reported. It is likely that a satisfactory classification will emerge only when the nature of these mystical perceptions (and our everyday perceptions too) is better understood. In the meantime, attempts at classification will be tentative, and care should be taken in assigning mystical experiences to this or that category. It is very easy to go astray in classifying mystical experiences. For example, in *Mystical Encounters*, I took an experience described by John Franklin to be an example of extrovertive (that is, this-worldly) mystical experience, but it turns out that his experience cannot be straightforwardly regarded as such.[55] John informs me that although he felt "'one' with everything," it was not a feeling of unity with nature or with the universe as ordinarily understood. Rather, he felt "translated into a different world or milieu," the details of which he cannot recollect, but which was very different from the universe we ordinarily know.[56] Perception there did not depend on the physical senses, and so the experience was certainly not of the sensate this-worldly type. It may not even have been trans-sensate this-worldly, for there was no sense of contact with the universe as ordinarily understood, and so may have been other-worldly.

I am, however, able to provide one example of mystical experience that was trans-sensate and had a strong this-worldly character. My own mystical experience, which occurred when sensory contact with the world had been left behind in sleep, appeared to give me unprecedented vision and knowledge of the universe.

2

The Land Beyond the Sea

> Only when we awake do we know it was a dream.
> By and by comes the Great Awakening,
> And then we find this life is the Great Dream.
>
> —Zhuangzi

ONE MORNING IN THE EARLY 1980s, I awoke from sleep and felt an almost inexpressible afterglow of emotion and meaning. The feeling, which had something to do with "wholeness," seemed to be connected with events in a dream. Standing on a sandy beach by the edge of the sea, I was pulled with tremendous force across the waters, as if toward a land beyond the horizon. On waking, I remembered the dream and realized there was a connection between the extraordinary feeling and the irresistible pull across the sea, but I had no inkling of the destination. In time, details returned to me: it was as if a traveler had taken photographs on a visit to a distant land, and these, viewed after an interval of weeks, brought back the marvelous sights of a forgotten country. However, the land beyond the sea was no *terra incognita*, no remote or irrelevant condition beyond human concern. Rather, it was the universe in which we live, the everyday world, but understood as a whole.

It is remarkable that the moment in my life when I have felt most awake and alive should have occurred while I was asleep. It is also remarkable that the details of an event of such personal significance should have been so easily forgotten. But eventually I recalled a few details, and in the present chapter I describe the experience and the circumstances in which it came about, and consider the peculiar fact that it was initially forgotten and then remembered to some extent.

Drawn into the Light

At the time of the experience I was an undergraduate student, taking courses in physical sciences and mathematics. In addition to my scientific interests, I had long-standing literary aspirations, and in my spare time I was engaged on what was going to be my great novel (alas, never completed). I bring up this writing activity because it came to mind during the mystical experience, and the plot I was working on, which centered on tireless efforts to wake an unconscious man, had affinities with the mystical experience, which was itself a kind of awakening. The novel begins with the central character driving aimlessly along the never-ending, circuitous roads of a great city. There is no hint of who the man is or where he has come from, and he himself probably does not know. Suddenly he is involved in a traffic accident, which shakes him from his trance, a splash of bright red on the car windscreen piercing the dull gray of the morning. He has knocked a pedestrian to the ground, and for a little while the normal functioning of the street is disrupted, although quickly restored by the emergency services.

The world goes on as if nothing has happened, but the protagonist has been affected. He visits the unconscious accident victim in the hospital and gradually takes over the young man's life, his name, lodgings, girlfriend, job in a metallurgical laboratory—a duplication of identity, and no one recognizes the substitution.[1] In the lab, there is a joke about a machine in the United States that can polish metal so finely that anyone who looks into the reflective surface will see the face of God. To find a means of waking the unconscious young man, the protagonist explores the life, arts, and sciences of the city, but to no avail. At the climax of the story, he gives up the search as futile and back at work goes about measuring the hardness of a highly polished sample with a diamond-tipped testing machine. As the diamond plunges toward the metal surface, an important but unspecified change takes place. I had no idea what that change might be and was uncertain how to end the story. I could not decide what to do with the young man: does he remain comatose, pass away, or wake up? The novel drew on my pre-university work experience in a lab, but in writing the story, which played with themes of identity and unconsciousness, I could see that I was working with symbols without really understanding what they meant or where they were taking me. The mystical experience was to provide an answer.

A month before the mystical event, I had my first "out-of-body" experience—another case of self-duplication. Again, this is worth mentioning, for it bore a slight resemblance to the mystical experience. In both instances, I was drawn toward a light and was able to see my own sleeping face. In the case of the out-of-body experience, I had fallen asleep on the bed in my college room and was surprised to find myself looking down on my face, eyelids closed, as if from a vantage point about a foot above. Although this was surprising, it was not a complete shock to me because about seven years before, at the age of thirteen, I had become interested in the possibility of out-of-body travel after reading about it first in a women's magazine article. My interest was especially piqued because my mother, commenting on the article, told me of her own out-of-body experience. Years before, while staying in Switzerland, she had cut her finger and slumped to the ground in a faint. But instead of unconsciousness, she found herself shooting up into the sky, high above the nearby mountains. At the time I was very much the budding experimental scientist, having become enthused by chemistry lessons in the previous school year, and so I attempted to travel out of the body to study the phenomenon for myself. This involved deep relaxation before going to sleep. I had no success and gave up after a few months, embarrassed at my credulity in taking the possibility of out-of-body travel seriously. However, even though I had quickly lost interest in the matter, I did acquire the habit of deep relaxation before going to sleep and continued to use the technique over the following years, a practice that may have laid some groundwork for what was to come.

Now, at last, I found myself in what seemed to be the out-of-body condition. There was a light a few feet behind my vantage point in the room, located where the desk lamp would have been in waking life, and I had the sensation of being pulled sideways toward this light. I thought that if I looked into it I would wake up, but I could not resist the pull, and I did indeed wake up. In later months, when I had further experiences of this kind, the concentration of light was sometimes present again, dimming if I attempted to look into it. In this first out-of-body experience, the luminosity in the darkened room brought the light of ordinary consciousness, for I woke from sleep upon moving toward it. In the mystical experience that was to follow a month later, I was again in effect drawn toward a light and also "woke up," but now into a much heightened state of luminosity and wakefulness.

A couple of months before the mystical experience, I had joined the university karate club and so came to read a little about Zen Buddhism in popular books. I was attracted by the talk of awakening, spontaneity, tranquility, and harmony with nature, and was intrigued by a mirror-polishing simile that reminded me of the metal-polishing imagery in my novel.[2] I also admired the prominence supposedly given by this form of Buddhism to experience and investigation over doctrine and religious trappings. In my reading, I came across mention of the psychologist Carl Jung and thought I should follow up the lead. When the university term gave way to the quiet of a holiday break, I had the opportunity to read some of Jung's *Memories, Dreams, Reflections*.[3] This work impressed me with its psychological sophistication and the richness of inner life it portrayed, and I was inspired to pay attention to my dreams. One that I recorded at the time suggests dissatisfaction with the way pleasant times come to an end, even if one tries to hold on to them. In the dream I resort to the authority of an unknown power to bring this process to an end. The attempt to remedy the unsatisfactory state of affairs was perhaps an intimation of the new phase of my life that was about to begin:

> I am Fig, the Spirit of Sweetness, who goes around very large dining tables, engaging diners in enchanting conversation and adding sweetness to their meals; but I also exist as two other spirits who follow me on my journeys round the tables, one of whom is the Spirit of Poison. As the Spirit of Sweetness, I linger as long as possible to delay the coming of the Spirit of Poison. Eventually, I go through protracted stages of interaction with people employed in the dining hall, demanding to see the management, which I eventually do. I force these people, who are my superiors in the catering set-up, to stop the poisoning side of things. This I do through some higher reference of which I myself do not know the nature.

I did not know or remember the identity of the third spirit involved in the cycle. The idea of three spirit-components may have been suggested by the Zen reading, if I had come across the Buddhist analysis of the forces behind the samsaric round of becoming, the "afflictions" (*kleśa*) or "three poisons" (*triviṣa*), greed, hatred, and delusion.

The mystical experience followed shortly after. It took place early one morning when I was asleep, probably between two dreams, although given the obscurity surrounding the eventual appearance of detailed memories, there is some room for doubt over the exact sequence of events. On waking, I remembered only the two dreams and felt that "wholeness" had been touched—a tremendous wholeness. But the central experience was not recalled. I was unaware of the details, being left with only a largely inexpressible feeling associated with a peculiar dream image. In the dream that led into the experience I may have been a child again, playing with friends, although I cannot be absolutely sure. It is possible that I have confused this recollection with dreams that followed in subsequent weeks. Whatever the case, I was certainly with friends on a sandy beach. Suddenly I was distracted from my activities:

The light is faint. Dunes and grass lie to one side, the sea to the other. Suddenly my attention is caught and I break away from the others. I stand at the edge of the water, still and upright, facing out to sea. In my hands I hold an object, a flat, wedge-shaped sliver of material, wider at the end closest to me. I gaze along the wedge and out to sea.

On waking, I was able to remember that the object was associated with a very strange and powerful feeling, one that I had not had before, except perhaps, I thought, in a very mild form as the nervous excitement of writing my novel. The feeling in the dream was connected with the flight along the taper, the sense of being drawn across the ocean. A few days later, I struggled to express the experience in the following note, written weeks before I had remembered the full extent of the experience:

> It's very difficult to say what it was I felt; in fact, on waking from the dream, I remembered the details, the sea, the shape and the fact that I had the feeling (it was not a feeling in the usual sense; I mean it's something I haven't had before, except perhaps in creative flows . . . but much stronger). What shall I say it was that I felt? There was nothing at all intellectual, conscious, thinking involved. This was so obvious when I woke up and found myself totally divorced from the experience. The intellectual reaction to it was with such terms: 'totality', 'wholeness', 'no going further', 'ultimate', and that sort of thing, but this intellectuality was miles off from the actual experience. The object was about a foot long and I was holding it with both hands in front of me at waist level with the rounded end towards me and the other end pointing over the ocean, or rather (and this is where, I think, lies my difficulty in remembering what the other end was like) the other end was not perceived – I was looking down on the shape and was drawn with an irresistibility along it, and in this drawing-along-towards lay the feeling-experience which was so unreproducible on waking.

Although the central experience was not remembered at the time, I was able to recall a subsequent dream that involved frantic efforts to cut strips from thin metallic sheet and paper, using a pair of scissors. On waking, I realized that the strips were imitations of the tapering object in the first dream, and that the imagery was taken from my work experience in the metallurgical laboratory, which had involved preparing strips of metal for experimental testing. In the dream, the frantic activity probably expressed a desire to regain the feeling associated with the taper in the first dream. But the method was hopeless: it was the attempt of a man who strives to regain something he has lost, but who does not realize that he is asleep, and therefore does not know who he is and what he seeks. The man frets to no purpose, chasing after dream images, when all he need do is wake up.

It is difficult to say when I remembered the central events between the two dreams and came to understand that the main experience, the source of the sense of wholeness, lay at the end of the flight along the taper. Initially I had thought that the experience was indescribable and very different from thinking ("There was nothing at all intellectual, conscious, thinking involved"), for I was left with a feeling that I could barely liken to anything else I had experienced. The only suggestion of an intellectual aspect to the feeling was perhaps the sense of wholeness, but I had no suspicion at the time that the sense derived from an experience that was in fact highly intellectual in nature, although of a quality far above anything I had previously known. The ineffability was therefore partly due to the difficulty of expressing an unfamiliar feeling but also to forgetfulness—I could not describe what I could not remember.

I think that the memories filtered through gradually and without much notice, for I cannot recall suddenly realizing that I had remembered the experience. In retrospect, it seems to me that some features of the experience were making an impression on my dreams before I was able to remember them at a conscious level—an example will be given in chapter 9. I refrained from recording the core experience at the time or mentioning it to others except in very vague terms, because it was felt to be too private and important to commit to writing or discuss. The only exception was a brief note, written about four months after the experience:

> All was known, understood, yet not as the 'I' understands. There was immense relief. 'No more searching', the 'I' said. All the worries of life dropped away, were found to be nothing. Yet there was resistance – the 'I' found its desires, hopes, works, aspirations to have the same phantom nature. I did not remember this side of it when I wrote [the first note], only the 'feeling'. C.f. Jung's vision-dream in 'M, D, Ref'.

The reference at the end is to Jung's near-death experience in 1944, recounted in *Memories, Dreams, Reflections*.[4] Administered oxygen and camphor after a heart attack, Jung found himself looking down on the Earth from high above. His attention was drawn to a great block of stone floating nearby in space, hollowed out to form a temple. Approaching the entrance, he experienced a painful shedding of his aims, desires, and thoughts, a feeling with which I could readily empathize.

It was not until about six or seven years after the experience that I attempted a detailed description. The testimonies of others show that reticence is common in such matters, for several reasons. A strong sense of privacy held me back from talking about the experience, a fear that the intensely meaningful experience would be trivialized and stripped of its significance if it were discussed with others. I was also intent not to fall into the error of describing the remarkable occurrence for no other reason than to impress others—the absurdity of this sort of exercise had registered with me very clearly during the experience itself over another matter of self-expression, my novel writing.

The following account, then, derives for the most part from the description set down a few years after the event when I was beginning to think that it would be valuable to look at the experience in greater depth. At that time, I had read hardly any accounts of mystical experiences and had not registered any notions of "cosmic consciousness" and the like. The delving into comparable experiences and the study of mysticism followed a little later, and then I was often surprised to find similar thoughts and feelings expressed.

No More Searching

The first thing I remember is gazing out upon a vast, resplendent world and thinking, with enormous relief, "no more searching," as if I had at last found what I had always been looking for. The thought surprised me because I had not been aware that I was still searching for anything. The next thing I realized was that there was no possibility of feeling pain in this state. Close to my vantage point were small, elongated patches, and I understood that for pain to be felt they had to be joined together. These patches were separated and could not come together in the present condition. The absence of pain was very attractive indeed.

Then there was the realization that I knew everything, understood everything, could see everything. It was vision, a world of light spread before me, a vast space of shining, transparent formations, densities of light making up endless shapes and figures. There was complete understanding of what it was all about, and it was so simple, so obvious. I retain images of certain figures nearby, human I think, standing out like unfinished statues, not fashioned in an opaque material, but as a translucency containing fine, interior detail. The universe stretched into the distance, but I can't say how far it extended or indeed if it went on without end. The luminous contents were not disposed uniformly, not equally in all directions: perhaps the best way I can describe the appearance is to liken it to the view from an aircraft just above a layer of clouds, a magnificent sea of shining clouds spreading toward the horizon. However, the "clouds" of my vision were translucent patterns of light, and I was situated among them, not above them. There was an immense amount of detail to be seen in the farther regions, and I had great difficulty taking it all in, understanding what I saw. The space seems to have included a temporal span, for at some stage I was looking into the distance and could see persons in other times. My attention was drawn to a group of people, spiritual practitioners I think, situated many, many years ago. Despite their remoteness, they were not far off compared with the great spaciousness of the world. I saw others too, closer in time, including one who stood out for some reason. I had the most personal sense of the nearest ones I could see, seemingly located in the most recent past.

After the discovery of the universal extent of my knowledge, there was a focus on specifics. I became aware of a "transformation" in a lower space of my visual field, like a flickering along consecutive states, creating a sense of movement. Whether there was actual movement or the motion was simply the presence of the multiple images, I am not sure. When I later saw Doré's etching of the lovers in Dante's underworld, showing a trail of images through the sky, I was reminded of the effect.[5] I recognized the whirl of images to be myself, my body, including head and face, seen from above. It was a shock to see myself like this, a hollow, flimsy shell whose life was in the whirl of the images and completely dependent on the great life and intelligence of the world. Yet it was also I who in some sense was the sole basis of everything. I was the mind from which everything derived and in which everything had its existence. There was nothing but myself, or rather nothing but the mind I had discovered myself to be, the intelligence and power sustaining the world.

There was tremendous relief to be had in this altered understanding of myself. My worries had no foundation now that I knew who I was. For instance, it was clear that there was no need to be anxious about the outcome of my university studies. In fact, I think that at this stage of the experience I had some knowledge of what was to follow in my life, and I was therefore able to understand that my studies had little relevance to what lay ahead. The details of this knowledge of the future were not, however, recalled when memories of the experience later surfaced, and I have remained ignorant of my future. But alongside the relief, there was also a mixture of dismay and humor. My narrow self-preoccupations were seen to be just as empty as my fears, and I found this hard to accept. I remember, in particular, seeing with unsettling clarity that my novel-writing efforts—a visual picture of the activity was involved in the understanding—were heavily motivated by an urge to reach out to others for recognition. The motivation appeared all the more absurd because it was seen to rest on a misunderstanding of the audience for whom I had been performing. Now everyone, audience included, was absorbed into the mind that was myself. It was both shocking and amusing. Whom was I trying so hard to impress? There was no one but myself.

Then, as if to remedy an incomplete understanding, my attention was drawn to the left and took in a vertical stretch or "board" of translucent luminosity on which I could see what appeared to have the form of "rings"— little circles or some very similar rounded shape. As the vision moved in further, it concentrated on two of these rings, one at the left, and one at the right, a little higher up. Concentrating on the right circle, I understood that it was a living being, and another circle too, further in the distance, was understood in the same way, indicating to me that all these circular things were living beings. Although they were part of my all-encompassing mind, they were distinct from me in that they were beings in their own right, but they were also like myself because they too were the immense mind. It was a wonder, a perplexity, that these little things likewise encompassed everything. A tremendous feeling of love arose, an intense, all-pervading love that reached out, streamed out to all. I was overwhelmed by the discovery that such powerful, all-inclusive love is possible. I realized how impoverished is my usual capacity to love, compared with the great love I now felt, but I was also overjoyed by the knowledge that it would be possible to love others so in my ordinary life. There was a visual impression associated with this realization, with love appearing to stream out from the center of my human body like rays of light.

But I felt extremely impure, unworthy, uncomfortable, defiling the pure love by my presence, and I thought I would have to cleanse myself deeply before ever wanting or daring to return here. I remember that at this point, intensely conscious of my impurity, I was apprehending a vast region of space and could observe several features in it. I may have been attending to an upward direction, compared with the previous focus. I seemed to know the presence of something greatly superior to myself, but the recollection is very hazy. Was it at this stage that the experience came to an end? I cannot be sure, but it seems possible that the feelings of intense unease in the presence of the great love may have precipitated the clouding-over. Whatever the case, there is one further unsettling feature to note, which may also have brought the experience to a close.

As I have said, there was, I think, knowledge of my life to come, although no specifics were later recalled. There were views of the more distant future too, of several ordinary people living in different times, connected with myself. Who the persons were in relation to myself, I don't know with absolute certainty, but I think I understood them to be lives to come. I had the impression that they belonged to a series that included me too. I remember a specific scene in which a man walks along a path that leads across fields. He is a very down-to-earth, centered individual, and I have the impression that he is myself in another life. In this viewing of myself and future lives, I was struck by the sheer ordinariness of myself, by how unremarkable I am and always shall be, now and in those lives to come, which was a disappointment to me, but which on reflection I understood to be a blessing. It is a humbling, deflating experience, but gives a healthy appreciation of what is possible and desirable, a loving, balanced way of life, in tune with the way things are, in contrast to the immature condition in which I had found myself to be.

But in viewing the series of lives, there was something outside my grasp. I could not understand the end to which the series led, for there was a conclusion that I could not fathom, which seemed to involve an absence of myself, although again the recollection is very hazy. Nowhere in the universe was I to be found. Maybe it was with the fear of an eventual conclusion to my individual selfhood that the state began to dim, and I felt it slipping away. I desperately wanted to stay, but the change could not be halted. I had never known clarity of this degree before, had never been so alive or felt such intense "realness," but now I was sinking fast, falling asleep, swooning into darkness and dreams.

It was into the strip-cutting dream that I have supposed the descent led, and it was not only in this dream that I rushed around foolishly. As I began to remember what had happened, the immediate desire was to recapture the state, and I tried to induce a recurrence through ill-conceived meditation exercises. A few disturbing dreams suggested to me that this was not the way to proceed. Needless to say, precipitous experiments in altered states of consciousness, whether through forced meditation, drugs, or other means can be dangerous, and the results are likely to be transient. The gate of human personality is usually rusted up through long neglect and should not be forced open, for damage to self and others is a possible outcome. The "experience" and the urge to recover it had dominated at first, when it was the message that needed to be absorbed. Even if I had managed to find my way back to the luminous state, I would not have been able to endure it for long, given my comparative immaturity. It would have been far too overwhelming, as I had recognized during the experience itself, when in the face of the immense love I had felt great discomfort.

Some Observations

In subsequent chapters, I shall look in depth at several aspects of the experience, but for the moment it may be useful to draw attention to and comment in brief upon certain points.

1. *This world.* It never crossed my mind that the luminous world might be a realm of existence other than the one we ordinarily know, for I could see my own body there and also other people, including some of my "other lives" as a human being, or so it seemed. It was the same universe I had always known but apprehended differently.

2. *No pain.* It is remarkable that I found the absence of physical pain so noticeable, for pain was not a particularly significant feature of my life then, and at the specific time of the experience I was not, as far as I know, in any pain at all, being fast asleep in bed. It is much more understandable that persons in the middle of near-death crises should experience the analgesic effect, as indeed they tend to do: typically, the intense pain caused by cardiac arrest, road accident, or similar trauma disappears as the near-death experience begins and returns when the experience comes to an end. It can be speculated that in the course of our everyday experience, there is a background level of bodily pain to which we are normally habituated (like background noise we stop noticing after a while), and it is only when the pain ceases that we become aware of its former presence, through its absence. Another point of interest here is the visual impression of the "patches" that in combination were understood to be necessary for experience of pain. Is it possible that I was observing some neurophysiological phenomenon in my sleeping brain, a biochemical substrate of pain (and perhaps even of ordinary perception in general) that had been interrupted, broken up into its component parts in the altered state of consciousness?

3. *Out of the body.* There is a possibility that my center of awareness had slipped out of my body during the experience, for I was able to see the body, including my head and face, from above. In chapter 1, I have noted several examples of mystical experience in which the center of perception seems to have left the body in connection with an expansion of consciousness, and it is a commonly reported feature of near-death experiences. In fact, my experience is reminiscent of the more mystical near-death experiences, an observation to be developed in chapter 3.

4. *Spatial orientation.* In my recollections, the luminous world was spatially extended—far from being nonspatial, it was extraordinarily spatial, possibly even to the extent of including past and future happenings within itself. It is noticeable that I found it natural to use various directional

descriptions in my account, such as the "lower space of my visual field" and "attending to an upward direction." It seemed appropriate to carry over such directional terms from ordinary experience to describe orientations in my greatly expanded visual field. But I am not sure what acted as a reference for this directional sense, since I was not at first conscious of my body and then came to view it externally, "below" my vantage point. I have wondered whether some of the directional sense derived from the distinction between past and future states. I have also wondered if at one point I was viewing a higher-dimensional space, when I attended to what I described as "an upward direction" and apprehended the "vast region of space," which I believe was distinguishable from the first region I had noted, the one that stretched into the distance and was filled with the structures of light (see chapter 8, "Hypercosmic Spaces"). But this is very speculative.

5. *Two facets of time.* It is difficult to say exactly how time was experienced, as my recollections depend on memory processes that may not have represented this elusive aspect of the experience very well. On the one hand, the experience seems to have had an "eternal" side to it, with contents of the past being open to inspection in a greater spatiality, as well as views of what I understood to be future lives. On the other hand, the experience seems to have involved temporal passage, with shifts from one insight, thought, and feeling to the next. I am not sure what to make of the awareness of a "transformation" in my visual field, which I describe as "like a flickering along consecutive states, creating a sense of movement." There appear to have been multiple images close by, giving a sense of "static movement," but my impressions of this are now very hazy indeed. This effect led me to wonder if our everyday sense of time flow is the result of a combination of temporal states in each moment, in each so-called specious or psychological present.[6]

6. *Two facets of self.* The experience of self seemed to have two sides. First, there was my usual self, responding to the disclosures with relief, incomprehension, dismay, amusement, awe, humility, and so on. Second, there was the world-encompassing, all-comprehending mind that in some sense was also myself. I shall have more to say about this intriguing two-foldness in chapter 4.

7. *Figures of light.* Everything was made of light, or, to put it more accurately, objects existed as the contents of my luminous field of experience. The persons I could see were statue-like in the sense that their bodies were motionless and fashioned out of the luminosity, and their life, like mine, was not their own but belonged to the whole in which they were little parts. It is possible that the figures I saw nearby were my parents asleep in the adjoining bedroom, since I was at home at the time.

8. *Other lives.* The experience seems to have brought awareness of other lives, specifically of ones to come. Some of the persons I saw in the past may have been other lives too, but I do not remember recognizing them as such. The awareness was not a *memory* of other lives but a *seeing* and *knowing* of them. Prior to the experience, I had been skeptical of the idea of reincarnation, probably because I still carried the assumption that consciousness is extinguished when the brain dies. Thus, when I was reading about Zen Buddhism a couple of months before the experience, I was not impressed by some of the more "religious" themes I found there, such as the idea of rebirth, which, although supposedly understated in Zen according to my reading matter, made no sense to me. I supposed that the belief must be a superstition carried over from primitive Buddhism into an otherwise appealing philosophy of life. However, my experience left me with the impression that reincarnation does take place, and the topic will receive some attention in chapter 10.

9. *The vision of the rings.* The ring-shaped beings were puzzling to me at the time, for I could not understand how these tiny things could be the same as the vast, all-inclusive mind that was myself. I put this aspect of the experience aside for several years. However, it became of considerable interest when I found parallels in the writings of Plotinus and Thomas Traherne, and in the *Avatāmsaka Sūtra*. The identity of the ring-shaped beings will be explored in chapters 5 and 6. Indeed, the enigma they have presented to me is the raison d'être of the current book, as I have noted in the Preface.

10. *All in the mind.* I was astonished to find that the universe had its existence in and derived from the great mind I now understood myself to be. The discovery was so outside my previous understanding that I initially struggled to put it into words. However, the view that the universe is "mind-dependent" in some fundamental way has been asserted by idealist philosophers for a long time. "Idealism" is a broad term, applied not without controversy to very different philosophies, including those of Plato, Plotinus, Berkeley, Leibniz, Kant, Fichte, Schelling, Hegel, Bradley, Royce, and Whitehead, and to some Asian schools and texts, Buddhist (e.g., Yogācāra) and Hindu (e.g., Advaita Vedānta, nondual Kashmir Shaivism, the *Yogavāsiṣṭha*), to name just a few prominent examples.[7] When I came across the philosophies of Leibniz and Plotinus, I was strongly drawn to them: they seemed to resonate with aspects of my experience and with puzzles I had come up against in my undergraduate study of physics.[8]

There are several routes to idealist philosophy. One is epistemological, through skepticism about knowledge of the world and the ensuing quest for certainty in experience. The emergence of idealism after Descartes, in thinkers such as Berkeley, is often read in this way. Another route is metaphysical, through mind–matter or source–product discontinuity problems generated by dualism. If matter is taken to be very different from mind, as it was by Descartes, then their interaction becomes mysterious. Similarly, if it is supposed that the creative or emanative source of the world is spiritual/ mental, then it is puzzling how a material world could come from it or be supported by it. In both cases, discontinuity is overcome by taking the material world to be itself spiritual/mental in nature. Mathematical physics can also be a route to idealism, the "unreasonable effectiveness of mathematics in the Natural Sciences" suggesting to some the reality of number in itself and therefore of "Idea" in a Pythagorean-Platonic sense.[9] Modern physics can point to idealism too, relativistic theory being a case in point.[10]

Another route is altered states of consciousness, including meditation and lucid dreams (e.g., "dream yoga"), mystical experiences, and, as we shall see below, "anesthetic revelations." At the very least, extraordinary experiences can encourage questioning of materialist assumptions and exploration of new possibilities.[11] Historical examples include philosopher and psychologist Gustav Fechner, whose visionary experience of the soul life of plants may have helped him toward a dual-aspect metaphysics, and philosopher Ernst Mach, whose unitive nature experience was a factor in his progress toward a neutral monist philosophy.[12] A modern example is neuroscientist Marjorie Hines Woollacott, whose profound experience during meditation prompted her to investigate evidence that consciousness is no mere product or function of the brain.[13] Sometimes a specifically idealist perspective develops out of extraordinary experiences, as I myself can attest, having been led by my own experience to the view that mind is fundamental. Another contemporary example is the distinguished microprocessor pioneer Federico Faggin, who had a mystical experience similar in some details to my own, including a cosmic expansion of love. Faggin has developed a philosophy in which units of consciousness emerge through ultimate reality's awareness of itself, and these units bear some resemblance to Leibniz's monads.[14]

An earlier example of great interest is the Cambridge philosopher John McTaggart Ellis McTaggart (1866–1925), known to generations of philosophy students for his proof of the unreality of time. It is likely that McTaggart's monadological idealism, which has a community of mutually perceiving, eternal selves at its heart and which places great emphasis on personal love, owes something to the mystical experiences of unity and love he occasionally enjoyed.[15] But McTaggart's approach to metaphysics was to construct purely deductive arguments that would arrive at the conclusions he had mystically intuited, such as the unreality of time, the reality of persons, and the centrality of love. In this regard, it has been observed that McTaggart was like a schoolboy who, tackling an algebra problem, has "a glimpse of the answer at the end of the book" and now tries to derive the answer "by patient, honest, application of the accepted methods."[16] McTaggart worked out his arguments without overtly drawing on the data of mystical experience. Nor did he draw on the natural sciences, including the new physics that was catching the attention of some philosophers at the time, including his student Bertrand Russell. McTaggart did not regard empirical investigation as relevant to metaphysical inquiry. By contrast, I have hoped for a mutually beneficial synergy of metaphysics, mystical experience, and the natural sciences that can take the discussion further than each on its own.[17]

Forgetting and Remembering

A puzzling feature of the episode is the way that memories of the core experience eluded me at first. This amnesia is worth considering because it has a bearing on questions the reader is entitled to ask and indeed should ask. Was there in fact a core mystical experience or were the memories that later surfaced just confabulations invented to make sense of the two strange dreams? Even if there were a core experience, how can I be sure that the memories which eventually appeared are reliable? I have to concede that doubt must remain on both counts, and I am unable to offer evidence other than the account itself and whatever agreement it may have with the testimonies of others who have had mystical experiences. I have not had serious doubts about the general accuracy of the memories, but opinion means little when it comes to establishing the truth of a matter. In practice, I have assumed that the memories do reflect an experience that really took place, and I have tried to act accordingly over the years, if not particularly consistently or effectively, often out of touch with the revelation of love that overawed me at the time.

However, my own acceptance of the authenticity of the memories does not mean that I am fully satisfied with the account I have given. I would not be surprised if some details, particularly the order in which I have set them down, have become confused in the process of recollection and description, and I have tried to indicate major uncertainties within the account. It is disconcerting that an experience of great personal significance should be known through memories that are even more open to doubt than the usual kind, for they are memories of an event that occurred while I was asleep. However, traces of the experience were left on waking, namely the memories of the two framing dreams and the afterglow feeling with its powerful sense of "wholeness." I made notes of these traces within a few days, and the jottings reassure me that the more detailed memories which surfaced in later weeks are based on a chronologically identifiable event. Furthermore, the general agreement between the contents of my recollections, the mystical accounts I have since come across, and the teachings of some mystical philosophies encourages me to think that I really did experience a condition of profound wakefulness, only to fall asleep again, first into private dreams, and then into the shared "waking dream" of everyday life.

There was one account of extraordinary experience that I had quite possibly read just a few days before my own experience, and it could be speculated that this had provided material out of which a "false memory" was constructed. This was Jung's account of his near-death experience in *Memories, Dreams, Reflections*, which I mentioned above. I was later to find Jung's account of his "exfoliation" at the rock temple reminiscent of my own humbling experience. Might I have unconsciously woven parts of his description into my own personal context? Jung himself, following Théodore Flournoy, recognized the phenomenon of "cryptomnesia," a process by which previously encountered material is unconsciously reconstructed into an apparently original production.[18] On the surface, explanations invoking cryptomnesia or false memories might seem credible, but the presence of novel elements in my recollections would have to be explained. I was able to remember many features that are not mentioned in Jung's account, and, more importantly, our experiences were not particularly similar, Jung's being more dreamlike and symbolic in character. I therefore think it more likely that Jung's account, if I had indeed read it before my own experience, acted as a stimulus, an "invitation to my psyche," rather than as the source of its contents. The same is probably true of the popular Zen literature I had been reading, which was superficial and unlikely to have supplied me with the detailed contents of my experience.

If a mystical experience truly occurred, how is the late emergence of memories to be explained? It might be conjectured that the forgetfulness was a repression of disturbing experience, as amnesia is sometimes said to be in the more mundane traumas. Overall, the experience was positive, and I wished to remain in this very attractive state when I felt it slipping away, but it is also true that there were some profoundly unsettling aspects, such as the exposure of motives and the feeling of inadequacy before the great love. The amnesia could therefore have acted in a self-protective way, allowing a gradual reintroduction of insights that would otherwise be disturbing. That there was some purpose behind the amnesia may be suggested by my inability to remember one detail of the experience: I could remember having knowledge of the future course of my life but could not remember specifics. The selectivity of the amnesia may suggest a purposeful censoring, for recall of such sensitive information might have interfered with the natural course of development and my ability to make choices freely (in so far as they can ever be made freely). The occurrence of the mystical experience while I was asleep can also be viewed in a similar light, as a protective measure. Contained between dreams and therefore placed at a distance from everyday life, and remembered without much ado after a delay of weeks, memories of the experience were able to enter waking consciousness unobtrusively, without bringing major disruption. I was able to continue my life and studies as normal. If the experience had occurred while I was awake, it would probably have had a far more disruptive effect.

Another line of approach is to suppose that the mystical amnesia was related, if only in part, to the kind of forgetfulness that customarily attends waking from sleep, when dreams disperse in the light of day unless efforts are made to preserve them. I wonder if some memories of the experience were still active when I awoke from sleep, memories that might have contributed to the afterglow feeling of "wholeness." If there were such memories, they must have faded very rapidly, and I had no opportunity to rehearse and stabilize them. I have been intrigued to find other accounts that suggest a loss of mystical insight through an inability to remember. Perhaps Dante refers to the phenomenon in *The Divine Comedy*. While striving to express the highest reaches of mystical ascent, Dante bemoans the loss of memory that made descriptive efforts defective: it was as if a single moment of forgetfulness had brought a deeper oblivion than the passage of twenty-five centuries (*Paradiso* XXXIII, 94–96).[19] If the poetry reflects a personal experience, Dante's illumination seems to have disclosed the unity of an ordinarily fragmented world (XXXIII, 85–93):

> In its depth I saw ingathered, bound by love in one single volume, that which is dispersed in leaves throughout the universe: substances and accidents and their relations, as though fused together in such a way that what I tell is but a simple light. The universal form of this knot I believe that I saw, because, in telling this, I feel my joy increase.[20]

Dante's inability to describe the experience—the ineffability so often reported by mystics—was joined by *a failure of memory*. That which could be remembered was like the feeling left by a dream that has evaporated. The feeling remained, but not the details (XXXIII, 55–63):

Thenceforward my vision was greater than speech can show, which fails at such a sight, and at such excess memory fails. As is he who dreaming sees, and after the dream the passion remains imprinted and the rest returns not to the mind; such am I, for my vision almost wholly fades away, yet does the sweetness that was born of it still drop within my heart.[21]

The "forgetting" of deep truths has been a recurrent theme in Western philosophy and literature, appearing whenever Platonic thought has found a receptive audience. The doctrine of *anamnēsis* ("recollection" or "remembrance") was first explained by Plato as recollection of knowledge previously acquired by the immortal soul in its wanderings from life to life (*Meno* 81c–d). Plato later adjusted the idea to accord with his emerging theory of Forms: anamnesis now refers to reacquaintance with a fundamental level of knowledge, the Ideas or Forms, forgotten at birth but recovered in part through reminders presented in sense perception (*Phaedo* 72e–77e). The return to the higher level of knowledge is portrayed in Plato's famous Allegory of the Cave (*The Republic* 514a–519b), which tells of human beings confined to an underground cavern, who mistake shadow-images projected on the walls for the originals. Those liberated from subterranean life are initially blinded by the light, but they come to see the true source of things and do not want to return to the former life, with its limited knowledge and trivial honors. If compelled or persuaded to return to the cave, they will have difficulty accommodating to the darkness and may seem clumsy and ridiculous to those who do not understand their plight. It is not far-fetched to conjecture that Plato's story has a basis in mystical experience and its aftereffects. The shift from comparative ignorance to knowledge and perception, from darkness to light, is suggestive of mystical expansions. So too is the loss of interest in the usual prizes offered by the world, the reluctance to go back to the dim state of consciousness, and the confusion and sense of confinement that follows.

It is not known for sure whether Dante's poetry and Plato's philosophy drew on personal familiarity with mystical experience (I hazard a guess they did), but mystical forgetting and remembering are certainly described in modern accounts. The novelist Margaret Prescott Montague (1878–1955) vividly conveys something of the mystical breakthrough to reality and the amnesia that can follow on return to the "cave." On regaining consciousness after a knock to the head, she was left with the impression that a great truth had been discovered, but she was unable to remember what it was. The lid of her mental "box" had sprung open for a few moments to reveal a greater world and a "larger self":

Here in this life we are like Jack-in-the-box. Our spirit is squeezed into something that is too small for it, with the lid hooked down tight, but every now and again, through the pressure of some high emotion, the lid flies off, we shoot up to our full height, and gaze with delighted eyes on a lovely new world. Once, through an accident, I think that the lid flew off for me. I received a violent blow on the head which knocked me insensible for a short time. When I regained consciousness, I brought back with me a feeling that I had been where the real things are, and as though this life here were hardly more than a dream. In those few moments of unconsciousness I had waked into truth. What truth is, and where I had found it, I do not know. All I brought back with me, like a trailing cloud of glory, was the conviction of having been a wanderer returned, a mirage-chaser looking at last upon reality. I had been where I belonged, and where the permanent things are to be found, and this life appeared, when I awoke, to be unreal to the point of absurdity. There was, indeed, the vague sense of a joke about the whole experience, as though the same trick — the trick of being made to believe that material life is all — had been played upon me, or I had played it upon myself, many times before. Then life in this world picked me up again and squeezed me inexorably back into my small self, like Jack being squeezed into his box.[22]

Another woman, C.R.P., recounted the most wonderful experience she had ever had, but could not remember anything about it:

I awoke one morning with the intense joy, the bliss, of some ineffable Experience flooding my whole being. Yet I had no memory of what had happened, though I struggled desperately to get back, unmindful of the duties that awaited me; for in comparison, they did not matter—nothing mattered. This wonderful sensation of joy and bliss remained with me for a couple of days. I only wanted to get back.[23]

The inability to recall information after a change in state of consciousness has commonly been discussed in terms of *state-bound* cognition: state-bound memory, learning, retrieval, and knowledge.[24] The phenomenon is not confined to the mystical contexts discussed here, being common in more familiar changes of consciousness, involving sleep, emotions, and intoxicants. For instance, dream material forgotten soon after waking may sometimes come back into awareness when a sleepy state of mind next sets in. It is also the case that mystical forgetting is not restricted to experiences that occur in sleep, dreams, or swoons into unconsciousness. Following exceptional

experiences that occur under a variety of consciousness-altering circumstances—quiet rest, meditation, physical and mental trauma, illness, drugs,
childbirth, dying—it may be felt that profound knowledge of the world or
a great universal secret has been momentarily revealed, only to slip away.[25]
Typically, the subject has a greatly deepened understanding that vanishes
when the experience ends, leaving only the memory that there had been a
special understanding, but with no sense of what was understood.

Outstanding examples of "state-bound" insight have been described by
individuals subject to anesthetic intoxication. Dissociative anesthetics such
as nitrous oxide and ketamine are known to induce effects other than the
pain relief and unconsciousness for which they are usually administered.
These side effects may include pleasurable sensations, involuntary laughter,
sharpened perceptions, synesthesia, hallucinations, and occasionally out-
of-body and mystical experiences. Typical of the more developed nitrous
oxide cases is transformation in the experience and understanding of thought
processes: there is an acceleration of thought, a rush of ideas, and a sense of
gaining new insights, including insights into the process of thinking itself.
An impressive example, induced by nitrous oxide inhalation on a visit to
the dentist, was recounted by the actor, dramatist, broadcaster, poet, and
novelist Richard Heron Ward (1910–1969).[26] Ward's account is notable for its
remarkably full presentation of deepening levels of awareness, yet it seems
that Ward had to struggle with his memory before the details returned to
him. Amnesia is a common outcome of nitrous oxide revelations (and of
ketamine ones too).[27] William James, who conducted inhalation experiments
after reading philosopher and poet Benjamin Paul Blood (author of *The
Anæsthetic Revelation and the Gist of Philosophy*, 1874), noted that nitrous
oxide illumination often ends by "losing the clue." Illumination changes into
bewilderment, insight into nonsense:

> as sobriety returns, the feeling of insight fades, and one is left staring
> vacantly at a few disjointed words and phrases, as one stares at a cadav-
> erous-looking snow peak from which the sunset glow has just fled, or at
> the black cinder left by an extinguished brand.[28]

During intoxication, a torrent of thoughts exhibited to James an identification of opposing concepts, "fused in the fire of infinite rationality." This was
the key insight of James's experience, the reconciliation of opposites in a
higher unity, with all contradictions revealed as degrees of difference in an
unbroken continuity. In the intoxicated state, James had the strong conviction
that Hegel's logic of the synthesis of opposites was true after all and "that we

are literally in the midst of *an infinite*, to perceive the existence of which is the utmost we can attain."[29] However, as sober consciousness returned, the emotional import invested in the realizations drained away, leaving a sense of empty abstraction, of "vertiginous amazement at a meaningless infinity."[30] James believed that the nonsense or triviality of anesthetic revelations is exposed in the cold light of ordinary consciousness, which suggested to him the equally nonsensical character of Hegel's idealist philosophy.

Eighty years before James's Hegelian experience, another thinker had intimations of idealist metaphysics in the peculiar effects of nitrous oxide intoxication. This was Humphry Davy (1778–1829), later president of the Royal Society and a prominent figure in the development of modern chemistry. Though empirically minded, Davy was also something of a Romantic thinker and poet, and an opponent of materialism. He was keenly aware of the beauty, simplicity, and unity of nature, and, even without the help of nitrous oxide, he could feel a mystical unity with the natural world, as occurred on one occasion when he rested by the sea. But the idealist insight came through nitrous oxide. As a young researcher at Thomas Beddoes's Pneumatic Institute in Bristol, Davy investigated the medicinal possibilities of the recently discovered gases, including nitrous oxide. On one occasion, in 1799, Davy inhaled substantial quantities of nitrous oxide and experienced a dramatic change to his thought processes:

> By degrees as the pleasurable sensations increased, I lost all connection with external things; trains of vivid visible images rapidly passed through my mind and were connected with words in such a manner, as to produce perceptions perfectly novel. I existed in a world of newly connected and newly modified ideas. I theorised; I imagined that I made discoveries.[31]

As the effects subsided, Davy felt the need to communicate his insights, but he could barely remember the new ideas, which were now "feeble and indistinct." Only one "collection of terms presented itself," sentences that he exclaimed with "the most intense belief and prophetic manner" to his companion Dr. Kinglake: *"Nothing exists but thoughts!—the universe is composed of impressions, ideas, pleasures and pains!"*[32] This declaration is reminiscent of Bishop Berkeley's idealist assertion that "to be is to be perceived," a philosophy Davy had encountered in his youthful readings of the British empiricists.

Idealist insight was even more pronounced in the anesthetic revelations of another prominent chemist, William Ramsay (1852–1916), who in 1904 received the Nobel Prize for his discovery of the "inert" gases. In the 1880s, over a period of several years, Ramsay self-experimented with anesthetics, including ether, chloroform, and nitrous oxide. Under partial anesthesia, he would invariably experience the "same curious delusion" that "the Universe centres itself" in him and "evolves out" of his own mind.[33] This he took to be Berkeleian, but it could equally be Leibnizian—and not quite either when examined closely. Although remaining skeptical, Ramsay admitted that his experiences led him to think that Berkeley's idealism deserves "a little more consideration" than is usual (see Box, "The Berkeleian hypothesis").

Subanesthetic doses of ether (and ethyl iodide, but not chloroform) conferred similar metaphysical insight upon another experimenter, Ernest Dunbar, for whom the "only logical position was subjective idealism" when he was under the influence of the gas:

> I began to realise that I was the One, and the universe of which I was the principle was balancing itself into completeness. All thought seemed struggling to a logical conclusion; every trifling movement in the world outside my consciousness represented a perfectly logical step in the final readjustment.[34]

Whereas James described his thought-trains as proceeding in a fashion consonant with Hegel's logic, Dunbar invoked the earlier German idealist philosopher Fichte, and, while admitting that there is nothing illogical in the Fichtean viewpoint, he expressed surprise that mere inhalation of ether should lead to the "ultimate realisation" of this viewpoint.

The anesthetic experiences of Davy, James, and Dunbar may well have brought insights into thought processes, but it is not clear if deep levels of mystical insight were reached. Ramsay's anesthetic experiences also seem to have fallen short of full mystical insight: he realizes that there is something illusory about space and time, he is overcome by the unassailable certainty that reality has been contacted, and he discovers that his world is a projection of the self, yet there is no sign that his experiences take him beyond his own personal, perceptual, and cognitive "orbit" to a deep engagement with self, other, and world. Certainly, he found the experiences very disappointing:

> My feelings are sometimes those of despair in finding the secret of existence so little worthy of regard. It is as if the veil that hides whence we come, what we are, and what will become of us were suddenly rent, and as if a glimpse of the Absolute burst upon us. The conviction of its truth is overwhelming; but it is painful in the extreme. I have exclaimed — "Good heavens! is this all!"[35]

➷ The Berkeleian hypothesis ↭

Ramsay on his anesthetic experiences: "An overwhelming impression forced itself upon me that the state in which I then was, was reality; that now I had reached the true solution of the secret of the universe, in understanding the secret of my own mind; that all outside objects were merely passing reflections on the eternal mirror of my mind; some more, some less transient.... The main and impressive fact for me was that *I* was self-existent, and that time and space were illusions. This was the real *Ego*, on whose surface ripples of incident arose, to fade and vanish like the waves on a pond.... I do not think that I am a follower of Bishop Berkeley in my ordinary every-day existence; my tendency of mind is, by training, and by the nature of my daily avocations, to suspend judgement—a condition of scientific scepticism. But under the influence of an anæsthetic all doubts vanish; I *know* the truth of Berkeley's theory of existence, and I also believe, because I know with absolute certainty, that self-existence is all that any reasonable man can be convinced of; that all fellow-creatures are products of my consciousness, and that, although they may be real to themselves, and have each a world of his own, to me they are merely parts of my thoughts, and, moreover, not very important elements in my chain of life.

"The theory attributed to Bishop Berkeley is a perfectly consistent one, and can be disputed only on grounds of what we term "common-sense." I do not, in my ordinary state of mind, attribute any importance to this theory, beyond regarding it as a somewhat improbable, but incontrovertible speculation; but I confess that, since my experiences with anæsthetics, I am disposed to regard it as worthy of a little more consideration than it usually receives. The difficulty in accepting it is our practically absolute certainty of the existence of our fellow-creatures; and the deduction that if A and B receive the same impression at the same time, that impression must be caused by some *thing*, external to both. But in my anæsthetic state, this objection presents no difficulty to me; I conceive each ego to have his orbit, and to stand absolutely alone, conscious of, but un-interfered with by, the other egos. To choose a crude illustration:—two mirrors reflect, but do not influence each other in any mechanical or material sense.... The fact remains that, while anæsthetised, my belief in that theory of existence which we may call for short the Berkeleian hypothesis, is immeasurably more firm and decided than in my normal state is my belief in the ordinarily accepted views of matter and motion which regulate the lives of most human beings."[36]

From William Ramsay, "Partial Anæsthesia," *Proceedings of the Society for Psychical Research,* **9 (1894), 236–44. With permission of the Society for Psychical Research.**

Ramsay's difficult feelings here are similar to those stirred up by psychedelic experiences that were arrested at an incomplete stage of development (e.g., William Braden's mescaline experience, to be described in chapter 4).

By contrast, R. H. Ward's anesthetic experience seems more fully mystical in development. Like Davy, Ward realized that "all was idea," and he discovered new connections between ideas.[37] Like James, he found that "things which we should call wholly different from one another became one another," a transformation that reached its conclusion in the reduction of ideas "by an incalculable series of combinations and cancellings" to a perfect unity.[38] This is recollected by Ward as the culmination of his experience in a supreme light. Overtly mystical features accompany the passage through deepening levels of consciousness, such as unity of subject and object, light experience, insight into suffering, and a sense of the eternal in the instant. There may therefore be good reason to suppose that in some cases the "anesthetic revelation" does indeed reveal more than the workings of subjective mental processes or chemically disorganized thought, and reaches a deep mystical level.

As ordinary consciousness began to assert itself, Ward experienced a visual pattern that he took to be a geometrical symbol or representation of the "meaning" of the universe, life on earth, and man:

> The sum of things appeared before my inward eye as *a living geometrical figure*, an infinitely complicated and infinitely simple arrangement of continually moving, continually changing golden lines on a background of darkness. ('Geometry', it has often been recorded, is a common form for such visions to take.) These golden lines were all that was left of the pure lucency of the 'region of light', yet, mere shadows of that original glory, they still conveyed something of its perfection. This living geometrical figure seemed to be telling me that *everything is in order*, that everything works according to an ineluctable pattern.[39]

Even this symbolic image began to fade, as the forgetting and ideational "nonsense" reported by others took hold:

> I was once more able to think normally, to say to myself . . ., 'So that's what it all means,' and even as I said it to forget what it all means . . . . Yet a dim and apparently nonsensical echo of 'what it all means' did remain in my head. 'What it all means,' I was urgently telling myself in the attempt to frustrate the swamping forgetfulness, 'is "Within and within and within and . . ." repeated like a recurring decimal.'[40]

An "aura of meaning" still attached to the apparently nonsensical phrase "within and within and within" as Ward left the dentist. It is notable that the sense of meaning *increased*, rather than decreased, as time went by and was partly regained through Ward's subsequent efforts to understand the experience. In consequence, Ward was able to give a fairly detailed account of the experience. It seems that knowledge lost at the close of a profound experience can find its way into ordinary consciousness after a delay. Examples not involving intoxicants include the experiences of Iris Skinner and Muz Murray. Skinner comments that months were to pass before she could recall more than fragments of the deeper part of her mystical experience.[41] Murray remembered much of his mystical experience in the immediate aftermath, but years later he felt that information was still "filtering through" into his awareness in the form of minor revelations.[42]

In my own case, memories also appeared after a delay. How is the delay to be explained? Suggestions can be made but will be vague and speculative. For instance, it might be supposed that time was needed for unconscious processes to work memory traces into an accessible, organized, and coherent form, a process that may have taken rather longer than usual because of the unfamiliar character of the experience. Other explanations might stress the contribution of conscious activity. I had been left with a puzzle that demanded attention, and deep interest in the event may have stimulated memories to emerge. I think that the dream-recording activities in which I engaged, encouraged by my reading of Jung, helped my powers of recall. The discipline rapidly improved my ability to remember and record dreams, and produced a wealth of material. The "training" provided by dream recording allowed my waking awareness to spread a little into the dreaming state and perhaps gave access to "state-bound" knowledge locked away in the subconscious.

Connected with the mysteries of the initial forgetting and the later partial recall is the problem of how memories could be generated in the first place. It is a puzzle how specific details can be discriminated from a vast field of knowing, making particular information available at the time and also for later recall. Without the ability to discriminate particulars, the mystic would be confronted with a panorama of knowledge too vast to be memorized as a whole—nothing could be brought back except perhaps the memory of expansive knowing having occurred. This often seems to be the case, but on occasions specific insights are recorded, suggesting that some discriminative processes are at work during the experiences. In my own case, I retain a few visual images: there is an overall view of the translucent world stretching into the distance, and some specific scenes too.

I also have memories of thoughts, understandings, and feelings that arose during the experience. In fact, it can be speculated that for substantial memories of content-rich mystical experiences to be generated, personal discriminations and reactions during an experience are important. These thoughts and feelings constitute familiar and easily memorized features that can later be recalled without too much difficulty, and therefore act as reminders of the less familiar material. In my own recollections, there are several personal reactions associated with particular insights, such as relief, discomfort, feelings of impurity, humility, and so forth, and it might be the presence of these that helped me to remember. If individual responses, including interpretations, during mystical experiences help to shape what is remembered, it would follow that individuals come back with their own stories and particular observations, colored by personal reactions and idiosyncratic tendencies to notice certain details. Although descriptions may have much in common, differences should be expected.

Having given an account of my own mystical episode and explored the peculiar way in which it was forgotten and then partly remembered, I now turn to another point of interest—its apparent connection to experiences at the brink of death.

3

Into the House of Death

I held it truth, with him who sings
To one clear harp in divers tones,
That men may rise on stepping-stones
Of their dead selves to higher things.

—Alfred Tennyson

NEAR-DEATH EXPERIENCE RESEARCHER Kenneth Ring makes the important observation that it is possible to have experiences very similar to those that occur near death even when no near-death crisis is involved. To put it bluntly, you don't have to be on the verge of death to have a near-death experience.[1] Ring points out that near-death crisis is just one circumstance in which the experiences occur. He lists some others: meditation, childbirth, personal crisis, church services. To these can be added, among others, beautiful scenery, relaxation, sleep, feelings of love, thoughts about profound matters, reading literature, listening to music, and lovemaking. It follows that explanations which try to account for near-death experiences (NDEs) *exclusively* in terms of the traumatized psychology and physiology of the dying brain are most likely incorrect, for it is possible to have similar experiences when the brain is in perfectly good condition. For example, Warner Allen's experience in the concert hall, described in chapter 1, is like some near-death experiences, with its tunnel-like passage to luminous reality, but it took place when there was no threat of death.

My own experience, taking place during sleep, also illustrates Ring's point. It had several features reminiscent of the more mystical type of NDE, even though it occurred without any hint of a near-death medical emergency in progress. I was simply asleep in bed. There is, for example, a parallel between my preliminary dream of the twilight sea-crossing and the journeys that are sometimes reported in the early stages of near-death experiences, which can involve a passage from a darkened state toward a luminous one, say, through a tunnel or over a bridge. In near-death experiences, the light at the end of the journey can take various forms, including paradise-like landscapes and deceased relatives, but in some cases the destinations are similar to the luminous world I found at the end of my own sea journey, namely a cosmic expanse full of knowledge, meaning, and love, bringing a new understanding of what is truly important in life. For example, Ring gives the case of a fourteen-year-old boy who, close to drowning in a flash flood, drifted along a tunnel toward an intense brightness:

> As I reached the source of the light I could see in. I cannot begin to describe in human terms the feeling I had at what I saw. It was a giant infinite world of calm, and love, and energy and beauty. It was as though human life was unimportant compared to this. And yet it urged the importance of life at the same time it solicited death as a means to a better, different life. It was all being, all beauty, all meaning for existence. It was all the energy of the universe forever in one immensurable place.[2]

This account reads very much like a description of mystical experience, with its references to beauty, meaning, love, calm, expansiveness, and an altered perspective on the significance of life. Another striking example is the near-death experience described by Reinee Pasarow.[3] A strong allergic reaction precipitated an out-of-body experience, a view of the Earth from high above, the feeling of a departed uncle's presence, a "vibrant light" permeated by music, and then a "vast light" into which she felt "irresistibly drawn." Unity with this light brought some mystical features: love, comprehensive knowledge, meaning, and old concerns exposed as trivial. Again, a near-death emergency had resulted in a mystical experience, presumably because physical traumas (that is, trauma to the body) constitute one kind of circumstance in which the everyday flow of consciousness is sufficiently interrupted to allow deeper levels to emerge.

But if some near-death experiences can rightly be regarded as mystical experiences, the converse also seems to be the case. In a sense, mystical experiences are a type of death experience, even if there is no question of biological dying taking place. Mystical experiences can be understood as journeys into death, metaphorically and psychologically, in the temporary subjugation of limited self-understandings they bring and in the long-term transformations of self they invite. They may even give a hint of the kinds of experiences that await us at death. It was therefore appropriate that my own mystical experience should have been prefaced by imagery long associated with the death transition.

Death and the Sea Journey

On a visit to the coast, it is easy to be impressed by the vastness of the scene. The huge watery expanse stretching to the horizon is, like mountain scenery or the starry heavens, an exterior immensity that intimates a vastness within. For the land dweller, the sea is a place of mystery, a zone of transition from the known to the unknown, an uncharted region that begins where the terrain of everyday life breaks off. The sea may strike the onlooker as a boundary zone that separates the familiar lands on this side of the waters from unknown regions on the other side. The coast can be a place of great beauty, with its expanses of water and sky, wave and cloud, and ever-shifting patterns of light, from subtle gradations to the more dramatic illuminations of storms, and sunrises and sunsets. As well as evoking expansive calm, the sea in other moods may suggest immense power and unplumbed depths, and therefore danger and death to the land dweller, who is tiny and insignificant in comparison, at the mercy of towering waves and hidden currents. Given the feelings of awe, wonder, and immensity the sea evokes, it is not surprising that coastal locations are fairly common settings for mystical experiences of nature and that they have sometimes furnished symbolic imagery for the dreams that accompany some mystical experiences.

In the dream that preceded my own experience, I was pulled *across* the sea, suggesting a particular type of symbolism: here the sea is a region to be traversed in order to reach the farther side. Ananda Coomaraswamy (1877–1947), that industrious explorer of common ground between the symbolisms of religious traditions, observed that the water journey can take various forms.[4] In one, the traveler proceeds up a river to its beginning, symbolically returning to the source of life. In another, the journey goes downstream to the sea. Here the sea stands for the spiritual totality, the placid ocean of eternity into which the individual life-streams pour. Finally, there is the river or sea as a stretch of water to be crossed, from one bank or shore to the other. The means of crossing are varied and might involve a bridge or some kind of vessel, such as a raft or ship. In the case of celestial journeys through the planetary spheres, the sky becomes a heavenly sea to be traversed. The waters are the "waters of death," and the land beyond the sea is the land to which the dead proceed, toward an afterlife in a dark, underworld realm or the sunny lands of paradise. In psychological terms, the journey can be interpreted as a descent into the unconscious, into the deeper, ordinarily hidden recesses of the mind, as Jung suggested:

> The night sea journey is a kind of *descensus ad inferos*—a descent into Hades and a journey to the land of ghosts somewhere beyond this world, beyond consciousness, hence an immersion in the unconscious.[5]

The sea journey to the realm of the dead is an ancient motif, dating back at least as far as the Mesopotamian *Epic of Gilgamesh*, in which the hero-king travels across the waters in search of immortality. Similar is the journey of Odysseus across the river of Ocean to the underworld, although diverging in some details.[6] It is interesting, with regard to the theme of "forgetting and remembering," that Gilgamesh's search for eternal life was brought to nothing when, after Gilgamesh fell asleep, a snake carried off the plant of immortality he had briefly won. For the Egyptians, the great sun-barque, once the vehicle of the sun god Rā and divinized kings alone, carried many through the nighttime realm of death, a "boat of millions."[7]

In the Indian sphere, the symbolism of "crossing the waters" has had a long history, often referring to the passage from the present condition of human life, the Hither Shore, to the firm ground of liberation, the Yonder Shore.[8] In early Buddhism, the latter was *nirvāṇa*, "the unconditioned" beyond *saṃsāra*, the cycle of life and death. In Jainism, the twenty-four teachers who appear in the fourth phase of our six-phase half-cycle of decline are called *tīrthaṅkaras*, "ford builders," masters of the spiritual life who show the way across the ocean of existence.[9] The sea to be crossed is this world itself, and so it has the characteristics of the Hither Shore. In a Buddhist collection of sayings, the waters are "the flood of will, birth, opinion, and ignorance."[10] In the Neoplatonic exegesis of the Odysseus myth, the waters are the mutable "sea of time and space," the world of matter in which souls are drowning, buried, or asleep, contrasted with the dry, sunlit homeland of eternity.[11] Thus, whether the sea represents a barrier between this world and the next, or this world of ignorance itself, the sea crossing is a death passage to true life. Usually the other shore is attainable only at the death of the body, although the shaman or yogin can travel there while still alive, if correctly initiated and able to surmount the dangers of the crossing. The perils of sea travel reflect the difficulties and terrors of the death journey, which again are highlighted in myths and religious practices.

My own "sea journey" took place after my attention had been drawn toward the ocean. Something had distracted me from my activities on the beach and caused me to stand by the water's edge and look into the distance.

It was most probably the sun located at the horizon that drew my attention, and I was then drawn along the tapering object toward it, into the realm of light. The positioning of the taper at waist level and the sense of being pulled along it most likely have a sexual quality, suggestive of the phallus. The taper was a route across the waters, and it is interesting to note that bridges, which also act as pathways to the other world, have been construed as phallic.[12]

But instead of following interpretations that view the "oceanic feeling" in plain sexual terms or as a regressive return to infantile unity with the mother (and even to intrauterine undifferentiation),[13] I think it more promising to follow the lead of those who view sexual desire as just one expression of a basic pull toward deeper realities, a desire or *eros* that in its higher forms is directed toward the blissful totality in which the divided achieve wholeness and even beyond to the source of things.[14] I shall have much more to say about this *eros* in due course. Sexuality in all its developmental forms, from infancy to adulthood, could then be viewed as the manifestation and localization of cosmic and divine "energies," a fundamental desire channeled into, appropriated by, and driving the procreative, social, cultural, artistic, and spiritual activities of human life. In contracted form, detached from understanding, these fundamental energies all too easily take on distorted and destructive forms but have many healthy and lofty expressions too. The phallus fascinates, enthralls, overpowers, pulls in directions one may or may not want to go, from rapacious violence and squalid obsession through banal allurements to tender feelings and aspirations toward love and communion.[15] The interpretation of the taper as a divinely oriented phallus is perhaps strengthened by the observation that the traditional night sea journey corresponds to the journey of the sun.

Through the Sun Door

It has sometimes been said that the journey of the hero is an imitation of the sun on its daily passage over the world and its nightly descent into the depths. In mythological terms, the traveler emulates the Sun God's passage through the underworld, which in its negative aspect is a place of terror, dissolution, and death, but in its positive aspect is the blissful return to the feminine for renewal, for resurrection into new life, for initiation and rebirth. If we take the dream scene to hint at the mythic journey of the solar hero, then the taper can be viewed as a trail of reflected light, the so-called glitter path produced by the ocean-crossing sun as it dips toward the horizon. Like the tunnel of the near-death experience, the glitter path leads to the fabled "Sun Door," the gateway to the other world. The subdued quality of the light in the dream gives a temporal reference to the scene, for it is neither the darkness of night nor the brightness of day, but a light in between, a transitional or liminal luminosity. It is twilight, a balance of light and dark, a temporal meeting of opposites that matches the spatial meeting of opposites in the dream scene, expressed in the symbol of the beach, as interspace between land and sea, and in the convergence of sea and sky at the horizon. In symbolic terms, the twilights of dawn and dusk are two openings in the cycle of time through which the eternal realm can be entered with relative ease.[16] This is so because twilight is a juncture at which the opposites are momentarily in balance, an equalization that allows one to step off the revolving circumference onto the still center of time's wheel. In chapter 9, I shall suggest that this wheel is the cycle of subject–object separation and unification, the journey of the self in its relations with the other. To put it another way, at twilight the Sun Door is more accessible than usual because it is located at the horizon, neither hidden in the darkness below nor inaccessible on high.

If, in the dream, the twilight marked the approach of dawn, then my attention was drawn to the rising sun in the East, and the symbolism was of the dawn type, stressing reemergence and rebirth, as in the solar mythologies of the Buddha and related figures, who, with the aid of a feminine principle, achieve their goal at the end of a hazardous night journey. In the yogic milieu in which the Buddha myth took shape, the journey had been interiorized as a night passage through meditative states, including encounters with the Lord of Death, prior to enlightenment at dawn. But if the twilight in the dream was dusk rather than dawn, then the symbolism places the scene at the outset of the night journey, and my attention was caught by the embers of the setting sun, and I was drawn, in mythological terms, into the lands of the dead, the Beautiful West or Duat of the Egyptians, the Greek and Celtic Isles of the Blessed, or the garden of the Hesperides, where the golden apples of immortality are to be found.

Discussing the coincidence of the opposites, the "Meeting of the Sun and Moon" in the twilight union, Joseph Campbell remarked that the theme constitutes a major development of the mythologizing of the first millennium BCE. In particular, the sunset of the night sea journey represented an "inward turning of the mind" that would "culminate in a realization of an identity *in esse* of the individual (microcosm) and the universe (macrocosm)."[17] To arrive at the Sun Door, according to this line of thought, is to meet a luminous higher self—a self none other than oneself, or a double or twin (see chapter 4). The flight of the "spiritual arrow" from darkness to "realms of spiritual light" is a journey of self-discovery, as Coomaraswamy observed.[18]

In the Indian sphere, there is early textual support for this view in the *Jaiminīya Brāhmaṇa* and *Jaiminīya Upaniṣad Brāhmaṇa*. The question posed at the Sun Door by the gatekeeper is "Who are you?" and is to be answered along the lines "I am you," to demonstrate recognition of one's essential nature as the higher self.[19] Passage through the Sun Door—the door into the realm of light—requires that one die to one's mortal self. Failure to do so will lead to rebirth, entry into the immortal realm having been refused.[20] As the *Muṇḍaka Upaniṣad* (1.2.11) puts it, the passage through the Sun Door leads to "where that immortal Person is, that immutable self."[21]

The cosmology behind these ideas takes the heavenly vault to be a surface that encloses our world of birth, death, and rebirth. The only way out is through a hole in the sky covered by the sun.[22] In the *Chāndogya Upaniṣad* (8.6.1–6), the proceedings have a physiological dimension: it is stated that colored rays travel between the veins of the heart and the sun, and that at death the soul ascends through one of the veins to the crown of the head, whence it travels to the sun, the door to the immortal realm.[23] The *Bṛhadāraṇyaka Upaniṣad* (4.4.8–9) also describes the path to the heavenly abode:

> There is an ancient path
> extremely fine and extending far;
> It has touched me, I discovered it!
> By it they go up to the heavenly world
> released from here,
> wise men, knowers of *brahman*.
>
> In it are the white and the blue, they say,
> the orange, green and red.
> By *brahman* was this path discovered;
> By it goes the knower of *brahman*,
> The doer of good, the man of light.[24]

The wise person who has traversed the path and discovered the true self will know that "I am he," the maker of everything, the possessor of the world, and indeed the world itself (4.4.12–13).

The combination of death journey, subtle physiology, luminosities, and call for self-recognition found in the ancient Indian scriptures recurs many centuries later in the elaborate tantric ideas and practices directed toward liberation at death, most famously in the Tibetan Buddhist and Bon religious sphere. The dying are urged to recognize the profound luminosity that manifests at the moment of death, the Clear Light, as their own true nature, and the subsequent postmortem visions that confront them, beautiful or terrifying, as projections of this true nature. Failure to recognize the Clear Light will be a missed opportunity to achieve liberation, and worse still, may lead to unfavorable rebirths if the enticing dull lights that subsequently manifest are followed instead. Within Buddhism, the liberating identification with the true nature is complicated by the fact that Buddhist philosophy typically attempts to steer clear of the idea of a permanent, essential self, such as the *ātman–brahman* of the *Upaniṣads*. The Clear Light may therefore be explained as a figurative expression for the liberating insight into "emptiness" (*śūnyatā*) understood as the interdependence or lack of inherent existence of things. Sometimes, however, the Clear Light has been understood as a permanent essence, the pure, experientially luminous Buddha-nature or "wisdom mind" undisturbed by defilements and limiting ideas.[25]

An early Western correlate of the "true identity" question posed during the death transition is suggested by instructions inscribed on gold leaves found in tombs located in southern Italy, Thessaly, and Crete.[26] One early gold lamella from Hipponion in southern Italy, dated to about 400 BCE, instructs the parched soul who enters the House of Hades to avoid the spring water at the white cypress tree and drink instead the water that flows from the Lake of Memory. The latter is obtained by correctly answering questions posed by mysterious guardians:

> Guardians stand over it who will ask you in their sensible mind why you are wandering through the darkness of corruptible Hades. Answer: I am a son of the earth and the starry sky; but I am desiccated with thirst and am perishing; therefore give me quickly cool water flowing from the lake of recollection.[27]

On another gold leaf, the question is posed by the Well of Memory itself: "Who are you? Where are you from?" Those who answer appropriately to questions of this kind will be greeted warmly with the words, "You are become god from man." Presumably the drink to be avoided is the water of forgetfulness, the antithesis of the sought-after water from the Lake of Memory. The deceased secure the revivifying water by declaring their purity ("pure I come from the pure") or their divine kinship as offspring of the primordial parents ("I am a child of Ge and Ouranos"). Precisely what follows is not clearly or consistently indicated across the twenty or so lamellae so far discovered, but some kind of rebirth into blessed company, immortality, and divinity seems to be envisaged, if not a permanent escape from a cycle of transmigration.[28] Concepts of transmigration were abroad at the time, most obviously in Pythagorean circles, but it is not known for certain if the gold leaves were produced by religious communities in which beliefs in reincarnation were held.

Why should the mystical experience have been introduced by a dream that involved imagery traditionally linked with death? One explanation would take death to be a metaphor for any transition that clears away the old in preparation for the new. The experience certainly had a transformative effect, suggesting to me that there was more to myself and the world than I had previously imagined. More specifically, the central experience involved a partial, temporary psychological "death," a disruption of ordinary self-cognitions, for during the experience I understood myself in a very different light, finding I was much less and much more than I had believed. It was a weakening of the familiar self-identifications to reveal unsuspected depths that made my usual physical and mental existence seem very insignificant, an insight that was both liberating and disturbing, joyful and shocking.

It was only after some time had passed that the death symbolism of the sea journey became obvious to me, but dreams after the experience continued to affirm an association with ego-death and my resistance to it. For instance, in one dream, a skeleton came out of the sea and motioned to me to return with it, but I was too fearful to acquiesce. In another, I knocked furiously on the door into a strange kingdom surrounded by a high wall, desperate to meet the girl who lived there, but when her father eventually opened the door to let me in, he turned out to be Death, and I backed away in fear. The most vivid example was a lucid dream, a journey to a Temple of Death, perhaps not unrelated to Jung's visit to the rock temple in his near-death vision:

> Lying in bed asleep, I decide to get up into the lucid state, which I do, and go over to the curtains, and draw them aside slightly. In the garden there is a tree covered in red and golden leaves, and a woman's voice appears in my mind, singing a beautiful song about the tree, although after a while her voice fades away, becoming my own. Then, still looking through the window, I notice giant, primaeval statues on the distant hillside, arranged side-by-side in groups of twos and threes, and also see a temple next to them. I decide to explore and walk across the valley, talking to an oldish man on the way, and find that the terrain on the other side is rather bare. As I reach the building I approach cautiously, because of the primitive, archaic feel of the place. I knock a couple of times on the large wooden door of the temple and go in when there is no reply. Passing across successive thresholds into rooms where men are having their heads shaved

in preparation for sacrifice, I begin to worry that I will be torn apart if I go into the next room, which I imagine will be dark. I don't want this to happen, and go through other rooms, and meet an old priest. He shows me around outside, and I see a graveyard nearby, with children playing by the tombstones. The priest says that beyond the graveyard I could meet a very interesting man and find the giant statues there too. But I am not keen to go and discuss it with the priest, and he is understanding – in fact, I get the impression that I am really discussing the matter with myself. I feel it is time to return to ordinary consciousness, and set off back across the valley, and I have a bird's-eye view of the scene on the way back.

The autumnal coloring of the tree in the garden and the bare terrain on the opposite valley side suggest a movement toward winter, and therefore, symbolically, toward death. The tree itself, about which the beautiful, female voice sang, is perhaps akin to the phallic taper of the beach dream. The statues made me think of gods or archetypal beings, arranged in male-female dyads and in triads. The children playing by the tombstones perhaps corresponded to the children on the shore in the preliminary dream (if there had indeed been children in that dream), and the "very interesting man" beyond the graveyard is perhaps the higher aspect of self that one may encounter on "the other side."

Now it is true that symbols of death can be rather exotic and potentially frightening, as in this dream, and the religious practices that have developed around such images can be grotesque and terrifying, as in shamanic rituals, Tibetan *chod* offerings, medieval *memento mori*, and festivals of the dead, but the act of dying in question here can be understood in a more prosaic and direct manner, in which sacrifice of self is internalized and "dying" becomes just a matter of yielding to an open, loving, nongrasping way of attending to the world. Dying, then, is understood in its psychological essence as a letting go from moment to moment of the thoughts and concerns that obstruct awareness of the mind's inherent wisdom, love, and inclusivity. As these attachments are often centered on limited self-understandings and self-concerns, the letting-go is a kind of death, a sacrifice of neurotic self-preoccupation. Perhaps Krishnamurti intended something along these lines when he discussed the possibility of entering "the house of death" while living, by letting go of the accumulated known. In the awareness of the moment, there is an awakening of "intelligence" and a freedom from past conditioning.[29] In the idea of freedom through the death of self-preoccupation in the present moment, there is an echo of the ancient understanding of the philosophical life as a preparation for death. For some philosophers, dying meant living in the joyfulness of the present moment through a shedding of the selfhood and vain passions that bind the soul to its narrow understandings and anxieties.[30] To rise above these distractions is to become great in soul, universal in thought, and present in each moment to the entire cosmos, perhaps even to the whole of time.[31]

"Dying" in its essential, experiential nature, then, does not require the terminal, bodily event which the word usually denotes, or even symbolic, imitative practices involving impressive self-mortifications and grisly rites. A simple shift in mental poise seems to be all that is required, a shift to apprehending the world and its inhabitants with a loving, inclusive, uncluttered mind. Thus mystical experiences are sometimes brought about when the "sound and fury" of self-centered dramas subside a little, quietened perhaps by the beauty of nature, a sense of fellowship with others, or some other feeling that breaks through the narrow mindset and connects with a deeper level of knowing and feeling.

If it is appropriate to understand my experience as an "other-worldly journey"—and the dream imagery of the sea-crossing from one land to another suggests that there is justification for this label—I would qualify the terminology by pointing out that the world I reached was none other than the world we ordinarily know but understood more expansively. The other-worldly journey was in fact a this-worldly journey, to "this world" understood more deeply. The Yonder Shore was no other than the Hither Shore but now apprehended in a radically different way.

The Judgment Scene

Journeys to the threshold of death, whether in near-death crises or the many other circumstances in which mystical experiences occur, can be very attractive, bringing love, knowledge, meaning, bliss, joy, freedom from anxiety, liberation from confinement, and so forth. However, the experiences can also be very uncomfortable. In my case, there were at least three sources of discomfort that I have found reported by others in their accounts of mystical and near-death experiences.

1. *Feelings of insignificance:* deflation of the ordinary self, its ambitions, and its attachments to the body.

Normally the chief player on the stage of life, the ego finds its concerns exposed for their relative unimportance, and the body may be revealed as "empty" or "dependent," as if flat, cartoon-like, lifeless in comparison with the great, living mind and universe. In my experience, the body on which my usual self-conceptions are based appeared lifeless, as if a movie had stopped running and was seen to consist of still frames. Perhaps there is a connection here with R. M. Bucke's observation that in cosmic consciousness "instead of men being, as it were, patches of life scattered through an infinite sea of non-living substance, they are in reality specks of relative death in an infinite ocean of life."[32] This kind of discovery may have been expressed in the Indian context in the graphic comparison of the universe to a funeral ground littered with corpses, and the associated tantric internalization of the "cremation sacrifice" as the "conflagration" of limited self-identifications.[33] Life belongs to the totality, of which the everyday self is a very small part, no longer a special focus of concern. In the universal context, the issues that usually take center stage become much less important, which can be shocking as well as liberating.

2. *Loss of others:* expansion of self with no recognition of others.

The cosmic self-expansion can bring a solipsistic lack of awareness of the social dimension of reality. In my case, it was a temporary phase that was corrected by the discovery of equals and the subsequent expansion of love. The loss of others, which can bring feelings of loneliness, seems to belong to an incomplete stage of development in which knowledge and unity have yet to progress to love and community. A woman whose consciousness had expanded until it encompassed everything came to feel very lonely:

> I was everything that is. It seemed curious at first, but then turned into a feeling of being very much alone. I thought surely there must be something or somebody outside of me, but I searched and searched and could find nothing that was not a part of me. Desperately, I wanted someone to share my existence. Finally, the loneliness became overwhelming and I snapped back into my usual little self.[34]

This arrested kind of self-expansion, in which there is no shift toward the social insight, seems more likely to occur in experiences induced by drugs, as I shall note again in chapter 4. Dramatic examples have been recounted by William Braden and John Horgan,[35] and there is an interesting near-death instance reported by a woman who underwent a very difficult childbirth. She felt she had become a light in heaven and contained in herself all mankind, yet she was a little ball of light, screaming, spinning, and profoundly alone.[36]

3. *Self-judgment:* a sense of impurity, shame, guilt, unworthiness
    or inadequacy that comes from recognition that one's actions,
    attitudes, and general mindset have been out of step with the
    deeper nature of things, specifically with love.

With the social dimension of reality and intimate connection between its members revealed, love comes to the fore, and hurtful actions against others weigh heavily. In the course of life, there are usually opportunities to develop empathy and compassion, to understand others as similar to oneself in needs, sufferings, and aspirations. But ordinary social intercourse gives limited preparation for the discovery of just how intimately related we are.

For myself, the "self-judgment" occurred when I experienced the great love that embraced all. The sense of impurity made me feel that I would not want to be exposed to such an experience again until I had changed and would be able to live more easily with the powerful love. I do not remember viewing any specific deeds over which I felt shame or remorse; rather; the feeling of impurity seems to have arisen from the contrast between the general condition of my everyday personality and the newfound state of mind. This feeling of impurity may be similar to the self-evaluations reported in some modern accounts of near-death experience. Here self-judgments are sometimes linked to a "review" of past events, actions, and motives. The individual comes face-to-face with past attitudes and actions, and self-judgments take place, bringing feelings of shame, guilt, regret. The "truth of love" emerges as the most important realization to be brought back to the world of the living and communicated to those who will listen.[37]

These judgments are often "internal," self-originated rather than inflicted by an external arbiter or impersonal law, unlike in many traditional postmortem scenarios.[38] Although the latter are often similar in that they involve a presentation of past deeds to the deceased, the assessor or impersonal justice is usually considered external. It might be thought that the role played by conscience and guilt in modern experiences reflects the psychologizing tendencies of our age. However, the internalist view of the judgment scene is not a recent development. Carol Zaleski finds a trace in the story of a soldier's near-death vision, told by Gregory the Great.[39] The journeying dead must cross a test-bridge to reach beautiful meadows, but the *guilt* of the unjust makes them stumble and fall into the murky river below, whereas a pilgrim sincere in life crosses the bridge with assurance. The model for the story is the ancient Persian postmortem scene at the bridge of Chinvat. Zoroaster himself had warned: "They shall be tortured by their own soul and their conscience when they come to the Bridge of the Separator."[40]

Gregory's story gives the merest hint of an internal, psychological dimension to the judgment scene. But the idea that postmortem judgments and punishments come from the conscience and are not simply imposed from outside was entertained by several early Christian thinkers, some of whom were unable to square belief in a loving God with the idea of divinely imposed, retributive, eternal damnation. If the loving nature of God is given preeminence, then a doctrine of universal salvation (*apokatastasis*) is a more logical position, and so too postmortem judgments and sufferings that are self-inflicted, permitted only temporarily by God, for purgative and educative purposes, making possible the eventual salvation of all souls. It seems that in their more private thoughts, the Alexandrian theologians Clement and Origen hoped for the purgative and temporary nature of postmortem sufferings, and Origen sometimes spiritualized the judgments and punishments through allegorical interpretation. Here he understands the hellish fire of Gehenna as the fire of the guilty conscience, fueled by sins.[41] In *De Principiis* (2.10.4), Origen takes a passage in Isaiah (50.11) as expressive of an inner, spiritual meaning to the fires of hell:

> By these words, it seems to be indicated each sinner kindles himself with his own fire, and is not immersed in another fire, which was previously kindled by someone else, or which pre-existed.[42]

The fire is not inflicted by outside agencies but arises internally as a disturbed conscience fed by sins. Origen draws an analogy with the disturbed body, made feverish by the intemperate intake of nourishment, perhaps, it has been suggested, drawing on the Stoic idea of the "fever of the passions."[43] According to Origen, the process depends on the capacity of the divinely empowered conscience to recall evil acts:

> when the mind of the conscience, by divine power, recalls all the actions, whose various imprints and forms were impressed on it when it was sinning will set out before its eyes a kind of story (*historiam*) of every single evil deed, of every foul, disgraceful or impious act that it has done. Then the conscience is agitated and pricked by its own stings, and becomes the accuser and witness against itself.[44]

There is, therefore, a divine contribution to the fire of suffering. However, this contribution is not an externally originated, divine judgment but the divinely infused power of the conscience to recall sinful actions. In addition, Origen describes a purgative fire of God through which all must pass: this fire is God Himself, who purifies repentant sinners, burning up their evil thoughts and actions. The relation between the two fires in the education of the soul is not too clear. Perhaps it is the fire of Gehenna in the troubled conscience that enables sinners to turn through remorse to the fire of God for subsequent purification.

Origen's understanding of self-judgment and his hopes for universal salvation resurfaced with the Cappadocian fathers—intermittently with Basil of Caesaraea and Gregory of Nazianzus, but more confidently with Gregory of Nyssa.[45] Ambrose of Milan echoed the Origenist position, and several other Christian thinkers have entertained alternatives to eternal damnation and have been inclined toward more internalist understandings of the postmortem judgment. Even the abrasive Church Father Jerome was capable of understanding the punishments meted out in hell as a metaphor for the self-recriminations of the sinner's guilty conscience. Before his turn against Origenist theology, Jerome occasionally raised the idea, and even later he was not completely dismissive.[46]

The view that afterlife judgment, punishment, and suffering are to some extent self-inflicted has been a minority position, but it has had some notable representation among mystical writers, presumably because personal experiences acquainted them with the self-recriminatory feelings that the knowledge and love of mystical experience can bring about. In *The Way to Christ* (1622), Jacob Boehme (1575–1624) portrays the soul's reaction when the revelatory wisdom of the Virgin Sophia manifests:

> Before Her the soul is frightened in its impurity so that all its sins are first awakened and before Her they are horrified and trembling. Then judgement comes over the sins of the soul so that it turns back in its unworthiness ashamed of its beautiful lover; it turns into itself and rejects itself as altogether unworthy to receive such a treasure. We who have tasted this heavenly treasure understand this but no one else does.[47]

It is not Sophia who recoils at the soul's impurity: she has pledged herself to the bridegroom soul and will infuse him with love, bringing great joy and turning the dark fire of vain selfhood into white light.[48] Likewise, Teresa of Ávila does not think God forsakes sinners. She wishes they could see how visible are their sins in the diamond-clear vision of the world:

> It was a terrifying experience for me, in so short a space of time, to see so many things at once in the clear depths of that diamond, and whenever I think of it, it is a most piteous reflection, that so many foul things, like

my sins, should have been pictured in that clearness and purity. So, whenever I remember this, I do not know how to bear it and at that time I felt so ashamed that I did not seem to know where to hide myself. Oh, that someone could reveal this to those who commit the most foul and dishonourable sins and could make them realize that their sins are not hidden.[49]

It is not God who pulls away in disgust or judgment but the soul in shame. Teresa marvels at the mercy of God: even though He knows all our sins in the greatest clarity, He continues to bear with us. The feelings of shame or unworthiness follow from the exposure of sins in the mirror-like knowledge. Failings are revealed, including every thought and action that one would prefer hidden. There are therefore two contributions to the judgment: the soul judges itself, but it does so in the revelatory light presented to it, like the conscience of Origen, divinely empowered to recall evil actions.

Some writers stress the central role of love in the fire encountered by the soul: it is not simply revelatory knowledge that causes the soul to burn. It burns because it finds that its thoughts and actions have worked against love. Isaac of Nineveh (d. ca. 700 CE) explains that love is intensely painful to those who have sinned against it but joyful to those who have lived by it. Like Origen's fire of God, the fire of love presents no obstacle to saints, while sinners suffer dreadfully:

> As for me, I say that those who are tormented in hell are tormented by the invasion of love. What is there more bitter and more violent than the pains of love? Those who feel that they have sinned against love bear in themselves a damnation much heavier than the most dreaded punishments. The suffering with which sinning against love afflicts the heart is more keenly felt than any other torment. It is absurd to suppose that sinners in hell are deprived of God's love. Love . . . is offered impartially. But by its very power it acts in two ways. It torments sinners, as happens here on earth when we are tormented by the presence of a friend to whom we have been unfaithful. And it gives joy to those who have been faithful. That is what the torment of hell is in my opinion – remorse.[50]

Here there is a tendency to merge the two fires of Origen—hell's fire and God's love—into one fire, a love that delights the good but distresses sinners. It is in the divine love that sinful deeds are revealed, remorse stirred, and the soul purified. Thus, for St. Catherine of Genoa, in her *Treatise on Purgatory*, the purifying fire is none other than the divine love, source of great joy and suffering, for it renders the soul conscious of its impurity and so purifies it.[51]

Self-judgment in the face of love also manifests in the well-regulated afterlife society envisioned by Emanuel Swedenborg (1688–1772), although his account is decidedly spiritualist rather than mystical in feel. When a person dies, the soul is revived and greeted by welcoming angels. These angels love all souls equally and wish to lead them to the heavenly regions of the afterlife. At first, souls may not recognize that they have passed on, and they become upset upon understanding their situation. However, they are happy with the welcoming reception provided by good spirits, a joy represented by the character of the ambient light, a white turning into yellow. Those who have not felt at ease in the company of good people during life cannot tolerate for long the loving spirits, and they gravitate to less exalted company in which they feel more comfortable and are able to resume their previous ways of life.

From here, there are further steps to the societies of heaven or hell, constituting the "Last Judgment" of each person.[52] "The Lord casts no one down into hell, but everyone does so to himself,"[53] and it is the discomfort of the impure soul before the mutual love of the heavenly state that makes the soul eager to retreat.[54] It is the soul's own feelings, thoughts, and habits that take it away from the blissful state, not the judgment of an external authority. Swedenborg, tutored by his angelic informants, is able to appreciate this, but the average soul may not so readily understand the self-originated direction of the postmortem journey. Hence the importance sometimes attached to holding onto awareness of one's divine kinship or identity in certain expositions of the postmortem journey: know that you are a child of divine parents; recognize that the alluring or frightening images confronting you are products of your own mind.

However, if judgments are not really external to oneself, it does not follow that they are merely arbitrary, personal reactions, subject to the relativisms of different upbringings and ethical codes or lack thereof. The evaluation seems to depend on a disparity between the usual self-position and the underlying loving nature, a basis that is far from arbitrary. Cultivation of an amoral position, a mind without conscience "beyond good and evil" in order to sidestep terminal self-evaluations and feelings of impurity, might fail very badly if there is indeed a basis for morality in the expansive loving mind and its community of beings, or indeed even in its "supernoetic" basis. In Plotinian philosophy, this is the One, which can be considered "beyond good and evil," for it transcends dualities, but it is nevertheless called "the Good" because it is the ultimate good of all the beings who derive from it. On the other hand, it is conceivable that personal self-judgments in the mystical, near-death, and postmortem mirrors of revelation could be excessive if one has been inclined in the ordinary course of life toward making harsh appraisals, of oneself or of others. One form of "pathology of the sublime" is excessive self-criticism.

There are other possible sources of discomfort in mystical and near-death experiences in addition to ego-deflation, solipsistic isolation, and self-judgment. For instance, in St. Teresa's account there is something of the sublime terror that is occasionally mentioned in descriptions of mystical experience, most often but not exclusively in connection with drug-induced states, such as Rosalind Heywood's "sheer excess of glory" (mescaline) and R. H. Ward's "barbaric splendor" (LSD). In St. Teresa's case, the greatness of the vision seems to have contributed to her fear, alongside the shame produced by moral revelations. She was overcome by seeing "so many things at once" in absolute clarity. The terrifying impact of the cosmic beauty is mentioned by Plotinus as a feature of less experienced contact with the divine mind. The intelligible cosmos is not something ordinarily known and can be disturbing when it is first discovered. This is perhaps why drug-induced experiences are more likely to bring sublime terror, being chaotic or uncontrolled introductions to the state, rather than skillful disclosures.

However, for the accomplished, the Beautiful may even appear boring in comparison with its source, the One or Good: the bored soul "falls flat on its back," says Plotinus (*Ennead* VI.7.22).[55] But for those with less experience, the Beautiful will be awesome, and for the "thoughtless" it is likely to be painful and can lead the inexperienced away from the deepest realization, the One. Beauty "brings wonder and shock and pleasure" and can breed painful desires (*Enn.* V.5.12).[56] In contrast, the Good, which is the source of Beauty in the intelligible world, is not frightening but "gentle and kindly and gracious," and there is no surprise or amazement when it is discovered, for we always aspire to the Good, and it is always present to us in its simplicity, whether we are asleep or awake (*Enn.* V.5.12). However, the discovery of the Good can itself be unsettling, not through awe, beauty, and subsequent unfulfilled desires, but through the incomprehensibility of this unthinkable reality (*Enn.* VI.9.3):

> But in proportion as the soul goes towards the formless, since it is utterly unable to comprehend it because it is not delimited and, so to speak, stamped by a richly varied stamp, it slides away and is afraid that it may have nothing at all. Therefore it gets tired of this sort of thing, and often gladly comes down and falls away from all this, till it comes to the perceptible and rests there as if on solid ground; just as sight when it gets tired of small objects is glad to come upon big ones.

The everpresent simplicity of the Good may not come as a great surprise, in contrast to the extraordinary, immensely complex feeling-cognition that is the Beautiful, but unlike the Beautiful it is beyond comprehension.

Plotinus's warning about the dangers of Beauty at the cosmic level are not intended to detract from the glory and value of the intelligible world, which he regularly asserts. Rather, they are probably meant to warn of the dangers involved in the discovery of the Intellect by the inexperienced lower soul. These dangers include ignorant, painful lusting after Beauty that leads away from reality, and inflatory efforts to rival Beauty. Intriguingly, Plotinus's cautions appear to be echoed in the warnings given by Boehme's Sophia. She describes two dangers faced by the soul who has glimpsed her and is desirous of more: the darkening of the Virgin's pearl in earthiness and the self-aggrandizement of Luciferian pride.[57]

Warnings about the inflatory dangers of mystical experience raise questions about the nature of self. Exactly how is the greater self that seems to be disclosed in some mystical experiences to be understood? Is there truly a self to be found in the depths of reality, and if so, how is it related to the ordinary self?

4

Who Do You Think You Are?

> He should be searched out, Him one should desire to understand.
> He obtains all worlds and all desires who
> has found out and who understands that Self.
>
> —*Chāndogya Upaniṣad*

IT WOULD APPEAR THAT MYSTICAL EXPERIENCE can be a "death" of the everyday self, not a total annihilation but a temporary, partial suppression, a challenge to old self-understandings, and an occasion for disquieting self-judgments. Indeed, the most transformative insights to be gained from mystical experience are those that call for a reassessment of oneself and one's relation to others. Discoveries of unity, enhanced vision, all-inclusive knowledge, the eternal now, and cosmic luminosity are undeniably remarkable and possibly of great interest for their philosophical and scientific implications, but mystical experiences are of most pressing concern for their impact on self-understanding. But what more precisely do the experiences reveal about self?

If the quotidian self is shown to be not as central and independent as it ordinarily appears, is there reason to suppose it is rooted in a deeper, more substantive self?[1] The guardian at the doorway into the realm of light seems to think so when he challenges visitors with the simple question, "Who are you?" Unlike the sphinx of Oedipus, who merely posed a riddle about mortal man condemned to pass from infancy to old age, the divine gatekeeper looks for the Eternal Self to show its face. Passage through the Sun Door, whether at actual death, in the near-death experience, or in the mystical ascent, requires that the everyday self be put in its place. Thus, the ancient gold tablets advise travelers in the afterworld to refrain from declaring their mortal identities: the gatekeeper will not be won over by humdrum replies of the kind "I am Mr./Mrs./Ms./Dr./Prof. So-and-so from such-and-such a place." Misidentification and weighty baggage keep the traveler from the sunny lands of eternity. The door clicks shut, and the sea of mutability beckons again.

How, then, might the divine janitor's challenge be answered? The declaration "I am a child of the earth and the starry sky" inscribed on those gold foils in the ancient tombs of Italy and Greece merely asserts divinity by *kinship* and is therefore relatively mild and innocuous. The Indian "I am you" to be uttered at the Sun Door is far stronger, with its assertion of divinity by *identity* with the supreme reality. Perhaps it is too strong, if not properly understood, for there is a danger of overstepping the mark in these matters. It is not the everyday self that is to be identified with the ultimate reality, but a higher self or soul. Mr. So-and-so is not the supreme reality; rather, his essential self or *ātman* is *brahman*. But how seriously should we take the idea of an essential self? Does mystical experience disclose an intrinsic "I-ness" in the depths of reality, or is mystical self-expansion just a case of ego-inflation, with everyday self-identifications inappropriately transferred to the cosmic sphere and beyond? There are no unanimous answers to be had from the teachings of mystically informed religious traditions, and in this chapter I touch upon the matter with no expectation of reaching any definite conclusions. It is probably only through extensive and deep familiarity with a range of mystical experiences that the status of self beyond its everyday expressions can be adequately gauged.

However, if it is correct to suppose that a certain kind of selfhood or "I-ness" is intrinsic to the cosmic level of experience, there are suggestions that such a cosmic self is *social* in character. Psychologists have long maintained that the self cannot properly be abstracted from its social contexts. Our relationships with others contribute much to what we consider ourselves to be and what we become. Similarly, cosmic mystical experiences sometimes point to a self that is fundamentally social in character. Self-discovery, far from excluding or subsuming others, seems to reveal a community of distinguishable yet intimately connected individuals. In particular, revelations of the significance of love point to an expansive self-experience that is not merely a unity with a world of objects, that is, a simple unity of cosmic knower and cosmic known, which, though certainly remarkable in itself, is likely to be a coolly impersonal, ultimately tedious, and therefore unsatisfactory state of affairs. Rather, there seems to be a loving communion of equals, and so it could be said that to know yourself truly is to love your neighbor deeply.

Know Thyself

Daring assertions of identity with the divine have been made now and again in the history of religious thought. The Greek philosopher Empedocles of Acragas (fifth century BCE) is said to have announced his elevation to divine status and deliverance from the cycle of transmigration with the words, "I tell you I am a god immortal, no longer a mortal."[2] But Empedocles had merely become one of the company of gods, not the supreme God with whom mystics have sometimes claimed identity in their moments of self-deification or "autotheism." In a state of ecstasy, al-Bistāmī (d. ca. 875 CE) is said to have uttered, "Praise be to Me! How great is My Majesty!" and al-Hallāj (d. 922 CE) has often been credited with the assertion "I am the Truth."[3] One version of al-Hallāj's famous lines of poetry would have delighted the keeper at the Sun Door with its forthright assertion of divine identity:

I saw my Love with the eye of my heart,
And He said, 'Who are you?' I said, 'You!'[4]

The pseudo-Eckhartian treatise *Schwester Katrei* (fourteenth century CE) contains a memorable autotheistic declaration. In this work, we meet Sister Catherine as she tries to attain union with God. After achieving oneness on a couple of occasions, she exclaims to her confessor, "Father, rejoice with me, I have become God!"—a rather incautious way of expressing the unity she had temporarily attained.[5] Prior to these moments of oneness, she had reached a condition of incorporative unity in which she found the created world within herself, as those turned toward God and the "mirror of truth" tend to do: "all the works God had created in heaven and on earth were within me."[6] But her moments of oneness with God now made heaven and earth too small for her, and she persisted in her spiritual strivings. Retreating from all created things, she entered into a deathlike trance for three days and emerged permanently "established" in the Godhead.

Expressions of divine self-identification are likely to exasperate the sober-minded and lead to accusations of heresy or, in modern secular contexts, invite psychiatric labels. Within mainstream religion, even comparatively acceptable doctrines of "becoming godlike," of acquiring divine characteristics, such as the concept of "deification" (*theosis*) in Christianity, may create unease. Careful expression of spiritual self-transformation or self-discovery is necessary if difficulties are to be mitigated. On the one hand, mystics are liable to be misunderstood and persecuted by those who hear their extraordinary pronouncements. They are particularly open to accusations of "antinomian libertinism," dissolute behavior alleged to result from the conviction that deification takes one beyond good and evil, beyond moral law. One may do as one wishes because one's will is now the divine will. However, this is far from an inevitable outcome, as the story of Sister Catherine is intended to convey: she is not tempted to be other than "a poor person" until she dies.[7] But mystics may misunderstand their own experiences, and some no doubt have had exaggerated estimations of their accomplishments and indulged in exploitative behavior driven by all-too-human motives and desires, as modern-day reports of guru–disciple abuses can suggest.

Two potential misunderstandings, touched upon before, are *inflation* and *deflation* (fig. 4.1). In the former, the ordinary self is taken to be more than it really is, invested with greater importance than it has or crudely identified with a deeper reality of some sort, such as God, a god, a higher self, or cosmic mind, like the Gnostic demiurge Ialdabaoth, who, after creating the world, ignorantly and arrogantly declares "I am God and there is none other beside me," little realizing that he is not the supreme being.[8] Conversely, in the deflationary mode, the ordinary self and everyday life are dismissed as worthless, insignificant, insubstantial, illusory, in comparison with the newly discovered reality.

Exclamations of identity with God, Brahman, Śiva, Buddha, the World, and so forth can be startling pointers to a profound truth, and they have had a role as teaching expedients, the audacious claims drawing attention to truths that might otherwise be missed. When the Ch'an Buddhist teacher Linji Yixuan (Jpn., Rinzai Gigen; d. 866 CE;) told his students that they were the "Patriarch-Buddha" and lacked nothing, he was expressing the Mahāyāna

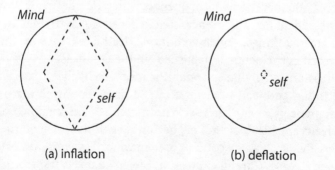

(a) inflation   (b) deflation

Figure 4.1   Two potential misunderstandings: (a) everyday self overestimated through misidentification with Mind; (b) everyday self excessively diminished in comparison with Mind.

doctrine of the Buddha-nature (*buddhatā*) or inherent Buddhahood in a particularly dramatic, pointed fashion, intended to rouse students to look to themselves, to the perfect nature they already possessed, instead of wasting effort in pursuit of externals.[9] But presented in isolation, exclamatory assertions of identity with greater realities do not engage with the complexities of personal identity and human nature, and fail to consider in what ways these realities are connected with the everyday self. It is a tricky matter to give adequate expression to the relation between the "little self" and the realities it believes it has encountered, especially since it is often far from clear what that relation is and indeed what those realities are.

The pursuit of balanced self-knowledge treads a difficult path between inflation and deflation. On one side lies the danger of appropriating too much to the ordinary self, pumping it up with grandiose delusions, while on the other lies the danger of rejecting the little self in the face of the overpowering divine. Balance means keeping a hold on the familiar, keeping sight of the person, while acknowledging the mystical depths. The importance of balanced self-knowledge has long been recognized, although the avoidance of self-inflation was perhaps the first to be emphasized in Greek religion. The commandment to "Know Thyself" (*gnōthi seauton*), inscribed on the temple of Apollo at Delphi, called for self-knowledge, but with the ambiguity typical of the Pythian oracle, it left the nature of this knowledge open to interpretation.[10] It is possible that initially the injunction demanded knowledge of one's character and skills, and, most importantly, knowledge of one's limitations. In this sense, the Delphic maxim warns mortals against inflation, against a usurpation of divinity: *know that you are a man and not a god* is the message.[11]

As a more interior understanding developed, the meaning ascribed to the Delphic maxim seems to have reversed in a most spectacular fashion, turning from pious expressions of humility before the gods, jealously possessive of their exalted status, to the recognition of the divinity within, as if a Prometheus had bestowed the fire of divine self-knowledge upon humankind. With the Socrates of Plato's dialogues, the shift is perhaps already evident: self-knowledge, although still a necessity for proper human conduct, acquires a divine aspect. Man must make himself the primary object of study, which means knowledge of the true self, the immortal soul. Plato goes some way toward portraying man's self-nature as it relates to the ethical life and the revelation of the divine. In the soul's tripartite constitution, reason is to bring spirit and appetite into harmony, like a charioteer controlling two contending horses, thereby enabling the soul to ascend to the vision of the Forms. The charioteer analogy in the *Phaedrus* is notable for its depiction of the soul as a *composite* of the lower and higher passions with a rational element, and for giving all three parts a role in the ascent to godlikeness, through which the soul becomes divine by apprehending the divine.

The idea that true self-knowledge requires the discovery of an inner, divine essence—*to know thyself is to know the divinity within*—became more definite and pronounced in later Platonic developments and was explicitly connected with the Empedoclean view that "like is known by like." This influential dictum, when applied to the spiritual sphere, implies that only by the presence of the divine in oneself is one able to know the divine at all. Already in the Platonic dialogue *First Alcibiades*, perhaps composed in the generation after Plato, true self-knowledge is understood to be knowledge of God and the highest part of the soul.[12] Just as the eye sees itself mirrored in another eye, so the soul will know itself by looking at the divine and discovering that its highest part resembles God. The theme was taken over by the Stoics, who often stressed the connection between God and the governing part of the soul, the *hēgemonikon*.[13]

With Plotinus, the inward path to self-knowledge and higher realities becomes very pronounced. The discovery of the ultimate reality, the One or the Good, is the climax of an unfolding of self-knowledge through the levels of the soul. Of the levels distinguished by Plotinus, the highest is identified with the Intellect, which means that the soul at its apex is a great intellect or mind eternally engaged in unitive contemplation of the intelligible cosmos. Thus, *to know thyself is to know the Intellect and its spiritual universe.* The lower part of the soul, which derives its rationality from the Intellect, is sometimes subdivided into the rational part and a part sunk in sensory experience. The mystical ascent reveals to the soul its higher nature in the Intellect proper, and perhaps even in the loving Intellect eternally in union with the One.[14] The soul, however immersed it may appear to be in sensory becoming, is nevertheless rooted in the highest realities, the Intellect and even the One.

By the time of the later Neoplatonists, the attainment of self-knowledge was well established as the first step in the philosophical life and was even equated with philosophy itself, as the path to the divine or to knowledge of the divine. But later Neoplatonists, notably Iamblichus and Proclus, were not to follow Plotinus's high estimation of the soul's constitution, according to which the soul is never really fallen from its contemplation of the Forms. By contrast, Iamblichus took the soul to be fully descended into the material world, the fall into matter alienating it from its lofty origins. However, Iamblichus scholar Gregory Shaw has argued that this move actually encouraged a more positive, less dualistic view of the soul and its relation to the material world, and a willingness to employ embodied, ritualistic practices on the spiritual path.[15]

In Jewish, Christian, and Muslim developments, the call to "know thyself" and the Empedoclean "like is known by like" could be blended with the belief that man is made in the Image of God or contains the divine breath: *to know thyself is to know thy Lord* because man contains the *imago Dei*. That true self-knowledge is knowledge of God might be taken to indicate a divine essence, core, ground, apex, point, or spark of the soul (*scintilla animae*, Eckhart's *Seelenfünklein*), the part of the soul that remains when all that is not of God has been stripped away, and perhaps valued at the expense of the human vessel that contains it. A comparable notion in Hindu religion is the *ātman*, while in the Buddhist sphere the Buddha-nature can have a similar function if understood as an intrinsic endowment hidden by the personality aggregates. The pursuit and attainment of self-knowledge would be like rummaging through one's home and finding a great treasure hidden in the attic. The house itself may be considered relatively worthless, but the treasure is greatly valued.

More inclusive interpretations were possible too, which took man to be a composite or a microcosmic image. In this case, the entire "house of man" could be regarded as the image of divinity, although the usually disordered state of the dwelling hides its temple-like nature. After some tidying, disinfestation, and restorative work, the presence of God would be evident throughout the house, not only in the attic but also in the living quarters and even in the cellar. In the notion of the microcosm, of man as representative of all things, there has been the possibility of understanding self-knowledge broadly. Man could seek out God not only in the essential self, at the soul's apex, but in the mortal self too, body included. In the words of Alexander Altmann, the microcosm motif extended "the base of the desired knowledge of God to include the body beside the soul."[16] There is something truly divine and cosmic about the individual constitution. As one old Jewish text (*Avot de-Rabbi Nathan*) puts it, to save one person is to save the entire world, and to destroy one person is to destroy the entire world, for all the ten creative divine powers are concentrated in the human microcosm.[17] *To know thyself as the little world is to know the great world.*

In the idea of the microcosmic nature or composite soul, the lowly elements of the human personality could be given a valued place alongside the heights. There was another way in which the everyday world could be considered an object of self-knowledge: *to know thyself is to know the entire created world as God knows it.* For example, self-realization in a famous Hermetic text (*Corpus Hermeticum*, Book XI) involved a form of "cosmic consciousness," a perceptual and cognitive apprehension of the universe in the way that God knows it. In Jewish and Christian contexts, the idea could be framed thus: *to know thyself is to know the world as Adam knew it before the Fall*. Having been made in the Image of God, the first man Adam had godlike perception and knowledge of the natural world. This was lost at the Fall, but the mystic, achieving self-knowledge through restoration of the divine Image, would acquire the prelapsarian, Adamic powers. Interestingly, this mystical notion was to have an influential counterpart in early modern science. In the sixteenth and seventeenth centuries, the belief was current that the emerging experimental sciences would provide a means of recovering Adam's lost capacities and knowledge. The belief was a motivating factor in the early modern scientific enterprise, being one of several ways in which religion encouraged rather than hindered the rise of science.[18] For a few thinkers, the scientific recovery of Adam's knowledge was blended with occult or mystical aspirations. A notable case is that of the physician-chemist J. B. van Helmont, for whom the scientific quest for knowledge of the natural world and the mystical path to self-knowledge were not distinct endeavors (see Box, "Physician, know thyself").

The Twofold Soul

The idea of dual self-identity—the twofold or "dual-aspect" soul[19]—has sometimes been couched in the picturesque imagery of the "two men." Discussing the soul's levels, Plotinus refers to an original, unbounded "higher man" and a "lower man" who has intruded upon and obscured the former, making man a dual thing (*Enn.* VI.4.14).[20] There were related conceptions of *homo duplex* in the ancient world. The *Corpus Hermeticum* claimed for man two natures, mortal in body, immortal in the "essential" man,[21] and Zosimos of Panopolis, an alchemist of the late third century CE, distinguished between the external, terrestrial Adam, the "man of flesh" (*sarkinos anthrōpos*), and the inner man Phos, the "man of light" (*phōteinos anthrōpos*).[22] The latter designation, suggestive of the luminous epiphany that is divine self-disclosure, depends on a play of words, the Greek *phōs* in slightly different forms meaning "light" or "man." For Jewish interpreters of Genesis 1.3 in Greek translation, the divine command "Let there be *phōs*!" could be understood to summon into existence a luminous celestial man, the cosmic anthropos, a demiurge-like being who assists God in the creation, identified with God's manifest "glory" (*kavod*) and with the cosmic Adam, and thus with the Image of God itself, as April DeConick explains.[23]

⮞ Physician, know thyself ⮜

In his labors to reform medical practice, the Flemish iatrochemist Johannes Baptista van Helmont (1579–1644) engaged in pioneering chemical experimentation, including quantitative work. But unlike most present-day medical researchers, van Helmont also regarded mystical contemplation and dreams as valid experiential sources of knowledge. He hoped that the self-knowledge thereby obtained would aid research by bringing awareness of personal bias in observations, and, more importantly, by uncovering a hidden component of the human constitution, the higher intellect (*mens*), the image of God, which has all-encompassing knowledge of reality, including nature. Thus the pursuit of self-knowledge promised not only the closeness to God sought by mystics but also knowledge of the natural world, which was to be used for the benefit of the poor and sick. Medicine practiced in the right spirit is a work of divine love.[24]

According to van Helmont, the intellect possesses its immense knowledge because all things are linked in cosmic sympathy through their shared origin in God's primordial creative act, and the human creature, as the last created thing, contains in essence all that came before.[25] Because the intellect contains all things, it knows all things by its unity with them.[26] It follows that the soul, by understanding itself, can understand all other things—a great benefit of self-knowledge. This direct type of knowing has been obscured since the Fall by the sensitive soul (*anima sensitiva*), with its misleading sense images and reasonings. However, the intellect can be felt in dreams, when the sensitive soul is less active, and it can be reached, with God's grace, through contemplation.

As a student, van Helmont was inspired by the mystic Johannes Tauler (ca. 1300–1361), and the influence of the Rhineland mystics is indeed evident in van Helmont's thought. Meister Eckhart had described the ideational presence of all things in the intellect,[27] and Tauler had said that man is as it were "three men," with animal, rational, and essential natures. God can be found by rising above the first two to the third, made in the image of God. For van Helmont too, sense and reason must be transcended through silence and self-surrender if the divine essence is to be found within. But van Helmont also sought knowledge of the natural world in the core of the soul, a this-worldly orientation that reflects intellectual currents of his day—Paracelsian alchemical mysticism in the service of medicine, and efforts scientific, occult, and mystical to recover Adam's knowledge of the world lost at the Fall. But when van Helmont's quest for self-knowledge finally brought a glimpse of his own soul, the vision was not as informative as he had hoped it would be (see chapter 5).

Man was created in the image of this luminous cosmic being. Although the divine Image was lost when Adam fell, it can be recovered. One way is through mystical vision of the divine Image, which impresses the Image on the soul.[28] The soul is made divine by apprehension of the divine, as Plato had explained in the *Phaedrus*.

If the first step is to recognize a higher level of soul, the next is to place it adequately in relation to the lower. It is possible to set up a great divide between the two, even to the point of envisaging two distinct souls in the one person, one good, one evil.[29] Plotinus does not take this path, but his "two men" imagery is not flattering to the lower man, an impostor who has "wound himself about us, foisting himself upon the Man that each of us was at first," the original Man that we all are in essence, but who is almost absent in effect, if not in actuality (*Enn.* VI.4.14). Like many of his time, Plotinus tended to undervalue the mortal and ephemeral, expressing embarrassment at his embodied form, but he avoided the grosser exaggerations of the period, taking pains to distance himself from the anti-cosmism of some gnostic contemporaries. As a follower of Plato, Plotinus acknowledged the beauty and divinity of the world of Becoming, and looked upon it as an image of the higher realities. In the practical sphere, he did not lose sight of the Platonic ideal of the philosopher engaged in the world, concerned with the care and education of others.

One way to suggest a more intimate relation between the "two men" is to represent them as *twins* or *doubles*, which points to their sameness but also their difference, a one who is two, or two who are one. Here the *doppelgänger* or *alter ego* is not modern depth psychology's false self or shadow figure, but the soul in its higher aspect—the Intellect, Mind, Self, divine Image, man of light, cosmic Adam, living Jesus. It is a feature of the body of Christian literature associated with St. Thomas, more fully Didymus Judas Thomas, who in the tradition was the twin of Jesus, and the apostle entrusted with the mission to Mesopotamia and India ("Didymus" and "Thomas" mean "twin" in Greek and Syriac respectively). The Thomas literature includes *The Gospel of Thomas*, unearthed in 1945 in the Nag Hammadi trove, and also *The Acts of Thomas*, one of the New Testament apocrypha. Inserted in two of the surviving manuscripts of the *Acts*, there is an older work that goes under the title *Hymn of the Pearl* (or *Hymn of the Soul*). In the *Acts*, the hymn is recited by Judas Thomas as he languishes in an Indian prison. It tells of a young prince who, near the end of a long quest, catches sight of his double in a mirror-like robe (see Box, "The robe of glory"). In the Thomas literature, the divine double is Jesus, the twin of Thomas, "the inner divine light or 'living Jesus.'"[30] More particularly, it seems that we each have our own

❧ The robe of glory ❦

An intriguing case of double identity can be found in *The Hymn of the Pearl*, a poetic fable that perhaps dates from the second century CE. The hymn has an attractive, childlike quality in both plot and style. Narrated in the first person, it recounts a young prince's quest to retrieve a pearl of great value.[31] Unburdened with overt theological teachings, it nonetheless seems to carry a message of great spiritual import.

From a palace in the East, the young prince is sent forth by his parents to the land of Egypt to recover a pearl guarded by a fearsome serpent. Before departing, the boy is required to take off his cherished robe, with the promise that it will be returned when the goal is attained. On reaching Egypt, he puts on the local attire to avoid arousing suspicion, but the Egyptians recognize him as a foreigner. Under the soporific influence of their cuisine he forgets his royal parentage and falls into a deep sleep. Aware of this unhappy turn of events, his parents send their son a letter, in the form of an eagle, to wake him from his sleep and remind him of his true identity, the robe, and the mission. Roused by this talking eagle-letter, the prince charms the serpent and secures the pearl. Abandoning his filthy clothes, he leaves Egypt, the radiance of the letter lighting the way home. Now he catches sight of his treasured robe, decorated with precious materials, brightly colored, rippling with gnosis, adorned with the image of the King of kings, and he sees himself in it:

> But when suddenly I saw my garment reflected as in a mirror,
> I perceived in it my whole self as well,
> And through it I recognized and saw myself.
> For, though we derived from one and the same we were partially
>   divided; and then again we were one with a single form.[32]

Lovingly reunited with his robe, the prince comes home, goal attained.

But what exactly has been achieved? On the face of it, a young prince has shown himself a worthy heir to his father's kingdom. But the story looks like spiritual allegory, employing such familiar symbols as the pearl, the serpent, and sleeping and waking. Precisely how the story is interpreted depends on the lens through which it is read, Thomasine, Manichaean, Mandaean, or other.[33] For many, divine self-knowledge is the message. As Bentley Layton observes, in respect of the Thomas literature, "to know oneself was to know one's divine double and thence to know god."[34]

preexistent, heavenly counterpart, invisible to the senses but discernible in the visionary encounter when we have returned to the light that is our source. Commenting on Saying 84 of the *Gospel of Thomas*, DeConick explains:

> each person has a heavenly eternal *eikon*, an Image which came into existence before the human body, the *eine* or 'resemblance' of the person. This heavenly image is concealed from the person because the person is living in a fallen condition, separated from his or her transcendent self.[35]

According to DeConick, the idea of an Image specific to each person belongs "to the early Jewish tradition of a divine twin, guardian angel, or image from which one was separated as the result of Adam's Sin."[36] It may also be indebted to the Greek and Roman *daimōn* or *genius*, a kind of guardian spirit.[37] It is hardly surprising to find that vision of one's heavenly Image and unification with it, although redemptive, may not be exactly agreeable, as Saying 84 seems to indicate: "how much you will suffer!"[38] Mystical self-revelations can be challenging, as noted in chapter 3, and Saying 84 perhaps alludes to this in its tersely cryptic way.

Although the divine Image was to remain a focus of Christian spiritual aspiration, its rendering as the divine twin in the Thomas literature was not to become part of the dominant orthodoxy established in the Christian West—a missed opportunity, perhaps, for the imagery of the "double" hints at a particularly close relationship between the individual and the divine, offering the possibility of deification through that intimate connection.[39] However, a Thomasine-like spirituality appears to have survived in the Christian East, contributing to a mysticism in which union with the divine Image has special prominence.[40] Furthermore, the divine double was to receive elaborate treatment in Iranian Sufism, identified there with the "man of light," as Henry Corbin explored in detail, and it was carried over from early Jewish tradition into the Kabbalah.[41]

The double also had a presence in Manichaeism, the religion founded by Mani (ca. 216–276 CE), a younger contemporary of Plotinus. Mani seems to have understood his own spiritual mission through the example of the prince in the *Hymn of the Pearl*: he relates that at the end of his twenty-fourth year he was visited by his divine Twin and guide-companion (*syzygos*), a mirror-like being in whom Mani's true identity was reflected, an identity from which he had been alienated by involvement in the body. In Mani's understanding, the Twin was peculiar to himself, as prophet and savior. By contrast, the Plotinian higher man, the soul-level that is divine Intellect, is a common identity open to discovery by all.[42] The Plotinian account makes

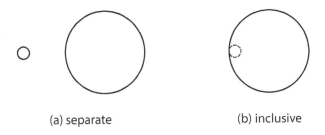

(a) separate   (b) inclusive

Figure 4.2   Experiences of the divine double, as separate or inclusive.

the higher man a deeply communal affair, a One-Man (see chapter 6). However, it is possible that Manichaeism did extend divine twinship to the faithful in general, reunion with the divine counterpart being possible after death, as Charles Stang has pointed out in his recent, in-depth study of the divine double in Plato, the Thomas literature, Mani, and Plotinus.[43]

The figure of the "two men" (and the "double" or the "twin") is clearly more than theological speculation about the constitution of the soul, for it is presented, at least in the instances noted here, as an experiential discovery and one of great salvatory importance. Precisely what it means to be "double" is open to interpretation, and no doubt varies across the traditions. For myself, the strength of the figure lies partly in its evocative power and its capacity to work from a subconscious level, as in dreams and visions, irrespective of how it is interpreted in rational terms. It also well captures two aspects of the spiritual encounter, identity and difference, unity and separation. Difference is more evident when the double is still experienced as the numinous Other (fig. 4.2a), whether guide, companion, messenger, doorkeeper, beloved, even if this Other does have one's semblance, as in those dreams in which a wiser version of oneself pays a visit. Identity becomes more pronounced in full-blown mystical states, but it seems that even here difference can have a place. Disclosure of the higher identity does not necessarily obliterate the everyday one. They are found to coexist, permitting constructive interaction and even relationship. Moreover, the former, if it is an all-inclusive whole, will be found to incorporate the latter (fig. 4.2b).

Some modern-day mystical accounts exemplify the coexistence. When Warner Allen came out of his "timeless moment" in the concert hall, he brought back with him the old forgotten secret: "I am not 'I', not the 'I' I thought."[44] But Allen noted that the disclosure of his newly remembered identity left the customary sense of ego intact, and he quoted Plotinus (*Enn.* v.3.4) to express the coexistence of the two: "He who has learnt to know himself is a two-fold person."[45] In his anesthetic revelation, R. H. Ward also found a twofoldness, recognizing in the realm of ideas a double identity, not just the old spectator or the newly rediscovered, all-inclusive subject, but the two together. This, he felt, was his rightful condition:

> One knew and understood this different world as a spectator of it, recognizing it as the object of one's apprehension, but at the same time knew and understood that it existed within oneself; thus one was at once the least significant atom in the universal whole and that universal whole.[46]

My own self-experience had a twofold character too. My everyday sense of self persisted, and I was able to react to the unfolding experience from the perspective of my ordinary personality, with shock, incomprehension, relief, amusement, feelings of impurity. Yet there was also the sense that I encompassed everything by virtue of the omniscient Mind that was also myself (a mind so expansive that it would be churlish to deny it a capital "M"). In the weeks following the experience, when memories appeared, I struggled to understand the event but found the language of "mind" a helpful way of indicating that the condition was not so very different from my usual "mental" life of perceiving, knowing, and loving, but vastly extended and deepened. The Mind that was myself was a whole, a totality, so that the world was within rather than without (fig. 4.3).

My account of the experience shifts to and fro in the identity that it expresses. In places, I feel and think from the perspective of my usual self. But I also find my identity in the Mind that sustains and holds everything in itself, and for which there can be no fear or petty ambition. Thus, two perspectives seem to operate alongside each other, the account sometimes

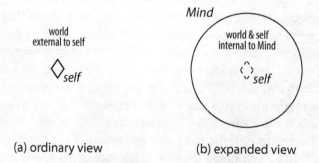

(a) ordinary view   (b) expanded view

Figure 4.3   (a) ordinary view: self prominent, world externalized, and Mind unknown; (b) expanded view: Mind prominent, world and everyday self internalized (self and Mind coexist).

expressing the one, sometimes the other. Even though the disclosure of the expansive Mind undermined my usual sense of self for the duration of the experience, the overall experience was affirmative of ordinary life. Humbled, deflated, and with motivations exposed, I was still able to observe a place for myself in all my ordinariness, which also involved loving in the way I had discovered to be possible. It seems that the everyday self is not intrinsically at odds with the deeper nature of things but can become so when it is ignorant of its roots.

It is therefore reasonable to suppose that spiritual practices should not be undertaken to *eliminate* the everyday self, harshly judged as an impostor, but rather should aim to *harmonize* this normally isolated and relatively ignorant self with the underlying reality, so that conscious integration is achieved. Presumably the everyday personality would then be infused with and transformed by the qualities of the underlying reality, including knowledge and love. In this integrated condition, the "little self" would not disappear, at least if it continues to be supported by a body of some sort, but it would now operate with an awareness and understanding of its place in the greater reality, and would be transformed by this awareness and understanding. There is, however, considerable room for debate over what such an integrated condition would be like and indeed whether it is really possible. Some support for the idea can be found in religious traditions that have envisaged a state of "living liberation," "enlightenment," or "sagehood" achieved by the virtuosi of the spiritual life.[47]

Aspiration toward a higher self has become commonplace in recent times, a staple of New Age spiritualities, fed by nineteenth-century currents of thought, including Romanticism, psychological concepts of the subconscious and subliminal Self, interest in Hindu philosophy, and Theosophy.[48] But it has had unwitting or disguised modern manifestations too. Jeffrey Kripal has explored the subject in his discussions of the "bimodal model of consciousness" and "the Human as Two," drawing on psychological theory, mysticism, and popular culture. He finds the bimodality expressed, for instance, in the superhero comic genre, with its protagonists who have secret identities and special, godlike powers, sometimes acquired through trauma and consequent dissociation from the everyday self, a factor also evident in cases of mystical experience.[49]

The nineteenth century added a new dimension to understandings of spiritual integration, for the sought-after unity of everyday self and the deeper reality could now be envisaged as not merely the sporadic accomplishment of a privileged few but as an increasingly common event, the outcome of a natural, agelong *evolutionary* climb through nature toward what R. M. Bucke called "the duplex individuality of the Cosmic Conscious person—i.e., the self conscious self and the Cosmic Conscious self."[50] Edward Carpenter elaborated on the idea in a lucid way: he described two consciousnesses in each person, "more or less distinct and separable,"[51] the first occupied with the individual life, the second with the universal, common life. We are all engaged in the long, arduous, evolutionary enterprise of bringing these together in such a way that neither is compromised:

> To attain this fusion of the individual and universal consciousness—so
> that, still remaining individual, one should partake and be aware of the
> universal life—this is the long effort and upward climb of humanity, worth
> all the struggles and disasters and failures by the way that may attend it.[52]

The labor of giving birth to universal consciousness in the individual can bring great inner tension, as Carpenter could vouch from his own experience, but, once the fusion has taken place, harmony is restored, and "real life and happiness are possible."[53]

But is it correct to suppose that the higher component of the twofold constitution is a "self"? From my own limited exposure to the condition, I would not like to conclude categorically that the expansive mind I discovered can properly be regarded as a greater self, although it is true that in my account of the experience, self-identification with the Mind is expressed. I recount experiencing the Mind and its world as myself, not as an "other," not as an entity distinct from myself:

> Yet it was also I who in some sense was the sole basis of everything. I was
> the mind from which everything derived and in which everything had its
> existence. There was nothing but myself, or rather nothing but the mind
> I had discovered myself to be, the intelligence and power sustaining the
> world.

Do self-identifications such as these provide evidence of selfhood intrinsic to the expansive mind, or have everyday self-labeling tendencies been confusedly applied to a new, unfamiliar domain of experience?

What would make the expansive mind a self? Unfortunately, this question is not easy to answer, for "self" is a notoriously difficult concept to pin down. In everyday usage, self is likely to be credited with a combination of features such as consciousness, perception, knowledge, thought, emotion, will, agency, personality, memory, and body. The expansive mind, as I remember it, certainly involved consciousness, perception, and knowing.

It might have involved thinking if the mind's "support" of the universe were understood to be a form of thinking. There was some verbal and image-based thinking activity too, but this could be attributed to a lower level of mind, which continued to function. The expansive mind involved love, which made my ordinary self feel very impure. However, it is notable that I became aware of the great love only as the experience developed. I have no idea if the Mind had any intrinsic will and agency, and I do not remember personality in the sense of a set of distinctive, individualized character attributes. Memory is often cited as a requirement for a continuing sense of self, but in this condition memory would be superfluous because there seemed to be knowing of the past—no need for memory traces if access to time in its entirety is available. I did not interpret the expansive field of experience as a "cosmic body," although sometimes experiences of this kind do bring a feeling of body extension, even cosmic in extent (see chapter 1), and the mystical literature contains some fine expressions of aspiration toward cosmic embodiment. Thomas Traherne put it thus: "You never enjoy the world aright, till the Sea itself floweth in your veins, till you are clothed with the heavens, and crowned with the stars" (CM I.29). Utpaladeva, a philosopher of the Pratyabhijñā school of Kashmir Shaivism, sings of his aspiration toward the supreme self in terms of bodily transformation:

> May my body blossom into your true nature,
> The worlds become my limbs. (Śivastotrāvalī 8.7)[54]

According to this Shaiva tradition, the entire emanated universe is the body of the supreme self, the self that is the ultimate source of all, and anyone who recognizes this superlative self as their own essential self will discover that they too possess the emanated cosmic body at all levels or steps (tattvas) of manifestation.[55]

However, a minimalist definition would not require that self have emotion, will, agency, personality, and body. For a subject to be a self, it need only be conscious of itself. In this bare sense, the expansive mind would be a self if it were a self-conscious or self-knowing subject, a reflexive subject. In the case of human beings, self-consciousness and self-knowledge show most obviously in thoughts and feelings about oneself, which are underpinned by concepts of self, of "I" as subject and "me" as object. Can the same be said of cosmic mind? In chapter 9, I shall have cause to note some philosophies informed by mystical experience that do attribute reflexive consciousness to deeper levels of reality—these are the philosophies of Plotinus and the Pratyabhijñā school.

The Social Self

I suspect that "self" can be applied in a meaningful and more than minimal way to the expansive mind. For evidence, I would look in particular to the social character of Mind, with its community of beings and ambiance of love, which makes it more than an impersonal, solitary intellect. The Mind knows and loves itself in relationship with the other minds it knows and loves. My own discovery of community took place when I was presented with the sight of others in the form of small "rings." These beings were contained within the expansive mind, yet they were also known to be beings in their own right, on a par with the great mind despite their diminutive size. Prior to this revelation, my understanding had taken a solipsistic turn, for other selves had been absorbed into the expansive mind that was "I." It was only when my attention was drawn to the little rings that "you" and "we" returned, making the social character of the experience extraordinarily evident (fig. 4.4).

It is noteworthy that some expansive experiences do not proceed to social insight and love but remain in what seems to be a transitional stage of development. This is perhaps more likely to occur when an experience is induced by drugs, as for instance was the case with William Ramsay's "disappointing," indeed "painful," anesthetic revelations, in which other persons had become mere parts of his thoughts and "not very important elements" in his self-centric "chain of life" (see chapter 2). Consider, for example, a mescaline experience described by journalist William Braden (1930–2008) in *The Private Sea*. Braden was uncertain whether the experience had really

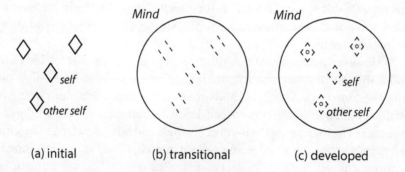

Figure 4.4 Transformation in social understanding: (a) self has no awareness of Mind and misconceives others as fully separate; (b) Mind dominates, with self and others not properly discriminated and understood; (c) self and others recognized as contents of Mind, and others known to be in essence Minds too.

penetrated to the truth: he felt that there was something "wrong" with it, not that it was necessarily untrue, but that he was not ready for it—the time was not right. The experience could certainly be described as a "bad trip," as Richard T. Wallis remarked in his comparison of Braden's drug-induced revelation with experience at the level of the Plotinian cosmic mind (Nous).[56] As the effects of the mescaline deepened, Braden felt apprehension but could not yet work out its source:

> Although I knew nothing, I felt that some awful truth was about to be revealed to me. It was lurking somewhere just beyond the borders of my comprehension, and very soon now I should come face to face with it. . . . I was starting to remember something, and it seemed to have some connection with sunlight and a cradle. But what could it be?[57]

Earlier in the account, Braden explains that since childhood he would sometimes experience a change of state, lasting a few seconds, in which "time would stop, all objects would lose their names, and the world would seem somehow peaceful and perfect."[58] His earliest memories of infancy, of lying in a cradle in sunlight, would be stirred by these moments, which suggested to him that similar feelings of peace and perfection had been felt at these times in his infancy. But the mood was very different in the mescaline experience. Braden was remembering the old, forgotten secret of deeper self-identity, but instead of it being a joyful realization, it was the first disturbing aspect of the "awful truth." The discovery brought no positive emotion, no relief, joy, or wonder, and was unwelcome:

> Then it came to me that I was gradually remembering my own identity, like an amnesia victim who slowly recovers his past. Finally it all fell together, and I remembered who I was. And it was so simple, really. I was life. I was Being. I was the vibrant force that filled the room, and was the room. I was the world, the universe. I was everything. I was that which always was and always would be. I was Jim [a helper present during the experiment] and Jim was me, and we were everybody else; and everybody else was us, and all of us put together were the same thing, and that same thing was the only thing there was. We were not God. We were simply all that there was, and all that there wasn't God. It was us, alone. And we were each other, and nowhere anywhere was there anything but us, and we were always the same, the one and only truth. . . . Having been reunited with the Ground of my Being, I wanted urgently to be estranged from it again as quickly as possible.[59]

The experience was disturbing for several reasons: loss of God, loss of the little self, fear of being everything, and anxiety about nonexistence. But most disturbing of all was the loss of truly real "other selves":

> I said that I was frightened by what I had gained, and this was true. But I had lost something, too, and it was more important to me than my wretched self, and more important even than God. For along with my own self I had lost all the other selves as well. I had lost other people. And I missed them very much.
>
> I wanted there to be someone else. Anyone else. And if there had been just two of us—really two of us—and we two were All That There Was, that would not have been so hard. But there was no one else; there was only the One.[60]

Braden's experience can be compared with another mescaline experience, one described by psychical researcher Rosalind Heywood (1895–1980). The cosmic oneness, interrelatedness, and endless movement finally became too much for her: "I felt that in another second I should be disintegrated by sheer excess of glory. 'Human kind cannot bear too much reality.'"[61] But she felt that something was missing in the relentless, impersonal cosmic splendor and managed to hold on long enough to ask the "magic" question:

> And then, just at cracking point, it dawned on me that with all that Cosmic Perfection, there was still something lacking. Everything, everywhere, was clearly interrelated in that vast Unity. But – it did not know it! The Universe did not know that it was one. At that staggering discovery I somehow pulled myself together and fumblingly, quiveringly, asked a question: 'Is there no conscious communication in all this inter-weaving Unity? Where is Love?'[62]

In response, a messenger appeared "out of the gold," the world of pure spirit.[63] It was the "Divine Mother," clothed in shades of blue, green, and purple. Her symbols were pearls: "She was like a pearl coming into a world of diamond."[64] Heywood was now able to see the universe through the eyes of divine love, a love that was "infinitely far from possessive doting, quite unsentimental, yet warm and comforting – and, above all, personal."[65] It had a gaiety to it, far beyond "any scherzo or even of wind-blown daffodils or sunlit seas."[66] The Divine Mother brought a message: the universe remains unaware of its own unity until love comes into it. She explained: "You were being shown the universe before the principle of communication, which is love, has been injected into it. Now you see the next job."[67] It was the appearance of the Divine Mother, symbolized by pearls, that transformed Heywood's experience. In my case, the revelation that disposed of the incomplete understanding was the recognition of like-minded beings in the form of "rings" (perhaps not so different from pearls), which sparked off feelings of universal love. The living other, lost for a moment in the perceptual-intellectual expansion, was recovered. In this way, the communal nature of the mind was suggested, through the recognition of others and the powerful feeling of love that reached to all, a love that, importantly, was understood not to be the exclusive preserve of the expanded condition but transferable to ordinary life.

Love Thy Neighbor

It seems, then, that other selves, social connectedness, and love are not necessarily recognized immediately, if at all, in cosmic mystical experience, and that some prompting may be necessary. Is the delay due to a lack of perceptiveness on the part of the "little self," love going unnoticed in the initial expansion of perception and knowing, but present nonetheless? Or is the delay indicative of something about the cosmic mind itself, as Heywood's account could be taken to suggest? She learned that the diamond-like intellect is incomplete until the "communicatory principle" of love has been injected into it. This may mean that there are different stages of cosmic mind, the more immediately accessible one being a cool, impersonal intellect, in contrast to a more advanced, socially conscious, loving mind. It might even mean that the latter emerges out of the former, perhaps dependent on agelong evolutionary and personal growth toward a more developed, loving type of consciousness, a process in which pointy intellects become well-rounded souls, in which diamonds become pearls (see chapters 10 and 11).

Whatever the case, it seems likely that mystical expansion and self-knowledge will be incomplete and potentially misleading if they do not show the world to be a social reality in which love is paramount. The communal nature of the expanded condition and the significance of love have a direct bearing on self-understanding: it might therefore be said that *he who knows himself loves with the love of his Lord*. In the light of this revised self-knowledge maxim, a celebrated passage in Book XI of the *Corpus Hermeticum* looks decidedly one-sided. Here we are told to make ourselves like God, who has all within himself as thoughts, for in true Empedoclean fashion like can be known only by like. But the instructions for this assimilation to divinity call for just perceptual and intellectual expansion, with no mention of love expansion:

> Make yourself grow to immeasurable immensity, outleap all body, outstrip all time, become eternity and you will understand god. Having conceived that nothing is impossible to you, consider yourself immortal and able to understand everything, all art, all learning, the temper of every living thing. Go higher than every height and lower than every depth. Collect in yourself all the sensations of what has been made, of fire and water, dry and wet; be everywhere at once, on land, in the sea, in heaven; be not yet born, be in the womb, be young, old, dead, beyond death. And when you have understood all these at once – times, places, things, qualities, quantities – then you can understand god.[68]

It is noticeable that there is no call here to love like God. Others have supposed that assimilation (*homoiōsis*, "making like") to God must involve the attainment of divine love. St. Augustine explains that we must be "loving in thought" like God,[69] and Marsilio Ficino asserts that "love unites the mind more quickly, more closely, and more stably with God than does knowledge," for while knowledge distinguishes, love unifies: "love transforms us into the beloved God."[70] Jacob Boehme describes the all-encompassing nature of love, which lifts us up to God, outward to the entire world, and down into hell itself. Love is as "high as God," raising us to unity with God, and it "enlarges the soul as wide as the whole creation of God."[71] We shall experience this enlargement when the throne of love has been set up in our hearts. Love is so great that it leaves the divine sphere and reaches even into the misery of the world and hell. Thomas Traherne, in *Christian Ethicks* (1675), recommends that we love each person in the world with the love of God:

> THE best Principle whereby a man can stear his course in this World, is that which being well prosecuted will make his Life at once honourable and happy: Which is to love every man in the whole World as GOD doth. For this will make a man the Image of GOD, and fill him with the mind and spirit of Christ.[72]

One must love with the mind of God, not just know with the mind of God. Traherne relates that during his years of alienation he was separated from love but through long application came to know it well: "I was once a stranger to it, now I am familiar with it as a daily acquaintance" (CM IV.61). Having witnessed the works of love in heaven and on earth, he was able to report that in heaven there is nothing simpler nor more natural than to love, while here love is frustrated by many impediments. However, love under these adverse conditions is all the more wonderful. Furthermore, Traherne realized that self-love as well as love of others is important. We cannot love others unless we love ourselves:

> That pool must first be filled that shall be made to overflow. He was ten years studying before he could satisfy his self-love. And now finds nothing more easy than to love others better than oneself: and that to love mankind so is the comprehensive method to all Felicity. (CM IV.55)

Only the self-love of God can truly satisfy, and this divine self-love is a love of all creatures. Assimilation to God requires that one replace one's selfish love with the all-inclusive self-love. Thus, it seems that self-love, commonly acknowledged in recent times as important for everyday psychological well-being, is also desirable in the mystical context, for here it is realized that all beings are intimately connected with oneself. To love oneself is to love all others; to harm another is to harm oneself. We might imagine the world to be a fabulous beast with many heads, like the mythical Hydra. Ordinarily, through a certain stiffness of the neck, these heads are unable to look down and recognize that they all sprout from one body. Ignorant of their common identity, they all too readily work against one another, exploiting, tyranniz-ing, murdering, pursuing individual gain and aggrandizement. Alliances are formed, but these tend to be of an exclusive nature, based on self-interest and limited notions of kinship and community. In contrast, the heads that have managed to relax their necks a little come to a perception of their mutual identity as outgrowths of the one body, and they can do nothing other than work for one another and for the good of all. This fabulous creature's self-love, if based on accurate perceptions of itself, will be all-inclusive.

Love cannot exclude anyone, for like the sun it shines on all. Traherne tells us that in the "interminable sphere" of the soul, love is infinite and extends undiminished to the farthest regions of space and time:

> Thence also it can see into further spaces, things present and things to come; height and depth being open before it, and all things in Heaven, Eternity, and Time, equally near. (CM IV.66)

That the soul is an active source of love, like the sun radiating light, makes the soul much more akin to God than would otherwise be the case. Traherne wonders whether the soul's outpouring of love throughout the world is the loving effusion of God directly present in the soul, or whether it is an image of God's love, a reflection of the divine love in the mirror-like soul (CM IV.83–84). The former way would be the "more precious," placing God in the soul, while the latter would be the "more marvellous," the soul containing the divine Image as a mirror contains the sun, and giving out love as the mirror reflects the sun's rays. But Traherne is willing to accept that the soul is, in its own right, a source of love. The soul is no simple mirror, reflecting God's love, but is able to love independently of God. This Traherne believes is shown by the soul's inconstant love, ranging from the feeble or misdirected love of our usual condition to the full love of the Kingdom of Heaven, where the delights, interests, and sacrifices, normally directed to just one beloved, are extended to all souls and reciprocated by all souls, "All there being like so many Suns shining upon one" (CM IV.85).

Souls in their outflow of love are also like fountains (CM IV.85), an analogy that underlines their variability and independence from God, for a fountain may be "shut up" (CM IV.85). Similarly, souls are like eyes, "mirrors with lids" (CM IV.86), capable of obstructing the beams of light and love they are designed to reflect and receive. The "lid of ignorance or inconsideration" shuts in the soul's love and shuts out the love of others. It is responsible for the greatest of evils, loss of communion with God in the kingdom of mutually loving creatures. It is the ruin of a soul to lose a world that was created for its enjoyment and honor, a deprivation God has sought to overcome at great cost, the sacrifice of His Son.

To "sin against infinite love" is to make oneself "infinitely deformed" (CM II.4). To cut oneself off from the natural, universal condition is to lose everything: "you bereave yourself of all" if you cannot accept the divine love and the world it gives you (CM IV.48). The rejection of love and its cosmic gift "blots out all at one dash, and bereaves you of a whole world in a moment" (CM IV.16). As a result, vision is "muddied, and blended, and confounded," the whole "lost and buried in ruins" and "nothing appearing but fragments, that are worthless shreds and parcels of them" (CM IV.54). Without divine love and its objects, "we live to no purpose," and "life is cumbersome and irksome to us" (CM II.4). Traherne strives to lead "crumpled-up" souls from the deformities of limited knowledge and love to the vision of the entire world and the felicity it brings.[73] Love is the key to recovering the "entire piece" (CM IV.54), so we would be wise to make room for it.

But how is this love to be expressed in the difficult conditions of ordinary life? It will show in the heartfelt desire that all should be happy, a happiness that ultimately can be nothing less than the felicity of the whole. It will be a universal love that does not lose sight of the individual:

To love one person with a private love is poor and miserable: to love all is glorious. To love all persons in all ages, all angels, all worlds, is Divine and Heavenly. To love all cities and all kingdoms, all kings and all peasants, and every person in all worlds with a natural intimate familiar love, as if him alone is Blessed. . . . The greatness of this man's Love no man can measure; it is stable like the Sun, it endureth for ever as the Moon, it is a faithful witness in Heaven. . . . Which however lofty and divine it is, is ready to humble itself into dust to serve the person beloved. (CM IV.69)

All this might sound hopelessly idealistic and scarcely achievable in a world so full of obstacles as our own. Traherne, however, insists that this kind of love is achievable, even if it may take years to nurture.

It goes without saying that genuine love cannot be forced or manufactured, but its natural expression can be encouraged, through nurture of personal relationships, reform of social, economic, and political conditions obstructive toward love, and practice of contemplative exercises. Mystical experiences sometimes give the impression that love is already freely available, waiting to be discovered and liberated, like the heat and light of the sun temporarily obscured by clouds. It would be presumptuous of me to expatiate further on these matters, but there is one detail I can usefully discuss. I was once ushered into the mystery by a vision of ring-shaped beings, and it is to those enigmatic heralds of love that I now turn.

5

Soul Spheres

Wherefore he made the world in the form of a globe,
round as from a lathe, in every direction
equally distant from the centre to the extremes,
the most perfect and the most like itself of all figures.

—Plato

UPON ITS RELEASE IN 2003, the motion picture *21 Grams* sparked interest in one of the more bizarre scientific experiments of the twentieth century. In 1907, Dr. Duncan MacDougall reported his experimental attempts to weigh the soul by measuring the weight changes of terminally ill patients as they expired on a specially constructed bed.[1] The reasoning went as follows: if the soul is a "ponderable" substance, capable of being weighed, then a decrease in body weight should register on sufficiently sensitive scales when the soul leaves the body at death. One patient lost three quarters of an ounce ("21 grams") at the moment of death, and a few others lost roughly similar amounts. MacDougall waited for his ailing human patients to pass away in their own good time, but his fifteen canine subjects in a similar experiment were not so fortunate, and unlike the human patients they showed no weight loss at death, suggesting to MacDougall a "physiological difference" between humans and dogs (and "probably" all other animals).

There are stories of earlier experimentalists who applied even more rudimentary practical techniques and fallible interpretative skills to their quantitative investigations of the soul. In what was most likely an attempt at character assassination, a story was told of Emperor Frederick II of Hohenstaufen (1194-1250), an early exponent of experimental science: he is alleged to have had a man sealed in a wine cask to ascertain whether a material soul leaves the body at death. After the man had suffocated, a hole was

made in the barrel. Because no soul-breath was observed to exit, it was concluded that no material soul leaves the body at death.[2] Clearly, the emperor
had neglected to run the experimental design by his ethics committee. Earlier
and equally gruesome investigations of this type are recorded in Buddhist
and Jaina texts in connection with the skeptical materialist Prince Pāyāsi,
who, as well as anticipating the barrel experiment attributed to Frederick,
is said to have ordered a criminal to be weighed before and after execution.
It seems that Pāyāsi took the apparent change in weight—an increase in
this case—as evidence for a material transformation at death, rather than
a spiritual one.[3] Fortunately, modern-day attempts to weigh the soul have
employed nondestructive techniques, using out-of-body experiences rather
than terminal death events, but the results have been uninformative.[4]

If the soul does have measurable attributes, there is one that could be of
special interest to scientific investigators. For reasons that will be elaborated
in some detail in the next chapter, there may be a direct link between the soul
and the universe, a correspondence that extends to their respective shapes.
This connection will introduce some precision to my use of the word "soul,"
which for the moment I leave in its commonly ill-defined state. To investigate
the shape of the soul, one can draw upon anecdotal reports of soul sightings.
In these, it is no great surprise to find that the souls of human beings are
often perceived to have the shape of the human body, sometimes in miniature form, a tendency that Carol Zaleski has called "somatomorphism."[5] For
example, Johannes Baptista van Helmont's quest for self-knowledge, which
I touched upon in chapter 4, eventually led him to a vision of his own soul.
The soul turned out to be human in shape, in both its innermost kernel and
outer covering (see Box, "In the figure of a man").

But it is perhaps surprising to find the departed occasionally described as
balls, globes, orbs, or spheres. Some observations of globular beings belong
to the tradition of fireball stories, in which hovering, apparently sentient
concentrations of light, witnessed in graveyards, bogs, and other locations,
have long been interpreted as visitations by departing souls, fairy folk, and
the like, and which at times seem malicious in intent, luring travelers into
danger. In western folklore, the will-o'-the-wisp (*ignis fatuus*, "spooklights")
belongs to the tradition, and there are many equivalents round the world.
For instance, in Japan there is the *hitodama*, the soul of a person separated
from the body, usually around the time of death, and sometimes described
as a hovering ball of blue light, although other colors are observed: "Fireballs
are usually reported to be in the shape of a circle, an ellipse or a ball with a
trail. Their colors are commonly reported as bluish white, or occasionally
yellow or red."[6] At places of great religious significance, fireballs are likely

❧ In the figure of a man ❧

One day in 1610, after thirteen years of contemplative striving, Johannes Baptista van Helmont finally caught a glimpse of his soul. The vision took place in a dream. On falling asleep, he found himself in a dark hall. To the left stood a bottle of liquor, which spoke to him, asking if he desired honors and riches. To the right was a chink in the wall through which a dazzling light shone. What van Helmont saw there was beyond expression, so he turned back to the beguiling drink and woke up in horror just as he was about to partake of it. Working in seclusion for years, van Helmont pursued chemical researches and remained hopeful of acquiring knowledge of his soul.[7] In due course, his theories and polemical style drew him into conflict with the Jesuits, and he fell foul of the Inquisition. It was at this time of "anxious afflictions" in 1633, twenty-three years after the first sighting of his soul, that van Helmont had a further glimpse:

> It was a transcendent light, in the figure of a man, whose whole was homogeneous, actively discerning, a substance spiritual, Crystalline, and lucent by its own native splendor. But enshrined it was in a second nubilous part, as the husk or exterior *cortex* of it self.[8]

The cloudy husk—the sensitive soul—had sexual characteristics, unlike the sexless kernel, the immortal, crystalline intellect. Van Helmont took this human-shaped intellect to be made in the Image of God, which suggested to him that God, as the original, must also be human-shaped. But he subsequently gave up his quest to know the soul, for despite the beauty of the vision, it gave him no lasting "perfection," unlike other visions of the intellectual type that had brought him knowledge.

The somatomorphism of the vision contrasts with a much earlier dream in which van Helmont found himself to be a *bubble* of celestial proportions. As a student, he was drawn to Stoicism, but a dream pointed to its weakness compared with the Christian revelation: "I seemed to be made an empty Bubble, whose Diameter reached from the Earth even to Heaven," positioned between a dark abyss and a sarcophagus, interpreted by van Helmont to signify Hell and death respectively. He concluded that Stoicism had made him haughty, "an empty and swollen Bubble," while Christianity impressed on him the need for divine grace.[9] The dream's bubble imagery was perhaps inspired by the spherical soul or vehicle mentioned in Stoic and Platonic writings.

to be venerated as divine manifestations and to confirm the sacredness of the sites. An outstanding example is that of the luminous globes and other light phenomena observed at the Wutai Mountains in north China, which have been a site of Buddhist monasticism for a very long time, associated with Mañjuśrī, the bodhisattva of wisdom. John Blofeld recounts an incident during a visit in the 1930s: from a high tower at night, numerous fireballs were seen to float past, indicating the presence of the bodhisattva. Blofeld comments: "Fluffy balls of orange-colored fire, moving through space, unhurried and majestic—truly a fitting manifestation of divinity!"[10]

An interesting example of a deceased person seen in the form of a luminous ball is the case of Louisa "Weesy" Coppin, at the time of writing the only individual in the *Oxford Dictionary of National Biography* whose occupation is stated as "ghost"—or rather, "supposed ghost."[11] In 1849, four-year-old Louisa died from gastric fever, but the remaining children of the Coppin family, aged between two and nine and a half, soon became aware of her presence, describing her as a "ball of bluish light."[12] The children's father, William Coppin, a surveyor of ships, was away at the time, but on his return he was informed of the remarkable sightings. At this point, a lady visitor arrived at the family home, and both she and Mr. Coppin, who was rather susceptible to mysterious happenings,[13] witnessed the luminous ball in the drawing room, in a corner near the ceiling. The ball was "distinctly visible" for the full quarter of an hour of the meeting. Afterward, Mr. Coppin went upstairs to the parlor, where he found Mrs. Coppin reclining on a sofa in a state of weakness, with the ball of bluish light just above her head, again near the ceiling.[14]

The children had identified the luminous ball as Louisa, but in the narrative the deceased girl is attributed a more conventional form too, for she is seen standing by walls and sitting at the dining table,[15] and even sitting on her aunt's knee, "dressed in robes of indescribable beauty and radiantly bright."[16] The case was made public forty years later, in 1889, when it was revealed that the deceased girl, questioned through the intermediary of her seven-year-old sister, had provided information on the whereabouts of Sir John Franklin's naval expedition, which in 1845 had set out to find the Northwest passage but had gone missing. The information was discovered to be surprisingly accurate when traces of the expedition were eventually found.[17] The case is made additionally interesting by this last aspect, which if true might indicate that something paranormal was afoot, whether or not it involved the ghost of Little Weesy.

Nowadays, sightings of luminous balls are likely to be explained in terms of combusting marsh gas, ball lightning, earthquake lights, St. Elmo's fire, incandescent meteors, and so on.[18] Not very long ago there was considerable interest in digital photographs that show "orbs," circular images sometimes understood to be pictures of souls, ghosts, and the like, but which are more convincingly explained as artifacts produced by out-of-focus specks of dust or rain drops.[19] More relevant to the present discussion are sightings of circular and spherical beings in *altered states of consciousness*, including out-of-body, near-death, mystical, and meditative states.

As the work of Jeffrey Kripal has impressed upon me, "unidentified fly-ing object" (UFO) sightings and "alien abduction experiences" (AAEs) can be added to this list, if they show signs of having occurred during altered states of consciousness and/or have a paranormal quality.[20] While many UFO sightings have an objective, "out there" feel and may indeed have involved meteorological phenomena or actual flying craft (if not extraterrestrial in origin), others look very much as if they depended on a shift of consciousness on the part of the observer, exhibiting characteristics reminiscent of altered states, including special lights and changes to time perception. In particu-lar, some AAEs exhibit the sleep paralysis and hypnagogic/hypnopompic kind of imagery typical of transitions between wakefulness and sleep (see below), and so are comparable to the "night hag" visitations of folklore.[21] Kripal points out that interpretation of UFOs in terms of altered states and the paranormal neither detracts from their reality nor rules out bodily and environmental manifestations, since the paranormal has an "expressive" as well as "receptive" side to it, as in psychokinetic "mind over matter" and poltergeist phenomena. The boundary commonly set up between inner mental states and the outer physical world becomes blurred in the face of certain extraordinary phenomena, including synchronistic "coincidences" and UFOs, as Jung emphasized.[22]

Kripal raises the case of aircraft pilot Kenneth Arnold, whose sight-ing in June 1947 of nine flying objects, emitting bright blue-white flashes, was instrumental in establishing UFOs in the modern public imagination. Kripal rightly finds fascinating the comment by Arnold's daughter Kim that her father came to the view that those objects he observed in 1947 were not machines but were alive, and that they were from another plane of existence, perhaps from the world "we enter when we die."[23] From this perspective, the foundational modern UFO sighting becomes a spiritual experience. Kripal discusses a few modern experiences of luminous, seemingly conscious balls, including the intriguing case of a triangular formation of golden orbs that appeared during a spontaneous shift in consciousness, announced by a "thick black haze" clouding the field of vision from the periphery inward, creating a kind of tunnel vision. The orbs, which were not so much seen externally as experienced within, induced "an overwhelming calm and a peculiar serenity." [24]

I have found reports of encounters with disc-like or ball-like beings in altered states of consciousness interesting because my own "abduction" into the land of the dead—the mystical state of unitive consciousness that was a kind of "ego-death"—brought such an encounter. Who or what were the circular beings I met? As it turns out, they were not "alien" at all, not different from myself, being both a part of me and the same as me. In the present chapter, I take a look at some precedents in the spiritual literature with the hope of shedding light on the matter.

Sea of Love

The "vision of the rings" was a turning point in my experience, for it led directly to the expansion of love. I had found my attention drawn to a "board" or strand of light in which ring-like shapes were positioned, and I understood these little things to be beings who were equivalent to "myself," that is, to the expansive mind I had become, a mind that contained the world within itself. The little beings were similarly endowed with the all-inclusive knowledge, and the recognition of them triggered the all-embracing love. I have yet to come across exact parallels to this triggering effect in the mystical literature. The closest I have found is a description, by St. John of the Cross, of the inflaming action of angels on the soul, which will be noted below.

The living beings were round in shape, and the ones I saw on the luminous board were, I think, arranged in a zigzag fashion (fig. 5.1). I described them as "little circles or some very similar rounded shape," by which I meant that their form was certainly rounded and could have been properly circular. I had the impression of a ring, which could be produced by a circle viewed face on or alternatively a sphere viewed from any direction. A sphere, especially a translucent bubble, might easily be viewed as a ring or circle. As several of these objects were seen in the same way, a spherical interpretation may well be justified, for views of several circles might be expected to include at least some with an oblique orientation to the vantage point, which I do not remember being the case. The matter is uncertain, and in the remainder of the chapter I shall concern myself with round forms described or depicted in the mystical and religious literature, whether they are circular or spherical.

Another point of interest is the observation that the ring-beings were very tiny parts of the overall vision. This lay at the root of my puzzlement:

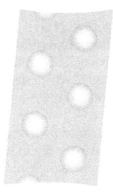

Figure 5.1   The "rings" in zigzag formation on a strand of luminosity (approximate depiction only).

it was paradoxical that a being equivalent to my expansive consciousness could be experienced as a tiny part of it. The paradox of a "part equal to the whole" may be the key to understanding the enigma of the rings and will receive special attention in the next chapter. As I was to discover, the notion of "parts that are the whole" is to be found in several traditions, including Neoplatonic, Jewish, Christian, Islamic, Hindu, Buddhist, and neo-Confucian.

But first, what is to be made of the love-engendering effect of viewing the ring-like beings? Plotinus mentions a passionate movement of the soul toward other members of the intelligible cosmos, a love that is an indirect expression of the love that draws the soul to its ultimate source, the One (*Enn.* VI.7.22). Christian discussions of the aspirational love toward God also found divine love reflected in the soul's relationship with other members of the heavenly community. In the love-inspiring power these beings exert on the soul, they are reminiscent of the rings that ignited my own, all-too-brief experience of universal love. In traditional Christian angelology, following the Christian Neoplatonist Pseudo-Dionysius (late fifth to early sixth century CE), it is the seraphim, burning with the love of God, who inflame the soul: being closest to God, they have the "capacity to stamp their own image on subordinates by arousing and uplifting in them too a like flame."[25] The angelic hierarchy was to receive its most famous literary depiction in *The Divine Comedy*, in which Dante first sees the hierarchy reflected in the eyes of his beloved Beatrice. Medieval writers were able to draw on *The Celestial Hierarchy* of the Pseudo-Dionysius for angelological details, finding there explanations of the many-eyed, many-winged cherubim full of knowledge and seraphim rapt in love.

St. John of the Cross gives a fine description of the inflaming action of a seraph in *The Living Flame of Love*. There is mention here of a point inflaming the soul to a love of cosmic proportions. Using the love metaphors of burning, wounding, and healing, St. John first describes one exalted type of love's transforming activity, which confers on the soul a knowledge of everything, but which does not involve any images or intellections.[26] St. John also acknowledges types of love-wounding that do incorporate forms, and he relates one sublime way involving an intellectual figure: this is the assault by a seraph with a dart enkindled in the fire of love, which pierces the soul to its heart. The wound is experienced as a point, a minute point like a mustard seed, which expands into a cosmic sea of love:

> Herein it feels its heat to be increasing and to be growing in strength and its love to be becoming so refined in this heat that it seems to have within it seas of loving fire which reach to the farthest heights and depths of the spheres, filling it wholly with love. Herein it seems to the soul that the whole universe is a sea of love wherein it is engulfed, and it can descry no term or goal at which this love can come to an end, but feels within itself, as we have said, the keen point and centre of love.[27]

The soul, having experienced itself engulfed in a universe of love, may now understand the comparison in the Gospels between the Kingdom of Heaven and the mustard seed that grows into a great herb: "For the soul sees that it has become like a vast fire of love which arises from that enkindled point in the heart of the spirit. Few souls attain to a state as high as this, but some have done so."[28] St. John has in mind St. Francis of Assisi, wounded by a seraph, but he may also be referring to St. Teresa's transverberation by a spear tipped with a point of fire and wielded by an angel. The angel is of the highest order, burning with divine love, but Teresa herself is unsure of the terminology in her own telling of the experience and thinks that the angel might have been one of the cherubim.[29] Some have understood Teresa's "transverberation of the heart" by the spear in sexual and erotic terms,[30] and there may well be good reason for finding erotic undertones in mystical "points of fire" and indeed in inflaming rings, circles, and spheres.

However, there is a danger that such interpretations will be back to front if they fail to recognize that human desire may be a channeling and dilution of transpersonal "energies," an expression of a deeper *eros*. The interpretation of certain mystical phenomena in erotic terms, then, is not incorrect if it acknowledges that desire, including sexual desire and its objects and their shapes, straight or curved, has a transcendent dimension, as appreciated in some spiritual traditions, including Platonic, Kabbalistic, tantric, and Daoist, and emphasized in recent years by Jeffrey Kripal in his construction of "the erotic" as a category that includes yet goes beyond the personal domain of human sexuality.[31] Moreover, it is notable that sexual experience has been known on occasions to provide an entry point to that greater "beyond."[32]

Spiritual Sphericities

There are many references to circles/spheres in the religious literature, and some are relevant to the present discussion because they are associated with mystical and near-death experiences. Sometimes the rounded forms in these experiences are just patterns of light, without seeming to have any further significance. For instance, during a medical emergency that involved great loss of blood, a woman experienced a "big kaleidoscope with white, silver and purple circles," followed by a life review from childhood onward, consisting of a succession of images, then a manifestation of "purple and silver orbs of light floating" in front of her, and finally a bright light that grew stronger but then dimmed, before the return to waking consciousness.[33]

Sometimes, however, the circles and spheres are understood to be conscious, intelligent, even spiritual beings, such as souls or guiding spirits. Circular forms observed in altered states can also be astronomical objects, such as the Earth seen from high above, stellar bodies, or the universe viewed as a whole, as in "celestial flight" experiences (see chapter 7). Near to death, Julian of Norwich (b. ca. 1342) had a vision of "a little thing, the size of a hazel-nut" in the palm of her hand—"it was as round as a ball."[34] This was "all that is made," and although it was very small, Julian understood that it—the universe—endures because God loves it.

Circular forms can also be experienced during meditative practice. For instance, various colored lights and luminous orbs manifest on the journey to the higher self described by the Sufi mystic Najm al-Dīn Kubrā (d. 1221 CE).[35] Another sophisticated example comes from the Bon and Buddhist traditions of Tibet, in the Dzogchen practice known as *thod rgal* ("leap over"), which is said to depend on the subtle physiology and "light channels" of the body, and which is intended to facilitate *spontaneous* luminous manifestations. It therefore differs from the deliberate practice of visualization. One method employs the dark retreat: sensory deprivation brings first simple luminosities, then iconic forms, and then complex visionary and psychical experiences, as Tenzin Wangyal's account of a forty-nine-day dark retreat well illustrates.[36] In the second week, he experienced visions of rays, spheres (*thig le*), rainbows, and symbolic forms, but then more realistic images began to appear, and Wangyal found himself immersed in them. Toward the end of the retreat, he had what seemed to be a clairvoyant vision too. As a practitioner of Dzogchen, Wangyal understood the luminous phenomena to be manifestations of his own mind. However, his understanding is not to be interpreted in merely psychological terms, for the luminous mind of Dzogchen is the immaculate Primordial Basis of all phenomena. It is therefore a luminous reality in the tradition of the *tathāgatagarbha* (Buddha-potential) and *dharmakāya* (truth-body) doctrines of Buddhism.

Thod rgal practices bring the "four visions."[37] First, little spheres, discs, or "drops" (*thig les*) of spectral light manifest, individually or in chains and other formations, and they grow in size and become more numerous as the first three stages unfold, before dissolving in the fourth. Visions appear in the discs: these can include views of the impure realms of existence, the wrathful and peaceful deities, the Buddha-families, and the pure lands.[38] It seems that the visionary contents depend to some extent on one's previous experience and so have a conditioned or "contextual" dimension to them, as Wangyal explains, for those without prior practice see images that are not described in the texts.[39] However, familiarity with the traditional imagery is presumably advantageous, supplying visionary forms recognizable and valuable to practitioners. The visions are not sought for their own sake but are approached with an attitude of nonattachment. The aim is to realize firsthand how all phenomena, including everyday sense perceptions, arise from the primordial ground of gnosis (*rigpa*), and through that realization to attain to the ground itself or at least to lay the foundations for liberation during the death transition, when similar but more intense visions arise and are to be recognized then as projections of one's own mind-nature. Thorough familiarity with the phenomena in the present life prepares the practitioner for similar experiences at death and the potentially liberative encounter with reality in the supreme light.

The *thod rgal* practice yields a sequence of luminous manifestations reminiscent of phenomena well known to psychological science, namely entoptic lights and hypnagogic-type imagery. "Entoptic" phenomena are said to originate within the eye or, if defined more broadly, anywhere within the visual nervous system, including the visual cortex. They include fields of light and geometric patterns that are universal in occurrence, found across cultures. The phenomena appear in a number of circumstances, including darkness, electrical stimulation, and pressure applied to the eyeball. Closely related to the entoptic phenomena experienced under these conditions are the lights and patterns that appear in drug-induced states, in the hypnagogic transitions between sleep and wakefulness, and, as already noted, during meditation. Here again, dots, circles, zigzags, grids, and other patterns can manifest (fig. 5.2). The luminous phenomena of hypnagogia and other altered states sometimes develop through a sequence of stages, beginning with the lights and patterns, and proceeding to images (as in the *thod rgal* practice). For example, hypnagogia may begin with simple luminosities, including the light fields and patterns, pass through sensations of floating and drifting, accompanied by faces, figures, and scenes, to imagery (including "auto-symbolic" representations of the mental and bodily state of the observer), and finally to dreamlike sequences in which the observer is immersed.[40] A similar progression has been observed in some drug-induced experiences, and it has been claimed, controversially, that entoptic phenomena engendered in shamanic altered states of consciousness, in which drugs often play a role, gave inspiration to the geometric designs of Palaeolithic rock art, which can include circles, grids, and zigzag patterns.[41]

As noted above, the *thod rgal* practice is intended, at least in part, to prepare the meditator for death, at which time the luminous phenomena will be experienced again in more intense form. Modern reports of near-death experience confirm that a succession of luminous phenomena can appear as death approaches. It has been claimed, however, that these luminous manifestations during NDEs, such as the lights, tunnel, and imagery, are *nothing but* biologically originated entoptics progressively elaborated into personally and culturally shaped hallucinatory images of increasing complexity. Ronald K. Siegel proposed such a theory, utilizing his research with THC, psilocybin, LSD, and mescaline.[42] Drawing on Louis Jolyon West's "perceptual release theory" (itself rooted in nineteenth-century theories of hallucination), Siegel supposed that there is a background of neurologically stored memories that is normally kept out of consciousness by the dominating influx of sense perceptions. When that sensory input diminishes, as a result of, say, sensory deprivation or disruption by hallucinogens, then the brain makes up for the loss by releasing its stored contents as hallucinatory images.[43] Applied to near-death experiences, Siegel's theory reduces them to biological and psychological factors alone, for it has no place for released contents of transpersonal origin.

Figure 5.2   Some entoptic patterns.

While it is necessary to be alert to the presence of entoptic phenomena and person-sourced or culture-sourced imagery in altered states of consciousness, including mystical experiences, there is the danger that this kind of theory prematurely excludes the possibility of transpersonal contributions. It is difficult to understand how biology and psychology alone, as currently formulated, could explain the expansive perceptions and profound knowing that mystical experiences seem to bring, as well as the psi cognitions of telepathy and precognition. Such phenomena—and others too—invite a "filter" type of theory proposed by William James, Frederic Myers, and others over a century ago, according to which transpersonal as well as personal contents of the subconscious can, when released, find their way into consciousness.[44] We should certainly be attentive to the presence of entoptic luminosities and personal, cultural, and religious imagery in mystical experiences, but it would be premature to claim that these phenomena exhaust the experiences. In considering my own "vision of the rings," I do have to take seriously the possibility that it involved entoptics, yet if the experience were a purely biological and psychological affair I would find it difficult to understand why it had the profoundly noetic, meaningful quality, the sheer expansiveness of consciousness, the clarity of wakefulness, and my recognition of the little circles as living beings equivalent to my world-encompassing mind, entities capable of inspiring the most inclusive kind of love. This is not typical of entoptic light displays and hallucinatory images.

Diagrams and pictures with circular designs abound in the literature and art of religion, but few illustrations I have seen remind me of the rings in the zigzag formation I observed. One interesting example that I have come across is the pictorial representation of the visions of the twelfth-century mystic St. Hildegard of Bingen, visions that included fiery soul-globes. Interestingly, the experiences on which these illustrations are based have sometimes been put down to migraine, a condition that can bring visual patterns and imagery very similar to entoptic phenomena. However, the globes of Hildegard—like my own little rings—were, it seems, rather more than mere shapes of light: as we shall see below, they are presented as all-knowing souls. Kabbalistic trees of the *sefirot*, which can show circles arranged in columns (see fig. 9.4) are a little reminiscent, but these diagrams represent the successive emanation of divine powers from the supreme source. Halos around heads and the aureolae enclosing the entire bodies of saints and deities in several religious traditions are also reminiscent in so far as they link intelligent beings with a circular form. Pictures that show eyes arranged on the wings of seraphim are reminiscent too, especially if the narrowness of the wings constrains the eyes into a zigzag formation.

Indeed, eye imagery is very relevant to the present discussion, for it brings together seeing, knowing, light, and sphericity, as several examples in the present chapter will show. I myself did not interpret the rings as eyes, neither during the experience nor afterward, but I appreciate that ocular imagery would have expressed their combination of rotundity and perceptual quality. One important but obscure employment of eye imagery in the mystical literature is to be found in the writings of Jacob Boehme and his followers.[45] Boehme dwelt on the idea of the divine eye, its reflexive self-knowledge, and its archetypal relation to the soul. Because the soul is a copy of the divine eye, the ocular and therefore globular character of the soul follows. Boehme writes: "So we must understand that the soul is in the form of a round globe, according to the eye of God," a globe of fire divided into two eyes arranged back-to-back, one of fire and one of light.[46]

Boehme's commentator Dionysius Andreas Freher (1647–1725) found confirmation that the soul "in its spiritual figure is a globe, not a triangle nor a square" in a visionary account furnished by Boehme's editor Johann Georg Gichtel (1638–1710).[47] A friend of Gichtel had killed himself, and Gichtel, inquiring into his fate by entering a trance state, observed the friend's soul "in the figure of a little globe, so contracted, astricted and narrowed, that it had as to appearance no life, and no ability to exert any of its powers and faculties."[48] The soul was trapped in the cold, dark, saturnine property that is the first of Boehme's seven "source spirits." Each night for a year, Gichtel endured grueling trance sessions in order to help his friend's soul progress through the first few source-spirit properties and regain its vitality.

Some modern accounts of near-death, out-of-body, and mystical experiences refer to round shapes in connection with the self or soul. Raymond Moody, in *Life After Life*, gives a few examples. In one, a traffic-accident victim found that his "being," "self," or "spirit" exited through his head.[49] He felt a "density" to his new form, which "was small, and it felt as if it were sort of circular, with no rigid outlines." In another case, a man felt like a round ball: "When my heart stopped beating . . . I felt like I was a round ball and almost maybe like I might have been a little sphere—like a B-B—on the inside of this round ball. I just can't describe it to you."[50] A case of inclusive double identity, it would seem—see figure 4.2b. Commenting on the arrangement of the little sphere in the larger ball, Jungian scholar Marie-Louise von Franz found here "an especially striking image, for it seems to describe the 'correct' relation of the ego to the Self, that is, the ego is a part of the whole and is at the same time one with the whole."[51] Jung himself commented on "parapsychic visions of luminous globes" and associated symbols of the Self in dreams and fantasies.[52] Moreover, the mandala as a symbol of wholeness was one of Jung's preoccupations.[53] Also recounted in Moody's *Life After Life* (and noted by von Franz) is the case of a man in great pain who first saw a ball of light ("no more than twelve to fifteen inches in diameter") in his room, and then, exiting from his body, he found himself to have the same globular form.[54] The first ball acted as a guide or higher self.

Other near-death examples include Eben Alexander's experience of orbs of light (see chapter 7), and Jean Renee Hausheer's encounter with "a wondrous, brilliant ball of the unimaginably whitest light from which emanated perfect love and peacefulness," a light with which she "became one and the same."[55] Also of interest is Jurgen Ziewe's prolonged out-of-body journey in August 1980.[56] After shedding his self-disguises, Ziewe found himself to be one of millions of sparkling orbs "bobbing along on a vast expanse of coloured light."[57] These orbicular souls were attached by filaments to bodies in a "distant darkness" (perhaps reminiscent of Plutarch's tethered minds—see below), but they were largely unaffected by whatever their far-off "counterparts" were doing. Ziewe's guide, his higher self, manifested now as a luminous orb, now as a beautiful face, now as a presence unified with the surroundings. A condition of unity, peace, and clarity had been attained, but this was not the end of the journey, for after further developments the essence of reality was reached, consisting of light, love, and intelligence, a knowing of all by being all.

The experiences of spheres described in modern accounts are quite varied, and some of the rounded shapes seem to be entoptic in character, or dream-like and symbolic, or just expressive of the amorphous luminosity that sometimes manifests in out-of-body and near-death experiences. However, the association made between spiritual beings and sphericity is worth pursuing, for there are interesting antecedents in traditional writings, some of which may help shed further light on the matter. Sphericity has been associated with soul, spirit, and divine realities in several ways, often in connection with light or fire. In approximate order of increasing strength, these associations can be classified as follows:

Soul is composed of spherical atoms

According to the ancient Greek philosopher Democritus, atoms have all kinds of shapes, but those that make up fire and soul are spherical. Soul is able to move things because it is itself capable of movement. The smooth, round shape of its constituent atoms allows the soul to extend easily through a body and exercise its animating power.[58] In this theory, soul and fire are linked, but the connection is indirect, through the common spherical shape of their atoms. It should be stressed that the soul is not itself spherical.

Rather, the atoms that make up the soul are spherical, and the soul adopts the shape of the body it permeates and moves. However, the association of soul, fire, and sphericity here could have encouraged later thinkers to make connections between the three.

Souls are hidden in a spherical blaze of light

Souls are not themselves spherical, but they may appear so if the blaze of light around the soul is mistaken for the soul itself. The seemingly globular form of the soul is described by Dante in the *Paradiso*, the third canticle of *The Divine Comedy*, completed shortly before his death in 1321. At one stage in the heavenly ascent, Dante is directed by his guide Beatrice to a group of a "hundred little spheres" (*cento sperule*), a multitude of luminous globes that irradiate and beautify one another with mutual love (XXII.23).[59] The brightest of these "pearls" is St. Benedict. Later, in the heaven of fixed stars, Dante sees further soul-radiances, and some become visible as "spheres," *spera* here perhaps meaning rings of circle-dancing souls.[60] Dante does not take the spherical shape to be the true form of the soul: rather, the lights are dazzling luminosities that conceal a human form. Dante must wait till his sight has been purified before he can look upon the unmasked forms of heavenly beings. Now the straight river of time becomes a circle of eternity, and Dante is ready for the unobstructed vision of the white-robed souls in the Empyrean.

It is possible that a story told about St. Francis of Assisi belongs to the same category, although in this case it is not clear that the dazzling sphere of light hides a human form. One night, when Francis was away from home and his friars were either resting or praying, a fiery chariot entered their house and turned around two or three times. A "huge globe of light" rested above the chariot, illuminating the night. The brothers concluded that it was the soul of Francis that was "shining with such great brilliance."[61]

Souls are lifted heavenward in a fiery sphere

It is appropriate that St. Benedict (ca. 480–540) should have appeared to Dante as shrouded in a luminous sphere, for Benedict himself was credited with a vision of a soul enclosed in a fiery globe. The story is told in the second book of Gregory the Great's *Dialogues*, which recounts the life and miracles of Benedict. In what has been described as "perhaps the most famous non-biblical vision of the early Middle Ages,"[62] Benedict saw the entire world as if it were "gathered together" in a single ray of light (*Dialogues* II.35). In this unifying light—the divine light that enlarges the soul's interior—Benedict saw the soul of Germanus, Bishop of Capua, carried heavenward. On an earlier occasion, Benedict had seen the soul of his twin sister Scholastica fly to heaven in the form of a dove. However, in the unifying light Benedict observed the soul of the bishop to ascend "in a fiery sphere" (*in spera ignea*), carried aloft by angels. Note that the soul of Germanus is not itself spherical. Rather, it is surrounded by a fiery sphere, carried above by angels. Scholars have suggested a number of sources for Gregory's story of Benedict's cosmic vision, including some that may have contributed to the detail of the fiery globe, such as Cicero's *Dream of Scipio*, Macrobius's commentary on the *Dream*, and stories about St. Martin of Tours (see below).[63]

Souls rise heavenward in flamelike bubbles

In one of the great classical accounts of near-death journeying out of the body, souls are seen to rise heavenward in luminous spheres, but here the globular envelope is a bubble in the surrounding atmosphere, the shining aether through which the soul ascends. Plutarch (ca. 45–ca. 125), biographer, historian, Platonic philosopher, and priest at the Delphic temple of Apollo, relates two stories of disembodied experience, the "myth of Thespesius" and the "myth of Timarchus." The former tells of Aridaeus, a dissolute inhabitant of Soli who fell from a height, hit his neck, and was thought dead. This Aridaeus, renamed Thespesius during the out-of-body excursion, recovered three days later at his funeral and told his tale:

> He said that when his intelligence was driven from his body, the change made him feel as a pilot might at first on being flung into the depths of the sea; his next impression was that he had risen somewhat and was breathing with his whole being and seeing on all sides, his soul having opened wide as if it were a single eye.[64]

In Plutarch's theory of the human constitution, the soul has two clearly distinguished parts, the soul submerged in the body, caught up in passions, pleasures, and pains, and the mind (*nous*) located external to the body or capable of moving outside the body, attached to it by a cord, like a buoy or cork float.[65] It is the mind or "daemon"—intelligence unclouded by bodily involvement—that is driven forth when Aridaeus falls, although it is still connected to his body by the anchor of the soul. As an early account of disembodied experience, the testimony is interesting for several details that recur in later postmortem, out-of-body, and heavenly visions, but in the present context we can note the great expansion in perception, a panoramic form of vision that invites description of the disembodied intellect as a "single eye," like the all-seeing eye of divinity.

The released intellect of Aridaeus/Thespesius rides on light beams radiated by the stars and sees souls rising from below. These are enveloped in bubbles as they push through the air:

> They made a flamelike bubble as the air was displaced, and then, as the bubble gently burst, came forth, human in form, but slight in bulk, and moving with dissimilar motions. Some leapt forth with amazing lightness and darted about aloft in a straight line, while others, like spindles, revolved upon themselves and at the same time swung downward, now upward, moving in a complex and disordered spiral that barely grew steady after a very long time.[66]

The ascending intellects are not themselves bubbles but are enclosed in bubbles that burst to release human forms within. An explanation of the complex, disordered spiral motions of some intellects is given in the Timarchus myth. At one point, Timarchus sees many stars, and these are observed to sink into a dark abyss or rise up from it. His unseen guide explains that these are the intellects rising and falling between rebirths. The extinguished stars are those intellects who fall to earth and sink into bodies, and the reillumined stars are those who have shed the mud of embodiment. Some of the latter show a "confused and uneven spiral" motion because their souls, still in the body, are unruly and pull them about, "as though jerked about on a tether."[67]

Balls of fire rise above the heads of the holy

It has been suggested that the miraculous stories of St. Martin of Tours (ca. 316–397) may have contributed to Gregory's account of Benedict's vision. Sulpicius Severus (ca. 363–ca. 420) describes the heavenly ascent of his friend Martin, witnessed in a lucid dreaming state: Martin, who appears to Severus with face ablaze, hair glowing red, shoots into the heavens, carried up on a cloud. On waking, Sulpicius is told that Martin had recently died.[68] However, the detail of the ascending *ball* of fire occurs in a different story told by Sulpicius and not in a postmortem context. As Martin stands before a large congregation, a few present see "a ball of fire dart out from his head, so that, as it rose in the air, the flame drew out into a hair of enormous length."[69] Sulpicius is unable to say why only a few persons witnessed the phenomenon, and he offers no explanation of the mysterious occurrence. There is no suggestion that the fiery ball is Martin's soul or a sheath of radiance enclosing his soul.

But some modern accounts of mystical and near-death experiences do describe feelings of passage through the top of the head, and there is a belief

among the Tibetans that at death the departing awareness exits through
the crown in a blaze of light, if only in the case of meditators who have
performed the necessary preparatory work and are on the verge of liberation or a rebirth that will lead to it.[70] The story is told that at his death the
Tibetan yogin Marpa (1012–1090 CE) sent an egg-sized, five-colored sphere
of light from the crown of his head into the sky to show the procedure to
his disciples.[71] In the Hindu Tantra, such cranial egresses and projections of
light are associated with the body's subtle anatomy. Of the various centers
of power (*cakra*) said to be positioned along the central axis of the body,
one has commonly been placed at the crown, the internal *sahasrāra* or
dvādaśānta, while another has sometimes been placed higher still, twelve
fingerbreadths above the crown, the cosmic *sahasrāra* or *dvādaśānta*. The
activation of this extracranial center is said to bring realization of the Self
and cosmic expansion of consciousness.[72] Swami Muktananda (1908–1982)
relates that a drop (*bindu*) of blue light, the "Blue Pearl" of his Siddha yoga
meditations, radiated out from his *sahasrāra*.[73] Muktananda explains that the
Blue Pearl is the house of the Self, the abode of God. Like the "space within
the heart" of the *Chāndogya Upaniṣad*, it is as small as a seed yet contains
everything within—the heavenly, mundane, and hellish worlds.

Souls come to occupy spherical resurrection bodies

Jorge Luis Borges, in *The Book of Imaginary Beings*, conjures up the charming
image of blessed souls brought back to life in the form of spheres that roll
into Heaven.[74] Souls released from their bodies are not themselves spherical,
but the glorious bodies they will come to occupy at the time of resurrection will be so. The spherical resurrection body is associated with Origen,
although it is probable that he held no such view and that it arose through
a confusion over Origen's stand against grossly material, anthropomorphic
conceptions of resurrection. Origen had argued against an understanding
of resurrection that makes the soul reoccupy exactly the same human body
it once informed, down to the same material parts that once constituted it.
However, there is no evidence in Origen's extant works that he thought the
resurrection body would be spherical.[75] He did subscribe to the view, current at the time, that the stars are spherical bodies animated by souls, but
this is not the same as to suppose that souls will come to occupy spherical
bodies at the resurrection.[76]

It is therefore likely that the idea of the spherical resurrection body was
either introduced by followers of Origen or was conjured up by his opponents. The first hint of a tendency to misread Origen's rejection of gross
anthropomorphism occurs with the anti-Origenist Methodius of Olympus

(late third century CE): he pokes fun at the idea of a resurrection body that is not human-shaped by listing some simple geometric alternatives: "Will it be in the shape of a circle, or a polygon, or a cube, or a pyramid?"[77] The next recorded instances come from the time of the first major Origenist controversy, around the close of the fourth century, again from a critic of Origen. During a ferocious attack on John of Jerusalem, Jerome (ca. 341–420) comments that the transfigured Lord did not appear "in the roundness of the sun or of a sphere."[78] By the time of the sixth-century Origenist controversy, the idea of the spherical resurrection body had become firmly attached to Origen and his later followers Evagrius of Pontus (ca. 345–399) and Didymus the Blind (313–398). In 543, the doctrine was anathematized in the Roman emperor Justinian's *Letter to Mennas*, and a decade later the condemnation was repeated under the auspices of Justinian in the tenth of fifteen anti-Origenist anathemas associated in a less than clear way with the Fifth Ecumenical Council at Constantinople. The belief that the body of the Lord after the resurrection was "ethereal and spherical in form" was condemned, and likewise the view that all other resurrection bodies will also be ethereal and spherical.[79]

Souls occupy a spherical container, body, or vehicle

Anti-Origenists such as Jerome and Justinian assumed that the attribution of sphericity to the resurrection body was a pagan importation and imposition. Indeed, there are some notable classical associations of sphericity with divinity, mind, and soul. In Cicero's *Dream of Scipio* (*Somnium Scipionis*, part of *De republica*, written between 54 and 51 BCE), the elder Scipio explains that men are endowed with souls made out of the celestial fires, the spherical stars animated by the divine mind.[80]

The work survived in a commentary by Macrobius (early fifth century CE), in which the relationship between the stars, divine mind, and human beings is developed. When Soul created the world, it infused divine minds into the spherical bodies of the stars, for only a spherical container is capable of holding the divine mind.[81] In the lower regions of the cosmos, the human body sustains a measure of the divine mind, and human beings stand out for their powers of mind, the ability to reason. This is because the erect human posture allows the heavens to be viewed, and the brain has the likeness of a sphere and is therefore able to house the divinely originated power of reason.[82] In *The Saturnalia*, Macrobius explains that the animating "vital principle" is "naturally spherical" and "comes to us from on high," and so resides in that part of the human body which is spherical and high, the brain.[83] From here the vital principle illuminates the body. Macrobius stresses that it is not the corporeal, celestial fire that animates human bodies, but the divine mind, infusing both the fiery star-spheres and the human brain.

By linking sphericity and divinity, Macrobius and others followed in the footsteps of the ancient philosophers who had attacked anthropomorphic conceptions of God (Xenophanes) or who had associated divinity with the spherical universe—the well-rounded, eternal Being (Parmenides) and the cosmic sphere unified by Love (Empedocles). Plato attributed sphericity to the universe (*Timaeus* 33), reasoning that the sphere is the most appropriate shape for a living being that contains all living beings and has nothing outside itself. As a self-contained whole, there would be no need for external limbs and organs that disturb the smoothness and symmetry of its spherical shape. He also forged a link between cosmic and human sphericity in the entertaining myth told by Aristophanes in the *Symposium* (189a–193d): human beings were originally endowed with circular bodies, derived from their celestial parentage of Earth, Sun, and Moon, but the bodies were split in half by the gods as punishment for arrogance, and human beings have ever since sought to recover their former wholeness through physical union: "love is simply the name for the desire and pursuit of the whole."[84]

Not unexpectedly, the idea of a spherical body or vehicle appears in the writings of Plato's followers. But in the case of Plotinus, the reference is incidental, occurring in a discussion of memory and the continuity of personal identity: he thinks it reasonable to suppose that souls who rise from the sensible world to the starry heavens will still be able to recognize one another, whether they have bodies similar to their earthly ones or have taken on spherical star bodies (*Enn.* IV.4.5). The latter possibility is no doubt an acknowledgment of Plato's story of newly created souls allotted to their own stars "as in a vehicle" prior to incarnation and their return to their native stars after leading a good life (*Timaeus* 41d ff.). More interesting is the conclusion that can be drawn from Plotinus's suggestion that we try to imagine the intelligible cosmos as an illuminated, transparent globe on which all things are displayed, albeit a globe shorn of materiality (see chapter 6). Since Plotinus considers the soul in its higher, undescended reaches to be this intelligible cosmos, it surely follows that we can likewise gain an impression of the undescended soul by imagining an illuminated sphere in the same way.

However, it is with the concept of the soul's "vehicle" (*ochēma*) or subtle body that soul, light, and sphericity come together explicitly in Neoplatonism.[85] The vehicle acts as an intermediary between the incorporeal soul and its gross, corporeal body, and makes possible various characteristics of the soul, such as its mobility, spiritual perceptions, and postmortem experiences. Two vehicles were sometimes described: a perishable pneumatic vehicle and an immortal one that is luciform (*augoeides*) and starlike (*astroeides*). There appear to have been contrasting views on the effect of gross embodiment on the soul's vehicle. According to the late Neoplatonist Damascius (ca. 462–540 CE), there is no essential change to the immortal body, just some deviation from its sphericity and luminosity.[86] Iamblichus (ca. 242–327 CE) envisaged a more serious outcome, a separation of the soul from its spherical vehicle. As Gregory Shaw puts it, "the soul's fall from the *Nous* was equivalent to its loss of circularity," a loss of its capacity to complete within itself its activities.[87] Spiritual progress involves the recovery of the star-vehicle and its circular motion. Through theurgic ("god-working") practices advocated by Iamblichus, aspirants can assimilate their souls to the celestial gods and reacquire the spherical vehicles and their heavenly revolutions, thereby becoming godlike in both form and motion, and therefore fit vessels of divinity.[88]

Souls are themselves spherical in their free or undisturbed state

Whereas Platonists made a distinction between the incorporeal soul and its body and vehicles, Stoic thinkers such as Cleanthes (ca. 331–ca. 232 BCE) and Chrysippus (ca. 280–ca. 207 BCE) eliminated the ontological gap between soul and body by taking soul itself to be corporeal. Thus soul itself has shape. It was argued that the soul would be incapable of binding with a corporeal body or partaking in its sensations and movements if it were of an essentially different, incorporeal nature. The soul too is a body, and for the Stoics the soul–body was breath (*pneuma*), the universal carrier of life, extending from its seat in the heart through the human frame and joining with the cosmic breath.[89] It is reported that Chrysippus believed the soul becomes spherical when it leaves the body, presumably because this is the shape that *pneuma* naturally assumes when unconstrained by a container.[90]

The spherical soul finds its most developed Stoic depiction in the writings of Roman Emperor Marcus Aurelius (121–180 CE), who draws on the conceit that a harmonious and self-sufficient person is "round." Horace, in his *Satires* (ca. 35 BCE), had said of the man who is free from the slavery of internal and external disturbances: "The wise man ... is complete in himself, smooth and round, so that no foreign element can adhere to his polished surface."[91] In the *Meditations*, Marcus Aurelius similarly represents the stable, inner condition of the wise man as spherical, but perhaps does so in a more than figurative sense, and he makes an explicit connection between the sphericity of the divine cosmos and the shape of the harmonious soul. The universe of Empedocles—in the condition of sphericity that prevails when

Love dominates in the cosmic cycle—is made a symbol of the equanimity of the Stoic sage. The spherical shape, equal in all directions, characterizes the harmonious soul, undisturbed by the passions of the body and the assaults of outer events:

> The soul attains to her perfectly rounded form when she is neither straining out after something nor shrinking back into herself; neither disseminating herself piecemeal nor yet sinking down in collapse; but is bathed in a radiance which reveals to her the world and herself in their true colours. (xi.12)[92]

Once attained, the condition cannot be upset by externals: "The globe, once orbed and true, remains a sphere" (xiii.41).[93] It is notable that in this state of invincible, spherical equilibrium, the soul is said to acquire a light in which both the outer world and the soul's inner condition are truly exhibited. In this way, the illumined, clear-seeing, fully rational soul-globe has a bearing on another matter that concerns Marcus Aurelius, namely the morally corrective power of cosmic vision, which puts worldly matters in perspective. The soul is able to rise above the vicissitudes and vainglories of life by encompassing the universe and its cyclical repetitions (as described by Stoic cosmology). It is to the rounded condition of the soul, educated in the lessons of universal vision, that the troubled emperor exhorts himself: he wishes to become "what Empedocles calls a 'totally rounded orb, in its own rotundity joying'" (xii.3).[94]

The All-Knowing Soul-Globe

The material outlined above shows that there has been a long association between soul and sphericity. In particular, the soul either occupies a globular body, vehicle, or envelope, or can itself be spherical. In Stoic thought, the distinction is blurred because the soul and body come together in doctrines of spiritual body or "corporeity," which attempt to overcome soul–body substance dualism. As in modern near-death reports, some of the historical material is presented as informed by visionary and mystical experiences, as for instance Plutarch's two stories of near-death experience and St. Gregory's telling of St. Benedict's mystico-clairvoyant vision. This is also true of some reports from the late Middle Ages. These are interesting because they attribute all-vision and all-knowledge to the soul-globe.

Two cases are preserved in a popular work of the thirteenth century by the Cistercian monk Caesarius of Heisterbach (ca. 1180–ca. 1240). This

Dialogus miraculorum is a collection of stories, set in dialogue form, that was intended to strengthen the resolve of novices. Soul-globes make an appearance in two stories. The first describes the near-death experience of an abbot of Morimond, a story conveyed to Caesarius by Dom Herman of Marienstatt, who had known the abbot.[95] As a young student in Paris, the future abbot had acquired great learning through the machinations of the devil, the fiend having thrust a knowledge-conferring stone upon the reluctant youth. After showing off his newly acquired learning and debating skills, the young man fell ill, confessed to the sin, and died. His soul was carried by demons into a deep ravine, where they hurled it from side to side, as if playing ball. This was a most painful experience, but fortunately a messenger of the Lord intervened, and the soul was allowed to return to the body and reanimate it. The soul was spherical, which no doubt facilitated the demons in their game of ball: "he said that his soul was like a glassy spherical vessel, that it had eyes both before and behind, that it was filled with all knowledge, and nothing could escape its range of vision."[96]

The increased power of vision had enabled the youth's soul to witness the activities of his fellow scholars at the funeral bier, observations that he later recounted to the great surprise of his auditors. It is notable that the youth attained to omniscience in his globular soul-state, an expanded knowledge that mirrors the earlier, misappropriated scholarly expertise that he had acquired with the aid of the diabolical stone. Furthermore, the soul was not a solid sphere but a glassy *vessel* filled with all knowledge. Jung refers to this detail in connection with the alchemist Zosimos and the round alchemical vessel, the *vas Hermeticum*,[97] and it is possible that some disparaging allusion to alchemy may have been intended, for the youth had acquired his learning through a stone that the devil had given, presumably a reference to the *lapis philosophorum*.

In the second story, told by the abbot of Brumback to the abbot of Caesarius's monastery, a girl has her spiritual doubts removed by a vision of angels and the blessed.[98] The beautiful but obstinate maiden had resisted her wealthy parents' request that she marry. Instead she desired to retire to a cell in order to devote herself to Christ. The spirited girl was soon overcome by melancholy at her confinement, wavered in faith, and fell ill. In this condition of spiritual and corporeal peril, she had the effrontery to question the abbot of Brumback: "Who knows if there be a God, or any angels with Him? or any souls, or any kingdom of heaven? Who has ever seen such things, who has ever come back to tell us what he has seen?"[99]

It was clear to the astonished holy man that the girl's despair was the work of the devil, and he advised her to continue with her devotions for another week. Prayers were said, and when the abbot returned he found the girl happy and transformed:

> Father, I have seen with my own eyes those whose existence I doubted; after you left me, my soul was rapt from my body, and I saw holy angels, I saw the souls of the blessed, I saw the rewards of the just. I saw also with the eyes of my soul my own body lying on the floor of my cell, as bloodless and pallid as withered herbage whose sap was all withdrawn.[100]

Asked about the soul's appearance, the girl attested to its sphericity:

> she said that it was a spiritual substance, that its form was spherical, something like the globe of the moon, and that it was full of eyes. She said further that when either an angel or a soul appeared to any one who was still in the body, the apparition always assumed a material form. But when a soul is delivered from the burden of the flesh, then it appears actually as it is to any other soul in the like condition.[101]

Here it is made clear that the soul is seen in its true globular form when viewed spiritually in the out-of-body condition.

It is notable that the soul-globe has *many* eyes. In chapter 7, I shall have reason to look at the common motif of ocular plurality, but for the moment it suffices to observe that the imagery of "many eyes" suggests heightened powers of perception and knowing. These powers can include various supernormal perceptions, including clairvoyant views of distant regions ("telescopic" vision) or enlarged detail ("microscopic," "magnificatory"), and the ability to see into and through normally opaque objects ("X-ray," "penetrative"). The "many eyes" imagery is particularly apt for two kinds of supernormal perceptions: (1) objects are seen simultaneously from front, back, top, and bottom, indeed from numerous directions ("multiperspectival"); (2) vision takes in the entire surroundings all at once ("spherical," "360-degree," "panoramic," "ambient"). The latter kind of perception is hinted at in the near-death story of the abbot of Morimond, for the spherical soul had "eyes both before and behind," and presumably could see all around. Like the other types of supernormal perception noted above, spherical perception is reported in some modern accounts of near-death and out-of-body experiences.[102]

Interestingly, supernormal perceptions can take place in the waking state without impeding ordinary sensory contact with the environment, and sometimes in conjunction with *a pervading luminosity*. For example, a special light gave penetrative vision to Buddhist monk Xuyun (1840–1959) when his evening meditation period came to an end:

> I opened my eyes and suddenly perceived a great brightness similar to broad daylight wherein everything inside and outside the monastery was discernible to me. Through the wall, I saw the monk in charge of lamps and incense urinating outside, the guest-monk in the latrine, and far away, boats plying on the river with the trees on both its banks – all were clearly seen.[103]

In his autobiography, the Indian yogi Paramhansa Yogananda (1893–1952) described several such incidents in the context of kriya yoga, which utilizes breathing exercises and works on the subtle physiology.[104] On one occasion his guru Lahiri Mahasaya slapped him on the chest, over the heart. In the ensuing silence, Yogananda experienced panoramic vision of his surroundings, which were now lit up by a "mellow luminescence," like the glow of flame under ash.[105] On a later occasion, Yogananda was praying to the Divine Mother when he found that he could look through walls, whether eyelids were open or shut, and that he could read the thoughts of his brother-in-law, who was nearby. Objects were surrounded by a mellow light of "white, blue, and pastel rainbow hues."[106] The fact that the spherical vision persisted when he closed his eyes suggested to Yogananda that it operated independently of the ordinary senses. On another occasion, the clairvoyance took on a decidedly mystical cast. After his guru Sri Yukteswar tapped him over the heart, Yogananda's sense of identity was no longer limited to the body, and his vision became spherically panoramic and penetrative. Objects appeared as if melted into a unifying, quivering sea of light, which expanded to embrace the entire universe. Moreover, Yogananda discovered that the creative light that sustains the universe issued from his heart.[107]

Another early twentieth-century case of penetrative, spherical perception also took a mystical turn. This is described by W. L. Wilmshurst.[108] It took place during a church service, as the *Te Deum* was being sung:

> At a single visual act, and without need of glancing from one point to another or from this object to that, the building I stood within and the whole surrounding landscape were in view, and all was garnished with this ultra-natural light [a violet haze]. What was locally behind me was equally perceptible with what was before me; what was above my head and about my feet was seen equally well at the same moment. I saw from all parts of my being simultaneously, not from my eyes only. I suppose it

was my soul that saw, and the soul is not bound by our conditions of space
or the laws of bodily vision.[109]

Soul-vision, it would seem, is spherical and reaches through opaque barriers,
including very solid church walls.[110] It is noteworthy that the experience
went on to take a mystical turn, with the blue haze changing into a "golden
glory," and there appeared directly overhead an "immense globe of bril-
liancy," radiating pulses of luminosity throughout space and into the depths
of the earth.[111] This central sphere of light and its surrounding corona or
"photosphere" were filled with a procession of distinct but interpenetrating
heavenly creatures:

> But the most wondrous thing was that these shafts and waves of light, that
> vast expanse of photosphere, and even the great central globe itself, were
> crowded to solidarity with the forms of living creatures . . . a single coher-
> ent organism filling all space and place, yet composed of an infinitude of
> individuated existences.[112]

It seemed that "two worlds" had come together, the church and its human
congregation singing the *Te Deum*, intermingled with the "heavenly hosts,"
the angelic choirs between God and man.[113] The experience deepened further
into a unitive state ("unified with all there is"), with consciousness of the
surroundings lost, and space, time, and form transcended.[114] Like Warner
Allen's experience in the concert hall, the entire episode can have lasted only
a few moments, for the rendition of the *Te Deum* was still in progress.[115]
And like Bucke's famous experience of "cosmic consciousness," the episode
began with a colored mist.[116]

It is difficult to know what to make of reports such as these, in which
vision supposedly reaches through objects, extends great distances, and
even becomes panoramic. Discussing vision through opaque bodies, Albert
Farges (1848–1926) warned against pseudoscientific explanations, such as
the hypothesis that the eyes project a special light that penetrates objects,
but he then made an equally flawed suggestion of his own: the human
retina is sensitive to X-rays and other invisible radiations.[117] Nowadays,
psychological explanations are likely to be given or even physical ones that
invoke extra dimensions (see Box, "A visual world behind the head"). As for
Wilmshurst's luminous globe, its nature is open to speculation. Positioned
at the "zenith," it is suggestive of a *kuṇḍalinī* expansion of consciousness
above the head, which itself would suggest that the preceding clairvoyant
phenomena were also associated with *kuṇḍalinī* (explicit in Yogananda's

A visual world behind the head

In your mind's eye, try to visualize everything around you all at once—not so easy! But according to one approach, this is just what spherical perception is: a 360-degree visualization of the environment, a hallucination that draws upon and vividly brings into consciousness a "cognitive map" or "internal representation" of the surroundings and the world further afield. This inner map is a "representational space" that we each construct and continuously adjust to help orient ourselves in the world and direct our actions there. If such an inner cognitive model exists, it raises the possibility of a "cycloramic visual field" that includes "a visual world behind the head," as psychologists Fred Attneave and Paul Farrar put it.[118] Neurologist James Austin drew upon this psychological theory to explain "ambient vision" in Zen meditation, including his own experience of it.[119] However, Austin had spherical awareness not of his surroundings but of a void, a silent, infinite, timeless, circumambient expanse of "crystalline, jet blackness."[120] Austin's representational space, if this is what it was, contained no representations apart from a small red maple leaf that he later realized was a memory image of a leaf he had seen weeks before.

Explanation of spherical and other supernormal types of perception in terms of representational space is analogous to explanation of out-of-body experience (OBE) in terms of cognitive modeling.[121] According to this approach, those who wander around bedrooms or intensive care units in the "out-of-body" condition are really exploring their own mental models of the surroundings, their own representational spaces. Such explanations readily account for the discrepancies often observed between features of the environment encountered in the OBE and in the waking state. However, even if spherical vision and OBEs are based on representations, the possibility remains that genuine, nonordinary modes of cognition are operative during them, supplying some of the details incorporated within the experiences.[122]

A very different approach—physical rather than psychological—calls on an extra spatial dimension to account for supernormal perceptions. It is a relatively old idea, dating back to late nineteenth-century psychical research, but has been applied more recently to the multiperspectival and spherical types of perceptions. According to Jean-Pierre Jourdan, displacement of the observer into an extra dimension, beyond the familiar three of space and one of time, can account for these and other extraordinary perceptions that arise during near-death experiences.[123]

kriya-yoga experiences). But as a globe filled with transparent beings, it is perhaps reminiscent of hypnagogic phenomena and the *thig les* of Dzogchen *thod rgal* practice (see above).

References to spherical perception predate the modern and medieval periods. We have noted that Plutarch's intellects, released from the body and enclosed in spherical envelopes, are endowed with panoramic vision, "seeing on all sides" like a single eye. Another striking example draws on the biblical vision of Ezekiel, with its four living creatures or cherubim and the four wheels-within-wheels full of eyes, later associated with a class of angels called the ophanim or "thrones" (fig. 5.3). In the *Homilies* of Pseudo-Macarius, a Syrian monk of the fourth century CE who combined Origenist and Messalian thought, Ezekiel's vision is interpreted as a foreshadowing of how the *soul* will appear once it has become the throne of the Holy Spirit. The soul that has "received its Lord" becomes "all light, all face, all eye":

> There is no part of the soul that is not full of the spiritual eyes of light. That is to say, there is no part of the soul that is covered with darkness but is totally covered with spiritual eyes of light. For the soul . . . is in every part on all sides facing forward and covered with the beauty of the ineffable glory of the light of Christ, who mounts and rides upon the soul.[124]

Like the eye-bedecked creatures and wheels of Ezekiel, the soul faces forward in all directions simultaneously. It is spherically percipient.

The spherical-soul stories preserved by Caesarius in the early thirteenth century have a significant twelfth-century precedent in the writings of the Benedictine abbess Hildegard of Bingen (1098–1179). Her descriptions are particularly interesting because they are quite detailed and are given pictorial representation in a series of illuminations. Hildegard relates that in "the third year of her life" she saw a great brightness, an experience that she could not express to others because of her young age.[125] Visions continued through her early years into adulthood, but it was only at the age of forty, a year after she had been made the abbess of her community, that she felt a powerful calling to make her visions known. Hildegard explains that she saw them in a cloud of light that attended her at all times and that the visions left her normal vision unaffected. The experiences included views of distant or invisible things, prophetic insights into the future, and visions of spiritual realities and symbolic scenes. Her visions often involved a divine voice in association with the light and, it seems, contained dazzling, shimmering formations, including stars, sparks, concentric circles, and castellations. We are fortunate that her book of visions, the *Scivias* ("Know the Ways [of the

Figure 5.3 Ezekiel's throne vision of God, with creatures and wheels full of eyes.[126]
Courtesy of the Pitts Theology Library, Candler School of Theology, Emory University.

Lord]"), contains not only descriptions and interpretations but also illuminated illustrations. The *Scivias* comprises twenty-six visions, each of which is described briefly and then interpreted in allegorical fashion.

Toward the end of her life, Hildegard provided a valuable explanation of the manner in which she received her visions, in a letter to an inquisitive admirer, Guibert of Gembloux.[127] She was able to distinguish two types of luminosity, one being a reflection or shadow of the other. Hildegard explained that since infancy her spirit had been able to ascend into the airy heights and dilate itself into distant regions. This manner of seeing things would also occur when she gazed at created things, such as transforming clouds. As the visions took place, she was not swooning into unconsciousness, for her physical senses would remain active, her eyes open. There was a brightness in which her visionary revelations appeared, a manner of imaging she compared to the reflection of sun, moon, and stars in water. This brightness she called *umbra viventis luminis* (or *lucis*), "the shadow of the living light," or perhaps "the reflection of the living light," depending on how *umbra* is translated,[128] and she described it as much brighter than a cloud surrounding the sun. Remarkably, the luminous "shadow" in which she saw her visions was a permanent presence, never absent. It was like gazing into "a starless firmament within a lucent cloud."[129] Speech in the visions was not like the words of men, but had a visual quality, being compared to a sparkling flame and a cloud stirred by air. The shadow of the living light provided Hildegard with answers to specific questions posed by her visitors. In modern terms, we could say that the light brought her, among other gifts, the psi perceptions, notably clairvoyance and precognition. Within the shadow of the living light, she occasionally saw another light, "the living light" itself, the *lux vivens*, a sight that would remove all the pain and misery of her old age.

Hildegard's shadow of the living light is somewhat reminiscent of the luminous *qaumaneq* of the Iglulik Inuit shamans, the "lighting" or "enlightenment" that gave them vision of things distant "as if the earth were one great plain,"[130] as well as things hidden, secret, spiritual, or even yet to happen:

> a mysterious light which the shaman suddenly feels in his body, inside his head, within the brain, an inexplicable searchlight, a luminous fire, which enables him to see in the dark, both literally and metaphorically speaking, for he can now, even with closed eyes, see through darkness and perceive things and coming events which are hidden from others; thus they look into the future and into the secrets of others.[131]

It also bears comparison to the luminosities noted above in connection with supernormal types of perception described in modern reports, a light that can bring penetrative, telescopic, and spherical vision. Like the shamanic experiences, Hildegard's involved feelings of ascent: her spirit would soar into the heavens and "shifting winds," and range "among various peoples, even those very far away."[132] Hildegard, as "shamanic" visionary, psychic, and healer, appears to have been exceptionally strong in *qaumaneq*, but questions inevitably arise as to why the light endured without interruption for so many years and why it appeared spontaneously at so young an age. Apprentice shamans have to undertake rigorous practices, including dark retreats, before they acquire their *qaumaneq*.

The soul-globe makes an appearance in the Fourth Vision of the First Book of the *Scivias*. This vision describes one soul's entry into its body at birth and the departure of another soul at the time of death, and it traces the journey of a soul through a dangerous world of desire and oppression as it looks for safety with the help of God. Hildegard's descriptions and interpretations provide some interesting details. The soul appears as a fiery globe, with no human features or members, and it resides in the heart, animating and ruling the body it inhabits. The globe, which is endowed with reason, intellect, and will, is fiery because it "burns with a fire of profound knowledge."[133] It "discerns whatever is within the circle of its understanding," and, by knowing God, it knows heavenly as well as earthly things.[134] Like the spherical, pneumatic soul of the Stoics, seated in the heart and controlling the body, Hildegard's globe is the breath in the creature: "I am the living breath in a human being, placed in a tabernacle of marrow, veins, bones and flesh, giving it vitality and supporting its every movement."[135]

The soul-globe encased in the body loses its sight and knowledge rather easily, being subject to disturbing whirlwinds, which are desires, temptations, and doubting and deceiving thoughts that bring confusion and misery.[136] The soul, however, can resist the disturbances, raising itself up through feelings of remorse and by heavenly inspiration. The fiery globe leaves the body at death, although the illumination depicting the scene shows a small *human* form emerging from the mouth of the body. Pictorial divergences from the text are found in other places in the *Scivias*, where the "somatomorphic" human form more typical of medieval literature is used to depict souls or divine presences. Hildegard describes her vision of the soul's emergence from the body: "Another of the globes freed itself from the lineaments of the form it was in and united all its bonds, and with a groan drew itself out of them, and broke away lamenting from its abode."[137] The released soul encounters spirits of light and darkness, who signify the moral qualities, meritorious or sinful, of the soul during its embodied life. These catch up with the soul at death and take it along its future path:

> And when it had thus freed itself, there came certain spirits, some of light and some of darkness, who had been its life's companions according to its behaviour in its abode, and who waited for its release so that they could lead it away with them.[138]

Hildegard also has a vision of a soul's embodiment before birth. The account of the soul's possession and animation of the fetus is made particularly interesting by a visionary sequence that precedes it and by a miniature that depicts the process. Hildegard's vision begins with a heightened understanding she calls "the knowledge of God."[139] It is "radiant with the most profound clarity" and views all things in the four corners of the world. There is a second radiance too, with the splendor of dawn and a purple brightness, interpreted by Hildegard as the Son born from the Virgin, and His sacrifice

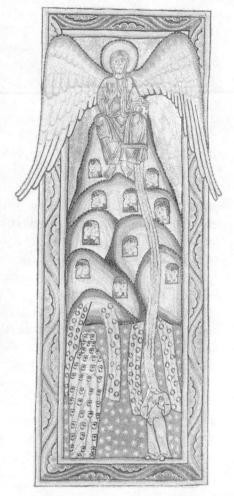

Figure 5.4   (a) Book 1, Vision 4; (b) Book 1, Vision 1.
Hildegard of Bingen, *Scivias*-Codex from the Benedictine Convent Rupertsberg,
Bingerbrück, Landesbibliothek (Cod. 1, Wiesbaden) (Photos: © Rheinisches Bildarchiv
Köln, rba_mfo13325 and rba_mfo13322).

and shedding of blood: "I saw a most great and serene splendor, flaming, as
it were, with many eyes, with four corners pointing toward the four parts
of the world, which was manifest to me in the greatest mystery to show me
the secret of the Supernal Creator; and in it appeared another splendor like
the dawn, containing in itself a brightness of purple lightning."[140]

The miniature that depicts the vision of divine, radiant knowledge
(fig. 5.4a) shows a kite shape, with the corners pointing in the four directions, signifying the all-encompassing extent of the knowledge. The kite is

filled with eyes and is divided along its vertical diagonal by a strip or tube in which are inscribed what appear to be several soul-globes and perhaps a single human face. The accompanying text describes the vision of a soul-globe entering and vivifying the body of an unborn child:

> And I saw the image of a woman who had a perfect human form in her womb. And behold! By the secret design of the Supernal Creator that form moved with vital motion, so that a fiery globe that had no human lineaments possessed the heart of that form and touched its brain and spread itself through all its members.[141]

In Hildegard's account, the body in the womb has already grown into a form that is recognizably human before the soul-globe enters it, contrary to theories that place the time of soul-entry at conception. In the illustration, the strip of circles narrows as it exits from the kite and descends into the womb and then into the body of the unborn child, perhaps acting as a channel through which a fiery soul-globe descends into the fetus or as a link between the soul-globe embodied in its earthly tabernacle and its true divine home in the heavenly tabernacle.

There is undoubtedly a good deal of consciously employed symbolism in Hildegard's visionary accounts. They are not unelaborated descriptions of visionary/mystical experience, and there is no need to resort to psychopathological explanations to account for the visions of eyes, such as the "knowledge of God" as a kite filled with eyes. The eye is a traditional symbol of divine knowledge, and its multiplicity symbolizes omniscience and omnipresence. Hildegard is familiar with eye symbolism and uses it in other visions too, and her familiarity with the Book of Ezekiel, from which she quotes several times in the *Scivias*, suggests that she knew well the prophet's vision of the divine throne, with its mysterious living creatures and wheels. Hildegard understands her vision of eyes in terms of angels around God: the radiant clarity and eyes in the heavenly kite correspond to cherubim or seraphim, and the dawn-like second splendor corresponds to the angelic order of the thrones. The connection is brought out two visions later, in Vision Six of the First Book, in a description of the three highest angelic orders.

What is to be made of the vertical strip in the kite, which contains the single face and the circles, presumably the soul-globes described in the text? The strip is shown in the illumination but is not mentioned in the text. Why are several globes shown linked to the child's body in the womb if only one is needed to vivify a body? Is an entire group of globes linked to the body, or is the tube a heavenly reservoir of preexistent souls, from which one

Figure 5.5   Book 3, Vision 1.
Hildegard of Bingen, *Scivias*-Codex
from the Benedictine Convent
Rupertsberg, Bingerbrück,
Landesbibliothek (Cod. 1, Wiesbaden)
(Photo: © Rheinisches Bildarchiv
Köln, rba_mf013340).

soul descends to animate a body? Or might the multiple globes represent just one soul in a state of motion, descending in a zigzag fashion? Similar depictions, containing circles in strips or ribbons, are shown in the illumination that accompanies the very first vision of the *Scivias*, a vision of God at the summit of an iron mountain, which represents the strength and stability of the eternal Kingdom of God (fig. 5.4b). Four strips of circles in zigzag formation descend from the base of the mountain. The strips are positioned at the sides of two figures, one "an image full of eyes on all sides, in which, because of those eyes, I could discern no human form," and the other a child.[142] Hildegard interprets these figures as her reaction to the bright light of God and His Kingdom. The many-eyed figure represents the fear provoked by seeing the justice of God, and the child symbolizes humility of spirit. However, in the text of the *Scivias*, there is no clear reference to the strips of circles shown in the accompanying miniature.

While there is no reason to doubt that Hildegard took inspiration from her visionary experiences, there are also many traditional elements woven into the *Scivias*. It is therefore necessary to ask whether Hildegard's account of the all-knowing soul-globes drew upon traditional sources. Is it possible that Hildegard knew of earlier references to soul-spheres, perhaps transmitted through Christian writers? In some respects, her soul-globes are reminiscent of the animating, rounded souls of the Stoics and perhaps even of Plutarch's flamelike bubbles, with the intellect tethered by a cord to the embodied soul (compare Hildegard's kite). Hildegard's globes are pushed around by the whirlwinds of passions and thoughts, and Plutarch's intellects are jerked about by their unruly souls. There is another detail in Hildegard's visions reminiscent of Plutarch. Hildegard describes falling stars and sparks that become extinguished in an abyss of darkness (fig. 5.5).[143] The light of the sparks is not lost but returns to God for other uses. In Hildegard's Christian telling, the stars and sparks are the fallen angels, who fell as a result of pride. In Plutarch's pagan myth of Timarchus, the sparks that fall into and rise from the abyss are souls participating in a cycle of reincarnation.

What, then, is to be made of Hildegard's intriguing vision of soul-globes, which combines overtly symbolic and allegorical elements with a supposed vision of the knowledge of God? Do we catch in Hildegard's descriptions a glimpse of the spherical soul or just a skillful reworking of traditional Christian and classical ideas, or perhaps a combination of the two? There is still another possible contribution to consider, the biological, the neurophysiological, which takes us back to the question of entoptics, those luminous phenomena said to be generated within the visual nervous system.

Migraine, Filters, and the Imagination

It has been suggested that Hildegard suffered from migraine and incorporated the visual phenomena ("aura") associated with the condition into her writings and the illuminations. The theory was advanced in 1917 by Charles Singer, a historian of science who had initially trained as a pathologist.[144] It was repeated by Oliver Sacks in his popular book on migraine[145] and more recently by Sabina Flanagan in a more developed form.[146] Singer interpreted the shimmering points, sparks, and stars (including the ones that fall into the abyss) as "symptoms of scintillating scotoma," and the visions of shining, castellated ramparts of the Heavenly City as "fortification figures."[147] Epilepsy can also involve a visual aura, but scotomas and fortification spectra are apparently not common in epilepsy,[148] and so it was understandable that the Hildegard miniatures should have been interpreted in terms of migraine rather than epilepsy. Sacks suggested that the occasional emergence of the "living light" from the "shadow of the living light" was a "second scotoma" that followed "in the wake of an original scintillation."[149] However, Hildegard's "shadow of the living light" was an everpresent, cloudy brightness, not a scintillation, which casts doubt on this aspect of his explanation. As for the vision of the falling, extinguished stars, Sacks interpreted it as a "shower of phosphenes" followed by a negative (dark) scotoma. Presumably, the fiery soul-globes would be interpreted in a similar manner, as phosphenes or some other feature of the migrainous visual aura.

Flanagan took the migraine theory further by interpreting illnesses in Hildegard's life as migrainous in nature, and she attempted to address some shortcomings of the migraine theory, which does not readily account for the *continuous* presence of the "shadow of the living light" or Hildegard's ability to approach the light at will to seek answers to questions. If Hildegard suffered from migraine, it was clearly a most unusual kind, marked by a permanent luminosity. Flanagan's efforts here were not entirely convincing: she conjectured that Hildegard had found a means of producing the migrainous photisms at will or that the photisms were provoked whenever questions were posed.[150] In this reading, the light was not continuously present but could be induced as required. It is not known with absolute certainty that the miniatures in the Rupertsberg *Scivias*, which are the primary source of evidence for the migraine theory, were supervised by Hildegard herself. The differences between Hildegard's text and the illuminations, such as the depiction of a soul-globe as human-shaped in one illustration, could suggest that Hildegard was *not* involved in their production. It is possible, then, that the strongest evidence for the migraine theory is actually fairly weak,[151] and it may not be possible to decide with any confidence whether migraine contributed to Hildegard's visions.

There is, however, another case of extraordinary light experience in the religious literature that bears some comparison to Hildegard's psychical and visionary "shadow of the living light," and which more clearly was associated with a migraine-like condition, but again atypical because of the persistence of the light. At the age of twenty-one, Anna Maria Taigi (1769–1837), an Italian woman, began to experience a mysterious light that was to endure without intermission until her death forty-seven years later, an everpresent globe or "sun" located one foot above her head and four feet in front (fig. 5.6). It is reported that she also heard divine locutions and acquired powers of healing. Initially, the disc was a matte gold and its radiance the color of "flame," but in due course the disc became much brighter, exceeding "seven suns."[152] The disc was surrounded by rays and what were described as "thorns" at the top and sides, and in the center there was the luminous image of a beautiful, seated woman.[153] It is said that in the light of her "mirror of divine wisdom" Anna Maria was able to inspect the entire world in minutest detail, not piecemeal but "all at a single glance," like St. Benedict in his brief illumination.[154]

The disc was constantly at her disposal, but Anna Maria would not attend to it continuously. When she did glance toward it and directed her thoughts to a particular matter, she would be rewarded immediately with all she wished to know. In the rays of the disc—but not in the disc itself—she would discern a great variety of things, symbolic and actual, including objects and persons, and happenings often of a calamitous nature, including events distant in space and in time, and the hidden thoughts of others, far as well as near, and the moral condition of persons, and the fate of the dead.

Although there are significant differences, the similarities between Hildegard's and Anna Maria Taigi's lights and the gifts they are said to have bestowed are clear to see and have been noted before in passing.[155] Anna Maria was often very ill too, and in her case a diagnosis of a migraine-related condition seems unavoidable given the combination of symptoms described: sick-headaches; great sensitivity to light, sound, and smell (she would "literally smell sin"); a bitter taste in the mouth; afflicted sense of touch in one hand (her "healing" right hand); perspirations; regular incapacity.[156] Moreover, some of her light experiences are suggestive of migrainous visual aura, such as the interwoven "thorns" above the disc, narrowing at the sides, and frequent visions of "black globes flying in the air, which suddenly took fire and covered the earth with a dense smoke."[157] Must we conclude that all the special gifts attributed to Anna Maria, including clairvoyant, telepathic, and precognitive perceptions supposedly verified on numerous occasions, were just symptoms of migraine (and perhaps a lesion in the retina or cerebral cortex, or some related condition),[158] misinterpreted in a pious, medically backward era? Perhaps so, but for a fair hearing it would be necessary to

Figure 5.6   Anna Maria Taigi gazes at her marvelous "sun."[159]

evaluate the quality of the original documentation that details Anna Maria's abilities and not prejudge the matter. This is outside my expertise, but I can follow another line of inquiry, which is to look more closely at migraine.

Until quite recently, migraine was commonly believed to be a vascular disease, caused by dilated blood vessels in the brain impinging on pain-sensitive areas, but now migraine with aura ("classical migraine") is recognized to be a neurological disorder of some complexity that involves disruption to the electrophysiological activity of the cerebral cortex, and which has much in common with epilepsy.[160] Although the mechanisms are not fully understood, it is believed that some initiating event, such as stress, low blood sugar, flickering lights, or a chemical trigger, sets off cortical spreading depression (CSD), a ripple of increased activity in the cortical neurons that leaves depressed activity in its wake. If the ripple begins at the back of the brain, in the occipital cortex (responsible for visual processing), it will be associated with the spreading visual aura that precedes migrainous headache. The ripple itself corresponds to luminous scintillations, and its trail of inactivity to the dark scotoma.

To explain the more unusual visual phenomena, regions of the cortex beyond the primary visual area have to be called upon, including extrastriate and temporal regions.[161] If the ripple passes through the somatosensory region in the parietal cortex, then tingling and numbness may be felt. The rate of progress of the ripple through the visual cortex and somatosensory cortex (graphically represented by Wilder Penfield's "homunculus")[162] corresponds well with the associated changes in the visual and somatosensory auras, underscoring the intimate connection between the biology and the experience.[163] When the motor region is affected, limb fatigue and loss of coordination may result. It is not too clear how the migrainous headache ensues, but it is thought that the meninges around the brain, the trigeminal nerve system, and the brain stem are involved.

It may be significant that the symptomatology of migraine and the phenomenology of kuṇḍalinī overlap to some extent, pointing to a degree of commonality in the brain regions involved. Both migraine and kuṇḍalinī arousal can bring vivid luminosities, headaches, and debilitating somatic disturbances, such as progressive numbness of the limbs, and feelings of hot or cold. It could therefore be speculated that kuṇḍalinī practices, such as breathing exercises and visualization of the somatic centers, can induce electrophysiological excitations and depressions in the visual, somatosensory, and motor regions of the cortex, leading to some migraine-like side effects. Gopi Krishna's kuṇḍalinī awakening, induced by meditation, brought a luminous expansion of consciousness but then left him with disturbing inner lights, weakness in the limbs, and even the bitter taste and lack of appetite reported of Anna Maria. The bitter taste also features in a Daoist equivalent to *kuṇḍalinī* practice, namely "inner alchemy," where it has been interpreted as a sign that the life force is on the move.[164]

Careful comparison of migrainous and epileptic symptomatologies with the phenomenology of *kuṇḍalinī* experience and related practices, such as those of the Buddhist Tantra, Daoist inner alchemy, and the *!kia* experience of the *!kung* people,[165] would be worth pursuing in order to facilitate "differential diagnosis" and thus provide insights into similarities and differences in the neurological mechanisms that may be involved. The idea that cortical sensory and motor mapping has a role to play in *kuṇḍalinī* experiences was pioneered by Itzhak Bentov in his mechanical-physiological theory, according to which mechanical vibrations stemming from the heart and aorta stimulate the sensory cortex, polarizing tissue there and setting up currents and magnetic fields.[166] While the details of Bentov's theory are likely to be wide of the mark, his suggestion that *kuṇḍalinī* experience is associated with electrical changes in the cortex, including the somatosensory "body map," is interesting, and not so different from the present-day understanding of the migraine aura in terms of CSD.

However, it is important to recognize that neurological mechanisms may be only part of the story, and so explanations in terms of migraine and related conditions, if applied to the experiences of Anna Maria, Hildegard, and other visionaries and mystics, could be incomplete in very significant ways and therefore misleading.[167] "Medical materialism," as William James called it,[168] reduces spiritual phenomena in their *entirety* to medical and psychiatric conditions, with no acknowledgment that those conditions may not so much *produce* some of the phenomena as *permit* them to manifest. More generally, it can be supposed that the brain does not so much create our experiences as condition them, regulating their contents by selectively including or excluding material from wider fields of consciousness, from a "subconscious" of great, even unlimited extent.

The idea that consciousness is not produced by our biology but regulated by it came to prominence in the late nineteenth century, discussed by such thinkers as James, Frederic Myers, and Henri Bergson, as noted above in the present chapter.[169] This "filter" or "transmission" theory of brain action has recently been investigated at length in the two edited collections spearheaded by Edward Kelly, *Irreducible Mind* and *Beyond Physicalism*, and applied there to a range of phenomena, normal and supernormal. I have discussed it in *Mystical Encounters with the Natural World* in relation to mystical states of consciousness.[170] Filter theory reminds us that experiences associated with organic and/or psychological disturbances need not be *entirely* reducible to those disturbances, which may act in part as releasing triggers rather than productive causes. The experiences may therefore exhibit a mix of characteristics, some deriving from the precipitating disturbance (say, migrainous photopsias stimulated by an occipital spreading depression) and some from a different source (say, a deeper luminosity intrinsic to the fabric of reality). It can be conjectured that the extreme, uncommonly prolonged migraine-related condition suffered by Anna Maria (and Hildegard too if she were similarly afflicted), worked in this manner, bringing pathological symptoms but also capabilities that were not inherently pathological. From the perspective of filter theory, and in view of the complex neurological character of migraine, it is conceivable that some mechanism involved in the condition can act to change filter behavior in extreme cases and so allow influxes of a transpersonal nature, luminous, noetic, affective. The net result will be experiences that combine biologically conditioned phenomena with genuinely transpersonal phenomena, psychical and mystical.

More specifically, it can be conjectured that Anna Maria's condition gave her *continuous access to a creative, image-making capacity of mind more commonly seen at work in altered states of consciousness*, such as meditation, transitions between waking and sleeping, dreaming, entheogenic drug use, and near-death experiences, but which is also more widely at work in everyday moments of creative inspiration. Some features of Anna Maria's experiences, from entoptic nets, necklaces, precious stones, and golden showers, to the faces and scenes witnessed in the disc's corona, and the autonomous development of her visions, are highly reminiscent of visual phenomena that manifest in altered states, following the familiar pattern of simple luminosities developing into images and scenes, as described above ("Spiritual Sphericities").[171]

It is true that the elaborate visual contents that manifest in altered states of consciousness are not typical of the migraine aura, but it seems that on rare occasions migraine can bring "complex visual hallucinations," as the medical terminology puts it.[172] Apparently these complex visions can include landscapes, persons, faces, animals, and strange creatures, as well as paranormal and religious figures, such as ghosts, angels, and spiritual personages.[173] Even the little folk ("Lilliputian hallucinations")—merry, dancing, and gaily attired—more commonly associated with folklore, alcohol withdrawal, and psychedelic experience, can make an appearance.[174] Migraine, then, would appear to be just one circumstance in which a range of visual phenomena, from the simple to the complex, can occur, and which are exhibited in a broad group of experiences that are not inherently pathological, namely *altered states of consciousness.* In the exceptional cases of Anne Maria and Hildegard, a migraine-related condition may have conferred a permanent field of luminosity in which complex imagery could arise. Whereas the average seer gazes into mirrors, crystals, glass balls, water, fire, clouds, and so forth to encourage the requisite state of mind for clairvoyance, it is possible that Anna Maria and Hildegard were gifted by their debilitating conditions with an inbuilt, ever available "scrying glass," an everpresent *qaumaneq.*

The "creative, image-making capacity of mind" I refer to above is, of course, the *imagination,* but an "imagination" understood as more profound and far-reaching than the term commonly signifies. And by "image," I do not mean just visual images, but contents in any of the sensory modalities, including auditory and olfactory. While "imagination" commonly refers to the process by which images and ideas are formed of things that are not immediately present to the senses (e.g., "a plate in the cupboard") or which do not even exist ("a unicorn on the moon"), a deeper understanding takes it to be more than an essentially mechanical process responsible for sifting, associating, extracting, and combining fragments of personal memory into new forms. The higher conception of the imagination, which has its forebears in Romanticism but a much older history too, takes it to be a creative power that can go beyond personal memories and the senses to weave its creations, having a transpersonal, even transcendent reach. Imagination so understood provides access to realities and knowledge not available by conventional means.[175] Working as it does creatively through images, this higher imagination may not furnish direct intuitions, but it does perform a mediatory function, expressing deeper truths through images and symbols accessible to everyday consciousness. The point to take away from all this is that organic and psychological conditions may sometimes bring into play an imaginal capacity that is not hallucinatory but revelatory.

Why Spherical?

The rotundity exhibited by what are sometimes taken to be souls or other spiritual beings in mystical, visionary, and near-death experiences can be understood in several ways. I shall summarize these understandings here and comment briefly on their applicability to my own experience:

- Neurophysiologically generated simple luminosities and geometric patterns in altered states of consciousness, including hypnagogia, and in some medical conditions are misinterpreted as spiritual beings.

Circular and spherical patterns of light do appear in altered states of consciousness, particularly in the early stages, and it is possible that they could be interpreted as conscious beings. However, as simple, round patterns of light, they would not have characteristics that obviously demand such interpretation, including responsiveness to the observer and, in some cases, the ability to engage in communication, as is sometimes reported in accounts of near-death experiences. I do have to take seriously the possibility that the "rings" I observed were the simple lights of an altered state of consciousness or, less likely, the photopsias of a migraine aura, and I have therefore devoted some attention to these phenomena in the present chapter.[176] However, I continue to be impressed by my realization at the time that the rings were all-knowing minds just like "myself," a mind that supported and contained the universe, and by the overall feel of the experience, with its great clarity and wakefulness, highly noetic quality, expansion of love on recognizing the rings as other living beings, and the tremendous sense of wholeness that was left when I woke up. As far as I know, these features are not typical of the entoptic stages of altered states or of the migraine aura.

- Inflaming points, circles, and spheres are erotic images misinterpreted as spiritual beings.

As previously noted, the erotic and the spiritual are not mutually exclusive categories. The erotic may be more deeply integral to reality than ordinarily suspected and ultimately traceable to the beauty and allure of the divine, as Platonists and tantrists have long avowed. For Plato's Socrates in the *Symposium*, tutored by the wise woman Diotima, *erōs* as sexual attraction toward a beautiful body is just the first step in a progression that culminates in the apprehension of the divine Form of Beauty. It may be helpful to follow Alan Soble and reserve the term *erotic* for sexual attraction, given the word's commonplace usage, and use *erosic* instead to cover the entire spectrum of love and desire of valued objects, mundane and transcendent.[177] At an exalted level, erosic love is "the desire and pursuit of the whole," as Aristophanes puts it in Plato's *Symposium*, a divine wholeness or unity from which one has been sundered.[178] In later chapters, the idea of an erosic pull toward the object to seek fulfillment, appetitive, erotic, spiritual, will become important. As regards my mystical episode, I can perhaps find an erosic pull in the dream induction, when I was drawn across the sea into the condition of wholeness, and perhaps in the mystical experience itself, when the vision of the rings drew me to a recognition of equals, triggering a universal expansion of love, a love that included all.

- Circles and spheres have a symbolic function, standing for the Self, psychological equilibrium, wholeness, and so on.

This approach, taken up in recent times by Jung and his followers, is certainly applicable to experiences and activities in which *symbolic* imagination is at work, such as dreams, daydreaming, imaginal visions, and creative inspiration, artistic, literary, religious. But it may not be so applicable to the deeper mystical states, those that go beyond symbol to reality, beyond mediatory imagination to the things themselves. My own experience had the quality of an encounter with reality, and I think the rings I observed could well have been more than symbolic.

- The body has subtle anatomical structures, some of which are round in shape, including one located above the head.

Some modern-day accounts of mystical experiences do describe "energy" flows up and down the body, and consciousness exiting the body through the cranium. My own experience had one feature that may be related to "energy centers," namely the universal expansion of love, which was pictured as radiating from the center of my body. But the rings themselves, a multiplicity of knowing beings out in the world at large, would seem to require a different understanding.

- The soul is not literally spherical, but its omnidirectional vision and expansive knowledge mean that it is readily called "spherical."

In my experience at least, the observed beings were literally round, that is, circular or spherical. However, there is reason to think that their round shape could be linked to their perception and knowing of the world, which was as encompassing as my own. The nature of this link will hopefully become clear in the next chapter.

- The soul itself is not spherical, but it appears so because it is shrouded in a glow of light.

- The soul itself is not spherical, but it can occupy a spherical bubble, vehicle, or body.

- The soul or an inseparable soul–body unit is spherical, perhaps by virtue of an intimate connection with a universe that is spherical.

Of these three traditional positions listed above, it is the last that catches my attention. I had found myself to be a mind that supported and contained the universe, and the rings were recognized as living beings equivalent to myself. There seems, then, to have been a connection between the universe and the "round" living beings. The next step will be to bring out in detail the logic behind the connection.

6

The Logic of Unity

if each Spirit be an intire World,
all Spirits are in each Spirit

—Jeremiah White

How is it possible for a tiny part of the whole to be that selfsame whole? The "vision of the rings" was the most puzzling feature of the experience I describe in chapter 2. It made no sense to me that those little beings within my expansive mind were themselves minds that embraced all things in their knowings. This feature was mystifying, and I put it aside for several years, my attention drawn instead to less puzzling aspects of the experience, such as the expansive knowledge, love, and spatiotemporality. I had no inkling that others might have had comparable experiences or that some philosophies would be able to shed light on the perplexing detail. In fact, it turns out that the vision of "parts that are the whole" is an essential feature of Plotinus's account of the intelligible cosmos, a level of reality that is said to be accessible through contemplation. What is more, Plotinus attempts to explain how a tiny part can be the entire whole. In this chapter, I take a look at Plotinus's intelligible cosmos and the reasoning that makes the paradox of whole cosmic parts understandable, even logical.

However, there is a problem to be faced. As a follower of Plato, Plotinus understood the intelligible cosmos to be a level of reality *above* the world of the senses. It is other-worldly, not this-worldly, to use the terminology introduced in chapter 1. My own experience of "whole parts," however, seemed to be situated in our everyday world, for I could see familiar things, such as my own body and other people. It is therefore instructive to look at a much later philosophy that is probably indebted to Plotinian thought but which brings the all-inclusive, all-knowing units of reality "down to earth." This is Leibniz's philosophy of monads, which again makes the idea of whole cosmic parts comprehensible, especially if it is modified to agree with the insights of mystical experience.

The Small Is Immense

Greek cosmic religion, particularly in its Stoicized form, had looked upon the universe as an organic whole in which the parts are harmonized with one another and share in the life and intellect of the whole. For the Stoics, all beings, in so far as they are rational, are joined in kinship and work together for the common good, like parts of one body. All are members of a city that has none of the usual civic boundaries: the Stoic city is a world city, the *kosmopolis*, in which natural self-preservative instincts (*oikeiōsis*, "self-love") have been extended from the individual, family, and immediate community to the entire human race, so that all are included in the universal love.[1]

In the philosophy of Plotinus, the organic universe and community of citizens were enlarged to include a higher level of reality described by the followers of Plato, the intelligible cosmos (*kosmos noētos*), but the extension was no mere reworking of Stoic ideas, for the interrelatedness of beings was understood in terms of an interpenetration of knowing and loving minds. The Stoic doctrine of material interpenetration gave way to a theory of intellectual interpenetration, a doctrine of mutually knowing intellects.[2] This community of intellects is not a collection of abstract ideas. It is a community of intimately related living minds that can be discovered through contemplative ascent. Although diversified, the intelligible cosmos is close to its source, the One, and its members show an accordingly high degree of integration and unity. In fact, each member expresses the total presence of the One and derives its light, life, and beauty from that source, so that the community reflects the One individually as well as collectively.

Plotinus likens our usual ignorance of the cosmic unity to an outward-looking vision that sees many faces. If we were able to turn round and see with the soul's higher vision, we would discover only one head behind the many faces (*Enn.* VI.5.7). The realization of common identity does not exclude the many, for the faces, divided from one another in the sensory realm, are found again in the intelligible world, but now joined in a unity, as pure souls knit into a whole. To gain an impression of the intelligible realm, Plotinus suggests that we imagine intellectual light radiant upon "a living richly varied sphere" or "a thing all faces, shining with living faces" (*Enn.* VI.7.15). But Plotinus reminds us that to picture the realm in this fashion is still to take an outside view. The truly inside view is to contemplate the realm by *being* it, through the unity of the knower and the known.

The unity of the intelligible community goes rather deeper than a coexistence of its members in one whole, for each is found to contain all the others. Each living mind is not only an individual member of the noetic community but also the entire community of minds. Each is a "star" that is the sun and all the other stars, suggesting an infinite interreflection of lights within lights:

> Each there has everything in itself and sees all things in every other, so that all are everywhere and each every one is all and the glory is unbounded; for each of them is great, because even the small is great; the sun there is all the stars, and each star is the sun and all the others. A different kind of being stands out in each, but in each all are manifest. (*Enn.* v.8.4)

Without suffering diminution, the Intellect of the entire intelligible universe is also the intellect of each part, and so each part is the entire whole. Yet no parts are shared between the intellects (*Enn.* v.8.9). Each member is a whole in its own right: "But this, the [intelligible] All, is universal power, extending to infinity and powerful to infinity; and that god is so great that his parts have become infinite" (*Enn.* v.8.9). The whole is not an aggregate of unconnected and arbitrary items, a "heap casually put together" (*Enn.* III.8.8), but a deeply interconnected unity of whole parts, each of which has the power of the Intellect.

Plotinus invites us to grasp the interpenetration of beings through a visualization that leads from the external view to an inner manifestation. Again we are to imagine a spherical form, at first the sensible universe of sun, stars, earth, sea, and all living things, as if displayed within a transparent globe (*Enn.* v.8.9). We are then asked to transform the spherical image by dematerializing it, and to call on God to come, bringing his universe with its gods, beauty, and radiance. The members of the intelligible cosmos—gods and souls—are each the whole yet distinct from one another, seeing not as spectators from outside but containing the vision within as self-knowledge (*Enn.* v.8.10). It is conceivable that the visualization points to a meditative exercise employed in Plotinus's circle to guide inexperienced aspirants toward intellectual vision and true self-knowledge, for Plotinus seems to advise the novice to aim toward the intelligible by forming mental impressions of it (*Enn.* v.8.11). This in itself is not particularly remarkable, for contemplative exercises designed to lift the soul from its petty concerns to the vision of the whole—to magnanimity or "greatness of soul"—had worthy precedents,[3] and were expressed in the extensive "soul-flight" literary genre. Nor is the linking of the spherical universe with its dematerialized, intellectual original particularly remarkable, for Plato, in the *Timaeus*, had described a spherical universe modeled on the Perfect Intelligible Living Creature, which is also spherical. It has been suggested that spherical contemplative aids may have been used in "mystical Neoplatonic rites," but it is has been questioned whether such rites took place and whether contemplation specifically employed spherical aids.[4]

But the Plotinian contemplation of the intelligible cosmos *is* remarkable for the interpenetration it finds between members of the intelligible community, each containing all the others. Although there were earlier notions of "all in all," in the thought of Anaxagoras, Platonists, and Christians, the Plotinian concept is remarkable for its clearly experiential basis, being presented as a vision attainable through contemplation. It stands out too for its philosophical understanding of how the interpenetration comes about, through the unity of many knowers with a common object of knowledge (see "Identity and Difference" below). There is little unambiguous evidence of similar realizations expressed in Western thought before Plotinus, and certainly no comparable philosophical elaboration. There may be hints in near-contemporary Gnostic literature, but the fragmentary passages in question do not elaborate on the vision and show little interest in developing a philosophical understanding. Plotinus was concerned to expose the Gnosticism he knew for its poor estimation of the sensible world and for its lack of appreciation of the sensible world's rootedness in higher ontological levels. However, there are similarities between the Plotinian description of the intelligible cosmos and certain Gnostic equivalents, the *barbēlō* realm or the *plērōma* ("fullness"), the perfect and ordered realm of beings (*aeons*) around the Godhead.[5] Resemblances can be put down to comparable mystical inspiration, parallel development of a common inheritance of Greek philosophy, or to a Gnostic application of the Christian "all in all" to the intelligible cosmos of Middle Platonism.

The fact that Plotinus gives particularly detailed attention to the intelligible world and its community of interpenetrating beings in sections of his anti-Gnostic writings (which include *Enn.* v.8, "On the Intellectual Beauty") suggests that he may have attempted to distinguish his position from Gnostic ideas that on the surface might have been confused with his own. *Zostrianos*, a Gnostic text of visionary ascent dating from the late second century or early third century CE,[6] contains phrases that would not be out of place in

Plotinus's *Enneads*, on the distinctness yet agreement of the members of the divine community, and their mutual inclusivity:

> They are not crowded against one another, . . . existing in themselves and agreeing with one another, as they are from a single origin. All of them exist in one, dwelling together and perfected individually in fellowship and filled with the aeon which really exists.[7]

Zostrianos is a text in the genre of pseudonymous spiritual reminiscences that recall flights to higher realms. The prophet recounts how his journey began in crisis, depression, and attempted suicide. An angel intervened and directed him to rise through the layers of the cosmos. At the exalted level of the self-begotten aeons, he saw that each member of the *barbēlō* community is associated with an eternal world that contains familiar things—living elements, imperishable trees, fruit, souls, men, creatures, gods, angels.[8]

While *Zostrianos* expresses a negative attitude toward the sensible world, another work containing hints of communal interpenetration, *The Tripartite Tractate* (early to mid third century CE),[9] is more positive in attitude, and unlike *Zostrianos* it clearly has a Christian background, probably a development of the theology formulated by Valentinus (second century CE). It seems that the "Son" of the indivisible source, the "Father," is clothed in aeons, the "Totalities," in such a way that each is also the Son that contains them and therefore all the others too, having a shared identity in the Son:

> All of them exist in the single one, as he clothes himself completely and by his single name he is never called. And in this unique way they are equally the single one and the Totalities. . . . He is each and every one of the Totalities forever at the same time.[10]

The congregation of aeons in the Son is a social representation of the Father, "a single representation although many."[11] The aeons preexisted in the Father as hidden thoughts, as the "Church," without separate existence from the source until they emerged in their own right. The position of *The Tripartite Tractate* here is probably closer to the Middle Platonism of Albinus and Numenius than to Plotinian doctrine in its understanding of the supreme source,[12] although Plotinus can be interpreted as allowing some kind of nonintellective presence of things in the One (see chapter 9). When the separated aeons are permitted to know the Father (too speedy a revelation would lead to the aggrandizement or destruction of the aeons), they aspire in love toward him as a collective, as the "pleromatic congregation." The Father has planted this longing in the aeons, and he himself reaches out toward them. In this depiction of the pleromatic community of the Son, joined in loving relationship with the Father, we can see a reading of Christian teachings on community in Christ and mutual indwelling. Influenced by the widespread Hellenistic preoccupation with spiritual self-knowledge and by Middle Platonic doctrines of divine intellect, *The Tripartite Tractate* seems to have transformed the Christian heavenly kingdom into a realm that bears at least a superficial resemblance to the Plotinian intelligible realm in which the parts contain the whole.

Loving aspiration at the communal level also has an important place in the Plotinian account of the return to the One, for the soul rises on the wave of loving Intellect, taking part in the Intellect's aspiration toward its source (chapter 9). The soul's discovery of the community of minds at its higher level brings to an end the solitary path of inward contemplative retreat and yields the opposite of isolation. At last divested of its loneliness and self-ignorance, the soul discovers its membership of the most inclusive community possible, the universal whole, in which all are united by identity-in-difference. A. H. Armstrong suggested that Neoplatonic and derivative conceptions of the spiritual community have counteracted exclusive, sectarian notions of kinship, including those separating human and nonhuman life.[13] Membership of the spiritual community does not belong to any special elect or creed. Indeed, all beings strive in contemplation toward the vision of unity, not only rational beings, but animals, plants, and even the earth that supports them (*Enn.* III.8.1). Armstrong emphasized the importance of the spiritual community in the contemplative return to the source: it is from the communal integration that the final step of ascent proceeds, for the mystic stationed in the fellowship of the intelligible order is poised to forgo cosmic self-knowledge and rise on the wave of loving Intellect that eternally aspires to its source.

Although Neoplatonism ceased to exist as a distinct school of philosophy in the sixth and seventh centuries CE, the Plotinian account of the interpenetrating divine community continued to exert an influence in the West, through the works of Christian theologians and philosophers who had access to the *Enneads* in the Greek original compiled by Porphyry or in the Latin translation of Marius Victorinus. The translation failed to survive into the Middle Ages, and the *Enneads* had to wait until 1492 for its next rendering into Latin, by Marsilio Ficino, who added a commentary. However, Neoplatonic ideas were available through other channels, including the Pseudo-Dionysian theology and Proclus's *Elements of Theology*, the latter passed off in the West as an Aristotelian work entitled *Liber de Causis*.

Plotinian and Neoplatonic ideas were also available in a few pagan works that had an influence into the medieval period, such as Macrobius's commentary on Cicero's *Dream of Scipio*.

In the East, sections of the *Enneads* survived in Aristotelian guise, and significant parts of the treatises v.8 and vi.7, which contain the impressive descriptions of the intelligible cosmos, were included in the *Theology of Aristotle*, a work thought to have been translated into Arabic in the ninth century CE. The *Theology* came to Europe in the early sixteenth century after its discovery in a Damascus library and was published in Latin in 1519.[14] The description of interpenetration in the *Enneads*, quoted above ("Each there has everything in itself," *Enn.* v.8.4), has a slightly more elaborate form of expression in the *Theology*:

> *Thus each one of them sees the things in its own being and in the being of its neighbour, and therefore they are all of them inside all of them, and the whole is in the whole* and the one is in the whole and the whole is in the one *and the one of them is the whole and the light which falls on them is infinite and therefore each one of them is immense,* for the great among them is immense *and the small is immense.*[15]

Thus, through Arabic translation and amplification, the Plotinian vision of the spiritual community passed to Muslim and Jewish thinkers. It is possible that a well-known Sufi text is indebted, if only indirectly, to the *Theology of Aristotle* for its depiction of the mutual identities revealed in the vision of the community. In *The Conference of the Birds* (*Manṭiq al-ṭair*), composed by Persian poet, mystic, and apothecary Farīd al-Dīn ʿAṭṭār (ca. 1145–1221 CE), several birds engaged on a quest gain entry through a kind of Sun Door into the kingdom of their Lord and are confronted there by puzzling mutual identities (see Box, "None understood such a thing"). The vision takes to a new level the mirror-like disclosure of identity we have already seen in the Thomas literature and other traditions. There, to look in the mirror was to discover one's divine doubleness; here, to look in the mirror with one's companions is to discover, additionally, a communal dimension of identity.

Identity and Difference

Like the birds in ʿAṭṭār's tale, who gaze uncomprehendingly into the face of the supreme and ask for "the solution of You being us and being You,"[16] we must now ask how it can be that "all are in all."

❧ None understood such a thing ❦

In 'Aṭṭār's *Manṭiq al-ṭair*, a wise hoopoe addresses the parliament of birds and invites his fellows to search for their king, the Sīmurgh, a mythical bird described in Persian literature, related to the griffin, phoenix, and garuda. Only thirty of the many thousands of birds make it to the end of the arduous journey over seven valleys, symbolic of the purification of the self. The survivors are dazzled and bewildered by a light brighter than thousands of suns, moons, and heavens of stars, but their loving devotion toward the goal overcomes all doubts, and with some difficulty they persuade the doorkeeper—a messenger from on high who at first interrogates and rebuffs—to let them through. The birds are admitted into the king's throne room, where they are instructed to read a scroll that describes in detail the events and actions of their lives, a "life review" that distresses the birds because they realize that in the past they have betrayed their spiritual natures. This final purification through shame allows the thirty to rise to the vision of the sunlike Sīmurgh, in whose shining face they see themselves not just as individuals but as the group and even as their Lord. It is a moment of self-revelation. 'Aṭṭār uses a pun to express the identity of the birds with one another and with their divine ground: in Persian, *si* means "thirty" and *murgh* means "bird," and so *sīmurgh* is both the king of the birds (*sīmurgh*) and the thirty birds (*sī-murgh*) themselves. There are mutual identities between the individuals, the collective, and the Lord, but distinctions remain:

> They saw themselves Sī-murgh in all; and Sīmurgh was in all Sī-murgh. When they turned their eyes to the Sīmurgh, it was veritably *that* Sīmurgh which was there in that place. When they looked at themselves, here too it was Sī-murgh. And when they looked both ways at once, Sīmurgh and Sī-murgh were one and the same Sīmurgh. There was Sīmurgh twice, and yet there was only one; yes, one alone, and yet many. This one was that one; that one was this one. In the whole universe none understood such a thing.[17]

Passing beyond the vision of mutual identity in the mirror of Majesty, the birds lose their individuality in the ultimate nothingness, an annihilation from which they recover after more than a hundred thousand centuries to find their selfhoods restored. Having revived from annihilation (*fanā*), they now subsist (*baqā*) in the divine—"permanence after extinction."

In everyday life, it is usual to have some degree of empathy with others, but mystical experiences can take empathy to a new level:

> Then, as the fishermen came abreast of me, one fish, alive, flapped up and seemed to stand on its tail and bow. I felt great compassion for the fish.
>   Suddenly everything was transformed, transfigured, translated, transcended. All was fused into one. I was the fish. The sun sang and the road sang. The music shone. The hands of the stall-keeper danced. The branches of the trees danced. All in time with the same music. They were the music and I was the music and I was the fish, the fishermen, the hands of the stall-keeper, the trees, the branches, the road, the sun, the music: all one and nothing separate. Not parts of the one but the one itself.[18]

The mystic discovers that in some sense all beings are "one," intimately connected in their identities, so that harming another is tantamount to harming oneself and everyone else too. The maltreated child, the rival eliminated through deceitful scheming, the trembling animal dragged to the slaughterhouse—in some sense they are all oneself, and their sufferings are one's own too, if only one knew it. This can be understood at the familiar level of compassionate empathy that joins beings together in a recognition of similar needs, aspirations, joys, fears, and miseries, but it also seems to be more deeply rooted than might ordinarily be suspected, in a shared identity. Realization of the underlying connection hopefully encourages more compassionate attitudes and, in the sphere of religion, provides an antidote to harsh doctrines of eternal damnation or selfish approaches to salvation, for the unity implies that none can be truly saved unless all are saved, as any good bodhisattva knows. The nonconformist minister Jeremiah White (1629–1707) put it thus:

> For if each Soul be a Unity, a Figure, a Shadow, of the Supream Unity (not a dead but a living Shadow) and that all Lines of Being, and Beauty meet in *this Apex*, and unity of the intellectual Spirit; no such Individual Soul can be for ever abandoned; *but the whole nature of things* must Suffer therein, as it did when Christ was crucified . . . . If so many Millions of these Intellectual Substances be never look'd upon, or visited with Redemption, not one Saint is *completely Saved*, for if each Spirit be an intire World, all Spirits are in each Spirit; as the Soul is in every part of the Body.[19]

There can be a temptation to trace the commonality to an absolutely unitary ground at the core of each individual, to the One or Godhead understood as innermost center. The ultimate root is one and the same for all: the many, stripped of individual differences, disclose a common core, the ground and source in which all differences are annihilated. But as illustrated by White's passage above, a qualified oneness can be posited at a describable, intermediate level that allows for difference as well as identity. There is no need to cast aside difference and multiplicity to find a common identity, and indeed difference must be admitted if individuality and a community of individuals are to be retained.

Unlike the unitary, ultimate ground, the cosmic mind in unity with the world of multiplicity provides a common but diversified source of identity for all beings. At the cosmic level of their constitutions, all beings are identical with one another, or to be more precise, they are nearly identical. It is an argument that can be found in the Plotinian discussion of Nous, the divine Intellect at the apex of each soul. The argument relies on the special kind of knowing that is attributed to the Intellect, the direct, nondiscursive knowledge whereby the Intellect *is* what it knows, the self-thinking thought of Aristotelian philosophy given a mystical twist, in which knower and known come together in an experiential unity:

> Of what is There we have direct knowledge, not images or even impressions; and to know without image is to be; by our part in true knowledge we are those Beings; we do not need to bring them down into ourselves, for we are There among them. Since not only ourselves but all other things also are those Beings, we all are they; we are they while we are also one with all: therefore we and all things are one.[20] (*Enn.* VI.5.7)

The reasoning can be summarized thus: as the nondiscursive knowledge at the summit of my soul, I am the cosmos of intelligible beings. But not only I, for you and all others know and are the intelligible cosmos at the summit of your souls. Thus, by our unity with a common intelligible world, we are all one another at the summit of our souls. You are the Whole; I am the Whole; therefore you and I are one another, and we are united in our Wholeness.[21] Edward Carpenter was to employ similar reasoning in his discussion of the Self, explaining how its universality follows from the identity of the knowing subject and the known object, an identity that he believed had been declared by many witnesses:

> If then we accept their evidence we must believe the final and real Self to be *one and universal*. For if A knows his essential identity with all the objects *a, b, c,* &c.; and B also knows the same; then A and B know their

essential identity with each other, even though they may never have seen each other. And so on. All our 'selves' consequently must be one, or at least united so as to be branches of the One—even though for a time deluded by the idea of separation.[22]

Taking O to represent the universe of things ("*a, b, c*, &c."), the logic proceeds thus: if A = O and B = O, then A = B.

Interest in the propositions "all souls are one" ("monopsychism" or the "unicity of the soul") and "all intelligences are one" ("mononoism" or the theory of *unitas intellectus*) has had a long history, inspired by the Neoaristotelian and Neoplatonic philosophers who brought the ideas to prominence in Western philosophy.[23] This was achieved by focusing attention on Aristotle's identification of intelligence with its objects, and on the problem of the relation between human intelligence and a higher, divine intelligence. Concern with the ideas persisted through medieval Jewish, Islamic, and Christian philosophy, and the unicity of intelligence became a subject of controversy, brought to a head in the doctrines of the Islamic philosopher Ibn Rushd (Lat., Averroes; 1126–1198 CE). Ibn Rushd denied individuality to souls distinct from their bodies and drew the conclusion that souls have no individual existence after death. Only the common, active intelligence is eternal, not the passive intelligence of individuals.

It is, perhaps, not surprising that the sophisticated but sometimes opaque discussions of souls, intelligences, and unity that we find in the Neoplatonists should be open to misunderstanding or simplification. Incautious statements that assert the complete identity of God with individual persons or objects might easily emerge from a mystic acquainted with the rudiments of Neoplatonic philosophy and draw charges of blasphemy or pantheism. The more acute philosophers had taken care not to suppress the individuality of things in doctrines of unmitigated oneness, and had acknowledged some principle of individuation that permits differences between things. The identification that gives oneness must be qualified by a differentiation that allows for multiplicity. If Plotinus asserted that all souls are one, he also maintained that they are distinct and many. Unqualified oneness is attributable only to the ultimate ground, while the existence of many beings at derivative levels calls for some kind of differentiating principle. All are identical at the very root of their natures because there is only one root in monotheistic or monistic doctrines of the ultimate, but it does not follow that all are identical at the derivative levels of the great minds and the little minds. For if the many are to be given a place in reality, the logic of unity must include difference as well as identity. Indeed, there can be no unity without difference if unity is a relation between distinguishable things. Absolute unicity excludes unity.

For Plotinus, unity of the many souls at their lower levels is possible because each one implies the common whole or potentially includes the whole, like the elements of a scientific system or the propositions of geometry (*Enn.* IV.9.5). But unity is much more evident among the souls in their higher reaches, at the level of the Intellect, for here the souls really are wholes, that is, intellects in union with the intelligible cosmos. But the unity here does not mean that "all minds are one": there is unity but not absolute oneness, for the wholes are distinguished from one another in some way, and it is this difference that permits multiplicity. The one mind is a multiplicity of distinguishable minds, each containing all the others. In *Ennead* v.8, Plotinus describes the interpenetration of beings in the intelligible realm: each contains all, so that everywhere there is all. Significantly, Plotinus adds: "A different kind of being stands out in each, but in each all are manifest" (*Enn.* v.8.4). In another passage, he explains that the Intellect is all, but so is each particular thing within it: "For it is not one thing and they another; nor is each individual thing in it separate; for each is the whole and in all ways all, and yet they are not confused, but each is in a different sense separate" (*Enn.* I.8.2). There is something that distinguishes the wholes from one another: an element that "stands out" (v.8.4), a difference "in their powers," "apart in a position without separation" (*Enn.* v.8.9), participation "in what it is capable of" (1.8.2), and having "its particular power in the whole," like a theorem in a body of knowledge (v.9.8).

The idea of dominant characteristics that distinguish like things had been present in earlier Platonic thought and even before Plato in Anaxagoras's doctrine of parts that contain something of everything but in varying proportions.[24] Hair, according to Anaxagoras, derives its hairlike quality through parts that predominate in hair-content, but which contain all other materials too. The Anaxagorean theory of differentiating predominance, applied to material objects, is very different from the Plotinian one, but differentiation by predominance had been posited at the level of the intelligible world before Plotinus, in the thought of Numenius. It seems that Numenius, like Plotinus, supposed that individual souls contain the intelligible cosmos in different ways.[25] The identity and difference were expressed in a principle that was to be much employed in Neoplatonic philosophy and later religious thought, for several purposes, and which has been called "the principle of participation" and "the principle of correspondence."[26] It is the idea that "all things are in all things, but in each after its own fashion." It is not known whether Numenius understood the principle through mystical experience, but it is certainly possible that Plotinus found support for its validity in his own visions of the intelligible cosmos.

Applied to the wholes of the intelligible world, which are Intelligences or living Forms, we may wonder how the differentiating principle of predominance is supposed to distinguish them: what makes the wholes different from one another, given that each is all things? I am unsure what Plotinus understood the predominance to be, and how it served to distinguish between the Intelligences. The explanation will depend on what the intelligible members of his cosmos are taken to be (universal Forms, living minds, perhaps even Forms of individuals) and in what sense they contain one another. If Plotinian intelligible members are interpreted as Platonic Forms such as Justice, then one Form or Idea would have to contain or imply all the others: Justice would include Beauty and so on, yet predominate in Justice. If cosmic vision of fellow intellects is emphasized, then each living mind contains all the other living minds as the contents of its knowledge, and yet is distinguished from these others in some way.

Living Mirrors

The source of differentiation becomes clearer in a later philosophy that posits a multiplicity of beings who are cosmic in scope. In his mature philosophy, Leibniz held that the world consists not of inert matter and its motions but of *perception* and its transformations. There is some debate over the proper interpretation of Leibniz's late metaphysics, but as the starting point for my own speculative efforts, I shall adopt a common but contested reading, according to which his metaphysics is a form of idealism that reduces matter to mind or the mindlike.[27] In this reading, the world consists of many parallel sequences of perceptual states. Each of these *monads* expresses the entire universe from its own sequence of perspectives, from its own changing points of view. In logical terms, a monad is a "complete concept," a subject that contains all its predicates, but the monad is no mere abstract entity. It is a living world of perception, a "living mirror" whose internal states express the universe. There is no universe apart from these internal, cosmic representations. We are, each one of us, such a self-evolving perceptual sequence, one of the monads, the simple substances of Leibniz's world-system, fundamental units of nature created and sustained by God, yet transforming and developing by virtue of an inner force or desire (*appetition*).

In this scheme, the "billiard ball" atoms of mechanical philosophy have been replaced by living centers of activity and perception. A. N. Whitehead put it well: "Lucretius tells us what an atom looks like to others, and Leibniz tells us how an atom is feeling about itself."[28] Monads, as simple substances without parts, are at least as robust as the universe they express and cannot be destroyed by natural means. They have existed since the Creation, and so we, as monads, are as ancient as the universe. Leibniz famously described the monads as having "no windows" through which anything can enter or leave. This is just a way of expressing their wholeness and causal self-sufficiency: since monads express the entire universe, they are all-inclusive wholes, and there can be no inflow or outflow. In this respect, they are like the organic cosmos of Plato's *Timaeus*, a living, thinking creature that has no need of external limbs, orifices, and sense organs because it contains everything within itself.

If monads express the same universe, what distinguishes one from another? Attentive to the concerns of medieval philosophy, including criticisms of Ibn Rushd's doctrine of the unicity of intelligence, Leibniz felt the need to establish a convincing principle of individuation. It emerged as the "Principle of the Identity of Indiscernibles," the idea that things exactly alike are one and the same. The logic utilizes the basic principle of identity ($A = A$) to remove tautology: A and B, but $B = A$, therefore only A. The principle implies that there cannot be a multiplicity of monads and a world made out of them unless the monads are distinguishable from one another. In Leibniz's theory, the *point of view* of a monad contributes toward its individuality: each state of a monad is a version of the world organized from a unique perceptual vantage point. Monads are therefore distinguished in part by their spatiotemporal organization, unique to a specific place at a specific time. It should be stressed, however, that the monads themselves are not located in space and time; rather, their internal representations express the monads in their "spatiotemporal" relations with one another, that is, in their relations of coexistence and succession. But it is not only unique perceptual perspectives that distinguish monads. Their perceptions are also characterized by different degrees of confusion and distinctness.[29] For the majority of monads, only a small part of the cosmic representation is consciously registered. Monads may be omnipercipient, but much of the perception is below the threshold of awareness.

The distinctness of perception is determined by the kinds of bodies associated with monads, that is, by the bodies they represent themselves as having at their points of view. By governing the degree of perceptual distinctness available, these bodies serve to place monads in a hierarchical classification. At the lower end of Leibniz's monadic Chain of Being, there are very many insentient monads, which have rudimentary bodies and therefore only highly confused perceptions of the universe. Collectively, these "bare" or "simple" monads give the appearance of being inert matter, but it would be better to describe them as dormant, asleep, or unconscious, since nothing is truly dead in the Leibnizian universe, and even the most basic monad is a living being (*vita*), endowed with perception and appetition, the former highly confused and the latter "insensible." A lump of rock is, roughly speaking, packed with many such monads, and lacks a central or dominant monad. In fact, matter in general is just the representation of configurations of these simple monads in the perceptions of another monad. This is a special kind of panpsychism or panexperientialism, a panperceptualism in which the elementary units of nature are perceptual and appetitive.

Further up the scale, above the mineral and plant kingdoms, there are monads associated with bodies equipped with sense organs. These bodies confer sentience, memory, and more complex, "sensible" appetitions in the form of perceptible appetites and desires, and their dominant monads are properly called animal "souls" (*anima*). In attributing sentience to animals, Leibniz departs from Descartes, who had asserted that animals are soulless automata. Monads with human bodies are more advanced still, with rationality, reflective consciousness (*apperception*), volitional appetition, and yet greater activity. They are rational souls (*anima rationalis*), spirits (*espirit*), minds (*mens*). They also differ from the subrational animals by having access to a priori necessary truths and abstract ideas grounded in God. It follows that rational souls are not only expressive of the world, as all monads are, but also directly expressive of God.

Human beings are not the only creatures blessed with reason, for an infinite gradation of rational beings continues all the way to God. Leibniz thought it credible to suppose that these superhuman beings include extraterrestrial creatures. Life on other planets in the solar system and beyond had become a matter of speculation in the seventeenth century, inspired by the new cosmology and the old principle of plenitude (maximal actualization of possibilities).[30] Leibniz's superhuman category also includes good and evil genii (*génies*), angels and demons who, though commonly regarded as supernatural, are not really so different from human beings, for they too must be associated with bodies, undergo transformation, and participate in the interconnected system of nature in which their monadic souls are units. Leibniz muses that the angels will have a more "a priori," less sense-dependent kind of knowledge, closer to God's entirely a priori knowing, and that their bodies are likely to be of a subtler kind, able to penetrate gross obstructions and transform at will. But they are still created, embodied beings. There are no sharp divisions between the monadic classes: Leibniz's adherence to the

Principle of Continuity leads him to speculate that there will be intermediate classes, such as the zoophytes between plants and animals. Similarly, the more advanced animals will approach humans by having basic powers of reasoning. But God, as the primitive "monad" at the summit of the hierarchy, is not a monad in the way that other beings are, for God is the creator of the system, not an embodied creature within the system.

Unlike Descartes, Leibniz recognized unconscious as well as conscious states, and in this respect he follows Plotinus, whose theory of the levels of the soul involves gradations of intellection, with the clearest at the summit of the soul in the Nous and its intelligible realm. For Plotinus, perceptions in the sensible realm are "Intellections of the dimmer order," while intellections in the intelligible realm are "vivid perceptions" (*Enn.* VI.7.7). It is possible that Plotinian philosophy was among the currents of thought that influenced the monadology, either directly (for Leibniz knew the *Enneads*) or indirectly through some intermediary such as Nicholas of Cusa, but it is important to recognize differences between the cosmic beings discussed by the two philosophers.

First, the universe expressed by Leibnizian monads is our everyday world of flowers, trees, birds, human beings, mountains, planets, and stars. In fact, monads are intimately involved in this everyday world, for, as we have already seen, they indirectly go to make up its material constituents. Matter, approximately speaking, consists of aggregates of monads, and so monads are the "true atoms of nature." The Plotinian intelligences, on the other hand, mirror an intelligible world of living Forms, a world that is not quite the one we experience in our sense perceptions, and they are not in any sense the constituents of matter. The relationship is one of original to image, the sensible world being a copy of the intelligible.

However, it can seem that Plotinus brings the two worlds closer together than is usual in Platonism. The intelligible cosmos of Plotinus sounds rather like our own universe experienced at a deeper level of unity, containing plants, animals, and men: "For all There is heaven; earth is heaven, and sea heaven; and animal and plant and man; all is the heavenly content of that heaven" (*Enn.* V.8.3). If there is an intelligible realm above the perceptual world in Leibniz's thought, it is not the Plotinian one: the contents of Leibniz's "intelligible realm" is the mind of God thinking *possibilities* and not actualities, ideas of creatures that will be brought into being only if they contribute to the perfection of the world. In contrast, the Plotinian intelligible realm contains actualities; it is not a plan conceived by the One, like a model used by a craftsman, a Platonic theory that Plotinus explicitly rejects. Leibniz's understanding of the intelligible world is more akin to theories of prefiguration in a divine mind, prior to the emergence of the world into the concrete existences of derivative realms.

Second, Leibnizian monads differ from Plotinian intellects by being *separate*, isolated perceptions interconnected indirectly through a pre-established harmony arranged by God. Moreover, it is not clear (to me, at least) whether Leibnizian monads represent one another *fully*: although they certainly represent one another by expressing the universe, it is not made explicit that a monad represents within itself the interior, perceptual details of the other monads. By contrast, Plotinian intellects are parts of one all-encompassing Intellect, and it is clear that they reflect one another fully: each "has everything in itself and sees all things in every other, so that all are everywhere and each every one is all and the glory is unbounded" (*Enn.* v.8.4). However, the gap between the two accounts can be closed. A Leibnizian monad would be more Plotinian if it were made explicit that the mirroring of other monads were truly complete. The monad would then have a highly communal inner nature, containing full representations of all the other monads within itself. At the same time, to make the Plotinian account more Leibnizian, we would have to say that the intellects are differentiated at least in part by their point of view: in effect, there would be many versions of the intelligible cosmos organized from many different experiential vantage points.

Third, a further difference between Leibnizian monads and Plotinian intellects is the manner in which temporality is understood in the systems. In their conscious and unconscious perceptions, Leibnizian monads are in *flux*. Each monadic state is a momentary state of the universe. Plotinian intellects, by contrast, are not in flux. They reflect the eternal realm of Being, and only the lower levels of the soul are sunk in Becoming, in temporal flux. However, both the monads and the intellects do at least have in common a reach beyond the present, the monad being full of the past and pregnant with the future. Monadic perceptions express past and future, as one might expect of truly complete concepts.

Fourth, the systems of Leibniz and Plotinus are notable for their rationality and attention to logic, but Plotinus, unlike Leibniz, unmistakably infuses his metaphysics with mystical insights. The Plotinian levels of reality are also stages in the mystical ascent, and the realm of intellects at the apex of souls is accessible to anyone who follows the journey of moral purification and contemplation, a journey that Plotinus knows well. Leibniz's system, although almost certainly influenced by mystical insights conveyed through Platonic, Kabbalistic, Hermetic, and Christian channels, is not itself a mystical philosophy. There is no very good evidence that Leibniz himself had mystical experiences,[31] and his monads do not have an explicitly mystical character. True, they are complete, interconnected, and all-perceiving, but not in a way open to conscious experience. In contrast, the Plotinian account of experience at the higher level of the soul is explicitly mystical, describing some typical mystical features, such as the unity of subject and object, luminosity, beauty, and transcendence of time. But if mystical feeling is absent from the monadology, Leibniz was at least able to express wonder at the capacity of the infinitely small to represent the infinitely great.[32]

This difference between the two philosophers shows in their contrary understandings of omniscience and the unconscious. Plotinus, as an experienced mystic, knows that when he turns away from his relatively clouded sense perceptions he experiences not a diminution of consciousness but vastly expanded knowledge and vision. The mystic rises from the relatively dim sense perceptions to the vivid noetic perceptions at the apex of the soul. Plotinian souls are omniscient at this deeper, noetic level, although at their lower levels they will not be aware of this vast, interior knowing unless they have practical training in philosophy. By contrast, most Leibnizian monads are confusedly omniscient. Although they perceive everything, they know everything only very confusedly, with their cosmic contents remaining largely unconscious: "Each soul knows infinity, knows everything, but confusedly."[33] Leibniz attributes distinctness only to those perceptions of a monad that its body is able to present to it clearly. Bodies "feel the effects of everything that happens in the universe" but present most of this to their dominant monads in an indistinct fashion.[34]

Leibniz's system does allow for some expansion of a monad's distinct perceptions when its body matures from seed form into a full-grown organism (see chapter 10 for details), but there is no suggestion that a soul in its current life would be able to attain to significantly clearer perceptions of the world, other than the temporary improvements afforded by use of artificial aids—say, magnifying glasses, microscopes, telescopes. I think, therefore, that the metaphysics of Leibniz may have something to learn from the familiarity with higher states of consciousness that informs the philosophy of Plotinus. I develop this suggestion a little further in the next section (and in chapter 9, I shall turn to Plotinian philosophy once again, to explore how monads derive from their source, a matter that Leibniz does not address in any depth). Conversely, it is possible that the interpenetrating, spiritual universe of Plotinus would benefit from the kind of treatment it seems to have received from Leibniz, namely its transformation into our everyday universe. Leibniz transfers to the material universe the mirroring of beings found in the Plotinian heaven.

Omniscience Confused and Distinct

Some mystical experiences bring great expansions of perception, knowledge, bliss, and love, and a feeling of unity with the universe. Monadology, if suitably revised, may help to shed light on such experiences. R. C. Zaehner, a scholar of mysticism who was not fond of cosmic mysticism, thought it a ridiculous contravention of logic to suppose that a limited human being could be united with the universe.[35] However, Leibniz's monadology tells us that we, as monads, do express the entire universe. Thus, identity with the universe is perfectly logical and natural. We are and always have been cosmic wholes. Mystics who experience "cosmic consciousness" are merely discovering the ordinarily hidden, cosmic dimensions of their own souls, and mystics who go beyond the universe to a simple oneness are perhaps encountering the source of the cosmic souls, the origin of the monads, the One or Godhead.

However, Leibnizian monadology as it stands does not explain how we can have our intervals of cosmic lucidity. Although the human soul is a relatively advanced kind of monad, it still has perceptions of the universe that are largely confused. It can distinguish only a small portion of the world clearly. However, some mystical experiences suggest that we can have our moments of clarity while still human, which implies that a revision of Leibniz's system may be needed, one that brings it closer to some of its mystical and esoteric sources. Leibniz performed an immense service by weaving together insights from these and other sources, including the sciences of his day and a variety of philosophies, into a beautifully streamlined system constructed in accordance with logical principles, but something of the original mystical vision was lost in the process, including the recognition that vastly expanded cognitions and perceptions are available to human beings in the here and now. Plotinus knew from his own experience that the soul in its higher reaches is a vast realm of knowing and seeing in which subject and object are united: "we are each one of us an intelligible universe" (*Enn.* III.4.3). By withdrawing from the senses, the soul can discover this level of intellection or clear perception.

More broadly, mystical philosophies have often recognized that some kind of superior knowledge or intellectual intuition—such as Greek *gnōsis* and Indian *jñāna*—is attainable by human beings. An example of particular relevance in the present context is Jainism, which has gone further than most other religious traditions by making the omniscience of souls one of its foundational tenets. Every soul (*jīva*) can in principle attain to effortless knowledge and trans-sensate vision of all things in the universe. This special knowledge, *kevalajñāna* ("knowledge isolated [from karmic obscuration]"), is described as perfect, complete, unique, absolute, pure, all-comprehensive, and infinite. It is a natural capacity, for the essence of the soul is knowledge, but it is usually obscured by external factors, the particles of karmic matter that cling to the soul.[36] Although *kevalajñāna* is said to be exceedingly difficult to uncover, its accomplishment by human beings is nonetheless regarded as possible when world conditions allow, as exemplified by the omniscience attained by the most recent of the Jaina ford-makers, Vardhamāna (Mahāvīra, "great hero"), when he achieved the status of Jina ("conqueror"). Interestingly, Jainism shares with Leibniz's monadology a taxonomy of beings based on perceptual–cognitive sophistication. The Jaina one ranges from single-sensed living beings, including plants, through animals with more senses, and then humans, the gods, and finally the liberated souls (see chapter 10). The Jaina taxonomy of life-forms, expounded for its motivational value on the path to liberation, is said to draw on the unlimited knowledge of the ford-makers.

Although itself rooted to some extent in mystical thought, the Leibnizian scheme seems to be out of touch with a number of insights offered by mystical experience. First, mystical experiences can give the impression that expansive knowledge and crystal-clear perception are freely available and just need to be accessed. Leibnizian monads, however, do not have this intrinsic noetic endowment: the perceptions of most monads, human souls included, are largely confused. Without this confusion, a monad "would be a deity" (*une Divinité*),[37] a possibility Leibniz discounts. He does allow himself to call the rational monad "a minute divinity within its own sphere" and a "little" God,[38] but by this he simply means that a rational monad has some degree of rationality, creativity, and free will within its limited domain. Monads, even exceptionally rational ones, cannot be truly godlike in knowledge and perception. For Leibniz, most monads are confusedly omniscient; only God is truly omniscient.

Second, in the Leibnizian scheme, the distinct perceptions of a monad are those that are mediated by the body with which it is associated. While a monad's perceptions are mostly confused, there is a limited degree of perceptual distinctness, furnished by the representation of its immediate environment, its organismic body. Leibniz says of monadic representation:

> It can only be distinct in regard to a small part of things, namely those that are nearest or most extensively related to each monad. . . . Thus, although every created monad represents the entire universe, it represents most distinctly the body which is especially bound to it.[39]

Representation is distinct only for those objects nearby or most related to the monad and therefore most evident in the monad's representation of its own body. By contrast, it is one of the enduring themes of mystical philosophy that the body and its sense organs conceal more than they reveal. Profound encounters with reality are usually thought to require withdrawal from the limited, potentially misleading apprehensions furnished by the senses.

Third, the dependence of distinct perceptions on the body and its sense organs in the Leibnizian scheme implies that during the life of an organism there can be no significant perceptual expansion. The only way to enhance perception in this life would be to employ instruments that aid the senses, such as microscopes and telescopes. A more permanent enhancement of perceptual range and acuity can take place only if, after death, a monad were to regrow a body markedly *superior* to its former one, with more powerful sensory and cognitive systems—a possibility not endorsed by Leibniz (see chapter 10). By contrast, mystical experiences suggest that expansions of knowledge and perception are possible now in this lifetime.

Fourth, Leibnizian monads are in flux, having momentary states that express the current state of the universe, with each present state implying or even expressing previous and future states of the universe. However, one lesson of mystical experience is the realization that all time exists in the moment, in an "Eternal Now" that embraces past, present, and future. It is therefore tempting to suppose that monadic states are not fleeting things, but are "permanent" in the eternal sense and fully inclusive of the entirety of time. Each state of the revised monad would then be a complete spatiotemporal perspective on the universe, a complete "spacetime" in modern scientific parlance. The fact that modern physics has cast doubt on a universe-wide present moment is further reason to question Leibniz's momentary monadic states and make each state spatiotemporally inclusive.

Fifth, mystical experience of souls as extended bodies may suggest that *represented* monads are not dimensionless points but have size and shape, a possibility to which I shall return in the final section of this chapter.

In summary, let me recommend the following revisions, *pace* Leibniz:

1. A monad's cosmic perceptions are perfectly distinct.

2. Confusion pertains to the monad's sense perceptions.

3. In principle, monads are able to go beyond their confused sense perceptions and access their perfectly distinct cosmic perceptions.

4. A monad's perceptual states do not perish.

5. Represented monads have size and shape.

Thus, monads at all levels of advancement always have perfectly distinct perceptions of the universe, although these are not apparent at the everyday level of consciousness. With this background lucidity, monads are no longer confusedly omniscient: they are truly omniscient. This is not to say, however, that their all-knowingness makes them equal to God, for they are still dependent, created things, emanated from their common source. In addition to their cosmic, *noumenal* perceptions, monads have perceptions that are dependent on their bodily sense organs. These *phenomenal* sensory experiences are not the monad's most distinct perceptions: rather, they are relatively confused and limited, and, metaphorically, constitute a perceptual "veil" that conceals more of the world than it reveals.

With the evolutionary development of sense organs and brains, these confused perceptions can improve in quality up to a point, but they will always be limited by the limitations of sensory channels and cognitive processing. But in addition to these circumscribed sense perceptions, there is always the deeper level of crystal-clear, trans-sensate perception of the universe. The accessibility of these noumenal perceptions in some mystical states means that the monads can increase their perceptual range and acuity without having to become associated with new, improved bodies. Perfectly lucid experience is intrinsic to every monad and need only be accessed, directly in mystical states and perhaps indirectly in the mediated form of psychical cognitions such as telepathy, clairvoyance, and precognition.[40]

The suggested revisions to the monad's perceptual constitution make the system consonant with mystical evidence that vastly expanded perceptions of the universe are available to human beings, waiting to be discovered behind the veil of the senses. Similarly, the revised scheme is now better able to support notions of the "twofold soul," "divine double," and so forth, raised in chapter 4. The Leibnizian monad is onefold, consisting of perceptions that are inherently indistinct or "minute" (*petites perceptions*), but some of which attain to distinctness in combination with one another, through a summation and amplification carried out by the monad's organismic body.[41] This state of affairs is shown in figure 6.1a: very indistinct perceptions of the universe, but a few relatively distinct perceptions of a nearby tree, mediated by the monad's body. In the Leibnizian scheme, only more advanced monads, endowed with sentience (more distinct perceptions, with memory), are properly called "souls."[42] Yet more sophisticated bodies bring thinking capacities and even self-consciousness, making monads "selves."

By contrast, revised monads are twofold in their constitution, having two clear-cut zones of perceptual contents (fig. 6.1b). There are, again, the contents mediated by the monad's organismic body, and attendant psychologi-

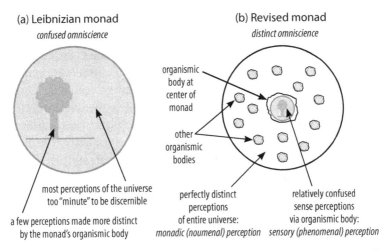

(a) Leibnizian monad
confused omniscience

(b) Revised monad
distinct omniscience

organismic body at center of monad

other organismic bodies

most perceptions of the universe too "minute" to be discernible

a few perceptions made more distinct by the monad's organismic body

perfectly distinct perceptions of entire universe: *monadic (noumenal) perception*

relatively confused sense perceptions via organismic body: *sensory (phenomenal) perception*

Figure 6.1   Perceptual constitution of Leibnizian monad and revised monad.

cal functioning and self-consciousness in the more advanced monads. But in addition to this phenomenal kind of experience, with its circumscribed self-identifications, the revised monad also has perfectly distinct perceptions of the universe. The monad at this level is an all-knowing, all-perceiving mind, and may even be a *self*, and a social self too, involving a community of selves. By revising Leibnizian monads so that they are a little more like Plotinian intellects, we can understand them to be selves, that is, to have intrinsic "apperception" or self-consciousness at the cosmic level. This self-awareness is a social awareness, for a monadic self represents within itself all the other monadic selves. While these other selves in a monad can be called "representations," the word does not convey the living reality of the beings as intuited in mystical experience. They are not just images of external monads, but, it would seem, living beings in their own right, and could be described as "guests." A monadic self is host to all its monadic guests and is, in reciprocal relationship, a guest in all its monadic hosts.

In the revised scheme, then, it is appropriate to call every monad a "soul" and even a "self," and to distinguish at least two soul-levels, namely the phenomenal zone of experience, including sense perceptions, and a noumenal zone that ordinarily goes unnoticed. Translating this understanding of the monad into traditional religious categories, we could say that the monad in its deeper nature equates, if only approximately, to such spiritual concepts as the higher self, the divine double, even the divine Image. This last designation is not as far-fetched as it may sound, for the monad can be construed as an intellective image of its divine source, generated through a primordial reflexivity, as will be explored in chapter 9.

The suggested revision of the monad is also in better agreement with the evidence of near-death experience. In Leibniz's scheme, the death transition is likely to be a period of prolonged unconsciousness because the body breaks down to leave a more basic organism, the animalcule, which has a more primitive body and therefore even dimmer perceptions.[43] Only if the nervous system and sense organs regrow in a subsequent life will the more distinct perceptions return. By contrast, in the revised scheme, the disruption of sensory perception and cognitions at or near the moment of death exposes the monad's previously hidden, perfectly distinct perceptions, like clouds parting to reveal the sun, figuratively speaking. The fact that near-death experiences sometimes do bring these expansions of vision and knowledge, and encounters with a higher self, stands in favor of the revised scheme.

A Newish Theory of Perception

As a way of reconciling mind and matter, Leibniz's monadology is often taken to be a form of idealism, an approach to the mind–body problem that sets up mind as primary and matter as derivative. As such, the monadology and George Berkeley's immaterialist metaphysics are likely to be mentioned in the same breath as examples of *idealist monism*, for both systems propose just one kind of "substance" (mind only). By contrast, the various forms of *substance dualism*, whether interactionist, epiphenomenal, or parallelist, posit two substances (mind and matter). *Materialism*, as a monism, has just one substance (matter only), as do two other monisms frequently discussed in the philosophical literature, *dual-aspect monism* (mind and matter as "aspects" of one substance) and *neutral monism* (one neutral substance, neither mind nor matter in itself, but giving rise to each).[44]

Of the monistic alternatives to materialism, idealism is the only one to rid itself completely of the materialist conception of matter that gave rise to the mind–body problem in the first place. The story has been told before.[45] Early modern science, preoccupied with the readily quantifiable qualities of extension and motion, followed the example of ancient Greek atomism and attributed only these "primary" or "geometric-kinematic" qualities to matter and so split it off from experience, even though extension and motion are inseparable from other qualities of experience. This is most obviously the case with the visual qualities, for color patches have extension, shape, and relative size (see chapter 8, "The Spatiality of Experience"). Materialists abstracted matter, space, and time from experience and set them up as realities more fundamental than experience, but they were then unable to explain how matter and void so conceived could give rise to something as different as experience, with its colors, sounds, flavors, and smells. Although the physical picture of the world has become more complex, with the introduction of forces, fields, mass, energy, spacetime, and so on, a similar segregation of qualities and similar abstractions remain. Only idealism fully critiques these splits and abstractions, and so reintegrates matter, space, and time into experience. The other monist alternatives to materialism do not do so fully, exhibiting residual dualism in their talk of mind and matter as "dual aspects" of one substance or distinct products of a "neutral" substance.

Although they are idealist monisms, the systems of Leibniz and Berkeley are also pluralisms in the sense that they package the one "mental substance" into a multiplicity of individual minds, Leibniz's perceptual monads and Berkeley's "minds and their ideas." But it is worth noting that there is room for debate over the precise classification of Leibnizian monadology, even as it has commonly been interpreted, for its monads are not in general sufficiently advanced to qualify as "mind" and are better called "mindlike." The majority of monads—the simple monads—have very confused perceptions, with none of the animal soul's perceptual distinctness, memory, and ability to reason, nor the rational soul's advanced rationality and self-consciousness. If Leibnizian monadology is not a fully fledged idealism, it might be called a *perceptual* or *experiential monism* instead. These classificatory uncertainties, however, do not apply to the revised monadology introduced above, for all monads are now thoroughly mind, being endowed with omniscient mind, and so the monism is unreservedly idealist.

As we have seen, this revised monadology posits two basic kinds of perception, the perfectly distinct cosmic perceptions that escape our notice except in some mystical and near-death experiences, and the relatively confused, everyday sense perceptions that are dependent on the sense organs and nervous system. How are these two kinds of perception related? Although I am open to suggestions, I think that a representative theory of perception—also commonly known as "representative realism" and "indirect realism"—is well suited to sketch out the nature of the connection. In standard representative realism, the objects displayed in sense perception are understood to be *mental representations* of objects that exist in a *material external world* (fig. 6.2). But in the idealist context of the monadology, the external world is not the material world of dualism and materialism but the cosmic contents of the monad's own noumenal perceptions. In fact, sense perceptions will just be special contents of these cosmic perceptions, mediated by the representational activities of the sense organs and brains that are themselves contained in the cosmic perceptions.

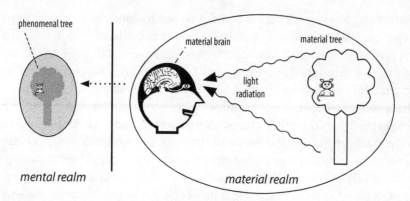

Figure 6.2   Dualist representative realism. (© Paul Marshall, 2005, p. 263, fig. 8.3 (modified), from Ch. 8, *Mystical Encounters with the Natural World: Experiences and Explanations*. By permission of Oxford University Press.)

To better understand this idea, consider a representative account of perception. Suppose you see a cat in a tree. According to the representative theory, your perception of the cat and tree is indirect. What you experience directly is the phenomenal *representation* of the cat and tree. The cat and tree in the external world are perceived indirectly through this mental representation. Exactly how the representation comes about is far from clear in the finer details of the brain processes, but in broad terms it is supposed that, in the case of vision, light rays from material objects arrive at each eye and are focused by a lens into an image on the light-sensitive retina. Electrical impulses are transmitted along the optic nerves into the recesses of the brain, first to the lateral geniculate bodies in the thalamus and then to the occipital cortex in each brain hemisphere, where they are subject to processing, with further processing in other parts of the brain.[46] Mental images of the external world come forth, including representations of the cat and tree. This representative theory has commonly been framed in dualist terms: external material objects come to be represented in mental impressions (fig. 6.2). However, the dualist version is faced by a grave problem, the discontinuity between the physical processes at work in the material brain and the mental representations they are supposed to produce. The leap from matter to experience is puzzling, to put it mildly.

Naturally, materialists dislike the idea of *mental* representations and reject the dualism of the standard representative theory, and so they may either dismiss the representative approach out of hand or reinterpret it in a materialist framework, turning mental representations into material brain states. Material objects in the external world are represented within material

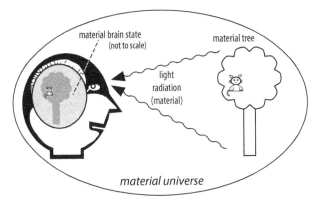

(a) A materialist version of representative realism.

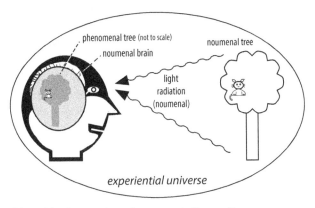

(b) An idealist version of representative realism.

Figure 6.3 **Monist versions of representative realism.** (© Paul Marshall, 2005, p. 264, fig. 8.4 (modified), from Ch. 8, *Mystical Encounters with the Natural World: Experiences and Explanations*. By permission of Oxford University Press.)

brain states alone (fig. 6.3a). By contrast, mental representations, being mental, are not anathema to idealists, and they can remodel the representative theory in idealist fashion by making the external world mental and perceptual. Contents of this experiential world are represented in sense perception. In the language of the revised monadology, the objects perceived *directly* in noumenal perception are perceived *indirectly* through the representations afforded by the senses, and these sense perceptions are just special, little patches in the greater noumenal perception (fig. 6.3b).

Where are the phenomenal patches located? One approach is to suppose that the patches exist in a "phenomenal space" distinct from physical space. This is a dualist theory because it posits two distinct realms, the phenomenal and the physical. John Smythies has advocated such an approach (see chapter 8). In monist metaphysics, however, there is no such radical distinction and therefore no motivation to separate phenomenal patches into a separate realm or space. In idealist metaphysics, the brain itself can be regarded as experiential in nature, a content of the great noumenal field of perception, and so it makes sense to situate the phenomenal patches in the brain, in some relatively large-scale structure or perhaps in a single brain cell, or even reproduced in several neurons.[47] There is also the possibility that the phenomenal patches may be located in a distinct unit that can detach itself from the brain, as in those old theories of the soul's subtle bodies, such as the luminous and pneumatic vehicles (*ochēma*) of Neoplatonic philosophy.[48] I mention this possibility because of those out-of-body experiences and some near-death experiences in which one seems to leave the body and yet has experiences very similar in character to ordinary sense perceptions. If these "out-of-body" perceptions are similar to sense perceptions, then they too are likely to be mediated, perhaps dependent on a subtle body with its own organs of perception. It is, of course, open to debate whether out-of-body experiences provide perceptual access to the environment, and whether anything really leaves the body during the experiences.

This, then, is the "newish" theory of perception in bare outline, a theory that is not entirely new because it takes old-fashioned representative realism and reworks it by transforming the material external world of dualism and materialism into a perceptual and mental world, into the noumenal hinterlands of the monad. Despite it being idealist, this version of the representative theory is still a form of realism in the sense that it continues to assert the reality of objects in a world external to human minds, albeit in an "external world" now *interior* to monadic minds. In summary, there are (at least) two kinds of perception in the monadic universe, both of which involve representation. The theory of perception can therefore be called *double representative realism* (table 6.1). First, there is our familiar sensory type of

DOUBLE REPRESENTATIVE REALISM			
type of perception	*directly perceived*	*indirectly perceived*	*type of representation*
sensory *phenomenal* "outward feel"	sensory representations of objects within the monad	objects within the monad	sensory: image formation via signals and nervous system
monadic *noumenal* "inward feel"	objects within the monad, and representations of other monads	other monads	monadic: mutual representation

Table 6.1   Two types of representative perception: phenomenal and noumenal.

perception, phenomenal in character, made possible by signal transmission, sense organs, and the activities of the nervous system. It provides indirect access to a world of objects (including trees and cats) via direct perceptions of mental representations. It feels like "outward" perception, perception of things external to the observer (except in some this-worldly mystical experiences when unity and inclusiveness take hold). Second, there is monadic perception, noumenal in character, which is trans-sensate and experienced as "inward" perception, a discovery of the contents of one's own expansive mind. Here the objects within the monadic mind are perceived directly, being known without intermediaries. However, monadic perception can be said to be representative and indirect in the sense that monads express the universe and so *represent* one another within themselves.

The statement that there are two kinds of perception in the monadic universe needs qualification. First, as noted before, sensory perception is really a development *within* monadic perception, and so the latter is the more basic of the two. Sensory perception is derivative and limited, dependent on the senses and revealing indirectly and dimly a few contents of the monadic perception. Sensory percepts—transient, opaque, and outward in feel—are specialized, phenomenal contents of noumenal, monadic percepts, eternal, inclusive, and inward in feel. It seems that in some mystical experiences (described as "mixed" in chapter 1), sensory contact with the world is maintained in conjunction with the more expansive noumenal kind, giving rise to a sort of "double vision," appropriate to a twofold soul.

Second, it would be a mistake to assume that sensory perception is the only kind of mediated, phenomenal perception. Mention can be made of the psi perceptions, consisting of clairvoyance, telepathy, precognition, and retrocognition, for which there is good but disputed evidence.[49] These perceptions are "extrasensory," not dependent on the familiar senses, yet neither are they direct, unmediated perceptions, as some mystical perceptions have a claim to be. I have discussed elsewhere how psi phenomena might fit into a monadological scheme, drawing on speculations by philosopher H. H. Price that raise filter theory.[50] More generally, the faculty of imagination in its higher range may constitute a form of perception, operative in psi, dream, hypnagogic, entheogenic, and other imaginal experiences. Although utilizing images derived from sensory experience, the imagination seems capable of weaving them together into experiences whose contents are not "imaginary" but genuine representations, often symbolic, of objective conditions. This "imaginative" or "imaginal" perception has been valued in some contexts, religious and otherwise, as more profound than the sensory kind, as I have noted before (chapter 5).

The Shape of the Soul (again)

Finally, let us return to the question of the soul's shape, now that the soul has come to be defined as a monad that expresses the entire universe in its perceptions. Exactly how Leibniz understood monads to be represented within one another is not clear to me. It is possible that he understood the representations to be unextended, dimensionless points because he maintained that monads themselves, considered externally, have no parts and are therefore unextended, indivisible, and without shape.[51] A monad may therefore represent other monads as unextended and without shape.

However, there is another, more interesting possibility: a monad may represent the other monads as they are in their internal nature, that is, as total perceptions of the universe. A monad would then contain within itself a multiplicity of full representations of the universe. There is some mystical justification for taking this approach: for instance, we have seen that experience at the cosmic level, as in the Plotinian noetic vision, can reveal others who are themselves the entire cosmos. It may therefore be appropriate to understand *represented* monads not as dimensionless points but as extended things with parts and an overall shape, yet still "atomic" in the sense of "uncuttable" or "unsplittable" because they are representations of the cosmic totality. As representations of the universe, they will have whatever contents, dimensionality, mass, angular momentum, and shape the universe possesses, but appropriate to their scale. Thus, a clear-perceiving monad would be able to observe its own overall cosmic shape by observing the shapes of the monads it represents or "hosts" within itself.

The idea that the part mirrors the whole because it is also the whole is evident in Plotinus's understanding of the intelligible cosmos: "There each comes only from the whole and is part and whole at once: it has the appearance of a part, but a penetrating look sees the whole in it" (*Enn.* v.8.4). In the *Theology of Aristotle*, the idea is even more explicit. You need only look at the part to see the whole, and you need only look at the whole to see the part: *"If each part of them is a part and a whole, then when you see the part you have seen the whole*, and when you see the whole you have seen the part."*[52] Now, at last, we are in a position to fathom the shape of the soul. Perceived souls, as whole parts—whole by virtue of their identity with the totality—mirror the whole and have whatever shape the whole possesses. For Plotinus and any thinker steeped in ancient Greek thought, it was natural to attribute sphericity to the cosmic totality, following the observations of the early astronomers and the speculations of the pre-Socratic philosophers. Thus, within the context of premodern astronomy, there was good reason to attribute rotundity to the soul: a spherical universe really does imply a spherical soul.

However, there have been alternatives, and the whole–part logic has even been applied to the human form. In mythological and religious thought, the cosmos has occasionally been pictured as human in shape, either in its enduring form or temporarily at some early, cosmogonic stage. For example, later Jaina cosmology sometimes depicted the inhabited space of the universe (*loka-ākāśa*) as human-shaped, with liberated souls occupying the upper-most region.[53] These omniscient souls are said to have the form of their last incarnation, for the Jaina soul takes on the shape of the body it fills, and the final body provides the template for the final soul-shape. But perhaps the deeper view is that such matters are beyond description, the Jaina ford-builder Mahāvīra having reputedly stated that the liberated, unconditioned soul is "not long nor small nor round nor triangular nor quadrangular nor circular."[54] In fact, Jainas have been more interested in the *color* of the soul than its shape, for the color is indicative of its moral and karmic condition.[55] In other words, Jainas have been more interested in the *moral shape* of the soul, given the social and salvatory importance of ethical behavior.

In the *Zohar*, a Jewish mystical text of the thirteenth century CE, it is not Plato's world-sphere that is the perfect shape that contains all shapes, but the human form,[56] and, in sixteenth-century Lurianic Kabbalah, Adam before the Fall was "an all-encompassing cosmic being" who contained all souls arranged into groups and subgroups.[57] An echo of these Jewish speculations can be found in Emanuel Swedenborg's portrayal of heaven, which explicitly calls upon the whole–part logic. Here the human-shaped world is not the universe but the heaven of angelic societies. According to Swedenborg, heaven, its societies, and angels all resemble one man, a great man, a macranthropos whom the angels call the Grand Man or Divine Man, which is also the name given to the heaven as a whole. The shape is not observed directly by angels, for their vision does not extend to the entire heaven, which is vast. Angels are, however, able to infer the shape of the whole from the shape of one of its societies: "For in the most perfect form, the whole is similar to the parts and the parts to the whole, the only differ-ence between them being that they differ in magnitude."[58]

Although presented as revelations from the heavenly and spirit worlds, and supported by references to the New Testament, there are elements of Swedenborg's discussion that most likely derive from Neoplatonic and Jewish mystical sources. The angels employ a suspiciously Neoplatonic turn of logic when they infer the shape of heaven, invoking the mutual likeness of wholes and their parts (a theme also present in the Kabbalah). It seems

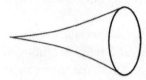  

Figure 6.4　The shape of the soul: trumpet, spherical dodecahedron, spherical truncated icosahedron?

that Swedenborg was familiar with Plotinian thought, through the *Enneads* and the *Theology of Aristotle*, and he may have absorbed the logic of mystical unity from these sources.[59]

If the human form is a rather unlikely candidate for overall shape of the universe, being just one irregular and physically unremarkable shape among many, then what might the universal shape be? Recent cosmological theorizing has suggested a number of candidate global geometries. For example, not so long ago it was suggested that the universe may be shaped like a trumpet, similar to a medieval horn, narrow at one end and bell-shaped at the other.[60] This "Picard topology," which has an infinite, hyperbolic geometry, implies a trumpet-shaped soul with an infinitely extended tail and a bell-shaped head (fig. 6.4). The Church Father Methodius, who scoffed at the idea of a resurrection body other than one that is human in form ("Will it be in the shape of a circle, or a polygon, or a cube, or a pyramid?"), would not have been amused by the thought. But the logic of unity, based on the soul's identity with the totality, tells us that souls in their essential form share the cosmic figure. If the universe is funnel-shaped, then represented monads will be funnel-shaped. If the universe is pyramidal, then they too will be pyramidal. If the universe is a five-dimensional spacetime hypersphere, then so too will be the represented monads. By virtue of their identity with the universe, souls are universe-shaped and will be represented as such in the deep experiences of other souls.

Another fairly recent cosmological model has spacetime wrapped round into a so-called soccer-ball or football universe.[61] According to this suggestion, the universe has a finite, hyperspherical geometry. More specifically, it is a "Poincaré Dodecahedral Space," which has been described as a "multiply connected variant of the simply connected hypersphere."[62] We can now understand why the two demons in the story recounted by Caesarius were so keen to play ball with the poor youth's soul: it was shaped like a regulation football. To be precise, though, footballs are commonly made in the form of the spherical truncated icosahedron, with its twelve pentagonal and twenty hexagonal faces, not the spherical dodecahedron, with twelve pentagonal faces (fig. 6.4). However, the Poincaré Dodecahedral Space belongs to the binary icosahedral group, which provides some justification for applying the "soccer ball" or "football" moniker to this cosmological model.

But humor aside—and however implausible it may sound—the logic of mystical unity implies that when cosmologists inspect the microwave background radiation to investigate the shape of the universe they are also exploring, unbeknown to themselves, the lineaments of their own souls. Early empirical investigators of the soul, such as MacDougall and (allegedly) Frederick II and Prince Pāyāsi, used techniques that were far too crude to be of any value, but modern cosmologists are in a better position to measure the soul's physical attributes. Conversely, when mystics have caught sight of the essential shape of the soul in a profound state of consciousness, then the logic of unity dictates that they have also perceived the shape of the universe, and their observations may provide useful information if they are able to remember, interpret, and express accurately what they have experienced. In my own case, the observed beings were round, and so it follows from the whole–part logic of unity that if these little ones represented the universe (and were not simply entoptics, migrainous phenomena, erotic imagery, symbols of wholeness, and so on), then the universe too is round in some way. It is intriguing that sphericity keeps turning up in accounts of mystical and related experiences, as we shall find again in the next chapter.

One final point. We have seen that if the universe has a certain shape then the soul will have that shape too at its cosmic level, given the identity of one with the other. But we need to inquire a little further and ask why the universe has the shape it has. In cosmology, Einstein's general theory of relativity currently provides the framework for understanding cosmic structure. Matter (mass-energy) is said to bend spacetime and the resultant curvature to govern the accelerative motions of matter that were previously attributed to gravitational force.[63] As John Wheeler put it, "Spacetime tells matter how to move; matter tells spacetime how to curve."[64] Since matter bends spacetime, the shape of the universe is influenced by the density and distribution of matter. The question arises whether there is enough matter in the universe to bend spacetime into a "closed" type of geometry, such as the hypersphere (fig. 6.5). If not, the geometry will be "open," meaning endless expansion. Since the late 1990s, it has been thought that cosmic expansion is accelerating, driven by a mysterious "dark energy." The acceleration points to an open geometry but does not rule out a closed one, for conditions could change in the long-term evolution of the universe, and physics is open to revision in the light of new observations and better theory.

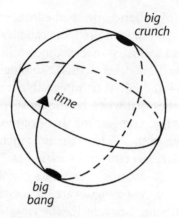

Figure 6.5   Big Bang to Big Crunch: the universe as the spacetime surface of a hypersphere (just one spatial dimension shown).

Matter influences cosmic shape by "bending" spacetime. But *why* is there this association between mass-energy distribution and spacetime curvature? The question is more metaphysical than physical at present: it is not addressed by the general theory of relativity, and the answer will depend on what matter, spacetime, and spacetime curvature are understood to be. In monadological metaphysics, matter boils down to the representation of groups of monads in a monad, and spacetime and its curvature would most likely be understood relationally, following the Leibnizian critique of Newtonian absolute space and time.[65] Space and time do not exist in themselves but are, respectively, the order of coexistences and the order of successions. However, considered *internally* to a monad, spacetime can be equated with the monad's perceptual field or "space" in which other monads are represented. To explain the bending of spacetime by matter, then, we would have to understand the way in which the structure of a monad's perceptual field depends on the monad's representation of other monads as bodies in motion. I shall have a little more to say about this in chapter 8, when I take a look at monadology and physics. But at present, the relevant point is that the shape of the soul, as the shape of the universe, depends on the soul's representation within itself of other souls. The shape of the soul is a communal affair.

7

Worlds Within Worlds

> In a single atom
> They see all worlds;
> If sentient beings should hear of this,
> They'd go mad in confusion.
>
> —*Avataṃsaka Sūtra*

IT WOULD BE ENCOURAGING at this point if I were able to furnish the reader with accounts of mystical experiences that lend support to the highly speculative ideas introduced in the previous chapter. There I outlined a revised form of Leibnizian monadology that takes perceptual perspectives to be the basic units of the world. But how extensive and convincing is the experiential support for a universe organized along such lines, a world of minds that represent one another in their entirety and constitute the ultimate basis of matter?

There are plenty of contemporary mystical accounts that describe features compatible with a universe so organized, such as expansive perceptions, all-inclusive knowledge, and interconnectedness, but there are not so many that plainly describe the signature characteristics of monadological organization. If mystical experiences really do give access to a universe of the kind sketched in the previous chapter, then we would expect them to reveal telltale signs of monadological representation, that is, "minds within the mind," "worlds within worlds," and "world as particle." A few modern accounts do describe such features. My own experience is a case in point: it seemed to disclose an all-encompassing mind that included within itself minds that were equally encompassing. This minds-within-the-mind discovery could also be construed as a worlds-within-the-world discovery, since the mind in question had the world as its contents. Mind and world—knower and known—are not experienced as distinct at this level, and so representation of the mind within itself is also representation of the world within itself.

In the course of my research into mystical experience, I have not come across many contemporary accounts that clearly describe the telltale signs. Why should this be? Two explanations come to mind. First, the monadological approach is misguided and will not be supported by the evidence. Second, the approach is sound, but evidence will be in short supply for some reason, perhaps because it is very difficult to enter the requisite state of consciousness or to remember and describe what has been experienced there. Support for the second explanation comes from experiences that seem to head toward a monadological insight but do not quite get there, offering only a glimpse of monadic organization or just a symbolic representation of it. It may be felt that progress to deeper insight is hindered by some obstruction, one that may take the form of a guardian at the threshold, like the custodian at the Sun Door we met in chapter 4, the deity who guards the way to the afterlife realms of true knowledge and liberation, and who is perhaps none other than one's own divine double. At its simplest, this "guardian" manifests as an anxiety or a warning that further progress will bring death, whether understood figuratively or literally—this is the "point of no return" mentioned in some near-death and mystical accounts. Interestingly, when the guardian is perceived, it may have attributes reminiscent of the revelation it guards, experienced as a bright luminosity or as a being with many eyes. By definition, monads are all-perceiving, interreflecting units of perception, and so a universe of monads is fittingly symbolized as a being with a multiplicity of coordinated eyes.

Although I have not come across many unambiguous, contemporary accounts of direct relevance, some historical texts informed by mystical and contemplative experiences are of considerable interest. Indeed, highpoints of both Greek and Buddhist philosophy in the first millennium CE incorporate experiential insights suggestive of monadological organization. The Plotinian account of the intelligible universe, which most likely acted as one source of inspiration for Leibniz's system, has already been described in the previous chapter,[1] and from roughly the same era there is the interpenetrating cosmos portrayed at length in the Buddhist *Avataṃsaka Sūtra*, later given philosophical systematization by the Chinese Huayan school, and influential in Korea and Japan. Advanced meditators are said to perceive the world as the omniscient Buddha perceives it, with the smallest particles found to contain the entire system of worlds. The authors of the Sutra were well aware that ordinary folk would be confounded by the idea of "worlds within particles," and the story goes that when the Buddha preached the *Avataṃsaka* teachings after his awakening the audience was largely baffled by his uncompromising depiction of reality.[2] But the visionary cosmology of the *Avataṃsaka Sūtra*, including its descriptions of the entire universe within the smallest particle, makes perfect sense in a monadological framework. Another historical example of great interest is the interreflective "souls-within-the-soul" experience of Leibniz's older contemporary, Thomas Traherne, who was so overwhelmed by the discovery of his own all-encompassing, mirror-like soul—the restored divine Image—that he could think, speak, and write of nothing else for two weeks.

The God with a Thousand Eyes

A number of contemporary accounts point toward monadological organization of experience, although there is often insufficient detail for conclusions to be drawn. For example, one account of psychedelic experience describes what seems to be a transformation of the agglomerated minute perceptions of ordinary, sensory experience (what Leibniz called *petites perceptions*) into clear, highly detailed perception, as well as a hint of the "cosmic relativity" of perspectives:

> The dominant impression was that of entering into the very marrow of existence. . . . It was as if each of the billion atoms of experience which under normal circumstances are summarized and averaged into crude, indiscriminate wholesale impressions was now being seen and savored for itself. The other clear sense was that of cosmic relativity. Perhaps all experience never gets summarized in any inclusive overview. Perhaps all there is, is this everlasting congeries of an infinite number of discrete points of view, each summarizing the whole from its perspective.[3]

Other experiences have also pointed to multiple centers of perception. For example, a couple of accounts raised in previous chapters are relevant here. The experience of Flora Courtois (chapter 1) brought knowledge that the universe has multiple centers: "Feeling myself centered as never before, at the same time I knew the whole universe to be centered at every point."[4] The statement is too concise for its meaning to be clear. However, it is the case that a universe structured along monadological lines will have a multiplicity of centers, the primary center from which a monad's perceptual contents are organized and the numerous secondary centers of perception that it represents within itself.

In Rosalind Heywood's account of mescaline experience (chapter 4), there is mention of "focuses of consciousness" or, as she also calls them, "eyes." Perhaps these are related to the "pearls" of the Divine Mother that Heywood also mentions, whose appearance on the scene when Heywood posed the "magic" question was to transmute the cosmic experience from the impersonality of intellect to the gaiety of love:

> I got far enough "in" — that is the only word I can use — to feel that I was in contact with aspects of the universe — focuses of consciousness — I don't know what words to use — so that it wasn't a matter of *my* knowing *them*. One was entirely swamped by their transcendency.[5]

Heywood was not permitted to remain for long in the condition, but she managed to have a little glimpse of how the world looks from the perspective of the transcendent "eyes" or foci of consciousness:

> I was not allowed to continue looking "up" at the transcendent — what shall I call them — entities? (Yet they were all-pervasive). Well, in each case they switched me round to face away from them, so that I could look "out" at the universe with a minute fraction of their eyes. It was astounding to look "out" with a compassion and understanding utterly beyond one's own capacity. One can't hold the attitude, of course. But one can faintly, *very* faintly, remember it, or rather an echo of it.[6]

Heywood was permitted only the briefest glimpse of the paradoxically all-pervasive yet focal centers of consciousness, but she was given some slight indication of how these entities perceive the universe, with compassionate love and understanding. It is also of interest that the world she perceived was in some sense spherical: "Such words as here or there, far or near, up or down, then or now, were simply not applicable in a world where everything seemed to be in a sphere – a non-spatial one."[7]

Heywood's experience had been triggered by a psychedelic drug, and it does seem to be the case that experiences induced by drugs are rather prone to the restrictions on progress to deeper insight that Heywood reports.[8] Drugs can be a quick route to profound levels of consciousness; indeed, they are likely to be too swift, plunging delicate, unprepared egos into overwhelming experiences. It can therefore be conjectured that the barrier to further development that sometimes intervenes in drug-induced cases is ego-protective, averting exposure to revelations of distressing and potentially destructive intensity. There is also the possibility that the barrier intervenes because the revelations are undeserved. The "storming of heaven," whether deliberate or accidental, is rebuffed. Entry has to be earned.

Whatever the case, there are a few accounts of drug-induced experience that describe the intervention of an obstructing factor before or during an encounter with a multitude of eyes. Toward the end of a protracted out-of-body experience stimulated by the smoking of cannabis, Susan Blackmore felt her body was progressively expanding to encompass the Earth, moon, solar system, galaxies and finally the entire universe, which seemed four-dimensional and spherical (compare with David Spangler's "out-of-body" expansion noted in chapter 1).[9] When she strained to reach beyond the universal boundary, the experience became "religious" in character, no longer simply an out-of-body experience. Her efforts to reach a higher vantage point, to ascend between what seemed to be two white, shining cliffs, were met with great resistance, as if she were "swimming against a current."[10]

But some progress was made, and it was as if a new "set of dimensions" were opening up to her. At the top, she caught the briefest glimpse of what were "either hundreds of eyes, or one huge eye, staring at me from every direction at once," but without seeming to take any notice of her. Yet Blackmore also reports that she had the feeling that from this newfound place her "little struggles were being kindly and laughingly watched."[11] Again, the multifocal, omnidirectional character of the glimpse, presumably experienced here in symbolic guise, is compatible with a monadological organization of perception, as is Blackmore's uncertainty over the multiplicity or unicity of the "eyes," which were many or one, perhaps like the bewildering Sīmurgh noted in chapter 6, the being who is equally many and one.

David Luke has also described an encounter with many eyes at the threshold of greater revelations. In the course of his experiments with the psychedelic drug DMT (N,N-dimethyltryptamine), Luke gained the impression that he was "intruding upon a cosmic gathering" to which he had not been invited.[12] In a final session with the drug, the impression was powerfully reinforced:

> I found myself breaking through the veil like a gatecrasher into a party of swirling, smiling eyeballs all attached to snake bodies, which were as startled to see me as I was to be there. The whole ordered assortment of eyes and snakes acted as one being. In the brief moment before it reacted to my arrival, I managed to catch a glimpse over what might loosely be described as "the shoulder" of this strange entity and instantly realized that I had seen something I should not have—a brief glance at the truly forbidden.[13]

The creature's eyes blocked any further view beyond the entity, and for the remainder of the trip Luke was hypnotized into a state of passive submission. After the experience, he was unable to remember what he had glimpsed, except that it was "both ineffable and highly illegal for mortal minds."[14] It is notable that the eye-snakes, although multiple, were coordinated, acting as one creature, which once again points to a unity in multiplicity, a being that is many yet one. Luke raises other accounts in which multiple eyes are described, and he points out several parallels in the religious literature, including the cherubim of Ezekiel's vision and the fierce, ever-vigilant protector deity Za Rahula of Tibetan Buddhism. One of these accounts quoted by Luke describes another many-eyed guardian of the threshold. Again, the experience took place under the influence of DMT. The guardian is appropriately styled "it/they," a One-Many:

> I noticed what seemed to be an opening into a larger space, like looking through a cave opening to a starry sky. As I approached this I saw that resting in the opening was a large creature, with many arms, somewhat like an octopus, and all over the arms were eyes, mostly closed, as if the creature were asleep or slumbering. As I approached it the eyes opened, and it/they became aware of me. It did not seem especially well-disposed toward me, as if it did not wish to be bothered by a mere human, and I had the impression I wasn't going to get past it, so I did not try.[15]

What do the many-eyed sentinels guard? Luke makes a connection between these beings and the guardians who oversee entry into *the realm of the dead*, and I think there is good reason for him to do so. A revealing case in point is the dragon Ladon, endowed with a hundred heads (and therefore with numerous eyes), who in Greek myth guards the tree of golden apples in the garden of the Hesperides, situated in the far west, where the sun sets each evening. This location unequivocally places the all-seeing guardian at the Sun Door, the entrance to the afterlife, pointing to a connection between the guardian and the luminous realm of liberation approached in the soul's death journey and in the flight of the shaman or yogin.

Ananda Coomaraswamy, in his essay "Le corps parsemé d'yeux," contends that divine beings associated with multiple eyes, such as Argos, Puruṣa, Indra, Varuṇa, Mitra, Horus, and Christ, are solar in nature.[16] The Sun God is thousand-eyed because it is thousand-rayed: in primitive understandings of vision, a ray implies an eye from which the ray is emitted, and so many rays imply many eyes. Shining forth its rays everywhere, the solar divinity has many eyes, seeing all, knowing all. We have noted before that it is the

Sun God who guards the portal of death and liberating knowledge, and so it makes mythological sense that a brightly shining or many-eyed sentinel should be found stationed at the threshold. It also makes monadological sense if the sentinel is taken to be representative of the reality it guards, a luminous world of multiple, harmonized, total perceptions, a universe of mutually perceiving "eyes." And we have seen that the way to win over this potentially intimidating sentinel is to shed limited self-identifications and rigidly dualistic consciousness, thereby recognizing that the sentinel and the reality it guards are none other than one's own deeper nature, one's higher identity and divine double: "Who are you?"—"I am you."

Journeys to the Edge

Susan Blackmore's journey to the edge of the universe is similar in some respects to other modern-day "celestial flight" experiences. Blackmore, we have noted, felt her body expand to encompass the universe, and, straining to go further, she caught a glimpse of an eye that was many or one. Colin Hannaford also describes a celestial journey and a meeting at the threshold. In a moment of emotional crisis, Hannaford knelt down and asked for help. He immediately lost contact with his mundane surroundings and felt propelled with increasing velocity out of the solar system and through galaxies. The flight came to an end in darkness, in a void state, as if he had reached a boundary or threshold. Slowly, Hannaford became aware of a vast presence that was familiar to him but which he found difficult to describe: "simultaneously it was expanding from a centre which was discrete and distant, and yet it was also all around. . . . It had a vastness and a centrality."[17] Once again, the being encountered at the threshold has a paradoxical quality: it has a single, discrete center, yet is pervasive too, "all around."

The presence made itself known to be a kindred being, bringing with it a feeling of strong, tender love and comradeship. It asked Hannaford what he wanted. Desperate to know what to do, Hannaford received the response, "BE HONEST," and he found himself back in his room. Initially Hannaford had thought that, unlike the celestial leg of the journey, the encounter at the threshold had not involved visual impressions, but he came to understand otherwise:

> But slowly I realised that my memory did contain a definite impression. I think now it had been there continually; but was so strange and uninformative that I had not noticed it – or I had even refused to notice it.

Indeed, I could make no sense of it then as I examined it. I rejected it and sought again for something that would make sense. But all of this was to no avail. . . . What I saw was an intensely black sphere, neither radiating nor reflecting light; not completely free, but as if a third enclosed from the base in the darker background apparently of space itself.[18]

This reminds me a little of my own reaction to the tiny but all-inclusive "rings" I saw embedded in the board of light: those beings seemed so out of my range of comprehension that I passed over them for several years.

Significantly, Hannaford does not insist that his flight through the solar system and galaxies was a genuine celestial journey: he appreciates that it might have been a journey "out of the picture that we have of the universe," an "allegorical" rather than a real trip through the heavens.[19] Blackmore had a similar suspicion: she had come to encompass the "Universe as my limited understanding of cosmology would have it – though I may be wrong there."[20] Hannaford and Blackmore were right to be cautious about the literal "reality" of their journeys, for the astronomical contents of celestial journeys tend to reflect the prevailing cosmological models, whether the ancient concentric planetary spheres (e.g., Cicero's *Dream of Scipio*) or the modern-day galaxies, Big Bangs, and latest multiverse scenarios.[21]

They can also include improbable events that are best understood symbolically, as I myself can attest. On one occasion, a few months after my mystical experience, I had an out-of-body/lucid dream in which I ranged over the Earth and shot up into the starry heavens. However, I was not left with the impression that I had really traveled anywhere. For one thing, some contents were obviously symbolic. At one stage, perhaps on Earth but more likely on a distant planet, I came across dinosaur-like creatures in a desolate landscape, and, having transformed into an eagle, I became involved in a life-or-death struggle with an aquatic reptile, very much like a plesiosaur in appearance. As the eagle, I strained to lift the reptile by its long, snake-like neck out of a pool of water, with the intention of decapitating it. The scene had a mythic quality, and the eagle–serpent battle is indeed a common mythological motif.[22]

The upshot seems to be that celestial journeys of this kind, although imaginal, may yet include deeply meaningful symbolic contents, and so should not be dismissed as mere dream or fantasy, for the imaginal has a truth of its own. Moreover, celestial "flights of the soul" are possibly analogous to the classic "passage through the tunnel" that can occur in the early stages of near-death experience. The unadorned experience of rapid motion through darkness can be enriched symbolically as a flight through celestial regions to a reality beyond the everyday universe. I would put my own night sea journey in the same category—rapid transition through a dark scene toward an "other-worldly realm," although one that turned out to be this-worldly. In my case, the imaginal phase came before and during the flight, in the form of the beach scene and the sea journey, whereas in some cases the imagery continues beyond or commences at the end of the flight, the passage through the luminosity at the tunnel end giving way to dreamlike images.

The following two examples of "flight" to a reality beyond the familiar universe took place in near-death circumstances. The first is the widely publicized case of neurosurgeon Eben Alexander, who in late 2008 fell into a coma as a result of bacterial meningitis. Alexander's flight may not have included a celestial leg in the manner of Blackmore's and Hannaford's, but it was certainly more than a simple passage through a dark tunnel.[23] At first, he was unaware of who or what he was, experiencing himself as a center of awareness in a murky, red-brown environment, as if buried in mud and roots, and he remained ignorant of his human identity throughout the entirety of his near-death experience. The next phase began when he flew through a luminous opening into a beautiful landscape. In this "Gateway" phase, Alexander found himself to be a disembodied speck on the wing of a butterfly, one of many butterflies passing along an idyllic valley, with fields, streams, waterfalls, flowers, trees, adults, children, and even dogs. He was accompanied by a beautiful girl, a "guardian angel" dressed in simple clothing, who reassured him that he was loved and had nothing to fear.

Not unlike the conclusion to Hannaford's celestial journey, Alexander's flight ended in an infinite black void "outside of the entire physical universe,"[24] where he became conscious of two distinct presences, the loving creator God and a mediating orb of light that illuminated the darkness. Alexander thinks the orb was connected with (and may even have been) the girl who had accompanied him on the butterfly wing, a girl he was later to identify as his deceased sister. In this "Core" phase of the experience, the void entities conveyed "lessons," which included the centrality of love in all the many universes that exist.[25] The lessons would often involve Alexander becoming what he was viewing, including the luminous orb and indeed the entire universe, a unitive tendency that gives his experience a mystical feel in places. The Core phase seemed to bring much cosmic knowledge, but Alexander has struggled to "unpack" it since his return to mundane consciousness,[26] and it is therefore not possible to gauge whether he was privy to specifically monadological insights. There is no detailed description of cosmic or microphysical structures in Alexander's book *Proof of Heaven*, but elsewhere he has described the "higher-dimensional multiverse" as a "big, very complex, corrugated ball," with time "wrapped up very tightly deep inside of the loop or point."[27]

The second case of near-death experience to be noted here did involve a celestial flight and provides more structural detail. I came across it on the Internet and have not investigated its provenance in any detail, although it does have a ring of authenticity. The account, attributed to Mark A. Horton, is rich in detail and should be studied in its entirety, but it is of particular interest to us here for its description of a spherical universes-within-universes structure.[28] Dangerously ill and comatose in hospital on New Year's Eve 1992, Horton experienced a blazing light and was lifted up high, becoming "pure intellect." In this new condition, he could travel wherever he wished and eventually found himself moving away from the Earth, solar system, star systems, and galaxy. Relaxing further, Horton experienced an explosion of love, knowledge, and unity, the celestial flight taking a decidedly mystical turn. His intellect encompassed everything, including past and future, and the love was overwhelming. The journey continued, with several celestial features observed, such as colliding galaxies and holes in space that were not really holes, for they were filled with something, a feature Horton could not properly understand. The spherical shape of the universe soon became apparent: "I began to discern a curvature to the scene before me and realized that the universe was really a large sphere containing all the galaxies. It became more and more apparent as I moved (still backwards) into the 'darkspace' beyond the sphere of galaxies."[29]

After slowing down and passing through a barrier, Horton was able to observe the sphere around the universe, finding it to be "at once transparent and slightly opaque." But the journey had not yet come to an end:

> I was still moving outward and could now make out around the shrinking curvature of our universe, other spheres which could only be other universes. These seemed to be arranged in some sort of order, a spherical shell of universes around a core that I could not see. And beyond this shell, another, towards which I was now speeding. The overall impression I'm left with is of something like those little carved "spheres within spheres" of ivory that one used to see in import shops.[30]

Pulled back to his body in the hospital bed, Horton felt great loss at the disappearance of the love, knowledge, and unity. At first, memories of the experience were suppressed, but they came back after a year had passed.

Horton understood the spheres outside the spherical universe to be other universes and found that these spheres were themselves arranged on a sphere. There were, in effect, both many spheres and one big sphere out-side the universe. This structure seems to have been repeated in some way at ever-increasing scales, creating a "Russian Doll" effect.[31] But it should be noted that Horton's spheres were just universes, with no suggestion that they were also monadic units of perception and the basic units of matter. And while Horton seems to describe universes within universes, this is also not clearly monadological because Horton does not indicate that the spherical universes were representations of one another. They seem to be universes completely unrelated to our own, whereas in a monadological scheme they could be representations of our own universe.

The following is perhaps a comparable experience, for it also brought unending repetition of spheres within spheres, arranged around a center. The experience was described by "a successful executive in his early fifties" who took part in the psychedelic research conducted by Jean Houston and Robert Masters:

> I experienced a shattering thunderbolt of ecstacy and my body dissolved into the flow of matter or energy of which the universe is made. I was swept into the core of existence from which all things arise and into which all things converge. Here there is no distinction between subject and object, space and time, or anything else. Here everything simply *is* and there is no beginning and no ending—only becoming. . . .
>
> In form, the ultimate reality seemed at times to have four corners, but this may have been a transitional stage of vision prior to reaching the center. I recall describing the core as a sphere composed of an infinite number of small spheres revolving in a spiral toward a center which itself is infinite, and that each of the small spheres is composed of still smaller spheres also revolving toward an infinite center and so on. How this concept came to me I do not know, as I do not have a clear recollection of such an image. It may be that at the ultimate point one is within the core and can no longer observe.[32]

But there is no suggestion here that the fractal-like spheres-within-spheres were universes-within-universes, as they were in Horton's account, and it is unclear whether it was our world that was observed to have this repeating structure or some other realm at or near the core of reality.

Finally, let us note an experience described by Martin Israel. It differs from Horton's in several ways, for it was not a near-death experience, and there was no visual experience of flight through the universe, although there was a feeling of ascent. Nevertheless, the case is relevant because in the period leading up to the experience, Israel had been concerned with the problem of the extent of the universe and whether anything existed outside it. If there were a reality greater than the universe, what would it be like and would it enclose the world?[33] These concerns with the limits of the familiar universe, and its relation spatial or otherwise to a greater reality, were to be answered by the experience.[34] At the time, Israel was a sixteen-year-old schoolboy. He had returned home, upset by a disappointing exam result, and had retired to bed. Listening to the overture of Weber's opera *Oberon* on the radio, Israel noticed a change of perception—the music became "blurred and indistinct" and an "iridescent radiance" filled and obliterated the room.[35] He felt he was being drawn up by a beneficent, luminous power into "the realm of eternal life":

> I was no longer in the universe at all, but in the realm of eternal life which is neither past nor future but only ever-living present. I had been lifted to a height above all measurable heights. I was able, in this situation, to perceive the entire created world, for I was outside it.[36]

From this exalted vantage point, suffering and death were seen in context, conferring upon Israel an optimistic perspective on the struggles and tragedies of life (see chapter 11). However, the point of interest to us here is the semblance of the universe that was presented to him:

> The entire created universe was shown to me symbolically as a gigantic sphere whose movement was discernible as a minute turn of a wheel, but this movement encompassed countless generations of human beings over a vast time-scale.[37]

Once again, the universe perceived from the outside was found to be spherical, if only in symbolic form.

Worlds in a Grain of Sand

The above examples, with their miscellaneous references to multiple centers of perception, coordinated eyes, spherical universes, and endless repetitions of spheres within spheres, are certainly intriguing, but they hardly qualify as solid, experiential support for a universe organized along monadological lines. The finer details of monadological structure are not overtly described, and so the experiences cannot be regarded as specifically monadological.

However, some accounts do go further. Perhaps the best modern example that I have come across is Bernard Roseman's worlds-within-the-world vision at a Navajo peyote ceremony. As the drug took effect, Roseman lost contact with his surroundings, and an obscuring velvet curtain opened to reveal parts that contain the whole:

> All about were the most perfect cogs, too perfect to be known in my everyday world. These cogs were spinning in opposing directions to one another, with no other purpose than BEING. The universe was enclosed in a huge round dome and contained millions of replicas of the same world, each representing a different plane of consciousness. These worlds were forever missing each other by inches; and as I mentally moved them up a degree where they met and formed the one complete world, the state of PERFECT ORDER BECAME. I laughed at my former prejudices and what I had considered sin in myself and others. I saw all this as being my own manifestations, and only because I considered it sin had made it so.
>
> I was living in a timeless pulsation that bridged the gap between all barriers. I reached many eternities, and felt akin with infinity. At long last I knew the relation all things had for one another!
>
> All objects seemed to be complete in themselves; as I searched the depth of an object I would see many worlds buried in it. And as I examined each world, I saw that each had objects of its own which were seen as worlds and objects endlessly.[38]

As the experience drew to a close, the "velvet curtain of confusion" reasserted itself, and Roseman found himself once again a "victim of sense objects and emotions."[39] In the above description, it is made clear that the little worlds are replicas of the full-size universe enclosed in the "huge round dome," and they are understood to be individual "planes of consciousness," which gives the account a monadological feel.

A rather different case of interest is cited by Pearl Hawkins in her book *Dr Bucke Revisited*, this time unconnected with mind-altering drugs.[40] A woman ("MG") had been going through a very difficult patch, and now recovered she was grieving one night for those hurt by recent events. She felt a love toward them, and the love became more inclusive, extending to all people, and she fell asleep weeping. Then, in the morning, MG woke up and felt peculiarly well. Morning light was shining through the window onto a table near her bed, illuminating glasses on a tray. The glasses were seen to emit particles of light that "were conscious and joyful, and somehow singing."[41] Each dancing particle was found to include all the others: "to contain in itself all other lights and also the source of all of them."[42] When MG looked out of the window, the same effect greeted her: everything was made of the conscious, luminous particles. The experience then took a more clearly mystical turn, with feelings of joy, timelessness, love, unity, complete understanding, and a sense of coming home. The particles of light were no longer in view, but the "implication of their consciousness, joy and constant renewal were all there."[43]

In the present context, the experience is of interest because it seems to have disclosed material constituents that were centers of consciousness *and* which contained one another. In a monadological approach, matter consists of representations of monads, and so in a monadic universe we would indeed expect the ultimate constituents of matter to be centers of consciousness. Furthermore, in the revised monadology introduced in the previous chapter, these centers are complete representations of the universe and so they would include within themselves all other centers: each particle contains all the others. MG commented that she later found connections with modern particle physics. It is possible that she had come across Fritjof Capra's *The Tao of Physics*, which describes the old S-matrix "bootstrap" theory of subatomic particles (superseded by the quark model). Capra explains: "In the hadron bootstrap, all particles are dynamically composed of one another in a self-consistent way, and in that sense can be said to 'contain' one another."[44] But MG's description of her experience is not simply a duplication of Capra's wording: she goes further by stating that each light contained not only all the other lights but also the *source* of all the lights.

MG's experience is a little reminiscent of William Blake's vision on the sands at Felpham in the early 1800s. Here he had a vision of conscious, luminous particles:

> In particles bright
> The jewels of Light . . .
> I each particle gazed,
> Astonish'd, Amazed;
> For each was a Man
> Human-form'd.[45]

In Blake's Swedenborg-tinted understanding, the particles of light are anthropomorphized and constitute the "One Man," the "Divine Humanity" or "Jesus," a community of beings seen from afar as one person. They "reflect each in each," so in effect the community of Minute Particulars is present in each Particular.[46]

Blake's most celebrated lines on the Minute Particulars are, of course, those in *Auguries of Innocence*:

> To see a World in a Grain of Sand
> And a Heaven in a Wild Flower,
> Hold Infinity in the palm of your hand
> And Eternity in an hour.[47]

Further afield, "worlds within worlds" appear in Indian philosophy. An intriguing example is the *Yogavāsiṣṭha*, a work now identified as a version of the *Mokṣopāya* (Kashmir region, tenth century CE), adapted to fit an Advaita-Vedāntic worldview but originally, it would seem, a text with its own distinctive viewpoint, drawing on but critical of other traditions.[48] Taking consciousness alone to be real, the *Yogavāsiṣṭha* endlessly asserts the illusory, dreamlike, nonexistent nature of the world, making the assumption that to be a product of mind is to be unreal (unwarranted in my opinion—see chapter 11). It is explained that the world is in the soul in the manner of a dream, and that the atoms of this dreamworld themselves contain dreamworlds. The world that exists in the mind contains other minds, and these minds contain their own worlds, and so on:

> Multitudes of worlds are contained in a grain of the brain of the mind; as the long leaves of the plantain tree are contained in one of its minute seeds. All the three worlds are contained in an atom as the intellect, in the same manner as great cities are seen in a dream; and all the particles of intellect within the mind have each the representation of a world in it.[49]

> Each world has its people, and all peoples have their minds. Again each mind has a world in it, and every world has its people also.[50]

B. L. Atreya, an early twentieth-century scholar of the *Yogavāsiṣṭha* (and parapsychologist who contributed to research into past-life memories), saw in its philosophy an anticipation of western idealisms and understood the "worlds within worlds" to follow from intersubjective representation, which makes the scheme sound rather Leibnizian.[51] My soul's dreamworld represents in itself the dreamworlds of others within it: "In this way, in every universe are contained millions of other universes, and this process goes on *ad infinitum*."[52] But these dreamworlds can vary greatly, and so the scheme is not properly monadological, lacking the full objectivity that comes from monadic expression of a common universe.

However, for the most striking, extensive, and elaborate references to worlds within worlds and particles, it is necessary to turn to the great sutras of Mahāyāna Buddhism, with their oceans upon oceans of beings and worlds, characterized by all-pervading luminosity, knowledge, and compassionate activity. More specifically, the voluminous compilation of texts commonly known as the *Avataṃsaka Sūtra* or *Flower Ornament Scripture*—of Indian origin but preserved in full only in translation (China, from fifth century CE; Tibet, ninth century CE)—is unparalleled for the sheer vastness of its cosmological sweep and descriptions of "worlds within worlds." In passages of visionary cosmology, the texts set out a universe of many world-systems. The smallest particles in these systems contain infinite oceans of worlds yet retain their distinctness. Webs of light, containing all lands and the countless Buddhas and bodhisattvas, extend throughout each world-system, and in each world-system the entire universe and all the Buddhas and bodhisattvas are to be found.

Numberless lands exist in a point the size of a hair-tip, yet these lands exist together without impinging on one another or causing the point to expand. The lands in a particle are themselves constituted of particles, but "the atoms in these lands are even harder to tell of." [53] Each particle contains all particles, for each particle contains all world-systems and their particles. Several analogies were used to convey this multiplication of worlds, particles, and Buddhas. One is the Jeweled Net of Indra: each gem in the net is distinct yet displays within itself reflections of the entire net, the individual gems, and all the reflections displayed in each gem. [54] Another is the Tower of Vairocana's Adornments (see Box, "As measureless as the sky"), described in the final chapter of the *Avataṃsaka Sūtra*, "Entry into the Realm of Reality," which circulated in its own right as the *Gaṇḍavyūha Sūtra*, composed some time during the first three or four centuries CE.

Multiple mirrors can be arranged to give an impression of the interpenetration of things. It is said that Fazang (643–712 CE), a patriarch of the Huayan tradition of Chinese Buddhism (Jpn., Kegon; Kor., Hwaŏm), which took the *Avataṃsaka Sūtra* as its chief scriptural source, employed mirrors to illustrate the philosophy to the female emperor Wu Zetian. The story goes that a room was lined with mirrors on the four walls, ceiling, floor, and corners, and a figure of the Buddha and a torch to illuminate it were positioned at the center. The interreflection of mirrors and the multiplication of Buddha images demonstrated the principles of "one in all" and "all in one." To illustrate how the small contains the large without obstruction, Fazang produced a crystal ball: in this, all the mirrors and their reflections were seen imaged. Fazang explained that the unobstructed interpenetration of spaces

❧ As measureless as the sky ❧

The *Gaṇḍavyūha Sūtra* details the journey to enlightenment of the young pilgrim Sudhana as he visits diverse spiritual guides, fifty-three in number. Toward the end of his quest, Sudhana questions Maitreya, the future Buddha, about the bodhisattva path, and Maitreya advises him to enter his abode. At the snap of Maitreya's fingers, the door to the tower opens, and Sudhana is allowed in. There, astonished, the youth beholds its enormous interior, far larger than its exterior appearance would suggest: "immensely vast and wide, hundreds of thousands of leagues wide, as measureless as the sky, as vast as all space, adorned with countless attributes."[55] The tower represents the visionary cosmos of the *Avataṃsaka* literature, the *dharmadhātu*, realm of the dharmas, the world as it is experienced by a Buddha. Here each thing contains every thing, without compromising its own distinctness or the distinctness of other things. Sudhana's entry into the tower represents the opening of the mind to unhindered vision and blissful experience of the *dharmadhātu*. The tower, as vast as the universe, contains within itself similar towers, equally vast, and each tower is reflected in the objects in every tower, yet the towers remain distinct. Sudhana sees himself too in all the towers, endlessly multiplied throughout.

The Buddha whose adornments fill the great tower is Vairocana, "the illuminator," "the resplendent one," the sunlike cosmic Buddha of whom the innumerable Buddhas in the *dharmadhātu* are emanations. Thus, to become a Buddha is to see oneself as Vairocana. In esoteric Buddhism, Mahāvairocana, "the great illuminator" (Jpn., Dainichi Nyorai, "the Great Sun Buddha") is the universe and its source, immanent in all things yet their transcendent ground too. Buddhist art sometimes shows Vairocana's cosmic body decorated with sun and moon, or radiating a nimbus of oceans.[56] The cosmic magnitude of Vairocana's manifestation is conveyed too by architectural and statuary immensities. The *stūpa* at Borobudur in Java, the largest Buddhist temple in the world, is a cosmic mandala that includes scenes from Sudhana's journey. And modern-day pilgrims who visit Nara, one-time capital of Japan, will likely join the throng of tourists, school parties, and sacred deer on the way to Tōdaiji temple. Passing through the Great Southern Gate, they will first pay their respects to the fearsome guardians housed inside. Then, in the Great Buddha Hall, the largest wooden building in the world, they will come face to face with a colossal statue of Vairocana, fifteen meters tall, seated on a lotus pedestal engraved with images of the Lotus Repository World.[57]

is easily demonstrated in this manner, but the unobstructed interpenetration of times is much harder to show. All things are mutually implicated, however remote they may be from one another in time as well as in space.

Sole Heirs to the Universe

A few years before Leibniz took his first steps toward a philosophy of monads in the 1670s, the experiential discovery of all-inclusive soul perception was expressed at length by the Anglican churchman, mystic, and poet Thomas Traherne.[58] His thinking has a monadological feel because it describes a universe of all-inclusive, interreflecting souls, but it is not properly monadological because it has no perceptual theory of material constitution. Traherne's atoms or "physical monads" are just dimensionless points, infinitely small, unchanging, mobile, passive units of matter that go to make up extended bodies.[59] In their materiality and passivity, Traherne's atoms are not so different from the atoms hypothesized by mechanical philosophers of the period, influenced by the revival of Democritean and Epicurean atomisms.[60] By contrast, Leibniz's "true atoms of nature" are perceptual and appetitive, and matter consists of perceptual representations of configurations of monads. While Traherne drew analogies between atoms and souls, and understood both to be points at which God is wholly present (and therefore infinite and all-embracing in their own ways), he did not go so far as to identify his material point-atoms with his spiritual soul-centers.[61]

Nevertheless, Traherne's characteristic doctrine of "sole heirdom" does portray a structuring of experience highly reminiscent of monadology. Traherne's souls, solitary yet highly communal, are reminiscent of Leibniz's monads, windowless yet interreflecting and mutually representative. The impetus behind Traherne's thinking is undoubtedly his own experience, but he explained and elaborated his insights with ideas available to him, principally Christian, Platonic, Aristotelian, and Hermetic, an intellectual background that he shared with Leibniz. Traherne believed that God had given him the task of showing "Immortal Souls the way to Heaven" (SM III.83),[62] and a greater part of the truth he hoped to convey in order to fulfill his mission was the knowledge that "the world is ours" (CM II.3).[63] More precisely, he insists that each one of us *individually* possesses God's Kingdom and its innumerable objects. There could be no greater act of love than to help others really know this truth. Traherne's message hinges on an exalted notion of the soul's "inheritance," which is the divine Image. To recover this inheritance—to become a "Possessor of the Whole World" (CM I.3)—is to achieve an unimaginably glorious end, which is to live in communion with God and all souls, and thereby enjoy the heights of felicity and love.

Notions of common possession are standard fare in Christianity, going back to the communal practices of sharing goods and the Pauline promise of the heavenly inheritance through resurrection in Christ. The New Testament contains several references to heirdom that later writers would find mystically pregnant: each one of us is an "Heir of the World" (Romans 4.13), a "Coheir with Christ" (Romans 8.17) and an inheritor of "all things" (Revelations 21.7). In Traherne's mystical reading, the inheritance follows from the soul's assimilation to God: we possess that which God possesses when we make ourselves like God, and so the Kingdom becomes ours too. But Traherne developed the idea in a way that made others question his sanity:

> Becaus it is a new Doctrine, and too great to be Believed, that a man upon Earth should be the Heir of All Things, not only in Heaven, but in Earth, in Ages, Kingdoms, Time and Eternitie: and som have been ready to Say to me, as Festus said to S. Paul, *Much Learning hath made thee mad.*[64]

Traherne's unsettling "new Doctrine" has several features that distinguish it from more conventional understandings of divine heirdom. First, Traherne is not willing to defer full inheritance to the post-resurrection state but regards it as attainable in the present life. Traherne knew from his own experience that even the infant is heir to God's Kingdom, and that although the infant's inheritance has been lost it can be recovered later in life. Meditations on the Kingdom of God afford not just glimpses of the life to come but also reveal the inheritance now in its full glory. Second, Traherne claims that the inheritance includes all things, not only the heavenly world to come but also the world we currently know. In fact, our world is a part of the spiritual Kingdom, and heaven is a *state* not a *place*, available here and now.[65] Third, Traherne makes the paradoxical assertion that we are all *sole* inheritors, a claim that contributes to the monadological atmosphere of his thought. Fourth, Traherne supposes that self-concern and greed, customarily lambasted by moralists, aid recovery of the inheritance if properly directed.

Heaven Here and Now

In Christian thought, heaven is principally a feature of "eschatology," the doctrine of the end of things, except in so far as it is the current abode of the angels. For human beings, full membership of the heavenly community must wait until the time of the resurrection and the formation of the new heaven and the new earth. This is not to say that glimpses of heaven in the present life are impossible, and Christian eschatology can be of the "realized" type, if it supposed that the Kingdom has already been inaugurated by the life, death, and resurrection of Christ.

In Traherne's day, spiritual exercises were available that were intended to afford glimpses of heaven. "Divine meditation," consisting of sustained intellectual, imaginative, and devotional reflection on religious topics, underwent a revival in England at the beginning of the seventeenth century, aided in no small part by the efforts of Joseph Hall (1574–1656).[66] The topics deemed suitable for meditation were quite varied and could include the passion of Christ, scriptural passages, and daily events and observations. The spiritual world was also an object of divine meditation, and the aspects that were contemplated might include the life of the saints, the heavenly life to come, and the city of God.[67] Heavenly meditations were sometimes employed to underscore the rewards of leading a Christian life and to loosen the hold of worldly attractions. In an early work, *The Arte of Divine Meditation* (1606), Hall had illustrated the various meditative stages with a step-by-step meditation on the eternal life, the life of the saints, and in his old age, he devoted an entire volume to heavenly meditation. In *The Invisible World* (1652), Hall expressed a wish to share glimpses of heaven and its community of angels, saints, and glorified souls, little glimpses obtained "by often and serious meditation,"[68] hinting that he himself had obtained some small knowledge of heaven through contemplation. Hall felt that he was not yet ready for the vision of God and therefore limited his aspiration to a vision of the heavenly world.

Hall's meditation provides few surprises: blessed souls live in a luminous heaven, enjoying sanctity, charity, knowledge, joy, entire union, and felicity. "All shine alike in their essential glory," but show the Augustinian differences of degree in their glory, a state of affairs that does not diminish satisfaction or arouse envy.[69] Each is sovereign of the Kingdom as well as subject, having a right to all. Each feels its own joy and the joy of others "in a mutual interknowledge, enjoying each others' blessedness."[70] The saints enjoy the presence of God in one another, and God is as "All in All."[71]

Traherne's depiction of the spiritual vision reflects similar Augustinian and Pauline themes—heirdom, God filling "all in all," and the Trinity in every soul as the divine Image (CM 1.69). Likewise, there is nothing unusual in the fact that Traherne gives Christ an exalted place at the center of the vision, the redemptive sacrifice on the Cross being the most valued element (CM 1.54–63). But like other seventeenth-century Protestants, Traherne believed that the meditation on the Passion was insufficient in itself and needed to be developed into a meditation on Christ in his heavenly glory.[72] In particular, Traherne felt the need for a more extensive consideration of divine love, and his answer was to transform the Passion meditation into a meditation on the greatness of Christ's soul and the Kingdom that is inherited through the sacrifice (CM 1.5, 1.64). The Passion remains at the center of the vision, as the pivotal, redemptive event in history, holding everything together in bonds of love, and open to view in the eternal vision of ages past and future (CM 1.80). But Traherne's real enthusiasm lay in the contemplation of the greater implications of the sacrifice: the eternal inheritance, the heavenly community of souls engaged in mutual knowing and loving.

A special feature of Traherne's heavenly meditation—which distinguishes it from many contemporaneous efforts—is the degree to which it integrates the envisioned heaven with the world in which we currently live. Traherne's Kingdom is no other-worldly place of divine existence to come, foreseen briefly in this life by a few. This limited understanding of the Kingdom, according to Traherne, is a great "Misapprehension" that deprives the soul of all happiness.[73] Rather, the Kingdom is the entire world properly understood, a spiritual universe that includes within itself our little world, earth as well as heaven, time as well as eternity, human beings as well as angels. It is not merely a trace of God or foretaste on earth of heavenly existence, traces that conventional "occasional meditations" on earthly happenings and objects were intended to reveal. Rather, heaven in its entirety can be found in the world, not as a trace or image, but as a spiritual reality that can be present in this life.

It is easy to gain the impression that heaven and its loving community are this-worldly for Traherne, to be found and enjoyed in the world we know. Heaven is with us here and now, if only we had the clarity to see and prize what we already have, for the same world is a paradise to some and a hell to others (CM 1.36; 1.46–50). With the right frame of mind, heaven will be with us here and now. Traherne was suspicious of Christians who deferred wisdom and true happiness to the next life, for he regarded the delay as contrary to the wishes of divine love and desire. Rather, we should aim for real happiness now, which "consisteth in the enjoyment of the whole world in communion with God," the parts we already know envisioned alongside those vastly more extensive regions that encompass all times and places.

Why was Traherne so sure of the full accessibility of the Kingdom right here and now? Presumably it was a result of his own experiences. In the *Centuries*, a work that seems to have been written toward the end of his life (possibly ca. 1670–71), Traherne gives the reader a glimpse of his childhood apprehensions of the universe, revealed in the divine light that accompanied him "from the womb" (CM III.1). It is as if St. Peter Damian's bejeweled paradise of golden streets, verdant fields, and imperishable crops had manifested in the Hereford of Traherne's infancy. The city "seemed to stand in Eden, or to be built in Heaven" (CM III.3). All was eternal, without birth and death. The trees were ravishingly beautiful, the dust of the streets was as precious as gold, and the inhabitants were like angels:

> The Men! O what venerable and reverend creatures did the aged seem!
> Immortal Cherubims! And young men glittering and sparkling Angels, and
> maids strange seraphic pieces of life and beauty! Boys and girls tumbling
> in the street, and playing, were moving jewels. (CM III.3)

The prose passages in the third section of the *Centuries* are deservedly famous for their outstanding beauty, and, along with parallels in verse form, such as "The Salutation" and "Wonder," have created the impression that Traherne is a poet of mystically transformed nature and pure childhood vision lost through contact with the corrupting ways of the world. In this role, Traherne is likely to be mentioned in the same breath as the Romantics. However, Traherne regained his spiritual sight in later life, the innocence of the original vision, oblivious of the world's evils, maturing into an appreciation of life's variegated character and an understanding of the vision. In Traherne's case, the regained vision clearly went far beyond a mysticism of the immediate environment, of nature and town, and attained to universal extent.

Precisely at what age Traherne regained his clear vision is unknown, although the autobiographical details he provides in the *Centuries* show that the recovery took place after he had completed his undergraduate education at the University of Oxford, and can therefore be dated sometime in the late 1650s or early 1660s, when Traherne was in his early to mid-twenties. After his university studies, Traherne retreated to the solitude of the countryside and applied himself to the search for happiness or "Felicity" (CM III.46), a subject no tutor at Oxford had "professly" taught (CM III.37). But the search was eventually successful. Traherne relates that he found himself "seated in a throne of repose and perfect rest. All things were well in their proper places, I alone was out of frame and had need to be mended" (CM III.60). The infant visions were vindicated, everything appearing "sublimely rich and great and glorious," all creatures, every blade of grass, understood to be the full exertion of God's power (CM III.62). Speaking of King David's experience that he found described in the Psalms, Traherne attempted to depict the spiritual universe and community, including the presence of spiritual companions.

The soul, having recovered its "pristine liberty," can see through "the mud walls of flesh and blood" to the regions of the world invisible to the senses:

> While his body therefore was inclosed in this world, his soul was in the temple of Eternity, and clearly beheld the infinite life and omnipresence of God: having conversation with invisible spiritual, and immaterial things, which were its companions, itself being invisible, spiritual and immaterial. Kingdoms and ages did surround him, as clearly as the hills and mountains. (CM III.95)

It seems that Traherne found himself present with angels, saints, and others, engaged in the communication of love throughout all times and places, a community that includes saints of "noble and benevolent natures" who live among us but who are well hidden and not easily observed (CM I.82–84). They can be of great benefit as spiritual teachers and companions to seekers who are sufficiently good to merit finding them. Traherne warns that we should expect "infirmities" even in these great souls, and their failings should not be ignored in a cowardly way or passed over lazily, but should be brought to their attention in "a divine and illustrious manner" by "chiding them meekly." Traherne may be thinking of his own weaknesses as a spiritual aspirant and teacher, including his self-acknowledged overtalkativeness,[74] or of the weaknesses of friends he encountered in the world of expanded vision, or the failings of companions he had met in his life at Credenhill or during his further studies at Oxford.

Traherne had found his way back to the Kingdom of God in a prophetic vision or "prevision" of what will be seen in Heaven (CM III.96) and is already seen by God and those who share His vision of all time in eternity (CM III.65). The vision left a powerful impression:

> This Endless Comprehension of my Immortal Soul when I first saw it, so wholy Ravished and Transported my spirit, that for a fortnight after I could Scarsly Think or speak or write of any other Thing. But Like a man Doteing with Delight and Extasie, Talk of it Night and Day as if all the Joy of Heaven and Earth were Shut up in it. For in very Deed there I saw the Divine Image Relucent and Shining. (SM IV.3)

It is not clear whether the experience left Traherne in the happy state permanently, time and eternity always viewed together, or required further contemplative efforts to make stable. In the *Select Meditations*, which is thought to have been written in the early to mid-1660s, and therefore fairly soon after the recovery, there is a suggestion that Traherne had difficulty holding onto the vision when removed from nature into the company of men. However, by the time Traherne composed the *Centuries*, he seems to have been able to see "on both sides of the veil or screen," witnessing love on earth and in heaven (*CM* IV.60).

What was it that so excited Traherne that he could think and speak of nothing else for a fortnight? What, experientially, might the discovery of the relucent and shining divine Image have been? In the section of the *Centuries* alluding to the recovery of the vision, Traherne's description of the powers of the Image suggests that a vision of all times and places was involved, a sense of containing all things within, and a feeling of love that actively encompassed all. A soul restored to the Image, a creature most like God, is "able to see all eternity with all its objects, and as a mirror to contain all that it seeth: able to love all it contains, and as a Sun to shine upon its loves: able by shining to communicate itself in beams of affection and to illustrate all it illuminates with beauty and glory: able to be wise, holy, glorious, blessed in itself, as God is" (*CM* III.61). The soul is now known to be a greater self, a "Secret self" enclosed within,[75] an infinite "sphere" or "eye":

> O Wondrous Self! O Sphere of Light,
> > O Sphere of Joy most fair;
> O Act, O Power infinit;
> O Subtile, and unbounded Air!
> > O Living Orb of Sight!
> Thou which within me art, yet Me! Thou Ey,
> And Temple of his Whole Infinitie!
> O what a World art Thou! a World within.[76]

There is an interior, all-encompassing, luminous self, "Thou which within me art, yet Me!"—a higher center of identity that makes the self double. Traherne says, "There is in a man a Double selfe, according as He is in God, or the world" (*SM* II.92). In the world, man is confined, but in God, he is everywhere, the soul being "All eye and sight." Thus, there are two kinds of sight (*SM* III.14), one viewing things *externally* with the bodily eyes, the other *internally* in the infinite sphere of the soul, in the "inclusive sphere" where all things are apprehended.[77] It would appear that the "Endless Comprehension" of Traherne's soul was an act of seeing, knowing, and loving that grasped infinity and eternity, his soul finding the universe within, an infinite room of treasures and joys, with "the dimensions of innumerable worlds . . . shut up" in it:

> Where it should lodge such innumerable objects, as it doth by knowing, whence it should derive such infinite streams as flow from it by Loving, how it should be a mirror of all Eternity, being made of nothing, how it should be a fountain or a sun of Eternity out of which such abundant rivers flow, it is impossible to declare. (*CM* IV.81)

But the impossibility did not stop Traherne from attempting again and again to explain how the soul can be so great as to contain its immense Kingdom.[78] The capacity is clearly related to the soul's "Endless Comprehension," for the soul contains its objects by "knowing" them and is present to them by "understanding," as "light is in a piece of crystal" (*CM* II.76). Understanding, a "lively pattern and Idea" of God's infinity, permits all things to be, containing and enjoying them (*CM* II.24). The soul "by understanding becometh all Things" (*CM* II.78). We must "think well," have thoughts like God's and "a mind composed of Divine Thoughts." In fact, the mind of God must be ours (*CM* I.10, I.13). In these respects, the soul—as an ideational pattern or intelligible mirror of the infinite God, a condition for things to be, and as a subject containing its objects by knowing them—is comparable to a Neoplatonic or Christian Platonic divine mind that intelligizes its contents.

Yet Traherne's soul, with its knowledge of the world of creatures throughout all times and places, including all sensory modifications, shares similarities with the Hermetic soul that has made itself into the likeness of God, in accordance with the instructions in Book XI of the *Corpus Hermeticum* (see chapter 4). Here Hermes is directed to contemplate God as holding "all the whole World in himself, as it were all Thoughts or Intellections," and to become equal to God in order to understand God. Traherne urges his reader to be present with creatures by an "act of understanding" (*CM* II.76), an exhortation reminiscent of the Hermetic text. Traherne knew the *Corpus Hermeticum*, both in the English translation of John Everard and in Ficino's Latin version, and he quoted extensively from Book XI in more than one of his works.[79] Traherne must have been impressed by the passages in Book XI to quote them at length, and it is easy to understand why, given their depiction of a world-encompassing divine mind to which one can attain likeness.

The Divine Image

Chief among the ideas employed by Traherne to explain how we have such great and God-like souls is the doctrine of the divine Image, a natural choice for a mystic in the Christian tradition and particularly attractive to one with

Platonic leanings. Traherne elaborated the doctrine of the divine Image in his own way, interweaving it with other traditional ideas, Neoplatonic and Christian, to show how the Kingdom is constituted in its finer details. These ideas include the Plotinian doctrine of total, divine omnipresence at each point, the Neoplatonic principle of plenitude, the Pauline fullness of "all in all," the valorization of the small and humble, the soul as mirror, and God or the universe as an infinite sphere whose center is everywhere and circumference nowhere.

Traherne says that he worked out the implications of the *imago Dei* on his own, during his search for happiness, but later found that he had not been as original as he had imagined. Traherne had worked out "the way of communion with God in all Saints" for himself, and then found it described by others, first in the Psalms, and then throughout the Bible and in many of the Church Fathers (*CM* III.66). For Traherne, the creation of man in the image and likeness of God makes possible a divine assimilation in which the attributes and ways of God become ours too (*CM* III.58–59). With our souls restored, our minds "in frame," we have not become God but have regained the status of being His most perfect creation, which is His Image (*CM* III.61)—it was, after all, the "Divine Image Relucent & Shining" that Traherne claimed to have discovered when his mystical vision returned. Thus, we shall know and think as God knows and thinks, love as He loves, see as He sees, be omnipresent as He is omnipresent, enjoy His divine happiness and kingdom of treasures as He enjoys them, and "be Holy towards all and wise towards all, as He is" (*CM* III.97). Traherne's employment of a mystical doctrine of the divine Image leads him to adopt a mirror metaphor: "man is made in the Image of God, and therefore is a mirror and representative of Him" (*CM* II.23). Man can see God imaged in his own mirror-like soul, and the presence of the Image gives him divine qualities, including the love that "can extend to all objects," and an understanding that

> is an endless light, and can infinitely be present in all places, and see and examine all beings, survey the reasons, surmount the greatness, exceed the strength, contemplate the beauty, enjoy the benefit, and reign over all it sees and enjoys like the Eternal Godhead. (*CM* II.23)

What, we may wonder, is the God whose likeness we should attain? God is "one infinite Act of KNOWLEDGE and WISDOM," made infinitely beautiful by the "many consequences of Love" (*CM* II.84). He is an "infinite eternal mind," luminous wisdom, knowing all things, present to all things, seeing all things, "all eye and ear." God is active, creating the world by thinking it into being, and wishing the good of all. In this concept of a supreme principle that is a perfect, productive mind, Traherne is at home in the tradition of Christian thinkers who have not maintained a rigorous apophatic theology, tending instead to bring God and his Mind together. Traherne's merging of the transcendent God with the thinking and loving Mind is reflective of a general Christian tendency to soften the distinction between the supreme source and its mind, although distinctions were of course made between God the Father and Christ the Son as Mind, while admitting their unity in the Trinity with the Holy Spirit.

Having It All

The inheritance includes everything: it is "All Things," not merely the gift of a heaven to come after the old order has passed away. Rather, the entire world is Traherne's inheritance, which includes the familiar earth and the visible universe ("this little Cottage of Heaven and Earth," CM I.18), fair in themselves, but only a very small part of a much larger spiritual world that we do not ordinarily see. In fact, the world properly understood is of infinite extent and content, an "illimited field of Variety and Beauty" encompassing all times and places, celestial powers, saints, angels, and treasures that are not localized in any one place ("some here, and some there" CM I.18), but which exist in full everywhere (reminiscent of the *Avataṃsaka Sūtra's* visionary universe). Traherne frequently emphasizes the smallness of the familiar world in comparison with the amplitude of the eternal Kingdom that the soul can encompass in its knowledge.[80] But despite the negligible extent of the "little Bubble" that is our familiar universe,[81] Traherne welcomes it as a beautiful part of the greater whole and argues that it must be valued if we are to value the whole: "If you be not faithful in esteeming these; who shall put into your hands the true Treasures?" (CM I.21). It is ingratitude to despise the common things of the world that are beautiful and which serve us well, such as the sun, the seas, and the body.

For Traherne, even the smallest things, including the material atom, are full of wonders, full of God, which becomes clear when they are observed in their proper places, in eternity (CM III.55). They might appear little on the outside, "rough and common," but, recalls Traherne, "I remember the time when the dust of the streets were as precious as God to my infant eyes, and now they are more precious to the eye of reason" (CM I.25). Womankind, the body, the senses, even covetousness, desire, and self-love—aspects of earthly existence regularly demeaned in religious worldviews—are valued by Traherne and explained with a turn of thought that cuts through the usual stock of moral platitudes, while upholding a truly spiritual ethic. Thus, with a Platonic appreciation of transcendent Beauty reflected in the world, Traherne does not dismiss love of a "fair woman," who is an heiress of the world, and who in her beauty is God's image. In fact, the problem with the besotted man is that he does not love the woman enough, with "ten thousand beauties" in the woman going unnoticed. She is to be loved more than she is at present, and all other persons equally well, and God above all (CM II.68). It is the limited compass of our love that Traherne criticizes: we do not love all sufficiently and equally well. Traherne's attitude to desire and wants is similar: they are not to be rejected but understood for their integral and necessary role in the economy of happiness.

Traherne's conception of existence is therefore remarkably unified and world-affirming, integrating the oft-devalued earthly life, with its transient beauty, loves, and desires, into a grand conception of the world's true unity, one no longer split by "churlish boundaries and divisions" (CM III.3). Again, this feature of Traherne's understanding of the divine inheritance probably owes something to his mystical experiences in infancy and adulthood, which did not obliterate the world but showed it in its full extent and richness, spatial, temporal, and eternal, and in which he found that the world so experienced is the perfection of beauty, the complete satisfaction of desires, and the greatest of felicities.

Sole Heirdom

The third unusual feature of Traherne's understanding of possession, and one of the most distinctive themes of his writings, is the curious notion of *sole heirdom*, of the solitary yet communal nature of the inheritance. Traherne complicates the simple assertion that we inherit the world by attaining to the likeness of God with his paradoxical insistence that we are each a *sole* heir of the world. Even in his infant visions—at least as Traherne was to recollect them in adulthood—everything in the universe was felt to belong to himself alone:

> The streets were mine, the temple was mine, the people were mine, their clothes and gold and silver were mine, as much as their sparkling eyes, fair skins and ruddy faces. The skies were mine, and so were the sun and moon and stars, and all the World was mine; and I the only spectator and enjoyer of it. (CM III.3)

Although the inheritance is the possession of all and a highly communal affair, it is also the possession of each, to be enjoyed alone, as Traherne supposed was the prototypical case with Adam, a man alone at his creation: "By making one, and not a multitude, God evidently shewed one alone to be the end of the World and every one its enjoyer. . . . So that I alone am the end of the World: Angels and men being all mine" (CM I.14, 15). Traherne quotes Seneca: "God gave me alone to all the World, and all the World to me alone" (CM I.15).

It has been observed in previous chapters that mystical experience may have a solipsistic flavor if the discovery of the all-encompassing mind obscures the existence of other minds. Does Traherne's mystical apprehension slip into solipsism when he claims that the world and its treasures are the sole possession of the one who apprehends them, as if the whole creation has been brought into existence for that one alone? The apparent solipsism of Traherne's sole heirdom resonates with the apparent solipsism of comments Leibniz makes about the causal self-sufficiency of the monad, "as if there existed nothing but God and itself," Leibniz here noting that he takes this expression from "a certain lofty-minded person, famous for her sanctity," a reference to St. Teresa of Ávila.[82] But Leibniz's solipsism is only apparent, for a monad is one of many monadic perceivers, each of which expresses the same universe—it is only *as if* nothing but God and an individual monad exist. At the very least, Leibniz can deploy his Principle of Sufficient Reason to argue for the multiplicity of monads: there would be no reason for God to create just the one monad and not all the many it represents.[83]

What about Traherne's assertions? Taken out of context, they do appear solipsistic or at least highly egocentric, and they might draw the accusation that Traherne's mystical experience was arrested at an incomplete stage, at the partially expanded self-concept in which the entire world is understood as self, but others are not yet recognized on an equal footing. Traherne's complete "possession of the world" would then correspond to a self-concept that has absorbed everything into itself, everything having become "me" or "mine." It is known that Traherne encountered some resistance to his statements, complaining in the Select Meditations that "here I am censured for Speaking in the Singular number, and Saying I" (SM III.65). How different it will be in heaven: "There it shall be our Glory and the Joy of all to Acknowledge, I. I am the Lords, and He is mine. Every one shall Speak in the first Person, and it shall be Gods Glory that He is the Joy of all" (SM III.65).

But Traherne is aware that the usual condition of self is far from the selfhood he is discussing. The self that is sole heir of the world is not the usual self, which has been lost in "the multitude of Wonders and Delights" of the infinite world (CM I.18). A sole heir is a soul that has attained to likeness with God. It is a happy loss to "find GOD in exchange for oneself," which we do when we "see Him in His Gifts, and adore His Glory" (CM I.18).

If Traherne avoids ego-inflation, can the same be said about solipsism? The answer has to be affirmative yet paradoxical: he understands that there are *many* sole heirs—"everyone shall speak in the first person." The world is not only my possession but everyone else's too. If true of one, then true of all: if God makes one the end of the world, he makes every one the end of the world (CM I.15). "Thou hast made All for me, & Me for All,"[84] and "Thou has made me the end of all things, and all the end of me. I in all, and all in me" (CM I.69).

How this may have been experienced is suggested by a passage as celebrated as the reminiscences of childhood vision. Traherne pictures the cosmically expansive soul, adorned with the great world as body and garment, and inclusive of others who are all sole heirs too, a condition that makes oneself much more than one would otherwise be (CM I.29). That the presence of many sole heirs adds to the glory of the vision and to the wealth of all is made very clear in Traherne's *Christian Ethicks* (published posthumously in 1675), which gives a remarkable picture of the members of the heavenly community in the vast, eternal universe, engaged in mutual knowing and loving, as if radiating luminous beams of love to one another:

> THE very sight of other mens Souls, shining in the Acts of their Under-
> standing throughout all Eternity, and extending themselves in the Beams
> of Love through all Immensity, and thereby transformed (every one of
> them) into a Sphear of Light comprehending the Heavens, every Angel
> and every Spirit being a Temple of GODS Omnipresence and Perfection;
> this alone will be a ravishing spectacle to that Goodness, which delights
> to see innumerable Possessors of the Same Kingdome:[85]

To convey the idea of many sole heirs, Traherne employs variations on a common medieval and Renaissance metaphor: God or the universe is a "sphere whose center is everywhere but circumference nowhere." This pseudo-Hermetic metaphor emerged during the revival of Platonism in the twelfth century and was to be repeated many times.[86] Traherne finds the *soul* to be such a sphere: "Every man is alone the centre and circumference of it. It is all his own, and so glorious, that it is the eternal and incomprehensible essence of the Deity" (CM V.3). Traherne observes that "We never Apprehend the World aright till we see it as a Sphere or Univers of Glory in which our selvs are the only Centres."[87] He understands that he is not the only sole heir or center, but finds many within the sphere of light, love, and knowledge into which he has been transformed: "I have found man to be a Centre in [a]World of felicitie, and my self a Sphere of infinit Centres."[88]

The pseudo-Hermetic metaphor gives Traherne a traditional expression for conveying the idea of multiple sole heirdom, but the key to understanding how this is possible, and how the smallest things, even the material point-atom, are a great treasure, is the doctrine of the total omnipresence of God in the part. By arriving at the cosmically enlarged self-knowledge, made possible only through the presence of God, we discover one another equally enlarged, for God is fully present in all:

> The fruition of thy self being infinite in me,
> but multiplyed infinitely in all thy Creatures.
>   In all thy Saints, in all thy Sons, shall I see thine Eternity
> wholly enjoyed, thine omnipresence wholly in every Bosom.[89]

Thus, Traherne's vision of the Kingdom of God reveals that God is fully present in all, a total omnipresence that establishes a community of God-images, of souls who know and love one another. God's omnipresence, his communication of himself "wholly in every centre" (CM II.82), ensures that each soul is a plenitude:

> For by the Indwelling of GOD all Objects are infused, and contained within. The Spiritual Room of the Mind is Transcendent to Time and Place, because all Time and Place are contained therein: There is a Room in the Knowledge for all Intelligible Objects: A Room in our Esteem for all that is worthy of our Care and Desire. I confess this Room is strange and Mysterious. It is the Greatest Miracle perhaps in Nature. For it is an Infinite Sphere in a Point, an Immensity in a Centre, an Eternity in a Moment. We feel it, tho we cannot understand it.[90]

Here perhaps we catch a glimpse of what it is like to see another soul in its fullness, an "Infinite Sphere in a Point," which is something hard to grasp but is nonetheless experienced. Infinite love is expressed in the smallest space and the smallest moment of time (CM II.80), and this space or center seems to be spherical, an "Infinite Sphere in a Point," like the vision of the spherical cosmos, a "Living Orb of Sight,"[91] a "Living Endless Ey," "an Inward *Sphere of Light*," "an Interminable Orb of *Sight*."[92]

It is possible that Traherne discovered the other sole heirs were also spheres, "spherical eyes" like his own spherical soul-vision, for in the

"Temple" of his infant mind, all the hearers were found to be eyes.[93] In the living temple of the adult mind, souls and minds appear with the seraphim, "like Spheres of Bliss," made infinite by love, sight, joy, thanksgiving, and praise.[94] However, at one point Traherne seems unsure whether his soul was truly a sphere:

> Twas not a Sphere
> Yet did appear
> One infinit. Twas somwhat evry where.[95]

Presumably this "strange mysterious sphere" that is not a sphere, infinite and everywhere, was the sphere unlike any other sphere, the infinite sphere whose center is everywhere and circumference nowhere.

Traherne's language for the expanded state is preeminently visual: the soul acquires God's sight as its own, finding the world to be a "valley of vision" in which "all the nations and kingdoms of the world appear in splendour and celestial glory" (CM III.84). A creature, made in the divine Image and having the divine sight, is like a mirror, containing within itself the eternal world, "able to see all eternity with all its objects, and as a mirror to contain all that it seeth" (CM III.61). Vision is expanded to infinite depths because the soul contains other souls who are equally mirror-like, leading to a multiplication of vision within the one vision. The full vision of one soul is made utterly full because it contains the full vision of all souls. These souls, which contain what they see, are able to encompass one another without obstruction, allowing an infinite multiplication of complete visions within each complete vision. Although the members of the spiritual community are infinite expressions of God's glory, they manage to remain distinct from one another, "without Confusion, or Diminution, every one distinctly enjoying all, and adding to each others fruition."[96] For Traherne, it is the deepest of wonders that a soul can "measure" not only one other soul, which would be equal to itself in its infinity, but all infinite souls, "wholly and fully" (CM II.71). The great world is so organized that an infinity is not restricted to equaling just one other infinity, but can encompass many such infinities:

> This is an infinite wonder indeed. For admit that the powers of one soul were fathomless and infinite: are not the powers so also of another. One would think therefore that one soul should be lost in another: and that two souls should be exactly adequate. Yet indeed my soul can examine and search all the chambers and endless operations of another: being prepared to see innumerable millions. (CM II.71)

It is a wonder that is "infinitely infinite," each soul seeing all souls in every other soul:

> one soul which is the object of mine, can see all souls, and all the secret chambers, and endless perfections, in every soul: yea, and all souls with all their objects in every soul. Yet mine can accompany all these in one soul: and without deficiency exceed that soul, and accompany all these in every soul. (CM II.72)

Traherne uses the analogy of many, interreflecting mirrors to convey the multiplication of one soul in other souls and its enjoyments: "And as in many mirrors we are so many other selves, so are we spiritually multiplied when we meet ourselves more sweetly, and live again in other persons" (CM II.70). In the Pauline metaphor (II Corinthians 3.18), it is the image of the Lord that is multiplied in the many mirrors. In the Augustinian heaven, God "will be seen by each of us in each of us." Traherne too finds God mirrored in souls but also understands souls to be mirrored in one another, rather like the beings in the Plotinian intelligible realm. But Traherne expands the eternal heaven to include our transitory realm, and a "worlds within the world" multiplication is implied because the souls mirrored in one soul contain all times, places, and objects within their secret chambers.

Wanting It All

One sole heirdom incorporates all souls and therefore the heirdoms of all others, maximizing the inheritance of each. Not only does mutual possession add to the glory of the Kingdom, it resolves a conflict between two human traits ordinarily set against each other, the self-interested, acquisitive tendency and the desire to promote the happiness and well-being of others:

> If they [the treasures of the Kingdom] are all ours wholly and solely, and yet nevertheless every one's too, it is the most delightful accident that is imaginable, for thereby two contrary humours are at once delighted, and two inclinations, that are both in our natures, yet seem contradictory, are at once satisfied. The one is the avaricious humour and love of propriety, whereby we refer all unto ourselves and naturally desire to have all alone in our private possession, and to be the alone and single end of things. This we perceive ourselves because all universally and everywhere is ours. (CM II.79)

The insatiable urge to acquire more and more, and the ambition to be the center of attention, are at last satisfied in the mystical comprehension of the world. The trouble with our desires is that they usually settle on hopelessly limited things, and we then toil for more and more because the infinite needs of the soul are left unsatisfied by anything less than communion with God in the Kingdom. As Ficino had explained, intellect, will, and love are not satisfied by anything short of God and move on until they possess the infinite good.[97] Traherne compares us in our desire for the whole to Alexander the Great, of whom it was said, "that young man sat down and cried for more worlds to conquer" (CM I.22).[98] We are so insatiable that "millions of worlds" would not satisfy us, for they are like "so many tennis-balls" in comparison with the true greatness of the soul (CM I.22). Covetousness, when abused, brings only misery, but correctly employed is a "noble inclination" (CM I.23) that leads us to the divine inheritance and harmonizes with that other tendency of human nature, "the communicative humour":

> whereby we desire to have companions in our enjoyments to tell our joys, and to spread abroad our delights, and to be ourselves the joy and delight of other persons. (CM II.79)

Covetousness and social feeling coincide because the sole possession is, happily, the possession of all, a common inheritance: "For thousands enjoy all as well as we, and are the end of all: and God communicateth all to them as well as us" (CM II.79).

In the mid-seventeenth century, the philosopher Thomas Hobbes had argued that human beings seek their own good exclusively: human nature is fundamentally self-centered—egotistic rather than altruistic. Traherne, like many contemporary men of religion, vigorously opposed Hobbes's ideas, but as we see here, Traherne's mystical understanding allowed him to respond to the challenge in an ingenious way, by acknowledging that self-interest and the desire for more are fundamental to the soul, but then interpreting these as inclinations toward the recovery of the divine whole and its community. Like the Stoics, he viewed self-love as an essentially healthy tendency that can be extended to the cosmos of beings. But Traherne raised the idea to a mystical level: self-interest in its pure form, not distorted into greed for "tinselled vanities," is compatible with social virtue because the deeper self, the expansive soul, is a social self.

8

The Physics of Experience

I have lingered on Leibniz's system, because I believe
that it contains hints for a metaphysic compatible
with modern physics and with psychology, although
of course it will require very serious modifications.

—Bertrand Russell

THE CHARITABLE READER may look upon the kinds of experiences described in the previous chapter, and the various ideas informed by them, as suggestive of a universe organized from multiple, experiential perspectives. However, it is unlikely that the evidence furnished by such experiences alone, no matter how plentiful and detailed, will ever be entirely convincing. Questions will be raised about the authenticity, accuracy, and interpretation of the testimonies, but beyond such justifiable queries and concerns, there may be a reluctance to concede that mysticism has anything at all to say about the natural world. If mystical experience is dismissed as mere hallucination or some other kind of mental or biological aberration, there will be no reason to take it seriously as a genuine source of knowledge. The same will be true if mystical experience is viewed as a product of "conditioning." According to one influential school of thought, mystical experiences are constructed entirely out of the ideas and images acquired by mystics from their religious and cultural backgrounds. If this is true, mystical insights into the natural world will simply be regurgitations of information absorbed from science education, science fiction, and the mass media.[1]

Even if it is allowed that mystical experiences can be a genuine source of insight, it does not follow that they provide insight into the natural world. It has been claimed that mysticism and physics have legitimacy only in their own domains, the realms of spirit and matter respectively. Mysticism and physics—and more generally religion and science—are said to be examples of what Stephen Gould famously called "nonoverlapping magisteria."[2] According to this position, religion and science neither agree nor conflict with each other because they are concerned with very different matters, the former with values and ultimate meaning (the "why" questions), the latter with empirical fact (the "how" questions). Likewise, it is claimed that mysticism and physics have nothing to contribute to each other because they differ in their respective domains, spirit and matter. Some authorities otherwise sympathetic toward mysticism have adopted this line of argument, contending that mysticism has nothing to contribute to an understanding of the natural world because it addresses a different domain.[3]

Healthy skepticism is, of course, to be welcomed, as it is all too easy to go astray in speculative endeavors, and it is true that efforts to make connections between mysticism and physics have, by and large, had serious shortcomings. All too often, modern-day mystics and authors of popular science–mysticism books have drawn parallels between a hotchpotch of mystical philosophies and scientific ideas in a way that inspires no confidence among specialists in science, history, philosophy, and religion. Nevertheless, some of the parallels—such as those to do with holistic interconnectedness and the eternalistic "block universe" view of time and space—are sufficiently interesting to deserve further investigation, and attempts to forge links between mysticism and physics should not be rejected out of hand from the mere prejudice that there can be no overlap of their respective "magisteria."[4] Indeed, the fact that there are mystical experiences of the natural world may suggest that "spirit" and "nature" are not so distinct as some assume them to be.

It is therefore intriguing to observe that not only mystical experiences and associated spiritual ideas point toward a universe structured from interconnected centers of perception. It just so happens that the hardest of the hard sciences may point in the same direction, for in the early twentieth century the sober discipline of physics showed signs of "going Leibnizian" after its long Newtonian apprenticeship. Both Newton and Leibniz were outstanding contributors to the emergence of physics as a modern scientific discipline in the late seventeenth and early eighteenth centuries. Newton is rightly celebrated for his laws of motion, theory of universal gravitation, and work in optics. Leibniz helped to clarify basic concepts in the study of motion, such as energy and force, and, like Newton, he came up with the calculus, a mathematical tool essential to modern physical science.

Newton's physics and its underlying metaphysics of absolute time, space, and motion initially dominated the field, whereas Leibniz's monadology was easily dismissed as a flight of fancy by critics of speculative metaphysics from the eighteenth century onward. But the monadology was anchored in the actualities of experience. It rejected the space–time–matter abstractions of the mechanical philosophers and looked instead to perception and its "perspectival" character as indicative of the deeper nature of things, with the world structured experientially from multiple points of view. It drew inspiration from or found apparent corroboration in both mysticism (Christian, Neoplatonic, Kabbalistic, Helmontian, neo-Confucian) and the empirical sciences of the day, physical and biological.

The scientific support now available for the kind of metaphysics proposed by Leibniz is stronger than it was in his own day. In the twentieth century, physics began to exhibit telltale signs of a monadological universe, notably a relativity of space and time, and a degree of holistic interconnectedness unimagined and unimaginable in the Newtonian world-picture. Two profound developments—relativistic and quantum physics—have led many to believe that Newton's metaphysical presuppositions were incorrect. Some have speculated that Leibniz's relational approach to space and time was on the right track, and a few have even drawn inspiration from his underlying metaphysics of monads. Ordinarily regarded as the science of matter and its motions, physics then becomes a science of the structural contents of multiple perceptions and their coordinated transformations.

Surface and Depth Theories

Before we take a look at the strange new physics that undermined the Newtonian worldview, it will pay to distinguish two kinds of theories in the sciences and place them in relation to the branch of philosophy called metaphysics. First, there is the *surface theory*, which stays close to the phenomena under investigation. Surface theories have the form of laws or principles that serve as generalized descriptions, condensing a mass of observational data into concise statements of a descriptive and predictive character, usually expressed in mathematical equations that link measurable quantities. The second kind of theory, the *depth theory*, is likewise grounded in observational data and employs mathematical formulae but also purports to give some insight into the workings of nature. Whereas the surface theory provides only superficial explanation at best, the depth theory has the appearance of offering deep explanation even if it does not. Depth theories invoke underlying objects and processes that are not immediately obvious, such as the unobserved microphysical constituents of objects and the causal chains of events that make up processes. Depth theories confer a sense of understanding, especially when they provide visualizable depictions of what may be going on behind the scenes.

Simple examples of surface and depth theories in physics come from the study of gases. For example, one of the gas laws, the Pressure Law, states that the pressure exerted by an ideal gas on the walls of its container is directly proportional to its absolute temperature. This law is a surface theory. It correlates measured quantities but offers at best only superficial explanation: "Why did the pressure in the container rise? Because the container was heated, the temperature of the gas inside increased, and the gas tried to expand." In contrast, the kinetic theory of gases is a depth theory: it allows the Pressure Law and the other gas laws to be derived from assumptions about the hidden constitution of gases. According to the kinetic theory, gases are made up of constantly moving particles that collide elastically with themselves and with the walls of their containers. The theory allows us to visualize a gas as a swarm of particles and to understand changes in the measurable, macroscopic gas properties, such as temperature, pressure, and volume, in terms of the motions and collisions of these microphysical particles.

Depth theories often call upon unperceived entities and processes, such as the gas particles and their collisions in the kinetic theory. More broadly, depth theories have invoked molecular, atomic, and elementary particles, and waves, ethers, forces, and fields. However, reference to such entities does not necessarily make a theory "deep," as the classic case of Newton's law of universal gravitation illustrates. This theory calls upon a "gravitational force" to account for the phenomena of gravity, such as the weights of bodies, ocean tides, and planetary motions. Newton's law tells us that the strength of gravitational force between bodies is proportional to the product of their masses and the inverse square of the distance between them.

Critics, Leibniz included, admired the power of the mathematical treatment, but were quick to point out that Newton's gravitational force was explanatorily empty, like the hidden or "occult" qualities employed in premodern philosophy. Although seeming to offer an explanation of gravitational phenomena, Newton's law does not say what gravitational force is and how it acts. Leibniz hoped to go beyond descriptive and predictive laws to nontrivial dynamical explanations, to depth theories that reveal the inner workings and powers of nature. Newton responded to his critics in the second edition of the *Principia* (1713), asserting that he had never intended to give a deep, causal explanation: "But hitherto I have not been able to discover the cause of those properties of gravity from phenomena, and I frame no hypotheses; for whatever is not deduced from the phenomena is to be called an hypothesis; and hypotheses, whether metaphysical or physical, whether of occult qualities or mechanical, have no place in experimental philosophy."[5] Newton moved tentatively toward a depth theory of gravity when, in his later thought, he speculated that there might be an all-pervading, perhaps corpuscular ether that supports gravitational attraction as well as other physical processes.

The distinction I have outlined above, between depth and surface theories, was made by Albert Einstein, although he called them *constructive theories* and *theories of principle* respectively:[6]

> [constructive theories] attempt to build a picture of complex phenomena out of some relatively simple proposition. . . . When we say that we understand a group of natural phenomena, we mean that we have found a constructive theory which embraces them.[7]

> [the] starting-point and foundation [of theories of principle] are not hypothetical constituents, but empirically observed general properties of phenomena, principles from which mathematical formulae are deduced of such a kind that they apply to every case which presents itself.[8]

Einstein remarked that constructive theories have the merit of comprehensiveness, adaptability, and clarity, while principle theories have logical perfection and secure foundations. That is to say, constructive (depth) theories offer clear understanding and can be applied to a whole range of phenomena. Principle (surface) theories allow phenomena to be deduced logically from the observationally intuited principles, and, by staying close to the phenomena, they make no fallible assumptions about deep structures and processes. Einstein understood his special theory of relativity to be a surface theory, and, as we shall see, it exhibits the associated strengths and weaknesses of surface theories. It is untroubled by the complexities in which depth theories become embroiled, but it is unsatisfying for those who seek understanding because it builds upon foundational principles without inquiring into their basis.

Physics and Metaphysics

I renamed Einstein's two types of physical theories to emphasize the point that some physical theories purport to shed light on the *deep* workings of nature whereas others remain close to the phenomenal *surface*. By invoking underlying mechanisms and forces, the depth theories of physics have some affinity and overlap with the branch of philosophy called *metaphysics* and its subbranch *ontology* (fig. 8.1).

Metaphysics addresses fundamental questions about the nature of things, including questions to do with reality and appearance (including the realities or *noumena* behind phenomena), causality, space, time and matter, the self, the mind–body connection, and freewill and determinism. Ontology is a branch of metaphysics that deals specifically with the nature of existence and its fundamental categories. The boundary between scientific depth theories and metaphysics/ontology is rather fuzzy, although in modern times scientific theories have generally been heavily experimental, quantitative, and mathematical, unlike traditional metaphysical efforts. Another difference is that scientific depth theories, with the possible exception of the modern-day "Theories of Everything" that aspire to unify all the forces of nature, do not usually claim to give a comprehensive, fundamental picture of reality. For example, the kinetic theory of gases is limited in its aspirations, dealing with only gas-related phenomena, and there is no pretense that its picture of gas as made of simple, elastic particles in motion through space is an accurate representation of the ultimate constitution of gaseous matter. A metaphysical theory, by contrast, would inquire into the very heart of matter in all its forms and into the nature of space, time, and motion too.

Even if depth theories do not seem particularly metaphysical, they rest upon metaphysical assumptions about space, time, matter, and causality, and the same can be true of surface theories. For example, Newton's laws of motion and his theory of universal gravitation rest on metaphysical suppositions about space, time, matter, and motion. Newtonian time is absolute, flowing uniformly and independently of matter and space. Material bodies are made up of impenetrable particles or "corpuscles" in the void, held together by forces of attraction. These composite bodies and their constituent particles are either at rest or in motion through space, which like time

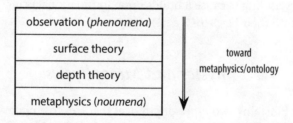

Figure 8.1   **Between phenomena and noumena: two kinds of physical theory.**

is absolute. Newtonian space is "absolute" in the sense that it provides an immovable background container in which bodies move. The absoluteness of space was important to Newton because it provided a fixed background against which his laws of motion were valid. However, Newton's absolute space and time are featureless, so in practice measurements of position and motion are relative, made between bodies.

Leibniz's take on space and time was very different, and so too his understanding of matter at its most fundamental level.[9] Leibnizian space and time are not independent substances, existing in themselves. Rather, his space and time are relational: space is the order of coexistent phenomena; time is the order of successive phenomena. Leibniz's relational understanding of space and time in his physics integrates well with his monadological metaphysics, for the temporality of a monad is its succession of perceptual states and its spatiality is its inner perception of the concurrent states of other monads. As for matter, Leibniz gave particular emphasis to its *intrinsic* force character, far more so than Newton. Again, the physics links with the metaphysics, for the ultimate units behind the phenomena of matter and force are the active, self-actualizing monads. However, for a long time Leibniz's monadology was not translatable into a quantitative, mathematically expressed, scientific depth theory, and there was no strong data to support it. Only in the twentieth century had experimental observation and mathematics each advanced sufficiently to make a physics rooted in Leibnizian or neo-Leibnizian metaphysics an attractive and perhaps viable proposition.

One factor that complicates the distinction between depth and surface theories is the strongly divergent attitudes to metaphysics over the past two hundred years or so. There has been a widespread distrust of speculative metaphysics in modern philosophy, a mistrust that has also colored attitudes toward scientific theory. Kant poked fun at Leibniz's monadology and pathologized mystical and psychical claims to supersensible knowledge, with Swedenborg's reports from the spirit world primarily in mind.[10] Kant attacked "dogmatic metaphysics" but erected in its place a dogmatic epistemology in which the noumena—the "things-in-themselves" behind phenomena—are unknowable, forever screened from view because human minds impose their inbuilt categories upon experience. Some philosophers have merely wanted to limit traditional metaphysical ambitions; others have rejected metaphysics altogether, for a variety of reasons, philosophical and ideological. Variants have included scientific positivism, pragmatism, philosophical behaviorism, logical positivism, Wittgenstein's linguistic rejection of traditional philosophical problems as "meaningless," and neo-pragmatist, post-structuralist, postmodernist, and feminist critiques. In recent decades there has been a return to metaphysics in the philosophical mainstream, but not often to metaphysics in the grand style. In conjunction with the fall from grace of speculative metaphysics in philosophy, there was a drive to expunge metaphysics from science. This showed in "anti-realist" interpretations of science. Scientific realists believe that scientific theories afford some insight into what really takes place in nature, and they are often willing to accord at least some reality to the objects and processes described in depth theories, such as particles and fields. In contrast, full-blown anti-realists have regarded depth theories as just complicated surface theories: they are useful stories that pretend to tell us what is going on but are just complex tools for describing and predicting phenomena.

The Relativity Revolution

In the two centuries after Newton and Leibniz made their pioneering contributions, the physical understanding of the world underwent major changes, but its metaphysical assumptions continued to follow the Newtonian example. In the eighteenth century, Leibnizian physics had some impact through the work of Rudjer Boscovich, who combined Newton's intercorpuscular forces with Leibniz's active point-centers of force, an idea also worked on by Kant. With the development of field theory in the nineteenth century, attention shifted from the point-centers to the surrounding medium, the "ether" by means of which forces of attraction and repulsion act. With the success of the wave theory of light in the mid-nineteenth century and James Clerk Maxwell's realization that light is intimately related to electricity and magnetism, the hypothesized carrier of light waves—the *luminiferous ether*—took center stage.

However, there were problems. First, the properties required of this light-bearing ether were very odd indeed. The ether has to be constituted in such a way that it offers no noticeable resistance to the motion of the planets yet is sufficiently rigid to support the extraordinarily rapid side-to-side vibrations of the fast-moving light waves. It also has to be incompressible in the direction of travel because light, unlike sound, exhibits no vibratory motion in its direction of travel. It was very difficult to reach an understanding of what the ether is and how it works. Second and more importantly, it proved impossible to detect the motion of the Earth through the ether on its yearly journey round the Sun. Motion through the light-carrying ether should affect optical phenomena in a measurable way, but a number of optical experiments failed to detect any such motion, including the extremely sensitive "ether-wind" experiment conducted by Michelson and Morley in 1887. Several interpretations of these unexpected and perplexing "null" results were suggested:

1. As the Earth revolves about the sun, it drags a portion of the ether with it, so optical experiments on the Earth will not detect motion through the ether (*ether-drag theory*).

2. The velocity of light is determined not by a luminiferous ether but by the immediate source of the light in the ether-wind experiments. In general, light is emitted at its velocity *c* relative to its source (*emission theory*).

3. Experimental apparatuses undergo deformation as they move through the ether, a deformation that leads to the null results (*deformation theory*).

4. The null results follow from two principles, the relativity principle and the light principle (*special theory of relativity*).[11]

The first interpretation was ruled out because other observations, notably stellar aberration, seemed to exclude an ether drag. The second, although consistent with stellar aberration, was undermined by observations of double stars and by some other considerations. The third, arrived at independently by George FitzGerald and Hendrik Lorentz, and developed into a mature form by Lorentz in 1904, maintains that the apparatus used to detect the Earth's motion is subject to deformation as it passes through the ether. If the cohesive forces between the constituent particles of bodies are electromagnetic in nature, it is not far-fetched to conjecture that bodies deform as they pass through the ether, the carrier of electromagnetic force. It turns out that nature is so constructed that electromagnetic methods, including optical experiments, cannot be used to detect the motion of a body through the ether. In Lorentz's approach, Maxwell's equations of electromagnetism are truly valid only in the stationary ether frame. Likewise, light travels at its true velocity *c* only with respect to this rest frame. However, observers in motion through the ether will arrive at exactly the same equations of electromagnetism and measure the same light velocity *c* because nature "conspires" to hide the differences from them.

Lorentz's theory was a depth theory, positing behind-the-scenes realities: his ontology consisted of two distinct entities, the luminiferous ether and the electrically charged microphysical constituents of matter, the "electrons." The theory retained Newtonian metaphysical assumptions, namely the concepts of universal time and the absolute rest frame. Lorentz's ether was stationary, and so, at the beginning of the twentieth century, physics still had an absolute rest-frame available to it. The luminiferous ether, bearer of electromagnetic waves and force, had taken over from Newton's space as the immobile, universal background to the ever-shifting dance of matter and radiation. At this point, in 1905, Albert Einstein turned matters on their head.

Unlike Lorentz's theory, Einstein's *special theory of relativity* (as it was later to be called) has the appearance of a surface theory, and Einstein regarded it as such. His theory dispenses with the underlying ether and its deformational effects on moving bodies as superfluous. Instead, it takes two simple claims as foundational principles, drawn partly from experimental results and partly from Einstein's intuition. In their original form (in 1905), these principles or postulates were stated as follows:

> *Relativity Postulate:* "the same laws of electromagnetics and optics will be valid for all frames of reference for which the equations of mechanics hold good."
>
> *Light Principle:* "light is always propagated in empty space with a definite velocity c which is independent of the state of motion of the emitting body."[12]

The principles can be stated in a more concise form that refers to *inertial* observers or frames of reference, that is, to observers who move at constant speed in a straight line relative to one another and therefore have no relative accelerations:

> *Relativity Principle:* the laws of physics are the same in all inertial frames of reference.
>
> *Light Principle:* the velocity of light c in empty space is the same in all inertial frames.

This form of the Light Principle highlights the strange fact that observers arrive at the same numerical value for the velocity of light, however fast they themselves are traveling. Whatever you take your own velocity to be, you will always measure the velocity of light in empty space to be 186,282 miles per second relative to yourself.

To the Relativity and Light Principles, the special theory attaches a measurement-based definition of simultaneity, a way of specifying whether events happen at the same time when they occur at different places. The upshot is that events one observer measures to take place at the same time are not simultaneous for another observer in relative motion (the *relativity of simultaneity*). There is no longer a universal "now" applicable to all observers, no "present state" of the universe, and the temporal order of at least some events will be judged differently.

Einstein's two principles can be derived from Lorentz's ether theory, but in Einstein's ether-free theory they have the status of unquestioned starting postulates, with no explanation of how they come about. From these postulates, several surprising effects can be deduced with considerable ease, including *time dilation* and *length contraction*. In simple terms, Einstein's theory predicts that observers will measure lengths to shorten and time intervals to expand in systems moving relative to them. This is a reciprocal effect: if you and I are in relative motion with each other, I will measure your rulers to contract and your clocks to run slow, and you will measure my rulers to contract and my clocks to run slow.

These surprising results and others, including the equivalence of energy and mass expressed in that most famous of equations $E = mc^2$, have since been confirmed many times by experiment, and they follow directly from Einstein's principles and his definition of simultaneous events. They are also in agreement with Lorentz's mature ether theory, explained there as consequences of the deformation of moving bodies and the retardation of signal emissions when bodies move through the ether. But in Lorentz's theory, measured length contractions and time dilations have the status of mere appearance if the bodies are actually at rest in the stationary ether. Only bodies in motion through the ether are subject to real deformation and retardation effects. By contrast, Einstein's theory has no concept of an absolute state of rest, and it therefore gives equal status to the contractions and dilations measured by observers in relative motion.

The theories of Einstein and Lorentz are empirically equivalent, sharing the same mathematical structure ("formalism") and making the same predictions. But in Lorentz's theory, space and time are still the absolutes they were in Newton's mechanics, while in Einstein's theory the Newtonian metaphysics of space and time is passed over along with the ether. But does Einstein's theory provide an alternative metaphysics of space and time to replace the Newtonian one? If Einstein's approach were a pure surface theory, it would *not* trace its results to the fundamental structure of space and time. However, it is very easy to read into Einstein's theory an ontological claim about space and time, one that moves the theory from its surface status to depth explanation and even toward metaphysics. It is often claimed that Einstein's theory presents a new, non-Newtonian understanding of space and time in which the two are inextricably joined, and that it is from this unified, four-dimensional spacetime that relativistic effects derive. The geometry of the spacetime is said to be "pseudo-Euclidean" because it is similar to but not exactly the same as the space in which Euclid's axioms of geometry hold. In Euclidean space, the overall spatial separation between things is given by the Pythagorean theorem, which combines the component distances (Δx, Δy, Δz) along the three spatial dimensions in the following way:

$$(\text{spatial separation})^2 = \Delta x^2 + \Delta y^2 + \Delta z^2$$

In Euclidean space, this spatial measure of separation (i.e., "distance") is the same or "invariant" for all observers. But in the pseudo-Euclidean Minkowski spacetime of special relativity, the measure of invariant separation, the so-called invariant interval, must include the time interval (Δt) between events, and it does so in a way that is not exactly "Pythagorean," having a minus sign in the equation:

$$(\text{invariant interval})^2 = \Delta x^2 + \Delta y^2 + \Delta z^2 - (c\Delta t)^2,$$
$$\text{where } c \text{ is the velocity of light}$$

The presence of the minus sign means that even if two events are very widely separated in space and time, say millions of miles and millions of years apart, their separation in Minkowski spacetime will nevertheless be zero if they lie on the path of a light signal, for the distance and time components will then exactly cancel out.

As early as 1908, the mathematician Hermann Minkowski introduced this unified concept of spacetime, declaring that "Henceforth space by itself, and time by itself, are doomed to fade away into mere shadows, and only a kind of union of the two will preserve an independent reality."[13] Einstein's theory, given a Minkowski cast, becomes a space–time theory and therefore no longer qualifies as a pure surface approach. Michel Janssen has put it thus:

> For Einstein special relativity was a theory of principle. With the introduc-
> tion of Minkowski space-time, however, it became a constructive theory.
> Minkowski space-time is the structure responsible for all the effects deriv-
> able from special relativity alone.[14]

Relativistic effects, such as length contraction, can be explained by resolving absolute Minkowski spacetime into relative spacetime diagrams for each observer in relative motion and showing how the observers use different spatiotemporal cross sections to make their time and distance measurements. The move toward ontology was reinforced by Einstein's general theory of relativity (1916), which took up the idea of spacetime and accounted for gravitational phenomena by calling on spacetime curvature in the presence of matter. It is then left to philosophers to debate whether Minkowski spacetime and spacetime in general have substantive existence and are validly employed as a basis for deep explanation. Is spacetime just a way of talking about space and time relations or does it have a reality of its own?

Given the mathematical and predictive equivalence of the two theories, it is natural to ask why Einstein's special theory eventually came to dominate twentieth-century physics, while Lorentz's theory and its luminiferous ether were largely abandoned. The question is best left to historians and philosophers of science to answer in detail. Lorentz's depth approach had the advantage of making strange effects such as length contraction and time dilation comprehensible within a conventional Newtonian framework of space and time, whereas Einstein's surface approach had great simplicity and economy as a virtue, being untroubled by the complexities and uncertainties surrounding the composition of ether and matter. Lorentz's depth theory had vulnerable foundations in this respect, with its undetectable ether and conjectural picture of matter, even more so when quantum physics appeared on the scene, mixing further complications into the brew. Already at the beginning of the twentieth century, even before Einstein formulated his special theory of relativity, the first hints of quantum physics were making an appearance, bringing new, unexpected puzzles, including doubts about the wave nature of light and its ethereal support. Einstein himself contributed significantly to the emergence of quantum physics, for already in 1905 he had advanced the idea that light radiation is not continuous and wavelike but comes in localized energy quanta or packets. It has been said that his brush with quantum phenomena encouraged him to take a surface approach in his theory of relativity. Einstein himself was to recall:

> Reflections of this type made it clear to me as long ago as shortly after 1900, i.e., shortly after Planck's trailblazing work, that neither mechanics nor electrodynamics could (except in limiting cases) claim exact validity. By and by I despaired of the possibility of discovering the true laws by means of constructive efforts based on known facts. The longer and the more desperately I tried, the more I came to the conviction that only the discovery of a universal formal principle could lead us to assured results.[15]

As a principle approach, the special theory of relativity was able to float untroubled above the complexities of ether and matter, including the quantum puzzles that were just coming to light.

Quantum Puzzles

The beginnings of quantum physics are usually dated to 1900 when Max Planck concluded that the energy of heat radiation assumes discrete values or "quanta." The discovery that energy and other quantities are packaged in discrete values pointed to a fundamental condition of discontinuity in the makeup of the natural world: physical quantities do not vary continuously but proceed in leaps. In 1913, Niels Bohr quantized the electronic structure of the atom by placing electrons around the atomic nucleus in discrete energy levels. When an electron changes its orbital level, a quantum of energy is absorbed or released. But it is not just abstract quantities such as energy that come in discrete packages, for in this model the electron leaps from orbit to orbit without occupying intermediate positions. Thus, it appears that something as concrete as motion is discontinuous at the microphysical level, and it has even been suggested that space, time, and spacetime are "atomic," coming in discrete, indivisible units. Thus, the first peculiarity of quantum physics to note is the *discontinuity* it attributes to nature.

The second peculiarity—*wave–particle duality*—had come to be well recognized by the early 1920s, for experiments had shown that light and other forms of electromagnetic radiation have both particle-like and wave-like characteristics. Then, in 1923 Louis de Broglie suggested that matter as well as radiation has this wave–particle duality. The peculiar combination of wave and particle properties is illustrated by the famous two-slit interference experiment. Particles of matter (e.g., electrons) or electromagnetic radiation (photons) are directed toward a screen with two narrow, parallel slits. Beyond this screen, a detector is deployed to record where the particles end up after they have passed through the slits. As expected, the detector registers the destination of individual particles, but unexpectedly the pattern of detected particles assumes the form of an interference pattern, which to physicists is suggestive of a wave phenomenon.

In the early days of quantum physics, several interpretations were put forward. For example, in his "pilot-wave theory," de Broglie suggested that a wave guides particles along their paths. In the two-slit experiment, self-interference of the pilot wave occurs when its passes through the slits, and so the particles it guides are directed into an interference pattern. The theory was not popular, and the idea of particles guided by waves along definite trajectories lay dormant for twenty-five years until it was revived and developed by David Bohm in the early 1950s.

The pilot-wave approach was a depth theory: it attempted to explain wave–particle duality by setting up two ontological categories, pilot waves and particles, and by describing what is really going on in the experimental apparatus. In contrast, the theory that came to dominate quantum physics for many years was more like a surface theory. It had a pronounced anti-realist flavor, influenced by philosophies suspicious of metaphysics, such as positivism and pragmatism. For the most part, the interpretation that emerged in Bohr's circle in Copenhagen avoided ontological questions: there was to be no speculation about unobserved microphysical processes behind the observed macroscopic phenomena. Particles were equated with particle measurements, and the wave or "wave function" was interpreted mathematically as a probabilistic tool for predicting the outcomes of particle measurements. Bohr was not so extreme that he entirely abandoned classical ontological categories. He maintained that particle and wave descriptions are "complementary" in the sense that each is validly applied to different aspects of the quantum experiment, the particle picture being relevant to the localized particle measurements and the wave picture to the treatment of the system prior to measurement.

Nevertheless, the somewhat obscure and variously expressed interpretative approach that emerged from Bohr's group—the so-called Copenhagen or orthodox interpretation—gives center stage to the mathematical formalism and steers clear of deep explanation and vizualizable pictures of what may be going on behind the scenes. A step toward deeper explanation, initiated by John von Neumann, developed by Eugene Wigner, and taken further by Henry Stapp, gave a role in the quantum process to the consciousness of the observer, which collapses wave functions to determinate measurements.[16] In a very different vein, David Bohm's adaptation of the de Broglie pilot-wave theory was unashamedly realist and in the 1980s was appropriately christened the "ontological interpretation."[17] It describes particles with well-defined, causally determined paths. The particles are guided by a "quantum potential" that supplies "active information" about the entire experimental setup. Bohm went explicitly metaphysical when he speculated about implicate and superimplicate orders behind the surface physics and strived after the unification of mind and matter as two aspects of one reality.

A third peculiarity of quantum physics, and perhaps the strangest of all, was given special emphasis by Bohm but had also been highlighted by Bohr, namely *wholeness* or holistic interconnectedness. Physical systems, from experimental apparatuses up to the universe in its entirety, have to be considered as a whole at the microphysical level because their parts are intimately connected with one another and with the system as a whole. This far-reaching connectedness is referred to as *nonlocality*, Einstein's "spooky actions at a distance," and in some special situations *entanglement*. According to Einstein's special theory of relativity, the communication of physical effects cannot proceed faster than the velocity of light. However, quantum systems do exhibit faster-than-light connections between their parts, as theory predicts and experiments have now confirmed. It is as if each part is in contact with other parts of the system in a manner that does not involve the conventional transmission of effects at the maximal light velocity or less. The peculiar nature of nonlocality is emphasized by "delayed-choice" experiments in which the final arrangement of the apparatus is decided upon only after the experiment is underway. In these experiments, the end state of the apparatus seems to have an effect on events that took place earlier in the experiment, implying that events in the future can influence events in the past. Nonlocality seems to extend backward in time as well as across space. Some interpretations of quantum physics attempt to show how this strange retroactive effect takes place, such as John Cramer's transactional interpretation based on the Wheeler–Feynman Absorber theory of radiation, in which waves propagate backward as well as forward in time.[18]

Cherchez les monades

On the whole, scientists abhor an explanatory vacuum. When confronted with puzzling phenomena, such as particles that behave as waves, they would dearly love to peek behind the surfaces of nature and inspect the inner workings. Einstein was no exception. He regarded the lack of deep explanation in his own special theory of relativity as unsatisfactory. As a theory of principle, it afforded no understanding. In a letter (14 January 1908) to Arnold Sommerfeld, Einstein remarked:

> A physical theory can be satisfactory only if its structures are composed of elementary foundations. The theory of relativity is just as little ultimately satisfactory as, for example, classical thermodynamics was before Boltzmann had interpreted the entropy as probability.[19]

As a surface theory, special relativity was as explanatorily vacuous as the old gas laws before the kinetic theory came along. Similarly, the measurement approach to quantum physics, even when dressed up in Bohr's philosophy of complementarity, left much to be desired from an explanatory point of view, and unsurprisingly it had little appeal to Einstein's probing mind.[20]

We have seen that in both cases there have been moves toward depth theory and even metaphysics. It is often thought that the special theory was

PHYSICS			PHILOSOPHY
observation	*surface theory*	*depth theory*	*metaphysics*
relativistic phenomena	Einstein's special theory of relativity	Lorentz's ether	the "X" behind the phenomenon (noumena)
		Minkowski's spacetime (?) ↔	
quantum phenomena	Bohr's measurement approach	de Broglie's pilot wave	
		Bohm's quantum potential ↔	
		Cramer's advanced waves	

Table 8.1   Physics in search of metaphysics.

taken to a deeper explanatory level when relativistic effects were interpreted as consequences of a non-Newtonian spacetime structure, one in which space and time are fused into four-dimensional Minkowski spacetime. However, the ontological status of this absolute spacetime is uncertain, and it is open to debate whether the approach really offers deep explanation—hence the question mark in table 8.1. There are reasons to think that spacetime in its absolute form is just an abstract mathematical space that does no more than link distance and time measurements of observers in line with Einstein's theory.[21] For example, the fact that the invariant measure of separation in Minkowski spacetime can be zero for events widely separated in space and time smacks of mathematical abstraction.[22] It is possible that something more interesting, profound, and concrete hides behind the Minkowskian spacetime formulation, a fully-fledged scientific depth theory and even a metaphysics. Similarly, there have been several interpretations of quantum physics that go beyond the measurement-centered "orthodox" interpretation by attempting to explain how the quantum effects come about. David Bohm, we have seen, not only sought to provide a scientific depth theory but also delved into the metaphysics of matter and consciousness.

It will come as no surprise that the approach I wish to put forward for consideration takes the noumenal reality behind both relativistic and quantum phenomena to be a universe of all-inclusive, mutually expressive, perspectival perceptions, that is, a world of monads. I am by no means the first to suggest that Leibnizian monadology—or more likely a reformulation of it—may provide a suitable metaphysical framework for modern physics. Herbert Wildon Carr (1857–1931), a leading proponent in England of Henri Bergson's philosophy, raised the idea in several publications, finding in the theory of relativity a shift from the Newtonian worldview to one more in accord with Leibnizian monadology:

In effect we are proposing in mathematical and physical science to abandon
Newton's philosophy and adopt that of Leibniz.[23]

Science is turning, unconsciously it may be but surely, to the concept of
the monad.[24]

The principle of relativity is formulated to meet the fact, empirically
established, that there is no absolute system of reference, no system in
terms of which all movements can be standardized. This is the counterpart, expressed in physical terms, of the metaphysical doctrine of the
monadology.[25]

Carr believed two scientific developments of his day—relativity in physics
and Bergsonian creative evolution in biology—were not only consistent
with monadological idealism but could be used to reform it.[26] Carr kept the
monads "windowless" but traced their harmony not to a "divine artificer" but
to creative evolution and the coordinating activity of the monads themselves.

Leibnizian monadology was just as influential in the work of Alfred
North Whitehead (1861–1947), who like Carr addressed scientific developments of the day, devoting much attention to relativity.[27] Whitehead came
up with an approach to gravitation that diverged from Einstein's, and in
recent years there have been moves to bring Whiteheadian metaphysics
and quantum physics closer together.[28] Whitehead's philosophy has many
points of contact with classical monadology, but there are also very major
differences,[29] and his reformulation of monadology went much further than
Carr's. Both Leibniz and Whitehead extrapolate from their own experience
to provide insights into the nature of the world in general, and the procedure yields some commonalities. The most fundamental is that the world
is experiential in nature (Leibniz's "perception," Whitehead's "prehension"),
and so matter has to be understood in terms of experience. Accordingly, they
reject mind–matter dualism and materialist monism in favor of experiential
monism or *experientialism*.

Moreover, there is not just one experience or experiencing subject but a
multiplicity of them (*pluralism*), each the same in kind but unique in itself.
These experiential realities—Leibniz's "monads," Whitehead's "actual occasions"—are the basic units of nature (*panexperientialism*), and as such are
the units (*atomism*) that go to make up composite bodies, which are either
aggregates or organisms, the latter distinguished by having a "dominant
monad" (Leibniz) or "presiding occasion" (Whitehead) as unifying center.
In both systems, the experiential units are classified according to degree

of sophistication, with advanced mental functioning and consciousness manifesting in only the higher-grade units.

Unlike classical atoms, the units of both systems are complex unities (*many-in-ones*). A monad represents all other monads in its perceptual constitution, while an actual occasion synthesizes ("concrescence") prehensions of past actual occasions into itself. In both cases, the basic units are extensively connected to one another and the universe (*holism*), more so than classical atoms: a monad fully expresses the cosmic whole, representing all its fellow monads, with past and future implicit too; an actual occasion is not nearly so internally inclusive, but it does have "a perfectly definite bond with each item in the universe,"[30] that is, with all actual occasions in its causal past. From these bonds it selectively constructs itself. Because actual occasions are built exclusively from prehensions of past occasions, the form of connectedness can be called "cumulative penetration," the accumulation of the past in each present experience. The future is only weakly immanent in the present, in the form of anticipatory feelings. By contrast, the future is strongly immanent in a monad, and so its holism is closer to the spatially and temporally inclusive "interpenetration" exhibited by the dharma-units of Huayan Buddhism in which everything past, present, and future coexist.[31]

Leibniz and Whitehead suppose that their basic units are in process (*becoming*), monads passing from cosmic state to state, actual occasions growing, perishing, and informing subsequent occasions. In both cases, becoming involves a striving or goal-orientation (Leibniz's "appetition," Whitehead's "subjective aim"): as striving, experiential units, monads and actual occasions are modeled on living things rather than mechanisms (*organicism*). However, there is a major difference between their understandings of becoming, which stems from Whitehead's desubstantialization of Leibniz's transforming monadic *things* into process *events*. Whitehead gave great emphasis to the distinction, for his metaphysics abandons the traditional concept of "substance" that Leibniz's metaphysics largely preserves. A monad, as a substance, is a "being" or "continuant" that persists through change, while an actual occasion is a transient "happening" or "event" that arises and passes away.

Monads and actual occasions also differ significantly with regard to causation. Monads are more holistically connected than actual occasions through their cosmic representations, but, as self-contained wholes, there is no possibility or need of direct causal interaction between them. Instead, they are linked by preestablished harmony, and causation works internally ("immanent" causation), monads being self-evolving wholes that express the same universe, represent one another, and so conform to one another.

Whitehead, like many modifiers and updaters of monadology, was put off by the "windowlessness" of monads and attempted to introduce direct causation. An actual occasion affects another actual occasion directly if it is prehended by the latter and thereby contributes to its constitution. This is certainly a departure from Leibnizian monadology, for preestablished harmony and the appeal to a divine source of harmonization are abandoned, but it introduces mysteries of its own, such as the means by which an actual occasion prehends other actual occasions if they are external to it and how it reproduces some of their objectified content within itself. Leibnizian monads do not need to go outside of themselves because they hold everything within, represented internally in their perceptions.

Thus Leibniz's enduring, self-contained, and mutually accommodated monads are turned by Whitehead into fleetingly transient and directly interacting actual occasions.[32] This is a retreat from Leibniz's fully cosmic understanding of the experiential units of nature, which as all-inclusive and therefore self-contained wholes endure at least as long as the universe endures. Although sympathetic toward Whitehead's program, I think his reformulation of monads unnecessarily limits them in the quality of their perceptions and in their spatiotemporal inclusivity, making them even less able than Leibniz's monads to underpin the mystical and physical phenomena raised in this book, and also one of the psi phenomena, precognition, which process philosophy finds difficult to accept as genuine because the philosophy takes the future to be unformed.[33] Rather, I think that monads need to be reformulated in the opposite direction, making them *more* perceptually lucid and spatiotemporally inclusive than even Leibniz envisaged, in the manner outlined in chapter 6.

Among recent thinkers who have taken an interest in the application of Leibnizian philosophy to modern physics,[34] special mention should be made of Julian Barbour. Appreciative of the criticisms leveled by Leibniz and Ernst Mach at Newton's metaphysics of absolute space and time, Barbour along with the physicist Lee Smolin attempted to build a mathematical model based on Leibnizian monadology.[35] The approach utilized a feature of the monadology that is open to mathematical treatment in a fairly straightforward way, namely the requirement of "maximal variety" among created things, that is, the Neoplatonic principle of plenitude as employed by Leibniz.[36] Barbour and Smolin came to recognize that their approach would have a long way to go before it could claim to look anything like quantum mechanics or a quantum theory of gravity, but the spacetime relationalism that inspired their project lives on in Barbour's subsequent work on time and in Smolin's demand for "background independence" in his criticism of the superstring approach to quantum gravity and his advocacy of an alternative, relational approach called "loop quantum gravity."[37] And Barbour remained unequivocal in his appreciation of the potential relevance of Leibnizian monadology to contemporary physics:

> Leibniz developed what to many is a quite fantastical philosophy. To me, however, his philosophy is the one radical alternative to Cartesian-Newtonian materialism ever put forward that possesses enough definiteness to be cast in mathematical form – and hence to serve as a potential framework for natural science.[38]

I agree with the sentiment expressed here, for I think that monadology is open to detailed mathematical modeling, at least if it is significantly updated to take in modern developments. This is because monadology, unlike most other nonmaterialist approaches, has a very concrete perceptual-structural unit that is open to detailed mathematical treatment, namely the universe itself and its representations from multiple perspectives. So a fruitful mathematical investigation of monadology is likely to center on global cosmic structure and its representations and symmetries at macrocosmic and microphysical scales.

Monadology does seem to be peculiarly well suited to modern physics. To appreciate this, let us reinterpret Einstein's surface principles as depth statements, that is, statements about how things really are. The special theory of relativity then changes from a theory of measurement into a theory that makes statements about physical reality. In this form, it tells us that the laws of physics and the velocity of light are not *just measured* to be the same but *really are* the same for observers in uniform relative motion. Similarly, the same distances and time intervals are not *just measured* to be different but *really are* different for observers. But how can this possibly be? How, for instance, can one and the same object *really* be different in length for different observers? How can the time elapsed between the same two events *really* be different for these observers?

It is possible if observers possess their own versions of the world. Let us suppose that the world is irreducibly plural and relative in its construction. More specifically, let us suppose that it is constituted of monads. Frames of reference and observers, whether fully automated measuring devices or scientists armed with clocks and rulers, are to be understood as monadic perceptual perspectives. We carry around with us our own versions of the world and all its objects, organized from our individual centers of perception. Because our worlds are versions of exactly the same world, they transform

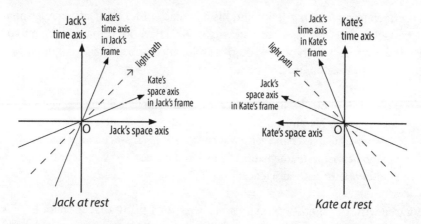

Figure 8.2   Jack and Kate at rest in their own relative spaces (just one spatial dimension shown).

in exactly the same way and are described by exactly the same laws of physics. And because light radiation will propagate in an identical way in our equivalent versions of the same world, the velocity of light will be the same. It is as if each one of us is endowed with a stationary luminiferous ether of our own, through which light travels at its maximal velocity c. In Lorentz's depth theory, there was just one stationary ether and one absolute time for all. In the absolute Minkowski ontology, there is just one spacetime, which can be resolved into multiple frames of reference to illustrate relativistic effects, into "an infinite number of spaces" as Minkowski put it, each with its own time axis defined by the temporal path of a point at rest in the space.[39] By contrast, in the monadological approach, the multiplicity of "frames" or "spaces" is taken to be a basic, ontological fact. The monads are multiple versions of the world with their own temporal sequences, and in this respect they are like the innumerable spaces into which Minkowski spacetime can be resolved. But in the monadological approach, there is just the multiplicity of monads and no absolute spacetime world.

To illustrate the difference between the Minkowski and monadological approaches, consider two astronauts Jack and Kate who fly past each other at event O with a relative velocity of half the speed of light. To depict their relative motion in the Minkowski approach, we have to resolve the absolute spacetime into two "spaces" and draw corresponding spacetime diagrams (fig. 8.2). Jack is shown at rest in one and Kate in the other. Note that Kate's motion through Jack's stationary frame is shown by her inclined time axis (and the same for Jack in Kate's frame). This is her path or "worldline" in Jack's frame. Now, in the monadological approach, these two diagrams do not depict "resolutions" of an absolute spacetime reality; rather, they express the essential multiplicity of the world, the plural, monadic character of its constitution, by illustrating the spatiotemporal perspectives of two monads.

In the monadological approach, relativistic phenomena such as length contraction and time dilation stem from the way the world is organized, as a multiplicity of mutually accommodated ("harmonized") versions. Quantum phenomena can also be understood to stem from monadic organization (and the structure and behavior of monads), if not so clearly and straightforwardly. Monads as the "true atoms of nature" have certain features that make them very different from classical particles, and it is conceivable that some of these features could lie behind quantum effects:

Monads are both continuous and discrete. In their inner constitution, monads are continuous fields of experience, but they confer upon the world a fundamental granularity or discontinuity because they are self-contained perceptions. Monads are discrete units in themselves and presumably in the way they are represented as matter in the inner constitution of one another. So we should expect the physics of matter in motion to exhibit discontinuities as well as continuities.

Monads are deeply interconnected. Although discrete units, monadic "particles" are not isolated from one another. They are intimately connected, being mutually accommodated and expressive of a common universe in their perceptions. Their behavior is correlated, and they are each informed by the entire universe. The "atomism" of the monadology is holistic, with fundamental particles intimately connected with one another through their representation of the whole. We may therefore expect the physics of matter to be far more holistic than was envisaged in the classical outlook.

The entire spacetime universe is represented locally in the monadic units of matter. The presence of the spatiotemporal whole in the part means that later states as well as prior states are immanent in the present state. This could mean that material behavior is not only conditioned by the past but is "future-sensitive" too, as the delayed-choice experiments can be taken to suggest.

Monads, being minds or mindlike, are active, appetitive, end-directed (i.e., not entirely passive), and they conform to more active monads. It follows that the behavior of *individual* units of matter will not be entirely describable and predictable using physical laws, and statistical and probabilistic treatments will have to suffice.

In the above, it is not difficult to see possible connections with some peculiar features of quantum physics, such as *discontinuity* and *nonlocality*. Moreover, there is the implication that purely physical description will be *incomplete* since it does not take into account the mind-like qualities of matter. There is also the promise that monadology, with its combination of the discontinuous and the continuous, can bring together quantum physics with its microphysical discontinuities and general relativity with its cosmic continuum.

But should we regard the apparent connections with quantum physics as more than superficial? The challenge is to show in detail how the metaphysics meshes with the physics, and this is no easy task. One challenge is to consider which of the above-noted monadological features may be particularly important for understanding quantum physics—not all may be equally significant. Another task is to examine points of contact between monadology and existing interpretations of quantum physics. For example, it is likely that there will be some overlap with Whiteheadian interpretations, if only to some extent given the metaphysical differences, such as the openness of the future in Whitehead's scheme. Monadic spatiotemporal inclusivity sits better with interpretations of quantum physics, such as Cramer's, that take the future to exist just as much as the present and which can therefore trace quantum effects to retrocausal or "backward-in-time" influence.[40]

As for other interpretations, monadology shares a realist outlook with those that treat particles as entities that follow definite trajectories, whether or not they are being measured, notably David Bohm's approach.[41] Bohm's physics and philosophy resonate with Leibnizian monadology in several ways, as Paavo Pylkkänen has pointed out, particularly in Bohm's concepts of the implicate order, enfoldment, and active information, and emphasis on nonlocality.[42] Monadology could also have a connection with interpretations that give consciousness a role in quantum processes, since monads are active subjects who can be the reasons for change in other monads, although monadology does not reserve subjectivity for an experimental observer but finds it widely distributed throughout nature. There may also be some connection with "relational" interpretations that adopt a core insight of relativistic physics by emphasizing the frame-dependence of observations, their relativity to the observer.[43] On the other hand, interpretations that are resolutely unmetaphysical, taking a positivist or pragmatist measurement approach, do not sit well with monadology. Finally, the many-worlds interpretation, which avoids the problematic wave function collapse by having all possibilities manifested, would be morally repugnant to classical monadology, for which only the "best of all possible worlds" is realized.

Another challenge is to work out how monadic matter is related to the elementary particles currently described by physics. One potential point of contact with the modern physical understanding of matter is the concept of extra dimensions, which in the 1980s and 1990s took center stage in attempts to achieve a unified physical picture of the world.

Multi-Dimensional Spaces

Physicists have made use of extra space dimensions in their recent efforts to integrate general relativity and quantum physics in a "theory of everything" and so unify gravity with the other known forces of nature, the electromagnetic, strong, and weak forces. To accomplish this, the supergravity and superstring theories introduced extra space dimensions that normally escape attention because they are curled up at extremely small scales. Supergravity theory used a total of eleven dimensions, the four familiar large spacetime dimensions and seven curled-up or "compact" space dimensions. Superstring theory added just six extra compact space dimensions to give a total of ten, and the development called M-theory increased this to eleven and beyond. More recently, in the late 1990s, the idea of additional *large* space dimensions emerged in theoretical physics. In one such theory, the universe is regarded as a membrane or "brane" located in a higher-dimensional space called the "bulk," with all forces apart from gravitation confined to the brane. In some theories, the bulk contains more than one brane. For instance, in the "ekpyrotic" model, two three-dimensional universes are situated along an extra space dimension and their collision gives rise to the event that is more conventionally interpreted as the Big Bang origin of the universe.

What might all this have to do with monads? Perhaps nothing, but it is noteworthy that extra dimensions are also a feature of the monadological scheme I have been proposing. This is because monads are *perceptual spaces* with their own sets of space and time dimensions, as I shall now explain.

The Spatiality of Experience

When Descartes made a sharp distinction between "extended thing" (*res extensa*) and "thinking thing" (*res cogitans*), he set up a dualism of matter and mind that is problematic for several reasons. For one thing, it is not at all clear how substances so very different from each other as extended matter and unextended mind can interact. For another, it is difficult to understand how unextended minds can have experiences with extended contents.[44] Many experiential contents are spatially extended, as is evident in our visual and tactile experiences of objects, whether in sense perception, dreaming, hallucination, or imagination. For example, if we picture to ourselves a cat in a tree, it is clear that both the imagined cat and the imagined tree are extended, having shape and relative size (fig. 8.3).

Whereas the extensional qualities of subjective experience are self-evident, the existence of an objective material world filled with extended bodies is uncertain and easy prey to skepticism. This observation, which dates back at least as far as George Berkeley's insistence that the primary qualities of "extension, figure, and motion" are in the mind, was given special emphasis in the early twentieth century by philosophers such as Bertrand Russell and C. D. Broad, who concerned themselves with what they took to be the indubitable "given" of experience, the directly known "sense-data," exemplified by extended color patches in visual experience. As Broad pointed out, the very idea of physical space is derived from acquaintance with visual experience, for the visual field is the exemplar of extendedness:

> [a visual field is] an extended whole of simultaneous parts; these parts, viz., variously coloured outstanding patches, do visibly have various shapes and sizes, and do visibly occupy various positions within the whole field.[45]

Because experiences commonly involve a dimensional arrangement of extended items (most obviously in the visual contents but also in connection with auditory and tactile sensations), it is possible to refer to experiences as *experiential* or *phenomenal spaces* or more particularly as *perceptual spaces* if the experiences are taken to be percepts of things. For example, if I were to dream of a unicorn, my phenomenal dream space would contain the figure of a creature with an equine shape and a single horn extending from its forehead. And if, in waking hours, I were to gaze out of the window into the garden, my perceptual space would consist of an extended field of variegated colors in the forms of trees, grass, flowers, birds, squirrels, clouds, and sky, seamlessly fused with sounds and body sensations that reinforce the sense of a spatial distribution of objects around myself, near and far.

Phenomenal/perceptual space is commonly taken to be three-dimensional. Objects seem to be extended and arranged in three independent directions, up and down, left and right, forward and backward, and we engage with objects as if they were so distributed, as when we reach out

Figure 8.3   The imagined cat and tree have qualities of extension.

to grasp hold of things or jump out of the way of oncoming vehicles. But the status of the forward-backward or "depth" component of phenomenal space is uncertain. Like the essentially flat images projected on the retina of the eye, visual experience is not multilayered in the depth direction, and like a painting on a canvas or a film projected on a cinema screen, it can be considered two-dimensional, being all opaque surface, with no proper transparency, no thick ordering of contents in the depth dimension. Psychology describes how the perception of depth and distance is interpretative, drawing on various types of cues, as illustrated by those "Magic Eye" or stereoscopic pictures that leap out of the flat page when we cross our eyes. But the question of dimensionality is nonetheless tantalizing because the phenomenal presentation of objects does have a definite 3-D feel, and it may be premature to explain away the sense of depth as mere interpretation. Although phenomenal space may be 2-D in the informational character of its contents, it is perhaps 3-D in its experiential actuality, with 2-D surfaces arranged in a truly 3-D experiential space.

Perspective Space

The concept of perceptual space can be taken in several directions. One possibility is to reformulate dualism in a way that unequivocally puts extension into the world of mind. In this form of dualism, the partner of the extended material realm is reconceived as an *extended* mental realm that incorporates the phenomenal spaces of experience, an approach taken by John Smythies for many years.[46]

Another path was followed by Bertrand Russell when he attempted to construct the material world of the physicists from perceptual spaces. In one phase of his long philosophical career, between 1912 and 1919, Russell took up the idea of 3-D perceptual spaces and developed it into a theory of 6-D perspective space. His intention here was to counter skepticism about the external world by forging a path from the certainties of the perceptual given, the sense-data as a sure ground of knowledge, to the far less certain public world of space, time, and matter discussed by physicists. A scientific *public space* was to be constructed from the *private spaces* of perceptual observers. In pursuing this project, Russell found inspiration in Leibniz's monadology:

> The theory to be advocated is closely analogous to Leibniz's monadology, from which it differs chiefly in being less smooth and tidy.[47]

> Let us imagine that each mind looks out upon the world, as in Leibniz's monadology, from a point of view peculiar to itself; and for the sake of simplicity let us confine ourselves to the sense of sight, ignoring minds which are devoid in this sense. Each mind sees at each moment an immensely complex three-dimensional world; but there is absolutely nothing which is seen by two minds simultaneously.[48]

Russell's idea was to take all the unique 3-D monadic private spaces, possible as well as actual, and arrange them as points in a continuous 3-D public space according to their "points of view." The resultant perspective space has a combined dimensionality of six, three from the private spaces and three from their arrangement in a public space. The characteristics of an object depend on the private spaces in which it is perceived. For example, a coin in one private space will be circular and silver, while in another elliptical and gray. An object in its totality is the class of all its relative aspects in the numerous perceptual spaces. In this approach, the 3-D public space and the basic constituents of matter described by physicists are "logical constructions" derived ultimately from the hard sense-data of perceptual spaces.

However, Russell did not consider himself to be espousing an idealism in which the material world is reduced to mind, in the manner of, say, Berkeley's immaterialism, according to which only minds and their ideas exist. For Russell, sense-data were not mental because he required the "mental" to be "aware of something." In fact, Russell in this period regarded the sense-data as "physical," meaning that they are "what is dealt with by physics," for in his theory they are the hard data from which the world of physics is constructed.[49] Nor did Russell regard his theory as phenomenalism. Whereas phenomenalism reduces material objects to actual and possible sense-data, Russell constructed material objects from sense-data without denying that the objects might exist regardless of the sense-data.[50]

Another kind of perspective space has been developed by cosmologist Bernard Carr in an effort to bridge the gap between "mind" and "matter"—between phenomenal spaces and the world of physics.[51] Carr's approach differs from Russell's in important respects, both in the philosophical underpinnings and in the details of the perspective space. For instance, Carr employs the concept of perceptual space in the tradition of Russell and others, but there is no suggestion that he is attempting to construct the universe of physics out of the certainties of sense-data, in the manner of Russell's method of "logical construction" (which Russell himself was to abandon as unworkable). Carr also takes a broader view of the kinds of phenomenal spaces that are to be located in perspective space. He is concerned not only with the perceptual spaces of sensory data but also with the "wild facts" in all their wildness, the phenomenal spaces of dreams, hallucinations, and a variety of extraordinary experiences, including out-of-body experiences, near-death experiences, psi phenomena, and apparitions, experiences of these kinds also being acknowledged to have extended contents. In fact, Carr broadens the meaning of "perception" to include all of these experiences and supposes that, like ordinary sense perception, they depend on sensors. Carr understands his perceptual spaces, ordinary and extraordinary, to be "projections" or "slices" of a higher-dimensional Universal Structure, which he equates with the higher-dimensional space recently discussed in physics, the "bulk" in which the familiar universe is said to be embedded as a "brane."

Carr's approach, like Russell's, is of interest here because a higher dimensionality follows from the combination of perceptual spaces into one, all-inclusive perspective space. However, I shall now suggest that monadology requires not a single perspective space but many perspective spaces, one for each monad, with dramatic consequences for the overall dimensionality of the world.

The Spaces Within the Soul

Russell believed that his theory of perspective space was "closely analogous" to Leibniz's monadology, but it diverges fundamentally in one very important respect: Russell's perspective space, like Carr's Universal Structure, integrates private spaces into a single, "all-embracing" spatial configuration.[52] But there is no such all-embracing structure in Leibniz's system, for the monads are primary units of reality and therefore are not located in an integrative superstructure.

Nevertheless, it is possible to apply the basic idea of a higher-dimensional perspective space to *each* monad. More specifically, the idea is applicable to the perceptual *interiors* of monads. Monads considered internally are perceptual representations of all the other monads, and so they *do* locate perspectives within a comprehensive structure, their own internal, experiential "space," "continuum," or "field," as it might be called. Thus, each monad is itself an all-embracing perspective space. For the revised Leibnizian scheme outlined in chapter 6, these perceptions can no longer be properly called "phenomenal spaces" because they are complete, perfectly distinct representations of the universe. They are not our everyday phenomenal perceptions. Rather, they are *noumenal spaces*, fully distinct noumenal perceptions of the universe.

As a starting point, we can suppose that the interior noumenal space of a monad involves a three-dimensional arrangement of objects, as suggested by the quasi 3-D representations of our phenomenal experiences. Monadic perceptual space, then, would be 3-D, with perceptual contents organized from the center of perception in three independent directions. But unlike phenomenal space, noumenal space will be "thick" with detail in the depth direction because monadic experience is a complete representation of the universe that, unlike sense perception, is not at the mercy of signal transmission from objects to eyes. Hence there are none of the opaque phenomenal surfaces with which we ordinarily have to contend, and genuine transparency and depth of contents will be the order of the day.

Now, if my 3-D noumenal space represents all the other 3-D noumenal spaces of my fellow monads, then the dimensionality of my noumenal space increases to six. So my monadic space is 6-D, like Russell's perspective space. However, the increase in dimensionality will not stop here because your noumenal space also represents my noumenal space and all the other noumenal spaces, and so it too is 6-D. Thus, when I represent your space, I also represent your representations of all the other spaces, which has the effect of increasing the overall dimensionality of my space to nine. In fact, mutual representation goes on indefinitely, like an infinite regress of reflections in mirrors, making for an unending repetition of perceptual spaces and their sets of dimensions. Hence, the dimensional structuring of the monadic universe is *nested*: perceptual spaces within perceptual spaces within perceptual spaces, sets of dimensions within sets of dimensions within sets of dimensions. For the basic 3-D noumenal space, this is expressed as an endless nesting of 3-D spaces within 3-D spaces, and so the overall dimensionality of the monad will be an infinite multiple of three.

However, we have seen that special relativity has given rise to the idea of a combined 4-D spacetime structure, and the introduction of spatialized time into the monad's perspective space would increase its dimensionality from six to eight at a first approximation, with 4-D spacetimes organized as points in a 4-D spacetime. Although there is no need to take the Minkowski version of spacetime seriously as an ontological reality, as I pointed out above, there may well be a role for spacetime conceived in non-absolute form, a plurality of real, monadic spacetimes rather than one abstract, monolithic spacetime. For one thing, spacetime does help to make sense of simultaneity, temporal ordering, time dilation, length contraction, and causal structure. Furthermore, general relativity makes use of the concept of spacetime to explain gravitation by attributing curvature to 4-D spacetime in the presence of matter and radiation. If this is interpreted in a strongly realist fashion, as indicative of the dimensionality of an actual spacetime world, then monadic perceptual space becomes 4-D spacetime with curvature.

The curvature of spacetime utilized by general relativity has not usually been taken to imply a real fifth dimension that "embeds" the curvature, except in popular expositions; rather, the fifth dimension has typically been regarded as an irrelevancy because the curved geometry of spacetime is treated as "intrinsic," with no external reference needed.[53] But perhaps it is hasty to dismiss the embedding dimension as an irrelevancy, particularly in the light of the recent bulk–brane cosmologies that do place the universe in a higher-dimensional space. So, to take one simple example, if the universe expands from a Big Bang and then collapses to a Big Crunch, it might take the form of a 4-D spacetime surface of a 5-D hypersphere, with the fifth dimension embedding the curvature. The monadic perceptual space would be a 5-D bubble with the contents of the universe and its temporal development spread over the surface (see fig. 6.5).

The dimensionality of the overall noumenal space, including all the mutual interrepresentations, would then be an infinite multiple of either four or five, depending on whether the embedding dimension of spacetime curvature is included. Note that because *spacetime* is interrepresented, not only are the three space dimensions multiplied but also the one time dimension. So in the above example of the 5-D hypersphere, time constitutes one component of the overall dimensionality of the sphere but is also wrapped round in the surface microstructure at ever descending dimensional levels. The dizzying multiplication of spacetime dimensions will sound bizarre to many, but it follows from the simple proposition that one perception represents another perception in full. It would not have seemed strange to, say, Plotinus, Thomas Traherne, and the authors of the *Avataṃsaka Sūtra* and the *Yogavāsiṣṭha*, who appear to have had experiential acquaintance with the multiplicatory characteristics of an interreflecting universe.

The Structure of Matter

An essential feature of monadology is its special understanding of matter. The "true atoms of nature" are the monads themselves. More accurately, bodies are made up of configurations of monads represented in other monads. So, in the simple case of the hyperspherical Big-Bang-to-Big-Crunch spacetime cosmos, each state of a monad would itself be a spacetime hypersphere and so too the fundamental units of matter represented in the monad. On close inspection, the hyperspherical particles would themselves be discovered to contain numerous hyperspherical particles within their surfaces, owing to the interrepresentational character of monads, and this would continue indefinitely at ever-decreasing dimensional levels, "wheels within wheels," ad infinitum. And being representations of the entire cosmic pattern, the spacetime particles at all dimensional levels would be interlinked. There is a far-reaching interconnectedness between the particles, extending even to the future if the particles are spacetime wholes and not merely spatial wholes. The particles are directly sensitive to everything in the universe, not only to events in the vicinity but also at great distances and even in the future, without requiring any signals transmitted to them at the finite velocities of special relativity.

There is one factor that may have to be considered in attempts to model the physics of monads. It may be necessary to pay attention to the immediate environment of a monadic particle, for it is possible that the particle has an impact on the spacetime environment in which it is embedded. This consideration is suggested again by the recent bulk–brane theories in theoretical physics, for in some of these the presence of a spacetime universe ("brane") is said to have a "warping" effect on the higher dimensional space ("bulk") in which it is embedded.[54] If this effect is represented at the microphysical scale, then matter would not be constituted solely of monadic particles but would also involve the warped spacetime environment in which the particles are set. It is then conceivable that the particles described by contemporary physics are expressions of the warped spacetime environment churned up, so to speak, by the coordinated dance of the monadic particles. In fact, it could even be speculated that the curvature of spacetime in the presence of matter (mass-energy) is a consequence of this warping around microcosmic monads. *This would mean that matter is not only the representation of configurations of monads but also the warped environment in the vicinity of represented monads.* However, I am well aware that my speculations here are running well ahead of my physical understanding, and I leave it to physicists to decide whether there may be any value in these ideas.

One further observation is worth making. In monadology, the fundamental particle mirrors the universe. More precisely, each temporal state of a particle mirrors the universe from its position in spacetime. So if the universe is of the kind that begins with a Big Bang, then from the temporal view each state of a *particle* also bursts into existence with a "bang." And if the universe ends with a Big Crunch, then each state of a particle collapses out of existence with a crunch. If the universe begins with a Bang and ends with a Crunch (fig. 6.5), then particles pulse in and out of existence as they leap from state to state. This will also be true of our own experiences in their cosmic fullness, if they express a universe that expands and contracts. From a temporal viewpoint, our cosmic experiences pulse in and out of existence, and this cosmic heartbeat is echoed in the fundamental units of matter. There is, of course, no guarantee that the Big Bang idea will survive developments in cosmology, and the Big Crunch fate of the universe has been out of favor for several years, a "Big Chill" scenario being favored by astronomical observations that point to a universe with accelerating expansion. But whatever form cosmic evolution is eventually found to take, this too will apply to the fundamental spacetime particles of the system.

Hypercosmic Spaces

When I first explored the idea of a universe represented in its own material microstructure, I wondered if monadic representation might also take place at ascending dimensional levels, at the macrocosmic level and above.[55] The worlds-within-worlds nesting of dimensions would then proceed "upward" and "around" the cosmic unit as well as "downward" at descending dimensional levels. The "Russian Doll" arrangement would then work both "up" as well as "down," with no end in view either way, so that we truly are "in the midst of an infinite" (to quote William James's phrase again). I was drawn to consider this possibility because, in the mystical experience described in chapter 2, I had the sense of looking beyond the luminous, highly detailed space that initially occupied my attention into another space, a vaster and emptier space which contained some details that made me feel very small. Since then I have come across several accounts of celestial flights to the edge of the universe, such as those noted in chapter 7, and these, even if they are symbolic, might again lead one to speculate about the possibility of structure beyond the cosmic unit, including repeating structure. In a monadological scheme, this would work as follows. Our spacetime universe is embedded in the spacetime of a very large representation of itself, and this greater spacetime contains representations of all the other monadic perspectives in our universe. Thus, if the cosmic unit were a hyperspherical bubble, we would find that our universe is embedded on the spacetime surface of a giant hypersphere and is surrounded on this surface by other spacetime bubbles, which are simply versions of our own universe represented from different perspectives. This macrocosmic representation might be repeated at ever-ascending hypercosmic dimensional levels, so that the world is infinite at both ever-ascending and ever-descending dimensional scales.

The idea of universes beyond the universe has become more acceptable in present-day cosmology, owing to multiverse speculations in general and more specifically to the kind of multiverse theory that places the universe ("brane") within a higher-dimensional space ("bulk"). In bulk–brane terminology, the expanded monadological worldpicture would view our brane as embedded in a bulk that is a large-scale representation of the brane, and this bulk would itself be a brane in a greater bulk, and so on, "brane in bulk" and "bulk as brane" indefinitely. All these would simply be representations of our own brane and therefore have the same spacetime dimensionality and geometry. So, if our universe were the spacetime hypersphere, then both its microphysical particles and the bulk in which it is embedded would be spacetime hyperspheres, and the physics that describes the universe in its bulk would be the same physics that describes the fundamental particle in its immediate spacetime environment.

I shall not take these ideas any further here, as they are truly in the realm of the fantastical, and I have no doubt already strained the reader's patience. However, it should be borne in mind once again that my extravagant conjecture is just an extension of the basic proposition that one full perception fully represents all other full perceptions.

9

Meet the World Parents

> One must study the genesis of the universe,
> that thereby we may be able to learn
> the nature of man.
>
> —Clement of Alexandria

THE PHILOSOPHY OF MONADS brings into sharp relief a long-standing metaphysical conundrum, the derivation of the Many from the One. How does a world of multiplicity arise from a first principle that is commonly taken to be singular? In Leibniz's monadology, the multiplicity of distinct yet harmonized cosmic perspectives points to a yet deeper level of reality, one that is their common source and ultimately responsible for their harmonized coordination. In Leibniz's theocentric system, this fundamental reality is God, the divine creator who, actualizing the best of all possible worlds, sets up, synchronizes, and sustains the monads in such a way that they express the same universe from their shifting perspectives. Leibniz does not explain in detail how God creates and sustains the monads, but it is clear that he envisages an emanational process. God "fulgurates" or flashes forth the monads, producing them like the thoughts of a thinker.[1] The monads are, in effect, parallel streams of perception of a supreme mind, poured forth from potentiality into luminous actuality by the power, knowledge, and will of this incomparable divine reality. It is as if God creates and sustains the world by thinking it from numerous points of view. Leibniz's emanationism is fitting given the mystical sources from which his monadology most likely drew some inspiration, and it is to mystical philosophies that we can turn to shed light on the emergence of monads from the common source that their coordinated multiplicity requires.

Schemes of world emanation can be very obscure and complex, and so I shall be selective in my approach, giving attention chiefly to one idea that I think is particularly valuable and which can be developed in interesting ways. This is the idea that a *reflexive* act of awareness, productive of certain kinds of self-consciousness, plays a fundamental role in the process of world creation and that the subject object dynamics initiated by this act, taking the form of a cyclical interplay of self and other, runs through the process of world creation and is woven into the fabric of the universe. In pursuing this idea, I shall examine the initial "moments" of world emanation in the systems of Plotinus and the Pratyabhijñā school of nondual Kashmir Shaivism. These systems are of special interest here for several reasons. First, they give overt attention to the role of subject and object in the emanative process. Second, they can be construed, although not uncontroversially, as forms of idealist metaphysics and are therefore well-suited to the idealist monism that I have advocated in previous chapters. They show how one can go about deriving a mentalistic universe from an ultimate reality that is itself mindlike in some way, albeit in a manner that largely transcends comprehension by derivative minds such as ours.

Third, these systems are informed by mystical experience and contemplative practice, and therefore have a clear experiential basis. Although they build on ideas received from tradition, they are also grounded in experiential familiarity with the realities discussed and are less likely to go astray than more abstract efforts. Hence I prefer to take them as my starting point, rather than, say, the post-Kantian idealisms of Fichte, Schelling, and Hegel, whose speculations on the creative subject and the progress of self-consciousness are certainly relevant to the matter in hand but are not, as far as I know, personally informed by deep mystical experiences. Engagement with the post-Kantian idealisms would undoubtedly be worthwhile, and these philosophies do have links with mysticism through the revival of interest in the subject during the Romantic period,[2] but I prefer to ground my discussion in philosophies more directly informed by mystical experience.

By presenting Plotinian and Pratyabhijñā ideas, and intimating certain parallels, I do not mean to imply that the systems as a whole are in detailed agreement with each other, for in-depth comparison would certainly bring out many differences. It also has to be admitted that my discussion will skirt around the interpretative difficulties that these philosophies present. Nevertheless, I believe that there are some interesting points of contact between them in their depictions of the early stages of world production. These include the importance given to subject and object, the idea that activity is at the very heart of reality, and the concept of the One-Many, a unified, cosmic level of experience between the One and the Many that mystics are able to access.

So that the discussion does not become overly dry, I devote some attention to that captivating goddess whose dualizing and multiplying mirror introduces certain kinds of self-consciousness by allowing the subject to take itself as its object, thereby making possible a universe of multiplicity and the various kinds of derivative self-knowledge that come with it. I then recount two dreams that may be relevant to the puzzle of how the Many come forth from the One. Finally, I tell a "twofold tale" about the dance of subject and object, of self and other, in cycles of separation and unification dominated by "Ego" and "Eros." But first a few words on *cosmogony*, the story of how the world comes to be.

The Origin of the World

Most present-day cosmologists subscribe to a Big-Bang model of cosmic evolution: the universe is said to have begun just under fourteen billion years ago in a condition of extreme density and temperature (the "Planck era"), expanding rapidly and cooling as it developed. According to one influential theory, a brief period of very rapid expansion took place in the early moments of the Big Bang, inflating the universe from minuscule size to several centimeters or meters in diameter ("inflation era"). For a very short time, a soup of quark and gluon particles dominated ("quark era"). Protons and neutrons then began to form ("hadron era"), and by three minutes they were combining into simple atomic nuclei ("nucleosynthesis era"). Hundreds of thousands of years later, the universe was sufficiently cool for atoms complete with electrons to form. Several hundred million years were to elapse before matter clumped together to form the first stars, making possible the synthesis of larger atoms. It is thought that our solar system and planet Earth came on the scene rather late, after nine billion years or so, with organic life in the form of simple cells developing on Earth several hundred million years later.

Theories about the origin of the universe are sometimes called "cosmogonies." One type of cosmogony, which includes modern scientific theories such as the Big-Bang model, aims to describe the temporal evolution of the early universe, setting out a timeline of events and "eras" such as those just described. However, there is another type of cosmogony, found in religious and philosophical contexts, that probes into the derivation of the universe from an ultimate source, that is, into its dependence on a ground reality.

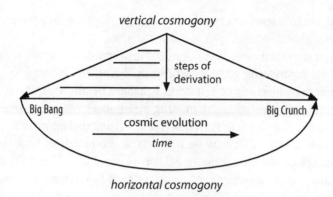

Figure 9.1   Horizontal and vertical aspects of cosmogony.

This latter type of cosmogony can be called "vertical," in contrast to the "horizontal" type that occupies modern-day cosmologists (fig. 9.1). It is vertical cosmogony that the mystic may seek to reverse in the mystical ascent, tracing back the steps of ontological derivation to the source.

The two types of cosmogony come together in a single scheme if attention is paid to both the vertical dependence of the universe on its ground and the horizontal evolution of the universe through time. In fact, the distinction between vertical and horizontal aspects of cosmogony can be viewed as a special case of a broader distinction between two kinds of causation, a vertical causation *behind* phenomena and a horizontal causation *among* phenomena. This is perhaps expressed in the Huayan Buddhist distinction between *li-shih wu-ai* (nature origination, *tathāgatagarbha* causation) and *shih-shih wu-ai* (conditioned origination, *dharmadhātu* causation). The former refers to the dependence of phenomena (*shih*) on principle (*li*), on the pure and immutable Mind, likened to the dependence of ocean waves on the ocean. The latter refers to the conditioned co-arising of phenomena, comparable to the interaction of the ocean waves, which in the holistic philosophy of Huayan is understood to involve the presence of the whole in the part. In the analogy, each wave entails or reflects every other wave and the entire ocean surface.[3]

Vertical cosmogony has often been understood to take place "out of time," to involve "eternal" or "logical" steps rather than temporal stages. Thus, many interpreters of Plato's *Timaeus* understood its cosmogony to be descriptive of a timeless construction of the world, a tenseless dependence of the lower ontological levels on their ultimate source. The temporal character of the account, couched in terms of a divine creator who fashions the world in time, is then regarded as an expository device.[4] The first few steps in the cosmogonies of Plotinus and the Pratyabhijñā school outlined below are to be taken in this spirit, for the sequence of steps laid out there are ontological and logically prior to the emergence of time. Another way of understanding vertical cosmogony is to suppose that it unfolds not atemporally but in a special time of its own, different from the time in which the familiar temporal evolution of the universe takes place.[5] There is, then, a "vertical time" of world production as well as the "horizontal time" of cosmic evolution. However, if this move introduces change into the heart of reality, it might be rejected as compromising the ultimate by destabilizing it.

The distinction between vertical and horizontal aspects of cosmogony is still valid if the "frozen" temporality of spacetime or the "block universe" is adopted. Take, for instance, the universe that begins with a Big Bang and ends in a Big Crunch. In the spacetime view, this might have the form of a spacetime hypersphere with the Big Bang at one "end" and the Big Crunch at the other (see fig. 6.5). Horizontal cosmogony would describe the causal sequences of events that spread out from the Big-Bang end of the hypersphere. By contrast, vertical cosmogony looks at the dependence of the entire spacetime hypersphere on deeper levels of reality, tracing the entire spacetime universe back to its "First Cause." Vertical cosmogony is active throughout all time, not just at an initial moment of temporal creation. Thus, if we go in search of the origin of the multiplicity we find around us, we may need to consider not only the temporal evolution of the universe but also its ongoing dependence on a ground reality that makes spacetime and matter possible in the first place. To the mystic, the steps of vertical cosmogony are accessible anywhere and anywhen in the spacetime universe, constituting an everpresent ontological ladder to the source reality.

In the theory of monads, horizontal and vertical aspects of cosmogony are both relevant. A monad involves the former because its perceptions express the universe and therefore represent its temporal evolution, including any temporal beginning and end it may have. But monadology also calls for vertical cosmogony, for the multiplicity of mutually accommodated cosmic wholes points to a common source. The derivation of monads must depend upon some procedure whereby multiple perceptions organized from different points of view emerge from a common, underlying source. According to some mystical cosmogonies, the route by which the Many come forth from the One involves a reflexive act of consciousness and a differentiation of subject and object. Monads, we can likewise conjecture, emerge through a perceptual-cognitive-affective "turning" of the ground reality toward itself, an act that generates a multiplicity of subjective stances and so creates a perceptual universe.

Reflexive Knowing

The process of world emanation can be understood to proceed by differentiation from an ultimate level A to two levels of perception B and C, which differ in kind and degree of subject–object discrimination:

A. *Ultimate level*
perfect identity of subject and object (?)

B. *Noumenal level*
cosmic subjects inclusive of their cosmic objects

C. *Phenomenal level*
limited subjects construing limited objects as distinct

The types of discrimination characteristic of the noumenal and phenomenal levels have already been shown diagrammatically in chapter 4 (figs. 4.3 and 4.4). While the subject–object structurings at these two levels are relatively unproblematic, there is uncertainty over the ultimate level from which the differentiation is commonly supposed to proceed. Is there a perfect subject–object identity prior to any differentiation, or is there pure subject without object, or even a complete absence of both subject and object?

To inquire into these questions and related matters, we can look at the emanation of the noumenal level from the ultimate level in the philosophy of Plotinus. In the Plotinian scheme, this is the derivation of Intellect or Nous and its multiplicity of intellects (*noes, noi*) from the One (*hen*). At the level of cosmic Intellect, subject and object are in a condition of duality-in-unity, distinguishable but not cognized as radically separate. The self-consciousness of the Intellect is not of the discursive kind with which we are familiar in our dualistic, conceptual mode of thinking. Because the Intellect is united with its intelligible objects (*noēta*), there is no representational gap between knower and known, and so there is none of the fallible, mediated self-knowledge that dominates at the sensory level. But the soul, aspiring to know itself, can attain to this knowledge through the experiential discovery of its rootedness in the Intellect.

However, the situation is not so clear at the ultimate level of Plotinian metaphysics, the One, the source of the Intellect and its multiple intellects. Although Plotinus often portrays the ineffable One by declaring what it is not, a passage in his *Enneads* offers a positive description that makes the One sound very much like a higher version of the self-knowing Intellect, but different in some way, presumably completely unified, with no hint at all of subject–object duality, not even the duality-in-unity and multiplicity-in-unity of the Intellect and its contents:

> it is not like something senseless; all things belong to it and are in it and with it. It is completely able to discern itself; it has life in itself and all things in itself, and its thinking of itself is itself, and exists by a kind of immediate self-consciousness, in everlasting rest and in a manner of thinking different from the thinking of Intellect. (*Enn.* v.4.2)

Taken at face value, the description attributes a special kind of self-awareness to the One, a consciousness that thinks itself in a special way, and perhaps even a sense of self, so that the One is an essential Self. It even seems to place all things in the One, presumably in such a way that they are not discrete, for the One is simple, not composite. If it makes sense to talk of subject and object at this level, they must be one and the same, and therefore completely indistinguishable. Alternatively it might be supposed that there is no object at all, if it makes sense to talk of a consciousness without an object, as John Bussanich has suggested: "absolute or infinite consciousness without an object, a nonrelational awareness that lacks intentionality."[6]

There has been much debate over the meaning of the above passage (v.4.2), which seems uncharacteristic of the Plotinian understanding of the One, although not unsupported by other passages.[7] However, if it is allowed that the One *is* mindlike in some way—aware and cognitive in some very special way that constitutes its inner life and activity—then the case becomes stronger for accepting the Plotinian metaphysics in its *entirety* as a form of idealism. Certainly, the One is such that it is able to produce the fair likeness of itself that is Intellect, and so it is probably not extravagant to suppose that there is something mindlike about the One, even though it may not be quite right to call it mind or intellect. There has been some controversy over whether any premodern philosophy, prior to the idealist critiques of Cartesian dualism, qualifies as idealism, but Plotinian metaphysics is perhaps one that does, and so too the nondual Shaivism of Kashmir.

Whatever the inner nature of the One might be, there is no doubt that the emanation of the Intellect and its intelligible cosmos from the One involves a reflexive turn. The path to Intellect has two phases, a going-forth and a turning-back that are to be understood as eternally coexistent rather than temporally successive, since time appears subsequently, further down the emanative sequence. In the first phase, an inchoate Intellect or pre-Intellect goes forth from the One, a procession (*prohodos*) of "infinite indeterminateness" that Plotinus describes as sight that has not yet grasped its object, "sight not yet seeing" (*Enn.* v.3.11). It is a subject that has yet to find its object. The idea owes something to an Aristotelian understanding of cognition and to Pythagorean-Platonic notions of an "indefinite dyad," interpreted by Plotinus as a streaming forth of infinite potentiality and life from the One. The inchoate or rudimentary Intellect emerges because of the "superabundance" of the One. The One is so generous in its plenitude that it "overflows" and "makes something other than itself," without diminishing itself (*Enn.* v.2.1). Behind the metaphorical language of emanation and flow is the idea that emerging Intellect is the One's external activity (*energeia*). This external activity derives from the One's internal activity, which is nothing less than the inner nature of the One.[8] The One, therefore, has twofold activity, one internal and essential and the other external and derivative, by which it is the "productive power [*dynamis*] of all things" (III.8.10, V.1.7, V.4.1, V.4.2).

By going forth, the inchoate Intellect leaves behind the One's perfect self-sufficiency and unity, and it therefore feels a deficiency and longs for that which is missing. Plotinus here makes use of the Platonic understanding of desire (*erōs*) as that which seeks to fill a want and which in its fulfillment begets.[9] The assertion of the subject, the inchoate Intellect, is a loss of sufficiency accompanied by a compensatory attraction toward the One as object. Here, at the very beginning of vertical cosmogony, Platonic "erosic" desire makes its first appearance, namely *the desire to possess a valued object to remedy a felt deficit in oneself.*[10] As an intellect, inchoate Intellect's nature is to know, and so it seeks to possess that which it desires by attempting to *know* it. Thus, the second phase of emanation, coincident with the first, is a contemplative reversion (*epistrophē*) of the inchoate Intellect toward the One, a turning-back of the subject to know an object (fig. 9.2). World emanation therefore begins with the going-forth of the One's external activity as intellective subject and its turning-back toward the One as its intended intelligible object.

The primordial dynamic of going-forth, felt insufficiency, turning-back in desire, and attempted possession is the prototype of all that follows in the process of manifestation. In their insufficiency, all derivative things desire after and seek to grasp the One and are drawn in contemplation toward it, which is therefore called their Good. But desire is readily diverted to objects less exalted and more easily grasped than the One and the Intellect, and in the shadier regions of the emanated universe, it readily latches on to substitutes that carry a trace of the divine luster, if only very dimly. Some of these are worthy stand-ins, elevating those whom they attract, while others are not so salubrious, dragging the smitten yet further from the light into labyrinths of image and shadow.

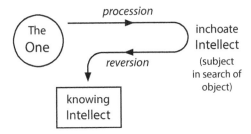

Figure 9.2   Procession and reversion: emanation of the knowing Intellect from the One via the inchoate Intellect.

It is the turning-back of the inchoate Intellect to know the One that generates intellectual seeing and begets Intellect proper, the knowing Intellect and its unified multiplicity. "Filled" by the One to which it has turned but unable to grasp this unthinkable reality, the inchoate Intellect crystallizes into knowing Intellect and its noetic universe, which, despite its beauty, grandeur, and wholeness, is nonetheless a dependent image of the One and therefore ultimately insufficient. The Beautiful is good, but the Good is better. The subject, the "sight not yet seeing," becomes a subject with a determinate object, "possessing the multiplicity which that sight itself made," a complexity generated in the attempt to contemplate the absolute simplicity (*Enn.* v.3.11). It is a self-thinking subject that has itself as object. In this self-thinking, the One is now known obliquely. The Intellect sees the One indirectly by seeing itself directly, the simple One being perceived via the complex mental representation that is the cosmos (perhaps an elevated "representative" perception additional to the ones discussed in chapter 6).

But does the sequence outlined above really explain how multiplicity derives from the One? How does the inchoate Intellect's attempt to know the One, in which a subject seeks to grasp an ungraspable object, generate complexity and multiplicity? Is it due to the nature of Intellect, the One's external activity, which must represent the One in its own diversifying way, or is it due to the intrinsic nature of the One, which is so "full" that it lends itself to representation as a multiplicity? Whatever the case, the subject's hankering after the object generates a cosmos of multiple subjects who have one another as objects.

From the now-established knowing Intellect, subsequent stages of world manifestation proceed through further rounds of procession and reversion, with subject and object losing much of their unity and becoming separated in sense perception and discursive thinking. The "double activity" doctrine is applied here too, with Soul following from the external activity

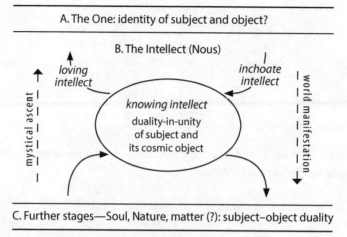

A. The One: identity of subject and object?

B. The Intellect (Nous)

loving intellect

inchoate intellect

mystical ascent

world manifestation

knowing intellect

duality-in-unity
of subject and
its cosmic object

C. Further stages—Soul, Nature, matter (?): subject–object duality

Figure 9.3   World emanation and mystical return (Plotinus).

of Intellect, and Nature from the external activity of the World Soul—but it is not clear whether corporeal matter originates in the same way, from the external activity of a prior reality.[11] In the Plotinian scheme, world emanation is hierarchical, proceeding from the One through rounds of procession and reversion, a procedure that generates a series of increasingly inferior simulacra of the original, like ever dimmer reflections in a series of mirrors. The Intellect is the first, clearest, and most fertile of these images; matter can be understood as the most remote and obscure, and it is completely sterile, having no external activity of its own and therefore no product.

But this is not the whole story. There is also a third phase of intellect, the loving Intellect (*nous erōn*), which is a feature of the Plotinian mystical ascent, the final stage of which begins in the realm of knowing Intellect (fig. 9.3). The beautiful cosmic kaleidoscope that is the Intellect, with its multiform images and interreflections, is the mystic's launching pad to the One, but the means of transport is the loving Intellect. In this final stage of the mystical ascent, the story of world manifestation comes full circle, passing from the emanated image that is Intellect to an unmediated, nonrepresentational encounter with the One, now finally attained.

The question arises whether the coming-home of loving Intellect in the mystical ascent can rightly be identified with the going-forth of the inchoate Intellect in the first "moment" of cosmogenesis. The inchoate and loving Intellects are similar in some ways, for they are both interposed timelessly between the One and the knowing Intellect, and they both lack subject–object seeing, harbor a desire for the One, and are "filled" by the One as they approach it. A case can therefore be made for identifying the two.[12]

The mystic on the ascent to the One would then encounter the first steps of world emanation. However, a good case can be made for distinguishing between the cosmogonic pre-Intellect and the mystical post-Intellect, for the pre-Intellect is an almost unconscious, diversifying, cosmos-manifesting intellect that seeks but fails to take possession of the One by knowing it, while the loving post-Intellect is a hyperconscious, unifying, cosmos-transcending intellect that successfully attains to the One by renouncing the Intellect's knowledge.[13]

Differentiation of subject and object down the Plotinian metaphysical hierarchy is couched in the language of luminosity and vision, and given Plotinus's mystical credentials, it is unlikely that the language is just metaphorical. In the Plotinian scheme, the One seems to involve a light without vision or seeing, a luminosity without subject–object differentiation, whereas the inchoate Intellect is vision looking but not yet seeing. The knowing Intellect is a light that sees itself, a subject that has the luminous cosmos as its object. The loving Intellect gives up seeing and is flooded by the light of the One. The language of light is a common feature of emanative systems, no doubt drawing on the universal experience of the sun as source of light and life. But a debt to mystical experience is surely undeniable, for the mystic, treading the path home to the source, does have experiences of luminosity, including a supreme light at the summit of the mystical ascent.

This is certainly true of the second scheme of world emanation to be considered here. In nondual Kashmir Shaivism, a complex grouping of traditions informed by consciousness-altering practices and situated within the Hindu Tantra, the highest reality is characterized by *prakāśa*, the primordial light of consciousness, the "Ancient Light," the source of all things eternally and from moment-to-moment, undiminished by its productions, illuminating them but not divided by them,[14] very much like the Plotinian One, luminous, self-sufficient, undiminished, immanent, transcendent. The process of emanation is explained as ultimately dependent on *vimarśa*, a reflexive awareness by which the light contemplates itself and produces the manifest universe through vibratory cycles (*spanda*) of consciousness.[15] The self-reflexivity of the light allows it to support the diversity of the cosmos, and in this capacity it is the power, the *śakti*, behind creation.[16]

The Pratyabhijñā ("recognition") school, positioned within nondual Kashmir Shaivism as its preeminent philosophical superstructure and associated with such figures as Utpaladeva and Abhinavagupta (tenth to eleventh centuries CE), has at its centerpiece the recognition "I am Śiva," which is to say that the luminous core of all beings is the supreme Self or God, the emanative source of the universe. According to this philosophy, there is a fundamental "I-ness" at the heart of reality, the luminous Self possessed of reflexive awareness that is the source and power behind all manifestation. Moreover, this perfect "I" is said to be the foundation of the everyday sense of self. Hence, the everyday ego is not to be dismissed as a mere construction to be abandoned on the way to liberation but is grounded in ultimate reality and is to be recognized as such in the mystical ascent: "For this mode of thinking, the human ego is an immanent expression of God's identity *that must be universalized and transfigured into its essential nature as perfect I-hood*," as David Lawrence has put it.[17]

In order to manifest the universe that it contains undivided in germinal form, the supreme consciousness, with its indistinguishable *prakāśa–vimarśa* or "I–This," goes beyond its perfect subject–object identity while remaining unaltered in itself. In the process of manifestation, Śiva contracts himself into limited selves without compromising his true nature, like an actor who takes on many roles, with the result that there is both Śiva unbound and Śiva bound. The process takes place through thirty-six steps or principles (*tattvas*). It begins with five pure stages of subject–object differentiation, the last three of which bring unified, cosmic experience, then proceeds through seven stages that bring a contraction from cosmic wholeness and a multiplication of limited selves. It is then completed through twenty-four impure stages attended by gross subject–object duality (table 9.1). The "impure" order is so called because it is marked by dualistic cognitions that radically distinguish subject and object. By contrast, unity prevails in the pure order, with consciousness aware that its objects are not separate from itself. Mystical ascent involves a reversal of these stages, from the gross dualities and concealments of the impure order, through the subtle differentiations of the pure, cosmic order, to the perfect identity of the supreme consciousness.

In this philosophy, divine self-consciousness is ascribed not only to the cosmic levels but also to the ultimate reality itself, the self-aware light that is *Parama Śiva*, luminous cognition with a very subtle vibrational quality. Plotinus, we have noted, openly ascribes self-consciousness to the One only when he departs from his usual reluctance to impose limits on the ultimate by pinning it down in words. But interestingly, both schemes do have in common an ultimate reality that is in essence activity, and also a subject in search of an object at the very beginning of world emanation. In the Plotinian scheme, this subject is the inchoate Intellect, the "sight not yet seeing." In the Pratyabhijñā scheme, it is the *Śiva tattva*, the "I" (*aham*) that is deprived of a "This" (*idam*). Whereas the supreme Śiva-consciousness is a perfect identity of "I" and "This," the *Śiva tattva* is deprived of "This" by means of its own power, the *Śakti tattva*. Note that *Śiva tattva* and *Śakti*

A. *Parama Śiva*	Undivided identity of self ("I") and its reflexive consciousness ("This")

B. The five principles (*tattvas*) of the pure (*śuddha*) order

1. *Śiva* 2. *Śakti* }	"I," with a lack of "This" (subject only, object negated)
3. *Sadāśiva*	"I am This," with emphasis on "I" (subject predominant)
4. *Īśvara*	"This am I," with emphasis on "This" (object predominant)
5. *Śuddhavidyā*	"I am I, This is This," equal emphasis (subject–object balance)

C. The thirty-one principles (*tattvas*) of the impure (*āśuddha*) order
"I" and "This" disconnected, and "This" no longer the universal "All-This" (seven principles)
Development of everyday self, and subtle & gross materiality (twenty-four principles)

Table 9.1   Emanation of the pure and impure orders.[18]

tattva, like the two phases of the Plotinian inchoate Intellect, are not successive moments in a temporal process of creation; rather, they are eternally coexistent with *Parama Śiva*, so that a triad exists prior to the real business of world manifestation.[19]

The negation of the object by *Śakti tattva*, which is a suppression of the divine fullness, is required for cosmic emanation to proceed. It allows *Śiva* "to feel the *want* of a universe," the subject to feel the absence of an object.[20] It is as if *Śiva* pretends to have lost the object in order to bring it forth again but no longer in germinal form. As a result, the object returns, now manifested as a cosmic multiplicity, an object in unity with its subject but clearly distinguishable from it, a duality-in-unity of the "All-This" and the "I" that is fully established in the last of the five pure principles, *Śuddhavidyā tattva*. This is the stage of fully achieved duality-in-unity and wholeness, with distinguishable but united subject and object, and the object experienced as a totality, the All-This. The experience has been characterized thus: "*I am all-this and all-this is mine as part and parcel of myself* and all this proceeds from and is created by me—I am the author of all this."[21] This statement well expresses the greater sense of selfhood I describe in my own account of mystical experience: "Yet it was also I who in some sense was the sole basis of everything. I was the mind from which everything derived and in which everything had its existence."

After the subject–object balance of the *Śuddhavidyā tattva*, the process of emanation continues with a second round of concealment, brought about by another power (*śakti*) of *Śiva*, the *Māyā tattva*, which introduces gross duality and multiplicity through a series of limitations, the five "veils" or "coverings" (*kañcukas*). These hide five prominent qualities of the divine reality, its omnipotence, omniscience, omnisatisfaction, eternity, and omni-

6.	*Māyā*	–	power of obscuration or veiling
7.	*Kalā*	–	limitation of authorship
8.	*Vidyā*	–	limitation of consciousness or knowledge
9.	*Rāga*	–	limitation of interest or satisfaction
10.	*Kāla*	–	limitation of temporal scope
11.	*Niyati*	–	limitation of spatial and causal scope
12.	*Puruṣa*	–	the finite, individual self

Table 9.2   The emergence of *puruṣa* through the activity of *Māyā*.

presence, resulting in a contraction from the cosmic expansiveness of the pure order to the limited subjects and their limited objects of the impure order, and leads to the sharp duality of subject and object with which we are ordinarily all too familiar. But the initial outcome of the activity of *Māyā* is the contracted spiritual self, the *puruṣa* (table 9.2). In fact, *Māyā*'s veiling produces many such limited *puruṣa*s demarcated from one another. There had been multiplicity in the pure order, but not of the individualized kind that now manifests, for the experiencers at each of the pure levels had in effect all been one and the same, with the same cosmic object as one another.[22] A multiplicity of subjects is already evident at the cosmic level, subjects who have the whole as their common object.

This is also the case in the Plotinian account, with its cosmic intellects, but I do not know if nondual Kashmir Shaivism anywhere elaborates so vividly on the cosmos of interpenetrating whole parts as Plotinus does and indeed the authors of the Buddhist *Avataṃsaka Sūtra*. But Kashmir Shaivism does recognize the presence of the whole in the part: by virtue of the presence of the infinite *Śiva* in each unit of the universe (totality, *kula*), the unit is a whole and therefore related to every other whole manifestation.[23] This results in the "coextensive unity" (*sāmarasya*) of all things. Abhinavagupta explains: "Just as 'sweetness' is present in its entirety in every atom of the sugarcane, so each and every atom [of the universe] bears within itself the emanation of all things."[24] Paul Muller-Ortega observes: "These doctrines of the essential interconnection of all things within the *kula* represent a transcription of yogic experience. Horrifying as these doctrines may seem to the tidy logician for whom a thing is itself and nothing more, they nevertheless must be understood if we are to penetrate the tantric mode of thinking about reality."[25]

Back now to *puruṣa*: it is inseparable from *prakṛti*, the first of the remaining twenty-four *tattvas*. The *prakṛti*s are the objective counterparts of the subjective *puruṣas* and come into being with them, the two together constituting a finite, dualized version of the comprehensive, unified subject and object of the cosmic *Śuddhavidyā tattva*. Through the limitations imposed by *Māyā*, the object is divided from the subject and perceived obscurely as a vague "something," and the subject is likewise only very dimly aware of itself. One interesting way of explaining the concealing activity of *Māyā* is to trace it to a suppression of the "I." At the beginning of the pure order, *Śakti tattva* had obscured the "This" (*idam*) component to prepare the ground for world manifestation. Now, at the commencement of the impure order, the *Māyā tattva* can be understood to obscure the "I" (*aham*), which in the preceding *Śuddhavidyā tattva* had existed in balance with the cosmic "All-This." With the "I" or divine experiencer obscured, the "This" rises to prominence and fills the void created by the veiling of the divine subject by developing its own, substitute "I"-components, the *puruṣas*.[26]

These selves are limited parts of the "All-This," and they take other limited parts of the "All-This" as their objects. In this crucial development, the self has become identified with highly circumscribed parts of the cosmic object, giving rise to a multiplicity of limited, spatially and temporally localized object-selves that take limited spatial and temporal portions of the whole as their objects. What we ordinarily take to be a subject attending to its object is really one part of the cosmic object taking another part of the cosmic object as its object. This misidentification is what nondual (*advaita*) philosophies sometimes call the "identification of the self with the not-self" or the "superimposition of the subject on the object." But nondual Kashmir Shaivism does not follow the example of some nondual philosophies by dismissing the object (whether the cosmic "All-This" or a tiny part of it) as unreal, for it is acknowledged to be a product of the creative divine consciousness.

In tracing the steps that lead from the sleepy, highly circumscribed *puruṣa–prakṛti* subject–object pairs through the remainder of the impure order to the fully elaborated condition that is our everyday experience of embodiment, perception, feeling, and thinking, nondual Kashmir Shaivism appropriates the twenty-five *tattva* scheme that had previously been enumerated in the Sāṃkhya philosophy. Similarly, the description of the first few steps of emanation, from *Śiva tattva* to *Māyā* and her five veils, takes its *tattvas* from the dualistic Śaiva Siddhanta philosophy and reinterprets them within a monistic framework in which everything derives from the self-aware light that is the supreme consciousness. In this manner, the cosmic drama and its innumerable participants are made entirely the product of concealments, differentiations, and multiplications grounded in a luminous consciousness that has an intrinsic subject–object dynamic.

Wisdom's Mirror

In the Hindu Tantra, the divine power *śakti* in its many forms, including the actively reflexive *vimarśa* of the supreme consciousness, the negating *Śakti tattva*, the concealing *Māyā*, and the *kuṇḍalinī* latent in the organismic body, is considered female, and the unity of consciousness with its power or activity is commonly depicted as sexual union. It is not surprising that accounts of world creation should "genderize" or "sexualize" the process, since the union of male and female is central to the human encounter with the mysteries of creation—hence the mating of the world parents and the elaborate family trees of gods and goddesses in ancient theogonies. But it would be hazardous to assert that human beings have merely projected their own experiences of desire, sex, and parenthood onto the inner workings of reality, especially if a worldview is entertained in which the human mind is taken to be rooted in a more profound mentality. Accordingly, it is possible that sexual and gender distinctions in biological and cultural spheres are based on distinctions in a greater sphere of life, although there is, of course, a danger of stereotyping in these matters, as for instance in the ascription of activity or passivity to one gender or the other. It is notable that the Hindu and Buddhist Tantras differ on this point, the former envisaging a union of passive, male consciousness (*Śiva*) and active, female power (*Śakti*), the latter a union of active, male skill-in-means (*upāya*) or compassion (*karuṇā*) and passive, female wisdom or insight (*prajñā*).

We have already met an example of female reflexivity in Boehme's "Virgin of Divine Wisdom." As partner of the active, masculine will of God, Boehme's passive, feminine mirror makes possible the eternal aspect of cosmogenesis by enabling the "threefold spirit" of God, the Father, Son and Holy Spirit, to know itself and gaze upon the creation prefigured there. Wisdom is called "virgin" because she reflects without giving birth to anything distinct from God.[27] From the potentiality displayed in the divine mirror, the spiritual creation unfolds atemporally by means of seven, interdependent "source spirits" or "qualities," the last of which is the fullness of God's corporeity, the "Kingdom of Heaven," the beautiful, harmonious whole in which the mirror's prefiguration is realized and all the qualities made visible. Boehme's portrait of divine Wisdom takes some of its inspiration from early Jewish sources, and his scheme is probably indebted to the Kabbalah. There is, for instance, an obvious parallel between Boehme's seventh spirit and the Kabbalah's tenth *sefirot*, the "great sea" of *Malkhut* ("Kingdom"), the consummation of the process by which the divine feminine presence (*Shekhinah*) and all preceding sefirotic powers are fully manifested. But

Wisdom was also a matter of personal experience for Boehme, the Virgin having "comforted" and "married" him in an hour of spiritual need.²⁸

It would be too great a detour to look into the prodigious career of divine Wisdom, including her varied appearances as the Gnostic "First Thought" (*Protennoia*) and fallen Sophia, the Buddhist "perfection of wisdom" goddess Prājnapāramitā, and the Holy Sophia of Eastern Orthodoxy and Russian sophiology.²⁹ But we can note that in one pattern of radiant engendering, the solar light of the divine masculine is received by a lunar, feminine equal or subordinate, eventually giving rise to the world in the cosmogonic process or the redeeming child in the drama of salvation. This primary female figure tends to be associated with wisdom and the reflective capacity. In Jewish thought, wisdom or *Hokhmah* initially had the role of personified, primal feminine, but in the Kabbalistic schemes *Hokhmah* was masculinized as the second *sefirah*. The feminine *Hokhmah* of early Jewish thought existed prior to the creation and played before Yahweh as if to entertain him (Proverbs 8.22–31). In Hellenized form, divine wisdom appeared as Sophia, and in *The Book of Wisdom* (first century BCE) she is the throne partner (*paredros*) of God, a radiance or reflection of the everlasting light, fairer than the sun, and "a spotless mirror of the working of God" (7.25–26).³⁰ She is active, taking the initiative in approaching humankind, acting as teacher, guide, and even lover, for God is to be approached and known through union with Wisdom.

Cosmogonically, psychologically, and mystically, the reflective Other can be understood as the bringer of self-consciousness, self-knowledge, and self-transcendence. On the downward path of manifestation, it is through the Other that the subtle and gross dualities of subject and object emerge. In human development, it is engagement with the Other—first with parents and family, and then in a wider sphere of relationships—that works to develop the knowledge of self as one among many selves. But the repose of the unfinished self is easily disturbed by the pull of the Other. The achievement of intimacy in close relationships brings some respite and hints at still deeper unities, for on the path home it is the Other who draws the mystic into the unity of the whole and perhaps even to an identity beyond all subject–object differentiation.

How One Became Three

My limited personal familiarity with mystical experience means that I have no firsthand insights to offer on the arcane matter of world derivation, at least none that I can remember. However, around the time of the mystical

expansion, I had two dreams that may be relevant. The first took place ten
months earlier, long before I had started to record my dreams. But this dream
was so vivid and luminous that I made a note of it:

> I fell asleep after lunch last Thursday and had a very vivid dream: I stood
> on the summit of a mountain, on a sloping plane of rock; about me was
> swirling fog, perhaps cloud, of a resplendent blue, illuminated grey colour.
> I was with someone, who I had in mind was my father. A small girl stood
> on a promontory of rock. She moved strangely into very sharp focus and
> seemed almost like a montage figure on the background of twisting cloud.
> I turned away, for no particular reason, and looked down the slope of rock
> into the fog. Shadows moved on the bluish surface, shadows of people,
> crossing, overlapping, growing, diminishing.

At the time, the dream was a mystery to me, although I recognized the
optical phenomenon displayed there, for I knew of the Brocken specter in
the Harz Mountains, the shadow of an observer cast on the clouds below.[31]
Later, when I delved into the world's religious traditions, I wondered if the
dream might have hinted at divine Wisdom. If the girl were the source of
the shadow figures, cast from her position on high, as seems to have been
the case, she could be interpreted as a feminine principle behind the shifting
multiplicity of creation, such as the *prakṛti* ("nature," "matrix") of Sāṃkhya
philosophy, likened to a dancing girl who performs before the *puruṣas*
("selves," "witnesses"), binding them with her enchanting show but finally
liberating them. But in the dream, the girl was peculiarly motionless, perhaps suggestive of her eternal nature, and her young age possibly indicated
her primordiality, her closeness to the luminous source. It is notable that
the shifting multiplicity seems to have come forth through obscuration, a
partial masking of the light, for the crowd consisted of shadows, which may
again point to the activity of a veiling Maya or Sophia.

The second dream, which took place a month or so after the mystical
experience, is perhaps more clearly cosmogonic. This was a lucid dream
in the form of an out-of-body experience, the first in the period after the
mystical experience. I was lying in bed one morning, conscious but not
awake, when an anatomically improbable lengthening took place, enabling
a "closing of the circle" in the manner of the *ouroboros*, the snake or dragon
that swallows its tail. This bodily act of self-reflexivity, I later discovered,
would not have been out of character for an Egyptian creator God, such as
Amun or Atum, or even the earth god Geb, grandson of Atum. Through
his solitary act, Atum creates the first male–female dyad of gods, Shu and

Tefnut: "he who had been one became three," adding two to the primordial oneness and setting the world creation in motion.[32]

With this extraordinary occurrence, my state of consciousness shifted. First I saw a pattern of fuzzy dots, and then I found myself out of bed, standing in the room and viewing it in perfect clarity, but realizing that I was dreaming even though I was "absolutely consciously awake," as I wrote afterward. The dream room was an accurate representation of the college room in which I was asleep, but the positioning of the furniture was slightly different, and the walls had fewer decorations and looked bare:

> I step over to the wall opposite the bed and examine some small posters on it. The one at the top is a skilfully drawn sketch of three cows standing in a field. Inexperienced with this sort of dream state, I go to my desk and pick up a scrap of paper and a pencil, with the intention of making a copy of the drawing, so that I can examine it at leisure when I wake up properly. But the image has changed before I can note it down – now there is a sketch of five human faces. I attempt to draw them too, but as I look again I notice that they have changed in some way. I look away, then back again, and realize that it is the facial expressions that have changed. I put down the pencil and paper, having given up trying to capture the changing dream images, and aware that it is pointless trying to record the details on dream paper. Instead I check to see if I can discern colour, and indeed I can see some reds and greens that look as realistic as any waking colour sensations.
>
> I look back at the poster – now hundreds of small faces are depicted, and mine is one of them. I do not recognize the others, and decide to find the face of a friend, which I do see when I start to look for it, suggesting to me that other people I know belong here as well as myself. There are some metallurgical formulations in the top right-hand corner of the diagram. Later I am looking at three posters, and one is now the dustcover of a book entitled *Five Case Studies by Freud*. I feel myself slipping from the state, and to stabilize the vision I have to look hard at the grainy patterns that have appeared on the wall. This happens again later and I am unable to hold on any longer, and wake up in my bed, in darkness, with eyes closed.

Poster images were to appear in some of my other out-of-body or lucid dreams, as if pictures rather than words were the more natural medium of communication for the condition of mind operative in this state. Shortly after I recorded the dream, it occurred to me that the drawing of the multitude of faces probably drew inspiration from a steel-manufacturing process I had studied just a few days before, the Q-BOP or "quiet basic oxygen process," in which oxygen is injected through the bottom of a furnace into molten iron to burn away the impurities. The bubbles of oxygen that rise through the iron had become faces in the dream picture, suggesting an upward movement of beings, ascending through a process of purification. I did not make a connection at the time between the bubble faces of the dream and the ring-like beings of the mystical experience; indeed it is possible that I had not yet remembered that feature of the mystical experience. It is therefore conceivable that through the lucid dream a fragment of the mystical experience was making its way into consciousness.

It is interesting that the picture of the bubble faces was preceded by drawings I cannot correlate with anything I remember from the mystical experience. The multiplication of beings, from the solitary sleeper who self-engenders the vision, through the three cows and the five transforming human faces, to a multiplicity of human faces (that is, from One to Three to Five to Many), suggests a cosmogonic diversification from an original oneness through a creative triad or trinity at an early stage, appropriately symbolized by the three cows, for the cow is a symbol of fertility and nurturing in many cultures. This cosmogonic interpretation is reinforced by the peculiar act that instigated the lucid dream, suggestive of a primordial creative act of self-impregnation that leads from the One to the Many, as in one version of the Egyptian creation myth.

In the early 1990s, when I first took an interest in mystical cosmogonies, it occurred to me that the dream posters, taken in sequence, are similar to diagrams used to illustrate cosmogony and theosophy, such as the "diagram of the Supreme Ultimate" (*taiji tu*) of the neo-Confucian Zhou Dunyi (Chou Tun-i, 1017–1073 CE), influenced by Daoist diagrams of cosmogony and inner alchemy.[33] There is also the Kabbalistic tree of the ten *sefirot*, which emerged somewhat later than the neo-Confucian diagram and bears some resemblance to it (fig. 9.4).[34] A primary group of three can be seen in both the neo-Confucian and Kabbalistic diagrams. In Zhou Dunyi's diagram, the triad consists of the Ultimateless (*wuji*), depicted as the empty circle at the top, and the Supreme Ultimate (*taiji*) shown as two interlocked halves, *yang* and *yin*, the two principles whose interplay produces the cosmos. Zhou Dunyi may have regarded the Ultimateless and the Supreme Ultimate as unmanifest and manifest aspects of one reality; by contrast, Daoist cosmogony tended to distinguish more sharply between *wuji* and *taiji*, placing the Dao, the Ultimateless or Infinite, prior to the beginning of the world that is the Supreme Ultimate.[35] *Wuji* is the One beyond difference, whereas *taiji* is the creative One whose components add up to three, for numerologically *yang* counts as one and *yin* as two:

The *taiji* is the One that contains Yin and Yang, or the Three . . . . This Three is, in Taoist terms, the One (Yang) plus the Two (Yin), or the Three that gives life to all beings (*Daode jing* 42), the One that virtually contains the multiplicity. The *taiji* is said to be the function of the Dao, whose substance is Chaos . . .; the *wuji* is the Dao as the metaphysical One, a neutral "no-number" that is before movement and quiescence (*dong* and *jing*), unity and multiplicity.[36]

The five circles in the cosmogonic diagrams of Zhou Dunyi and the Daoists represent the five transforming phases or agents (*wuxing*) of Chinese nature philosophy, and therefore match well with the five faces sketched on my dream poster, which were also transforming.[37]

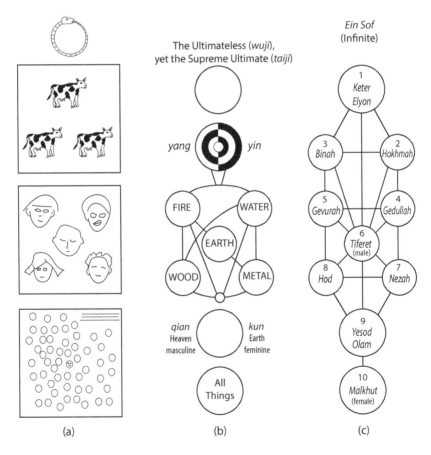

Figure 9.4   (a) the sequence of dream posters; (b) Zhou Dunyi's diagram of the Supreme Ultimate;[38] (c) a Kabbalistic tree of the *sefirot*.[39]

In the tree of the *sefirot*, the primary group of three consists of *Keter* ("crown"), *Ḥokhmah* ("wisdom") and *Binah* ("understanding"), the three hidden *sefirot*.[40] However, a grouping of the next *sefirot* into five (i.e., 3 + 5 + 2) is not a natural division of the tree, which is usually divided into 3 + 7, or 3 + 6 + 1, or 3 + 3 + 3 + 1, or even 5 + 5.[41] The lower sections of the Chinese and Kabbalistic diagrams represent stages of the cosmogonic process in which multiplicity is more advanced, in the production of the "ten thousand things" of Chinese philosophy and in the totality of the Kabbalistic spiritual "kingdom" of *Malkhut*, the final *sefirah*, the only one that is properly female. In my dream, a multiplicity of individuals was depicted in the third poster, the picture of the bubble faces.

In the Hindu sphere, cosmogonic progression from one through three and five to many has been described by the advaitin guru Ramaṇa Maharṣi (1879–1950). Here the three are the *guṇas*, the "strands" or qualities from which the universe is built, and the five are the elements:

> The one becomes three, the three becomes five and the five becomes many; that is, the pure Self (*satva*), which appears to be one, becomes through contact, three (*satva*, *rajas* and *tamas*) and with those three, the five elements come into existence, and with those five, the whole Universe. It is this that creates the illusion that the body is the Self.[42]

The illusion is dispelled by "Self-enquiry," and "the multiplicity resolves itself into five, the five into three, and the three into one."[43]

A further connection between the lucid dream and cosmogony may be evident in one aspect that concerned me a little at the time. This is the *Five Case Studies by Freud* illustrated book jacket, a title that suggested psychopathology, a distortion of the five mutable faces seen on the poster earlier in the dream. I wondered if it might be a comment on my own state of mind, but another interpretation, in keeping with the cosmogonic theme, is possible. If the five transforming faces correspond to cosmic agents or elements, then the Freudian "Five Case Studies" might imply a disorganization and disharmony of these elements. Something, it would seem, can go off kilter at the stage of the Five.

There is precedent for the idea in Zhou Dunyi's system, where evil emerges through the imbalanced reaction of the *five* principles of human nature to external phenomena.[44] More fundamental is the predicament described by Manichaeism, with its radically dualistic division of good and evil elemental *pentads*: a fivefold structuring of the light realm is irreconcilably at odds with its fivefold counterpart in the realm of darkness.[45] In contrast, the tantric Buddhist understanding avoids dualism: here the world is the expression of divine energies, and so the *five* deluded passions of wandering beings are recognized as derivative of the five pure wisdoms and five great elements, and as transformable into the wisdoms.[46] In the Lurianic Kabbalah, the Five manifest in the process of restoration after a calamitous turn of events in the cosmogonic process. Unable to contain the downward flow of light from the three supernal *sefirot*, the next six *sefirot* break into fragments, invigorating the forces of darkness. Restoration (*tikkun*) of the fallen light involves the reconstitution of the sefirotic vessels into *five* principal configurations or "faces" (*parzufim*),[47] and the gradual return of the exiled soul-sparks through a difficult but expiatory process of transmigration (*gilgul*) up the ladder of nature (see chapter 10). A parallel of sorts to this redemptive process can be read into the lucid dream: the "five faces" poster is followed by the sketch of the bubble faces rising through a metallurgical furnace, suggestive of an alchemical transformation of the world, an ascent through the vessel of nature. If the bubble-faces are equated with the ring-beings of the cosmic mystical experience, then the universe can be considered a vessel of transformation through which the ring-beings rise in order to bring about purification—of themselves and of the world at large.

The above is, admittedly, a rather cursory and perhaps strained attempt to enlarge upon the Freud book jacket detail—to "amplify" a dream image in the Jungian sense, exploring its possible meanings by placing it in broader mythological and religious contexts. However, the question that the various religions try to address here is certainly not trivial: whence comes evil? Why all the suffering in the world? The question will take center stage in chapter 11 when monadic evolution and the nature of God come under scrutiny, but it has a bearing too on the subject matter of the present chapter, for cosmogony can be understood to initiate a cyclical interplay of subject and object, as I shall now explain, a cycle that brings much sorrow and joy.

A Twofold Tale: Ego and Eros

I have taken up the idea that a reflexive act of awareness, involving the assertion of a primordial subject and an accompanying want of an object, sets the cosmogonic process going and brings forth the Many. Now I take the discussion further by exploring the subject–object *dynamics* generated by the initial cosmogonic act as it plays out through innumerable, interweaving cycles of consciousness in the world process. I use the word "dynamics" for good reason, because there are *forces* or *powers* at work in the cycles, driving them along, two basic forces derivative of the primordial dynamic in which the emerging subject seeks that which it lacks. The upshot is that any stark opposition between duality and nonduality, between dual and nondual states of consciousness, is a gross oversimplification, for there are intermediate steps between the two extremes. The construction of the world itself will depend on these steps of subject–object differentiation and unification.

In the previous section, I dwelt on the Three and the Five without attending properly to the Two whose interactions have often been regarded as essential to the cosmogonic process. Multiplicity requires contrast, distinction, difference, an observation sometimes expressed in the idea that the universe depends on opposites for its existence and transformations. Primordial pairs abound in creation myths, such as the earth and sky as world parents, whose separation powers creation. Ancient thinkers delighted in lists of contraries, no doubt inspired by the contrasts observable throughout nature: light–dark, male–female, father–mother, summer–winter, life–death, sun–moon, motion–rest, up–down, right–left, east–west, north–south, and so forth. Some opposites assume cyclical form, such as day and night, the round of the seasons, growth and decay, and it is not surprising that these revolving contrasts, along with the static ones, should be worked into comprehensive schemes of fundamental categories and correspondences, a common occupation of premodern thought. One of the most interesting of these schemes is the categorization of change set out in the *I Ching*, with its sixty-four transforming hexagrams derived from *yin* and *yang*. Originally denoting the shady and sunny aspects of a hill, *yin* and *yang* came to acquire the status of primary pair and gathered a range of associations, including dark and light, female and male, passive and active, receiving and giving, contracting and stretching.[48] When *yin–yang* and the five-agent teachings came together, perhaps in the third century BCE, the idea of a cycle powered by two primary complements emerged in Chinese thought.

A comparable idea had already been expressed in the Greek world in the "twofold tale" of Empedocles, whose Love (*philia*) and Strife (*neikos*) are the contrary forces that dominate alternating phases of the world and drive the four "roots," air, fire, water and earth. While Love unifies the roots into a spherical whole, Strife divides and separates them. It is through Strife that the soul is condemned to mortality, to wander through numerous reincarnations, as Empedocles himself could attest, having been "once a boy and a girl, a bush and a bird and a leaping journeying fish."[49] Empedocles drew a sharp distinction between the ingathering phase of unity and the separating phase of multiplicity, and took a dim view of the latter. By contrast, Heraclitus of Ephesus, who had flourished half a century earlier, held strife (*eris*) in high esteem, understanding it not as one of two alternately dominant powers or world phases, but as a *dynamical*, creative principle that underlies all change, operative *throughout* the cycle of transformation.[50] Even that which is apparently unchanging depends on a continuous, hidden struggle between mutually dependent contraries, as for instance in a strung bow, with its static balance of opposed forces.[51] Opposites are complements, mutually defining and inseparable from each other, neither capable of permanently gaining the upperhand.

At the beginning of the nineteenth century, the twofold tale of unifying and diversifying tendencies entered the modern age in the speculations of nature philosophers, idealists, and Romantics, notably F. W. J. Schelling (1775–1854), Henrik Steffens (1773–1845), Lorenz Oken (1779–1851), and S. T. Coleridge (1772–1834). It was not only the transformational worldviews of ancient philosophers and their alchemical successors that provided inspiration. Advances in chemistry, natural history, and especially magnetism and electricity in the late eighteenth century, underscored the significance of attraction, repulsion, and polarity in the world. In the wake of Kant, philosophers paid increased attention to the role of subject–object duality in the constitution of the mind, and on the mystical side, there was renewed interest in Boehme's ideas, including his vivid picture of two contrary forces that produce a rotation. Boehme had described an antagonism between the first two of his seven source spirits, dryness or contraction (alchemical salt, astrological Saturn) and expansion (alchemical mercury, astrological Jupiter). The tension between the two qualities drives a third, the anguished rotation (alchemical sulfur, astrological Mars). William Law (1686–1761) was to claim that Boehme's first three principles had inspired Newton's formulation of his mechanics and theory of planetary motion. In this reading, Boehme's contractive, expansive, and rotary principles correspond to the balance of gravitational-centripetal attraction and inertial-centrifugal resistance in the stable orbits of the moon and planets.[52] It seems that a similar claim was made by the theosophist Friedrich C. Oetinger (1702–1782), whose writings contributed to the emergence of German nature philosophy.[53]

When Coleridge came to tell a twofold tale in the 1810s, elaborated into triads and pentads, he took seriously the alleged influence of Boehme's mysticism on Newton's physics. Coleridge conceived of a centrifugal tendency toward "individuation" opposed by a centripetal tendency to "attachment," a struggle that runs through nature:

> We may suppose for instance, with Newton, that in nature there is a continual antagonism going on between an universal life and each individual

composing it. We will suppose that there is a tendency throughout nature perpetually to individuate, that is in each component part of nature to acquire individuality, but which is as harmoniously counteracted by an attempt of nature to recall it again to the common organization. . . . In short, there is through all nature, and we must assume it as a ground of all reasoning, a perpetual tendency at once to individualize and yet to universalize, or to keep <*a balance*> even as we find in the solar system a perpetual tendency in each planet to preserve its own individual path, with a counter tendency which of itself would lead it into the common solar centre.[54]

For Coleridge, individuation was not mere separation but evolutionary development through the differences that make a unified whole possible, a unity in multiplicity.[55] Coleridge's two tendencies, the individualizing and the universalizing, and his Heraclitean "polar logic" of creative, dialectical transformation have close affinities with ideas then current in German *Naturphilosophie*.[56] For example, Oken wrote:

Every living thing is twofold in character. It is one persistent in itself, and one immersed in the universe. In everything, therefore, are two processes, one individualizing, vitalizing, and one universalizing, destructive. By the process of destruction, the finite thing seeks to become the universe itself; by the vitalizing process, however, the variety of the universe, and yet with that to remain a Singular. That only is truly living which represents the Eternal, and the whole multiplicity of the universe in the *Singular*.[57]

Life individualizes, death universalizes, and the two work together to generate ever higher forms that better express the cosmic whole. The alchemical story of transmutation from base to noble through death and regeneration had found a place in early nineteenth-century evolutionism. Echoes of Romantic twofold tales were to reverberate in early twentieth-century thought, most famously in Freud's life and death instincts, Eros and Thanatos, but also in Jung's principles of relatedness and discrimination, the feminine Eros and the masculine Logos, and in his distinction between object-directed extraversion and subject-directed introversion and his theory of personality based upon the distinction.[58] It is evident too in Edward Carpenter's Love and Death, those "tyrannous and terrible over-lords of our mortal days" who are doors to a greater life.[59]

An aspect of *Naturphilosophie* of considerable interest in the present context, taking us back to the cosmogonic significance of subject and object, is the attempt to unite two legacies of Leibnizian thought, a reputedly idealist *metaphysics* that reduces matter to perceptual subjects and their objects, and a dynamical *physics* that reduces matter to active point-centers of attractive and repulsive force. Kant himself had contributed to the force-picture of matter, along with Rudjer Boscovich, John Michell, and Joseph Priestley, but his philosophy was obstructive toward a unification of physics and metaphysics. It confined scientific knowledge to the phenomenal realm, conditioned by the spatiotemporal and causal structuring imposed by the perceiving subject, and undermined traditional metaphysics by making the objects of perception unknowable in themselves. For post-Kantian idealists, critical of the epistemic dualism of phenomenal appearance and unknowable world-in-itself, the way forward was through a reappraisal of Kant's subject and its relation to the object. In a particularly fruitful move, the subject or its undifferentiated ground was transformed into the creative source of things, which opened the way to a potential unification of physics and metaphysics. Thus Schelling hoped to trace the polarity of attractive and repulsive forces constitutive of matter to the differentiation of the Absolute into subject and object, that is, to a cosmogonic act of self-consciousness, and thereby forge a link between matter and mind:

> Matter, too, like everything that exists, streams out from the eternal essence, and represents in appearance an effect, albeit indirect and mediate only, of the eternal dichotomizing into subject and object, and of the fashioning of its infinite unity into finitude and multiplicity.[60]

However, the enterprise was premature and its outcome unavoidably sketchy and qualitative, unlikely to impress the tough-minded scientific types who became increasingly common in the decades to come. Nineteenth-century nature philosophy lacked the data and mathematical tools that would make possible the derivation of physics and its forces from an idealist metaphysics of perceiving subject and its objects. Perhaps only in recent times, after revolutionary developments in mathematics and physics, can such a project be carried through, as intimated in chapter 8. The multidimensional perceptual spaces of subjects who take one another as their represented objects may now be open to modeling, for physicists have become accustomed to understanding the forces of nature in terms of symmetries and higher dimensional spaces.

Certainly, if mind or something akin to mind is given primacy, as metaphysical idealists believe it should, then the separation and creative interplay of opposites at the root of cosmogony will be mental in character, that is, perceptual, cognitive, volitional, affective, imaginal. More specifically, we can suppose that the interplay depends on a distinction between subject and object, perceiver and perceived, knower and known, self and other. The simplest way of envisaging the interplay is to suppose that *subject and object pass repeatedly through phases of felt separation and unification*, an alternately dualizing and unifying cyclical movement that will be ingrained in all that follows. The whole of creation will consist, then, of innumerable cycles of consciousness in which subjects are alternately detaching from and unifying with their objects in their feelings, perceptions, cognitions. Perhaps even the universe itself is one such cycle of cognition and feeling, a great, overarching pulse of luminous consciousness, containing within itself the many lesser pulses. The fundamental particles of matter could be such pulses too, by virtue of embodying the whole in monadic fashion, as I suggested toward the end of chapter 8.

The idea that the world proceeds through a cyclical interplay of subject and object has a notable precedent in nondual Kashmir Shaivism, which develops the idea of cycles of "emission" and "withdrawal" at great length in its Spanda ("vibration") and Krama ("sequence") teachings. Rotating wheels of divine creative powers are described, circles of goddesses that are cycles of cognition with spokes that range from one to infinity, and which evolve into ever greater complexity before withdrawal into the supreme consciousness from which they have emerged. Among these wheels, the twelve-spoked one ("the Wheel of the Absolute"), associated with twelve powers or goddesses, has been given special importance, perhaps through the prominence of the twelvefold division in the astrological wheel of time.[61]

These teachings, which provide a framework for advanced meditative practices, are too complex and obscure to look into here. Instead, let us treat the subject–object cycle in relatively simple fashion as a dynamic process of differentiation and unification driven by *restoring* forces. The alternately dualizing and unifying cycle of feeling-cognition will then exhibit restoring pulls, polarities, moments of balance, and critical turning points in the following manner (fig. 9.5a). From a condition of unity ①, the subject proceeds to differentiate from its object ② and becomes clearly distinguishable from it ③. At this moment of separation, an unconscious, restorative pull U toward the discarded condition of unity arises, but it is not yet sufficiently powerful to halt further subject–object differentiation ④, which continues until it reaches a limit ⑤, the subject cognizing itself as maximally distinct from its object yet moderated by the increasingly powerful restorative pull toward unity.

This pull is now very strong, and the subject *consciously* seeks to take hold of the object ⑥ and attain union with it ⑦. Subject and object are still

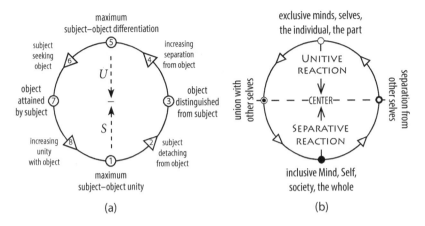

Figure 9.5   (a) the subject–object cycle; (b) the self–other cycle.

distinguishable but no longer cognized as radically distinct. Following this moment of union, an unconscious reactive pull S toward the condition of separation kicks in, but it is not yet sufficiently strong to halt further subject–object unification ⑧, which continues until it reaches a limit ①, with subject cognizing itself as maximally united with its object but poised to separate. A full cycle has been completed. The pull S toward separation has reached a maximum too, and the movement toward differentiation begins anew. In due course, the cycle of subject and object evolves into a well-elaborated cycle of self and others, some objects coming to be known as other selves. With ever more sophisticated cognitions, perceptions, feelings, and self-concepts, it becomes a cycle of the individualized self in a society of selves, even a cycle of the self in relation to the spiritual whole and Self (fig. 9.5b).

The cycle constructed here is dynamic, with two restorative, limiting forces alternately at play. As soon as the subject divorces itself from the object at ③, a restorative pull U toward unity arises, exerting a restraining influence that reaches a maximum at ⑤. The combination of duality and the counterpull toward unity characterizes the upper half of the cycle ③–⑦. This restorative pull toward the object—let us call it the *erosic pull toward unity*—can take several forms, dependent on the level of development of the subject and its current psychosomatic state. For example, the pull might consist of basic appetites, drives, or needs that direct the subject toward the externalized object or other self, such as hunger, thirst, sexual desire, and security needs. At a more developed level, it could be the desire for reassurance or recognition, the yearning for companionship and love, the allure of beauty in art and nature, and even a longing to reconnect with the whole and the ultimate ground. This erosic pull *and* the varied states of relatedness and unity to which it is directed can be subsumed under the category Eros.

Conversely, after the subject enters into union with its object at ⑦, a restorative pull *S* toward separation arises, exerting a restraining influence that reaches a maximum at ①. A combination of unity and the background counterpull toward separation characterizes the lower half of the cycle ⑦–③. Again, this pull—let us call it the *egoic pull toward separation*—might take several forms, ranging from simple aversion, retreat from pain, avoidance of a threatening object, assertion of self, the urge to escape from restrictive relationships or seek freedom from oppressive authority, the drive toward independence and self-determination, and perhaps even cultural and evolutionary imperatives, for progress may be made when the "crowd" or "herd" is left behind. This egoic pull *and* the various states of separteness and duality to which it is directed can be subsumed under the category Ego.

The subject–object cycle is fundamentally a movement of consciousness, but a crude physical analogy can be employed to bring across its dynamics. Consider an oscillating spring, alternately extending and compressing. When the spring enters its extended condition, a restoring force arises, checking the extensional motion most strongly at the point of maximum extension. When the spring enters its compressed condition, a restoring force arises, checking the compressive motion most strongly at the point of maximum compression. The picture combines an Empedoclean cycle of unity and division with Heraclitean dynamic opposition. Only at two points in the cycle are the restoring forces absent, at ③ and ⑦, when unity and division are momentarily in balance. And only at two points is the motion halted, at the moments of maximal unity and division, at ① and ⑤.

Where does the subject–object cycle begin, if indeed it has a beginning? How does the "spring" come to oscillate? The question takes us back to the cosmogonies of Plotinus and the Pratyabhijñā school, with their emerging subjects—the inchoate Intellect and the *Śiva tattva* respectively. We can follow their example and suppose that world emanation begins with the assertion of a subject who feels the lack of an object. The subject assertion can be understood to proceed in various ways. For instance, it might start from a state of subject–object *balance*, as numbered ③ in figure 9.5a. The cycle commences with the assertion of the subject from ③ to ⑤, with accompanying unitive counterpull to restore the original balance.

There are other possibilities, and I shall note just one (fig. 9.6). Let us suppose that the subject emerges from a complete subject–object *unity* ①, rather than a balance. If subject procession corresponds to the first quarter cycle ①–③, then reversion or "turning back" commences at ③, for here the

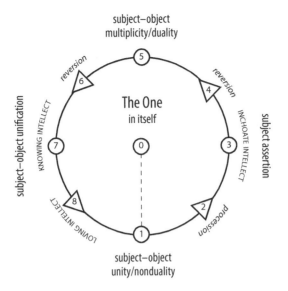

Figure 9.6   How the subject–object cycle commences: one proposal.

unifying pull toward the veiled object sets in, and continues to act all the way to ⑦, at which point the object is properly attained. If we squeeze the highest levels of Plotinian cosmogony and mystical return into this cyclical framework (perhaps inappropriately since these levels are atemporal, and procession and reversion are coincident, not successive), then procession and reversion of the inchoate Intellect could be equated to the three-quarter cycle ①–⑦, coming to fruition in the unity-in-duality of the knowing Intellect at ⑦. Here the subject, whose nature is to know, has found its determinate object not in the infinite, unknowable One but in a representation generated in the attempt to know the One. The loving Intellect, transporting the subject back to its emanative source, might then be equated with the final quarter ⑦–①, at the conclusion of which perfect unity is achieved.

But is it appropriate to locate the One itself in the cycle (at ①)? If the One is understood to be a perfect subject–object identity, then perhaps it is acceptable to do so. However, if the One is completely beyond subject and object, then a more appropriate location would be at the center of the cycle ⓪ (fig. 9.6). If the One in its internal activity is beyond subject and object, even subject–object identity, then it is better placed beyond the cycle at ⓪, whereas the One as primordial source characterized by perfect subject–object unity could be located at the start of the cycle, at ①. This distinction is perhaps similar to the Daoist one between the Ultimateless and the Supreme Ultimate, *wuji* and *taiji*.

The above discussion may sound rather abstract, and so it should be emphasized that the subject–object cycle is not just cognitive and perceptual. It is powered by feeling, the separation of subject from object engendering a unitive yearning for the object, and the suppression of the subject in their union in turn engendering a drive toward individual assertion and independence. It is, in bare outline, the story of *a subject who is never quite satisfied*, except perhaps at the fleeting moments of balance. In more complex, evolved form, it is the story of many selves in a dance of separation and union—the story of the universe. At the level of the discrete, contracted self, out of touch with the cosmic whole, the assertion of the subject is fraught with danger and anxiety, for the little self is a fragile, needy thing, self-serving in its struggle to survive and necessarily self-protective in the face of threats from a world that seems external to itself and often hostile.

But self-interest and concern for others need not be contraries, as the mutually supportive activities of creatures demonstrate, and there is the hope that the two tendencies of egotism and altruism—Traherne's "contrary humours"—can be reconciled in the mature self and the just society. Common empathy and mystical insight narrow the gap between selves, allowing self-interest to be other-interest.

An Evolutionary Preamble

The incessant cycling through duality and unity, ego-assertion and ego-surrender, indeed life and death, explored in the present chapter seems to be more than aimless meandering. On our planet at least, evolution has led to organisms of amazing complexity. Even the single-celled *amoeba proteus* is a wonder to behold, never mind multicellular masterworks such as the sparrow and the elephant. However, for many decades now, evolutionary biologists have usually insisted that while evolution may have directions or trends it does not urge *progress* (improvements) and even more so that it does not involve *purpose* (goal-directedness), two interlinked concepts that are unpalatably mentalistic for materialist science if taken to imply value and intent. The idea that evolution progresses toward goals is likely to be dismissed as a popular misconception carried over from earlier times, when progressionism in biological thought was widespread, influenced by theories of intellectual, moral, and social progress rooted in the Enlightenment.[62]

This is not to say that concepts of progress and purpose disappeared completely from biology, and it has been claimed that the idea of progress still has a hold on modern biologists, even if they are unwilling to admit it.[63] Evolutionary progress and purpose have been a subject of philosophical inquiry and controversy, one basic challenge being the difficulty of pinning down what "progress" might mean in the evolutionary context, if it is not mere increase in biological complexity or well-adaptedness ("fitness") to an environment.[64]

The idealist metaphysics I have developed here, drawing on Leibniz's unashamedly mindlike monads, does have basic units of nature that are progress-oriented and goal-directed, for they are appetitive and strive to realize their potential, if only obscurely for the most part. It is therefore incumbent upon me to explore how these purposive or "teleological" agents are to be integrated with biological evolution and its mechanisms, including natural selection, which will play a role in the long-term development of monads by making available to them bodies with sense organs, nervous systems, brains, perceptions, and mental capacities of considerable sophistication. The evolutionary biological "progress" of relevance here, then, is the emergence of bodies that supply monads with higher levels of phenomenal consciousness and associated behaviors and social relationships.

If my fraternizing with concepts of progress and purpose were not bad enough, monadology compels me to add another controversial ingredient to the mix: monads are just the kind of entity that could pursue their long-term objectives by navigating a series of lives in the various kinds of bodies that evolution makes available, for monads are able to pass intact through bodily death. Thus, I shall now consider how biological evolutionism can be integrated with a monadological metaphysics that envisages not only progress and purpose but also transmigration. What would such an evolutionary monadology look like? With cosmogony we labored over beginnings; now it is time to take to the road and seek out ends.

10

Where Do You Think You're Going?

Believe yourself a Whole, indivisible, indefeasible,
  Reawakening ever under these, under those, conditions . . .
   And made for love—to embrace all, to be united ultimately with all.

—Edward Carpenter

I F CONSCIOUSNESS, MEMORY, AND PERSONALITY depend entirely on brain processes, they will come to an end when those processes cease at death. However, there is some evidence that consciousness can exist independently of the brain and that memory and personality are preserved to some extent after death. The brain-independence of consciousness is suggested by its persistence and extraordinary intensification during near-death experiences, when brain function has been drastically compromised and perhaps even suspended in some instances. Postmortem survival is suggested by phenomena such as mediumistic contacts with the dead, crisis apparitions of the recently deceased, and memories of past lives.[1] The last typically involve young children who recall persons, places, and events from previous lives that often came to a violent end. Birthmarks and defects may be present that correspond to the injuries sustained at death.[2]

Painstaking investigations conducted by Ian Stevenson, Jim Tucker, Erlendur Haraldsson, and others have yielded well-researched evidence for reincarnation, although many details remain obscure.[3] For example, it is not known whether reincarnation is the general rule or applies only to certain individuals, such as those who have died violently or have urgent "unfinished business" for another reason. Nor is it known whether the process can operate across species, with transmigration between human, animal, and even plant embodiments, as some have believed it does. The means by which reincarnation takes place, the nature of that which reincarnates, and the possibility of intermediate phases between death and rebirth are open to speculation, as is the nature of the driving force behind reincarnation—impersonal law, external arbiter, one's own conscience, regrets, habits, desires, ambitions, choices, loves, enmities. On these and other questions, a variety of positions have been taken.

When I first came across the idea of reincarnation, I was very doubtful of it, in part because I was still under the sway of the materialist presumption that consciousness is generated by the brain, even though I did not consider myself a materialist. My outlook was that of a skeptic wary of dogmatic claims, scientific, religious, or otherwise. Moreover, I was of the opinion then (and continue to be so now) that belief in reincarnation and karma could be used in personally and socially manipulative ways. Nevertheless, following the experience described in chapter 2, I have been open to the possibility of reincarnation, and I would not be surprised if my present life were just one in a sequence of linked lives. As previously observed, it was not other-life *memory* as such—memories of being other persons—that arose during the mystical experience; rather, it was a seeing and knowing of others with whom I appeared to have a serial connection.

It is, of course, possible that the experience was hallucinatory or that I misinterpreted certain contents to be revelatory of other lives when they were not. But I would not be surprised if reincarnation really does take place, given the evidence from other sources and its compatibility with the neo-Leibnizian philosophy I have found attractive. Although Leibniz resisted the idea of reincarnation ("transmigration or metempsychosis of the soul"), the alternative he described ("metamorphosis") is rather similar, and his metaphysics is easily adapted to support reincarnation proper. There are features of the monadology that make it a natural companion to reincarnation doctrine. First, monads are extremely resilient, being to all intents and purposes indestructible. They express the universe and so can endure at least as long as the universe endures. As cosmic wholes, monads do not perish when their organismic bodies break down at death, and it is conceivable that they become associated with new bodies. Nothing so trifling as death can halt their progress.

Second, monadology sets out a classification of living organisms, a taxonomy that ranges from simple monads in crude bodies, through plants, animals, and humans with increasingly sophisticated bodies, to superhuman entities with very subtle bodies. In Leibniz's metaphysics, the taxonomy or "Chain of Being" is *not* a scene of transmigratory ascents and descents. Nevertheless, hierarchical classifications of this kind do lend themselves to such application, as in the ancient Indian religion of Jainism, which like monadology categorizes living beings according to their levels of sensory sophistication and consciousness. The present chapter begins with a brief account of the Leibnizian hierarchy and some comparison with the Jaina one. The Leibnizian scheme is fairly static: although monadic organisms aspire and develop toward perfection, monads are in the main restricted to the type of body with which they were created. The Jaina hierarchy is more flexible, for its souls are subject to transmigratory ups and downs through diverse embodiments. It is therefore a true ladder of nature, a hierarchy that can be traversed.

There is, however, an interesting fact about the ladder that was not appreciated until modern times: it is more a tree than a ladder, one that has been growing and branching over the ages, through the emergence of new species (that is, of new kinds of bodies) and the extinction of old ones. This realization, prompted by consideration of the fossil remains of extinct organisms, had yet to crystallize in Leibniz's day, but it was to achieve mature expression by the nineteenth century in the concept of *biological evolution*. There is overwhelming evidence that the diverse organisms alive today on earth, human beings included, are related by descent from common ancestors, the single-celled organisms that appeared several billion years ago.

While evolution has sometimes been depicted as antithetical to religion, it is only so when the two are conceived narrowly, evolution as entirely purposeless, and religion as inflexibly wedded to the belief that creatures have always existed in their present forms. Since the nineteenth century, evolutionism and religion have in fact come together happily in a variety of circumstances and continue to do so, and reincarnation has been given a role in some evolutionary spiritualities, including monadological ones. Evolution transplants reincarnation into a more complex world in which new kinds of embodiments become available over time, while reincarnation makes evolution relevant to the long-term development of individuals, which is advanced by the new kinds of bodies and mental capacities that evolution throws up.

But to what end, if any, is this development headed? Is there some meaning behind the ceaseless wandering, life upon life, and the harsh struggle for survival in the agelong evolutionary march? Is meaning to be found in the journey itself, in the destination to which it leads, or in both journey and goal? If, as I have suggested, monads are and always have been fully conscious, omniscient minds, what have they to gain from the long, difficult path they follow? In this chapter and the next, an attempt will be made to address these questions.

The Great Chain of Being

A degree of order can be imposed on the varied contents of the natural world by classifying them into a few basic categories, such as the traditional kingdoms of mineral, vegetable, and animal. These categories need not be arranged in hierarchical fashion, ranked one above the other, but very often they have been. In complexity of structure, development, and activity, and in other ways too, perceptual, cognitive, or spiritual, plants have typically been placed above minerals, animals above plants, and human beings above nonhuman animals. The elevated status humans immodestly award themselves in such rankings has been qualified to some extent by the admission of yet higher, superhuman classes, populated by angels, demigods, extraterrestrials, and the like, and often but not always by the installation of a supreme being at the very top of the scheme, as its source and perhaps its end. Natural history becomes spiritual ontology, a blueprint of creation, and even a road map to salvation.

Regrettably, hierarchical taxonomy can also be justification for speciesist attitudes, and for racist, classist, and sexist ones too when the stratifying tendency is carried over into matters of ethnicity, social role, and gender. The inner life of nonhuman beings is, of course, difficult to fathom, particularly the life of those very different from ourselves. It is therefore quite possible that rankings can be very misleading, even more so because they are based on anthropocentric values and concerns. For instance, it is likely that we commonly underestimate plant life.[4] It is notable that several of the mystical experiences noted in chapter 1 involved contact with plants.

When developed in a philosophical direction, hierarchical taxonomy becomes the "Chain of Being" or *scala naturæ*, the Ladder of Nature, characterized by fullness, continuity, and gradation of forms.[5] One such philosophical scheme is Leibniz's hierarchy of monads, ordered according to perceptual distinctness and ranging from the insentient monads in minerals and plants, through the sentient souls in charge of animal bodies, to rational human and superhuman souls, including the angelic and demonic spirits (*génies*), who have superior intellects and subtler bodies (table 10.1). Although all monads are omnipercipient, having total perceptions of the universe, they are to a great extent confused, and only God is truly omniscient. Monads with more advanced bodies gain some perceptual distinctness through their senses and mental faculties, and at the rational level may even partake of the divine knowledge.

In chapter 6, I drew on mystical hints to suggest a revised system in which monads are truly omniscient. These monads, from the most humble

Deus	omniscience—complete a priori knowledge (no body)
genius	perception, sensation, reason (rational souls in subtler bodies)
mens	perception, sensation, reason (rational souls in human bodies)
anima	perception, sensation (souls in animal bodies)
vita	perception (simple monads in minerals and plants)

Table 10.1 Leibniz's hierarchy of monads.[6]

to the most exalted, have perfectly clear perceptions of the universe. Indeed, their cosmic perceptions are intellections, being unmediated knowings, and so their omnipercipience is true omniscience. Ordinarily, however, the sense-based experiences of monads give no inkling of the immense *noumenal* depths within, but sometimes mystical experiences afford a glimpse. Although the revised monads are all equal in their inherent omniscience, they can still be arranged hierarchically in the manner of Leibnizian monads, for they are distinguished by the quality of their *phenomenal* perceptions and associated mental activities. Leibnizian monads, with their inherently confused perceptions of the universe, are ranked according to the degree of perceptual distinctness and mental clarity their organismic bodies confer. By contrast, the revised monads, which have inherently clear noumenal perceptions of the universe, are ranked by the degree of confusion that their phenomenal perceptions and minds introduce.

The suggested inversion brings the monadology into line with religious teachings that place the divine majesty and amplitude within. The aim of spiritual practice, then, is not to acquire that which one lacks but to uncover that which one already has. The treasury within is brimming with splendors, yet few realize it is there. Those who do may seek to enter but must first make themselves worthy. Thus, Plotinus, having undergone moral, intellectual, and contemplative preparation, takes leave of his senses and rises to the undescended part of his soul, which is the Intellect in unity with its intelligible cosmos, rooted in and illumined by the One. As a Christian Platonist, Thomas Traherne retires to his Self in a center and finds there the "Relucent & Shining" Image of God, the spiritual universe replete with kingdoms and ages, an inheritance that each possesses individually. Early Buddhism, wary of metaphysical essences, was not inclined to portray the spiritual path as an uncovering of an inherent nature, but the idea emerged strongly in some forms of Mahāyāna Buddhism, notably in the concept of the Buddha-nature, when understood as an inherent actuality rather than mere potentiality to attain Buddhahood:

At that time the Tathāgata with his unobstructed pure eye of wisdom
universally beheld all sentient beings throughout the universe and said:
'How amazing! How amazing! How can it be that these sentient beings are
fully endowed with the wisdom of the Tathāgata and yet, being ignorant
and confused, do not know it and do not see it?[7]

Spiritual practice brings out Buddhahood, dispelling the ignorance that
ordinarily conceals it. This perspective, which drew on *tathāgatagarbha*
("Buddha womb/embryo") doctrine, found expression in the teachings of
"original enlightenment" (Chin., *benjue*; Jpn., *hongaku*) developed in the
Huayan, Tiantai, and Ch'an schools of Chinese Buddhism, transmitted to
Korea, and highly influential in Japan, where it received further development.[8] Original enlightenment was even extended to include entities that
Indian Buddhism had not recognized in any explicit way as possessed of
sentience and consciousness, and which therefore had been excluded from
participation in the karma-driven round of samsaric rebirth and the path to
liberation in *nirvāṇa*.[9] Zhanran (Chan-jan; 711–782 CE), a patriarch of the
Tiantai school, contended that insentient beings, including grasses, trees,
and soil, possess the Buddha-nature and strive to actualize their original
enlightenment, an idea that was taken up in various ways by Japanese
Buddhists, including Saichō (767–822), Kūkai (774–835), Ryōgen (912–985),
and Chūjin (1065–1138).[10]

Jainism had from its earliest recorded period affirmed the intrinsic
omniscience of beings, and the life, sentience, and liberative potential of
plants and elements were not held in any doubt. All *jīvas*—the soul-units of
Jainism—have perception (*darśana*) complemented by knowledge (*jñāna*),
and so they are inherently conscious, indeed omniscient. However, from time
immemorial, karmic types of matter have acted to limit their perception and
knowledge. Removal of these obscurations by means of ascetic practices
liberates a *jīva* by uncovering its naturally unlimited perception, knowledge,
bliss, and energy. Jaina life-forms consist of *jīvas* in combination with their
bodies, the latter composed of matter (*pudgala*) that is ultimately atomic
in constitution. The life-forms can be classified in a hierarchy according
to the number of sense organs they are attributed and the quality of their
knowledge (table 10.2).

Although the Leibnizian and Jaina hierarchies have features in common,
such as the ranking of souls by level of perception and consciousness, they
also exhibit differences. For example, the Leibnizian monads found in minerals and plants are not attributed sensation, including it would seem pain
sensation. Pain, according to Leibniz, requires some degree of discrimina-

*siddha*s	–	unlimited knowledge, perception, power, bliss (no body)
gods	–	five senses, reason, superknowledges
hell beings	–	five senses, reason, superknowledges
humans	–	five senses, reason
animals	–	touch, taste, smell, sight, hearing, reason (born from womb or egg, including fish, reptiles, birds, mammals)
	–	touch, taste, smell, sight, hearing (born by coalescence of material particles)
	–	touch, taste, smell, sight (e.g., wasps, flies, scorpions)
	–	touch, taste, smell (e.g., ants, flees, termites)
	–	touch, taste (e.g., worms, leeches, snails)
plants	–	touch only (single-souled, such as trees and shrubs, and multi-souled, such as root vegetables)
elementals	–	touch only (souls with bodies of earth, water, fire, or air; pervade the universe but not found in the bodies of other organisms)
*nigoda*s	–	touch only (minuscule, plantlike, with no bodies of their own, exist in clusters, very short-lived; pervade the universe, including bodies of other organisms)

Table 10.2   Jaina hierarchy of living beings.[11]

tion, which the basic monads lack.[12] By contrast, the *jīva*s in element and plant bodies are taken to be sentient and are therefore thought capable of feeling pain, if not with much awareness or any understanding.[13] The pervasiveness of sentience in the Jaina universe underpins the characteristic Jaina attitude of universal nonviolence (*ahiṃsā*), for violence against any living being causes it suffering and harms one's own prospects of liberation.

The Jainas also go further in the attribution of rationality to the higher animals, going so far as to view those with reason as capable of moral choice and therefore subject to karmic consequences. For Leibniz, only human and superhuman souls are sufficiently rational to be moral agents and therefore subject to justice at the Last Judgment. But the most significant difference is clear to see at the very top of the two schemes. The Jaina hierarchy has liberated, godlike souls (*siddha*s) at its summit, but no creator God from whom the souls derive. Leibnizian monadology does have a creator God, fulgurating monads into existence at the Creation as fully expressive of the universe—hence their omnipercipience and harmonious coordination. Jainism, as far as I know, makes no attempt to explain why its *jīva*s are intrinsically omniscient or indeed why they exist at all, other than to say that they are knowers by nature and have been around for endless time. Unlike monads, *jīva*s are neither derivative things nor entities in which the universe has its concrete existence.

A Jaina argument against the existence of a creator God follows from the division of reality into two basic categories, soul/animate (*jīva*), which is of the nature of consciousness, and soulless/inanimate (*ajīva*), consisting of motion, rest, atomic matter, space, and, according to some Jainas, time. This metaphysical dualism takes matter to be a substance in its own right, and so it is asked: "how can an immaterial god create that which is material?"[14] Surely an immaterial god is unable to create something so very different from itself as matter? With the reality of matter taken for granted, the existence of an immaterial creator is rejected. Jaina philosophy faces the same kind of difficulty that besets Cartesian dualism: how can substances so different from each other as soul and matter interact, whether in the yoking of souls to their bodies or in the adhesion of karmic matter to the souls? But the mind–body problem is not so urgent for Jaina metaphysics, which neither separates soul and matter into distinct realms nor denies to matter the sensible qualities of color, taste, smell, and touch. By contrast, the matter of early modern science, such as Descartes' extended matter, lacked even the sensible qualities and so was even further removed from mind.

When the existence of the immaterial creator is assumed, as it was by Leibniz, the opposite conclusion offers itself, and idealist rather than dualist or materialist metaphysics can prevail. This was the case in a mystical forerunner of Leibniz's monadology, developed in the early 1670s by Anne Conway (1631–1679) and Francis Mercury van Helmont (1614–1698), son of Johannes Baptista van Helmont (whom we first met in chapter 4, on his quest for self-knowledge).[15] Like the Jaina philosophers, Lady Conway and van Helmont could not believe that an immaterial god creates something so utterly different from itself as lifeless matter.[16] But unlike the Jainas, Conway and van Helmont took the existence of the spiritual creator as a given and concluded that matter must be of the nature of spirit. Conway aimed her spiritual monism against Hobbesian materialism and Cartesian dualism, and also against Spinoza's pantheistic monism as she understood it.

Van Helmont explained how matter comes to be: God emanates spirits, some of whom contract from their original state of union, knowledge, and happiness to become unconscious monads. These monads do not feel pain, for they are insentient. Not all spirits fall to this level: they occupy numerous intermediate positions between God and the stuporous state. But those spirits who do fall into unconsciousness cling together, and their "coalition" is the matter that makes up bodies.[17] Matter, then, does not exist "by and of itself," not "positively," but "privatively" like a shadow. However, the sleeping monads can reawaken, loosen themselves from their mutual entanglements ("separation of sparks"), ascend through the degrees of knowledge, and return to union with God.[18] This is union, not identity, for van Helmont, like Conway and Leibniz, makes a firm distinction between creator and created. The Helmontian spirits are dependent products, exalted beings originally in union with God and capable of reunion, but still created things and not the divine essence itself.

Scaling Nature's Ladder

A further major difference between the Leibnizian and Jaina hierarchies concerns the mobility of souls up and down the ranks. A ladder is truly a ladder only if it can be climbed, but Leibniz's Chain of Being offers little or no opportunity for a lower-level monad to advance above its station. Leibniz believed that an all-powerful, benevolent deity had created the universe. It followed that the world is essentially good and indeed the best of all worlds that could have been created. There is no reason to try to escape from it or mend it, and so the Chain of Being is not a path to salvation or world repair. The hierarchy is taxonomic and metaphysical, explaining how the various things we observe in nature are related to the monads. By contrast, the Jaina taxonomy of living beings is steadfastly soteriological: it operates within a renouncer tradition that looks upon the world with dismay as an ocean of suffering through which souls wander in their transmigrations from body to body. The Jaina hierarchy sets out the kinds of embodiments to which souls proceed at death, depending on the quantity and character of the karmic matter that has adhered to them. It also promises the goal of liberation, escape from transmigration if the soul's intrinsic nature is unveiled.

As there is no essential difference between *jīvas*, each can in theory progress to higher births and ultimately to liberation. Even *nigodas*, at the bottom of the scheme, can progress to liberation, although it is said that many remain stuck in their condition for endless time. But when scaling the ladder of sentience and consciousness, it is important not to aim too high, for life in a heaven realm is just too pleasant to encourage desire for liberation, and the sufferings of hell are too obstructive. Only at the human level is there a helpful balance of suffering, mental capacity, access to teachings, and ability to take action. Human birth is very precious indeed, as other renouncer traditions have also insisted.

After many lives, some *jīvas* do manage to slough off their karmic matter and free their intrinsic omniscience to become *kevalins* while in the body. At death, these buoyant, fully purified souls rise to the summit of the many-storied universe, above the hells, earth, and heavens, to become and forever remain unembodied *siddhas*, resplendent in their unlimited perception, knowledge, bliss, and energy. But as Padmanabh S. Jaini points out, "this is not a theory of necessary evolution; the Jaina also accepts the possibility of retrogression, and thus of eternal bondage."[19] There are snakes as well as ladders, paths that lead down as well as up. In fact, the board game "snakes and ladders" has been used to illustrate the ups and downs of samsaric existence and the path to liberation.[20]

Although commonly associated with Indic religions, belief in transmigration has been fairly widespread. In the West, it was taught in the Pythagorean–Platonic traditions. Heraclides of Pontus (fourth century BCE), a student of Plato, tells a story about Pythagoras' recollections of his former lives, which included stints as a Trojan warrior and a fisherman as well as wanderings through animal and plant bodies. When transmigration is given a set sequence, it is presented as a cycle through the domains of the elements. The historian Herodotus (fifth century BCE) tells of a doctrine, implausibly attributed by him to the Egyptians, in which souls migrate from human embodiment through a 3,000-year round of terrestrial, aquatic, and aerial incarnations back to human form.[21] It is usually supposed that Pythagoras was one of those unnamed Greeks whom Herodotus says adopted this teaching. Empedocles may have been another, for he described a 30,000-season passage through his four elements by the exiled soul (*daimōn*) who, under the dominion of Strife, has shed blood or broken oaths: "The ethereal power . . . pursues souls to the sea, the sea spits them up onto the threshold of the earth, the earth into the rays of the bright sun, and the sun hurls them into the whirls of the ether: each receives them from another: all hate them."[22] Like his *saṃsāra*-renouncing Indian contemporaries, Empedocles urged escape from miserable wandering to blessedness and immortality.

In his *Dīwān-i Shams-i Tabrīzī*, Sufi poet Jalāl al-Dīn Rūmī (1207–1273 CE) writes of a linear progression through the mineral, vegetable, animal, human, and angelic realms toward God:

> From the moment you came into the world of being,
> A ladder was placed before you that you might escape.
> First you were mineral, later you turned to plant,
> Then you became animal: how should this be a secret to you?
> Afterwards you were made man, with knowledge, reason, faith;
> Behold the body, which is a portion of the dust-pit, how perfect it has
>   grown!
> When you have travelled on from man, you will doubtless become
>   an angel;

After that you are done with this earth: your station is in heaven.

Pass again even from angelhood: enter that ocean,

That your drop may become a sea which is a hundred seas of 'Omān.[23]

This passage and closely related ones in Rumi's *Dīwān* and his other major work, the *Mathnawī*, have received a variety of interpretations.[24] If Rumi believed in the transmigration of souls, as is sometimes claimed, then the above lines could well describe transmigration up the ladder of nature on the path toward God. But transmigration (*tanāsukh*) is not an orthodox Islamic teaching, for it is commonly deemed incompatible with belief in the bodily resurrection at the Judgement.[25] However, some offshoots, such as the Druze and Alawite traditions, do subscribe to it.[26] It has even been claimed that Rumi anticipated biological evolutionism in such passages, but scholars tend to be unimpressed by this modern gloss and explain the ladder as the descent and reascent of spirit's manifestations through hierarchical levels of reality, akin to Neoplatonic emanationism, with its divine fountainhead and ontological cascade.[27] Rumi often depicts the ascent as a progression through cycles of ingestion and assimilation: minerals are food for plants, plants for animals, animals for human beings. Nature's ladder is a food chain that leads to the divine, driven by a hunger that is in essence a longing for God.[28]

Plotinus had said that all things, including animals, plants, and soil, aspire in contemplation toward their source, a path of ascent from the sensible, through the intelligible, to the One, driven by the insufficiency and longing that departure from the source, the perfectly sufficient One, inevitably entails. In this scheme, there is no question that transmigration has a role to play: Plotinus, as a follower of Plato, had no qualms about incorporating and adapting the doctrine within the framework of his own metaphysics. While the undescended part of the Plotinian soul remains undisturbed in its contemplation of the Forms, the lower part transmigrates from life to life in the sensible realm, with the reincarnation determined by the body and character of the previous embodiment. The souls of human beings who take care of their rational qualities will continue to occupy human bodies. But those dominated by the senses and attendant desires will reincarnate as animals. If they have been especially dull-witted, they will be reborn as plants. Those who succeed in reconnecting with the higher part of their souls will rise to the Intellect and its gods, and ultimately to the One, no longer subject to transmigration. In this scheme, there is an ineluctable moral law of action and reaction that bears comparison to some Indian notions of karma. Tyrants will be reborn as slaves, murderers as the murdered.[29]

As we have seen, Leibniz's monadology departs from the philosophy of Plotinus in important respects, and here a further point of contrast emerges. Although well acquainted with transmigration doctrine, Leibniz rejected it as such. But his friend Francis Mercury van Helmont did subscribe to a theory of transmigration, "the revolution of souls," drawing inspiration from the Lurianic Kabbalah, which he had helped bring to the attention of Christian scholars, including Leibniz, through the publication of the *Kabbala denudata* (1677, 1684) with Christian Knorr von Rosenroth. This sixteenth-century development in Jewish mysticism, centered on Isaac Luria (1534–1572 CE) and his Safed circle, had detailed a process by which the repair of the fallen world is to be accomplished. In this labor of *tikkun*, the purification of souls or "raising of sparks" through a gradual ascent of nature's ladder was sometimes given a role:

> And the Holy One, blessed be He, gradually lifts them up, little by little, from level to level; first He places them in inanimate objects, and from inanimate objects to vegetation, and from vegetation to animals that do not speak, and from there to speaking beings—pagans and slaves—and from thence to Israelites.[30]

According to some Kabbalists, the souls of human beings may undergo transmigration (*gilgul*, "rolling") into animal, plant, and even mineral embodiments, if their sins so require. Reascent follows the food chain:

> Because first [such a soul] rises from the inanimate to the vegetative, as it grows from the earth and enters the vegetative. Then an animal that eats grass consumes it, and it rises to the level of an animal; after that, people slaughter it and eat it, and it becomes, once again, part of man's own body, and then is rectified, for man's consumption of it brings about its purification.[31]

The holy can assist the process if they eat heedfully, assimilating into their bodies the degraded souls in the food.

Although van Helmont believed that souls rise through many degrees of knowledge to union with God, even from the stuporous material condition, he does not appear to have subscribed to the Kabbalistic belief in interspecies transmigration. Leibniz reports that his friend believed transmigration takes place solely within the same species, which means that humans will always be reborn as humans.[32] Van Helmont outlined an inventive but contrived scheme of universal salvation in which each soul seeks perfection by migrating through 12 human incarnations over 1,000 years, with the possibility of an extra life for extreme sinners, who are born into the army of Gog and Magog at Armageddon and then suffer correction in hell for a very long but finite time, salvation being inevitable because God is love. Each of the 12 lives is like an hour of daytime, although one that lasts on average 83⅓ years, for the Psalmist (90.4) had said that 1,000 years is like a day in the sight of God.[33] As if to comply with his chronology, van Helmont passed away at the ripe old age of 84. When he attempted to demonstrate the conformity of his Kabbalah-inspired transmigration doctrine to Christian truths, van Helmont pointed out that the revolution of souls through 12 incarnations allows those who are still far from perfection, such as "Fools," "Naturals," "Abortives," "Monsters," and cannibals, to attain perfection, which is only fitting in a world created by the wise and loving Christian God.[34] Transmigration is to be valued for it leads to redemption and reunion with God.

Lady Anne Conway, van Helmont's partner in spiritual monism and apocatastatic speculation, was even more daring, arguing for the *transmutation* of individuals from one species to another. In this, she directly echoed the Kabbalistic belief in ascent through the food chain:

> For there are transmutations of all creatures from one species to another, as from stone to earth, from earth to grass, from grass to sheep, from sheep to human flesh, from human flesh to the lowest spirits of man and from these to the noblest spirits.[35]

Conway reasoned that all creatures are spirit and so differ only in mode, not in substance. Substance cannot be changed, but mode can, and so individuals can change species. A horse, having progressed over many lives, may transmute into a man, and a man, if he falls into bad ways, may change into a brute or devil. But if a man leads virtuous lives, his transmutation will be angelical.[36] Like van Helmont and the Kabbalists, Conway believed in the elevating power of suffering, which works to desolidify congealed spirits and hasten their return to God. Conway herself knew suffering all too well, enduring a chronic illness with severe headache as its chief symptom. The episodes started when she was about twelve, after a fever, and became more frequent, prolonged, and debilitating as she grew older. Symptoms included the headache, sometimes unilateral, with bouts lasting up to four days, incapacity, vomiting, and hypersensitivity to light, sound, and movement—a combination suggestive of migraine. Van Helmont's medical expertise was unable to effect a cure, although his engaging personality, stimulating ideas, and therapeutic approach, which recognized a psychosomatic component of illness and accordingly employed the psychological technique of *philalgia* (of taking a loving attitude to one's pain), helped her come to terms with the condition.[37] Viewed in the right way, Conway's pain could be seen as a divine gift bestowed on one who had sought higher truth:

> Rather did she yearn for joys not to be known by the senses of the flesh but by the mind. So at length Christ, descending suddenly from on high, came in his full glory bringing pain by the hand, who was clothed in consuming flame and fire and swift circles of blazing heat.[38]

Conway can be placed in the company of her fellow chronic sufferers Hildegard of Bingen and Anna Maria Taigi in view of the seemingly migrainous character of her ailment *and* its association with spiritual and psychical phenomena.[39] In the unpublished preface to Conway's *The Principles of the Most Ancient and Modern Philosophy*, signed by van Helmont, there is mention of Conway's "Supernatural Comforts and Refreshments after some of her greatest Agonies and Conflicts" and of her "strange Praevisions of things future."[40] Moreover, van Helmont is said to have taken down stories of Conway's "extraordinary visions," perhaps involving the psi perceptions of clairvoyance, telepathy, and precognition.[41] One story concerns her sister-in-law Dorothy Rawdon: Conway inexplicably knew that Dorothy had been laid low by the "falling sickness." Another story tells of the Earl of Norwich, who Conway intuited had come off his horse and sustained an injury, and was in need of a "liniment" in Conway's possession. It is reported that in both cases her intuitions were confirmed.

Leibniz's version of transformation, *metamorphosis*, does not allow such interspecies change, and there seems to be very little room for individual progress up his hierarchy. The overall picture is fixed. This is because Leibniz contends that a monad is pretty much tied to the kind of body with which it was initially created. He maintains that all monads preexist from the creation of the universe and continue to exist for its duration. At the creation, monads came into being in association with miniature, seedlike bodies that determine the types of full-sized bodies they will have. From these spermatic bodies, the macroscopic bodies of monads grow, endure for a time, and then decompose at death, dwindling back to the spermatic bodies. In the case of subrational monads, the spermatic bodies may regrow again into full-sized bodies, and the cycle can continue indefinitely.

This process may sound a little like transmigration, but Leibniz insists that it is metamorphosis, a gradual corporeal change in which the monad never completely divests itself of its body. While praising Pythagoras for his doctrine of the immortal soul, Leibniz disassociates his own position from those of Pythagoras and van Helmont by insisting that metamorphosis rather than transmigration takes place.[42] Leibniz does admit the theoretical possibility of transmigration, even into the bodies of other species "in the Brahmin or Pythagorean manner," if the transmigrating soul were to retain a rarefied body and shed only its coarse body, but his adherence to the Principle of Continuity inclines him to a decay-and-regrowth model rather than accept the major change that transmigration to a new coarse body would involve.[43] Drawing on contemporary microscopical investigations and theories of spermatic preformation, he supposes that during the death transition, an animal's body never entirely falls away. Rather, it dwindles to the spermatic animalcule and remains in this miniature form, with its more limited perceptions, until conception takes place again and regrowth begins. These spermatic bodies, like everything else in the universe, are in a state of perpetual flux and so can change to some extent, but not it seems to such a degree that they can transform into the seeds of macroscopic creatures of different species.

The process is not quite the same for rational monads, such as human souls, although here again the monad that will come to occupy a human body has preexisted from the Creation with an appropriate spermatic body. It has a miniature animal body, and so the soul of a human-to-be is just an animal soul, sentient but not rational, until conception takes place. After conception, the spermatic animal grows to become the body of a human being, and the soul becomes rational. Leibniz is unsure how this leap to rationality comes about, whether through some natural inbuilt propensity toward reason or through the intervention of God, who would elevate the soul by conferring reason upon it.[44] And while subrational monads are destined to pass through many lives and deaths in the corporeal waxing and waning that is metamorphosis, the destiny of a rational creature such as a human being is free from such cycles, for at death the soul's body reverts to an animalcule until the Last Judgment, after which time entry into Heaven or Hell follows, for rational beings as moral beings are subject to divine justice.

However, it is possible to gain the impression that Leibniz envisaged significant individual progress. Take, for instance, the following anecdote recounted by Michael Gottlieb Hansch:

> I remember that once, when Leibniz and I met in Leipzig and were drinking caffè latte [Caffée cum lacte], a beverage which he greatly savored, he said that in the cup from which he was drinking there might be, for all we know, monads that in future time would become human souls.[45]

By this speculation (which Kant took to be a joke),[46] Leibniz may just have meant that some members of his special class of potentially human spermatic animals were present in the tasty brew, without intending to suggest that *any* kind of monad there could progress to the rational level. Elsewhere Leibniz is clear that only a human spermatic animal can become human, and even then the transformation is not guaranteed: "Thus a mere animal will never become a man, and the human spermatic animals which do not pass into this great transformation through conception are mere animals."[47]

Although subrational monads will never become human, the possibility of departure from the human level sometimes appears to be suggested. In the following passage, Leibniz seems to admit both descent and ascent (*descendre et monter*), which would make his position closer to Conway's, which allows transmutation into animals, devils, and angels:

> It is just as reasonable that there should be substances capable of perception below us as above us, so that our soul, far from being the lowest of all, finds itself in the middle, from which one may rise or sink. Otherwise there would be a deficiency in order, or what some philosophers call a *vacuum of forms.*[48]

In a letter to Electress Sophie, Leibniz again seems to admit the possibility of a human soul's advancement to a higher class of rational being, although here he omits to mention the possibility of descent: "It ought to be believed that there are rational souls more perfect than us, that could be called *genies*, and we could well be of their number one day. The order of the universe seems to require this."[49]

But in the two passages just cited, which date from the same period (1704–1706), Leibniz's interest lies not in the possibility of ascent and descent. Rather, it is the *order* of the organismic hierarchy, for his Principle of Continuity requires that there be no gaps in it, no *vacuum formarum*, no "vacuum of forms." There would be such gaps if the human level were not intermediate between higher and lower classes of embodied souls, between the genii and the animal souls.

Climbing the Tree of Life

There is in my library a bulky volume entitled *The Natural History Book.*[50] Over many pages of exquisite photography, some 5,000 of the 1.9 million or so species cataloged by biological science at the time of the book's writing are depicted, testifying to the astonishing diversity and artistry of nature. Here one finds heliodor, a golden-yellow variety of beryl suggestive of crystallized sunbeams, the tiny seasparkle equipped with gas bag and tentacle, renowned for lighting up the ocean a ghostly blue, the traveler's tree of Madagascar sporting impressive fanlike foliage, the peacock mantis shrimp looking for all the world like a visitor from outer space, with its exotic coloring and queer eyes perched on stalks, the sandpiper *Philomachus pugnax* so elegant in its neck ruff, and the ground pangolin, with scaly coat that puts the workmanship of medieval armorers to shame.

The plan of the book is fairly traditional, proceeding from minerals and rocks through plants to animals, but with fossils and microscopic life slipped in before the plants, and fungi interposed between the plants and the animals. However, this volume is no guidebook to the antique ladder of nature, no Leibnizian paean to the finely graded plenitude of God's monadic creation or Jaina meditation on the destinations to which fettered souls transmigrate. As a twenty-first-century production, published just over 150 years after Charles Darwin's *Origin of Species* (1859), the book presents not a *scala naturæ* but an *arbor vitæ*, a tree of life that traces the evolutionary branching of organisms from single cells to complex, multicellular animals such as ourselves. Human beings no longer rank above the animals and a little below the angels: here male and female specimens of *Homo sapiens* are tucked away inconspicuously with the other great apes, the gorilla, the orangutan, the bonobo, and the chimpanzee.[51] The blandest of the family Hominidae, humans are noted for their bipedal posture, lack of body hair, and the "relatively large braincases" they have in common with the other great apes. Uniquely among the numerous specimens on display in the book, they are clad in swimsuits, the fig leaf having passed out of fashion some time ago.

Until the rise of modern biological evolutionism, it was believed that species had existed with no or very little change since the creation of the world—or from beginningless time if the world had no temporal origin. But nowadays it is appreciated that new species have been evolving out of older ones for billions of years, and that many have come into being and suffered extinction over the course of time, as the fossil record clearly shows. When organisms appeared on Earth a few hundred million years after the planet formed, they did so not all at once but gradually and with increasingly diverse forms. The plants and animals we observe today in great profusion and diversity are descendants of relatively simple, common ancestors, the unicellular organisms that first appeared between 3.5 and 4 billion years ago, at least according to current estimates. It has been speculated that these organisms, similar to bacteria, may have evolved out of systems of self-replicating molecules.

Transformism, the idea that new species evolve out of older ones, was by no means the brainchild of Darwin alone. It had been discussed in the eighteenth century in connection with the growing realization that the Earth has passed though epochs of formation over millions of years. It was set out in detail at the beginning of the nineteenth century by Jean-Baptiste Lamarck (1744–1829). Lamarck suggested that biological evolution is driven by two factors. First, there is an intrinsic, primary tendency toward complexity, an entirely natural and progressive "power of life" that spontaneously and continuously organizes simple life-forms out of inanimate matter and gradually shapes them into more complex forms. The fixed scale of nature was turned by Lamarck into a serial process of species transformism, *la marche de la nature*. But Lamarck's linear escalator was complemented by a tree-like branching of species. This deviation from the mainline was attributed to an extrinsic, secondary factor, again natural, but accidental and potentially disruptive rather than progressive, namely the impact of environmental change. Changes to habitats induce organisms to alter their habits, which strengthens some organs and atrophies others, somatic adjustments passed on and reinforced down the generations. It is this second mechanism, the "inheritance of acquired characters," to which the term Lamarckism is often applied (although apparently the idea was not original with Lamarck).

In the mid-nineteenth century a different evolutionary mechanism was proposed, arrived at independently by Darwin and Alfred Russel Wallace (1823–1913), although it won general acceptance only from the 1920s and 1930s, displacing neo-Lamarckism and other alternatives. This was *natural selection*, a mechanism that has since come to dominate evolutionary thinking. It has been widely supposed that the branching of the family tree into new species is an entirely natural, purposeless affair, driven by mutations and other sources of heritable variation (such as new genetic combinations through sexual reproduction, genetic drift, and horizontal gene transfer) in association with the sifting action of natural selection, which disposes of many variations before they become established while favoring a few. Organisms are more likely to survive if their inherited characteristics make them better able than their competitors to exploit the limited resources of their environments. And they are more likely to reproduce if inherited characteristics, such as the bright plumage of some birds, increase their chances of attracting mates ("sexual selection").

But environments change, sometimes rapidly, promoting previously unsustainable or insignificant kinds of variations. In a controversial move, natural selection has been shifted by some biologists to the genetic level, turning the gene and its DNA code into the unit of selection. Critics have responded by pointing out that the organism itself, not its genetic coding, is engaged in the struggles of life, and so is better regarded as the unit of selection.[52] Furthermore, many organisms are successful because they cooperate with one another in social groups or engage in mutually beneficial interactions with members of other species, and so the unit of selection can be understood even more broadly, going beyond the organism and its genetics into social, symbiotic, and even cultural spheres.

There is also some evidence that evolutionary processes may be more complex at the molecular level than commonly supposed, involving "epigenetic" factors, that is, factors outside the genes that control the expression of genes. In this connection, there has been a qualified yet controversial reengagement in recent years with Lamarckian inheritance of acquired characters, an idea eclipsed by the neo-Darwinian emphasis on emergence of new species ("speciation") through the mechanism of mutation and natural selection. In some instances, characteristics acquired during the life of an organism can be passed on to its offspring, a form of transmission now called "transgenerational epigenetics."[53] For instance, there has been considerable interest in the role played by epigenetics in the transmission of some medical conditions. Thus, not all variation of the more complex organisms depends on so-called random processes: it can stem from the life events of organisms, including their responses to environmental pressures, such as stress and lack of food. But it remains to be seen whether the science of epigenetics will one day lend credence to the archetypal speculations of Edward Carpenter and then Jung, which were based in part on the neo-Lamarckian idea that instincts are biologically inherited accumulations and condensations of ancestral life experience that unconsciously pattern behavior.[54]

There is another means, not recognized at all in mainstream science, by which the past might live on through the generations, a form of transmission that will depend on mechanisms other than genetic and epigenetic inheritances from ancestors. If it is allowed that reincarnation takes place and, as the evidence appears to suggest, carries over ingrained habits, memories, personality traits, learned skills, and even physical attributes, then some process must be responsible for the transmission. It has been suggested that reincarnation involves a substrate or "vehicle" that survives the gross disintegration of the organism and is capable of supporting the transmission of some characteristics to the new organism, initially by influencing the development of the embryo and fetus. Ian Stevenson referred to this hypothesized intermediary as the *psychophore* ("mind-carrier"), which he thought might be fieldlike in action.[55] The idea of a soul-vehicle that survives death has had a presence in religious thought since ancient times, expressed in the concept of subtle bodies.[56] In Leibniz's philosophy, there is a body that survives death, although it is not a subtle body in the traditional sense. This is the microscopic "animalcule" described above, which in the case of subrational monads acts as a seed for the regrowth of macroscopic bodies during the process of metamorphosis. Leibniz would be able to account for transmission of characteristics from one life to the next by supposing that the animalcule acts as a carrier of information.[57] But more generally, a past life will inform the present one because the monad, being omnipercipient, has impressions of all that has happened to it.

If transmigration does take place and operates widely throughout nature, then evolutionary theory is likely in need of some revision, at the very least to accommodate the transmission of psychological and physical character-istics suggested by the empirical evidence for reincarnation. For example, when an organism dies without offspring, some of its specific qualities may nonetheless survive, carrying over to the succedent incarnation and perhaps spreading from there to a wider population through reproduction. A grander picture is conceivable too, one in which reincarnation works in tandem with species evolution in a progressive manner directed toward ends. In premodern times, transmigration was typically viewed as a sorry business, a wearisome, potentially endless round from which escape is desirable, or somewhat more positively as a long journey home to a divine condition from which souls fell through heedlessness, moral lapse, or a catastrophic failure during the cosmogonic process (as in the Lurianic Kabbalah).

However, since the advent of evolutionary thought it has become pos-sible to reimagine transmigration as fundamentally creative and purposive, working over long ages toward world-building and person-making through the cultivation and ascent of a tree of life by transmigrating souls. Evolution, then, would not simply be the result of blind mechanisms or the handiwork of an external, supernatural designer. It would be shaped from *within* nature by those immersed in the world process, who according to the philosophical perspective taken in the present book are the monads. But monadology in its classical Leibnizian form had no place for advancement through transmigra-tion, as observed above. Nor did it entertain the possibility of advancement through the emergence of new kinds of bodies, that is, through species evolution. In the nineteenth century, however, transmigration, biological evolution, and monads were to come together in the progressive spirituali-ties of esoteric thinkers. Evolutionary monadology appeared on the scene, if only at the occult margins of evolutionary thinking.

Evolutionary Monadology

The idea of species evolution had not quite taken shape in Leibniz's day, and it is understandable that his philosophy has little or no concept of progress through speciation. Although a cutting-edge thinker, Leibniz was in many respects a man of his time, and he assumed that all species came into existence at the Creation as the types of bodies associated with monads, albeit in seed form. Nevertheless, it is possible that modern evolutionary thinking owes a debt to his metaphysics, if only indirectly. The Leibnizian God is noninterventionist, not given to interfering with nature once it has been set going. Monads are created as closed, energy-conserving systems, designed to proceed under their own steam. God's activity lies in setting up the monads, conferring upon them all that they need to proceed on their own (but Leibniz was not a complete laissez-faire deist, for he had God continuously sustain the monads too). It has been suggested that this feature of Leibniz's thought set the scene for the naturalistic evolutionism of later times by encouraging Enlightenment thinkers to view nature as self-organizing and self-sufficient.[58]

It has also been suggested that Leibniz anticipated modern biological evolutionism by recognizing the mutability of species. According to the historian of ideas Arthur O. Lovejoy, Leibniz was prominent among those who "temporalized" the Great Chain of Being, turning it from a static hierarchy of beings fixed for all time into a dynamic one in which more advanced biological forms progressively come into existence.[59] The Chain of Being was transformed into a "Chain of Becoming," a plenum of potentialities gradually actualized as the universe advances toward greater perfection. According to Lovejoy, Leibniz drew on fossil evidence to suggest that species transform over time, a view that departed from the long-standing Platonic, Aristotelian, and Christian preference for the immutability of species. It would be impressive if Leibniz had anticipated modern evolutionary theory in this one respect, but there is reason to think that Lovejoy overstated the case. It appears that Leibniz envisaged only limited changes within species rather than emergence of new ones.[60] If this is so, the Leibnizian universe offers very little opportunity for significant development, not only at the individual (*ontogenetic*) level but also at the species (*phylogenetic*) level.

But Leibniz's writings can give the impression that he envisaged real progress at the *cosmological* level, with the universe improving significantly as time goes by: "Further, we realise that there is a perpetual and a most free progress of the whole universe towards a consummation of the universal beauty and perfection of the works of God, so that it is always advancing towards a greater development."[61] This is a strong assertion of universal progress, but it is possible that the "progress" and "perfection" in question merely consist in the development of unripened spermatic bodies into their macroscopic forms, that is, the growth of bodies that have been seeds since the creation of the universe into full-grown organisms.[62] This is a somewhat limited notion of progress, being maturation rather than thoroughgoing transformation. Only if monads were able to develop beyond their preordained stations in the hierarchy, through transmutation, transmigration, or some other means of corporeal upgrade, would there be significant advancement.

Notions of human progress and perfectibility were to become all the rage in the Enlightenment, and, by the early nineteenth century, progressionism in the biological realm hung heavy in the air, due in part to German *Naturphilosophie* and the materialist French transformism of Lamarck and his supporters. There was talk of evolutionary transformation leading from "Monad to Man,"[63] evidenced it was supposed in the stages of species evolution seemingly exhibited in human embryological development, an idea summed up later in the century by Ernst Haeckel's slogan "ontogeny recapitulates phylogeny." Robert Grant, the leading proponent of Lamarckian thought in Britain and a teacher of Darwin at the Edinburgh Medical School in the mid-1820s, expressed it thus:

> He [the student] traces, in comparative anatomy, the human organs coming successively into being, and rising in complexness, from the *monad* [emphasis added] through all the grades of animal existence; and discovers, by the close resemblance which exists between the transient forms presented by man's organs during their development, and their permanent or adult forms in inferior orders of animals, that the plan of organization is everywhere the same, and man the climax of its development.[64]

Although the *biological* term "monad" may owe a debt to Leibniz's organicism, the entities in question were not his *metaphysical* units but primitive, microscopic organisms, the "infusoria" that transformists posited as the first step in the evolution of animals from inanimate matter.[65]

Transformism was a minority position, more popular with social reformers, anticlericals, materialists, and atheists than with naturalists, and it had powerful opponents. However, it came to widespread attention through a publishing sensation of 1844, *Vestiges of the Natural History of Creation*. This anonymous work of popular science, penned by the Edinburgh publisher Robert Chambers, brought together observations from several disciplines, including geology, zoology, and linguistics, to frame a scheme of planetary and biological development, a natural rather than theological history of creation.[66] The popularization of species transformism in the 1840s fed into an esoteric perspective on "monad-to-man" in the writings of the spiritualist, medium, occultist, sex magician, and antislavery campaigner Paschal Beverly Randolph (1825–1875).[67] Here species evolution is combined with transmigration and a metaphysical rather than biological concept of the monad in a story of aeonian progress up nature's escalator (see Box, "I was one of these monads").

Randolph embeds his discussion of monads in a highly digressive account of an extraordinary experience that befell him shortly after he had been contemplating a cosmogonic diagram sketched by his host Andrew Jackson Davis (1826–1910), "the Poughkeepsie Seer," spiritualist philosopher, and putative channeler of Swedenborg. Wandering off into the countryside, Randolph lay under trees and pondered the big questions, only to find his body succumbing to a "death-like state of insensibility." His soul thus freed, he became "all sight," including penetrative vision. His desire to see a soul resulted in a flight to a distant location, where his wish was granted.[68]

Randolph maintained that transmigration through the ascending kingdoms of nature comes to an end once human embodiment has been achieved. Thus, there is a great deal of transmigration but generally no reincarnation, if the latter is understood narrowly to mean a series of *human* embodiments, as it sometimes has been. Whereas French spiritualist thinkers such as Allen Kardec (1804–1869), founder of the "spiritism" movement, wholeheartedly embraced reincarnation in this sense, as a succession of human embodiments, the American and British spiritualists of the period followed Swedenborg's influential account of postmortem happenings by situating the afterlife progress of humans exclusively in the spirit world (or the "soul world" in Randolph's terminology), thereby ruling out repeated human embodiments.[69]

Randolph did envisage further human incarnation if embryological development is interrupted before human cerebral characteristics appear, arrested at a prehuman stage by either biological defect or abortion.[70] Thus Randolph would have agreed with van Helmont that "Monsters" and "Abortives" incarnate again as humans, but unlike van Helmont he was of the opinion that "Idiots" do not, for according to Randolph they have achieved a sufficient degree of cerebral development for progress to commence in the soul world. Similarly, gross deformity of body is no reason for further human incarnation, as long as some human cerebral functioning has been established, transforming the monad into a soul.

☙ I was one of these monads ❧

In *Dealings with the Dead* (1862), Paschal Beverly Randolph chronicles the evolutionary trek of his "deceased friend" and nom de plume "Cynthia," one of a sea of monads to have issued from God.[71] The monads, sparks of divine thought endowed with "capacities infinite in number and power," became enfolded in matter—not the Helmontian or Leibnizian matter that is composed of monads themselves but a condensation of light rays. Randolph tells of three light-emanations from the divine source: the rays that condense to form matter, the waves of an etherial, mesmeric fluid that bathes the worlds, and the monadic scintillae themselves.[72]

The journey home of the spiritual center latterly known as Cynthia to its lofty source was to be "circuitous and spiral,"[73] as it is for all monads, pursued through countless transmigrations in the evolving realm of nature. Ages were spent embedded in a molecule in the heart of a fiery comet that cooled to become the Earth.[74] Heaved to the surface by an earthquake, this monad passed through numerous embodiments, time and time again casting off its impermanent coverings to better express its hidden capacities, first shells of granite, then moss, plant, fish, bird, reptile, beast, and mammal bodies, at last approaching human incarnation through a string of primate embodiments, including the aye-aye, loris, mandrill, orang, chimpanzee, and gorilla. Finally the monad became a human soul, endowed with self-consciousness, intelligence, and a degree of intuition. "Thus it is seen how and why man is the culmination of nature, and is brother to the flower and the worm."[75]

Having become an individuated soul, the monad is no longer subject to transmigration unless its human embodiment has fallen short in some way, as a result of incomplete embryological development or, rarely, grave sin. But if all has gone well, the postmortem journey to God will continue in the soul world, that commodious realm within the soul that is a "fiery globe."[76] The soul is a spiritual universe, containing a hierarchy of angelic levels through which God can be approached. But the end result is not the annihilation that Randolph believes "the Brahmins and other orientalists" and Plato had envisaged: "Plato maintained that the soul was *Divinæ particulum auræ*, an emanation from God Himself, a portion of His immaculate Being, detached for a time only, and that after innumerable transmigrations it is re-absorbed into Himself again, and loses its own distinctiveness."[77] Rather, the monad that has become a soul will remain individual, godlike but not swallowed up in God, and so truly immortal.

Randolph's biographer John Patrick Deveney has observed that a similar constellation of ideas appears in *Isis Unveiled* (1877), authored by Helena Petrovna Blavatsky (1831–1891), cofounder of the Theosophical Society.[78] Although there are certainly differences, the similarities are so pronounced that it is difficult to resist the suspicion that Madame Blavatsky drew directly on Randolph's ideas, altering and embroidering them to some extent and linking them to Kabbalah and other sources, without properly acknowledging the debt to her fellow occultist—she merely refers to an unnamed "authority."[79] Like Randolph, Blavatsky raises embryological recapitulation theory when she supposes that transmigration generally comes to an end with human embodiment.[80] The exceptions include again "teratological" phenomena (congenital defects), "cases of abortion," and, on rare occasions, criminal acts.[81] But unlike Randolph, Blavatsky also makes exceptions of "congenital idiocy" and infant death, for she believes that the rational capacity has not developed sufficiently in these cases for the monads to become human souls.

By the time of her next major publication, *The Secret Doctrine* (1888), Blavatsky had turned to Eastern "masters" and had come to accept further human embodiment as the general rule, but with no possibility of backsliding into animal rebirths, contrary to Hindu, Jaina, and Buddhist teachings. Now the theory of monadic evolution is elaborated into a system of Rounds, Cycles, Chains, Globes, and Root-Races that defies concise review. These ideas continued to have a presence in Theosophy, as evidenced by the writings of Annie Besant, Charles Leadbeater, and Alice Bailey, and found their way into later occult and New Age literature.[82] Through Theosophy, they also featured in Rudolf Steiner's Anthroposophy, although significantly modified there.[83] Randolph's monadological ideas were also taken up by the Hermetic Brotherhood of Luxor (founded in 1884), which censured Blavatsky's turn to the East and consequent embrace of further human embodiments on earth, rather than postmortem life in the spirit world.[84]

In these various employments of monads, little use is made of the metaphysical details of Leibniz's monadology, such as the explanation of material constitution in terms of perception. Nor are the biological details of evolution of any great concern. What attracted these evolutionary occultists is, naturally enough, the lofty status of the monad as a divine spark, its aspiration toward its divine source, and the indestructibility that allows it to take part in a long process of development, including transmigrations through nature.[85] While not fully utilizing the resources of Leibniz's metaphysics, the early contributors did at least acknowledge the philosopher as a worthy forerunner, although one who had not quite possessed the truth. In *Dealings with the Dead*, Randolph refers to "the famous 'Monad Theory' of Leibnitz," in which the philosopher "came very near the truth, as has been seen,"[86] and in *The Secret Doctrine* Blavatsky echoes Randolph's words very closely:

> It is well known that Leibnitz came very near the truth several times, but he defined Monadic Evolution incorrectly, a thing not to be wondered at, since he was not an Initiate, nor even a Mystic, but only a very intuitional Philosopher. Yet no Psycho-physicist ever came nearer than has he to the Esoteric general outline of evolution.[87]

Randolph was clearly a pivotal figure among the occultists who came to espouse evolutionary monadologies, but it is not clear to me how he himself latched onto "monads." Was it simply through a creative misreading of biological "monad-to-man" evolutionism, or from contacts with fellow occultists and exposure to the ideas of earlier thinkers in which evolution and transmigration or related ideas had come together? Randolph had many contacts in the American spiritualist scene and beyond, including the British and French occultists he met during his travels in the 1850s, and he also visited the Middle East, apparently encountering the local traditions there that maintain a belief in transmigration.[88]

For the historian of science, the appropriation of monadology, albeit in very truncated form, by nineteenth-century and early twentieth-century occultists and Theosophists will be a fascinating chapter in the science-religion interactions provoked by the rise of biological evolutionism, illustrating again that, contrary to popular misconceptions, religious thinkers were not inevitably hostile to species evolution in some form or other, and indeed could incorporate it enthusiastically into their religious worldviews and even construct spiritualities in which evolution is central. Cultural historian Theodore Roszak referred to these evolutionary spiritualities as "metaphysical evolutionism":

> The metaphysical evolutionists do not simply accept the idea of evolution as received from the biologists; rather, they insist upon extending the idea to include the mind, the soul, and the entire universe. Rather than taking its place as a scientific discovery outside the perimeter of religion, evolution becomes the essential content of religion within a universe that is seen as a drama of progressively unfolding consciousness.[89]

While alert to the serious shortcomings and eccentricities of the "occult evolutionists" of the late nineteenth and early twentieth centuries (and their countercultural descendants in the 1960s and 1970s), Roszak was sympathetic toward the general thrust of their visions, seeing in them a resurgence of much earlier human aspirations toward transformation and transcendence, and an attempt to engage with the evolution of consciousness in a way that could do justice to it, unlike the biological evolutionism that had left meaning and purpose out of the account.[90] Similarly, Jeffrey Kripal, as a historian of religions, regrets the general lack of awareness of the "evolutionary esotericisms," as he calls them, alternatives to the simplistic opposition of science and religion promulgated by the now discredited "conflict thesis" of the late nineteenth century, or their strategic segregation as "nonoverlapping magisteria," or their unhappy union in literalist creation science. Kripal emphasizes the richness and variety of these neglected evolutionary esotericisms, the debts they can owe to unusual experiences and encounters, and the premodern traditions of spiritual progressivism they echo.[91]

However, the philosopher or scientist may not be so fascinated, dismayed perhaps at the speculative excesses of occultists and Theosophists, and unimpressed by "secret masters" as reliable sources of information. It would certainly be hasty to contrive a *detailed* evolutionary monadology before the facts of cosmology, particle physics, and biology have been established with any certainty, and care would have to be taken to avoid the sexism, racism, and speciesism into which evolutionary spiritualities can slip if they absorb the prejudices of their times.[92] Perhaps worthwhile exploration of possibilities can be had by attempting to update Randolph's fable of monadic evolution, drawing on present-day science and spirituality, but the project could easily end in foolishness. So too the annexation, fanciful elaboration, and monetization of these kinds of ideas by new religious movements.

Needless to say, Randolph's science is dated, commencing with a monad stuck in a fiery comet that later became the Earth.[93] Nowadays the monad's temporal journey will be given a much broader sweep, commencing at the Big Bang billions of years ago and proceeding through subsequent cosmic and geological eras. More speculatively still, the journey could be traced to prior universes from which the present one arose, if cyclic and multiverse models are adopted. Modern cosmology has yet to provide a definitive account of the origin and very early moments of the universe, and the same is true of the ultimate fate of the universe—Big Crunch, Big Bounce, Big Chill, Big Rip? It follows that the details of monadic evolution will be highly speculative at the moment, even more so since the relation between monads and the fundamental particles of modern physics has yet to be worked out.

However, some observations on the *impetus* behind monadic evolution can be made, taking up ideas raised in chapter 9. There I drew upon

Plotinian metaphysics to explore the dynamics behind the emergence of the Many from the One. According to this line of thought, multiplicity emerges through the secondary, reflexive activity of the One in primordial "moments" of procession and reversion. The assertion of the subject is accompanied by a turning-back to seek an object, for going-forth entails a loss of self-sufficiency and an erosic desire for its recovery. The attempt to grasp the One intellectually begets multiplicity, establishing the knowing Intellect and its multiple intellects that have the intelligible universe as their object, each in their own particular way. I suggested that this Platonic-Plotinian dynamic might provide a way of understanding the origin of monads, a multiplicity of subjects who take representations of one another as their cosmic objects, expressed from their unique points of view.

The basic dynamic of going-forth and turning-back, of subject in want of an object, applies to the *atemporal* dependence of the Many on the One ("vertical cosmogony"), but I would suggest that it can be understood to power the *temporal* development of monads too ("horizontal cosmogony"), including their participation in an evolutionary process. Like the One itself, the primordial dynamic that sets the subject–object wheel spinning is present to all subsequent things, and so it can be supposed that the appetition of monads—their tendency to pass from perceptual state to state as they strive toward more distinct perception and knowing—*is grounded in the primordial pull toward the One*, in the "looking" that strains to become "seeing." Species evolution will serve this groping for "vision" by making available new kinds of bodies, sensory systems, mental capacities, and therefore richer, more complex streams of phenomenal experience and activity, eventually yielding creatures who have the capacity to approach the One consciously.

All created beings, then, are drawn to fulfillment by appetition, by a desire intrinsic to their natures as divinely originated and oriented beings, the "erosic pull toward unity" that reaches for many things on the way but which cannot rest for long because those things always slip away and never quite satisfy, falling short of both the ultimate source and the cosmic whole that derives from it. The "egoic pull toward separation" steers their course too, at the most basic through aversive behaviors that protect limited subjects from external threats ("self-preservation," "survival instinct"). In due course, as individuals and their social interactions become more complex, the basic pulls diversify into the full range of social emotions at play in the self–other cycle. But at an early stage of evolution, as bodies acquire a level of complexity that requires upkeep, the root desire will still be unrecognizable for what it essentially is and ultimately will be, channeled into appetites that support sustenance and reproduction, regulated by the pains and pleasures that needs and their satisfactions involve. Hence hunger, thirst, sexual libido, and the like, but spiritual in origin and goal—Rumi's hungering after God through the food chain. It will persist in these guises, supporting the bodily needs of organisms, but find more varied, complex expression too as all manner of strange, beautiful creatures and their social groups emerge, giving different prominences to the phases of the self–other cycle, but all entangled in webs of competition and dependency, conflict and cooperation.

Certainly in that confused groping toward fulfillment there will be much selfishness, greed, and violence, conflicting appetitions that pull toward mutually obstructive goals, many twists and turns along the way, unlikely leaps forward, dead ends, long fallow periods, and developments that seem wildly off course, but sometimes preparing the ground for longer-term progress. Slowly and perhaps surely, monads build and climb a tree of life that leads beyond brute biology and crude psychology to bodies, minds, and societies better able to express and satisfy the root desire. The urge to grasp transmutes into friendship and communal love, a desire for the well-being and progress of fellow travelers, and even a love that embraces all. Monadology lends itself to this "Platonic" reworking of evolutionism, for the monad is just the kind of being that could undertake the journey, being essentially immortal and driven by inbuilt appetition toward its goal (*telos*), a striving that in its evolutionary maturation moves from "self-centeredness" to "Reality-centeredness" as its divine promise comes to be realized.[94] The full working-out of a monad's striving is made possible if we depart from classical monadology and introduce transmigration and species evolution, liberating it from its fixed station in a Chain of Being.

In the earlier stages of evolutionary development, the *telos* of monads who build and climb the tree of life can perhaps be approached solely through the opportunities afforded by natural selection operating on recognized sources of variation, including mutation and procreative sex (genetic shuffling). While mutations are random and directionless in themselves, natural selection is not, for it encourages the development of organisms with well-organized bodies, capable minds, and effective behaviors that promote survival and reproduction, although the persistence of defects is not ruled out as long as they are not so severe that the organism is entirely compromised. While natural selection may work to advance brute abilities to survive and reproduce in given environments, the evolutionary "arms race" has wider consequences, encouraging, it would seem, the development of bodies and minds through which monads can work toward their long-term ends. Perceptual and cognitive abilities, protective and nurturing feelings, cooperative and altruistic behaviors, and even sensitivity to beauty, may be furthered by natural and sexual selection, and so the intrinsic potentials of monads can be actualized in the long term.

The evolutionary *telos* of monads would be approached more directly by transgenerational epigenetics and transmigration, which in their own ways carry over the consequences of life experience to new generations. In a monadological world, there could be other factors at work too, although these, like transmigration, will be unpalatable to mainstream evolutionary biologists. Nevertheless, they are possible within a monadological framework and so should be noted, however improbable they may sound. One such factor is psi, including telepathy, clairvoyance, and precognition. There is significant but disputed evidence, anecdotal and experimental, that humans and some nonhuman animals (such as dogs and cats) have psi abilities, which in a monadological framework would be traced to the all-inclusive perceptions that are inherent to monads.[95] Evolutionary processes may have exploited this intrinsic, monadic omnipercipience, drawing upon it in psi abilities, if only to the extent that they can provide competitive advantages without compromising survival through information overload and distraction.[96] For everyday functioning, it is beneficial not to perceive and know too much (as Leibniz himself pointed out).[97] To be effective, psi may have to be limited and operate in a largely unconscious fashion most of the time.

If organisms do evolve psi abilities, these in turn could influence evolution through the special kinds of knowledge, communication, and action they confer. For example, apparently chance matings and predator–prey interactions that play a role in evolution could sometimes involve telepathy, clairvoyance, and precognition. Moreover, in a monadological world, material nature is responsive to mind, for matter is constituted of monads and therefore has mindlike qualities. It is not entirely passive and mechanical in behavior, and conforms to the mental states of higher-grade monads, thereby making psychokinetic "mind-over-matter" influence a possibility.[98] The upshot for evolution is that apparently random events, such as biological mutations and seemingly chance encounters, may sometimes originate in the conformance of material processes to the desires and volitions of monads and therefore would not be random at all. Nature, being monadic itself, can bend to and provide for the strivings of monads. But this, of course, is all very speculative and underdeveloped, and needs further consideration—and psi requires more resources for its investigation.

Equally controversial will be the idea of "higher interventions" in the evolution of species. In response to the apparent inability of natural selection to account for advanced mental life, Alfred Russel Wallace proposed a purposive evolutionism in which natural selection is complemented by

"Higher" or "Overruling" intelligence.[99] Natural selection is utility-oriented, geared toward the practicalities of survival, so Wallace pondered how it could yield the advanced capacities so evident in modern humans yet surplus to requirement when they first appeared in early humans. He concluded that the capacities were established in advance by guiding powers, in preparation for a time when they could be used. By "Overruling Intelligence," Wallace was not suggesting that a Supreme Being intervenes supernaturally. Rather, there are many "higher intelligent beings, acting through natural and universal laws."[100] The law of continuity suggests that there are such beings between the human and divine. Wallace put it thus in *The World of Life* (1910):

> But to claim the Infinite and Eternal Being as the one and only direct agent in every detail of the universe seems, to me, absurd. If there is such an Infinite Being, and if (as our own existence should teach us) His will and purpose is the increase of conscious beings, then *we* can hardly be the first result of this purpose. We conclude, therefore, that there are now in the universe infinite grades of power, infinite grades of knowledge and wisdom, infinite grades of influence of higher being upon lower. Holding this opinion, I have suggested that this vast and wonderful universe, with its almost infinite variety of forms, motions, and reactions of part upon part, from suns and systems up to plant life, animal life, and the human living soul, has ever required and still requires the continuous co-ordinated agency of myriads of such intelligences.[101]

While offensive to the scientific naturalism of his colleagues, Wallace's speculations are consistent with the qualified naturalism of classical monadology. The latter, we have seen, has a noninterventionist God who sets up the monads with the resources they need to develop on their own. It also has numerous grades of beings between humans and God, as required by the Principle of Continuity applied to the Chain of Being. These agencies exist and operate *within* the system of nature and are therefore "natural," not "supernatural." Like Wallace's "higher intelligences," Leibniz's advanced beings—the subtle spirits and superior extraterrestrials—could conceivably influence evolution on Earth, and personal, cultural, and spiritual development too.[102] Wallace's inclusion of guiding intelligences in his theorizing, and his suggestion that they act by the power of "mental impression,"[103] was no doubt encouraged by the spiritualist ideas and phenomena he had begun to study in the 1860s, and by his earlier involvement with mesmerism, but it was made possible by his perception of the inadequacies of natural selection as a mechanism for the emergence of higher mental capacities in humans.

In *The World of Life*, Wallace has a chapter entitled "Is Nature Cruel? The Purpose and Limitations of Pain." Here he discusses the utility of pain and evaluates animal suffering, concluding that it is not as deep as might be thought, and that it does not compromise a purposive evolutionary process. Natural selection had turned the spotlight on nature's dark side, about which religious skeptics were only too happy to wax lyrical, since it calls into question the character and even the existence of a creator God. It is to the problem of suffering and its implications for evolutionary spirituality and the nature of God that I now turn.

11

The Making of God

Do you not see how necessary a World of Pains and
troubles is to school an Intelligence and make it a soul?

—John Keats

EVOLUTIONARY MONADOLOGY paints a grand picture of beings headed individually and collectively toward some valued end. Yet this bright vision is blotted by a terrible darkness that threatens to undermine the integrity of the scheme. Evolution and life in general involve much pain and suffering, at least for those sufficiently advanced in sensation and mentality to be susceptible to them. Nature can be astonishingly beautiful, joyous, and nurturing, but it is also the scene of endless predation, violence, fear, sickness, loss, and death. The food chain, even if it does lead to God, is very grim indeed, as natural history documentaries never tire of showing. Human civilization, while promising a degree of insulation from basic hardship, introduces new levels of ingenuity and cruelty to the sufferings on offer. What are we to make of this sorry state of affairs? Does it take away from, even morally invalidate, the evolutionary enterprise? Can the suffering endured in the course of evolutionary development be justified, even if the outcome is truly wonderful? The journey may bring many joys and have a sublime end, but is it worthwhile, given all the suffering involved?

Questions such as these are even more pressing for theistic religions with a God who is deemed all-powerful, all-knowing, and all-good. Surely the existence of such a creator is logically inconsistent with a world so full of misery as our own? This, simply put, is the "theoretical" problem of evil, in which "evil" is understood broadly to cover the full range of ills, including bodily pain and mental suffering, and commonly divided into "moral" evils stemming from choices of free agents (such as slavery, racism, animal cruelty), and "natural" evils independent of such choices (including diseases and natural disasters).[1] The classic response is to argue that God as an all-good creator detests evils but permits them for *greater goods* in the present world and in the life to come. One greater good frequently raised is freewill: while it is true that freewill opens the door to moral evils, it makes the creation immeasurably superior to how it would otherwise be, a world of real persons, not of automata. Similarly, natural evils may be unavoidable if the world is to support persons, bodies, and the processes on which they depend, a world of complexity and change, of growth and decay, of birth and death—and therefore of pain and suffering.

Arguments such as these, here very briefly indicated, are open to refinement but also criticism, and a great deal has been written on the problem of evil. I shall not attempt to give this vitally important topic the detailed consideration it deserves, partly because I have not reached a settled position on the question myself, but it would be remiss of me not to highlight some ideas of special relevance to evolutionary monadology, since evils do present a challenge. As set out here, these ideas are not intended to constitute a vindication of the system, but they may provide some grist for the mill. The nature of God also receives attention, since the problem of evil raises significant difficulties for theistic religion, and classical monadology has a creator God at its center.

The Shaping of the Soul

One approach to the problem of evil is to argue that evils, moral and natural, are not regrettable, permitted accompaniments of a good creation but have a positive, even essential place there. Evils not only make greater goods possible, they can actively encourage them. If we were to look on the world from a higher vantage point, we would see that evils have a role in the great economy of things. Lady Conway, it has been noted, was able to find meaning in her own very considerable suffering by taking the view, shared with van Helmont, that suffering raises spirits out of their material stupor through ascending degrees of knowledge to God. Leibniz, in his *Theodicy*, or vindication of the justice and goodness of God, had a place for evils too. Setbacks do not detract from and indeed may contribute to the overall development of the world. Sometimes it is necessary to take a step backward to leap two steps forward. If current knowledge of prehistory had been available in

Leibniz's day, he might have cited the extinction of the dinosaurs as a case in point, a global catastrophe with long-term benefits—or so we mammals like to think. In Leibniz's opinion, the world appears ugly and dark only if we focus on small, unrepresentative parts of it and fail to look at the complete picture. Furthermore, in the best of all possible monadic worlds, which a supremely good God would surely create, all things are interconnected and work together, even the most trivial details, to make it the best world. Remove any detail, even a very great evil, and it will no longer be the best world. Leibniz's optimism—that of a mathematician whose moral calculus maximizes the good—made him an easy target, for it is simple enough to point to appalling natural and moral evils that make "best world" talk sound ridiculous, even if it is not (Voltaire, in *Candide*, invoked the Lisbon earthquake of 1755 and the Seven Years' War).

Evils can encourage goods, including fortitude, patience, moderation, generosity, compassion, indeed character-building in general—the *shaping* of the soul. The evils that attend evolution are no exception. Writing on the compatibility of science and spiritualism, Alfred Russel Wallace gave suffering a prominent role in the evolutionary worldview he had helped to develop. Evolution gives us our bodies, and the necessarily imperfect world in which evolution has operated then develops our souls:

> This world-life not only lends itself to the production, by gradual evolution, of the physical body needed for the growth and nourishment of the human soul, but by its very imperfections tends to the continuous development of the higher spiritual nature of man.[2]

The challenges presented by the natural world strengthen "man's intellectual nature," while moral evils strengthen "the higher sentiments of justice, mercy, charity, and love." For Wallace, this is the "best attainable solution of the great world-old problem of the origin of evil."[3]

Philosopher of religion John Hick (1922–2012) was to express similar ideas, setting out two stages of development in our challenging world: evolution yields the species *Homo sapiens*, and humans, now established, can then grow intellectually, morally, spiritually.[4] Hick attempted to construct a Christian theodicy consistent with modern cosmology and evolutionism, unlike the old Augustinian theodicy in which God creates paradise just a few thousand years ago, with perfect human beings in place at the outset, followed by a fall into sin and imperfection through misuse of freewill (and eventual admission to heaven for the saved). Instead, Hick has God create the world billions of years ago, not as a fully formed paradise but a challenging environment in which evolution yields early *Homo sapiens*—intelligent, social, religious, but still self-centered animals. In the next phase, which is our current stage, these imperfect, half-formed creatures have the opportunity to grow morally and spiritually toward divine "likeness" by meeting the challenges of life, without which there would be no impetus to grow. The world, then, is in the business of person-making. Hick describes the world as a place of "soul-making," drawing on poet John Keats (see Box, "The vale of Soul-making").[5]

Clearly one human life is too brief for much progress to be made, and evils are often so great that they act destructively, leading at least in the short term not to progress but the very reverse. Hick therefore supposes that opportunities for growth continue in the afterlife, "in another sphere of existence," through "many lives in many worlds,"[6] leading to the salvation of all—again a departure from the Augustinian account. While Hick acknowledges the possibility of reincarnation in our present world and puts reported cases of past-life memories in the "fifty-fifty probability category,"[7] his preference is for a series of future lives in *other-worldly* realms. He recognizes that the idea of further development in the afterlife, while not Christian orthodoxy, does resonate with spiritualist teachings.[8] Indeed, Hick's preferred concept of postmortem life is comparable to the spiritualist ideas of Randolph and Wallace—continued development not on earth but in the soul or spirit worlds. It follows that Hick too thinks there is just the one human life spent on earth, but unlike Randolph he admits no prior transmigrations through inorganic, plant, and animal realms leading up to the human birth. For Hick and Wallace, the human life on earth is the very first life, with no previous lives of any kind.

Hick's approach to the problem of evil meshes well with evolutionary monadology. Both are set within the modern scientific context of biological evolutionism and both recognize a challenging process of "soul-making" that leads to fulfillment. However, evolutionary monadology avoids at least some of the criticisms that can be leveled at Hick's scheme. The latter, like many traditional theodicies, suffers from anthropocentrism, envisaging only human salvation. Accordingly, Hick treats animal suffering in a less than satisfactory way, downplaying suffering in nonhuman animal life, as Wallace had in "Is Nature Cruel?" Moreover, it seems that only the human animal can progress toward spiritual maturity, and so the "universal salvation" is highly qualified, being universal only to humans. While this is an advance on many earlier views, it leaves the suffering of most creatures unredeemed. There is no chance of fulfillment for any of the innumerable nonhuman animals that have populated the world, including those from which *Homo*

❧ The vale of Soul-making ❧

All too familiar with tragedy in his short life, Keats was drawn to find meaning in suffering. Writing to his brother George and sister-in-law Georgiana in April 1819, he described an alternative to the common opinion that the world is a "vale of tears" from which we are to be saved. Rather it is a "vale of Soul-making," a "system of Spirit-creation," in which sparks of divine intellect are turned into individuated souls, into personalities:

> There may be intelligences or sparks of the divinity in millions—but they are not Souls till they acquire identities, till each one is personally itself. Intelligences are atoms of perception—they know and they see and they are pure, in short they are God—how then are Souls to be made? How then are these sparks which are God to have identity given them—so as ever to possess a bliss peculiar to each one's individual existence? How, but by the medium of a world like this? . . . Do you not see how necessary a World of Pains and troubles is to school an Intelligence and make it a soul? A Place where the heart must feel and suffer in a thousand diverse ways.[9]

The world is a "School" in which sparks of divinity are tutored to become souls "through the medium of the Heart."[10]

Hick too employs pedagogical analogies,[11] one of several features of his theodicy that has led to the suggestion that Hick's "patron saint" is *not* Irenaeus, the Church Father whom Hick adopted in preference to Augustine.[12] Hick's theodicy seems closer to Origen's, who looked on the world as "a school for souls" in which suffering is educative and therapeutic. Origen speculated that rational beings (*logikoi*) had turned away from contemplation of their Creator through "boredom" or a "cooling" of ardor, and so became souls (*psychai*). Their journey home through material embodiment will continue for many world ages, since one age is insufficient for the work of restoration. Origen hoped for a universal salvation, when God shall be "all in all."

Origen's thoughts on preexistence of souls, world cycles, remedial justice, and salvation contributed to seventeenth-century reappraisals of the afterlife and an interest in metempsychosis.[13] It is likely that the speculations of van Helmont and Conway owe a debt to Origen, with their spiritual monads who fall away from God to varying degrees but reascend through suffering, and who are guaranteed salvation because God is love.

sapiens evolved, and those very many exploited in cruel ways by humans on their paths to fulfillment. It seems that, in the great scheme of things, plants and animals are just fodder for the human project. To quote Wallace again, who anticipates Hick's anthropocentrism:

> Thus the whole *raison d'être* of the material universe—with all its marvellous changes and adaptations, the infinite complexity of matter and of the ethereal forces which pervade and vivify it, the vast wealth of nature in the vegetable and animal kingdoms—is to serve the grand purpose of developing human spirits in human bodies.[14]

And like Hick, Wallace articulates the intuition that human life is "preparation for a higher state of progressive spiritual existence,"[15] reflecting the spiritualist belief in *postmortem* development.

Evolutionary monadology avoids anthropocentrism because it accepts transmigration and therefore can understand *all* creatures to be on paths to fulfillment, building and climbing the tree of life together. Moreover, in a deeply integrated universe, where each partakes of all the others in a multiplicity-in-unity, fulfillment *must* be universal if any single creature is to be truly fulfilled (chapter 5). One man put it well, recalling a mystical experience in nature that left him with universalist convictions:

> Because of the experience I know that *everything* involved in this process is God, is Love, Light, Bliss . . . that everything is in migration, movement, towards the Great Awakening to That which, in essence, everything is. Nothing, nothing is excluded from the 'redemptive' process. Not only all men, but men and rocks and stars and trees are brothers, are divine, and carry within them the splendour awakening to Itself. After this event I somehow knew that this was the last time [of incarnate existence], that there would be no more Is for this soul's development . . . that it 'had crossed the line into the land of no to-morrows'. Yet I also realised that we cannot really go Home until everything goes Home again.[16]

Evolutionary monadology is advantageous in another respect. As we have seen, Hick takes the human life on earth to be the very first life, with no preceding lives at all, human, animal, or otherwise. This is problematic because it furnishes no explanation of the very different familial, economic, educational, and cultural conditions into which humans are born, and the different degrees of suffering to which they are thereby exposed. There is a very unequal, seemingly random distribution of evils and goods in the world. While the inequality does not, in Hick's scheme, deny any human being eventual fulfillment, it does call into question the justice of the system. Evolutionary monadology, by contrast, gives a human life a very long prehistory, in numerous previous lives, human, animal, and otherwise. The context, quality, and challenges of the current life are not then arbitrary, for they are conditioned by previous lives. This is not to assert a rigid law of moral cause and effect or an external arbiter who rewards and punishes; it may just mean that past lives condition the present one in some respects, through habits, desires, regrets, loves, animosities, conscience in the face of postmortem revelations, and perhaps even choices made prior to rebirth.

Evolutionary monadology may suggest some improvements to Hick's account of soul-making, being more able to address nonhuman suffering and the unequal distribution of goods and evils, but it too is confronted by a difficulty that Hick recognized as the greatest challenge to his own "teleological" theodicy, which gives so much weight to the achievement of a valued end. Do the ends really justify the means? Hick asks "whether all the pain and suffering, cruelty and wickedness of human life can be rendered acceptable by an end-state, however good?"[17] In the throes of suffering, the answer is likely to be an emphatic "no," and attempts at justification will sound hollow, platitudinous, even callous. Affirmation of meaning in suffering needs to be approached sensitively and cautiously, for it is very often impossible to see any meaning in specific instances, and while the overall thrust of suffering may be to advance creatures along their paths there may be very many instances in which sufferings are gratuitous, lacking any specific outweighing benefit. Furthermore, the idea that intense, prolonged suffering is *purposely* built into the world can give the creator the appearance of a cruel instructor who puts together an excessively harsh educational program for the "improvement" of the unfortunate students.

Yet in different moods, life can seem worth the pain and suffering it brings, even more so if it is understood to lead to a very great good. For instance, the beauty and wonder of nature, the joys of relationships, the satisfactions of creativity, exploration, and learning may in their various ways lead one to think that life, even with its worries, hardships, and many stupidities, is indeed worthwhile. The locus *par excellence* for optimism is mystical experience, which sometimes appears to reveal that all things do work together for the good:

> I was standing alone on the edge of a low cliff overlooking a small valley leading to the sea. It was late afternoon or early evening and there were birds swooping in the sky – possibly swallows. Suddenly my mind 'felt'

as though it had changed gear or twitched into another view of things. I still saw the birds and everything around me but instead of standing looking at them, I *was* them and they were me. I was also the sea and the sound of the sea and the grass and sky. Everything and I were the same, all one. It was the most peaceful and 'right' feeling imaginable and I knew without any smallest doubt that everything happened for a reason, a good reason, and fitted into everything else, like an arch with all the bricks supporting each other and their cornerstone without cement, just by their being there. I was filled, swamped, with happiness and peace. Everything was RIGHT.[18]

The passage reads like a mystical companion piece to Leibnizian optimism over the "best of all possible worlds" in which all the parts work together for the good. Suffering is not explicitly mentioned here but may be implied by the statement that "everything" happens for a good reason.

Some mystical experiences are more explicit about suffering, especially those that take place at challenging times, as if to bring some relief by showing how things look from a higher perspective. From there, suffering may be understood to play an indispensable role in spiritual evolution and lead to a great end, as one woman discovered when a long period of illness and unrest led to a mystical opening:

> The great truth that life is a spiritual evolution, that this life is but a passing phase in the soul's progression, burst upon my astonished vision with overwhelming grandeur. Oh, I thought, if this is what it means, if this is the outcome, then pain is sublime! Welcome centuries, eons, of suffering if it brings us to this![19]

The sense that everything fits together then arose: "What joy when I saw there was no break in the chain—not a link left out—everything in its place and time. Worlds, systems, all blended in one harmonious whole."[20]

In the next example, there is a clearer indication of the end to which spiritual evolution leads, and from the elevated vantage point suffering and death look quite insignificant in light of that great end:

> In my situation beyond creation I could divine the onward flow of life in the cosmos. I was aware of the perpetual cycle of life: countless generations of creatures lived, suffered, died, and were reborn. This cycle continued until the creature attained fullness of being. It was not simply an unending round of life, death, and rebirth, but rather one that had, as its end,

the perfect union of creature with Creator. This ascending spiral of life, death, and rebirth was seen to be the destiny of all living things in their progress towards completion. The struggle and termination of each life were comparable, in relation to divine reality, to the tearful resistance of little children who are put to bed by their parents, and who awake fresh the next day to advance on new adventures. I was filled with an irresistible sense of humour and delight when I realised that the pain borne by the creature was trivial in comparison with the glory that was to be revealed in him and in the whole world at the end of the human struggle. The entire created universe was shown to me symbolically as a gigantic sphere whose movement was discernible as a minute turn of a wheel, but this movement encompassed countless generations of human beings over a vast time-scale.[21]

This is Martin Israel's symbolic vision of the spherical universe, noted in chapter 7. The vision was followed by a transformation of personality: for the first time, Israel felt truly whole, in union with the entire creation and his "identity added to it."[22]

I cannot recall any comparable insights from my own mystical experience. While I may have been aware of future lives (and perhaps past ones too), I was unable to grasp the conclusion to which they led, and there were no insights I can remember into the role of suffering in my life or in the world at large. There may have been hints in the lucid-dream posters described in chapter 9, notably in the picture of the bubble faces rising through the purificatory blast furnace. However, a later dream did bring a powerful intuition of meaning in suffering. This again was a lucid dream, one that occurred at a time when I had become immersed in the seemingly intractable suffering of another. In the dream, which had the form of an out-of-body experience, I wandered out of the house and down the road toward the pub, and was having a conversation with an unseen person about suffering and its role in growth. As if to provide firsthand understanding of the matter, I found myself crushed under what I imagined to be a *wheel*, enduring utter destruction, total defeat, but the dreadful sensation was infused with meaning and could perhaps be called a rapture. It was very far from a rational understanding expressible in words, the meaning inseparable from the agony.[23]

Examples could be multiplied, but an important point at issue is whether extraordinary intuitions can be taken at face value as evidence that suffering is deeply meaningful, that all things really do work together for the good, and that the ends justify the means. For those who have had them, the experiences are likely to be "authoritative," as William James put it, and bring some assurance and consolation.[24] For those who have not, the descriptions may be interesting and suggestive but hardly decisive, and the usual doubts arise. Do mystical experiences provide genuine insights into reality? Assuming that they do, are mystics able to remember, understand, and convey those insights in a satisfactory manner? The belief systems of mystics may help them understand and express their experiences, at least up to a point, but they may also serve to distort, through omissions, additions, and unwarranted interpretations. More seriously still, it has been claimed that mystical experiences themselves, not just the descriptions of them, may be constituted of the background beliefs of mystics, reflecting back to them their own religious and cultural assumptions, as the "contextualist" or "constructivist" school of thought maintains. Then there are the claims that mystical experiences are just neurological or neuropsychological anomalies and therefore of little significance. Attempts to reduce mystical experiences entirely to religious conditioning and/or neurobiology have been unconvincing, and the possibility remains that mystical experiences do what mystics strongly feel they do, which is to reveal deeper aspects of reality.[25]

One final point about mystical experiences and suffering: with all their clarity, transcendence, light, and beauty, the experiences can give the impression that evils have no substantive reality—indeed, not only evils, but our everyday selves and the world in general. On return to ordinary consciousness, the mystic may feel that the world is inferior, unreal, illusory, dreamlike, an impression that can find its way into metaphysics, theodicies, and schemes of salvation. The idea of "world as dream" has had some currency in Asian thought, the previously noted *Yogavāsiṣṭha* being an outstanding example.[26] There are instances too in the West. A particularly beautiful one is due to the Christian Platonist and mystic Peter Sterry, who lived through the tumult of the English Civil War and its aftermath.[27] In a theodical story, Sterry portrays life in our world of suffering as the troubled dreams of souls who have fallen into a profound sleep, and God may be dreaming too. But the dreaming is no sad accident: souls voluntarily undergo the ordeal to bring about a great end, for themselves and for God, an end that was originally disclosed to them but which they do not presently understand.[28]

There are several dream characteristics on which the analogies draw: the felt realness of dreams while they are being dreamed; their immersive quality, so much so that there is usually no recognition that a dream is in progress; their transience, the contents melting "into thin air" on waking; their status as products of mind; the diminished awareness they usually involve, including limited understanding of one's identity; their sometimes oppressive atmosphere or terrifying contents, from which it is a relief to wake up; the unimportance of dream happenings from the waking perspective. It can seem that our waking lives have such dream qualities too, when viewed from a higher vantage point. In my mystical experience, I found that the worries and hopes of my everyday life had no foundation, as they were dependent on a severely limited concept of myself. From this vantage point, there was nothing to fear. Moreover, my frantic efforts to recover the expansive state in the subsequent dream were just that, the efforts of a man in a dream, when all I needed to do was wake up.

Doubtless there are lessons to be learned here, and dream analogies do have value.[29] But they can be misleading because waking experiences differ from dreams in significant ways. For instance, dreams are often inconsistent within themselves, and even more so with other dreams and across dreamers, whereas waking life is consistent throughout its course and for all. If waking life is a dream, it is clearly a highly coherent, collective one, which stretches the meaning of "dream" to breaking point. Moreover, a dream comes to an end when one wakes from it, but we are told that the world of waking life persists after mystical awakening—it continues to be experienced but is now known for what it is.[30] True, for metaphysical idealists the world is a mental production, like a dream, but they do not usually conclude from this that the world lacks objective existence or is unreal. To dismiss the world as unreal just because it is mental betrays a lingering materialism that dismisses mind and its products as not fully real.

Idealism can describe a world that is just as real as the one of materialism. In monadology there are multiple subjects who express a *common* universe, and the material structure that derives from their perceptions is just as concrete and enduring as it is for materialists and physicalists, perhaps even more so, for monads are effectively indestructible. Furthermore, if my idealist adaptation of the representative theory of perception is correct (chapter 6), the sense perceptions of the waking state are generally veridical, providing access to the noumenal contents of the world at large, albeit through representations limited in scope and introducing characteristics of their own. Nor should there be any suggestion that the goods and ills of the world are unreal, although it is true that they will look rather different from an elevated perspective, viewed in the context of the whole, as the mystical passages quoted above indicate. This is not to minimize the acutely felt sufferings of beings, which must be recognized as such and addressed as best one can, but to place them in perspective. From the viewpoint of creatures immersed in the world process, life can seem extremely burdensome, and it often is. From the elevated viewpoint, the formerly time-bound creature sees the old burdens drop away, and they can seem laughable, which they sometimes are. But each view on its own can bring distortions, the former wallowing in misery, the latter liable to dismiss it. It is surely important to bring the two perspectives together, valley floor and mountain top, so that they correct the excesses of each other, attentiveness to suffering working together with knowledge of what the world really is. There is a sense of this in the Buddhist yoking of compassion and wisdom, of active intent to relieve the sufferings of sentient beings working in combination with insight into non-Self and emptiness.

God-Making

The challenge presented by evil is acute for religions with an all-powerful, all-knowing, all-good creator God, although the kinds of arguments outlined above, such as the "greater good" appeals to freewill and soul-making, aim to show that there is no *logical* contradiction in an all-great creator on the one hand and a creation beset by evils on the other. Yet the sheer depth and seeming gratuitousness of much suffering still raises doubts about traditional characterizations of divinity. At the least, proponents of *classical theism*—those philosophies and theologies that posit the all-perfect creator God—may look for a more nuanced understanding of the divine superlatives. What does is mean to be "all-powerful"? Can God do absolutely anything? It is well recognized that it is unreasonable to expect even an omnipotent God to perform the logically impossible, such as create a square circle. And it might be unreasonable to expect God to create something entirely different in nature from God. For example, if God is of the nature of mind, God will create in a way that mind creates, by thinking, imagining, dreaming, willing, and its creations will be minds or the contents of mind.

This is the line of argument Conway and van Helmont took when they criticized materialism: Spirit cannot create something so different from itself as nonspiritual matter; it can create only a world of spirits, and so matter must be composed of spirits. Leibniz believed in an all-perfect creator, but his theodicy recognized limitation: he wrote of "original imperfection," for the created cannot be as perfect as the creator and is therefore deficient, even if the world is the best of all possible worlds. God cannot create an equal to God. There is a limit to divine power in this regard, and creatures are necessarily limited and prone to evils. But for Leibniz, to recognize the imperfection of the creation is not to take away from the perfection of God.[31]

Increasingly, there have been moves to develop alternatives to classical theist concepts of God, prompted by the challenge of evil and other spurs, such as a longing for a more personal, approachable, knowable, intimate, involved kind of God than classical theism seems to present. In these attempts, some of the classical attributes of divinity may be reinterpreted or abandoned, not only perfect power, perfect knowledge, and perfect goodness, but also aseity (self-sufficiency), impassibility (not affected by externals, not suffering), simplicity (not composite), immutability (not subject to change), eternality (not temporal), incorporeality (no body), and transcendence (distinct from the creation). God reconceptualized may be less than ultimate in power, knowledge, or goodness, more like a human person, subject to change, acted upon by the creation, immersed in the world as a participant, realized through the world, suffering along with creatures, and evolving with and through them. The world, then, is in the business of God-making as well as soul-making. Indeed, soul-making contributes to God-making if the shaping of souls adds to God in some way.

Many of these themes are present in an original manner in Whitehead's process philosophy and in process theisms inspired by it. The God of Whitehead has two aspects, the *primordial* and *consequent natures*. The primordial nature involves an everlasting prehension, ordering, and offering of possibilities open to actual occasions, the fleeting units of Whitehead's system (described in chapter 8). The consequent nature is a cumulative reception and synthesis of the possibilities actualized through the arising and perishing of actual occasions. Thus, God in the consequent nature is affected and augmented by the world. It is claimed this alternative concept of God eases the problem of evil because God is no longer the all-powerful, all-knowing, impassible creator of classical theism but a cocreator and participant with the actual occasions, who are themselves empowered to a degree and can go their own ways, resisting God's persuasive but not coercive influence. There is no great end to which the process leads, just an ongoing accumulation, synthesis, and reconciliation of experiences, good and evil, in God's consequent nature. As experiencing *subjects*, actual occasions perish, but they achieve immortality as *objects* prehended in the everlasting consequent nature of God. They exist after death as objectified contents of the divine memory, drained of subjective life—perhaps not a postmortem outcome to die for? There have been searching criticisms of Whitehead's concept of God as a response to the problem of evil, but this is not to say that some version of process theism, of which there have been several, cannot be more successful.[32]

My own speculations share with Whitehead's a background in the metaphysics of Leibniz, and so there is some common ground, including units of nature conceived as experiential, striving, and holistically connected. But there are major differences too, and these include the respective concepts of God. I do not pretend to have a very firm hold on the concept of God that would best suit my monadological speculations, but it will be different from Whitehead's, which does not assign God a productive and sustaining role. Whitehead's God guides and assimilates actual occasions, but it is not a source and ground that produces and sustains them. Rather, actual occasions are self-creating entities, drawing selectively upon prior actual occasions to construct themselves. In Whitehead's naturalistic philosophy, nature is a given, with nothing behind it, and God is a part of nature, a very special, everlasting actual entity among perishing actual entities. I have stayed closer to Leibniz by positing a source that produces, sustains, and harmonizes monads, and which therefore underlies nature. In this regard, the concept of God is closer to classical theism than process theism. The monadic units of nature, understood in Leibnizian fashion as all-inclusive wholes between which there can be no transfer of contents and properties (no "transeunt" causation), require a productive, sustaining, harmonizing ground.

Does this mean, then, that monads are best placed within a Leibnizian classical theism, as creations of an all-great God possessed of perfect power, knowledge, and will? Perhaps so, but it is unclear how Leibniz's God creates monads, and so in chapter 9 I turned to another concept of a productive, sustaining ultimate reality, the One of Plotinus. Unfortunately it is not possible to pin down the One in itself: its inner life evades description, unlike the complex, determinate things that derive from it, things we are able to know, think, and talk about. Plotinus, however, says it is possible to think about *ourselves* in relation to the One: for instance, *we* are dependent on the One, and it is *our* good. With this proviso in mind, quite a lot can be said about the One, and it then seems comparable, at least superficially, to the God of classical theism, having in common such attributes as simplicity, self-sufficiency, impassibility, omnipotence, omnipresence, all-goodness, transcendence, and immanence, although omniscience properly applies to the Intellect, the One's immediate derivative.[33]

Transcendent though the One may be in its self-sufficiency, it is not at all remote, being always and everywhere present as the source of things, available to those who turn to it, and intimate too it would seem, unlike the awesome Intellect, for the One is "gentle and kindly and gracious" (*Enn.* v.5.12), a surprising statement if the One is indifferent to its products, as seems to be the case.[34] Unlike the God of classical theism, the One does not providentially guide and control, providence coming into play only at a derivative level. Nor is the productivity of the One portrayed as a free, intentional act informed by consideration of possibilities, and the One is no demiurge who fashions the world according to a plan or model—again, demiurgic activity belongs to a derivative level. Rather, the One's productivity follows necessarily from its perfection (nevertheless, it would seem that talk of will and freedom in connection with the One is not inappropriate).[35] And while Plotinian and classical monotheisms have in common one ultimate, transcendent origin of things, the former as a pagan monotheism is accommodating to the many divine powers of polytheism, but now understood as derivative from and dependent on the One.[36]

The problem of evil may not be quite so challenging for a concept of the divine that omits deliberation and design at the highest level, but it is still a concern that evil seems to derive ultimately from the One. It would be too great a digression to look in detail at Plotinus's understanding of evil, but in a nutshell evil follows indirectly from the insufficiency entailed by departure from the One's self-sufficiency. In Leibnizian terms, "original imperfection" is there at the very beginning of the Plotinian productive path and is integral to creation, driving the cosmos of beings by drawing them erosically toward fulfillment at their source. The initial departure from sufficiency and perfection does not yet constitute "evil," for good is still very prominent in the derivative hypostases of Intellect and Soul, in which form and measure prevail. But at the outermost fringe of the scheme, which is matter, there is complete *absence* of good—of sufficiency, perfection, intelligibility, form, measure. Hence matter is the very opposite of good, and Plotinus identifies it with evil and understands moral evils to follow from the lower soul's involvement with it. The identification of matter and evil will sound strange to modern ears, given the very different, scientific understanding of matter that now prevails (which utilizes number and measure to the extreme), and it was even unattractive to Plotinus's Neoplatonic successors Iamblichus and Proclus, for whom matter was imbued with number and was essentially the divine product of a divine source.[37]

In view of my debts to Leibniz and Plotinus, the concepts of God they advance are of great interest to me. But the particular form of idealism I have advocated, including its take on monads, means that I may be unable to appropriate straightforwardly either of their concepts of God. It is true that a central place will remain for a productive, sustaining source, since the monads require it, and so there is reason to keep something like the Leibnizian God or the Plotinian One at the heart of the system, but the concept of God may need enlarging in light of the changes I have made. To be more specific, I shall join Whitehead by proposing that God has two natures but understand them in a very different way. The *essential nature*, as I shall call it, is the ultimate reality, God-in-itself, like the Plotinian One in its internal activity. If this essential nature has some kind of self-consciousness, then it is appropriately regarded as a "self," an "essential," "innermost," or "highest" self, or better the highest level of self. The *derivative nature* of God is dependent on the essential nature and comprises the entire creative process, comparable to the external activity of the One plus everything that follows from it, including the entire created universe. While there is considerable room for uncertainty over the appropriateness of "self" talk for the essential nature, it is more clearly applicable to the derivative nature, a "higher self" or better a higher level of self that I earlier characterized as a social or communal self (see chapter 4). Cosmic in scope, this noumenal level of self contains the everyday level of self too, all the little, local selves supported by their phenomenal experiences and bodies (fig. 11.1).

In setting out these two natures of God, I am not proposing two distinct Gods but distinguishing two levels of one God, a twofold God. To employ an analogy, if God is the sun, then the essential nature is the hidden solar interior, the core and its environs, while the derivative nature is the visible exterior, the surface and atmosphere. God is core and corona, and everything in between. The analogy is, of course, defective in several ways. For instance, the sun is just one celestial body among many, with a solar system and universe beyond it, whereas there is nothing beyond God as understood here. The "divine sun" includes everything, the core as hidden interior and all that derives from it as manifest exterior.

This concept of the essential nature is similar to (and inspired by) other notions of hidden or unmanifest God, such as those touched upon in chapter 9: *prakāśa–vimarśa* of nondual Kashmir Shaivism, *Ein Sof* of mystical Judaism, *wuji* of Daoism and neo-Confucianism. As precursors of modern, developmental concepts of a self-actualizing God, mention should also be made of Meister Eckhart's Godhead (*Gottheit*, "Godhood") or Abyss (*Abgrund*) from which emerges *Gottes*, the creative, trinitarian nature of God, and Jacob Boehme's *Ungrund* in which the threefold spirit of God develops prior to creation proper. While the various understandings of unmanifest reality have their own very distinctive features and are poorly treated if bundled together indiscriminately, in general terms they fall within the purview of "negative theology" or "apophatism," the path of negation, of saying by unsaying, knowing by unknowing, exemplified by Plotinus's treatment of the One. Within Christianity, negative theology has had a long history, made prominent there by the influential writings of the Pseudo-Dionysius. Theological apophatism blends well with practical mysticism, for engagement with the ultimate not only comes up against the limitations of language faced by the theologian but also presents a challenge

God {	*essential nature* essential Self (?) essential Mind (?)	God-in-itself, "Godhead," perhaps the highest level of self, if its activity involves self-consciousness
	derivative nature noumenal or monadic Self; derivative, cosmic, or global Mind	higher level of self, a cosmic One-Many, individual and communal, temporal and eternal, inclusive of the entire universe and its phenomenal ("little", "local") selves and minds

Figure 11.1   The two natures of God and corresponding levels of self.

to the mystic, the "formlessness" or "nothingness" bringing disorientation and perhaps even fear of annihilation, since there is nothing determinate on which the discursive mind can fasten.

Although heedful of negative theology, I think it important to make at least one positive characterization of the essential nature, in terms of "mind" or "consciousness." For in my idealist theorizing I have taken the universe to be of the nature of mind, a system of monadic minds, and to avoid a problematic source–product discontinuity, it will be expedient to take the essential nature, the ultimate ground of the monadic minds, to be mindlike in some way—mind or consciousness that presumably involves subject–object identity, like the self-reflexive light *prakāśa–vimarśa* or the Plotinian One described in positive terms as luminous, self-conscious, and self-intellective, but in a manner different from the derivative Intellect. This step unifies the two natures in common mentality: God is mind, essentially and derivatively (fig. 11.1). It would seem that little can be said about the mentality of the essential nature, but much can be said about the derivative nature or "derivative Mind of God," which includes everything ontologically subsequent to the essential nature, namely the entire creative process from beginning to end.

This creative process can be divided into three phases, making the derivative nature "triphasic": (1) *origination*, interplay of subject and object that establishes the monads, explored in chapter 9; (2) *development*, progress of monads through self–other interactions in the evolving system of nature they comprise, explored in chapter 10; (3) *fulfillment*, completion of the monadic journey and full realization of the derivative nature, possibly involving a unitive, communal return to the essential nature. Origination is equivalent to the "vertical cosmogony" of chapter 9, the derivation of the universe from an ultimate ground, often understood as atemporal in its first "moments."

The development phase includes the "horizontal cosmogony" of cosmic evolution, biological evolution, and psychological, social, cultural, moral, and spiritual growth, that is, the adventure of soul-making. Traditionally, fulfillment has been discussed in terms of "salvation," "deliverance," "liberation," "isolation," "restoration," "enlightenment," and so on, depending on the religious tradition, but I prefer "fulfillment" because it suggests that the journey is constructive, directed toward a consummation that is more than redemption, liberation, or recovery of a former condition, although deliverance from evils and liberation from sufferings are certainly to be welcomed as aspects of fulfillment.

Fulfillment in the monadological context will have individual, communal, and cosmic aspects, since monads are individuals who, representing one another, express the universe. The fulfillment of one monad will involve the fulfillment of all monads, since they are interdependent, and this collective, universal fulfillment could be construed as a "heavenly" community of sorts, perhaps along the lines described by Plotinus, Traherne, and others. Collective fulfillment presumably makes possible the unitive approach to the essential nature of God at the climax of the mystical ascent: the Plotinian mystic, it will be remembered, comes to receive the One by means of the cosmic community that is the Intellect, which divesting itself of its self-knowledge eternally aspires to the One as loving Intellect.

Together, the three phases constitute the derivative mind of God, a created, evolving, and consummated nature that adds to God, making God more than it is in its essential nature. The one God, two natures, and three phases are summarized in figure 11.2. Here the essential nature is shaded to represent its obscurity to the discursive mind—negative theology's "dazzling darkness" that is an excess of light. The triphasic derivative nature is represented by the unshaded region around the essential nature, consisting of the origination (o) and fulfillment (f) phases above the dotted line and the development (d) phase below it. Inscribed within the development region is a symbol of the subject–object and self–other cycles (c) through which development proceeds, shown as four quadrants and five cardinal points (four directions plus center), the wheel of joy and sorrow in the service of soul-making and God-making.

This expanded, developmental concept of God shifts the theological terrain from classical theism to *panentheism*, a type of theism in which God includes the universe but exceeds it.[38] Panentheism covers a range of positions, each with its own understanding of how the universe is *in* God. Panentheisms differ from classical theisms by asserting a stronger kind of immanence: God is not just present to the creation as its creator but "con-

Figure 11.2   One God, two natures, three phases (origination, *development*, fulfill-ment), four quadrants (i.e., subject–object *c*ycle).

tains" it in some way. The creation is a part of God. But panentheisms share with classical theisms a recognition of divine transcendence, and so differ from *pantheisms*, which identify God and the universe without remainder. On the other hand, panentheisms and pantheisms can have in common a developmental understanding of God. For if God is the universe (pantheism) or includes the universe (panentheism), then God or a part of God develops through cosmic and biological evolution, and through the psychological, social, moral, and spiritual development of created beings.

How does a developmental, panentheistic concept of God link with the evolutionary monadology I have been advancing here? If a monad expresses the universe, and the universe is the derivative nature of God, then a monad expresses the derivative nature from its particular sequence of perspectives. In fact there is no derivative nature of God apart from the monads, just as there is no universe apart from them. Thus, the life trajectory of a monad is not different from the origination, development, and fulfillment of the derivative nature of God. In this particular version of panentheism, which is idealist, panpsychic, and monadological, the universe is "in" God in the sense that it exists as the contents of monadic minds, in the multiply realized derivative nature of God. Conversely, God is "in" the universe not just by virtue of the omnipresence of its essential nature as ultimate source and power, comparable to the divine immanence of classical theism, but also through the representation of monads within monads, that is, of the derivative nature throughout itself. Matter consists of representations of monads, which means that the derivative nature of God is fully represented in each basic unit of material structure. The "Spiritual Eye" sees that a clod of earth, a speck of dust, the meanest atom in the universe, embraces the divine majesty and amplitude.[39]

It may seem odd to equate monads with the derivative mind of God, and it would be so if they were old-style, Leibnizian monads, but my suggested revision has transformed monads from largely confused cosmic perceptions into minds akin to Plotinian intellects, endowed with clarity of vision, unity of knower and known, omniscience, luminosity, and eternity (but see below). To look into the depths of one's monadic nature is to find there a divine mind, a luminous "higher self," a self that is a social self, a One-Many, with mutual identities linking all, as ʿAṭṭār's portrayal of the Sīmurgh nicely conveys. When this divine Self is encountered as the numinous Other, it may be perceived as guide, companion, beloved, not indifferent but approachable and responsive, perhaps open to entreaties and even active in making contact. But in a more unitive engagement, it is recognizable as one's own deeper self-identity, encountered at the Sun Door in meditative, mystical, near-death experiences, and during the death transition itself. This divine monadic mind, whether apprehended as the Other or as one's own Self, can be construed as the personal and communal dimension of God, contrasted with the essential nature clouded in unknowing, which in its simplicity is not evidently describable as personal and communal. But God considered as a whole is so describable, for it includes the derivative nature, in which the world and souls are fashioned, personalities nurtured, love and compassion actualized, and God augmented.

According to this line of thought, the higher self—the "divine double," "divine Image," "man of light," "cosmic Christ," "cosmic Buddha," as the derivative nature of God—comes to be what it is through a very long developmental process, through the cruciform wheel of joy and sorrow, the tutoring of divine sparks in "a World of Pains and troubles" where lessons of the heart are learned. However, time is most peculiar, and the fully evolved derivative nature of God, the labor of ages, is there at the *beginning* of the developmental phase, indeed at every step of the journey, an original and ongoing endowment that embraces the entire process. This would mean that fully realized love and compassion provide a background to the entire evolutionary process—surprising though it will seem.[40] Let's see how this can be. A revised monad is eternal as well as temporal: each monadic state is a noumenal spacetime whole organized from a particular spatiotemporal vantage point, timelessly permanent yet containing within itself the entirety of temporal development and the phenomenal patches of experience that give our everyday life its transient feel. In reformulating the monads, I collapsed the Platonic two-world distinction between an eternal, intelligible realm of the truly real and a temporal, sensible realm of appearances, yielding one world in which the eternal-noumenal and the temporal-phenomenal are inseparable, the latter being special contents of the former.

This may seem very unPlotinian, and it probably is. Plotinus is usually taken to uphold a firm distinction between the intelligible cosmos in which the undescended part of the soul resides and the sensible cosmos in which the descended part is sunk. It has sometimes been suggested that the two Plotinian realms are in fact one world apprehended in two different ways, although it is probably rather optimistic to ascribe such an integrative view to Plotinus. But the universe that has emerged here, through the blending of Plotinian and Leibnizian ideas, is of this kind, one world viewed in two different ways, one way noumenal, subtly dualistic, eternal in feel, whole, independent of the senses, and the other way phenomenal, grossly dualistic, transient in feel, fragmentary, dependent on the senses. I have been encouraged to take a "one world, two views" approach because some mystical experiences suggest that in addition to the familiar "outward" way of perceiving the world through the senses there is the more fundamental "inward," trans-sensate way, as I first noted in chapter 1 and then took further in chapter 6.

It is possible that at a certain stage of development the two views come together in *conscious* union, as Carpenter speculated when he supposed that the evolutionary journey ultimately brings a fusion of the individual consciousness and the universal consciousness, an integration in which the former is not obliterated by the latter, but transformed by it (see chapter 4). Carpenter explains that the everyday sense of self is modified by the discovery of the deeper self:

> The thoughts connected with separation and mortality—the greeds, the fears, the hatreds, the griefs fall off—and a new world, or conception of the world, opens—life is animated with a new spirit. The Me-conception (as far as that means isolation, mortality, "self-seeking") disappears, is broken up, is transformed; and the life is transformed accordingly.[41]

Of special interest in the present context is Carpenter's understanding that the deeper self, the "divine soul," is the *outcome* of an evolutionary, developmental process across many successive lives, through numerous reincarnations, and yet is inclusive of and witness to all those little selves and their embodiments, for its view of things is spatiotemporally all-embracing.[42] The eternal soul holds together in itself all the successive, temporal lives, overlooking and ordaining them "as from a mountain-top": from this high vantage we would "become distinctly aware of having relation to several bodies simultaneously," that is, to all our successive embodiments, known not through faint memories but in their actuality.[43] Carpenter's thinking here is consistent with the picture of monadic souls as spacetime wholes, as complete concepts, each monadic state being inclusive of the monad's entire temporal development, including all the serial lives through which it develops (and the parallel lives of all the other monads too).[44]

Each of the two ways of apprehending the world—eternal-noumenal and temporal-phenomenal—can be valued for its own qualities and contributions to the whole, and it would be a mistake to deprecate the phenomenal for its transience, limited scope, and the suffering it involves. After all, if the speculations here are correct, then it is through the phenomenal, with its incompleteness, temporal strivings, and many challenges, that the inclusive love and meaningful contents of the noumenal are established. Without phenomenal contents to give it depth, the noumenal would be a grand but empty light show, with spectacular pyrotechnics that signify nothing. The noumenal gains value from the phenomenal that develops within it. It may even be the case that the cosmos has been *set up* in such a way to encourage the emergence and development of organisms with rich phenomenal consciousness. Ideas of this kind have been much discussed under the heading of "the anthropic principle," which revolves around the observation that the universe seems to be finely tuned for the emergence of intelligent life.[45] I shall not broach this vexed topic except to note that one intriguing feature of the universe, the threeness of its large space dimensions, is said to be important for clear signal transmission and therefore for high-quality sensory representation and communication, which is ideal for the generation of sophisticated phenomenal experience and the advanced organisms that rely on it.[46]

The upshot of placing the totality of time in each moment is that the entire working-out of the creative process, from origination to fulfillment, from "alpha" to "omega," is eternally present in each moment, at every step of the journey. In the phenomenal view, fulfillment is a long way off, not at all suspected or just dimly intuited, but in the noumenal view, it is completely realized here and now, in the eternal present. God as fully evolved derivative nature and higher self—and indeed God as everpresent essential nature—is here and now at all moments of the universal process. Thus fulfillment is not limited to a distant future, an end time or "eschaton," since it is eternally realized in each moment, as Traherne insisted, the all-encompassing heavenly "Kingdom" and "secret self" already present and open to discovery by those who care to look.

Moreover, even if the ultimate fulfillment of a monad means that its appetitive striving and the suffering this involves cease, and the monad's sequence of experiential states and bodily transmigrations reach a terminus (perhaps comparable to a Buddha's *parinirvāṇa* at death), its entire life journey will remain since it is eternal, not as a desiccated museum piece drained of subjectivity, but as a living reality. It must be stressed that without the long, difficult journeyings of created beings there would be no fulfillment, no "eternal riches," no great universe, no meaning and inclusive love, no higher selves. In theological terms, this understanding of "final things" brings together two apparently contrary positions, a "realized eschatology" because the fulfillment is present here and now from the eternal viewpoint, and a "future eschatology" because it is here and now only by virtue of a process that has not reached its conclusion from the temporal viewpoint.[47]

Where now lies the problem of evil, after the introduction of a panentheistic concept of God into evolutionary monadology? On the surface, it could appear that panentheism makes evil more problematic for the theist than it already is, since it includes the universe in God and therefore includes all the ills of the universe in God, making God less than perfect. For the classical theist who is used to extolling the omniperfection of God, the situating of evils in God will be difficult to take. But the presence of evils in the universe and therefore in God should not be a concern. Panentheists, unlike pantheists, maintain that the universe is just a part of God, since God exceeds the universe. There is, then, a very significant part of God distinct from the world and its evils. Precisely how this is understood will depend on the way in which a panentheism goes about situating the universe "in" God. For the kind of panentheism sketched here, the universe with its goods and evils exists as the *derivative* nature, that is, as the evolving contents of the derivative mind of God, made up of monadic streams of experience, not as the *essential* nature. The latter provides a secure foundation and destination for all its dependents.

While this may provide reassurance to those troubled by the idea of the world and its evils being in God, it is not the most significant observation that can be made. More importantly, the problem of evil does not hinge on the "whereabouts" of the universe, on its internality or externality to God. Rather it is a question about the *responsibility* of God for a creation in which there are very serious evils. It is beside the point whether the creation is interior or exterior to God, for in either case the moral character of God calls for scrutiny, and similar kinds of justifications to those raised by classical theists, such as the appeals to freewill and soul-making, can just as well be raised by panentheists. Naturally, panentheists will not employ these arguments in quite the same way, since they are not out to defend the all-perfect God of classical theism. Rather they can use them to show that there are greater goods, such as freewill, soul-making, and even God-making, that outweigh and make sense of evils in God-the-universe, while at the same time understanding God-distinct-from-the-universe as rather different from the all-perfect God of classical theism and therefore not so difficult to reconcile with the depth of suffering evident in the world. But panentheists will go further and contend that the problem of evil is additionally eased by their concept of God, for God is no longer a separate entity outside the struggles of suffering creatures. God is here in the thick of it, suffering along with creatures or even suffering *as* those creatures, if ultimately it is God who undergoes the process, developing numerous personae in the evolutionary drama that is the universe. The derivative nature of God, which is none other than ourselves, evolves through numerous streams of experience, building the universe, cultivating the tree of life, developing love and compassion, bringing souls to fruition, and making God more than God would otherwise be.

Epilogue

An Infinit Light will appear in our Souls,
an Infinit Extent, an Infinit Kingdom . . .
a living Sphere of Infinit Blessedness,
a transelemented World of Glory.

—Thomas Traherne

WHEN, ALL THOSE YEARS AGO, I lay in bed fast asleep yet wide awake, astonished to find the universe in my mind, free of the concerns that ordinarily dominate, I thought to myself this is really important, I must try to hold on to it in my everyday life, *remember who I am*. As it turned out, I remembered almost nothing when I woke up, although the afterglow of wholeness suggested to me that something remarkable had occurred. But a few memories were to surface, and these I have recorded here. In the first place, then, the writing of this book, pursued on and off over many years, has been a labor of recollection, of self-remembering, an attempt to stay in touch with the experience and whatever it revealed—to drink water from the Lake of Memory, one might say. In the everyday course of life it is easy to forget, and most of the time I do forget, swept along by familiar ways of thinking and feeling. But if the experience brought genuine insight, as I think it did, then it is surely important to pay attention to its message: behind our apparently separate selves, there is a tremendous unity and knowledge, even a deeper center of identity, at once individual and communal, whose natural inclination is to love. This, if true, is worth remembering and acting upon.

But how can I be certain that the experience was no mere brain quirk or confabulation? I cannot be sure, but the character of the experience as I remember it—the clarity, wakefulness, and knowing quality of an order far above the ordinary—does make me think that the experience was genuinely revelatory, offering a glimpse into a reality that is itself extraordinarily clear, wakeful, and knowing. Those unfamiliar with experiences of this kind will be skeptical and point out that a sense of "realness" is no reliable guide to what is "real," for experiences that feel real can turn out to be dreams or hallucinations.[1] Still, I have been sufficiently impressed by the truly exceptional quality of the experience to try to understand it on its own terms.

In the second place, then, the current book follows my attempts at understanding through the exploration of religious, philosophical, and scientific ideas. Some parts of the study, especially in the early chapters, are descriptive, classificatory, and comparative, and so have stayed fairly close to the experience and should be relatively uncontroversial. I gave an account of the experience, identified it as mystical, likened it to the more profound kind of near-death experience, and explored historical parallels, including encounters with the higher self and sightings of the spherical soul. While some instances of the latter may be "entoptic" in nature, based in the visual nervous system, the tiny "rings" I observed came across to me as living beings equal to the vast mind I now understood myself to be, a perplexing equivalence of the small and the great that launched the turn to speculative philosophy in the chapters that followed.

There I developed a metaphysics inspired by Leibniz and Plotinus, a revised monadology that takes mutually representative units of perception to be the basic components of nature, striving, perceiving minds that are confused and limited in their sense-mediated "phenomenal" perceptions but perfectly distinct and comprehensive in their cosmic "noumenal" perceptions. It follows from this theory that when neuroscientists go in search of the "neural correlates of consciousness," as they have been doing with vigor in recent decades, they are more accurately exploring the brain correlates of *phenomenal* consciousness, without realizing that those correlates are contents of a greater *noumenal* consciousness. Phenomenal consciousness does have brain correlates and, along with the entire brain itself, is part of a much greater field of consciousness.

It was not only mystical experience that drew me toward a panpsychic, idealist metaphysics: some baffling features of modern physics, relativistic and quantum, become more comprehensible within the framework. Indeed, I have found monadology to be an unusually fertile approach, and it has opened up paths that I might not otherwise have explored, including questions about cosmogony, evolution, reincarnation, suffering, and the nature of God. These musings, in the final chapters, are admittedly highly speculative and go well beyond the mystical experience that originally prompted my thinking, but they do follow naturally, if not inevitably, from a monadological outlook.

It seems to me that empirical investigation of the ideas presented here can be taken forward in at least two ways. The first is the study of mystical experiences and related supernormal perceptions. Although I gathered a range of materials suggestive of a world organized from multiple centers of perception, including some impressive historical writings, contemporary accounts germane to the topic were not plentiful. It would help if further relevant accounts were available for study. Mystical experiences of sufficient depth to be informative do occasionally take place "spontaneously," without obvious triggers, but they are also prompted by near-death emergencies and entheogenic substances, and there may be rich seams of data to explore here. Also of interest are experiences that are not so profound but which exhibit the supernormal perceptions that sometimes precede full-blown mystical experiences, such as the penetrative, panoramic, and multiperspectival types of vision. It remains to be seen whether these strange perceptions admit of purely psychological explanation or call for a more profound understanding of the nature of perception.

Perhaps the most significant direction for further investigation will be the idea that monadology supplies a metaphysical framework in which relativistic and quantum physics become more comprehensible. This suggestion needs to be scrutinized and taken further by physicists and philosophers. Following recent developments in theoretical physics, including superstring theory and brane cosmology, physicists may now be in a position to construct models of the interrepresentational, multidimensional world of the monads and test these models against observation. Unlike most nonmaterialist varieties of metaphysics, monadology has an understanding of matter that is sufficiently concrete to be elaborated further and subjected to mathematical modeling and empirical investigation.

But what if scientific efforts were one day to uncover the fundamental structure of matter, and it turned out *not* to be monadological, despite the suggestive hints from relativistic and quantum physics? Monadology, for all its attractions, would have to be abandoned. Even then I think idealism will continue to best describe the relation between mind and matter, for only idealism fully critiques the needlessly austere concept of matter that gave rise to the mind–body problem in the first place, with its fixation on extension and motion to the exclusion of other experiential qualities, as I observed in chapter 6. So while I am open to the possible failure of specifically monadological idealism, I think that idealism will remain the most credible solution to the mind–body problem.

There are times, it must be admitted, when I fear I have been led to unwarranted speculations by an experience of uncertain status. But I do find reassurance in the intractability of the mind–body problem to those approaches that doggedly persevere with the materialist abstractions of matter, space, and time or retain vestiges of them. When I inspect my everyday experiences—vibrant, seamless fields of color, sound, aroma, flavor, body sensation, with feeling, desiring, willing, knowing, and meaning, and organized from a succession of vantage points—I cannot but think they tell me something fundamental about the world at large, that it too is of the nature of experience and mind. Idealism and its monadological variety then seem reasonable. Of course, extrapolation from the familiar can be risky. A fish in the sea would be mistaken to think that water is everywhere, but when it comes to a category as irreducible and inclusive as experience, the extrapolation is more compelling. While a fish may sink to the ocean floor below or leap into the air above, we never reach the limits of experience.

Ideas about the nature of reality are not of merely theoretical interest, for metaphysical positions, whether held knowingly or unwittingly, have an impact on the way we understand ourselves and engage with one another and the natural world.[2] It would be unfair to place the blame alone on materialism and dualism for the relatively alienated condition in which we human beings find ourselves, for the dualizing mindset, with its conceptual fragmentation of the world and extreme differentiation of the I and the not–I, presumably goes back long before the comparatively recent emergence of these philosophies and their shared concept of matter. Indeed, the mindset may well have its roots very far back in the evolutionary journey, even in the early moments of world creation, according to the ideas explored in chapters 9 and 10. But the materialist concept of matter, with its exclusion of experiential qualities, intrinsic values, and mind from the world at large, gives expression to and reinforces our deep-seated tendencies to overlook the experientiality of things and the unity that comes with it. It also encourages a narrow, anthropocentric approach to values, centered on the value of things to humans, with consequent exploitation of other humans, animals, plants, and the natural world in general.

Would it, then, be naive to hope that a philosophy that readmits excluded qualities, values, and mind into the world at large will not only unravel the mind–body problem but also foster less exploitative, more egalitarian attitudes? Metaphysics in itself will change nothing unless its ethical implications are brought out and actively incorporated into personal, social, economic, and political life. The kind of metaphysics advocated here does have ethical implications. At the very least, as a Leibnizian-style panpsychism, it tells us that the world is full of monadic beings who possess some level of consciousness and desire, and so encourages us to broaden our sense of kinship and empathetic connection. It calls on us to recognize those beings as not fundamentally different from ourselves, that is, to appreciate them as striving subjects, as fellow travelers on their own meaningful journeys, rather than things to be treated in any way we please. It tells us too that all beings are deeply interconnected, yet unlike some monist philosophies it does not submerge the individual in the whole. It strikes a balance between the individual and the collective, setting neither one above the other.

In such ways, idealist monadology has the potential to inform ecological, social, and political thinking, furnishing support to causes that aim to promote universal well-being and equality, such as environmental protection and animal welfare, access to education and healthcare, equal rights and opportunities, equitable use of resources, harmonious international relations, to name some areas of pressing concern.[3] No doubt these can be pursued through common empathy and compassion alone, but a philosophy such as monadology can lend support and give additional impetus through its big picture, grounding action in an understanding of how deeply related all beings are and supplying an antidote to worldviews that work in the opposite direction by splitting things up and isolating them.

Leibnizian monadology reenchants the world, ensouling nature and envisaging life in a process of unfoldment everywhere. The changes I have introduced take this revalorization further. Now even the humblest, seemingly most insignificant being has the perfectly clear, fully evolved divine consciousness within, and all are liberated from their fixed positions in a Chain of Being, free to pursue the far-reaching evolutionary development through which the gift of divine consciousness is made possible. This is a lofty vision, expressed in fine words, but what could it mean in the rough and tumble of life? Certainly, determined efforts to advance welfare and equality through social, economic, and political transformation—easier said than done, of course. And personal and spiritual transformation too, not distinct from those transformations in the public sphere, through work on Ego and Eros, transmuting selfish desire into altruistic love.[4] Cultivation of wonder, gratitude, reverence, tranquility, and a nondual outlook. Delight in the beauty and complexity of a world that is wholly yours and equally mine, as Traherne might have put it. Even conscious integration with a "higher self" or whatever reality lies behind our everyday selves, by growing in likeness to that reality and therefore becoming capable of receiving and enduring it. In these various endeavors, the spiritual traditions offer some guidance in their contemplative practices and ways of life, although probably not too much should be expected of such practices in the short term, and certainly not in isolation of broader personal and social growth. Lasting transformation is a slow business, with no set rules or single path.[5]

This book opened with Romantic regret at lost unity and limited vision, at the self cut off from nature and other selves, but also with Romantic hope for reconnection and wholeness, when habitual ways of thinking and feeling give way to wonder at the miracle of existence and to a unitive apprehension of the world. Accounts of mystical experiences offered some sense of that renovated vision, and the most transformative insights to be gleaned from the experiences have to do with "self." It seems that we are both much less and much more than we ordinarily take ourselves to be, and that we are all deeply interconnected. I have explored one way in which this connectedness can be understood: ours is a world of mutually accommodated minds that derive from a common source and which through long journeys home come to realize their potential. Alternative understandings merit exploration, but the basic message remains clear: we are intimately connected, far more deeply than surface appearances suggest, and so to love inclusively is the surest way to proceed.

Notes

PREFACE

Epigraph. Cicero, *De legibus* I, in Eliza Gregory Wilkins, *The Delphic Maxim in Literature* (Chicago: University of Chicago Press, 1929), p. 64.

1 Recent studies include *Panpsychism: Contemporary Perspectives*, ed. by Godehard Brüntrup and Ludwig Jaskolla (Oxford: Oxford University Press, 2017), and *The Routledge Handbook of Panpsychism*, ed. by William Seager (London: Routledge, 2019). See also David Skrbina, *Panpsychism in the West*, rev. edn (Cambridge, MA: MIT Press, 2017).

2 For literature on idealism, see below at chapter 2, n. 7.

3 *The Soul Hypothesis: Investigations into the Existence of the Soul*, ed. by Mark C. Baker and Stewart Goetz (New York: Continuum, 2011); Stewart Goetz and Charles Taliaferro, *A Brief History of the Soul* (Chichester, West Sussex: Wiley-Blackwell, 2011).

4 Paul Marshall, "Mystical Experience and Metaphysics," Esalen Center for Theory and Research website, *Beyond Physicalism* supplement, 2014 <https://www.esalen.org/sites/default/files/resource_attachments/Ch-2-Supp-MEM.pdf>, and "Mystical Experiences as Windows on Reality," in *Beyond Physicalism: Toward Reconciliation of Science and Spirituality*, ed. by Edward F. Kelly, Adam Crabtree, and Paul Marshall (Lanham, MD: Rowman & Littlefield, 2015), pp. 39–76.

5 On Whitehead and Russell, see chapter 8. Of the British monadological idealists, I mention J. M. E. McTaggart in chapter 2 and H. Wildon Carr in chapter 8.

6 Paul Marshall, *Mystical Encounters with the Natural World: Experiences and Explanations* (Oxford: Oxford University Press, 2005).

7 On the question of an essential self in Buddhism, see for instance the chapter on *tathāgatagarbha* doctrine in Paul Williams, *Mahāyana Buddhism: The Doctrinal Foundations*, 2nd edn (Abingdon, Oxon: Routledge, 2009). Also Miri Albahari, "Against No-*Ātman* Theories of *Anattā*," *Asian Philosophy*, 12 (2002), 5–20.

8 There is a sizable body of philosophical writing on "the self." For a starting point, see *The Oxford Handbook of the Self*, ed. by Shaun Gallagher (Oxford: Oxford University Press, 2011). Richard Sorabji takes a historical perspective in *Self: Ancient and Modern Insights About Individuality, Life, and Death* (Oxford: Clarendon Press, 2006). The views of some contemporary spiritual teachers and academics are set out in *A New Approach to Studies of the Self: Its Development, Function, and Relation to Consciousness*, ed. by Nini Praetorius and Simon Höffding, special issue of *Journal of Consciousness Studies*, 23.1–2 (2016).

9   Ian Hacking, *The Social Construction of What?* (Cambridge, MA: Harvard University Press, 1999), pp. 21–25.

10 Paul Marshall, "The Psychical and the Mystical: Boundaries, Connections, Common Origins," *Journal of the Society for Psychical Research*, 75.1 (2011), 1–13. A connection between psychical and mystical phenomena is brought out dramatically in the case of St. Joseph of Copertino, whose levitations were associated with mystical ecstasy. See Michael Grosso, *The Man Who Could Fly: St. Joseph of Copertino and the Mystery of Levitation* (Lanham, MD: Rowman & Littlefield, 2016).

11 Paul Marshall, "Why We Are Conscious of So Little: A Neo-Leibnizian Approach," in Kelly, Crabtree, and Marshall, pp. 387–422.

12 Paul Marshall, *The Living Mirror: Images of Reality in Science and Mysticism* (London: Samphire Press, 1992). Subsequent citations are to the 2006 revised edition.

1 MYSTICAL PERCEPTIONS

Epigraph. Ralph Waldo Emerson, *Nature* (Boston: James Munroe, 1836), p. 13.

1   *The Prose Works of William Wordsworth*, ed. by Alexander B. Grosart, 3 vols (London: Edward Moxon, 1876), III, 194.

2   Percy Bysshe Shelley, "On Life," in *Essays, Letters from Abroad, Translations and Fragments*, 2 vols (London: Edward Moxon, 1852), I, 181–88 (p. 185). In this essay, written in 1819, Shelley repudiates his earlier allegiance to materialism and gropes toward a nondual epistemology in which the thought and its object, and the "I," "you," and "they," are brought into unity as "modifications" or "portions" of thought, of the "one mind." It has been debated whether Shelley's philosophy, according to which "nothing exists but as it is perceived," is idealism, as the phraseology might suggest, or alternatively a skeptical empiricism, a common interpretation in recent times. See for instance Kenneth Neill Cameron, *Shelley: The Golden Years* (Cambridge, MA: Harvard University Press, 1974), pp. 150–58, and Hugh Roberts, *Shelley and Chaos of History: A New Politics of Poetry* (University Park: Pennsylvania State University Press, 2004), pp. 129–34.

3   Shelley, "On Life," p. 181.

4   Shelley, "On Life," p. 186.

5   Shelley, "A Defence of Poetry," in *Essays, Letters from Abroad, Translations and Fragments*, I, 3–49 (p. 44).

6   Citations to Traherne's *Centuries* are to Thomas Traherne, *Centuries of Meditations*, ed. by Bertram Dobell (London: Bertram Dobell, 1908), and are abbreviated CM.

7   From Traherne's poem "Walking." See Gary Kuchar, "Traherne's Specters: Self-Consciousness and Its Others," in *Re-Reading Thomas Traherne: A Collection of New Critical Essays*, ed. by Jacob Blevins (Tempe: Arizona Center for Medieval and Renaissance Studies, 2007), pp. 173–99.

8   For nonduality in religious and philosophical thought, see David Loy, *Nonduality: A Study in Comparative Philosophy* (New York: Humanity Books, 1998).

9   Andrew M. Greeley, *The Sociology of the Paranormal: A Reconnaissance* (Beverly Hills, CA: Sage Publications, 1975).

10 David Hay and Gordon Heald, "Religion Is Good for You," *New Society*, 80 (1987), 20–22.

11 Kathleen Raine, *The Land Unknown* (London: Hamish Hamilton, 1975), pp. 119–20.

12 RERC No. 004138, in *Seeing the Invisible: Modern Religious and Other Transcendent Experiences*, ed. by Meg Maxwell and Verena Tschudin (Oxford: Religious Experience Research Centre, 1996), p. 55. Accounts from the Alister Hardy Religious Experience

Research Centre, University Wales Trinity Saint David, Lampeter, UK, are designated "RERC" followed by the official archive number and also the publication reference if quoted from a published source.

13 Anne Bancroft, "A Crowning Clarity," in *The Light of Experience* (London: British Broadcasting Corporation, 1977), pp. 65–69 (pp. 66–67).

14 Bancroft, pp. 67–68.

15 Flora Courtois, "An Experience of Enlightenment," in *The Hazy Moon of Enlightenment*, by Taizan Maezumi and Bernard Glassman (Somerville, MA: Wisdom Publications, 2007), pp. 115–36 (p. 115).

16 Courtois, p. 117.

17 Courtois, p. 124.

18 Courtois, p. 125.

19 RERC No. 001481, from the archive of the Alister Hardy Religious Experience Research Centre.

20 RERC No. 002461, in Maxwell and Tschudin, p. 136.

21 Robert Wolf, "Seeds of Glory: An Interview," *Psychedelic Review*, 8 (1966), 111–22 (pp. 117, 118).

22 Wolf, p. 117.

23 RERC No. 000500, from the archive of the Alister Hardy Religious Experience Research Centre.

24 RERC No. 000500, from the archive of the Alister Hardy Religious Experience Research Centre. See also Edward Robinson, *The Original Vision: A Study of the Religious Experience of Childhood* (Oxford: Religious Experience Research Unit, 1977), pp. 28–29.

25 Case 27 (Mrs. A.), in Raynor C. Johnson, *Watcher on the Hills* (London: Hodder & Stoughton, 1959), p. 71.

26 RERC No. 004764, in Maxwell and Tschudin, p. 171.

27 RERC No. 000647, from the archive of the Alister Hardy Religious Experience Research Centre.

28 H. W. Yoxall, "Allen, (Herbert) Warner (1881–1968)," rev., in *Oxford Dictionary of National Biography* (Oxford University Press, 2004) <http://dx.doi.org/10.1093/ref:odnb/30385>.

29 Warner Allen, *The Timeless Moment* (London: Faber and Faber, 1946), p. 33.

30 Allen, p. 33.

31 Allen, p. 31.

32 Robert M. May, *Cosmic Consciousness Revisited: The Modern Origins and Development of a Western Spiritual Psychology* (Shaftesbury, Dorset: Element Books, 1993), p. 295.

33 May, p. 299.

34 Introductory books on comparative mysticism include Denise Lardner Carmody and John Tully Carmody, *Mysticism: Holiness East and West* (Oxford: Oxford University Press, 1996), Robert S. Ellwood, *Mysticism and Religion*, 2nd edn (Chappaqua, NY: Seven Bridges Press, 1999), and William Harmless, *Mystics* (New York: Oxford University Press, 2008). Harmless lists many relevant works in "Spirituality and Mysticism: Surveys & Introductory Works," Bibliographies for Theology, *Journal of Religion & Society* website <https://dspace2.creighton.edu/xmlui/bitstream/handle/10504/84491/Mysticism1.pdf>. For an overview of the modern study of mysticism, see Bernard McGinn, *The Presence of God: A History of Western Christian Mysticism*, I. *The Foundations of Mysticism: Origins to the Fifth Century* (London: SCM Press, 1992), pp. 263–343. For a philosophical overview, see Anthony N. Perovich, "Philosophical Reflection on Mysticism," in *A Companion to Philosophy of Religion*, ed. by Charles Taliaferro, Paul Draper, and Philip L. Quinn, 2nd edn (Chichester, West Sussex: Wiley-Blackwell, 2010), pp. 702–09. For a psychological

overview, see David M. Wulff, "Mystical Experience," in *Varieties of Anomalous Experience: Examining the Scientific Evidence*, ed. by Etzel Cardeña, Steven Jay Lynn, and Stanley Krippner, 2nd edn (Washington, DC: American Psychological Association, 2014), pp. 369–408. For empirical research, see Ralph W. Hood Jr, Peter C. Hill, and Bernard Spilka, "Mysticism," in *The Psychology of Religion: An Empirical Approach*, 5th edn (New York: Guilford Press, 2018), pp. 354–403. For a recent overview of work in Religious Studies, see Michael Stoeber, "The Comparative Study of Mysticism," in *Oxford Research Encyclopedia of Religion* (New York: Oxford University Press), online publication date September 2015 <https://doi.org/10.1093/acrefore/9780199340378.013.93>.

35 Louis Bouyer, "Mysticism: An Essay on the History of the Word," in *Understanding Mysticism*, ed. by Richard Woods (London: Athlone Press, 1981), pp. 42–55.

36 Ellwood, *Mysticism and Religion*, p. 39.

37 Marshall, "Mystical Experiences as Windows on Reality," p. 42.

38 McGinn, *Presence of God: Foundations of Mysticism*, pp. xvi–xvii.

39 R. C. Zaehner, *Mysticism Sacred and Profane: An Inquiry into Some Varieties of Præternatural Experience* (Oxford: Clarendon Press, 1957).

40 RERC No. 000388, from the archive of the Alister Hardy Religious Experience Research Centre.

41 Marshall, *Mystical Encounters*, pp. 206–10. See also Jeffrey J. Kripal, *Roads of Excess, Palaces of Wisdom: Eroticism and Reflexivity in the Study of Mysticism* (Chicago: University of Chicago Press, 2001), pp. 156–98.

42 Robert K. C. Forman, *Mysticism, Mind, Consciousness* (Albany: State University of New York Press, 1999), pp. 11–13. On pure consciousness, see also *The Problem of Pure Consciousness: Mysticism and Philosophy*, ed. by Robert K. C. Forman (New York: Oxford University Press, 1990), and *The Innate Capacity: Mysticism, Psychology, and Philosophy*, ed. by Robert K. C. Forman (Oxford: Oxford University Press, 1998). See Marshall, *Mystical Encounters*, pp. 145–75.

43 See also Marshall, *Mystical Encounters*, pp. 60–64.

44 Marshall, *Mystical Encounters*, pp. 84–102. For a recent study of triggers, see Steve Taylor and Krisztina Egeto-Szabo, "Exploring Awakening Experiences: A Study of Awakening Experiences in Terms of Their Triggers, Characteristics, Duration and After-Effects," *Journal of Transpersonal Psychology*, 49 (2017), 45–65.

45 See for instance Steve Taylor, *Out of the Darkness: From Turmoil to Transformation* (London: Hay House, 2011), and "The Peak at the Nadir: Psychological Turmoil as the Trigger for Awakening Experiences," *International Journal of Transpersonal Studies*, 32.2 (2013), 1–12.

46 e.g., Ann Wroe, *Being Shelley: The Poet's Search for Himself* (London: Jonathan Cape, 2007), pp. 15–16.

47 Pierre Hadot, *Philosophy as a Way of Life: Spiritual Exercises from Socrates to Foucault*, ed. by Arnold I. Davidson, trans. by Michael Chase (Oxford: Blackwell, 1995), p. 211.

48 *Upaniṣads*, trans. by Patrick Olivelle (Oxford: Oxford University Press, 1996), p. 167 [*Chāndogya Upaniṣad* 8.1.3].

49 Thomas Traherne, *Select Meditations*, ed. by Julia J. Smith (Manchester: Carcanet Press, 1997), p. 1 [I.81].

50 Traherne, p. 65 [III.27].

51 Gopi Krishna, *Kundalini: The Evolutionary Energy in Man* (Boulder, CO: Shambhala, 1971), p. 207.

52 Krishna, p. 208.

53 Irina Starr, *The Sound of Light*, 3rd edn (Ojai, CA: The Pilgrim's Path, 1991), p. 8.

54 Courtois, "An Experience of Enlightenment," p. 126.

55 Marshall, *Mystical Encounters*, p. 24; John Franklin, "A Spiritual Biography: An Account of Spiritual/Religious Experiences from a Small Child to the Present Moment," *De Numine*, 28 (2000), 14–17.

56 John Franklin, email correspondence with author in 2006 and 2009.

2 The Land Beyond the Sea

Epigraph. Chuang Tzŭ: Mystic, Moralist, and Social Reformer, trans. by Herbert A. Giles (London: Bernard Quaritch, 1889), p. 30 (modified).

1 In retrospect, I would interpret this doubling of self as a shift of consciousness from an unreflective "trance" condition to an awareness of the condition and an impulse to wake from it. On the self-impersonation genre, see Wendy Doniger, *The Woman Who Pretended to Be Who She Was: Myths of Self-Imitation* (Oxford: Oxford University Press, 2005).

2 I refer here to the famous mirror verses attributed to Shenxiu (d. 706 CE) and Huineng (d. 713 CE) in Ch'an Buddhism's *Platform Sūtra*. See for instance Peter N. Gregory, "The *Platform Sūtra* as the Sudden Teaching," in *Readings of the* Platform Sūtra, ed. by Morten Schlütter and Stephen F. Teiser (New York: Columbia University Press, 2012), pp. 77–108. On Buddhist mirror imagery, see Paul Demiéville, "The Mirror of the Mind," in *Sudden and Gradual: Approaches to Enlightenment in Chinese Thought*, ed. by Peter N. Gregory (Honolulu: University of Hawai'i Press, 1987), pp. 13–40 (first publ. in French as "Le miroir spirituel," *Sinologica*, 1.2 (1947), 112–37), and Alex Wayman, "The Mirror as a Pan-Buddhist Metaphor-Simile," in *Buddhist Insight: Essays by Alex Wayman*, ed. by George R. Elder (Delhi: Motilal Banarsidass, 1984), pp. 129–51 (first publ. in *History of Religions*, 13 (1974), 251–69). My own affair with mirror tropes culminated with *The Living Mirror*, in which I attempted to transmute the distorting mirror of materialist philosophy into a mirror that better reflects self and world.

3 C. G. Jung, *Memories, Dreams, Reflections*, ed. by Aniela Jaffé (London: Fount, Collins, 1977). On the problematic status of *Memories, Dreams, Reflections* as "autobiography," see Alan C. Elms, "The Auntification of C. G. Jung," in *Uncovering Lives: The Uneasy Alliance of Biography and Psychology* (New York: Oxford University Press, 1994), pp. 51–70, and Sonu Shamdasani, "Memories, Dreams, Omissions," in *Jung in Contexts: A Reader*, ed. by Paul Bishop (London: Routledge, 1999), pp. 33–50 (first publ. in *Spring*, 57 (1995), 115–37).

4 Jung, pp. 320–23.

5 Gustave Doré, *The Doré Illustrations for Dante's Divine Comedy* (New York: Dover Publications, 1976).

6 The trail of images that gave a sense of motion might be considered a form of polyopia or some such phenomenon (say, "visual trailing" palinopsia, cinematographic vision, transient akinetopsia), but not of the "objective" type through the eyes, since I was asleep. These visual phenomena are occasionally a feature of hypnagogia and the migraine aura, and they can be stimulated by hallucinogens. It is notable that the basis of pain too was "split" apart, separated into patches, which made the actual sensation impossible. I have not come across reports of a comparable occurrence in the mystical, psychological, or medical literature. For my thoughts on the sense of time flow and its relation to the specious present, see Marshall, *The Living Mirror*, pp. 110–12, 139–42, and "Why We Are Conscious of So Little," pp. 50–51.

7 For a survey of Western idealist philosophies, see Jeremy Dunham, Iain Hamilton Grant, and Sean Watson, *Idealism: The History of a Philosophy* (Durham: Acumen, 2011). There are many books on German Idealism and a growing number on Anglo-American Idealism: recent examples of the latter include *Anglo-American Idealism: Thinkers and Ideas*, ed. by James Connelly and Stamatoula Panagakou (Bern: Peter Lang, 2010), W. J. Mander, *British Idealism: A History* (Oxford: Oxford University Press, 2011), and David Boucher and Andrew Vincent, *British Idealism: A Guide for the Perplexed* (Continuum, 2012). In the English-speaking world, the most prominent metaphysical idealist of recent times was T. L. S. Sprigge, who argued for a panpsychic, "pantheistic" absolute idealism: see Sprigge, *The Vindication of Absolute Idealism* (Edinburgh: Edinburgh University Press, 1983) and *The God of Metaphysics* (Oxford: Clarendon Press, 2006), and the festschrift *Consciousness, Reality and Value: Essays in Honour of T. L. S. Sprigge*, ed. by Pierfrancesco Basile and Leemon B. McHenry (Frankfurt: Ontos, 2007). Two recent works of interest are *British Idealism and the Concept of the Self*, ed. by W. J. Mander and Stamatoula Panagakou (London: Palgrave Macmillan, 2016), and *Idealism: New Essays in Metaphysics*, ed. by Tyron Goldschmidt and Kenneth L. Pearce (Oxford: Oxford University Press, 2017). Idealism has had spirited advocacy outside the mainstream, including Peter B. Lloyd, *Consciousness and Berkeley's Metaphysics* (London: Ursa Software, 1999), and Bernardo Kastrup, *Why Materialism Is Baloney* (Alresford, Hants: iff Books, 2014). My own philosophical case for idealism (without appeals to extraordinary experience) was summarized in "Transforming the World into Experience: An Idealist Experiment," *Journal of Consciousness Studies*, 8.1 (2001), 59–76. As far as I know, there is no up-to-date survey of idealism in non-Western traditions, although discussions of specific thinkers and traditions are available. These often debate whether the Western category "idealism" is applicable and, if so, in what sense. To give two recent examples: on the vexed question of Buddhist "idealism," see Birgit Kellner and John Taber, "Studies in Yogācāra-Vijñānavāda Idealism I: The Interpretation of Vasubandhu's *Viṃśikā*," *Asiatische Studien/Études Asiatiques*, 68 (2014), 709–56 <http://www.ikga.oeaw.ac.at/mediawiki/images/d/dd/Kellner_Taber_2014_Yogacara_Idealism_I.pdf>; on Advaita Vedānta and British Idealism, see Ankur Barua, "The Absolute of Advaita and the Spirit of Hegel: Situating Vedānta on the Horizons of British Idealisms," *Journal of Indian Council of Philosophical Research*, 34 (2017), 1–17 <https://doi.org/10.1007/s40961-016-0076-4>.

8 See Marshall, *The Living Mirror*, "Preface to the Revised Edition," pp. vii–ix.

9 This is Eugene P. Wigner's phrase: "The Unreasonable Effectiveness of Mathematics in the Natural Sciences," *Communications on Pure and Applied Mathematics*, 13 (1960), 1–14. On "mathematical realism," see for instance Mark Colyvan, *An Introduction to the Philosophy of Mathematics* (Cambridge: Cambridge University Press, 2012).

10 e.g., Kurt Gödel, "A Remark about the Relationship between Relativity Theory and Idealistic Philosophy," in *Albert Einstein: Philosopher-Scientist*, ed. by P. A. Schilpp, Library of Living Philosophers (La Salle, IL: Open Court, 1949), pp. 557–62. For some early debates about idealist interpretations of relativistic theory, see José M. Sánchez-Ron, "The Early Reception of Einstein's Relativity among British Philosophers," in *Einstein and the Changing Worldviews of Physics*, ed. by Christoph Lehner, Jürgen Renn, and Matthias Schemmel, Einstein Studies, 12 (Boston: Birkhäuser, 2012), pp. 73–116. Also Thomas A. Ryckman, "Early Philosophical Interpretations of General Relativity," in *The Stanford Encyclopedia of Philosophy*, ed. by Edward N. Zalta, winter 2016 edn <https://plato.stanford.edu/archives/win2016/entries/genrel-early/>.

11 Jeffrey J. Kripal discusses many contemporary examples in his book *The Flip: Epiphanies of Mind and the Future of Knowledge* (New York: Bellevue Literary Press, 2019). Also of

considerable interest is Charles F. Emmons and Penelope Emmons, *Science and Spirit: Exploring the Limits of Consciousness* (Bloomington, IN: iUniverse, 2012).

12 See Marshall, *Mystical Encounters*, pp. 252–53.

13 Marjorie Hines Woollacott, *Infinite Awareness: The Awakening of a Scientific Mind* (Lanham, MD: Rowman & Littlefield, 2015).

14 Federico Faggin, "Requirements for a Mathematical Theory of Consciousness," *Journal of Consciousness*, 18.59 (2015), 421–38 <http://www.jofc.org/telas/home/arquivo.php?id=jofc_59_17_en>. See also articles on the Federico & Elivia Faggin Foundation website <http://www.fagginfoundation.org/category/articles-2/>.

15 G. Lowes Dickinson, *J. McT. E. McTaggart* (Cambridge: Cambridge University Press, 1931). McTaggart's two basic characteristics of mysticism emphasize unity: (1) *mystic unity*—the assertion of "a greater unity in the universe" than is recognized in ordinary experience or science; (2) *mystic intuition* of that unity—consciousness of unity in such a way that knower and known are brought closer and more directly together than in "ordinary discursive thought." See J. McT. Ellis McTaggart, "Mysticism," in *Philosophical Studies*, ed. by S. V. Keeling (London: Edward Arnold, 1934), pp. 46–68 (p. 47) (first publ. in *The New Quarterly*, 2.7 (1909), 315–39). For McTaggart on love, see W. J. Mander, "On McTaggart on Love," *History of Philosophy Quarterly*, 13 (1996), 133–47. For McTaggart as a monadological idealist, see Emily Thomas, "British Idealist Monadologies and the Reality of Time: Hilda Oakeley Against McTaggart, Leibniz, and Others," *British Journal for the History of Philosophy*, 23 (2015), 1150–68.

16 Peter Geach, "Cambridge Philosophers III: McTaggart," *Philosophy*, 70.274 (1995), 567–79.

17 Marshall, *The Living Mirror*, and "Mystical Experience and Metaphysics."

18 For example, Henri F. Ellenberger, *The Discovery of the Unconscious: The History and Evolution of Dynamic Psychiatry* (London: Fontana, 1994), p. 170.

19 Dante Alighieri, *The Divine Comedy: Paradiso*, trans. by Charles S. Singleton, 2 vols (Princeton, NJ: Princeton University Press, 1991), I, 377.

20 Dante, I, 377.

21 Dante, I, 375.

22 Margaret Prescott Montague, "Some Meditations of the Heart," *Atlantic Monthly*, 118 (1916), 746–55 (pp. 753–54).

23 W. Winslow Hall, *Recorded Illuminates* (London: C. W. Daniel, 1937), p. 194.

24 e.g., Roland Fischer, "State-Bound Knowledge: 'I Can't Remember What I Said Last Night, but It Must Have Been Good'," in *Understanding Mysticism*, ed. by Richard Woods (London: Athlone Press, 1981), pp. 306–11; Alan J. Parkin, *Memory: Phenomena, Experiment, and Theory* (Oxford: Blackwell, 1993), pp. 87–92. The state-boundedness of knowledge does not mean that investigation of altered states of consciousness from within is necessarily futile. Charles Tart has long advocated "state-specific sciences," that is, scientific investigation performed within altered states. See Charles T. Tart, "States of Consciousness and State-Specific Sciences," *Science*, 176 (1972), 1203–10. For background, see Charles T. Tart, "State-Specific Sciences: Altered State Origin of the Proposal," Charles T. Tart Blog, 2015 <http://blog.paradigm-sys.com/state-specific-sciences-altered-state-origin-of-the-proposal/>.

25 For some examples, see Carol Zaleski, *Otherworld Journeys: Accounts of Near-Death Experience in Medieval and Modern Times* (New York: Oxford University Press, 1987), pp. 132–33.

26 R. H. Ward, *A Drug-Taker's Notes* (London: Victor Gollancz, 1957), pp. 26–32. This book describes the author's supervised LSD sessions in the mid-1950s. In his first memoir, Ward tells of a formative encounter in a café with a mysterious and very Gurdjieff-like

"Monsieur X." At the time, in the late 1920s, Ward was a young student in Paris. See Ward, *Gallery of Mirrors: Memories of Childhood, Boyhood and Early Adulthood* (London: Victor Gollancz, 1956), pp. 205–14. The striking similarity between Monsieur X and Gurdjieff is noted in J. Walter Driscoll and the Gurdjieff Foundation of California, *Gurdjieff: An Annotated Bibliography* (New York, Garland, 1985), p. 204.

27 On ketamine and forgetting, see Ornella Corazza, *Near-Death Experiences: Exploring the Mind–Body Connection* (London: Routledge, 2008), pp. 112–13.

28 William James, "On Some Hegelisms," *Mind*, 7 (1882), 186–208 (p. 206). See also James's "Consciousness Under Nitrous Oxide," *Psychological Review*, 5 (1898), 194–96, and *The Varieties of Religious Experience: A Study in Human Nature* (New York: Longmans, Green, 1902), pp. 387–88.

29 James, "On Some Hegelisms," p. 206.

30 James, "On Some Hegelisms," p. 208.

31 Humphry Davy, *Researches, Chemical and Philosophical; Chiefly Concerning Nitrous Oxide, or Dephlogisticated Nitrous Air, and Its Respiration* (London: J. Johnson, 1800), p. 488.

32 Davy, p. 489.

33 William Ramsay, "Partial Anæsthesia," *Proceedings of the Society for Psychical Research*, 9 (1894), 236–44 (pp. 236–37, 242, 243).

34 Ernest Dunbar, "The Light Thrown on Psychological Processes by the Action of Drugs," *Proceedings of the Society for Psychical Research*, 19 (1905), 62–77 (p. 74).

35 Ramsay, p. 239.

36 Ramsay, pp. 237, 239, 243.

37 Ward, pp. 28–29.

38 Ward, pp. 29, 30.

39 Ward, p. 30. On webs and nets, see below at chapter 7, n. 54.

40 Ward, p. 31.

41 Iris Skinner, "The Gift of Love," *Light*, 115 (1995), 9–12 (p. 9).

42 Nona Coxhead, *The Relevance of Bliss: A Contemporary Exploration of Mystic Experience* (New York: St Martin's Press, 1985), pp. 31–33.

3 INTO THE HOUSE OF DEATH

Epigraph. Alfred Tennyson, *In Memoriam* (London: Edward Moxon, 1850), p. 1.

1 Kenneth Ring, *Heading Toward Omega: In Search of the Meaning of the Near-Death Experience* (New York: Quill, 1985), pp. 225–28. In *Beyond the Light* (New York: Birch Lane Press, 1994), P. M. H. Atwater introduced the term "near-death-like experience" to cover experiences similar to NDEs but not involving life-threatening circumstances.

2 Ring, pp. 54–55.

3 Reinee Pasarow, "Death – My Luminous Journey," *Fate*, 35 (1982), 65–69 (pp. 67–68). See also Pasarow's "A Personal Account of an NDE," *Vital Signs*, 1.3 (1981), 11, 14.

4 Ananda K. Coomaraswamy, "Some Pali Words," in *Coomaraswamy: Selected Papers*, ed. by Roger Lipsey, 2 vols (Princeton, NJ: Princeton University Press, 1977), II, 264–329 (pp. 324–27). See also Coomaraswamy, "The Sea," I, 405–11, and René Guénon, *Fundamental Symbols: The Universal Language of Sacred Science* (Cambridge: Quinta Essentia, 1995), pp. 233–35.

5 C. G. Jung, "The Psychology of the Transference: Essays on the Psychology of the Transference and Other Subjects," in *The Practice of Psychotherapy*, trans. by R. F. C. Hull, 2nd

edn, *The Collected Works of C. G. Jung*, 20 vols (London: Routledge & Kegan Paul), XVI (1964), 163–321 (pp. 245–46).

6   *The Epic of Gilgamesh*, trans. by N. K. Sandars, rev. edn (Harmondsworth, Middx: Penguin, 1972), pp. 37–39.

7   Philippe Derchain, "Death in Egyptian Religion," in *Greek and Egyptian Mythologies*, ed. by Yves Bonnefoy (Chicago: University of Chicago Press, 1992), pp. 235–39 (p. 236).

8   See Katherine K. Young, "Tīrtha and the Metaphor of Crossing Over," *Studies in Religion/ Sciences Religieuses*, 9 (1980), 61–68.

9   Paul Dundas, *The Jains* (London: Routledge, 1992), pp. 17–20.

10 Coomaraswamy, "Some Pali Words," II, 325.

11 Kathleen Raine, *Blake and Antiquity* (London: Routledge & Kegan Paul, 1979), pp. 3–16.

12 See Carl-Martin Edsman, "Bridges," *The Encyclopedia of Religion*, ed. by Mircea Eliade, 16 vols (New York: Macmillan, 1987), II, 310–14.

13 For example, Sigmund Freud, "Civilization and Its Discontents," in *The Standard Edition of the Complete Psychological Works of Sigmund Freud*, ed. by James Strachey, 24 vols (London: Hogarth Press, 1961), XXI, 57–146; J. Moussaieff Masson, *The Oceanic Feeling: The Origins of Religious Sentiment in Ancient India* (Dordrecht: Reidel, 1980). See William B. Parsons, *The Enigma of the Oceanic Feeling: Revisioning the Psychoanalytic Theory of Mysticism* (New York: Oxford University Press, 1999).

14 See Anthony Storr, *Solitude* (London: Flamingo, 1989), pp. 185–202.

15 Eugene Monick, *Phallos: Sacred Image of the Masculine* (Toronto: Inner City Books, 1987), pp. 25–27.

16 Coomaraswamy, "Symplegades," I, 521–44.

17 Joseph Campbell, *The Masks of God*, III: *Occidental Mythology* (Harmondsworth, Middx: Penguin, 1976), pp. 163–64.

18 Coomaraswamy, "The Symbolism of the Dome," I, 415–64 (p. 447).

19 Coomaraswamy: "Symbolism," pp. 445–51; "*Svayamātṛṇṇā*: Janus Coeli," I, 465–520 (pp. 472–74); "Bhakta Aspects of the Ātman Doctrine," II, 387–97.

20 Johannes Bronkhorst, *The Two Sources of Indian Asceticism* (Delhi: Motilal Banarsidass, 1998), p. 60.

21 *Upaniṣads*, p. 270.

22 *Upaniṣads*, pp. xlvii–xlviii.

23 *Upaniṣads*, pp. 170–71.

24 *Upaniṣads*, p. 66.

25 e.g., S. K. Hookham, *The Buddha Within: Tathagatagarbha Doctrine According to the Shentong Interpretation of the* Ratnagotravibhaga (Albany: State University of New York Press, 1991).

26 Walter Burkert, *Greek Religion: Archaic and Classical*, trans. by John Raffan (Oxford: Basil Blackwell, 1985), pp. 293–94; Radcliffe G. Edmonds III, *Myths of the Underworld Journey: Plato, Aristophanes, and the 'Orphic' Gold Tablets* (Cambridge: Cambridge University Press, 2004), pp. 29–110. For the texts and discussion, see Alberto Bernabé and Ana Isabel Jiménez San Cristóbal, *Instructions for the Netherworld: The Orphic Gold Tablets*, trans. by Michael Chase (Leiden: Brill, 2008), *The "Orphic" Gold Tablets and Greek Religion: Further Along the Path*, ed. by Radcliffe G. Edmonds III (Cambridge: Cambridge University Press, 2011), and Fritz Graf and Sarah Iles Johnston, *Ritual Texts for the Afterlife: Orpheus and the Bacchic Gold Tablets*, 2nd edn (Abingdon, Oxon: Routledge, 2013).

27 Burkert, p. 293.

28 Edmonds, *Myths of the Underworld Journey*, pp. 82–101.

29 Mary Lutyens, *The Life and Death of Krishnamurti* (London: Murray, 1990), pp. 107–08.

30 For a detailed discussion, see Hadot, *Philosophy as a Way of Life*.

31 Hadot, pp. 229–30.

32 Richard Maurice Bucke, *Cosmic Consciousness: A Study in the Evolution of the Human Mind* (1901; repr. New York: Arkana, Penguin, 1991), p. 73.

33 e.g., Mark S. G. Dyczkowski, *The Doctrine of Vibration: An Analysis of the Doctrines and Practices of Kashmir Shaivism* (Albany: State University of New York Press, 1987), pp. 143–44.

34 RERC No. 004764, in Maxwell and Tschudin, pp. 171–72.

35 William Braden, *The Private Sea: LSD and the Search for God* (Chicago: Quadrangle Books, 1967); John Horgan, *The End of Science: Facing the Limits of Knowledge in the Twilight of the Scientific Age* (London: Abacus, Little, Brown, 1998).

36 Bruce Greyson and Nancy Evans Bush, "Distressing Near-Death Experiences," in *The Near-Death Experience: A Reader*, ed. by Lee W. Bailey and Jenny Yates (New York: Routledge, 1996), pp. 209–30 (pp. 222–23).

37 See Zaleski, pp. 128–31, and Carol Zaleski, "Death, and Near-Death Today," in *Death, Ecstasy, and Other Worldly Journeys*, ed. by John J. Collins and Michael Fishbane (Albany: State University of New York Press, 1995), pp. 383–407 (pp. 394–98).

38 See Helmer Ringgren, "Judgment of the Dead," *The Encyclopedia of Religion*, ed. by Mircea Eliade, 16 vols (New York: Macmillan, 1987), XIII, 205–07.

39 Zaleski, *Otherworld Journeys*, pp. 29–30, 69, 73.

40 Zaleski, *Otherworld Journeys*, p. 66.

41 See Lawrence R. Hennessey, "The Place of Saints and Sinners After Death," in *Origen of Alexandria: His World and His Legacy*, ed. by Charles Kannengiesser and William L. Petersen (Notre Dame, IN: University of Notre Dame Press, 1988), pp. 295–312; Henri Crouzel, *Origen*, trans. by A. S. Worrall (Edinburgh: T. & T. Clark, 1989), pp. 242–46; Brian E. Daley, *The Hope of the Early Church: A Handbook of Patristic Eschatology* (Cambridge: Cambridge University Press, 1991), p. 56.

42 Hennessey, p. 307.

43 Hennessey, pp. 308–11.

44 Hennessey, p. 308.

45 Daley, pp. 81–89; Morwenna Ludlow, *Universal Salvation: Eschatology in the Thought of Gregory of Nyssa and Karl Rahner* (Oxford: Oxford University Press, 2009).

46 Daley, pp. 103–04.

47 Jacob Boehme, *The Way to Christ*, trans. by Peter C. Erb (New York: Paulist Press, 1978), pp. 56–57.

48 Boehme, pp. 58–62.

49 *The Complete Works of Saint Teresa of Jesus*, trans. and ed. by E. Allison Peers from the critical edn of P. Silverio de Santa Teresa, 3 vols (London: Sheed & Ward, 1946), I, 294.

50 Quoted by Olivier Clément, *The Roots of Christian Mysticism: Text and Commentary* (New York: New City Press, 1995), p. 303.

51 Crouzel, pp. 245–46.

52 Emanuel Swedenborg, *Arcana Caelestia*, trans. by John Elliott, 12 vols (London: The Swedenborg Society, 1984), II, §§2117–34.

53 Swedenborg, II, §2121.

54 Swedenborg, II, §§2130–02.

55 Unless otherwise stated, citations to Plotinus's *Enneads* are to *Plotinus: Enneads I–VI*, trans. by A. H. Armstrong, Loeb Classical Library, 7 vols (Cambridge, MA: Harvard University Press, 1966–88). Further references to the *Enneads* are abbreviated as *Enn*.

56 See J. M. Rist, *Plotinus: The Road to Reality* (Cambridge: Cambridge University Press, 1967), pp. 53–55, and A. H. Armstrong, "Beauty and the Discovery of Divinity in the Thought of Plotinus," in *Kephalaion: Studies in Greek Philosophy and its Continuation Offered to Professor C. J. de Vogel*, ed. by J. Mansfeld and L. M. de Rijk (Assen: Van Gorcum, 1975), pp. 155–63 (pp. 161–62) (repr. in A. H. Armstrong, *Plotinian and Christian Studies* (London: Variorum, 1979), chap. 19).

57 Boehme, p. 60.

4 Who Do You Think You Are?

Epigraph. The Thirteen Principal Upanishads, trans. by Robert Ernest Hume (London: Oxford University Press, 1921), p. 268 [*Chāndogya Upaniṣad*, 8.7.1].

1 I first broached this topic in *The Living Mirror*, pp. 75–81.

2 W. K. C. Guthrie, *A History of Greek Philosophy*, I: *The Earlier Presocratics and the Pythagoreans* (Cambridge: Cambridge University Press, 1962), p. 199.

3 Annemarie Schimmel, *Mystical Dimensions of Islam* (Chapel Hill: University of North Carolina Press, 1975), pp. 49, 66. However, on "I am the Truth," see Julian Baldick's observations in *Mystical Islam: An Introduction to Sufism* (London: I. B. Tauris, 1989), pp. 47–48.

4 Baldick, p. 47.

5 *Meister Eckhart, Teacher and Preacher*, ed. by Bernard McGinn (Mahwah, NJ: Paulist Press, 1986), p. 358.

6 *Meister Eckhart*, p. 360.

7 *Meister Eckhart*, pp. 13, 366.

8 Giovanni Filoramo, *A History of Gnosticism*, trans. by Anthony Alcock (Oxford: Blackwell, 1992), pp. 82, 89.

9 Heinrich Dumoulin, *Zen Buddhism: A History*, I. *India and China* (New York: Macmillan, 1988), pp. 191–92; *The Record of Linji*, trans. by Ruth Fuller Sasaki, ed. by Thomas Yū-hō Kirchner (Honolulu: University of Hawai'i Press, 2009), pp. 155–60.

10 My brief historical survey of "know thyself" is indebted to Alexander Altmann, "The Delphic Maxim in Medieval Islam and Judaism," in *Studies in Religious Philosophy and Mysticism* (London: Routledge & Kegan Paul, 1969), pp. 1–40. See also Gerard J. P. O'Daly, *Plotinus' Philosophy of the Self* (Shannon: Irish University Press, 1973), pp. 11–19; Chr. Gorm Tortzen, "*Know Thyself* – A Note on the Success of a Delphic Saying," in *Noctes Atticae: 34 Articles on Graeco-Roman Antiquity and Its Nachleben*, ed. by Bettina Amden and others (Copenhagen: Museum Tusculanum Press, 2002), pp. 302–14.

11 Altmann, pp. 4–5.

12 On self-knowledge in the *First Alcibiades*, see David M. Johnson, "God as the True Self: Plato's *Alcibiades I*," *Ancient Philosophy*, 19 (1999), 1–19.

13 Altmann, p. 6.

14 On the loving Intellect, see chapter 9.

15 Gregory Shaw, *Theurgy and the Soul: The Neoplatonism of Iamblichus* (University Park: Pennsylvania State University Press, 1995); Gregory Shaw, "Platonic *Siddhas*: Supernatural Philosophers of Neoplatonism," in Kelly, Crabtree, and Marshall, pp. 275–313.

16 Altmann, p. 19.

17 Moshe Idel, *Kabbalah: New Perspectives* (New Haven, CT: Yale University Press, 1988), p. 121.

18 Peter Harrison, *The Fall of Man and the Foundations of Science* (Cambridge: Cambridge University Press, 2007).

19 I borrow "dual-aspect" from the title of a conference organized by Gregory Shaw, "Esoteric Anatomies and Dual Aspect Soul," held at the Center for Theory and Research, Esalen Institute, California, in April 2015.

20 Even three or more selves—see Sorabji, *Self*, pp. 118–19.

21 Brian P. Copenhaver, *Hermetica: The Greek Corpus Hermeticum and the Latin Asclepius in a New English Translation, with Notes and Introduction* (Cambridge: Cambridge University Press, 1992), p. 3 [Book 1.15].

22 e.g., Henry Corbin, *The Man of Light in Iranian Sufism* (Boulder, CO: Shambhala, 1978), p. 14.

23 April D. DeConick, "What is Early Jewish and Christian Mysticism?" in *Paradise Now: Essays on Early Jewish and Christian Mysticism*, ed. by April D. DeConick (Atlanta: Society of Biblical Literature, 2006), pp. 1–24.

24 Berthold Heinecke, "The Mysticism and Science of Johann Baptista van Helmont (1579–1644)," *Ambix*, 42.2 (1995), 65–78 (pp. 68–69).

25 Walter Pagel, *Joan Baptista van Helmont: Reformer of Science and Medicine* (Cambridge: Cambridge University Press, 1982), pp. 22–33.

26 Jean Baptiste van Helmont, *Oriatrike, or, Physick Refined*, trans. by John Chandler (London: Lodowick Loyd, 1662), p. 25.

27 Reiner Schürmann, *Meister Eckhart: Mystic and Philosopher* (Bloomington: Indiana University Press, 1978).

28 DeConick, p. 22.

29 On the "two souls" doctrine, see R. Ferwerda, "Two Souls: Origen's and Augustine's Attitude Toward the Two Souls Doctrine. Its Place in Greek and Christian Philosophy," *Vigiliae Christianae*, 37 (1983), 360–78; also Benjamin P. Blosser, *Become Like the Angels: Origen's Doctrine of the Soul* (Washington, DC: Catholic University of America Press, 2012). Blosser calls the morally dualistic view the "conflict model," contrasting it with the "hierarchical model," which distinguishes between metaphysical levels, not moral natures. There is, of course, potential for a moral disjuncture between higher and lower soul-levels, but in the hierarchical scheme the lower soul is not by nature morally evil, even if it is rather easily misled.

30 Bentley Layton, *The Gnostic Scriptures: A New Translation with Annotations and Introductions* (London: SCM Press, 1987), p. 359.

31 My summary here draws freely on both the Greek and Syriac versions, which are not exactly the same. English translations from the Greek include Layton, pp. 366–75, and J. K. Elliott, *The Apocryphal New Testament* (Oxford: Oxford University Press, 2005), pp. 488–91. English translations from the Syriac include A. F. J. Klijn, *The Acts of Thomas: Introduction, Text, and Commentary*, 2nd rev. edn (Leiden: Brill, 2003), pp. 182–87, based on W. Wright, *Apocryphal Acts of the Apostles*, 2 vols (London: Williams and Norgate, 1871), II, 238–45. For English translations of both the Syriac and Greek texts, with the originals, see Johan Ferreira, *The Hymn of the Pearl: The Syriac and Greek Texts with Introduction, Translation, and Notes* (Sydney: St Pauls Publications, 2002).

32 Layton, p. 374. The "single form" is the "single royal symbolon," that is, the sign of the King. The sign also unites the two attendants who brought the robe to the prince, and so they likewise are two and one.

33 On the problem of interpretation, see Robin Darling Young, "Notes on Divesting and Vesting in *The Hymn of the Pearl*," in *Reading Religions in the Ancient World: Essays Presented to Robert McQueen Grant on his 90th Birthday*, ed. by David E. Aune and Robin Darling Young (Leiden: Brill, 2007), pp. 201–14.

34 Layton, p. 359.

35 April D. DeConick, *Recovering the Original Gospel of Thomas: A History of the Gospel and Its Growth* (London: T. & T. Clark, 2005), p. 215.

36 April D. DeConick, *Seek to See Him: Ascent and Vision Mysticism in the Gospel of Thomas* (Leiden: Brill, 1996), p. 164. In chapter 7, DeConick looks in detail at the background to the idea of a heavenly double, counterpart, or guardian angel.

37 DeConick, *Seek to See Him*, pp. 150–51.

38 DeConick, *Recovering the Original Gospel*, pp. 217–18.

39 Charles Stang suggests that the Thomas literature offered an alternative model of deification to the one that became part of the dominant orthodoxy. See Charles M. Stang, *Our Divine Double* (Cambridge, MA: Harvard University Press, 2016).

40 DeConick, *Recovering the Original Gospel*, pp. 241–42.

41 Corbin, *Man of Light*. On the Kabbalah, see DeConick, *Seek to See Him*, p. 154, drawing on Gershom Scholem's essay "*Tselem*: The concept of the astral body," in Scholem, *On the Mystical Shape of the Godhead: Basic Concepts in the Kabbalah* (New York: Schocken Books, 1991), pp. 251–73.

42 Leo Sweeney brings out this difference in his chapter "Mani's Twin and Plotinus: Questions of 'Self'," in *Neoplatonism and Gnosticism*, ed. by Richard T. Wallis (Albany: State University of New York Press, 1992), pp. 381–424. Sweeney notes the possible anachronism of discussing the higher natures in terms of "self" as nowadays understood.

43 Stang, pp. 178–83.

44 Allen, *Timeless Moment*, p. 31.

45 Allen, p. 187.

46 Ward, *Drug-Taker's Notes*, p. 29.

47 See for example *Living Liberation in Hindu Thought*, ed. by Andrew O. Fort and Patricia Y. Mumme (Albany: State University of New York Press, 1996); Stephen C. Angle, *Sagehood: The Contemporary Significance of Neo-Confucian Philosophy* (New York: Oxford University Press, 2009); Harold Coward, *The Perfectibility of Human Nature in Eastern and Western Thought* (Albany: State University of New York Press, 2012). The Indian holy man Ramaṇa Maharṣi has been regarded as a prime example of living liberation in modern times. See for instance Andrew O. Fort, *Jivanmukti in Transformation: Embodied Liberation in Advaita and Neo-Vedanta* (Albany: State University of New York Press, 1998), pp. 134–51, and Arvind Sharma, "*Jivanmukti* in Neo-Hinduism: The Case of Ramaṇa Maharṣi," *Asian Philosophy*, 15 (2005), 207–20.

48 e.g., Wouter J. Hanegraaff, *New Age Religion and Western Culture: Esotericism in the Mirror of Secular Thought* (Albany: State University of New York Press, 1998); Christopher Partridge, "Truth, Authority and Epistemological Individualism in New Age Thought," in *Handbook of New Age*, ed. by James R. Lewis and Daren Kemp (Leiden: Brill, 2007), pp. 231–54 (pp. 237–43).

49 Jeffrey J. Kripal, *The Serpent's Gift: Gnostic Reflections on the Study of Religion* (Chicago: University of Chicago Press, 2007); *Authors of the Impossible: The Paranormal and the Sacred* (Chicago: University of Chicago Press, 2010); *Mutants and Mystics: Science Fiction, Superhero Comics, and the Paranormal* (Chicago: University of Chicago Press, 2011; *Comparing Religions: Coming to Terms* (Chichester, West Sussex: Wiley Blackwell, 2014); *Secret Body: Erotic and Esoteric Currents in the History of Religions* (Chicago: Chicago University Press, 2017).

50 Bucke, *Cosmic Consciousness*, p. 185.

51 Edward Carpenter, *The Art of Creation: Essays on the Self and Its Powers* (London: George Allen, 1904), p. 253.

52 Carpenter, p. 254.

53 Carpenter, p. 254.

54 Constantina Rhodes Bailly, *Shaiva Devotional Songs of Kashmir: A Translation and Study of Utpaladeva's* Shivastotravali (Albany: State University of New York Press, 1987), p. 57.

55 David Peter Lawrence, *The Teachings of the Odd-Eyed One: A Study and Translation of the Virūpākṣapañcāśikā, with the Commentary of Vidyācakravartin* (Albany: State University of New York Press, 2008), pp. 15-18, 26-28; Gavin Flood, *Body and Cosmology in Kashmir Śaivism* (San Francisco: Mellen Research University Press, 1993), and *The Tantric Body: The Secret Tradition of Hindu Religion* (London: I. B. Tauris, 2006), pp. 146-54.

56 Richard T. Wallis, "ΝΟΥΣ as Experience," ed. by R. Baine Harris, *The Significance of Neoplatonism* (Norfolk, VA: ISNS, 1976), pp. 121-53 (pp. 140-41).

57 Braden, *Private Sea*, pp. 237, 238.

58 Braden, p. 230.

59 Braden, pp. 238-39.

60 Braden, p. 242.

61 Rosalind Heywood, *The Infinite Hive: A Personal Record of Extra-Sensory Experiences* (1964; repr. Harmondsworth, Middx: Penguin, 1978), p. 234.

62 Heywood, pp. 234-35.

63 Heywood, p. 235.

64 Heywood, p. 235.

65 Heywood, p. 236.

66 Heywood, p. 236.

67 Rosalind Heywood, "Mind and Mescalin: A Sceptical 'Guinea-Pig'," *Manchester Guardian*, 29 May 1954, p. 4 (repr. in Zaehner, pp. 208-10 (p. 210)).

68 Copenhaver, p. 41 [Book XI.20].

69 McGinn, *Presence of God: Foundations*, pp. 240-41.

70 Paul Oskar Kristeller, *The Philosophy of Marsilio Ficino* (Gloucester, MA: Peter Smith, 1964), pp. 264, 273. There has been long-running discussion of the comparative worth of knowledge and love on the mystical path, taking off from St. Paul's declaration that a man who knows all but lacks love is nothing (I Corinthians 13). See McGinn, *Presence of God: Foundations*, pp. 71-73 on Paul, pp. 118-27 on Origen, and pp. 257-62 on Augustine.

71 Jacob Boehme, "Of the Supersensual Life," in *The Signature of All Things* (Cambridge: James Clarke, 1969), pp. 225-75 (pp. 240-43).

72 Thomas Traherne, "Of Magnificence" (chap. 31), *Christian Ethicks: Or, Divine Morality Opening the Way to Blessedness, by the Rules of Vertue and Reason* (London: Jonathan Edwin, 1675), pp. 489-512 (pp. 503-04); critical edition: Thomas Traherne, *Christian Ethicks*, ed. by Carol L. Marks and George Robert Guffey (Ithaca, NY: Cornell University Press, 1968), p. 253.

73 "It is only Sin that Crumples up the Soul, which were it freely Spred abroad, would be as Wide and as large as the Univers"—Traherne, *The Kingdom of God*, in *The Works of Thomas Traherne*, ed. by Jan Ross, 9 vols (Cambridge: Brewer, 2005-), I (2005), 253-553 (p. 305) [XI.31-33].

5 Soul Spheres

Epigraph. B. Jowett, *The Dialogues of Plato*, 2nd edn, 5 vols (Oxford: Clarendon Press, 1875), III, 616 [*Timaeus*, 33].

1 Duncan MacDougall, "Hypothesis Concerning Soul Substance Together with Experimental Evidence of Such Substance," *Journal of the American Society for Psychical Research*, 1 (1907), 237-44.

2 Thomas Curtis Van Cleve, *The Emperor Frederick II of Hohenstaufen: Immutator Mundi* (Oxford: Clarendon Press, 1972), pp. 317–18.

3 Debiprasad Chattopadhyaya, *Indian Philosophy: A Popular Introduction*, 3rd edn (New Delhi: People's Publishing House, 1975), pp. 195–98; Dundas, *The Jains*, p. 81.

4 Bernard Carr, "Worlds Apart? Can Psychical Research Bridge the Gulf between Matter and Mind," Presidential Address, 2002, *Proceedings of the Society for Psychical Research*, 59 (2008), 92.

5 Zaleski, *Otherworld Journeys*, pp. 50–52.

6 Sébastien Penmellen Boret, *Japanese Tree Burial: Ecology, Kinship and the Culture of Death* (Abingdon, Oxon: Routledge, 2014), p. 183. See also Wikipedia contributors, "Hitodama," *Wikipedia, The Free Encyclopedia* <http://en.wikipedia.org/w/index. php?title=Hitodama>.

7 Jean Baptiste van Helmont, "The Image of GOD; OR, Helmont's Vision of the Soul, Englished," in *A Ternary of Paradoxes*, trans. by Walter Charleton (London: William Lee, 1650), pp. 121–47 (p. 127).

8 Van Helmont, "The Image of GOD," pp. 127–28. For an alternative translation, see van Helmont, "The Image of God," *Oriatrike*, pp. 714–23 (p. 716). See also "The Authours Confession," *Oriatrike*, pp. 8–11 (p. 9). For the Latin original, see Johanne Baptista van Helmont, *Ortus medicinæ, id est, Initia physicæ inaudita* (Amsterdam: Ludovicum Elzevirium, 1648).

9 Van Helmont, "The Authours Studies," *Oriatrike*, pp. 11–14 (p. 12).

10 John Blofeld, *The Wheel of Life: The Autobiography of a Western Buddhist* (Berkeley, CA: Shambhala, 1972), pp. 149–50. See Raoul Birnbaum, "Light in the Wutai Mountains," in *The Presence of Light: Divine Radiance and Religious Experience*, ed. by Matthew T. Kapstein (Chicago: University of Chicago Press, 2004), pp. 195–226.

11 Ralph Lloyd-Jones, "Coppin, Louisa (1845–1849)," in *Oxford Dictionary of National Biography* (Oxford University Press, 2004) <http://dx.doi.org/10.1093/ref:odnb/58880>.

12 J. Henry Skewes, *Sir John Franklin: The True Secret of the Discovery of His Fate*, 2nd edn with supplement (London: Bemrose, 1890), p. 71.

13 Skewes, pp. 226–43.

14 Skewes, p. 72.

15 Skewes, pp. 71, 73.

16 Skewes, p. 313.

17 R. Lloyd-Jones, "The paranormal Arctic: Lady Franklin, Sophia Cracroft, and Captain and 'Little Weesy' Coppin," *Polar Record*, 37.200 (2001), 27–34. The case was brought to my attention by Shane McCorristine's talk, "Mesmerism and Victorian Arctic Exploration," at the 2011 "Exploring the Extraordinary" conference, York, UK.

18 On fireballs, spectral lights, and related phenomena, including UFOs, see Antony Milne, *Fireballs, Skyquakes and Hums: Probing the Mysteries of Light and Sound* (London: Robert Hale, 2011).

19 For example, "All about orbs," Association for the Scientific Study of Anomalous Phenomena (ASSAP) <http://www.assap.ac.uk/newsite/htmlfiles/Orbs%20centre.html>.

20 Jeffrey J. Kripal, "The Soul Is a UFO," in Whitley Strieber and Jeffrey J. Kripal, *The Supernatural: A New Vision of the Unexplained* (New York: Tarcher/Penguin, 2016), pp. 262–81.

21 David J. Hufford, *The Terror That Comes in the Night: An Experience-Centered Study of Supernatural Assault Traditions* (Philadelphia: University of Pennsylvania Press, 1982).

22 See Roderick Main, *The Rupture of Time: Synchronicity and Jung's Critique of Modern Western Culture* (Hove, East Sussex: Brunner-Routledge, 2004).

23 Kripal, in Strieber and Kripal, p. 312. Apparently Ken Arnold's "spiritual" or "super-natural" interpretation of the sighting dates back to the early years (Kripal, personal communication).

24 Kripal, in Strieber and Kripal, p. 272. For another case of conscious balls of light, see Mark Fox, *Spiritual Encounters with Unusual Light Phenomena: Lightforms* (Cardiff: University of Wales Press, 2008), p. 87: for a week in 1938, a man had been praying regularly when one night, lying in bed awake, he witnessed "several globes of very bright light floating past at the other end of the room." They were "about the size of full moons," and floated through the walls. He was convinced that "they were living, conscious entities, existing on another plane, and apparently not a material one" (RERC No. 002058).

25 Andrew Louth, *Denys the Areopagite* (1989; repr. London: Continuum, 2002), p. 47.

26 Saint John of the Cross, *Living Flame of Love*, trans. and ed. by E. Allison Peers from the critical edn of P. Silverio de Santa Teresa (Garden City, NY: Image Books, 1962), p. 182.

27 Saint John of the Cross, p. 186.

28 Saint John of the Cross, p. 187.

29 Peers, *Complete Works of Saint Teresa of Jesus*, I, 192.

30 For example, James H. Leuba, *The Psychology of Religious Mysticism* (London: Kegan Paul, Trench, Trubner, 1925), pp. 143–45.

31 For an overview, see Kripal, *Comparing Religions*, pp. 177–206.

32 Jenny Wade, *Transcendent Sex: When Lovemaking Opens the Veil* (New York: Paraview Pocket Books, 2004).

33 Penny Sartori, *The Wisdom of Near-Death Experiences: How Understanding NDEs Can Help Us Live More Fully* (London: Watkins, 2014), p. 42.

34 Julian of Norwich, *Revelations of Divine Love*, trans. by Elizabeth Spearing (London: Penguin, 1998), pp. 7, 47.

35 Corbin, *Man of Light*. On the shared interest in photisms in Tibetan Yoga and Kubrā's Sufi order, see Tobi Mayer, "Yogic-Ṣūfī Homologies: The Case of the 'Six Principles' Yoga of Naropa and the Kubrawiyya," *The Muslim World*, 100 (2010), 268–86. This article also raises the "idealist" understanding of the internality of the world in Kubrā and his followers.

36 Tenzin Wangyal, *Wonders of the Natural Mind: The Essence of Dzogchen in the Native Bon Tradition of Tibet* (Barrytown, NY: Station Hill Press, 1993), pp. 10–19.

37 e.g., Wangyal, pp. 169–74; Shardza Tashi Gyaltsen, *Heart Drops of Dharmakaya: Dzogchen Practice of the Bon Tradition*, ed. by Richard Dixey, trans. by Lopon Tenzin Nam-dak (Ithaca, NY: Snow Lion, 1993), pp. 95–103; Padmasambhava, *Natural Liberation: Padmasambhava's Teachings on the Six Bardos*, trans. by B. Alan Wallace (Somerville, MA: Wisdom Publications, 1998), pp. 244–55.

38 For illustrations of *thig le* visions in *thod rgal* practice, see for instance Wangyal, p. 12, and Royal Library of Denmark, "Thod Rgal Kyis Dpe'u Ris (Drawings of Examples of Thögal), Tibet Early 20th Century," Department of Oriental and Judaica Collections, Jt 12, *Treasures in the Royal Library* exhibition, 2003–04 <http://www2.kb.dk/elib/mss/treasures/oja/jt_12.htm> [accessed 16 April 2015].

39 Wangyal, p. 171.

40 Andreas Mavromatis, *Hypnagogia: The Unique State of Consciousness Between Wakeful-ness and Sleep* (London: Routledge, 1987), pp. 78–80.

41 J. D. Lewis-Williams and T. A. Dowson, "The Signs of All Times: Entoptic Phenomena in Upper Palaeolithic Art," *Current Anthropology*, 29 (1988), 201–45.

42 Ronald K. Siegel and Murray E. Jarvik, "Drug-Induced Hallucinations in Animals and Man," in *Hallucinations: Behavior, Experience, and Theory*, ed. by R. K. Siegel and L. J.

West (New York: Wiley, 1975), pp. 81–161; Ronald K. Siegel, "Hallucinations," *Scientific American*, 237.4 (1977), 132–40; Ronald K. Siegel, "The Psychology of Life After Death," *American Psychologist*, 35 (1980), 911–31. See Marshall, "Mystical Experiences as Windows on Reality," pp. 66–67.

43 Sensory deprivation through dark retreats, meditation, flotation tanks, and such like, has a striking medical analogue in the condition known as Charles Bonnet Syndrome (CBS) or "visual release hallucinations": here simple and complex visual imagery is experienced by those who have impaired vision. The auditory equivalent of CBS has been called Musical Ear Syndrome. See for instance Edward F. Kelly and Michael Grosso, "Genius," in Kelly and others, *Irreducible Mind: Toward a Psychology for the 21st Century* (Lanham, MD: Rowman & Littlefield, 2007), pp. 423–93 (pp. 438–39). Instead of labeling CBS mere hallucination, Graham Dunstan Martin sees in it a hint of the immense, even world-creative power of mind—see his book *Does It Matter? The Unsustainable World of the Materialists* (Edinburgh: Floris Books, 2005), pp. 118–19. The syndrome is named after the naturalist Charles Bonnet (1720–1793), who in 1760 first described the condition, reporting experiences set down in great detail by his visually impaired grandfather Charles Lullin. See Dominic H. ffytche, "Visual Hallucinations and the Charles Bonnet Syndrome," *Current Psychiatry Reports*, 7 (2005), 168–79. Bonnet himself experienced the phenomenon as his own eyesight deteriorated.

44 See Marshall, *Mystical Encounters*, pp. 233–40; Kelly and others; Kelly, Crabtree, and Marshall.

45 e.g., Andrew Weeks, *Boehme: An Intellectual Biography of the Seventeenth-Century Philosopher and Mystic* (Albany: State University of New York Press, 1991), pp. 146–49; Julie Hirst, *Jane Leade: Biography of a Seventeenth-Century Mystic* (Aldershot, Hants: Ashgate, 2005), pp. 30–40.

46 Jacob Boehme, *The Forty Questions of the Soul* and *The Clavis*, trans. by John Sparrow (London: Watkins, 1911), p. 110.

47 C. Walton, "Experimental Theosophy.—'Singular Relation,'" *Notes & Queries*, 3rd ser., 4.99 (21 November 1863), 405–07 (p. 405).

48 Walton, p. 406.

49 Raymond A. Moody, *Life After Life* (New York: Bantam, 1975), pp. 47–48.

50 Moody, p. 49.

51 Marie-Louise von Franz, *On Dreams and Death: A Jungian Interpretation* (Chicago: Open Court, 1998), pp. 110–11.

52 C. G. Jung, "On the Nature of the Psyche," in *The Structure and Dynamics of the Psyche*, trans. by R. F. C. Hull, 2nd edn, *The Collected Works of C. G. Jung*, 20 vols (London: Routledge & Kegan Paul), VIII (1969), 159–234 (p. 199).

53 C. G. Jung, "Concerning Mandala Symbolism" and "Appendix: Mandalas," in *The Archetypes and the Collective Unconscious*, trans. by R. F. C. Hull, 2nd edn, *The Collected Works of C. G. Jung*, 20 vols (London: Routledge & Kegan Paul), IX.1 (1968), 355–84, 385–90.

54 Moody, pp. 102–03.

55 Jean Renee Hausheer, "My Unimaginable Journey: A Physician's Near-Death Experience," *Missouri Medicine*, 111 (2014), 180–83 (p. 181) (repr. in *The Science of Near-Death Experiences*, ed. by John C. Hagan III (Columbia: University of Missouri Press, 2017), pp. 49–54).

56 Jurgen Ziewe, *Multidimensional Man: A Voyage of Discovery into the Heart of Creation* ([Raleigh, NC]: [Lulu Press], 2008), pp. 191–211. My thanks to David Lawton for bringing this book to my attention.

57 Ziewe, p. 197.

58 G. S. Kirk, J. E. Raven, and M. Schofield, *The Presocratic Philosophers*, 2nd edn (Cambridge: Cambridge University Press, 1983), p. 427.

59 Dante, *Paradiso*, I, 247.

60 Dante, II, 384-85.

61 *St. Francis of Assisi, Writings and Early Biographies: English Omnibus of the Sources for the Life of St. Francis*, ed. by Marion A. Habig, 3rd rev. edn (London: SPCK, 1979), pp. 655-56.

62 Bernard McGinn, *The Presence of God: A History of Western Christian Mysticism*, II. *The Growth of Mysticism: From Gregory the Great to the Fifth Century* (London: SCM Press, 1995), pp. 71-74.

63 Th. Delforge, "Songe de Scipion et vision de saint Benoit," *Revue Bénédictine*, 69 (1959), 351-54; Pierre Courcelle, "La vision cosmique de saint Benoit," *Revue des études Augustiniennes*, 13 (1967), 97-117.

64 Plutarch, "On the Delays of the Divine Vengeance," in *Moralia*, trans. by Phillip H. De Lacy and Benedict Einarson, Loeb Classical Library, 16 vols (Cambridge, MA: Harvard University Press, 1927-2004), VII (1959), 170-299 (p. 273).

65 Plutarch, "On the Sign of Socrates," in *Moralia*, VII, 362-509. See John Dillon, *The Middle Platonists: A Study of Platonism, 80 B.C. to A.D. 220* (London: Duckworth, 1977), pp. 211-14.

66 Plutarch, "Divine Vengeance," pp. 273, 275.

67 Plutarch, "Sign of Socrates," p. 473.

68 *The Western Fathers: Being the Lives of SS. Martin of Tours, Ambrose, Augustine of Hippo, Honoratus of Arles, and Germanus of Auxerre*, ed. and trans. by F. R. Hoare (London: Sheed & Ward, 1954), p. 52.

69 *Western Fathers*, p. 103.

70 Lati Rinbochay and Jeffrey Hopkins, *Death, Intermediate State and Rebirth in Tibetan Buddhism* (London: Rider, 1979), pp. 53-54.

71 Chökyi Nyima Rinpoche, *The Mirror of Mindfulness: The Cycle of the Bardos*, ed. by Marcia Binder Schmidt, trans. by Erik Pema Kunsang (Hong Kong: Rangjung Yeshe Publications, 1987), p. 38.

72 Lilian Silburn, *Kuṇḍalinī: Energy of the Depths* (Albany: State University of New York Press, 1988), pp. 30-31; Flood, *Tantric Body*, pp. 141, 157-62.

73 Swami Muktananda, *Play of Consciousness: A Spiritual Autobiography*, 4th edn (South Fallsburg, NY: SYDA Foundation, 1994), p. 160.

74 Jorge Luis Borges, *The Book of Imaginary Beings* (London: Penguin, 1974), pp. 21-22.

75 Henry Chadwick, "Origen, Celsus, and the Resurrection of the Body," *Harvard Theological Review*, 41 (1948), 83-102; A. J. Festugière, "De la doctrine 'Origeniste' du corps glorieux sphéroïde," *Revue des sciences philosophiques et théologiques*, 43 (1959), 81-86.

76 Alan Scott, *Origen and the Life of the Stars: A History of an Idea* (Oxford: Clarendon Press, 1991), p. 163.

77 Chadwick, pp. 97-98.

78 Crouzel, pp. 252-53.

79 John Ernest Leonard Oulton and Henry Chadwick, *Alexandrian Christianity: Selected Translations of Clement and Origen with Introductions and Notes*, 2 vols (London: SCM Press, 1954), II, 232.

80 Cicero, *On the Good Life*, trans. by Michael Grant (Harmondsworth, Middx: Penguin, 1971), p. 345. Ciceronian and other classical sources of inspiration can be seen in Gustav Fechner's humorous case for the sphericity of superhuman beings. In his satirical work "The Comparative Anatomy of Angels," published in 1825 under the pen name Dr. Mises,

Fechner raises ingenious arguments to show that the anatomical irregularities of the human form ("countless corners, protuberant gnarls, growths, holes, cavities, etc.") are overcome in developmentally more advanced creatures, such as the eye-like, planet-like, spherical "angels" who orbit close to the Sun, legless, transparent bubble-beings filled with either oxygen (male) or hydrogen (female). The combustive union of the sexes generates sunshine. See Marilyn E. Marshall, "Gustav Fechner, Dr. Mises, and the Comparative Anatomy of Angels," *Journal of the History of the Behavioral Sciences*, 5 (1969), 39–58. For a translation of Fechner's text (from which the above quote is taken), see Gustav Fechner, "The Comparative Anatomy of Angels," trans. by Hildegard Corbet and Marilyn E. Marshall, *Journal of the History of the Behavioral Sciences*, 5 (1969), 135–51. My thanks to Gustavo Rocha and Jeffrey Kripal for reminding me of Fechner's piece, which I first found mentioned in Ellenberger, p. 215.

81 Macrobius, *Commentary on the Dream of Scipio*, trans. by William Harris Stahl (New York: Columbia University Press, 1966), pp. 143–44 [1.14.8].

82 Macrobius, p. 144 [1.14.9–10].

83 Macrobius, *The Saturnalia*, trans. by Percival Vaughan Davies (New York: Columbia University Press, 1969), p. 481 [XII.9.17].

84 Plato, *The Symposium*, trans. by Walter Hamilton (Harmondsworth, Middx: Penguin, 1951), p. 64.

85 e.g., E. R. Dodds, "The Astral Body in Neoplatonism," in Proclus, *The Elements of Theology*, trans. by E. R. Dodds, 2nd edn (Oxford: Clarendon Press, 1963), pp. 313–21; Richard Sorabji, *The Philosophy of the Commentators, 200–600 AD: A Sourcebook*, 3 vols (Ithaca, NY: Cornell University Press, 2005), I, 221–41.

86 *Damascius' Problems and Solutions Concerning First Principles*, trans. by Sara Ahbel-Rappe (Oxford: Oxford University Press, 2010), pp. 30–31.

87 Shaw, *Theurgy and the Soul*, p. 90.

88 In addition to the works by Gregory Shaw already cited, see his "Theurgy and the Platonist's Luminous Body," in *Practicing Gnosis: Ritual, Magic, Theurgy and Liturgy in Nag Hammadi, Manichaean and Other Ancient Literature*, ed. by April DeConick, Gregory Shaw, and John D. Turner (Leiden: Brill, 2013), pp. 537–57. Also Crystal Addey, "In the Light of the Sphere: The Vehicle of the Soul and Subtle-Body Practices in Neoplatonism," in *Religion and the Subtle Body in Asia and the West: Between Mind and Body*, ed. by Geoffrey Samuel and Jay Johnston (Abingdon, Oxon: Routledge, 2013), pp. 149–67.

89 Josiah B. Gould, *The Philosophy of Chrysippus* (Leiden: Brill, 1970), pp. 99–100, 126–37.

90 See Michael Lapidge, "Stoic Cosmology," in *The Stoics*, ed. by John M. Rist (Berkeley and Los Angeles: University of California Press, 1978), pp. 161–87 (p. 182).

91 Niall Rudd, *The Satires of Horace* (Cambridge: Cambridge University Press, 1966), p. 192.

92 Marcus Aurelius, *Meditations* (Harmondsworth, Middx: Penguin, 1964), p. 170.

93 Aurelius, p. 130.

94 Aurelius, p. 180.

95 Caesarius of Heisterbach, *The Dialogue on Miracles*, trans. by H. von E. Scott and C. C. Swinton Bland, 2 vols (London: George Routledge, 1929), I, 39–42 [Book I, Chapter 32]. Zaleski (*Otherworld Journeys*, p. 51) notes this exception to the "somatomorphic rule."

96 Caesarius, p. 42.

97 C. G. Jung, *Alchemical Studies*, trans. by R. F. C. Hull, *The Collected Works of C. G. Jung*, 20 vols (London: Routledge & Kegan Paul), XIII (1968) 86, 197–98.

98 Caesarius, pp. 235–37 [Book IV, Chapter 39].

99 Caesarius, p. 235.

100 Caesarius, p. 236.

101 Caesarius, pp. 236–37.

102 For example, Kenneth Ring and Sharon Cooper, "Near-Death and Out-of-Body Experiences in the Blind: A Study of Apparent Eyeless Vision," *Journal of Near-Death Studies*, 16 (1997), 101–47 (p. 139); Jean-Pierre Jourdan, "Near Death Experiences and the 5th Dimensional Spatio-Temporal Perspective," *Journal of Cosmology*, 14 (2011) <http://journalofcosmology.com/Consciousness152.html>. My thanks to Bernard Carr for drawing my attention to Jourdan's work.

103 Xu-Yun, *Empty Cloud: The Autobiography of the Chinese Zen Master, Xu Yun*, ed. by Richard Hunn, trans. by Charles Luk (Shaftesbury, Dorset: Element Books, 1988), pp. 38–39.

104 Paramhansa Yogananda, *Autobiography of a Yogi* (New York: The Philosophical Library, 1946; repr. New Delhi: Sterling, 2007).

105 Yogananda, p. 81.

106 Yogananda, pp. 205–06.

107 Yogananda, pp. 143–44.

108 Walter Leslie Wilmshurst, "The Vision Splendid," in *Contemplations: Being Studies in Christian Mysticism*, rev. and enlarged edn (London: Watkins, 1928), pp. 142–52 (first publ. in *The Seeker*, 9 (1914), 226–38). The account is relatively well known, abridged versions being available in Raynor C. Johnson, *The Imprisoned Splendour* (London: Hodder & Stoughton, 1953), pp. 305–07, and F. C. Happold, *Mysticism: A Study and Anthology*, rev. edn (Harmondsworth, Middx: Penguin, 1970), pp. 136–38. Mircea Eliade comments on it in "Experiences of the Mystic Light," in *The Two and the One*, trans. by J. M. Cohen (London: Harvill Press, 1965), pp. 19–77 (pp. 70–71). W. L. Wilmshurst (1867–1939), solicitor, mystical poet, and noted author of works on Freemasonry, informs the reader that he was given "permission to restate and publish" in his own words the anonymous author's narrative, but it quite possibly describes an experience of his own, given Wilmshurst's later inclusion of it in *Contemplations*, a collection of his own writings. As one reviewer stated, "The account is anonymous, but we are much mistaken if we are to seek far for the authorship"—from "Periodical Literature," *Occult Review*, 19 (March 1914), 174–77 (p. 176).

109 Wilmshurst, p. 146.

110 From the evocative description of the building and its environs, the church can be identified as the twelfth-century Church of St. Michael and All Angels, situated by the River Wharfe at Linton-in-Craven, near Grassington, North Yorkshire. From 1882, Wilmshurst lived in Huddersfield, pursuing a career in law. During his holidays he would explore the countryside, including the Yorkshire Dales, and he was especially fond of Wharfedale—see Antony R. Baker, "W. L. Wilmshurst: His World of Fallen but Living Stones," *Ars Quatuor Coronatorum*, 119 (2006), 40–105 (p. 43).

111 Wilmshurst, p. 147.

112 Wilmshurst, p. 147. The combination of separateness and overlap is reminiscent of the interpenetrating beings in the Plotinian intelligible cosmos, and the author draws on Swedenborg to convey this paradoxical state of affairs: "every angel *is* space in himself, is penetrable by and affords special accommodation to every other angel" (Wilmshurst, p. 148). On Plotinus and Swedenborg, see chapter 6.

113 Wilmshurst, p. 149.

114 Curiously, the term "photosphere" is to be found in an earlier description of penetrative, panoramic vision, although there it refers mainly to the blue, vaporous auras clairvoyantly seen around persons. Nineteenth-century occultism had recognized a luminous form of clairvoyance inducible by hypnosis: Emma Hardinge Britten's *Ghost Land*, which

purports to be the autobiography of a "Chevalier Louis du B.," contains a description of mesmerically induced, out-of-body clairvoyance supported by a luminous mist. "Above and about me, it was discernible as a radiant, sparkling mist, enclosing my form, piercing the walls and ceiling, and permitting my vision to take in an almost illimitable area of space, including the city, fields, plains, mountains, and scenery, together with the firmament above my head"—*Ghost Land; or Researches into the Mysteries of Occultism*, trans. and ed. by Emma Hardinge Britten (Boston: E. H. Britten, 1876), pp. 22–23. At one point (pp. 198–203), a clairvoyant vision of great scope is described, in which innumerable nature spirits are seen to fill the natural world, as well as angelic spirits in the worlds of the sun, which is described as "like an orb of molten gold" (p. 201).

115 Wilmshurst, p. 151.

116 Bucke, *Cosmic Consciousness*, pp. 9–10: "a flame-colored cloud."

117 Albert Farges, *Mystical Phenomena Compared with Their Human and Diabolical Counterfeits*, trans. by S. P. Jacques from the 2nd French edn (London: Burns Oates & Washbourne, 1926), pp. 408–18.

118 Fred Attneave and Paul Farrar, "The Visual World Behind the Head," *American Journal of Psychology*, 90 (1977), 549–63.

119 James H. Austin, *Zen and the Brain: Toward an Understanding of Meditation and Consciousness* (Cambridge, MA: MIT Press, 1998), pp. 470–01, 487–99.

120 Austin, p. 479.

121 e.g., Susan J. Blackmore, *Beyond the Body: An Investigation of Out-of-the-Body Experiences* (London: Heinemann, 1982).

122 On evidence for psi in OBEs, see Emily Williams Kelly, Bruce Greyson, and Edward F. Kelly, "Unusual Experiences Near Death and Related Phenomena," in Kelly and others, pp. 367–421 (pp. 400–03).

123 Jourdan, "Near Death Experiences." See also John Smythies, "Consciousness and Higher Dimensions of Space," *Journal of Consciousness Studies*, 19.11–12 (2012), 224–32. I am unconvinced that mere displacement of vantage point into a higher dimension would yield spherical, penetrative, and multiperspectival perceptions. Consider the Flatland analogue in which the vantage point is lifted from the 2-D plane where it is normally situated to a point in 3-D space above the plane. While ordinarily hidden features of 2-D Flatland will now be perceptible *below* (if there were a mechanism to support such perceptions), the vantage point is no longer *within* the plane and so there is no true spherical and penetrative vision, that is, no looking all *around* oneself *in* the plane and *through* opaque objects, and multiperspectival perception is not explained at all. These types of perceptions, if more than psychological constructions, perhaps fit better into a monadological scheme of the kind to be outlined in chapter 6, for monadic or soul perception will be by its very nature omnidirectional, unimpeded, and multiperspectival.

124 George A. Maloney, *Pseudo-Macarius: The Fifty Spiritual Homilies and the Great Letter* (Mahwah, NJ: Paulist Press, 1992), p. 37 [Homily 1.2].

125 Described in *Vita sanctae Hildegardis*—see Peter Dronke, *Women Writers of the Middle Ages: A Critical Study of Texts from Perpetua (†203) to Marguerite Porete (†1310)* (Cambridge: Cambridge University Press, 1984), p. 145.

126 "Ezeckielis visvm," *Biblia Sacra ex Sebastiani Castalionis postrema recognitione*, trans. by Sébastien Castellion (Basle: Pietro Perna, 1573), p. 1080.

127 Joseph L. Baird, *The Personal Correspondence of Hildegard of Bingen* (New York: Oxford University Press, 2006), pp. 135–41; see also Dronke, pp. 167–69.

128 See Barbara Newman, *Sister of Wisdom: St. Hildegard's Theology of the Feminine* (Berkeley and Los Angeles: University of California Press, 1987), p. 16 n. 15.

129 Dronke, p. 169.

130 Mircea Eliade, *Shamanism: Archaic Techniques of Ecstasy*, trans. by Willard R. Trask (Princeton, NJ: Princeton University Press, 1972), p. 61, quoting from Knud Rasmussen, *Intellecutual Culture of the Iglulik Eskimos*, trans. by W. Worster (Copenhagen: Gyldendalske Boghandel, Nordisk Forlag, 1929), pp. 112, 113.

131 Eliade, pp. 60–61 (Rasmussen, pp. 112–13).

132 Baird, p. 138.

133 Hildegard of Bingen, *Scivias*, trans. by Columbia Hart and Jane Bishop (Mahwah, NJ: Paulist Press, 1990), p. 120 [1.4.16].

134 Hildegard, p. 120 [1.4.16].

135 Hildegard, p. 113 [1.4.4].

136 Hildegard, pp. 113–14 [1.4.5].

137 Hildegard, p. 115 [1.4.8].

138 Hildegard, p. 115 [1.4.8].

139 Hildegard, p. 116 [1.4.9].

140 Hildegard, p. 109, and p. 116 [1.4.9].

141 Hildegard, p. 109, and pp. 119–20 [1.4.16].

142 Hildegard, pp. 67–69 [1.1].

143 Hildegard, p. 309 [III.1].

144 Charles Singer, "The Scientific Views and Visions of Saint Hildegard (1098–1180)," in *Studies in the History and Method of Science*, ed. by Charles Singer (Oxford: Clarendon Press, 1917), pp. 1–58; Charles Singer, "The Visions of Hildegard of Bingen," in *From Magic to Science: Essays on the Scientific Twilight* (London: Ernest Benn, 1928), pp. 199–239.

145 Oliver W. Sacks, "Appendix I: The Visions of Hildegard," in *Migraine*, rev. and expanded edn (Berkeley and Los Angeles: University of California Press, 1992), pp. 299–301.

146 Sabina Flanagan, *Hildegard of Bingen, 1098–1179: A Visionary Life* (London: Routledge, 1989).

147 Singer, "Scientific Views," pp. 51–55, and "Visions of Hildegard," pp. 230–34.

148 Sheryl Haut, "Differentiating Migraine from Epilepsy," *Advanced Studies in Medicine*, 5.6E (2005), 658–65.

149 Sacks, p. 301.

150 Flanagan, p. 208.

151 But see Madeline Caviness, "Artist: 'To See, Hear, and Know All at Once'," in *Voice of the Living Light: Hildegard of Bingen and her World*, ed. by Barbara Newman (Berkeley and Los Angeles: University of California Press, 1998), pp. 110–24. Caviness makes a case for Hildegard's supervision of the miniatures.

152 Edward Healy Thompson, *The Life of the Venerable Anna Maria Taigi, The Roman Matron (1769–1837)* (London: Burns and Oates, 1873), p. 102.

153 Thompson, pp. 224–25.

154 Thompson, p. 240. It seems that St. Joseph of Copertino knew this single glance too: he employed a mirror analogy to express the all-inclusive vision of the ecstatic, as noted by Grosso, p. 121.

155 J.-M. Curicque, *Voix prophétiques, ou, Signes, apparitions et prédictions modernes touchant les grands événements de la Chrétienté au XIXe siècle et vers l'approche de la fin des temps*, 2 vols (Paris: Victor Palmé, 1872), II, 154; Thompson, pp. 229–32.

156 Thompson, pp. 161–02.

157 Thompson, p. 238.

158 On migraine and cortical lesions, see Pari N. Shams and Gordon T. Plant, "Migraine-like Visual Aura Due to Focal Cerebral Lesions: Case Series and Review," *Survey of*

Ophthalmology, 56.2 (2011), 135–61 <https://doi.org/10.1016/j.survophthal.2010.07.005>. It is probably significant that Anna Maria's visions were associated with an eye that was *almost blind*: "nevertheless it was with that eye that she contemplated 'the sun of eternal wisdom,' but natural light had little effect on it except to cause the acutest suffering" (Thompson, p. 161). It is therefore conceivable that Charles Bonnet Syndrome may have contributed to the complex visual images she experienced. See above at n. 43; also Michael N. Block, "An Overview of Visual Hallucinations," *Review of Optometry* (2012) <https://www.reviewofoptometry.com/ce/an-overview-of-hallucinations>.

159 Reproduced from Thompson, frontispiece.

160 Marino Muxfeldt Bianchin and others, "Migraine and Epilepsy: A Focus on Overlapping Clinical, Pathophysiological, Molecular, and Therapeutic Aspects," *Current Pain and Headache Reports*, 14.4 (2010), 276–83 <https://doi.org/10.1007/s11916-010-0121-y>.

161 G. D. Schott, "Exploring the Visual Hallucinations of Migraine Aura: The Tacit Contribution of Illustration," *Brain*, 130 (2007), 1690–1703 <https://doi.org/10.1093/brain/awl348>.

162 On the "homunculus" representation and its limitations, see for example G. D. Schott, "Penfield's Homunculus: A Note on Cerebral Cartography," *Journal of Neurology, Neurosurgery, and Psychiatry*, 56 (1993), 329–33 <http://jnnp.bmj.com/content/56/4/329>, and Claudio Pogliano, "Penfield's *Homunculus* and Other Grotesque Creatures from the *Land of If*," *Nuncius*, 27 (2012), 141–62.

163 Michael A. Rogawaski, "Migraine and Epilepsy—Shared Mechanisms within the Family of Episodic Disorders," in *Jasper's Basic Mechanisms of the Epilepsies*, ed. by Jeffrey L. Noebels and others (Oxford: Oxford University Press, 2012), pp. 930–44.

164 Rudolf Pfister, "Phosphenes and Inner Light Experiences in Medieval Chinese Psychophysical Techniques: An Exploration," in *Concepts and Categories of Emotion in East Asia*, ed. by Giusi Tamburello (Rome: Carroci, 2012), pp. 38–58.

165 On the *!kia* experiences that follow from the boiling of the *n/um* "energy" in dance, see for instance Richard Katz, *Boiling Energy: Community Healing Among the Kalahari Kung* (Cambridge, MA: Harvard University Press, 1984), and the diagram in Edward F. Kelly and Rafael G. Locke, *Altered States of Consciousness and Psi: An Historical Survey and Research Prospectus* (1981; repr. New York: Parapsychology Foundation, 2009), p. 39.

166 Itzhak Bentov, "Micromotion of the Body as a Factor in the Development of the Nervous System," in Lee Sanella, *Kundalini – Psychosis or Transcendence?* (San Francisco: H. S. Dakin, 1976), pp. 71–95; Bentov, *Stalking the Wild Pendulum: On the Mechanics of Consciousness* ([London]: Fontana/Collins, 1978), pp. 171–94.

167 R. H. Elliot, "Migraine and Mysticism," *Postgraduate Medical Journal*, 8 (1932), 449–59 <http://europepmc.org/articles/PMC2532152>; on Blaise Pascal and others, including Hildegard, see Klaus Podoll and Derek Robinson, *Migraine Art: The Migraine Experience from Within* (Berkeley, CA: North Atlantic Books, 2008), pp. 2–14. The Wilmshurst experience could be interpreted similarly, as migraine aura (without headache), although very atypical in many ways, including brevity of development and duration, lasting only a few moments in total. The experience ended with a form of *teleopsia*, the surroundings appearing as if "at a remote distance, as when one looks out upon a scene through a reversed telescope" (Wilmshurst, p. 150). On teleopsia and migraine, see Podoll and Robinson, pp. 252–53. But as I explain in the main text, pathologies (including migraine) do not rule out genuinely transpersonal phenomena and may even facilitate them.

168 James, *Varieties of Religious Experience*, pp. 12–15.

169 G. William Barnard discusses the filter theories of James and Bergson in *Exploring Unseen Worlds: William James and the Philosophy of Mysticism* (Albany: State University of New

York Press, 1997) and *Living Consciousness: The Metaphysical Vision of Henri Bergson* (Albany: State University of New York Press, 2011).

170 Marshall, *Mystical Encounters*, pp. 233–40.

171 See also Marshall, "Mystical Experiences as Windows on Reality," pp. 64–68, including figure 2.1.

172 M. Manford and F. Andermann, "Complex Visual Hallucinations: Clinical and Neuro-biological Insights," *Brain*, 121 (1998), 1819–40.

173 Podoll and Robinson, pp. 214–26.

174 Podoll and Robinson, pp. 220–22; Prabhat K. Chand and Pratima Murthy, "Understanding a Strange Phenomenon: Lilliputian Hallucinations," *German Journal of Psychiatry*, 10 (2007), 21–24 <http://www.gjpsy.uni-goettingen.de/gjp-article-chand.pdf>.

175 See for instance Edward F. Kelly, "Toward a Worldview Grounded in Science and Spirituality," in Kelly, Crabtree, and Marshall, pp. 493–551 (pp. 510–13). On the power of imagination and the English Romantics, see for instance Jonathan Wordsworth, "The Romantic Imagination," in *Companion to Romanticism*, ed. by Duncan Wu (Oxford: Blackwell, 1998), pp. 486–94.

176 I say "less likely" because I am not subject to migraine attacks, and my experience more closely followed the pattern of an altered state of consciousness, especially the near-death experience (chapter 3). It was probably facilitated by the years of deep relaxation and prompted by my reading of Jung at the time, with accompanying resolution to pay attention to my dreams.

177 Alan Soble, *The Structure of Love* (New Haven, CT: Yale University Press, 1990). Soble makes erosic love conditional upon the perceived merits of the beloved, contrasting it with unconditional agapic love.

178 Platonic *erōs* has sometimes been caricatured as selfish desire—for a corrective, see McGinn, *Presence of God: Foundations*, pp. 26–28.

6 THE LOGIC OF UNITY

Epigraph. Jeremiah White, *The Restoration of All Things: Or, A Vindication of the Goodness and Grace of God* (London: N. Cliff and D. Jackson, 1712), p. 147.

1 e.g., M. R. Wright, *Cosmology in Antiquity* (London: Routledge, 1995), pp. 73–74.

2 A. H. Armstrong, *The Architecture of the Intelligible Universe in the Philosophy of Plotinus* (Cambridge: Cambridge University Press, 1940), p. 36.

3 See Hadot, *Philosophy as a Way of Life*, pp. 97–101.

4 See Danuta Shanzer, *A Philosophical and Literary Commentary on Martianus Capella's De Nuptiis Philologiae et Mercurii Book 1* (Berkeley and Los Angeles: University of California Press, 1986), pp. 138–42, 151.

5 On the *plērōma*, see Violet MacDermot, "The Concept of Pleroma in Gnosticism," in *Gnosis and Gnosticism: Papers Read at the Eighth International Conference on Patristic Studies*, ed. by Martin Krause (Leiden: Brill, 1981), pp. 76–81. On the *plērōma* in relation to the Platonic intelligible cosmos, see John Dillon, "Pleroma and Noetic Cosmos," in Wallis, ed., pp. 99–110, and Richard T. Wallis, "Soul and Nous in Plotinus, Numenius and Gnosticism," in Wallis, ed., pp. 461–82.

6 See John H. Sieber, "Zostrianos (NHC VIII,*1*): Introduction," in *Nag Hammadi Codex VIII*, ed. by John H. Sieber (Leiden: Brill, 1991), pp. 7–28 (p. 25).

7 *The Nag Hammadi Library in English*, ed. by James M. Robinson and Richard Smith, 3rd rev. edn (San Francisco: HarperSanFrancisco, 1990), p. 426 [VIII,*1*.115, 116].

8 *Nag Hammadi Library*, p. 416 [VIII,1.48].

9 *Nag Hammadi Library*, p. 58.

10 *Nag Hammadi Library*, p. 68 [1,5.67].

11 *Nag Hammadi Library*, p. 69 [1,5.68].

12 John Peter Kennney, "The Platonism of the Tripartite Tractate (NH I, 5)," in Wallis, ed., pp. 187–206 (pp. 200–02).

13 A. H. Armstrong, "The Apprehension of Divinity in the Self and Cosmos in Plotinus," in R. Baine Harris, pp. 187–98 (pp. 194–97).

14 On the origins and reception of the *Theology*, see chapters by F. W. Zimmermann, Paul B. Fenton, and Jill Kraye in *Pseudo-Aristotle in the Middle Ages: The* Theology *and Other Texts*, ed. by Jill Kraye, Charles B. Schmitt, and W. F. Ryan (London: Warburg Institute, University of London, 1986).

15 *Plotiniana Arabica*, trans. by Geoffrey Lewis, in *Plotini Opera: Tomvs II, Enneades IV–V*, ed. by Paul Henry and Hans-Rudolf Schwyzer (Paris: Desclée de Brouwer; Brussels: L'Édition Universelle, 1959), p. 385 [*Theologia* x.137]. In Lewis's translation, italics indicate text that is a fairly close paraphrase of the Plotinian original, while roman lettering indicates short deviations (and small lettering longer additions).

16 Farīdu'd-Dīn ʿAṭṭār, *The Speech of the Birds:* Manṭiqu't-Ṭair, trans. by Peter Avery (Cambridge: Islamic Texts Society, 1998), p. 378.

17 Henry Corbin, *Avicenna and the Visionary Recital*, trans. by Willard R. Trask (New York: Pantheon Books, 1960), pp. 201–02.

18 RERC No. 001284, in Maxwell and Tschudin, p. 48.

19 White, p. 147. On the Christian Neoplatonic theological background to this passage, see D. P. Walker, *The Decline of Hell: Seventeenth-Century Discussions of Eternal Torment* (London: Routledge & Kegan Paul, 1964), pp. 109–10. On the idea that the soul is wholly present in every part of the body, see Marshall, *Living Mirror*, pp. 166, 281–82.

20 This is Stephen MacKenna's translation: Plotinus, *The Enneads*, trans. by Stephen MacKenna, abridged edn (London: Penguin, 1991), p. 461.

21 e.g., Richard T. Wallis, *Neoplatonism*, 2nd edn (London: Bristol Classical Press, Duckworth, 1995), pp. 54–55.

22 Edward Carpenter, *Art of Creation*, p. 68.

23 Philip Merlan, *Monopsychism, Mysticism, Metaconsciousness: Probems of the Soul in the Neoaristotelian and Neoplatonic Tradition* (The Hague: Martinus Nijhoff, 1963), pp. 54–55.

24 Proclus, *Elements*, pp. 254, 346.

25 E. R. Dodds, "Numenius and Ammonius," in *Les Sources de Plotin* (Geneva: Fondation Hardt, 1960), pp. 3–61 (pp. 22–23); Paul Henry, "The Place of Plotinus in the History of Thought," in Plotinus, *The Enneads*, trans. by MacKenna, pp. xlii–lxxiii (pp. lxxi–lxxii).

26 See Dodds's note to Proclus's Proposition 103, in Proclus, *Elements*, p. 254; also Wallis, *Neoplatonism*, pp. 123–24.

27 Marshall, "Why We Are Conscious of So Little," pp. 388–89. It has been debated whether Leibniz's metaphysics is idealist and if so at what point in his philosophical career it became idealist, and whether the monadology retains aspects of Leibniz's earlier, Aristotelian understanding of the organism as a union of form and matter. If it does, the monad is a "substantial form" that in union with matter constitutes a "composite," "compound," or "corporeal" substance. See for instance Brandon C. Look, "Leibniz's Metaphysics and Metametaphysics: Idealism, Realism and the Nature of Substance," *Philosophy Compass*, 5 (2010), 871–79.

28 A. N. Whitehead, *Adventures of Ideas* (Cambridge: Cambridge University Press, 1933; repr. 1961), p. 136.

29 Leibniz contrasts "confusion" with "distinctness," and "obscurity" with "clearness." For simplicity, I shall ignore the subtleties and employ just the first pair of terms. See C. D. Broad, *Leibniz: An Introduction*, ed. by C. Lewy (Cambridge: Cambridge University Press, 1975; repr. 1979), pp. 135–36.

30 e.g., Philip C. Almond, *Adam and Eve in Seventeenth-Century Thought* (Cambridge: Cambridge University Press, 1999), pp. 60–64.

31 On Leibniz's supposed mystical experience, see Daniel J. Cook, "Leibniz on Enthusiasm," in *Leibniz, Mysticism and Religion*, ed. by Allison P. Coudert, Richard H. Popkin, and Gordon M. Weiner (Dordrecht: Kluwer, 1998), pp. 107–35 (p. 119).

32 Catherine Wilson, *Leibniz's Metaphysics: A Historical and Comparative Study* (Manchester: Manchester University Press, 1989), pp. 186–87.

33 G. W. Leibniz, "Principles of Nature and Grace, based on Reason," in G. W. Leibniz, *Philosophical Texts*, trans. and ed. by R. S. Woolhouse and Richard Francks (Oxford: Oxford University Press, 1998), p. 264 [§13].

34 Nicholas Rescher, *G. W. Leibniz's Monadology: An Edition for Students* (London: Routledge, 1991), p. 212 [*Monadology* §61].

35 See Marshall, *Mystical Encounters*, pp. 213–14.

36 Ramjee Singh, *The Jaina Concept of Omniscience* (Ahmedabad: L. D. Institute of Indology, 1974); Padmanabh S. Jaini, *The Jaina Path of Purification* (Delhi: Motilal Banarsidass, 1979), pp. 266–67; K. P. Sinha, *The Philosophy of Jainism* (Calcutta: Punthi Pustak, 1990), pp. 6–7, 130–44.

37 Rescher, pp. 209, 210 [*Monadology* §60]. See also Leibniz's *Theodicy*, §403.

38 Rescher, pp. 275, 276 [*Monadology* §83; *Theodicy* §147].

39 Rescher, pp. 209, 216 [*Mondadology* §§60, 62].

40 See Marshall, "Why We Are Conscious of So Little." For a more frugal but still panpsychic explanation of mystical perceptions of the natural world, see Anthony N. Perovich, "Taking Nature Mysticism Seriously: Marshall and the Metaphysics of the Self," *Religious Studies*, 47 (2011), 165–83.

41 Marshall, "Why We Are Conscious of So Little," p. 404.

42 Rescher, pp. 91–92 [*Monadology* §19].

43 Rescher, p. 94 [*Monadology* §21].

44 For overviews of approaches to the mind–body problem, see for instance Max Velmans, *Understanding Consciousness*, 2nd edn (Hove, East Sussex: Routledge, 2009), and Matthew Colborn, *Pluralism and the Mind: Consciousness, Worldviews and the Limits of Science* (Exeter, Devon: Imprint Academic, 2011), pp. 69–86. Idealism has often been omitted or poorly served by introductory works on the philosophy of mind, but an exception is Stephen Priest's *Theories of Mind* (London: Penguin, 1991). See also my overview in *Mystical Encounters*, pp. 240–57.

45 For a classic discussion of the distinction between qualities in early modern science, see E. A. Burtt, *The Metaphysical Foundations of Modern Physical Science: A Historical and Critical Essay*, 2nd rev. edn (1932; repr. London: Routledge & Kegan Paul, 1972). For my observations on the distinction, see Marshall, *The Living Mirror*, pp. 34–47, and "Transforming the World into Experience."

46 For an introduction to the visual system and the other senses, see David E. Presti, *Foundational Concepts in Neuroscience: A Brain–Mind Odyssey* (New York: Norton, 2016).

47 On "single-cell" or "single-neuron" theories of consciousness, see Jonathan C. W. Edwards, "Is Consciousness Only a Property of Individual Cells?" *Journal of Consciousness Studies*, 12.4–5 (2005), 60–76, and *How Many People Are There In My Head? And In Hers? An Exploration of Single Cell Consciousness* (Exeter, Devon: Imprint Academic,

2006); Steven Sevush, "Single-Neuron Theory of Consciousness," *Journal of Theoretical Biology*, 238 (2006), 704-25, and *The Single-Neuron Theory: Closing In on the Neural Correlate of Consciousness* (Switzerland: Palgrave Macmillan, Springer Nature, 2016).

48 See chapter 5, "Souls occupy a spherical container, body, or vehicle."

49 On the current state of research, see *Parapsychology: A Handbook for the 21st Century*, ed. by Etzel Cardeña, John Palmer, and David Marcusson-Clavertz (Jefferson, NC: McFarland, 2015). See also Imants Barušs and Julia Mossbridge, *Transcendent Mind: Rethinking the Science of Consciousness* (Washington, DC: American Psychological Association, 2017), Dean Radin's various books, beginning with *The Conscious Universe: The Scientific Truth of Psychic Phenomena* (New York: HarperEdge, 1997), and Charles T. Tart, *The End of Materialism: How Evidence of the Paranormal Is Bringing Science and Spirit Together* (Oakland, CA: New Harbinger Publications, 2009). For an annotated, introductory bibliography of psychical research, see Kelly and others, pp. 645-55.

50 Marshall, "Why We Are Conscious of So Little." On psi, mystical experience, and filters, see also Marshall, "The Psychical and the Mystical."

51 Rescher, p. 51 [*Monadology* §3].

52 *Plotiniana Arabica*, p. 387 [*Theologia* x.143].

53 Dundas, *The Jains*, pp. 77-80; Jaini, *Jaina Path*, pp. 127-30.

54 Dundas, pp. 37-38; Jaini, pp. 270-71.

55 Jaini, pp. 114-15; Kristi L. Wiley, "Colors of the Soul: By-Products of Activity or Passions?" *Philosophy East and West*, 50 (2000), 348-66.

56 Scholem, *On the Mystical Shape*, p. 45.

57 Scholem, pp. 228-32.

58 Emanuel Swedenborg, *Heaven and Its Wonders, and Hell: From Things Heard and Seen* (London: Dent, 1909), p. 27 [§62].

59 Signe Toksvig, *Emanuel Swedenborg: Scientist and Mystic* (New Haven, CT: Yale University Press, 1948), pp. 112-13, 294, 369 n. 3. See also Corbin, *Avicenna*, p. 54. On Swedenborg and the Kabbalah, see for instance Marsha Keith Schuchard, *Why Mrs Blake Cried: William Blake and the Sexual Basis of Spiritual Vision* (London: Century, 2006).

60 Stephen Battersby, "Big Bang Glow Hints at Funnel-Shaped Universe," *New Scientist* (15 April 2004) <https://www.newscientist.com/article/dn4879-big-bang-glow-hints-at-funnel-shaped-universe/>; Ralf Aurich and others, "Hyperbolic Universes with a Horned Topology and the Cosmic Microwave Background Anisotropy," *Classical and Quantum Gravity*, 21 (2004), 4901-26.

61 Jean-Pierre Luminet and others, "Dodecahedral Space Topology as an Explanation for Weak Wide-Angle Temperature Correlations in the Cosmic Microwave Background," *Nature*, 425 (2003), 593-95 <https://doi.org/10.1038/nature01944>; Luminet, "The Shape and Topology of the Universe," arXiv:0802.2236v1 [astro-ph], 15 February 2008 <https://arxiv.org/abs/0802.2236>; Luminet, *The Wraparound Universe*, trans. by Erik Novak (Wellesley, MA: A K Peters, 2008).

62 Luminet, "Shape and Topology," p. 15.

63 In the general theory of relativity, "matter" includes both particles and nongravitational fields (such as electromagnetism), and it is their *mass-energy* that is associated with spacetime curvature, "mass-energy" because of the equivalence of mass and energy in relativistic physics. To be even more precise, the quantity in question is the "stress-energy tensor" in Einstein's field equations, made up of energy, momentum, pressure, and stress.

64 John Archibald Wheeler with Kenneth Ford, *Geons, Black Holes, and Quantum Foam: A Life in Physics* (New York: Norton, 1998), p. 235.

65 *The Leibniz-Clarke Correspondence*, ed. by H. G. Alexander (Manchester: Manchester University Press, 1956); Jeffrey K. McDonough, "Leibniz's Philosophy of Physics," in *The Stanford Encyclopedia of Philosophy*, ed. by Edward N. Zalta, spring 2014 edn <https://plato.stanford.edu/archives/spr2014/entries/leibniz-physics/>.

7 Worlds Within Worlds

Epigraph. *The Flower Ornament Scripture: A Translation of the* Avatamsaka Sutra, trans. by Thomas Cleary, 3 vols (Boston: Shambhala Publications, 1985–87), II (1986), p. 271.

1 The Plotinian cosmic vision perhaps has a modern parallel in Sri Aurobindo's description of the Overmind and its "million Godheads," which may draw in part on his own mystical experiences. See Sri Aurobindo, *The Life Divine* (Pondicherry: Sri Aurobindo Ashram Publication Department, 2005), pp. 294–98 <http://www.sriaurobindoashram.org/ashram/sriauro/writings.php>. My thanks to Sean Kelly for bringing this passage to my attention. Comparative discussions of the philosophies of Plotinus and Aurobindo can be found in *Neoplatonism and Indian Thought*, ed. by R. Baine Harris (Albany: State University of New York Press, 1982), and *Neoplatonism and Indian Philosophy*, ed. by Paulos Mar Gregorios (Albany: State University of New York Press, 2002).

2 e.g., Neal Donner, "Sudden and Gradual Intimately Conjoined: Chih-I's T'ien-t'ai View," in Gregory, pp. 201–26 (p. 207).

3 Timothy Leary, "The Religious Experience: Its Production and Interpretation," *The Psychedelic Review*, 1.3 (1964), 324–46 (p. 332).

4 Courtois, "An Experience of Enlightenment," p. 125.

5 Edward Robinson, *This Time-Bound Ladder: Ten Dialogues on Religious Experience* (Oxford: The Religious Experience Research Unit, 1977), p. 67.

6 Robinson, p. 67.

7 Heywood, *The Infinite Hive*, p. 230.

8 However, Heywood mentions that under the "effect of natural beauty" she once had a similar experience of self-transcendence, restriction, yet partial view from the higher perspective (Robinson, p. 67).

9 Blackmore, *Beyond the Body*, pp. 1–5; Blackmore, "Out-of-the-Body, Explained Away, But It Was So *Real.....*," The Archive of Scientists' Transcendent Experiences (TASTE), Submission No. 00075 (26 January 2001) <http://www.issc-taste.org/arc/dbo.cgi?set=expom&id=00075&ss=1>.

10 Blackmore, "Out-of-the-Body, Explained Away."

11 Blackmore, *Beyond the Body*, p. 4.

12 David Luke, "Disembodied Eyes Revisited: An Investigation into the Ontology of Entheogenic Entity Encounters," *The Entheogen Review*, 17.1 (2008), 1–9 (p. 2) (repr. and ed., with a postscript, in David Luke, *Otherworlds: Psychedelics and Exceptional Human Experience* (London: Muswell Hill Press, 2017), pp. 101–26).

13 Luke, p. 2.

14 Luke, p. 2.

15 Quoted by Luke, p. 4, from Peter Meyer, "Apparent Communication with Discarnate Entities Induced by Dimethyltryptamine (DMT)," in *Psychedelic Monographs & Essays*, ed. by Thomas Lyttle, 6 vols (Boynton Beach, FL: PM & E Publishing Group, 1985–1993), VI (1993), 28–67.

16 Coomaraswamy, "Le corps parsemé d'yeux," in *Coomaraswamy*, I, 371–75 (first publ. in *Zalmoxis*, 2 (1939), 153–55), building on Raffaele Pettazzoni's "Le corps parsemé d'yeux,"

Zalmoxis, 1 (1938), 3–12. Jung also discusses multiple eyes ("polyophthalmia") and, more generally, the experience of multiple luminosities, interpreting them as signs of multiple consciousness in the unconscious ("On the Nature of the Psyche," pp. 190–99).

17 Colin Hannaford, "Ordinary Solutions: The Inspiration of Democracy," Daily Info—Your Guide to Oxford (1997) <http://www.dailyinfo.co.uk/polcaus/Han.html> [accessed 6 March 2005].

18 Hannaford, "Test," *Soldier* (chapter 3), The Institute for Democracy from Mathematics <http://http://www.gardenofdemocracy.org/pt3test.html> [accessed 6 March 2005].

19 Hannaford, "Test."

20 Blackmore, *Beyond the Body*, p. 4.

21 e.g., Mellen-Thomas Benedict, "Through the Light and Beyond," in Bailey and Yates, pp. 39–52. Note also that celestial soul-travel, if it were at all like the transport of ordinary matter, would be limited to the speed of light and involve extreme accelerations necessary to reach distant regions of the universe in a short time, and so would have an unfortunate consequence, namely the differential aging effect commonly discussed in relativistic physics as the "Twin Paradox." The intrepid soul-voyager, having journeyed for only a few minutes by its own measure, might return to Earth to discover that many years had elapsed and that its human body had long since perished.

22 The eagle is often taken to be a solar-hero symbol and its fight with the serpent a contest between "opposites," such as spirit and matter, reason and instinct, conscious and unconscious, evolved and primitive. For a vivid description of an eagle–snake encounter, see P. B. Shelley's *The Revolt of Islam*, Canto 1.

23 There is no mention of a celestial flight through the solar system and galaxies in Eben Alexander's book *Proof of Heaven: A Neurosurgeon's Journey into the Afterlife* (London: Piatkus, 2012). For Alexander's description of his entry into "the Core," see pp. 46–47. A documentary does employ graphics of receding motion through the universe to depict Alexander's travel to the Core: "Is There Life after Death," dir. by Kurt Sayenga, *Through the Wormhole*, season 2, ep. 1 (Science Channel, 8 June 2011) <http://www.imdb.com/title/tt1757576/>.

24 Eben Alexander, "Neurosurgeon Dr. Eben Alexander's Near-Death Experience Defies Medical Model of Consciousness," interviewed by Alex Tsakiris, 22 November 2011 <http://www.skeptiko.com/154-neurosurgeon-dr-eben-alexander-near-death-experience/>.

25 Alexander also perceived orbs just before he transitioned from the Gateway to the Void: high above clouds, there were "flocks of transparent orbs," silvery "shimmering beings" (*Proof of Heaven*, pp. 45–46), which perhaps were responsible for a booming chant he could hear. Alexander conjectures that these lofty, interpenetrating beings may lie behind "our culture's concept of angels" (p. 84). Compare with the angelic choirs of the Wilmshurst account.

26 Alexander, *Proof of Heaven*, pp. 48–49.

27 Eben Alexander, "Neurosurgeon Dr. Eben Alexander's Near-Death Experience"; Mary Montgomery, "Cyberweave: Spirituality and the Internet. A Neurosurgeon's NDE Leads to the Belief that Consciousness is the True Key to Reality," *The Monthly Aspectarian*, 33.6 (February 2012), 47–49 (p. 48) <http://content.yudu.com/Library/A1vlf3/TheMonthlyAspectaria/resources/7.htm>.

28 Mark A. Horton, "My Near Death Experience" <http://www.mindspring.com/~scottr/nde/markh.html> [accessed 20 June 1997]. The account continues to be available on the alt.consciousness.near-death-exp newsgroup: David G. Goggin, "Mark's NDE" (8 October 1996) <https://groups.google.com/forum/#!searchin/alt.consciousness.near-death-exp/horton/alt.consciousness.near-death-exp/tPRXS39Gtok/7vxkVk7_UZgJ>

[accessed 23 August 2017]. On Mark Horton, a founder of the newsgroup and a Linux expert, see Victoria Welch, "Mark Horton Passes Away," in Gary Moore, "Stop the Presses," *Linux Journal*, 32 (1 December 1996) <http://www.linuxjournal.com/article/241> [accessed 21 February 2010].

29 Horton, "My Near Death Experience."

30 Horton, "My Near Death Experience."

31 For another "Russian Doll" experience, see Corazza, p. 91.

32 Jean Houston and Robert E. L. Masters, "The Experimental Induction of Religious-Type Experiences," in *The Highest State of Consciousness*, ed. by John White (Garden City, NY: Anchor Books, 1972), pp. 303–21 (p. 307).

33 Martin Israel, *Precarious Living: The Path to Life* (London: Mowbray, 1982), pp. 28–29.

34 Israel, p. 33.

35 Israel, p. 29.

36 Israel, p. 30.

37 Israel, pp. 30–31.

38 Bernard Roseman, *The Peyote Story*, rev. edn (Hollywood, CA: Wilshire Book Company, 1968), pp. 19–20.

39 Roseman, p. 24.

40 Pearl Hawkins, *Dr Bucke Revisited: Cosmic Consciousness – Quantum Consciousness* (London: Athena Press, 2004), pp. 137–40.

41 Hawkins, p. 138.

42 Hawkins, p. 138.

43 Hawkins, p. 139.

44 Fritjof Capra, *The Tao of Physics: An Exploration of the Parallels between Modern Physics and Eastern Mysticism,* rev. edn (London: Fontana, 1983), p. 328.

45 William Blake, "Letter to Thomas Butts 2 October 1800," in *The Complete Writings of William Blake*, ed. by Geoffrey Keynes (London: Oxford University Press, 1966), pp. 804–06 (p. 804).

46 Marshall, *The Living Mirror*, pp. 286–88.

47 Keynes, p. 431.

48 See for instance *The* Mokṣopāya, Yogavāsiṣṭha *and Related Texts*, ed. by Jürgen Hanneder (Aachen: Shaker Verlag, 2005); Jürgen Hanneder, *Studies on the* Mokṣopāya (Wiesbaden: Harrassowitz, 2006); *Engaged Emancipation: Mind, Morals, and Make-Believe in the* Mokṣopāya (Yogavāsiṣṭha), ed. by Christopher Key Chapple and Arindam Chakrabarti (Albany: State University of New York Press, 2015).

49 *The Yoga-Vasishtha Maharamayana of Valmiki*, trans. by Vihari Lala Mitra, 4 vols (Calcutta: Kahinoor Press, 1891–99), II (1893), p. 6 [III.52.19–20 (*utpatti prakaraṇa*)].

50 *Yoga-Vasishtha*, Mitra, IV (1899), p. 316 [VIb.63.33 (*nirvāṇa prakaraṇa, uttarārdha*)].

51 B. L. Atreya, *The Philosophy of the* Yoga-Vāsiṣṭha: *A Comparative, Critical and Synthetic Survey of the Philosophical Ideas of Vasiṣṭha as Presented in the* Yoga-Vāsiṣṭha-Mahā-Rāmāyaṇa (Adyar, Madras: The Theosophical Publishing House, 1936), pp. 207–08, 555–56.

52 B. L. Atreya, "The Vedanta of the Yogavasishtha," *The Kalyana-Kalpataru or The Bliss*, 3.1 (1936), 230–42 (p. 233).

53 *The Flower Ornament Scripture*, II (1986), 204.

54 On the Buddhist metaphor, see Graham Priest, "The Net of Indra," in *The Moon Points Back*, ed. by Yasuo Deguchi and others (Oxford: Oxford University Press, 2015), pp. 113–27. On the metaphor extended beyond its Buddhist context, see for instance David Loy, "Indra's Postmodern Net," *Philosophy East and West*, 43 (1993), 481–510, and

William Joseph Jackson, *Heaven's Fractal Net: Retrieving Lost Visions in the Humanities* (Bloomington: Indiana University Press, 2004). In relation to Leibniz's monadology, see Ming-wood Liu, "The Harmonious Universe of Fa-Tsang and Leibniz: A Comparative Study," *Philosophy East and West*, 32 (1982), 61–76. Jude Currivan describes a hypnagogic "net of Indra" experience at the age of four, in which she "seemed to be at the center of a vast interconnected and pulsing web of rainbow light, which shimmered in geometrical shapes that repeated and mirrored each other from the smallest to the largest scales," patterns that made up "living forms of light"—see Currivan, *The Cosmic Hologram: In-Formation at the Center of Creation* (Rochester, VT: Inner Traditions, 2017), p. 232. Compare with R. H. Ward's liminal experience of the golden "living geometrical figure" and its aura of meaning "within and within and within"—see chapter 2. Also Rosalind Heywood under mescaline: "that inter-relatedness was symbolized by a delicate spidery web, like the filaments on a cactus, which linked everything to everything from atom to nebula. Not that there were solid objects or solid threads. Nothing was static. The entire Universe was in constant fluid movement" (*The Infinite Hive*, p. 235).

55 *The Flower Ornament Scripture*, III (1987), p. 365.
56 See Williams, *Māhāyana Buddhism*, p. 146.
57 e.g., Williams, pp. 147–48; Dorothy C. Wong, "The Art of Avataṃsaka Buddhism at the Courts of Empress Wu and Emperor Shōmu/Empress Kōmyō," in *Avataṃsaka Buddhism in East Asia: Huayan, Kegon, Flower Ornament Buddhism; Origins and Adaptation of a Visual Culture*, ed. by Robert Gimello, Frédéric Girard, and Imre Hamar (Wiesbaden: Harrassowitz, 2012), pp. 223–60 <http://www.virginia.edu/art/pdf/wong-articles/13.pdf>.
58 I wrote much of this section in the early to mid-1990s, before several of Traherne's manuscripts had been published in their entirety (or indeed had come to light), and I therefore made limited use of the full range of his writings. Moreover, my focus here is rather narrow, on Traherne's spiritual universe and his concept of sole heirdom, and so does not reflect his full range of concerns. For an accessible introduction to Traherne's oeuvre, including the recent manuscript discoveries, see *Happiness and Holiness: Thomas Traherne and His Writings*, ed. by Denise Inge (Norwich, Norfolk: Canterbury Press, 2008). Inge explores Traherne's theology of desire in *Wanting Like a God: Desire and Freedom in Thomas Traherne* (London: SCM Press, 2009). On Traherne in his historical contexts, see *Thomas Traherne and Seventeenth-Century Thought*, ed. by Elizabeth S. Dodd and Cassandra Gorman (Cambridge: Brewer, 2016). For a concise biography, see Julia J. Smith, "Traherne, Thomas (*c*. 1637–1674)," in *Oxford Dictionary of National Biography*, online edn (Oxford: Oxford University Press, 2010) <http://dx.doi.org/10.1093/ref:odnb/38074>.
59 "An Atom is a Physical Monad, or an Indivisible and Tangible Realitie, of No Dimensions parts, or powers, merely passiv, and a Seed of Corporietie"—Traherne, *Kingdom of God*, in Ross, I, p. 342 [XVIII.65–67]. It is possible that Traherne borrowed the term "physical monad" from philosopher Henry More, who came to refer to atoms by this name, distinguishing them from "metaphysical monads" or spiritual substances. See Frances L. Colby, "Thomas Traherne and Henry More," *Modern Language Notes*, 62 (1947), 490–92. On More's atoms, see Jasper Reid, *The Metaphysics of Henry More* (Dordrecht: Springer, 2012), pp. 44–51. For Traherne on atoms, see chapter 18 and the first part of chapter 19 in Traherne, *Kingdom of God*, in Ross, I, pp. 341–50, and "Atom" in Traherne's encyclopedic *Commentaries of Heaven*, in Ross, III (2007), 333–63. Leibniz's monads are "metaphysical points" or "atoms of substance," that is, true, indivisible unities, alive and perceptual; "mathematical points," the points of view from which monads express the universe, are also indivisible; "physical points" or "atoms of matter" are not strictly

points at all, being composed of parts—see Leibniz, "New System," in *Philosophical Texts*, pp. 143–52 (p. 149) [§11].

60 But Traherne's material atoms are unextended and therefore incorporeal, unlike the extended atoms/corpuscles of the early Galileo, Gassendi, Descartes, Boyle, and Newton (and More too). As dimensionless points, Traherne's atoms are more like mathematical atoms, the points or "indivisibles" that had sometimes been posited as constitutive of continua. The atoms of Galileo's later theory of matter were unextended—see for instance Carla Rita Palmerino, "Galileo's and Gassendi's Solutions to the *Rota Aristotelis* Paradox: A Bridge Between Matter and Motion Theories," in *Late Medieval and Early Modern Corpuscular Matter Theories*, ed. by Christoph Lüthy, John E. Murdoch, and William R. Newman (Leiden: Brill, 2001), pp. 381–422, and Susana Gómez, "From a Metaphysical to a Scientific Object: Mechanizing Light in Galilean Science," in *The Mechanization of Natural Philosophy*, ed. by Sophie Roux and Daniel Garber (Dordrecht: Springer, 2012), pp. 191–215. Dimensionless points were characteristic of Islamic atomism and had a significant presence in fourteenth-century European thought, including the ideas of Oxford indivisibilists Henry Harclay and Walter Chatton—see for instance Richard Sorabji, *Time, Creation and the Continuum: Theories in Antiquity and the Early Middle Ages* (London: Duckworth, 1983), and John E. Murdoch, "Infinity and Continuity," in *The Cambridge History of Later Medieval Philosophy: From the Rediscovery of Aristotle to the Disintegration of Scholasticism, 1100–1600*, ed. by Norman Kretzmann, Anthony Kenny, and Jan Pinborg (Cambridge: Cambridge University Press, 1982), pp. 564–91.

61 On Traherne's literary and theological uses of atomism, see Stephen Clucas, "Poetic Atomism in Seventeenth-Century England: Henry More, Thomas Traherne and "Scientific Imagination,"" *Renaissance Studies*, 5 (1991), 327–40, Elizabeth S. Dodd, *Boundless Innocence in Thomas Traherne's Poetic Theology: "Were All Men Wise and Innocent . . ."* (Farnham, Surrey: Ashgate, 2015), pp. 51–52, 169–71, and Cassandra Gorman, "Thomas Traherne and 'Feeling Inside the Atom,'" in Dodd and Gorman, pp. 69–83.

62 Citations to Traherne's *Select Meditations* (abbreviated SM) are to Thomas Traherne, *Select Meditations*, ed. by Julia J. Smith (Manchester: Carcanet Press, 1997).

63 Citations to Traherne's *Centuries* (abbreviated CM) are again to Thomas Traherne, *Centuries of Meditations*, ed. by Bertram Dobell (London: Dobell, 1908).

64 Traherne, "All Things," *Commentaries of Heaven*, in Ross, II (2007), 407–14 (p. 407).

65 "All Things," p. 414: "Heaven surely is a State and not a Place."

66 For background, see Frank Livingstone Huntley, *Bishop Joseph Hall and Protestant Meditation in Seventeenth-Century England: A Study with the Texts of* The Art of Divine Meditation *(1606) and* Occasional Meditations *(1633)* (Binghamton, NY: Center for Medieval & Early Renaissance Studies, 1981); Richard A. McCabe, *Joseph Hall: A Study in Satire and Meditation* (Oxford: Clarendon Press, 1982). For a concise biography of Hall, see Richard A. McCabe, "Hall, Joseph (1574–1656)," in *Oxford Dictionary of National Biography*, online edn (Oxford University Press, 2008) <http://dx.doi.org/10.1093/ref:odnb/11976>.

67 On Protestant heavenly meditation, see Barbara Kiefer Lewalski, *Protestant Poetics and the Seventeenth-Century Religious Lyric* (Princeton, NJ: Princeton University Press, 1979), pp. 165–88 (with special reference to Traherne, pp. 174–76).

68 Joseph Hall, *The Works of the Right Reverend Father in God, Joseph Hall, D.D.*, ed. by Josiah Pratt, 10 vols (London: Williams and Smith, 1808), IV (*Devotional Works*), 447.

69 Hall, p. 479.

70 Hall, p. 505.

71 Hall, p. 481.

72 On English Protestant mediation on the Passion, see Lewalski, pp. 157–58, 166.

73 Traherne, *Inducements to Retirednes*, in Ross, I, 3–43 (pp. 34–35) [ll. 1209–20].

74 e.g., *SM* III.65: "Too much openness and proneness to Speak are my Diseas." See for instance Anne Ridler, "The Essential Traherne," in *Profitable Wonders: Aspects of Thomas Traherne*, by A. M. Allchin, Anne Ridler, and Julia Smith (Oxford: Amate Press, 1989), pp. 9–21 (p. 11).

75 Traherne, "Nature," in Ross, VI (2014), 31–33 (p. 32) [l. 19].

76 Traherne, "My Spirit," in Ross, VI, 26–30 (p. 29) [ll. 110–17].

77 Traherne, "Misapprehension," in Ross, VI, 135–36 (p. 136) [l. 62].

78 For a metaphorical reading of Traherne's declarations of all-encompassing soulhood, see Harold Skulsky, *Language Recreated: Seventeenth-Century Metaphorists and the Act of Metaphor* (Athens: University of Georgia Press, 1992), pp. 87–93. Skulsky maintains that Traherne's seemingly metaphysical claims about the interiority of the world in the soul are just figurative: Traherne merely glorifies the wonder that is *ordinary, human representational thought*, which is able to frame ideas about all manner of things. While Skulsky's interpretation accords with Traherne's depiction of "thought" as ranging far and wide, it does not explain why Traherne would use such rapturous language to convey a somewhat banal observation, and it ignores his personal attestations to a *higher* level of cognition at which the soul can operate. It is not ordinary, discursive thought that holds the universe within, all things, all ages, all places, but the "Secret self" or "Immortal Soul," with its "Endless Comprehension," as Traherne was astonished to discover when he first glimpsed the divine Image. It seems that Traherne experienced a highly noetic, mystical expansion of some kind, perhaps an all-encompassing "cosmic consciousness."

79 Traherne, "Of Magnanimity" (chap. 28), *Christian Ethicks*, pp. 440–63 (pp. 444–47) (Marks and Guffey, pp. 226–27); *Kingdom of God* (chap. 37, "Of the Nature of Spirits"), in Ross, I, pp. 463–65. On Traherne and the Hermetica, see Carol L. Marks, "Thomas Traherne and Hermes Trismegistus," *Renaissance News*, 19 (1966), 118–31.

80 e.g., *CM* II.70: "The Ocean is but the drop of a bucket to it, the Heavens but a centre, the Sun obscurity, and all Ages but as one day."

81 Traherne, "Of Magnanimity," p. 442 (Marks and Guffey, p. 225).

82 Leibniz, "New System," in *Philosophical Texts*, pp. 143–52 (p. 150) [§14]. See also Leibniz, "Discourse on Metaphysics," in *Philosophical Texts*, pp. 53–93 (p. 84–85) [§32].

83 On Leibniz and solipsism, see for instance Fabrizio Mondadori, "Solipsistic Perception in a World of Monads," in *Leibniz: Critical and Interpretative Essays*, ed. by Michael Hooker (Manchester: Manchester University Press, 1982), pp. 21–44; Robert McRae, "As Though Only God and It Existed in the World," in Hooker, pp. 79–89; Jonathan Westphal, "Leibniz and the Problem of Other Minds," *Studia Leibnitiana*, 33 (2001), 206–15.

84 Traherne, *Church's Year-Book*, quoted in Carol L. Marks, "Traherne's Church's Year-Book," *The Papers of the Bibliographic Society of America*, 60 (1966), 31–72 (p. 67).

85 Traherne, "Of Eternal Love" (chap. 7), *Christian Ethicks*, pp. 82–99 (pp. 94–95) (Marks and Guffey, p. 55).

86 See Marshall, *The Living Mirror*, p. 238.

87 Traherne, "Apprehension," *Commentaries of Heaven*, in Ross, III, 169–82 (p. 181).

88 Traherne, "The Delights of Ages," *Commentaries of Heaven*, in Ross, II, 335–53 (p. 341).

89 [Thomas Traherne], *A Serious and Pathetical Contemplation of the Mercies of God* (London: Reverend Doctor Hicks, 1699), p. 128.

90 Traherne, "Of Righteousness" (chap. 10), *Christian Ethicks*, pp. 128–43 (p. 133) (Marks and Guffey, p. 73).

91 Traherne, "My Spirit," in Ross, VI, 29 [l. 114].

92 Traherne, "The Preparative," in Ross, VI, 11–13 (p. 11) [ll. 14, 17, 18]. On the eye, see Lewalski, pp. 208–09, 379–82.
93 Traherne "Dumnesse," in Ross, VI, 22–24 (p. 23) [l. 61].
94 Traherne, "In thy Presence (Thoughts. IV)," in Ross, VI, 73–75 (p. 75) [ll. 91–94].
95 Traherne, "My Spirit," in Ross, VI, 29 [ll. 100–02].
96 Traherne, "Of Eternal Love" (pp. 94–95) (Marks and Guffey, p. 55). The phrase "without Confusion, or Diminution" has a Plotinian ring, suggestive of the intellects of the intelligible cosmos (see chapter 6), but Traherne's all-encompassing souls, following the Hermetic example of self-expansion, include our everyday universe. On Traherne and Platonism, see Carol L. Marks, "Thomas Traherne and Cambridge Platonism," *PMLA*, 81 (1966), 521–34, and Sarah Hutton, "Platonism in Some Metaphysical Poets: Marvell, Vaughan and Traherne," in *Platonism and the English Imagination*, ed. by Anna Baldwin and Sarah Hutton (Cambridge: Cambridge University Press, 1994), pp. 163–77.
97 Kristeller, *Philosophy of Marsilio Ficino*, pp. 262, 268.
98 According to Plutarch, Alexander wept because he had not even conquered *one* world, never mind an infinite number: "Alexander wept when he heard Anaxarchus discourse about an infinite number of worlds, and when his friends inquired what ailed him, 'Is it not worthy of tears,' he said, 'that, when the number of worlds is infinite, we have not yet become lords of a single one?'" Plutarch, "On Tranquility of Mind," trans. by W. C. Helmbold, in *Moralia*, Loeb Classical Library, 16 vols (Cambridge, MA: Harvard University Press, 1927–2004), VI (1939), 163–241 (pp. 177, 179) [466D].

8 The Physics of Experience

Epigraph. Bertrand Russell, *The Analysis of Matter* (London: Kegan Paul, Trench, Trubner, 1927), p. 159.
1 So said Robert E. L. Masters and Jean Houston of psychedelic experience—see *The Varieties of Psychedelic Experience*, 2nd British edn (London: Turnstone Books, 1973), pp. 303–06. I discuss in detail the "constructivist" or "radical contextualist" understanding of mystical experience in Marshall, *Mystical Encounters*, pp. 176–97.
2 Stephen Jay Gould, "Nonoverlapping Magisteria," *Natural History*, 106.2 (March 1997), 16–22, 60–62
3 e.g., Ken Wilber, "Physics, Mysticism, and the New Holographic Paradigm," in *The Holographic Paradigm and Other Paradoxes*, ed. by Ken Wilber (Boston: New Science Library, 1982), pp. 157–86; *Quantum Questions: Mystical Writings of the World's Greatest Physicists*, ed. by Ken Wilber (Boston: New Science Library, 1984); Richard H. Jones, *Science and Mysticism: A Comparative Study of Western Natural Science, Theravāda Buddhism, and Advaita Vedānta* (Lewisburg, PA: Bucknell University Press, 1986).
4 I looked into the critical responses to the popular science–mysticism literature in Paul Marshall, "Mysticism and Physics: Completely Unrelated Endeavours or Potential for Constructive Interaction?" (unpublished master's dissertation, Lancaster University, 1997).
5 *Sir Isaac Newton's Mathematical Principles of Natural Philosophy and his System of the World*, trans. by Andrew Motte in 1729, rev. by Florian Cajori, 2 vols (Berkeley and Los Angeles: University of California Press, 1962), II, 547.
6 On Einstein's distinction, see for instance Harvey R. Brown, *Physical Relativity: Space-Time Structure from a Dynamical Perspective* (Oxford: Clarendon Press, 2005), pp. 71–73, and Don A. Howard, "Einstein's Philosophy of Science," in *The Stanford Encyclopedia of*

Philosophy, ed. by Edward N. Zalta, fall 2017 edn <https://plato.stanford.edu/archives/fall2017/entries/einstein-philscience/>.

7 Albert Einstein, "Einstein on his Theory: Time, Space, and Gravitation," *The Times* (London), 28 November 1919, pp. 13–14 (p. 13).

8 Einstein, p. 13.

9 There is, however, a point of contact in Johannes Baptista van Helmont, who influenced both Newton and Leibniz but in rather different ways. On Newton, see William Newman, "The Background to Newton's Chymistry," in *The Cambridge Companion to Newton*, ed. by I. Bernard Cohen and George E. Smith (Cambridge: Cambridge University Press, 2002), pp. 358–69. On Leibniz, see Walter Pagel, "J. B. van Helmont, *De Tempore*, and Biological Time," *Osiris*, 8 (1948), 346–417 (pp. 350–51).

10 Marshall, "Mystical Experience and Metaphysics," p. 3. For Kant's reaction to Leibniz, see Wilson, *Leibniz's Metaphysics*, pp. 314–22.

11 See for instance David Bohm, *The Special Theory of Relativity* (1965; repr. Abingdon, Oxon: Routledge, 2006), pp. 21–50.

12 Albert Einstein, "On the Electrodynamics of Moving Bodies," in *The Principle of Relativity: A Collection of Original Memoirs on the Special and General Theory of Relativity*, by H. A. Lorentz and others, trans. by W. Perrett and G. B. Jeffery (New York: Dover Publications, 1952), pp. 37–65 (pp. 37–38).

13 Hermann Minkowski, "Space and Time," in H. A. Lorentz and others, pp. 75–91 (p. 75).

14 Michel Janssen, "*COI* Stories: Explanation and Evidence in the History of Science," *Perspectives on Science*, 10 (2002), 457–522 (p. 506). For a different viewpoint, see Pablo Acuña, "On the Empirical Equivalence between Special Relativity and Lorentz's Ether Theory," *Studies in History and Philosophy of Science Part B: Studies in History and Philosophy of Modern Physics*, 46 (2014), 283–302.

15 Albert Einstein, "Autobiographical Notes," in *Albert Einstein: Philosopher-Scientist*, ed. by Paul Arthur Schilpp, 3rd edn (La Salle, IL: Open Court, 1969), pp. 1–94 (pp. 51, 53).

16 See Harald Atmanspacher, "Quantum Approaches to Consciousness," *The Stanford Encyclopedia of Philosophy*, ed. by Edward N. Zalta, summer 2015 edn <https://plato.stanford.edu/archives/sum2015/entries/qt-consciousness/>; Henry P. Stapp, *Mind, Matter and Quantum Mechanics*, 3rd edn (Berlin: Springer, 2009); Henry P. Stapp, *Mindful Universe: Quantum Mechanics and the Participating Observer*, 2nd edn (Berlin: Springer, 2011).

17 David Bohm, *Wholeness and the Implicate Order* (London: Routledge & Kegan Paul, 1980); David Bohm and B. J. Hiley, *The Undivided Universe: An Ontological Interpretation of Quantum Theory* (London: Routledge, 1993); F. David Peat, *Infinite Potential: The Life and Times of David Bohm* (Reading, MA: Addison-Wesley, 1997); Paavo T. I. Pylkkänen, *Mind, Matter and the Implicate Order* (Berlin: Springer, 2007).

18 John G. Cramer, "The Transactional Interpretation of Quantum Mechanics," *Review of Modern Physics*, 58 (1986), 647–87; Ruth E. Kastner, *The Transactional Interpretation of Quantum Mechanics: The Reality of Possibility* (Cambridge: Cambridge University Press, 2013). For a "popular science" introduction, see John Gribbin, *Schrödinger's Kittens and the Search for Reality* (London: Phoenix, 1996), pp. 233–47.

19 Einstein, quoted by John Stachel in *Einstein's Miraculous Year: Five Papers That Changed the Face of Physics*, ed. by John Stachel (Princeton, NJ: Princeton University Press, 1998), pp. 19–20.

20 On Einstein's search for a constructive theory of the quantum, see John Stachel, "Einstein and Quantum Mechanics," in *Conceptual Problems of Quantum Gravity*, ed. by Abhay Ashtekar and John Stachel (Boston: Birkhäuser, 1991), pp. 13–42.

21 See Harvey R. Brown and Oliver Pooley, "Minkowski Space-Time: A Glorious Non-Entity," in *The Ontology of Spacetime*, ed. by Dennis Dieks (Amsterdam: Elsevier, 2006), pp. 67–89.

22 Marshall, *The Living Mirror*, pp. 218–19.

23 H. Wildon Carr, *The General Principle of Relativity in its Philosophical and Historical Aspect* (London: Macmillan, 1920), p. 118.

24 H. Wildon Carr, *A Theory of Monads: Outlines of the Philosophy of the Principle of Relativity* (London: Macmillan, 1922), p. 347.

25 H. Wildon Carr, "The Reform of the Leibnizian Monadology," *Journal of Philosophy*, 23.3 (1926), 68–77 (p. 75).

26 Carr, "Reform," pp. 73–75.

27 As fellow members of the Aristotelian Society, Whitehead and Carr were in a good position to engage with each other's ideas. See for instance H. Wildon Carr, "Discussion: The Idealistic Interpretation of Einstein's Theory," *Proceedings of the Aristotelian Society*, New Series, 22 (1921–22), 123–38, in which Whitehead challenges Carr's association of the theory of relativity specifically with idealist metaphysics. Pierfrancesco Basile observes that Carr "must have been an important interlocutor for Whitehead," given their shared philosophical concerns—Basile, "Herbert Wildon Carr (1857–1931)," in *Handbook of Whiteheadian Process Thought*, ed. by Michel Weber and Will Desmond, 2 vols (Frankfurt: Ontos, 2008), II, 383–87.

28 e.g., *Physics and Whitehead: Quantum, Process, and Experience*, ed. by Timothy E. Eastman and Hank Keeton (Albany: State University of New York Press, 2003); Michael Epperson, *Quantum Mechanics and the Philosophy of Alfred North Whitehead* (New York: Fordham University Press, 2004).

29 For comparisons, see A. H. Johnson, "Leibniz and Whitehead," *Philosophy and Phenomenological Research*, 19 (1959), 285–305; Charles Hartshorne, "Whitehead and Leibniz: A Comparison," in *Contemporary Studies in Philosophical Idealism*, ed. by John Howie and Thomas O. Buford (Cape Cod, MA: Claude Starke, 1975), pp. 95–115; Timothy Mooney, "Whitehead and Leibniz: Conflict and Convergence," *Philosophical Studies*, 32 (1988–90), 197–212.

30 Alfred North Whitehead, *Process and Reality: An Essay in Cosmology*, ed. by David Ray Griffin and Donald W. Sherburne, corrected edn (New York: Free Press, 1985), p. 41.

31 Steve Odin, *Process Metaphysics and Hua-Yen Buddhism: A Critical Study of Cumulative Penetration vs. Interpenetration* (Albany: State University of New York Press, 1982).

32 For detailed discussion, see Pierfrancesco Basile's *Leibniz, Whitehead and the Metaphysics of Causation* (Basingstoke, Hants: Palgrave Macmillan, 2009), and his "Learning from Leibniz: Whitehead (and Russell) on Mind, Matter and Monads," *British Journal for the History of Philosophy*, 23 (2015), 1128–49.

33 David Ray Griffin, "Parapsychology and Philosophy: A Whiteheadian Postmodern Perspective," *Journal of the American Society for Psychical Research*, 87 (1993), 217–88. See Kelly, "Toward a Worldview," p. 527.

34 Recent monadological speculations include several articles in *NeuroQuantology*, 4.3 (2006) <https://www.neuroquantology.com/index.php/journal/issue/view/15/show-Toc>: David M. Harrison, "Quarks, Bootstraps and Monads," pp. 252–62 <http://dx.doi.org/10.14704/nq.2006.4.3.101>; Gordon Globus, "The Saltatory Sheaf-Odyssey of a Monadologist," pp. 210–21 <http://dx.doi.org/10.14704/nq.2006.4.3.103>; Teruaki Nakagomi, "Picture of the World as a Quantum Monadistic System," pp. 241–48 <http://dx.doi.org/10.14704/nq.2006.4.3.106>. Nakagomi's first article on the subject was "Quantum Monadology: A World Model to Interpret Quantum Mechanics and Relativity," *Open*

Systems & Information Dynamics, 1 (1992), 355–78. See also George Gale, "Chew's Monadology," *Journal of the History of Ideas*, 35 (1974), 339–48.

35 Lee Smolin, "Space and Time in the Quantum Universe," in *Conceptual Problems of Quantum Gravity*, ed. by Abhay Ashtekar and John Stachel (Boston: Birkhäuser, 1991), pp. 228–91; Julian Barbour and Lee Smolin, "Extremal Variety as the Foundation of a Cosmological Quantum Theory," arXiv:hep-Th/9203041v1, 1992 <http://arxiv.org/abs/hep-th/9203041>.

36 J. B. Barbour, "On the Origin of Structure in the Universe," in *Philosophy, Mathematics and Modern Physics: A Dialogue*, ed. by Enno Rudolph and Ion-Olimpiu Stamatescu (Berlin: Springer, 1994), pp. 120–31; Julian Barbour, "The Deep and Suggestive Principles of Leibnizian Philosophy," *Harvard Review of Philosophy*, 11 (2003), 45–58.

37 Julian Barbour, *The End of Time: The Next Revolution in Physics* (Oxford: Oxford University Press, 1999); Lee Smolin, *Three Roads to Quantum Gravity* (London: Weidenfeld & Nicolson, 2000); Lee Smolin, "The Case for Background Independence," in *The Structural Foundations of Quantum Gravity*, ed. by Dean Rickles, Steven French, and Juha T. Saatsi (Oxford: Oxford University Press, 2006), pp. 196–239.

38 Barbour, "Deep and Suggestive Principles," p. 47.

39 Minkowski, "Space and Time," pp. 79–80.

40 As well as Cramer's transactional interpretation, note for instance Mark Hadley's general relativistic theory described by Marcus Chown in *The Universe Next Door: Twelve Mind-Blowing Ideas from the Cutting Edge of Science* (London: Headline, 2001), pp. 62–81, and Michael Silberstein, W. M. Stuckey, and Michael Cifone's relational blockworld interpretation presented in their "An Argument for 4D Block World from a Geometric Interpretation of Nonrelativistic Quantum Mechanics," in *Relativity and the Dimensionality of the World*, ed. by Vesselin Petkov (Dordrecht: Springer, 2007), pp. 197–216. See also Huw Price, *Time's Arrow and Archimedes' Point: New Directions for the Physics of Time* (Oxford: Oxford University Press, 1996)—my thanks to Chris Nunn for drawing my attention to this book.

41 Marshall, *The Living Mirror*, pp. 309–10.

42 Pylkkänen, *Mind, Matter and the Implicate Order*, pp. 19, 134, 137–38, and "A Quantum Cure for Panphobia," in Seager, *Routledge Handbook of Panpsychism*.

43 See for instance Federico Laudisa and Carlo Rovelli, "Relational Quantum Mechanics," in *The Stanford Encyclopedia of Philosophy*, ed. by Edward N. Zalta, summer 2013 edn <https://plato.stanford.edu/archives/sum2013/entries/qm-relational/>.

44 Gary Hatfield, "Descartes' Physiology and its Relation to his Psychology," in *The Cambridge Companion to Descartes*, ed. by John Cottingham (Cambridge: Cambridge University Press, 1992), pp. 335–70 (p. 355).

45 C. D. Broad, *The Mind and Its Place in Nature* (London: Kegan Paul, Trench, Trubner, 1925), p. 203.

46 e.g., John R. Smythies, *The Walls of Plato's Cave: The Science and Philosophy of (Brain, Consciousness and Perception)* (Aldershot, Hants: Avebury, 1994); Smythies, "Space, Time and Consciousness," *Journal of Consciousness Studies*, 10.3 (2003), 47–56; Smythies, "Brain and Consciousness: The Ghost in the Machines," *Journal of Scientific Exploration*, 23 (2009), 37–50.

47 Bertrand Russell, "The Relation of Sense-Data to Physics," in *Mysticism and Logic, and Other Essays* (London: Longmans, Green, 1918), pp. 145–79 (p. 158).

48 Bertrand Russell, *Our Knowledge of the External World as a Field for Scientific Method in Philosophy* (Chicago: Open Court, 1914), p. 87.

49 Russell, "Relation of Sense-Data to Physics," pp. 149–52.

50 Sajahan Miah, *Russell's Theory of Perception 1905–1919* (London: Continuum, 2006), pp. 140–48.

51 See Carr, "Worlds Apart?" and especially Carr, "Hyperspatial Models of Matter and Mind," in Kelly, Crabtree, and Marshall, pp. 227–73.

52 Russell, *Our Knowledge of the External World*, p. 89.

53 Marshall, *The Living Mirror*, pp. 210–11.

54 e.g., Lisa Randall, *Warped Passages: Unravelling the Universe's Hidden Dimensions* (London: Allen Lane, 2005).

55 Marshall, *The Living Mirror*, p. 266.

9 MEET THE WORLD PARENTS

Epigraph. Clement of Alexandria, *The Writings of Clement of Alexandria*, trans. by William Wilson, 2 vols (Edinburgh: T. & T. Clark, 1867–69), I (1867), 392 [*Stromateis*, 1.60].

1 Leibniz, *Monadology* §47; *Discourse on Metaphysics* §14.

2 e.g., Andrew Weeks, *German Mysticism from Hildegard of Bingen to Ludwig Wittgenstein: A Literary and Intellectual History* (Albany: State University of New York Press, 1993), pp. 215–32; Glenn Alexander Magee, *Hegel and the Hermetic Tradition* (Ithaca, NY: Cornell University Press, 2001).

3 e.g., Peter N. Gregory, "What Happened to the 'Perfect Teaching'? Another Look at Hua-yen Buddhist Hermeneutics," in *Buddhist Hermeneutics*, ed. by Donald S. Lopez, Jr. (Honolulu: University of Hawai'i Press, 1988), pp. 207–30.

4 e.g., Philo of Alexandria, *The Contemplative Life, The Giants, and Selections*, trans. by David Winston (Mahwah, NJ: Paulist Press, 1981), pp. 13–17; Sorabji, *Time, Creation and the Continuum*, pp. 268–75.

5 e.g., Gershom Scholem, *Kabbalah* (New York: Dorset Press, 1987), p. 103; Elliot R. Wolfson, *Alef, Mem, Tau: Kabbalistic Musings on Time, Truth, and Death* (Berkeley and Los Angeles: University of California Press, 2006).

6 John Bussanich, "Plotinus's Metaphysics of the One," in *The Cambridge Companion to Plotinus*, ed. by Lloyd P. Gerson (Cambridge: Cambridge University Press, 1996), pp. 38–65 (p. 62).

7 See John Bussanich, *The One and Its Relation to Intellect in Plotinus* (Leiden: Brill, 1988), pp. 20–27.

8 On the double-activity doctrine, see Eyjólfur Kjalar Emilsson's *Plotinus on Intellect* (Oxford: Clarendon Press, 2007), and more recently his *Plotinus* (Abingdon, Oxon: Routledge, 2017), pp. 48–59. Also Dominic J. O'Meara, *Plotinus: An Introduction to the Enneads* (Oxford: Clarendon Press, 1993), pp. 62–65.

9 Plato, *The Symposium*, 206b–212a.

10 See John J. Davenport, *Will as Commitment and Resolve: An Existential Account of Creativity, Love, Virtue, and Happiness* (New York: Fordham University Press, 2007), pp. 95–96. Davenport stresses that there is more to Platonic erosic ("erosiac") love than attraction to the perceived merits of the beloved. Erosic love is a "need love," dependent on a *felt absence* that appropriation of the beloved's perceived merits promises to fill. It is lack seeking fulfillment.

11 See William J. Carroll, "Plotinus on the Origin of Matter," in *Neoplatonism and Nature: Studies in Plotinus' Enneads*, ed. by Michael F. Wagner (Albany: State University of New York Press, 2002), pp. 179–207; Jean-Marc Narbonne, *Plotinus in Dialogue with the Gnostics* (Leiden: Brill, 2011), pp. 11–53.

12 e.g., A. C. Lloyd, *The Anatomy of Neoplatonism* (Oxford: Clarendon Press, 1990), pp. 169–71, 176–77, and Pierre Hadot, "Neoplatonic Spirituality, Plotinus and Porphyry," in *Classical Mediterranean Spirituality: Egyptian, Greek, Roman*, ed. by A. H. Armstrong (New York: Crossroad, 1986), pp. 230–49 (pp. 242–44).

13 Bussanich, *The One*, pp. 100–01, 176–79, 231–36.

14 Dyczkowski, *Doctrine of Vibration*, pp. 59–68.

15 Dyczkowski, pp. 69–75 (on reflexive awareness, the Goddess, and the mirror in nondual Kashmir Shaivism, see pp. 66–68). On the vibrating light, see Paul Eduardo Muller-Ortega, *The Triadic Heart of Śiva: Kaula Tantricism of Abhinavagupta in the Non-Dual Shaivism of Kashmir* (Albany: State University of New York Press, 1989), pp. 118–19.

16 Muller-Ortega, pp. 95–99.

17 Lawrence, *Teachings of the Odd-Eyed One*, p. 12.

18 Based on Jaideva Singh's "Introduction" to Kṣemarāja, *The Doctrine of Recognition: A Translation of Pratyabhijñāhṛdayam*, trans. by Jaideva Singh (Albany: State University of New York Press, 1990), pp. 3–30 (pp. 6–13).

19 For Abhinavagupta, however, there is "time" (and sequence) above the limited time (*kāla tattva*) of the impure order. This is the divine pulsation *spanda* at the heart of the divine, and, more specifically, the first movement of divine will at the beginning of the creative process (there is sequence too in the unfolding of the pure order from the pure subject of the *Śiva tattva* to the subject–object balance of the *Śuddhavidyā tattva*). My thanks to Loriliai Biernacki for bringing Abhinavagupta's view to my attention—see Biernacki, "Panentheism and Hindu Tantra: Abhinavagupta's Grammatical Cosmology," in *Panentheism across the World's Traditions*, ed. by Loriliai Biernacki and Philip Clayton (New York: Oxford University Press, 2014), pp. 161–76 (pp. 172–74).

20 J. C. Chatterji, *Kashmir Shaivaism* (Albany: State University of New York Press, 1986), p. 22; Deba Brata SenSharma, *The Philosophy of Sādhanā, with Special Reference to the Trika Philosophy of Kashmir* (Albany: State University of New York Press, 1990), p. 32.

21 Chatterji, p. 34.

22 Chatterji, pp. 46–47, 106–07.

23 Muller-Ortega, pp. 101–02.

24 Dyczkowski, p. 55.

25 Muller-Ortega, p. 102.

26 SenSharma, pp. 37–38.

27 On the role of Boehme's mirror-like Virgin in the eternal production, see for instance David Walsh, *The Mysticism of Innerworldly Fulfillment: A Study of Jacob Boehme* (Gainesville: University Presses of Florida, 1983), pp. 74–78, and Weeks, *Boehme*, pp. 121–26.

28 Jacob Boehme, *Concerning the Three Principles of the Divine Essence*, trans. by John Sparrow (London: H. Blunden, 1648), p. 142 [chap. 14, §52].

29 See for instance Caitlín Matthews, *Sophia, Goddess of Wisdom: The Divine Feminine from Black Goddess to World-Soul* (London: Aquarian Press, HarperCollins, 1992).

30 *The Book of Wisdom: An English Translation with Introduction and Commentary*, trans. by Joseph Reider (New York: Harper, 1957), p. 117.

31 I had in my possession M. Minnaert's *The Nature of Light and Color in the Open Air*, trans. by H. M. Kremer-Priest (New York: Dover Publications, 1954), which mentions the Brocken specter in a section on the scattering of light by fog and mist (pp. 257–59).

32 Barbara Watterson, *The Gods of Ancient Egypt* (London: Batsford, 1984), p. 46.

33 See Fung Yu-lan, *A History of Chinese Philosophy*, trans. by Derk Bodde, 2 vols (Princeton, NJ: Princeton University Press, 1983), II, pp. 435–42; Isabelle Robinet, "*Taiji tu*, Diagram

of the Great Ultimate," in *The Encyclopedia of Taoism*, ed. by Fabrizio Pregadio, 2 vols (Abingdon, Oxon: Routledge, 2008), II, 934–36.

34 For detailed comparison of the neo-Confucian and Kabbalistic diagrams, and the question of influence one way or the other, see Martin Zwick, "The Diagram of the Supreme Pole and the Kabbalistic Tree: On the Similarity of Two Symbolic Structures," *Religion East & West*, 9 (2009), 89–109, and "Symbolic Structures as Systems: On the Near Isomorphism of Two Religious Symbols," in *Systems Theory and Theology: The Living Interplay between Science and Religion*, ed. by Markus Locker (Eugene, OR: Pickwick Publications, 2011), pp. 62–96. It is of interest that Zhou Dunyi's diagram of the Supreme Ultimate was reproduced in Rashīd al-Dīn's *Tānsūqnāma*, as part of a Persian translation of a Chinese medical treatise. See Johan Elverskog, *Buddhism and Islam of the Silk Road* (Philadelphia: University of Pennsylvania Press, 2010), p. 160. Rashīd al-Dīn (ca. 1247–1318), Jewish by birth but a convert to Islam, was vizier at the court of the Mongol Ilkhans in Iran and a major figure in the intercultural transmission of knowledge.

35 Wing-tsit Chan, *A Source Book in Chinese Philosophy* (Princeton, NJ: Princeton University Press, 1969), pp. 464–65; Isabelle Robinet, "*wuji* and *taiji*: Ultimateless and Great Ultimate," in *The Encyclopedia of Taoism*, II, 1057–59 (p. 1058).

36 Robinet, "*wuji* and *taiji*," p. 1058.

37 On the threefold and fivefold patterns in Taoist cosmogony and cosmology, see Isabelle Robinet, "Cosmogony, 2. Taoist Notions," in *The Encyclopedia of Taoism*, I, 48–51 (pp. 49–50), and "*sanwu*: Three and Five; 'Three Fives'," in *The Encyclopedia of Taoism*, II, 853–54.

38 See for instance Fung, II, 434–51.

39 See for instance Scholem, *Kabbalah*, pp. 106–07.

40 There is also a Kabbalistic doctrine of three lights ("splendors") from which the first three *sefirot* emanate, a primordial trinity of lights that are one—see Scholem, *Kabbalah*, pp. 95–96.

41 Scholem, *Kabbalah*, p. 108; Moshe Hallamish, *An Introduction to the Kabbalah*, trans. by Ruth Bar-Ilan and Ora Wiskind-Elper (Albany: State University of New York Press, 1999), pp. 139–41.

42 Ramaṇa Maharṣi, "Manifestation of the Self," 12 September 1947, in Suri Nagamma, *Letters from Sri Ramanasramam, Volumes I, II, and Letters from and Recollections of Sri Ramanasramam*, trans. by D. S. Sastri, 5th rev. edn (Tiruvannamalai, Tamil Nadu: Sri Ramanasramam, 2006), pp. 298–301 (p. 299).

43 Ramaṇa Maharṣi, p. 299.

44 Fung, II, p. 447.

45 See Timothy Pettipiece, *Pentadic Redaction in the Manichaean* Kephalaia (Leiden: Brill, 2009).

46 On Manichaean-Buddhist pentadic assimilation, see Samuel N. C. Lieu, *Manichaeism in the Later Roman Empire and Medieval China: A Historical Survey* (Manchester: Manchester University Press, 1985), pp. 208–10.

47 Scholem, *Kabbalah*, pp. 140–44.

48 A. C. Graham, *Disputers of the Tao: Philosophical Argument in Ancient China* (La Salle, IL: Open Court, 1989), pp. 330–01.

49 Kirk, Raven, and Schofield, *Presocratic Philosophers*, p. 319.

50 Guthrie, *History of Greek Philosophy*, pp. 437–54.

51 Note, however, that there is interpretational uncertainty over the bow analogy (and Heraclitus' philosophy of change in general), depending on whether the bow is considered to

be undisturbed or flexed—see Edward Hussey, *The Presocratics* (London: Duckworth, 1972), pp. 43–46. The flexed condition leads to the fertile idea of a backward-acting, restoring force.

52 "Isaac Newton and Jacob Boehme. An Enquiry," in *Selected Mystical Writings of William Law*, ed. by Stephen Hobhouse, 2nd rev. edn (London: Rockliff, 1948), pp. 397–422; Arthur Wormhoudt, "Newton's Natural Philosophy in the Behmenistic Works of William Law," *Journal of the History of Ideas*, 10 (1949), 411–29.

53 Karl Popp, *Jakob Böhme und Isaac Newton* (Leipzig: Hirzel, 1935); Hobhouse, p. 422; Wormhoudt, p. 413.

54 Samuel Taylor Coleridge, *The Philosophical Lectures of Samuel Taylor Coleridge: Hitherto Unpublished*, ed. by Kathleen Coburn (London: Pilot Press, 1949), p. 357.

55 See for instance Mary Anne Perkins, *Coleridge's Philosophy: The Logos as Unifying Principle* (Oxford: Clarendon Press, 1994).

56 See for instance Trevor H. Levere, *Poetry Realized in Nature: Samuel Taylor Coleridge and Early Nineteenth-Century Science* (Cambridge: Cambridge University Press, 1981).

57 Lorenz Oken, *Elements of Physiophilosophy*, trans. by Alfred Tulk (London: The Ray Society, 1847), pp. 23–24.

58 Sean M. Kelly, *Individuation and the Absolute: Hegel, Jung, and the Path Toward Wholeness* (Mahwah, NJ: Paulist Press, 1993).

59 Edward Carpenter, *The Drama of Love and Death: A Study of Human Evolution and Transfiguration* (London: George Allen, 1912), pp. 284–85.

60 F. W. J. von Schelling, *Ideas for a Philosophy of Nature*, trans. by Errol E. Harris and Peter Heath (Cambridge: Cambridge University Press, 1988), p. 179.

61 Dyczkowski, *Doctrine of Vibration*, pp. 115–28. Sixteen phases of perception are also described in nondual Kashmir Shaivism—see *The Stanzas on Vibration*, trans. by Mark S. G. Dyczkowski (Albany: State University of New York Press, 1992), pp. 275–77. Michael Whiteman described a sixteenfold cycle, which he considered to be an updated version of ancient ideas—see John Poynton, *Science, Mysticism and Psychical Research: The Revolutionary Synthesis of Michael Whiteman* (Newcastle upon Tyne: Cambridge Scholars, 2015), pp. 42–49.

62 See for instance Michael Ruse, *Monad to Man: The Concept of Progress in Evolutionary Biology* (Cambridge, MA: Harvard University Press, 1996), and Timothy Shanahan, *The Evolution of Darwinism: Selection, Adaptation, and Progress in Evolutionary Biology* (Cambridge: Cambridge University Press, 2004).

63 As claimed by Ruse in *Monad to Man*.

64 Philosophical discussions include *Evolutionary Progress*, ed. by M. Nitecki (Chicago: Chicago University Press, 1988). On the problem of defining evolutionary progress, see Francisco J. Ayala, "Can 'progress' be defined as a biological concept?" pp. 75–96, in the above collection. For a concise introduction, see Timothy Shanahan, "Evolutionary Progress: Conceptual Issues," *eLS* (Wiley, 2012) <http://www.els.net/WileyCDA/ElsArticle/refId-a0003459.html>.

10 WHERE DO YOU THINK YOU'RE GOING?

Epigraph. Edward Carpenter, "Believe Yourself a Whole," in *Towards Democracy*, complete edn (London: Swan Sonnenschein; Manchester: S. Clarke, 1905), pp. 490–91 (p. 491).

1 Edward F. Kelly, "Empirical Challenges to Theory Construction," in Kelly, Crabtree, and Marshall, pp. 3–38 (pp. 6–13).

2 Emily Williams Kelly, "Psychophysiological Influence," in Kelly and others, pp. 117–239 (pp. 232–36).

3 e.g., Ian Stevenson, *Twenty Cases Suggestive of Reincarnation*, 2nd edn (Charlottesville: University of Virginia Press, 1974) and *Children Who Remember Previous Lives: A Question of Reincarnation*, rev. edn (Jefferson, NC: McFarland, 2001); Jim B. Tucker, *Life Before Life: Children's Memories of Previous Lives* (New York: St. Martin's Griffin, 2008) and *Return to Life: Extraordinary Cases of Children Who Remember Past Lives* (New York: St. Martin's Press, 2013); Erlendur Haraldsson and James G. Matlock, *I Saw a Light and Came Here: Children's Experiences of Reincarnation* (Hove, East Sussex: White Crow Books, 2017); Peter Fenwick and Elizabeth Fenwick, *Past Lives: An Investigation into Reincarnation Memories* (London: Headline, 1999). In *Secret Body* (pp. 376–98), Jeffrey Kripal considers the implications of Stevenson's work for the study of religion. For theoretical studies of reincarnation and karma, see Gananath Obeyesekere, *Imagining Karma: Ethical Transformation in Amerindian, Buddhist, and Greek Rebirth* (Berkeley and Los Angeles: University of California Press, 2002), and Mikel Burley, *Rebirth and the Stream of Life: A Philosophical Study of Reincarnation, Karma and Ethics* (New York: Bloomsbury Academic, 2016).

4 There has been some discussion of "plant consciousness": see for instance Alexandra H. M. Nagel, "Are Plants Conscious?" *Journal of Consciousness Studies*, 4.3 (1997), 215–30, and Michael Marder, *Plant-Thinking: A Philosophy of Vegetal Life* (New York: Columbia University Press, 2013). My thanks to Alan Hunter for bringing the latter to my attention. There is also now the discipline of "Animal Studies," which investigates human attitudes toward and interactions with nonhuman animals. See Paul Waldau, *Animal Studies: An Introduction* (New York: Oxford University Press, 2013). For an overview of "animal consciousness," see Colin Allen and Michael Trestman, "Animal Consciousness," in *The Stanford Encyclopedia of Philosophy*, ed. by Edward N. Zalta, winter 2017 edn <https://plato.stanford.edu/archives/win2017/entries/consciousness-animal/>.

5 Arthur O. Lovejoy, *The Great Chain of Being: A Study of the History of an Idea* (Cambridge, MA: Harvard University Press, 1936).

6 For the Latin terms, see Miklós Vassányi, *Anima Mundi: The Rise of the World Soul Theory in Modern German Philosophy* (Dordrecht: Springer, 2011), p. 37.

7 Peter N. Gregory, *Inquiry into the Origin of Humanity: An Annotated Translation of Tsung-Mi's Yüan jen lun with a Modern Commentary* (Honolulu: University of Hawai'i Press, 1995), pp. 57, 182–83 (from the "Manifestation of the Tathāgata" chapter of the *Avataṃsaka Sūtra*).

8 Jacqueline I. Stone, *Original Enlightenment and the Transformation of Medieval Japanese Buddhism* (Honolulu: University of Hawai'i Press, 1999).

9 Lambert Schmithausen, *The Problem of the Sentience of Plants in Earliest Buddhism* (Tokyo: International Institute for Buddhist Studies, 1991); Ellison Banks Findly, "Borderline Beings: Plant Possibilities in Early Buddhism," *Journal of the American Oriental Society*, 122 (2002), 252–63.

10 Stone, pp. 9, 29–30. See also Knut A. Jacobsen, "Humankind and Nature in Buddhism," in *A Companion to World Philosophies*, ed. by Eliot Deutsch and Ron Bontekoe (Oxford: Blackwell, 1997), pp. 381–91; Robert H. Sharf, "On the Buddha-nature of Insentient Things (or: How to Think about a Ch'an *Kung-an*)" [1999] <http://kr.buddhism.org/zen/koan/Robert_Sharf-e.htm>; William LaFleur, "Enlightenment for Plants and Trees," in *Dharma Rain: Sources of Buddhist Environmentalism*, ed. by Stephanie Kaza and Kenneth Kraft (Boston: Shambhala, 2000), pp. 109–16; Matthew Hall, *Plants as Persons: A Philosophical Botany* (Albany: State University of New York Press, 2011).

11 Based on Dundas, *The Jains*, pp. 81–82, 90–91; Jaini, *Jaina Path*, pp. 107–11; *That Which Is*, Tattvartha Sutra: *A Classic Jain Manual for Understanding the True Nature of Reality*, trans. by L. M. Tatia (San Francisco: HarperCollins, 1994). For a presentation in the light of modern science, see K. V. Mardia, *The Scientific Foundations of Jainism*, 2nd rev. edn (Delhi: Motilal Banarsidass, 1996), and Kanti V. Mardia and Aidan D. Rankin, *Living Jainism: An Ethical Science* (Alresford, Hants: Mantra Books, 2013).

12 Broad, *Leibniz*, p. 160. Note however that insentient monads, like the more advanced, sentient ones such as ourselves, possess "rudiments or elements of suffering, semi-suffering," "imperceptible little urges," "insensible stimuli," a "disquiet" or *Unruhe*. See Gottfried Wilhelm Leibniz, *New Essays on Human Understanding*, edited by Peter Remnant and Jonathan Bennett (Cambridge: Cambridge University Press, 1996), II.20.6. We are not consciously aware of these "minute sufferings," which are the appetitional counterparts of the "minute perceptions." The semi-sufferings play a role in the appetitive process, unconsciously drawing monads toward "semi-pleasures" in their satisfaction—and toward conscious pleasures in the case of the more advanced monads.

13 Kristi L. Wiley, "Five-Sensed Animals in Jainism," in *A Communion of Subjects: Animals in Religion, Science, and Ethics*, ed. by Paul Waldau and Kimberley Patton (New York: Columbia University Press, 2006), pp. 250–55. However, it is sometimes alleged that *nigodas* suffer great pain, e.g., Surendranath Dasgupta, *A History of Indian Philosophy*, 5 vols (Cambridge: Cambridge University Press, 1922–55), I (1922), 190.

14 *Sources of the Indian Tradition*, ed. by Ainslie T. Embree, 2nd edn, 2 vols (New York: Columbia University Press, 1988), I, 80–82 (*Mahāpurāṇa*, 4.16–31, 38–40).

15 On Conway, see Sarah Hutton, *Anne Conway: A Woman Philosopher* (Cambridge: Cambridge University Press, 2004). On Francis Mercury van Helmont, see Allison P. Coudert, *The Impact of the Kabbalah in the Seventeenth Century: The Life and Thought of Francis Mercury van Helmont (1614–1698)* (Leiden: Brill, 1999). For points of contact between the "philosophical biologies" of J. B. van Helmont and Leibniz, including the Helmontian *archeus* and the Leibnizian dominant monad, see Pagel, pp. 350–51 n. 8. Also Coudert, *The Impact of the Kabbalah*, pp. 316–17.

16 Anne Conway, *The Principles of the Most Ancient and Modern Philosophy*, trans. and ed. by Allison P. Coudert and Taylor Corse (Cambridge: Cambridge University Press, 1996), p. 45; [Francis Mercury van Helmont], *A Cabbalistical Dialogue* (London: Benjamin Clark, 1682), p. 4. On Leibniz and this argument, see Stuart Brown, "F. M. van Helmont: His Philosophical Connections and the Reception of Later Cabbalistic Philosophy," in *Studies in Seventeenth-Century European Philosophy*, ed. by M. A. Stewart (Oxford: Clarendon Press, 1997), pp. 97–116 (pp. 113–14).

17 [van Helmont], *A Cabbalistical Dialogue*, pp. 9–11.

18 The scheme probably owes a debt to Origen. See chapter 11, Box, "The vale of Soul-making."

19 Jaini, *Jaina Path*, p. 111.

20 Jyotindra Jain and Eberhard Fischer, *Jaina Iconography*, Part 2: *Objects of Meditation and the Pantheon* (Leiden: Brill, 1978); "Jain Snakes & Ladders," Victoria and Albert Museum <http://www.vam.ac.uk/content/articles/j/snakes-and-ladders/>.

21 Jonathan Barnes, *Early Greek Philosophy* (Harmondsworth, Middx: Penguin, 1987), p. 86.

22 Barnes, p. 194.

23 *Selected Poems from the Dīvāni Shamsi Tabrīz*, ed. and trans. by Reynold A. Nicholson (Cambridge: Cambridge University Press, 1898), pp. 47, 49.

24 Schimmel, p. 322. For additional passages, see William C. Chittick, *The Sufi Path of Love: The Spiritual Teachings of Rumi* (Albany: State University of New York Press, 1983), pp. 77–82.

25 Paul E. Walker, "The Doctrine of Metempsychosis in Islam," in *Islamic Studies Presented to Charles J. Adams*, ed. by Wael B. Hallaq and Donald P. Little (Leiden: Brill, 1991), pp. 219–38.

26 Yaron Friedman, *The Nuṣayrī-'Alawīs: An Introduction to the Religion, History, and Identity of the Leading Minority in Syria* (Leiden: Brill, 2010), pp. 102–10.

27 Schimmel, pp. 320–23; also Annemarie Schimmel, *The Triumphal Sun: A Study of the Works of Jalāloddin Rumi* (Albany: State University of New York Press, 1993), pp. 289–32; Chittick, pp. 72–82.

28 Franklin D. Lewis, *Rumi, Past and Present, East and West: The Life, Teachings and Poetry of Jalâl Al-Din Rumi* (Oxford: Oneworld, 2000), pp. 416–17.

29 For a detailed discussion, see Obeyesekere, pp. 287–308. Also John Bussanich, "Rebirth Eschatology in Plato and Plotinus," in *Philosophy and Salvation in Greek Religion*, ed. by Vishwa Adluri (Berlin: de Gruyter, 2013), pp. 243–88.

30 Scholem, *On the Mystical Shape*, p. 237, from R. Joseph Solomon Delmedigo, *Noveloth Ḥokhmah* (Basle, 1631), summarizing Ḥayyim Vital. Also Hallamish, *An Introduction to the Kabbalah*, p. 301.

31 Hallamish, p. 302, from Ḥayyim Vital, *Sha'ar ha-Miṣvot*.

32 Leibniz, *New Essays*, II.27.6, 14.

33 [Francis Mercury van Helmont], *Two Hundred Queries Moderately propounded Concerning the Doctrine Of the Revolution of Humane Souls, And its Conformity to the Truths of Christianity* (London: Robert Kettlewell, 1684), pp. 52–53. On van Helmont's transmigration doctrine, see Walker, *Decline of Hell*, pp. 137–46, and Philip C. Almond, *Heaven and Hell in Enlightenment England* (Cambridge: Cambridge University Press, 1994), pp. 17–23.

34 Francis Mercury van Helmont, *The Paradoxal Discourses of F. M. Van Helmont, Concerning the Macrocosm and Microcosm, of the Greater and Lesser World, And Their Union* (London: Robert Kettlewell, 1685), part 2, chap. 4 ("Concerning the Revolution of Humane Souls"), pp. 106–07.

35 Conway, *Principles*, p. 65 (for discussion, see "Introduction," pp. xx–xxi).

36 Conway, pp. 32–33, 35–36.

37 Grace B. Sherrer, "Philalgia in Warwickshire: F. M. Van Helmont's Anatomy of Pain Applied to Lady Anne Conway," *Studies in the Renaissance*, 5 (1958), 196–206.

38 Sherrer, p. 205, trans. from a Latin poem "on the Love of Pain" (*de Amore Dolorum*), dedicated to Conway, in MS. Locke c. 32, fol. 47, perhaps authored by van Helmont himself, as Sherrer suggests.

39 Marjorie Hope Nicolson found much in common between Anne Conway and Hildegard, not only in a shared malady. See *The Conway Letters: The Correspondence of Anne, Viscountess Conway, Henry More, and Their Friends, 1642–1684*, ed. by Marjorie Hope Nicolson and Sarah Hutton, rev. edn (Oxford: Clarendon Press, 1992), xxvii.

40 Conway, p. 5.

41 See C. J. Langston, "Lady Conway and Valentine Greatrake, the Stroker," *Argosy*, 30 (July to December 1880), 378–87 (p. 381). Conway was supposedly "exercised by a series of extraordinary visions," as real as waking experience. Although Langston remarks that the stories were recorded by van Helmont, he omits to cite any documentation. Like other details in the article, the stories may have been conveyed through "family tradition"—on this and the identity of Langston, see Nicolson and Hutton, p. 247 n.

42 Gottfried Wilhelm Leibniz, "Considerations on Vital Principles and Plastic Natures" (1705), in *Philosophical Papers and Letters: A Selection*, ed. and trans. by Leroy E. Loemker (Dordrecht: Kluwer, 1989), pp. 586–91 (pp. 588–89).

43 Leibniz, *New Essays*, II.27.6.

44 Leibniz, *Theodicy*, §91, §397.

45 Hansch, 1728, quoted in Benson Mates, *The Philosophy of Leibniz: Metaphysics and Language* (New York: Oxford University Press, 1986), p. 204.

46 Immanuel Kant, *Dreams of a Sprit-Seer*, trans. by Emanuel F. Goerwitz, ed. by Frank Sewall (London: Swan Sonnenschein, 1900), p. 52.

47 Leibniz, "Letter to Remond" (11 February 1715), in Loemker, pp. 658–60 (pp. 658–59).

48 Leibniz, "Considerations on Vital Principles," p. 588.

49 Leibniz, "Letter to Electress Sophie" (6 February 1706), in *The Shorter Leibniz Texts: A Collection of New Translations*, ed. and trans. by Lloyd Strickland (London: Continuum, 2006), pp. 81–85 (p. 84).

50 *The Natural History Book: The Ultimate Visual Guide to Everything on Earth*, ed. by Becky Alexander and others (London: Dorling Kindersley, 2010).

51 Alexander and others, p. 549.

52 Samir Okasha, "The Levels of Selection Debate: Philosophical Issues," in *Philosophy of Biology: An Anthology*, ed. by Alex Rosenberg and Robert Arp (Chichester, West Sussex:Wiley-Blackwell, 2010), pp. 327–34.

53 e.g., *Handbook of Epigenetics: The New Molecular and Medical Genetics*, ed. by Trygve O. Tollefsbol, 2nd edn (London: Academic Press, 2017).

54 On Carpenter, Jung, and neo-Lamarckism, see Marshall, *Mystical Encounters*, pp. 125–27.

55 Ian Stevenson, *Where Reincarnation and Biology Intersect* (Westport, CT: Praeger, 1997), pp. 183–85.

56 See chapters 5 and 6. On the subtle body, see Samuel and Johnston.

57 Of interest here is the *palingenesis* ("rebirth") theory of Charles Bonnet, the naturalist after whom the medical syndrome is named (see above at chapter 5, n. 43). Bonnet, a great admirer of Leibniz, gave the Chain of Being a more developmental form by envisaging repeated but progressive recreation of the Chain through a series of catastrophes ("revolutions of the globe"), a process that enables, say, plants to become animals, through the unfolding ("evolution") of preformed structures. Bonnet's theory posits an indestructible, preexistent "germ of restitution," a "little ethereal machine" made of elements analogous, perhaps, to ether, light, fire, and electricity, and residing in the corpus callosum as seat of the soul. This germ survives gross bodily death and guarantees continuation of memory and therefore preservation of personality through repeated metamorphosis or "resurrection." On Bonnet and Leibniz, see for instance Olivier Rieppel, "The Reception of Leibniz's Philosophy in the Writings of Charles Bonnet (1720–1793)," *Journal of the History of Biology*, 21 (1988), 119–45.

58 Lester G. Crocker, "Diderot and Eighteenth Century French Transformism," in *Forerunners of Darwin: 1745–1859*, ed. by Bentley Glass, Owsei Temkin, and William L. Straus (Baltimore, MD: Johns Hopkins Press, 1959), pp. 114–43.

59 Lovejoy, *Great Chain of Being*, chap. 5.

60 Lloyd Strickland, "Leibniz on Whether the World Increases in Perfection," *British Journal for the History of Philosophy*, 14 (2006), 51–68.

61 Gottfried Wilhelm Leibniz, "On the Ultimate Origination of Things (23 Nov. 1697)," in *Philosophical Writings*, ed. by G. H. R. Parkinson (London: Dent, 1973), pp. 136–44 (p. 144).

62 Strickland, pp. 62–65.

63 Ruse, *Monad to Man*.

64 Robert Grant, "Address on the Study of Medicine, Delivered at the Opening of the Medical School, October 1st, 1833," in *The Lancet MDCCCXXXIII—XXIV*, ed. by Thomas Wakley, 2 vols (London: Wakley, 1834), I, 41–50 (p. 44).

65 On the Leibnizian background to the biological employment of the term "monad," see Justin Erik Halldór Smith, "Leibniz's Hylomorphic Monad," *History of Philosophy Quarterly*, 19 (2002), 21–42 (pp. 24–25).

66 See James A. Secord, *Victorian Sensation: The Extraordinary Publication, Reception, and Secret Authorship of* Vestiges of the Natural History of Creation (Chicago: University of Chicago Press, 2000).

67 On Randolph, see John Patrick Deveney, *Paschal Beverly Randolph: A Nineteenth-Century Black American Spiritualist, Rosicrucian, and Sex Magician* (Albany: State University of New York Press, 1997). On Randolph and sex, see also Hugh B. Urban, "Sex Power Is God Power: Paschal Beverly Randolph and the Birth of Sex Magic in Victorian America," in *Magia Sexualis: Sex, Magic, and Liberation in Modern Western Esotericism* (Berkeley and Los Angeles: University of California Press, 2006), pp. 55–80, and "Paschal Beverly Randolph and Sexual Magic," in *Hidden Intercourse: Eros and Sexuality in the History of Western Esotericism*, ed. by Wouter J. Hanegraaff and Jeffrey J. Kripal (New York: Fordham University Press, 2011), pp. 355–67.

68 On Randolph's experience, see Deveney, *Randolph*, pp. 108–09. Randolph describes his experience in [Paschal Beverly Randolph], *Dealings with the Dead: The Human Soul, Its Migrations and Its Transmigrations, Penned by the Rosicrucian* (Utica, NY: M. J. Randolph, 1861–62), p. 173 onward, and less elaborately but with more background detail in his earlier articles "Dealings with the Dead," No. 2 and No. 3, in *Banner of Light* 5.24 (10 September 1859), 3–4, and 5.25 (17 September 1859), 7, respectively.

69 Deveney, *Randolph*, p. 278; Lynn L. Sharp, *Secular Spirituality: Reincarnation and Spiritism in Nineteenth-Century France* (Lanham, MD: Lexington Books, 2006).

70 See [Randolph], pp. 146–49. The French Lamarckian Etienne Serres had observed that the brains of all vertebrates are similar at an early stage of development. According to recapitulation theory, the brain development of higher species recapitulates this common early stage and subsequent stages of development too. Serres and another eminent Lamarckian, Étienne Geoffroy Saint-Hilaire, explained "Monsters" in terms of arrested development during recapitulation, an idea that Randolph seems to have picked up.

71 This is "Cynthia Temple"—see Deveney, *Randolph*, p. 438 n. 50.

72 [Randolph], pp. 44–45.

73 [Randolph], p. 45. The "spiral" here, like several other details in Randolph's story, probably derives from his former acquaintance Andrew Jackson Davis. Davis inherited Swedenborg's predilection for the spiral form.

74 Davis had written of "baby suns and baby planets, commonly called 'comets'"—see Davis, *The Magic Staff: An Autobiography of Andrew Jackson Davis* (New York: J. S. Brown, 1857), p. 339.

75 [Randolph], p. 43.

76 [Randolph], pp. 49, 146, 191. Randolph is able to see luminous globes, ranging in size from a pea to four inches in diameter, "larger, smoother, and rounder" in "better," more intelligent persons, and centered on the corpus callosum (p. 196). On this last point, Randolph echoes those eighteenth-century thinkers who located the seat of the soul not at the pineal gland, as Descartes had, but at the corpus callosum, such as Bonnet (see above at n. 57) and, earlier, Giovanni Lancisi and F. G. de La Peyronie. The latter's investigations of impaired mental function associated with brain damage, by means of autopsy and surgical operation, led him to conclude that the immaterial soul exercises its functions at the corpus callosum. See Timo Kaitaro, "La Peyronie and the Experimental Search for the Seat of the Soul: Neuropsychological Methodology in the Eighteenth Century," *Cortex*, 32 (1996), 557–64. It would seem that Randolph's globe houses the monad, which in preformationist fashion

is human-shaped for a human and extremely small (p. 239). Randolph also describes an enclosing, slightly ellipsoidal globe, not more than fifty yards in vertical diameter, on the walls of which are displayed personal memories ("Memorama," pp. 50–51) and the effects of one's actions on others ("Phantorama," p. 68), reminiscent of near-death life reviews.

77 [Randolph], pp. 146, 166.

78 Deveney, *Randolph*, pp. 276–82. Deveney lists nine points of commonality between Blavatsky's early ideas and those of Randolph and fellow spiritualist and occultist Emma Hardinge Britten.

79 H. P. Blavatsky, *Isis Unveiled: A Master-Key to the Mysteries of Ancient and Modern Science and Theology*, 2 vols (New York: J. W. Bouton, 1877), I, 351. Deveney raises the alternative "hidden-hand conspiracy theory," according to which Randolph and Blavatsky (and Britten) derived their ideas from a common source, a secret society to which they may have belonged. See Deveney, *Randolph*, pp. 257–62.

80 Blavatsky, *Isis Unveiled*, I, 302–03, 388–09.

81 Blavatsky, *Isis Unveiled*, I, 351–02.

82 e.g., Annie Besant and C. W. Leadbeater, *Man: Whence, How and Whither: A Record of Clairvoyant Investigation* (Adyar, Madras: Theosophical Publishing House, 1913); C. W. Leadbeater, *The Monad; and Other Essays upon the Higher Consciousness* (Adyar, Madras: Theosophical Publishing House, 1920). Also I. K. Taimni, *Man, God, and the Universe* (Wheaton, IL: Quest Books, 1974)—my thanks to Alan Hunter for bringing this book to my attention. It has been pointed out to me that the "consciousness units" of the channeled, discarnate entity Seth bear some resemblance to monads—my thanks to Michael Brown ("Aspects of Reality and Mind," http://www.hg29hh.freeserve.co.uk/mindreal.htm [accessed 11 May 2001]). See Jane Roberts, *The "Unknown" Reality: A Seth Book*, 2 vols (Englewood Cliffs, NJ: Prentice-Hall, 1979).

83 e.g., Rudolf Steiner, "Lecture 22" (Berlin, 24 October 1905), in *Foundations of Esotericism*, trans. by Vera and Judith Compton-Burnett (London: Rudolf Steiner Press, 1983) <http://wn.rsarchive.org/Lectures/GA093a/English/RSP1982/19051024p01.html>.

84 Deveney, *Randolph*; Joscelyn Godwin, Christian Chanel, and John P. Deveney, *The Hermetic Brotherhood of Luxor: Initiatic and Historical Documents of an Order of Practical Occultism* (York Beach, ME: Samuel Weiser, 1995).

85 [Randolph], pp. 191–92.

86 [Randolph], p. 165.

87 H. P. Blavatsky, *Secret Doctrine: The Synthesis of Science, Religion, and Philosophy*, 3rd rev. edn, 2 vols (New York: Theosophical Publishing House, 1893), I, 680 (see pp. 687–94 for details). Blavatsky says that if the teachings of Leibniz and Spinoza were merged so that they corrected each other, then a "true spirit of Esoteric Philosophy" would remain (p. 690).

88 On Randolph's travels, see Deveney, *Randolph*.

89 Theodore Roszak, "Evolution," *The Encyclopedia of Religion*, ed. by Mircea Eliade, 16 vols (New York: Macmillan, 1987) V, 208–13.

90 Theodore Roszak, *Unfinished Animal: The Aquarian Frontier and the Evolution of Consciousness* (London: Faber and Faber, 1976), pp. 115–51.

91 Kripal, *Secret Body*, pp. 173–83.

92 Even a thinker as oppressed by racial prejudice as Randolph could not escape its allure. Randolph was conflicted: born of a white father and a black mother, he was subject to white racism on numerous occasions, yet he sometimes expressed racist views himself. See Deveney, *Randolph*, pp. 150, 160; Christine Ferguson, "Blended Souls: Paschal Beverly Randolph and Occult Miscegenation," in *Determined Spirits: Eugenics, Heredity and Racial Regeneration in Anglo-American Spiritualist Writing, 1848-1930* (Edinburgh: Edinburgh

University Press, 2012), pp. 114–41. On Blavatsky, Theosophy, and racism, see for instance Isaac Lubelsky, "Mythological and Real Race Issues in Theosophy," in *Handbook of the Theosophical Current*, ed. by Olav Hammer and Mikael Rothstein (Leiden: Brill, 2013), pp. 335–55. Roszak too comments on it (*Unfinished Animal*, p. 123).

93 Cometary theory of the Earth's origins significantly predates the nineteenth century, going back to seventeenth-century speculation, notably William Whiston's *A New Theory of the Earth* (1696), which has a chaotically constituted comet become our orderly Earth when its orbit round the Sun shifted from extreme eccentricity to circularity.

94 I borrow the terms self-centeredness and Reality-centerdness from John Hick, *An Interpretation of Religion: Human Responses to the Transcendent*, 2nd edn (New Haven, CT: Yale University Press, 2004), p. 301.

95 On animal psi, see for instance Rupert Sheldrake, "Animal Psi," in *Parapsychology: Research on Exceptional Experiences*, ed. by Jane Henry (Hove, East Sussex: Routledge, 2005), pp. 114–22. On understanding psi in a monadological framework, see my discussion of H. H. Price's ideas—Marshall, "Why We Are Conscious of So Little," pp. 394–98.

96 On psi and evolution, see Richard S. Broughton, "Psi and Biology: An Evolutionary Perspective," in Cardeña, Palmer, and Marcusson-Clavertz, pp. 139–48.

97 Leibniz says that the confusion of a monad's perceptions is advantageous, hiding distracting details and keeping unconscious the "minute sufferings" of the appetitional process (see above at n. 12): "That is why the infinitely wise Author of our being was acting in our interests when he brought it about that we are often ignorant and subject to confused perceptions – so that we could act more quickly by instinct, and not be troubled by excessively distinct sensations of hosts of objects which, necessary though they are to nature's plan, are not agreeable to us" (*New Essays*, II.20.6).

98 Marshall, "Why We Are Conscious of So Little," pp. 399–401.

99 [Alfred Russel Wallace], "Sir Charles Lyell on Geological Climates and the Origin of Species," *Quarterly Review*, 126 (April 1869), 359–94 (pp. 391–94).

100 Alfred Russel Wallace, *Contributions to the Theory of Natural Selection: A Series of Essays*, 2nd edn (London: Macmillan, 1871), pp. 372–72A ("Note A").

101 Alfred Russel Wallace, *The World of Life: A Manifestation of Creative Power, Directive Mind and Ultimate Purpose* (London: Chapman and Hall, 1910), p. 400.

102 Such ideas have been a staple of science fiction and other forms of speculative writing. Prominent examples include the Firstborn and their black monoliths in the *Space Odyssey* series of Arthur C. Clark, and the planet-seeding Engineers in the *Alien* movies. See various entries in the online *Encyclopedia of Science Fiction* (SFE) <http://www.sf-encyclopedia.com/>, including "Evolution," "Forerunners," "Origin of Man," "Transcendence," and "Uplift." Note also the "ancient astronauts" literature—see "Ancient Astronaut," Wikipedia, https://en.wikipedia.org/wiki/Ancient_astronauts. Jeffrey Kripal looks at evolutionary spirituality and mysticism as expressed in the science fiction and superhero comic genres—see his *Mutants and Mystics*, and *Secret Body*, pp. 169–83.

103 Wallace, *World of Life*, p. 395.

11 The Making of God

Epigraph. John Keats, *The Complete Poetical Works and Letters of John Keats*, ed. by Horace E. Scudder (Boston: Houghton, Mifflin, 1899), p. 370.

1 The distinction is not as clear-cut as may first appear: on the one hand, it has been much debated whether there are truly free choices; on the other, some apparently natural ills

may stem from the choices of moral agents (human or otherwise), such as extreme weather events due to anthropogenic climate change.

2 Alfred Russel Wallace, "Are the Phenomena of Spiritualism in Harmony with Science?" *The Medium and Daybreak*, 16.820 (1885), 809b–810b, available at The Alfred Russel Wallace Page website <http://people.wku.edu/charles.smith/wallace/S379.htm>.

3 Wallace, "Are the Phenomena of Spiritualism," p. 810.

4 But Hick does not mention Wallace in his major study *Evil and the God of Love*, 2nd edn (New York: Harper & Row, 1978). See also John Hick, "An Irenaean Theodicy," in *Encountering Evil: Live Options in Theodicy*, ed. by Stephen T. Davis, 2nd edn (Louisville, KY: Westminster John Knox Press, 2001), pp. 38–72.

5 Hick, *Evil and the God of Love*, p. 259 n. 1.

6 Hick, "An Irenaean Theodicy," pp. 51, 71.

7 John Hick, *The Fifth Dimension: An Exploration of the Spiritual Realm* (Oxford: Oneworld, 1999), p. 248.

8 John Hick, *Death and Eternal Life*, 2nd edn (Basingstoke, Hants: Macmillan, 1985), pp. 404–07, 414–22.

9 Keats, pp. 369, 370.

10 Keats, p. 370.

11 Wallace too: "The whole universe, in all its myriad forms . . . became to him *a vast school-room* [emphasis added], furnishing the materials needed for the development of all his hitherto unused faculties and for the gradual elevation of his intellectual and moral nature." Alfred Russel Wallace, "Evolution and Character," *Fortnightly Review*, n.s., 83 (1 January 1908), 1–24 (p. 23), available at The Alfred Russel Wallace Page website <http://people.wku.edu/charles.smith/wallace/S649.htm>. See also Wallace, *World of Life*, pp. 397–98.

12 Mark S. M. Scott, "Suffering and Soul-Making: Rethinking John Hick's Theodicy," *Journal of Religion*, 90 (2010), 313–34.

13 Walker, *Decline of Hell*.

14 Wallace, "Are the Phenomena of Spiritualism," p. 810.

15 Wallace, "Are the Phenomena of Spiritualism," p. 810.

16 Case 24 (J. P. W.), in Johnson, *Watcher on the Hills*, pp. 65–66 (p. 66).

17 Hick, *Evil and the God of Love*, p. 385.

18 RERC No. 001239, in Maxwell and Tschudin, p. 47.

19 Bucke, *Cosmic Consciousness*, p. 326.

20 Bucke, p. 326.

21 Israel, *Precarious Living*, pp. 30–31.

22 Israel, p. 31.

23 On the "turning wheel of terror-joy," see Joseph Campbell, *The Masks of God*, IV: *Occidental Mythology* (Harmondsworth, Middx: Penguin, 1976), pp. 405–28.

24 James, *Varieties of Religious Experience*, pp. 422–23.

25 See Marshall, *Mystical Encounters*, "Mystical Experiences as Windows on Reality," and "Mystical Experience and Metaphysics."

26 Arvind Sharma, *The World as Dream* (New Delhi: D. K. Printworld, 2006).

27 I had reason to look at Peter Sterry in *The Living Mirror*, pp. 284–85, in connection with Traherne and idea of the whole in the part.

28 Walker, *Decline of Hell*, pp. 115–18.

29 Moreover, dreams do not just stand for the unreal misunderstood as the real: they have positive associations too. Dreams can be venues for creativity and spiritual inspiration and communication, when the imagination and higher intellect are not so obscured by

sensory input and discursive thought, as the elder van Helmont had maintained (see chapter 4). Romantic medical doctor Gotthilf Heinrich von Schubert (1780–1860) put it thus, as quoted by Freud: "Der Traum sei eine Befreiung des Geistes von der Gewalt der äusseren Natur, eine Loslösung der Seele von den Fesseln der Sinnlichkeit"—the dream is a release of the soul from the fetters of the senses. Sigmund Freud, *Über den Traum* (Wiesbaden: J. F. Bergmann, 1901), pp. 307–08.

30 Sharma, pp. 205–07.

31 On Leibniz, original imperfection, creaturely limitation, and metaphysical "evil," see Michael Latzer, "Leibniz's Conception of Metaphysical Evil," *Journal of the History of Ideas*, 55 (1994), 1–15, Maria Rosa Antognazza, "Metaphysical Evil Revisited," in *New Essays on Leibniz's* Theodicy, ed. by Larry M. Jorgensen and Samuel Newlands (Oxford: Oxford University Press, 2014), pp. 112–34, and Samuel Newlands, "Leibniz on Privations, Limitations, and the Metaphysics of Evil," *Journal of the History of Philosophy*, 52 (2014), 281–308.

32 e.g., Nancy Frankenberry, "Some Problems in Process Theodicy," *Religious Studies*, 17 (1981), 179–97; Sprigge, *God of Metaphysics*, pp. 454–58.

33 On the One's attributes, see Lloyd P. Gerson, *Plotinus* (London: Routledge, 1994).

34 See John M. Dillon, "Signs and Tokens: Do the Gods of Neoplatonism Really Care?" in *Fate, Providence and Moral Responsibility in Ancient, Medieval and Early Modern Thought: Studies in Honour of Carlos Steel*, ed. by Pieter d'Hoine and Gerd Van Riel (Leuven: Leuven University Press, 2014), pp. 227–38.

35 John Peter Kenney, *Mystical Monotheism: A Study in Ancient Platonic Theology* (Hanover, NH: University Press of New England/Brown University Press, 1991), pp. 104–05. See J. M. Rist's discussion of *Enn.* VI.8 in his *Plotinus*, pp. 66–83.

36 John Peter Kenney, "The Platonic Monotheism of Plotinus," in *Models of God and Alternative Ultimate Realities*, ed. by Jeanine Diller and Asa Kasher (Dordrecht: Springer, 2013), pp. 775–81, and "The Greek Tradition in Early Christian Philosophy," in *The Pimlico History of Western Philosophy*, ed. by Richard H. Popkin (London: Pimlico, 1999), pp. 118–28.

37 Shaw, "Platonic *Siddhas*," pp. 288–89; John Dillon, "The Divinizing of Matter: Some Reflections on Iamblichus' Theurgic Approach to Matter," in *Seele und Materie im Neuplatonismus/Soul and Matter in Neoplatonism*, ed. by Jens Halfwassen, Tobias Dangel, and Carl O'Brien (Heidelberg: Winter, 2016), pp. 175–86.

38 Studies of panentheism include *In Whom We Live and Move and Have Our Being: Panentheistic Reflections on God's Presence in a Scientific World*, ed. by Philip Clayton and Arthur Robert Peacocke (Grand Rapids, MI: Eerdmans, 2004), and *Panentheism across the World's Traditions*, ed. by Biernacki and Clayton.

39 A reference to Peter Sterry—see Marshall, *Living Mirror*, pp. 284–85.

40 Compare with Adam Crabtree's adoption of Charles Sanders Peirce's concept of "evolutionary love" or *agape*. Following Peirce, Crabtree sees *agape* as the fundamental condition for all evolution but recognizes *eros* as the mechanism through which evolution is brought about. Crabtree, *Memoir of a Trance Therapist: Hypnosis and the Evocation of Human Potentials* (Victoria, BC: Friesen Press, 2014), pp. 165–80; "Continuity of Mind: A Peircean Vision," in Kelly, Crabtree, and Marshall, pp. 423–53; and especially *Evolutionary Love and the Ravages of Greed* (Victoria, BC: Friesen Press, 2017).

41 Carpenter, *Art of Creation*, p. 81.

42 Carpenter distinguishes several aspects of self. These include the *Race-life* and *Race-self* (comparable to Jung's collective unconscious understood as accumulated inheritance), the little, local *personality* of a single life (with a coarse, outer, animal personality, and a

subtler, inner "ego" personality in the case of developed creatures), the more extensive *individuality* of a string of personal lives, and a *Divine Soul* (or *All-self* of the universe) that emerges from the process but embraces all the phases in its all-inclusive spatiotemporality. This All-self, being universal, pervades the lives of the personal and individual selves, and transcends the Race-life. See Carpenter, *The Drama of Love and Death.*

43 Carpenter, *The Drama of Love and Death*, pp. 282–83, 286.

44 For a recent articulation of comparable ideas but drawing on Whitehead, Aurobindo, and others, see Sean M. Kelly, "Integral Time and the Varieties of Post-Mortem Survival," *Integral Review*, 4.1 (2008), 5–30. Whitehead and Aurobindo are also brought together in the context of reincarnation by Eric M. Weiss, *The Long Trajectory: The Metaphysics of Reincarnation and Life after Death* (Bloomington, IN: iUniverse, 2012).

45 For an overview, see for instance Patrick A. Wilson, "Anthropic Principle," in *Encyclopedia of Cosmology: Historical, Philosophical, and Scientific Foundations of Modern Cosmology*, ed. by Norriss S. Hetherington (New York: Garland, 1993), pp. 11–17.

46 John D. Barrow and Frank J. Tipler, *The Anthropic Cosmological Principle* (Oxford: Oxford University Press, 1988), pp. 266–69.

47 I leave it to Buddhism scholars to decide whether a comparable reconciliation of eternal and temporal views, drawing on the idea of a spatiotemporally inclusive "now," emerged in discussions of "original enlightenment" (*hongaku*) as Buddha-nature inherently possessed by all, set against "acquired enlightenment" (*shikaku*) achieved through spiritual cultivation across numerous lives. According to his biographers, the young monk Dōgen, who later established Sōtō Zen in Japan, puzzled over original enlightenment as it was taught by the Tendai Buddhist tradition in which he was training on Mount Hiei. Why do human beings need to engage in spiritual practice, he pondered, if they are inherently endowed with the Buddha-nature? The answer at which he arrived was an understanding of "the oneness of practice and attainment" informed by an expanded concept of time and space. See for instance Masao Abe, *A Study of Dōgen: His Philosophy and Religion*, ed. by Steven Heine (Albany: State University of New York Press, 1992), and Hee-Jin Kim, *Eihei Dōgen: Mystical Realist* (Somerville, MA: Wisdom Publications, 2004).

Epilogue

Epigraph. Thomas Traherne, *Kingdom of God*, in Ross, 1, p. 276 [v.276–77, 280–81].

1 Marshall, "Mystical Experiences as Windows on Reality," pp. 43–44.

2 See for instance Michael Grosso on the wider implications of materialism, in *The Man Who Could Fly*, pp. 3–5. For a classic discussion, see Morris Berman, *The Reenchantment of the World* (Ithaca, NY: Cornell University Press, 1981).

3 On Leibnizian thought as ecophilosophy, see Pauline Phemister, *Leibniz and the Environment* (Abingdon, Oxon: Routledge, 2016). On the relevance of panpsychism to environmental thinking, see Freya Mathews, *For Love of Matter: A Contemporary Panpsychism* (Albany: State University of New York Press, 2003), and Skribna, pp. 271–85.

4 Crabtree, *Evolutionary Love*. See also Traherne on the "avaricious" and "communicative" humors in chapter 7.

5 Robert K. C. Forman, *Enlightenment Ain't What It's Cracked Up To Be: A Journey of Discovery, Snow and Jazz in the Soul* (Winchester, Hants: O Books, 2011).

Selected Bibliography

This bibliography lists only a few of the works cited in the Notes, namely those that are cited more than once, with the subsequent, abbreviated citations at a remove from the original, full citation and therefore not straightforward to identify.

Abbreviations used for frequently cited works:

CM   Thomas Traherne, *Centuries of Meditations*, ed. by Bertram Dobell (London: Bertram Dobell, 1908)

SM   Thomas Traherne, *Select Meditations*, ed. by Julia J. Smith (Manchester: Carcanet Press, 1997)

Enn.   *Plotinus: Enneads I–VI*, trans. by A. H. Armstrong, Loeb Classical Library, 7 vols (Cambridge, MA: Harvard University Press, 1966–88)

Allen, Warner, *The Timeless Moment* (London: Faber and Faber, 1946)

Austin, James H., *Zen and the Brain: Toward an Understanding of Meditation and Consciousness* (Cambridge, MA: MIT Press, 1998)

Bailey, Lee W., and Jenny Yates, eds., *The Near-Death Experience: A Reader* (New York: Routledge, 1996)

Biernacki, Loriliai, and Philip Clayton, eds., *Panentheism across the World's Traditions* (New York: Oxford University Press, 2014)

Blackmore, Susan J., *Beyond the Body: An Investigation of Out-of-the-Body Experiences* (London: Heinemann, 1982)

Braden, William, *The Private Sea: LSD and the Search for God* (Chicago: Quadrangle Books, 1967)

Broad, C. D., *Leibniz: An Introduction*, ed. by C. Lewy (Cambridge: Cambridge University Press, 1975; repr. 1979)

Bucke, Richard Maurice, *Cosmic Consciousness: A Study in the Evolution of the Human Mind* (1901; repr. New York: Arkana, Penguin, 1991)

Cardeña, Etzel, John Palmer, and David Marcusson-Clavertz, eds., *Parapsychology: A Handbook for the 21st Century* (Jefferson, NC: McFarland, 2015)

Carpenter, Edward, *The Art of Creation: Essays on the Self and Its Powers* (London: George Allen, 1904)

—— *The Drama of Love and Death: A Study of Human Evolution and Transfiguration* (London: George Allen, 1912)

Carr, Bernard, "Worlds Apart? Can Psychical Research Bridge the Gulf between Matter and Mind," Presidential Address, 2002, *Proceedings of the Society for Psychical Research*, 59 (2008)

Conway, Anne, *The Principles of the Most Ancient and Modern Philosophy*, trans. and ed. by Allison P. Coudert and Taylor Corse (Cambridge: Cambridge University Press, 1996)

Coomaraswamy, Ananda K., *Coomaraswamy: Selected Papers*, ed. by Roger Lipsey, 2 vols (Princeton, NJ: Princeton University Press, 1977)

Copenhaver, Brian P., *Hermetica: The Greek* Corpus Hermeticum *and the Latin* Asclepius *in a New English Translation, with Notes and Introduction* (Cambridge: Cambridge University Press, 1992)

Corazza, Ornella, *Near-Death Experiences: Exploring the Mind–Body Connection* (London: Routledge, 2008)

Corbin, Henry, *Avicenna and the Visionary Recital*, trans. by Willard R. Trask (New York: Pantheon Books, 1960)

—— *The Man of Light in Iranian Sufism* (Boulder, CO: Shambhala, 1978)

Courtois, Flora, "An Experience of Enlightenment," in *The Hazy Moon of Enlightenment*, by Taizan Maezumi and Bernard Glassman (Somerville, MA: Wisdom Publications, 2007), pp. 115–36

Crabtree, Adam, *Evolutionary Love and the Ravages of Greed* (Victoria, BC: Friesen Press, 2017)

Crouzel, Henri, *Origen*, trans. by A. S. Worrall (Edinburgh: T. & T. Clark, 1989)

Dante Alighieri, *The Divine Comedy: Paradiso*, trans. by Charles S. Singleton, 2 vols (Princeton, NJ: Princeton University Press, 1991)

Dodd, Elizabeth S., and Cassandra Gorman, eds., *Thomas Traherne and Seventeenth-Century Thought* (Cambridge: Brewer, 2016)

Dundas, Paul, *The Jains* (London: Routledge, 1992)

Dyczkowski, Mark S. G., *The Doctrine of Vibration: An Analysis of the Doctrines and Practices of Kashmir Shaivism* (Albany: State University of New York Press, 1987)

Ellenberger, Henri F., *The Discovery of the Unconscious: The History and Evolution of Dynamic Psychiatry* (London: Fontana, 1994)

Ellwood, Robert S., *Mysticism and Religion*, 2nd edn (Chappaqua, NY: Seven Bridges Press, 1999)

Flood, Gavin, *The Tantric Body: The Secret Tradition of Hindu Religion* (London: I. B. Tauris, 2006)

The Flower Ornament Scripture: A Translation of the Avatamsaka Sutra, trans. by Thomas Cleary, 3 vols (Boston: Shambhala Publications, 1985–1987)

Gregory, Peter N., ed., *Sudden and Gradual: Approaches to Enlightenment in Chinese Thought* (Honolulu: University of Hawai'i Press, 1987)

Grosso, Michael, *The Man Who Could Fly: St. Joseph of Copertino and the Mystery of Levitation* (Lanham, MD: Rowman & Littlefield, 2016)

Guthrie, W. K. C., *A History of Greek Philosophy*, I: *The Earlier Presocratics and the Pythagoreans* (Cambridge: Cambridge University Press, 1962)

Hadot, Pierre, *Philosophy as a Way of Life: Spiritual Exercises from Socrates to Foucault*, ed. by Arnold I. Davidson, trans. by Michael Chase (Oxford: Blackwell, 1995)

Harris, R. Baine, ed., *The Significance of Neoplatonism* (Norfolk, VA: International Society for Neoplatonic Studies, 1976)

Helmont, Jean Baptiste van, *Oriatrike, or, Physick Refined*, trans. by John Chandler (London: Lodowick Loyd, 1662)

Heywood, Rosalind, *The Infinite Hive: A Personal Record of Extra-Sensory Experiences* (1964; repr. Harmondsworth, Middx: Penguin, 1978)

Israel, Martin, *Precarious Living: The Path to Life* (London: Mowbray, 1982)

Jaini, Padmanabh S., *The Jaina Path of Purification* (Delhi: Motilal Banarsidass, 1979)

James, William, *The Varieties of Religious Experience: A Study in Human Nature* (New York: Longmans, Green, 1902)

Johnson, Raynor C., *Watcher on the Hills* (London: Hodder & Stoughton, 1959)

Jourdan, Jean-Pierre, "Near Death Experiences and the 5th Dimensional Spatio-Temporal Perspective," *Journal of Cosmology*, 14 (2011) <http://journalofcosmology.com/Consciousness152.html>

Jung, C. G., "On the Nature of the Psyche," in *The Structure and Dynamics of the Psyche*, trans. by R. F. C. Hull, 2nd edn, *The Collected Works of C. G. Jung*, 20 vols (London: Routledge & Kegan Paul), VIII (1969), 159–234F

Kelly, Edward F., "Toward a Worldview Grounded in Science and Spirituality," in Kelly, Crabtree, and Marshall, pp. 493–551

Kelly, Edward F., Adam Crabtree, and Paul Marshall, eds., *Beyond Physicalism: Toward Reconciliation of Science and Spirituality* (Lanham, MD: Rowman & Littlefield, 2015)

Kelly, Edward F., and others, *Irreducible Mind: Toward a Psychology for the 21st Century* (Lanham, MD: Rowman & Littlefield, 2007)

Kirk, G. S., J. E. Raven, and M. Schofield, *The Presocratic Philosophers*, 2nd edn (Cambridge: Cambridge University Press, 1983)

Kripal, Jeffrey J., *Comparing Religions: Coming to Terms* (Chichester, West Sussex: Wiley Blackwell, 2014)

—— *Mutants and Mystics: Science Fiction, Superhero Comics, and the Paranormal* (Chicago: University of Chicago Press, 2011)

—— *Secret Body: Erotic and Esoteric Currents in the History of Religions* (Chicago: Chicago University Press, 2017)

Kristeller, Paul Oskar, *The Philosophy of Marsilio Ficino*, trans. by Virginia Conant (1943; repr. Gloucester, MA: Peter Smith, 1964)

Lawrence, David Peter, *The Teachings of the Odd-Eyed One: A Study and Translation of the Virūpākṣapañcāśikā, with the Commentary of Vidyācakravartin* (Albany: State University of New York Press, 2008)

Leibniz, G. W., *New Essays on Human Understanding*, edited by Peter Remnant and Jonathan Bennett (Cambridge: Cambridge University Press, 1996)

—— *Philosophical Texts*, trans. and ed. by R. S. Woolhouse and Richard Francks (Oxford: Oxford University Press, 1998)

Lovejoy, Arthur O., *The Great Chain of Being: A Study of the History of an Idea* (Cambridge, MA: Harvard University Press, 1936)

McGinn, Bernard, *The Presence of God: A History of Western Christian Mysticism*, I. *The Foundations of Mysticism: Origins to the Fifth Century* (London: SCM Press, 1992)

Marks, Carol L., and George Robert Guffey, eds., *Christian Ethicks* by Thomas Traherne (Ithaca, NY: Cornell University Press, 1968)

Marshall, Paul, *The Living Mirror: Images of Reality in Science and Mysticism*, rev. edn (London: Samphire Press, 2006)

—— *Mystical Encounters with the Natural World: Experiences and Explanations* (Oxford: Oxford University Press, 2005)

—— "Mystical Experience and Metaphysics," Esalen Center for Theory and Research website, *Beyond Physicalism* supplement, 2014 <https://www.esalen.org/sites/default/files/resource_attachments/Ch-2-Supp-MEM.pdf>

——— "Mystical Experiences as Windows on Reality," in Kelly, Crabtree, and Marshall, pp. 39–76

——— "The Psychical and the Mystical: Boundaries, Connections, Common Origins," *Journal of the Society for Psychical Research*, 75.1 (2011), 1–13

——— "Transforming the World into Experience: An Idealist Experiment," *Journal of Consciousness Studies*, 8.1 (2001), 59–76

——— "Why We Are Conscious of So Little: A Neo-Leibnizian Approach," in Kelly, Crabtree, and Marshall, pp. 387–422

Maxwell, Meg, and Verena Tschudin, eds., *Seeing the Invisible: Modern Religious and Other Transcendent Experiences* (Oxford: Religious Experience Research Centre, 1996)

Minkowski, Hermann, "Space and Time," in *The Principle of Relativity: A Collection of Original Memoirs on the Special and General Theory of Relativity*, by H. A. Lorentz and others, trans. by W. Perrett and G. B. Jeffery (New York: Dover Publications, 1952), pp. 75–91

Obeyesekere, Gananath, *Imagining Karma: Ethical Transformation in Amerindian, Buddhist, and Greek Rebirth* (Berkeley and Los Angeles: University of California Press, 2002)

Pagel, Walter, "J. B. van Helmont, *De Tempore*, and Biological Time," *Osiris*, 8 (1948), 346–417

Peers, E. Allison, trans. and ed., *The Complete Works of Saint Teresa of Jesus*, from the critical edition of P. Silverio de Santa Teresa, 3 vols (London: Sheed & Ward, 1946)

Plotiniana Arabica, trans. by Geoffrey Lewis, in *Plotini Opera: Tomvs II, Enneades IV–V*, ed. by Paul Henry and Hans-Rudolf Schwyzer (Paris: Desclée de Brouwer; Brussels: L'Édition Universelle, 1959)

Podoll, Klaus, and Derek Robinson, *Migraine Art: The Migraine Experience from Within* (Berkeley, CA: North Atlantic Books, 2008) Proclus, *The Elements of Theology*, trans. by E. R. Dodds, 2nd edn (Oxford: Clarendon Press, 1963)

Proclus, *The Elements of Theology*, trans. by E. R. Dodds, 2nd edn (Oxford: Clarendon Press, 1963)

Pylkkänen, Paavo T. I., *Mind, Matter and the Implicate Order* (Berlin: Springer, 2007)

Rist, J. M., *Plotinus: The Road to Reality* (Cambridge: Cambridge University Press, 1967)

Ross, Jan, ed., *The Works of Thomas Traherne*, 9 vols (Cambridge: Brewer, 2005–)

Ruse, Michael, *Monad to Man: The Concept of Progress in Evolutionary Biology* (Cambridge, MA: Harvard University Press, 1996)

Samuel, Geoffrey, and Jay Johnston, eds., *Religion and the Subtle Body in Asia and the West: Between Mind and Body* (Abingdon, Oxon: Routledge, 2013)

Schimmel, Annemarie, *Mystical Dimensions of Islam* (Chapel Hill: University of North Carolina Press, 1975)

Scholem, Gershom, *Kabbalah* (New York: Dorset Press, 1987)

——— *On the Mystical Shape of the Godhead: Basic Concepts in the Kabbalah* (New York: Schocken Books, 1991)

Seager, William, ed., *The Routledge Handbook of Panpsychism*, (London: Routledge, 2019)

Shaw, Gregory, "Platonic *Siddhas*: Supernatural Philosophers of Neoplatonism," in Kelly, Crabtree, and Marshall, pp. 275–313

——— *Theurgy and the Soul: The Neoplatonism of Iamblichus* (University Park: Pennsylvania State University Press, 1995)

Skribna, David, *Panpsychism in the West*, rev. edn (Cambridge, MA: MIT Press, 2017)

Sorabji, Richard, *Self: Ancient and Modern Insights About Individuality, Life, and Death* (Oxford: Clarendon Press, 2006)

——— *Time, Creation and the Continuum: Theories in Antiquity and the Early Middle Ages* (London: Duckworth, 1983)

Sprigge, T. L. S., *The God of Metaphysics* (Oxford: Clarendon Press, 2006)

Stang, Charles M., *Our Divine Double* (Cambridge, MA: Harvard University Press, 2016)

Traherne, Thomas, *Christian Ethicks: Or, Divine Morality Opening the Way to Blessedness, by the Rules of Vertue and Reason* (London: Jonathan Edwin, 1675)

Upaniṣads, trans. by Patrick Olivelle (Oxford: Oxford University Press, 1996)

Walker, D. P., *The Decline of Hell: Seventeenth-Century Discussions of Eternal Torment* (London: Routledge & Kegan Paul, 1964)

Wallis, Richard T., ed., *Neoplatonism and Gnosticism* (Albany: State University of New York Press, 1992)

Ward, R. H., *A Drug-Taker's Notes* (London: Victor Gollancz, 1957)

Weeks, Andrew, *Boehme: An Intellectual Biography of the Seventeenth-Century Philosopher and Mystic* (Albany: State University of New York Press, 1991)

White, Jeremiah, *The Restoration of All Things: Or, A Vindication of the Goodness and Grace of God* (London: N. Cliff and D. Jackson, 1712)

Williams, Paul, *Māhāyana Buddhism: The Doctrinal Foundations*, 2nd edn (Abingdon, Oxon: Routledge, 2009)

Wilmshurst, Walter Leslie, "The Vision Splendid," in *Contemplations: Being Studies in Christian Mysticism*, rev. and enlarged edn (London: Watkins, 1928), pp. 142–52 (first publ. in *The Seeker*, 9 (1914), 226–38)

Wilson, Catherine, *Leibniz's Metaphysics: A Historical and Comparative Study* (Manchester: Manchester University Press, 1989)

Zaehner, R. C., *Mysticism Sacred and Profane: An Inquiry into Some Varieties of Præternatural Experience* (Oxford: Clarendon Press, 1957)

Zaleski, Carol, *Otherworld Journeys: Accounts of Near-Death Experience in Medieval and Modern Times* (New York: Oxford University Press, 1987)

Index

Page references for Figures and Tables are italicized.

About the Author

Paul Marshall is an independent researcher with interests in mysticism, religion, philosophy, science, and their interactions. He studied Natural Sciences at the University of Cambridge and received his MA and PhD in Religious Studies from Lancaster University. He is author of *The Living Mirror: Images of Reality in Science and Mysticism* (1992) and *Mystical Encounters with the Natural World: Experiences and Explanations* (2005). With Edward F. Kelly and Adam Crabtree, Marshall coedited *Beyond Physicalism: Toward Reconciliation of Science and Spirituality* (2015).

CPSIA information can be obtained
at www.ICGtesting.com
Printed in the USA
LVHW090249201219
641206LV00004B/45/P

9 781538 124772